W9-BEA-362

Trees of
Western
North
America

Princeton Field Guides

Rooted in field experience and scientific study, Princeton's guides to animals and plants are the authority for professional scientists and amateur naturalists alike. **Princeton Field Guides** present this information in a compact format carefully designed for easy use in the field. The guides illustrate every species in color and provide detailed information on identification, distribution, and biology.

Birds of the Dominican Republic and Haiti, by Steven Latta, Christopher Rimmer, Allan Keith, James Wiley, Herbert Raffaele, Kent McFarland, and Eladio Fernandez

Birds of the West Indies, by Herbert Raffaele, James Wiley, Orlando Garrido, Allan Keith, and Janis Raffaele

Caterpillars of Eastern North America: A Guide to Identification and Natural History, by David L. Wagner

Common Mosses of the Northeast and Appalachians, by Karl B. McKnight, Joseph Rohrer, Kirsten McKnight Ward, and Warren Perdrizet

Dragonflies and Damselflies of the East, by Dennis Paulson

Dragonflies and Damselflies of the West, by Dennis Paulson

Mammals of North America, Second Edition, by Roland W. Kays and Don E. Wilson

Nests, Eggs, and Nestlings of North American Birds, Second Edition, by Paul J. Baicich and Colin J. O. Harrison

Trees of Eastern North America, by Gil Nelson, Christopher J. Earle, and Richard Spellenberg, Illustrations by David More, Edited by Amy K. Hughes

Trees of Western North America, by Richard Spellenberg, Christopher J. Earle, and Gil Nelson, Illustrations by David More, Edited by Amy K. Hughes

Trees of Panama and Costa Rica, by Richard Condit, Rolando Pérez, and Nefertaris Daguerre

Richard Spellenberg, Christopher J. Earle, and Gil Nelson

ILLUSTRATIONS BY DAVID MORE

Edited by Amy K. Hughes

Trees of Western North America

Princeton University Press
Princeton and Oxford

Copyright © 2014 by Richard Spellenberg, Christopher J. Earle, Gil Nelson, and
    Amy K. Hughes
Illustrations © 2014 David More

Illustrations of Coast Redwood tree (p. 53) and Giant Sequoia tree (p. 54)
© Robert Van Pelt

Requests for permission to reproduce material from this work should be sent to
Permissions, Princeton University Press

Published by Princeton University Press, 41 William Street, Princeton, New
Jersey 08540

In the United Kingdom: Princeton University Press, 6 Oxford Street, Woodstock,
Oxfordshire OX20 1TW

press.princeton.edu
Cover art © 2014 David More

All Rights Reserved

ISBN 978-0-691-14579-2
ISBN (pbk.) 978-0-691-14580-8

Library of Congress Control Number: 2013950318

British Library Cataloging-in-Publication Data is available

This book has been composed in Minion Pro

Printed on acid-free paper. ∞

Edited and designed by D & N Publishing, Baydon, Wiltshire, UK

Printed in China

10 9 8 7 6 5 4 3 2 1

CONTENTS

Introduction 6
About This Book 6
Taxonomy and Names 7
Gymnosperms and Angiosperms 7
Tree Biology 9
Forest Structure 18
Leaf Keys 19
   Key to the Gymnosperms by Leaf Type 20
   Key to Selected Angiosperm Trees
      by Leaf Shape 21

THE TREES

Gymnosperms 26
   Conifers 26
Ginkgoaceae: Ginkgo Family 27
Araucariaceae: Araucaria Family 28
Cupressaceae: Cypress Family 30
Pinaceae: Pine Family 55
Taxaceae: Yew Family 110

Angiosperms 112
   Monocots 112
Arecaceae: Palm Family 112
Asparagaceae: Asparagus Family 118

   Dicots 130
Adoxaceae: Moschatel Family 130
Anacardiaceae: Cashew Family 134
Apocynaceae: Oleander Family 148
Aquifoliaceae: Holly Family 149
Araliaceae: Ginseng Family 152
Asteraceae: Aster Family 152
Betulaceae: Birch Family 156
Bignoniaceae: Bignonia Family 172
Boraginaceae: Borage Family 176
Buddlejaceae: Buddleja Family 178
Burseraceae: Torchwood Family 178
Cactaceae: Cactus Family 180
Cannabaceae: Hemp Family 199
Celastraceae: Bittersweet Family 204
Cornaceae: Dogwood Family 206

Ebenaceae: Ebony Family 210
Elaeagnaceae: Oleaster Family 212
Ericaceae: Heath Family 216
Euphorbiaceae: Spurge Family 226
Fabaceae: Bean or Pea Family 230
Fagaceae: Beech or Oak Family 276
Garryaceae: Silktassel Family 320
Hamamelidaceae: Witch-hazel Family 324
Juglandaceae: Walnut Family 325
Koeberliniaceae: Allthorn Family 334
Lauraceae: Laurel Family 335
Malvaceae: Mallow Family 340
Meliaceae: Mahogany Family 346
Moraceae: Mulberry Family 346
Myoporaceae: Myoporum Family 352
Myricaceae: Wax Myrtle Family 353
Myrtaceae: Myrtle Family 354
Oleaceae: Olive Family 362
Papaveraceae: Poppy Family 378
Pittosporaceae: Cheesewood Family 379
Platanaceae: Planetree Family 381
Proteaceae: Protea Family 385
Punicaceae: Pomegranate Family 386
Rhamnaceae: Buckthorn Family 386
Rosaceae: Rose Family 402
Rubiaceae: Madder Family 454
Rutaceae: Citrus or Rue Family 456
Salicaceae: Willow Family 464
Sapindaceae: Soapberry Family 500
Sapotaceae: Sapodilla Family 514
Simaroubaceae: Quassia Family 516
Solanaceae: Nightshade Family 518
Staphyleaceae: Bladdernut Family 520
Styracaceae: Storax Family 521
Tamaricaceae: Tamarisk Family 522
Ulmaceae: Elm Family 528
Verbenaceae: Vervain Family 534
Zygophyllaceae: Caltrop Family 538

Acknowledgments 540
Abbreviations 541
Glossary 542
Index of Species 547

■ ABOUT THIS BOOK

This guide presents the trees that grow without the aid of human cultivation in the western portion of North America north of Mexico. This region is more or less naturally defined by the area between the eastern base of the Rocky Mountains and the Pacific Ocean. More precisely, we have chosen the 100th meridian as the division between East and West. In the United States this meridian defines the eastern border of the Texas panhandle, extends northward across the central portion of the Great Plains, and in Canada lies slightly east of the borders between Saskatchewan and Manitoba, and Northwest Territories and Nunavut. Southward, in Texas, there is a notable difference in the species composition of the woody vegetation that lies east or west of a dividing line that continues south from the panhandle's eastern border to Abilene, then curves eastward near the eastern edge of the Edwards Plateau, passing through Austin and ending at Corpus Christi on the Gulf of Mexico.

NATIVE AND INTRODUCED

We indicate in the tree descriptions whether a species is native or introduced to the region covered by this book. Most are "native," meaning they were already in North America before Europeans came to the New World. Since then, many trees have been introduced as ornamentals, to provide food, browse, or wood products, or for erosion control or windbreaks. Some of these trees are naturalized: They are reproducing and persisting as populations without the aid of horticultural practice. A few prominent cultivated street and garden trees are also included.

This guide covers the western United States and Canada as indicated on the map.

TAXONOMIC ORGANIZATION AND SEQUENCE OF SPECIES

Species are arranged in the book in a manner that reflects the general relationships among species and, at the same time, provides a sequence convenient for the user. The first part of the book covers gymnosperms (conifers and their relatives); the larger group of trees called angiosperms (flowering plants) follows, first with the monocotyledons, or monocots (among them palms and yuccas), then the dicotyledons, or dicots. See "Gymnosperms and Angiosperms," p. 7, for more on these groups. Within the gymnosperms, monocots, and dicots, the trees are organized into families, within each family into its genera (singular, *genus*), and within each genus the species that occur in the West. Anyone studying our flora will find it useful to learn to recognize families, or genera, as a route to identifying species. Families, genera, and species are presented in alphabetic order, except in a few instances in which a different arrangement simplifies identification (as in some of the gymnosperms, and the flowering plant families Fabaceae, Fagaceae, Rosaceae, Salicaceae, and Tamaricaceae).

NAMES

We use up-to-date scientific names, drawn from the *Flora of North America North of Mexico* (www. efloras.org), the USDA PLANTS Database (www. plants.usda.gov), and recently published technical literature. We use a unique scientific name for each species. We also provide at least one, and often several, common names, some of them regional. (See "Taxonomy and Names," below.)

DESCRIPTIONS

Each family, genus, and species has its own description, except when a genus has only one species in the West; in such a case there is only one inclusive genus and species description. Family and genus descriptions describe the group and provide some information on how the plants are used, their ecology, and, sometimes, on problems of classification.

Species descriptions begin with common and scientific names, including alternative names ("A.K.A."), if any. For all native species (and many introduced) we provide a "Quick ID," a short statement describing how to recognize that particular species. A more detailed description follows, providing information on habit (the plant's growth form), bark, twigs, foliage, flowers, and fruit. Descriptions vary in length depending on our assessment of the cultural or ecological importance of the tree as well as the extent of its geographic distribution. We indicate whether the species is native or introduced, and provide the usual flowering period, elevation and general habitat, and geographic distribution. When applicable, we explain how to distinguish the species from similar, usually closely related species. For nearly all native and some introduced species we provide a thumbnail map showing the geographic range of the species in North America north of Mexico.

■ TAXONOMY AND NAMES

Taxonomy defines groups of organisms, gives names to the groups, and arranges them in a hierarchy, thereby producing a classification. It is the oldest of biological sciences, originating in language that spoke of organisms in nature. Modern classifications use many lines of evidence, including morphology, chemistry, and DNA-based data, to classify organisms according to their evolutionary relationships. At the higher levels of the hierarchy, those relationships are still unclear; in this book we use traditional names such as angiosperms, gymnosperms, monocots, and dicots. At the lower levels of the hierarchy, we use the formal ranks of family, genus, and species, which form a useful framework for identification.

It is useful to learn to recognize plant families; knowing their characteristics makes identification easier and can give one some familiarity with local plants in any part of the world. Families are collections of genera that share a common ancestor. The use of DNA analysis in taxonomy, however, is producing ongoing changes in our understanding of some traditional plant families. The former maple family (Aceraceae), for example, does not appear in this book; maples (genus *Acer*) are now placed within a varied soapberry family (Sapindaceae). The iconic *Yucca* genus of the Southwest, once in the Agavaceae, is now allied with asparagus in the Asparagaceae. For the most part, we have adopted new family alignments, but in a few cases where it helps identification, we have maintained traditional families. We explain the newer, often tentative, classification whether we adopt it or not.

SPECIES NAMES

As strange as it may seem, the precise definition of a "plant species" has been argued for decades. For our use it is a group of populations that persists in nature, sufficiently distinct to bear a name. Most species have one or more common names, but common names differ among the world's many

languages, as well as regionally, and often do not indicate species relationships. Furthermore, one species may have several common names, or several different species may have the same common name. Conversely, all species are assigned a two-part scientific name that applies to only that species. It distinguishes by name one species from another, indicates some degree of relationship, allows international communication about organisms, and affords ready information retrieval from references. Scientific names inform us, for example, that Emory Oak (*Quercus emoryi*) and Valley Oak (*Quercus lobata*) are related, both in the genus *Quercus*; but Poison-oak (*Toxicodendron diversilobum*) and the she-oaks (species of *Casuarina*) are not related to each other or to *Quercus*, despite being called "oaks."

The scientific name is a Latinized name, Latin having been the primary language of science in the 18th century, when the system was devised. It is a two-part name, or binomial, composed of a genus name followed by a specific epithet. The first part is a noun, referring to a kind of plant (sumac, oak). The specific epithet is usually an adjective that describes the species or its habitat or commemorates a person. *Rhus glabra*, the scientific name for Smooth Sumac, provides an example: *Rhus* derives from an ancient Greek name for sumac; *glabra*, from the Latin for "bald," refers to the absence of hairs on plant parts. The names or abbreviations that follow the binomial indicate the author or authors who named and described the plant. *Rhus glabra* is followed by "L.," for Carolus Linnaeus, the Swedish botanist who is credited with having developed the binomial system 260 years ago. When a named species is later understood to belong to a different genus, the specific epithet may be moved from one genus to another. The name of the author who first named the plant is placed in parentheses, followed by the author who moved the name to a different genus. How names are applied and moved about is regulated by a set of rules, the *International Code of Nomenclature for algae, fungi, and plants* (www.iapt-taxon.org). The binomial, together with the author's name, is the complete scientific name for a plant.

■ GYMNOSPERMS AND ANGIOSPERMS

Two great groups of land plants bear ovules, which when fertilized produce seeds. The seed may be viewed as a little survival packet: It has an outer protective layer that surrounds a nutritive tissue, the *endosperm*, to be used by the germinating embryo that developed from the fertilization of an egg within the ovule. The seed plants are traditionally divided into angiosperms and gymnosperms. We retain those groups in this book.

The conifers and their allies, the Ginkgo, cycads, and gnetophytes, comprise the *gymnosperms*, a term derived from the Greek words for "naked seeds." The ovules of these plants are not protected within a closed ovary, as they are in the angiosperms, but are borne directly on structures that expose them to the environment at the time of pollination, although the ovules are often protected to some degree by overlapping scales. Technically, the endosperm in gymnosperms has a different origin than that of the angiosperms, that difference further helping to distinguish the two groups. Most gymnosperms are pollinated by wind, but many cycads are pollinated by insects. In conifers and gnetophytes, as in angiosperms, the pollen grain grows a pollen tube that conveys sperm to, or even within, the ovule, where the egg is fertilized. In Ginkgo and the cycads, however, fertilization occurs when motile sperm swim from the pollen grain into the ovule.

There is considerable ongoing scientific debate about whether or not the groups within the gymnosperms are more closely related to each other than they are to the angiosperms. All of the gymnosperm groups have an evolutionary history that goes back at least 200 million years, but the fossil record is too incomplete to determine evolutionary relationships, except in very indirect ways using modern plant material. It is clear, though, that the gymnosperms were formerly a highly diverse group, of which only a comparatively few families have survived to the present.

The other group of seed plants is the *angiosperms*, a term derived from Greek words meaning "vessel" and "seed," referring to a plant with seeds borne within an enclosure. Angiosperms evolved from gymnosperms around 200 million years ago, when a leaflike, ovule-bearing structure in a seed fern closed around its ovules (which when fertilized develop into seeds), producing a carpel. The flower, characteristic of angiosperms, became an organized reproductive structure consisting of carpels, stamens, petals, and sepals.

The *carpel* is the fundamental unit of the *pistil*, the pollen-receiving, seed-producing part of the flower. There are two types of pistils: those composed of a single carpel (a simple pistil); and those composed of two or more carpels joined together (a compound pistil). One can usually determine

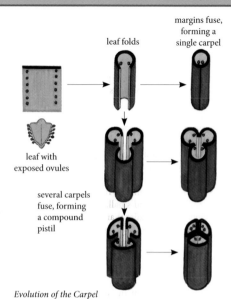

leaf folds   margins fuse, forming a single carpel

leaf with exposed ovules

several carpels fuse, forming a compound pistil

Evolution of the Carpel

the number of carpels in a pistil by counting the number of chambers (or locules), but because chamber walls are sometimes incomplete or absent in a compound pistil, the number of branches on the stigma (the pollen receptor at the tip of the pistil) is also usually a reliable indicator; two or more branches suggest a compound pistil. The diagram above illustrates the evolution of the carpel from an ovule-bearing leaf, and the development of a compound pistil from a fusion of several carpels. Two other features that distinguish angiosperms from gymnosperms are the seed-bearing closed fruits and the way the endosperm develops.

Angiosperms are divided into the Monocotyledoneae, or monocots, and Dicotyledoneae, the dicots. The names refer to the number of embryonic, often nutrient-storing leaves in the embryo within the seed; *monocots* typically have one, *dicots* typically have two. In addition, monocots usually have

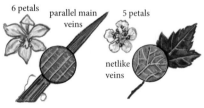

6 petals   parallel main veins   5 petals

netlike veins

Monocot Flower and Leaf   *Dicot Flower and Leaf*

flowers with parts in multiples of three and leaves with a number of conspicuous parallel veins. Dicots usually have flowers with parts in multiples of four or five, and net-veined leaves with main veins branching in a pinnate or palmate pattern, interconnected by a conspicuous net of minor veins.

■ TREE BIOLOGY

There is no scientific difference between a tree and a shrub, although a tree is generally understood to have a single woody stem (a trunk) and a well-defined crown of branches. In this book we include such plants, large and small, along with a number of plants generally taller than a human that may be thought of as shrubs, often growing with multiple woody trunks.

TREE GROWTH

A tree's growth is often seasonal, beginning in the spring and ceasing in the autumn, or beginning during the wet season and ceasing during the dry period. Trees may grow from seeds or from the roots or branches of existing trees. When a tree grows from a branch that is in touch with the ground, it is called *layering*; when it grows from roots of another tree, it is called *suckering*. Trees grow larger through the years as roots and twigs become longer, and the trunk, branches, and roots increase in girth.

At the tip of every twig and every root is a tiny patch of cells (the *apical meristem*) that divide, rapidly at the onset of the growing season and usually not at all during dormant periods. These divisions produce new cells behind the tip that enlarge, mature, and perform specific functions, at the same time adding length to the twig or root. The rate and direction of growth determines the shape of the *crown* of the tree. If the apical meristem on the main stem divides more rapidly than those at the tips of branches, the tree will be conical, as in firs and spruces. If all the meristems divide at the same rate and branches spread equally, the crown will be round. The shape of the crown, particularly of open-grown trees, is often useful in tree identification.

As a twig or young root matures, a new set of dividing cells forms beneath its outer layer. This is a continuation of a cylindric layer of dividing cells (the *vascular cambium*) that extends throughout the tree beneath the bark of the branches, trunk, and roots. Cells of this layer divide inward and outward. New cells produced inward mature into water-conducting cells and other cells of the wood; those produced outward mature into cells that conduct sugar produced in the leaves and into cells of the bark. As new wood cells are added by the cambium, the wood increases in volume, and the cambium and bark are stretched. The bark becomes fissured and cracked as it stretches and dies, producing patterns helpful in tree identification. The dead outer layer protects the inner living tissue from insects, fungi, fire, abrasions, and other hazards.

TRUNK AND CROWN

Above ground, a tree has a *trunk* from which grows an array of branches and leaves that form the *crown*. We describe, in general terms, crown shapes of trees growing in the open under moderate conditions. Local conditions, however, can influence the shape of the crown. In a crowded forest the crowns of trees may be narrow, the shaded lower branches small or lost, and the upper branches growing toward the light. Wind, salt spray, abrasion by wind-blown ice or sand, lightning, fire, and other environmental influences can injure or deform a tree's crown. On high windswept ridges, windblown ice crystals may kill exposed foliage, producing a forest of low, gnarled trees called *krummholz* (German for "crooked wood").

The *trunk* is the branch-free portion between the roots and the crown. In our descriptions we usually give its diameter, measured at a height of about 1.3 m. In some cases, as in arid regions, tree trunks may be very short; for those the diameter is estimated at about the midpoint between the ground and the first branches. When we describe a tree as having more than one trunk, it means the trunk divides at a height lower than 1.3 m, often at ground level.

BARK

Bark is the outer protective covering of the branches, trunk, and roots. It varies among species from paper-thin to very thick. As a tree increases in girth, the bark is stretched, producing patterns of cracks, ridges, and flat areas that are often characteristic of a species. Large vertical cracks are often called *fissures*, smaller ones *cracks*, and short cracks or crosshatching may be called *checks*. Closely adjacent fissures have *ridges* between them; when they are farther apart the intervening space may form *plates*. Bark may be papery, fibrous, corky, or hard and woody. The elements may wear bark away very slowly, and it may become thick and deeply fissured. Thinner bark may continually shed its outer layers in long shaggy strips, flaking scales, or in paperlike sheets. We describe the bark of most species, and illustrate its features.

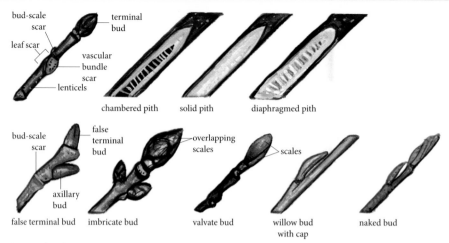

bud-scale scar

terminal bud

leaf scar

vascular bundle scar

lenticels

chambered pith   solid pith   diaphragmed pith

bud-scale scar

false terminal bud

overlapping scales

scales

axillary bud

false terminal bud   imbricate bud   valvate bud   willow bud with cap   naked bud

Twigs and Buds

TWIGS AND BUDS

Buds are composed of tiny patches of cells ready to divide and are usually covered by protective scales. A *terminal bud* forms at the tip of a twig each year as growth ceases. It is usually covered by external scales that protect dormant cells (the apical meristem) that are ready to divide and produce new tissue the next growing season. When growth begins, the bud scales fall away from the terminal bud, leaving *bud-scale scars* on the twig that mark the point as the beginning of that season's growth. A *twig* is the portion at the tip of a branch system produced by the current year's growth—that is, the part between the terminal bud and the bud-scale scars left from the previous year's terminal bud. One may determine the age of a young branch by counting the rings of bud-scale scars produced each year along the branch.

Terminal buds form at the tips of the twigs; *lateral buds* form in the *axils* of leaves along a twig; *false terminal buds* are lateral buds that appear to be at the tip of the twig but are slightly offset. When buds become active and begin to grow, they may give rise to a new twig with its new leaves, a flower, a flower cluster, or a cone.

The protective bud scales may be *imbricate*, overlapping like shingles; *valvate*, meeting only at their edges like a clamshell; or may consist of a *cap* formed by a single scale. If there are no scales at all, the bud is said to be *naked*. Buds and their scales may be covered by protective gummy or sticky substances, hairs, or minute glands.

Twigs provide many clues to the identification of a tree, useful in summer or winter. The place on a twig where leaves attach is the *node* (see "Leaf Arrangement," opposite). When the leaf falls, the twig bears a distinctively shaped *leaf scar*. Within the scar is a pattern of several small points where *vascular bundles* entered the leaf; the number of these *bundle scars* can provide identification clues, especially in winter. Twigs usually have a distinctive color, and the surface may have noticeable *lenticels*, patches of loose, usually pale, corky cells, varying from small dots to short dashes or even long lines. The twig surface may be hairless, variably hairy, or glandular, the glands stalked or not (see "Hairs, Glands, Wax, and Resin," p. 14), or it may be winged or thorny (see "Thorns, Spines, and Prickles," p. 14). In cross section a twig may vary from circular to angled (if four-angled, it is often described as "square"); in some cases the pattern or color of the twig's *pith*, or interior tissue, is important. In a number of trees we mention *short shoots*, twigs that grow very slowly and are much shorter than the faster-growing main branch; the short shoots may bear leaves or fruits (described and illustrated in "Leaf Arrangement").

LEAVES

Photosynthesis, which produces sugars from water and carbon dioxide using light energy from the sun, occurs in green tissues of plants. By this mode plants produce their "food," and ultimately provide support for almost all life on Earth. The complex chemical processes of photosynthesis operate best at different temperatures in different species, but always require sufficient water for cells to function. Leaves must neither dry out nor overheat, and their

Leaf Arrangement

shapes, lobing, and divisions help cope with their limitations. Each leaf has a lifetime during which it is productive, after which it falls. The presence or absence of leaves and their many shapes and arrangements provide important characters for tree identification.

Trees that are never barren of leaves are *evergreen*. Their leaves persist on the tree for one or more years, and new leaves are borne before old leaves drop. Most conifers and many kinds of angiosperm trees are evergreen. *Deciduous* trees are without leaves for part of the year. Many drop their leaves before the cold season; others may be *drought deciduous*, dropping leaves during the dry season. In either case, leaves are dropped when they can no longer function. In species of the cypress family (Cupressaceae), which are predominantly evergreen, entire twigs die and fall with all of their attached leaves, usually after three to four years.

LEAF ARRANGEMENT The arrangement of leaves on the twig is helpful in identification. Leaves are *opposite* when two are attached on either side of a node. When three or more are attached at a node, the leaves are *whorled*. When only one leaf occurs at a node, the leaves are *alternate*. (On leafless twigs, the leaf scars indicate the arrangement.) Alternate leaves show a *spiral* arrangement along the twig, discernible by tracing a line up or down a twig from one node to the next. The illustration above shows a *five-ranked* spiral, with the first five leaves tracing a spiral around the twig, and the sixth positioned directly above the first. Leaves may bend or twist upon their petioles to obtain maximum light,

in some species orienting on opposite sides of the twig in the same plane. Such leaves are *two-ranked*. In some conifers, such as firs, the arrangement of the needles on the shoot can look very different in sun foliage (sometimes resembling a toothbrush or bottlebrush) and shade foliage (which may appear two-ranked), even though the needles are actually spirally arranged. Some leaves grow in close clusters or bundles, called *fascicles*, usually from short shoots. The *pine-needle bundle* is a short shoot genetically programmed to grow only so long, to produce a certain number of needles for the species, and then to stop growing and after a few seasons to drop as a unit.

PARTS OF A LEAF Leaves vary in shape and size. A *simple* leaf has an undivided blade of leaf tissue. The leaf blade may be cleft or lobed, sometimes deeply, but not separated into leaflets, as in a *compound leaf*, discussed below. A common kind of simple leaf in dicots consists of a stalklike *petiole* and an expanded, flat *blade*. If leaves have a petiole, they are *petiolate*; if the petiole is absent and the blade attaches directly to the twig, the leaf is *sessile*. At the base of the petiole is often a pair of *stipules*; these may be small green leaflike structures, or may be a different color or modified into scales, bristles, or spines (called *stipular spines*). Conifer leaves are often scalelike or needlelike. Scalelike leaves are short, thick, and often closely appressed to the twig. Needlelike leaves are much longer than wide and divergent from the twig.

The edge of the leaf blade is the *margin*, the features of which are often important. Margins may be

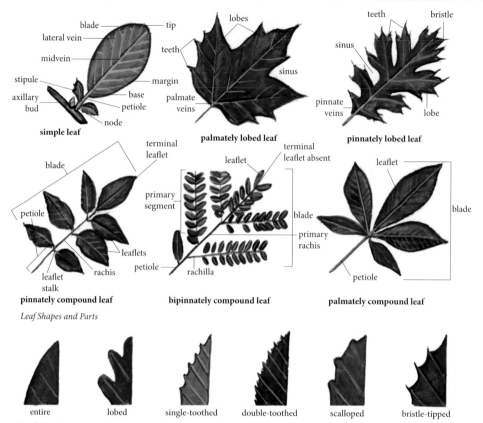

Leaf Shapes and Parts

Leaf Margins

entire, that is smooth and not incised or toothed; they may be *toothed* and have fine or coarse, sharp or blunt, bristle- or gland-tipped teeth; or they may be *scalloped* or more deeply cleft and thus *lobed*. The lobes can be round-tipped or pointed. Lobed leaves may be *pinnately lobed*, with a feather-like shape, as seen in many oaks; or *palmately* lobed, roughly hand-shaped, like most maples.

Leaves of monocots have *parallel veins* that run the length of the blade; additionally, tiny veins connect adjacent parallel main veins, often like rungs of a ladder. Most dicot leaves are *net-veined*, with tiny veins forming netlike interconnections between major veins, which usually form a prominent pinnate or palmate pattern. (Monocot and dicot venation is illustrated in "Gymnosperms and Angiosperms," p. 8.) A pinnately veined leaf has a *midvein*, or *midrib*, and several prominent *lateral veins* branching from it. Palmately veined leaves have several main veins originating from the same point at the base of the leaf. Veins may be relatively inconspicuous or, especially on the lower surface, may be raised well above the surface, often in a prominent netlike pattern.

COMPOUND LEAVES In a compound leaf the blade is divided to the midrib, which is then called the *rachis*. The blade consists of individual divisions called *leaflets*. If the leaflets are aligned along two sides of the rachis like the sides of a feather, the leaf is *pinnately compound*. If the divisions all join at the tip of the petiole, in the pattern of a hand with spreading fingers, the leaf is *palmately compound*. A palmately compound leaf has no rachis. Pinnately compound leaves may be *odd-pinnate* (with an odd number of leaflets because a terminal leaflet is present) or *even-pinnate* (terminal leaflet absent). The leaflets may be opposite one another or may be alternate on the rachis.

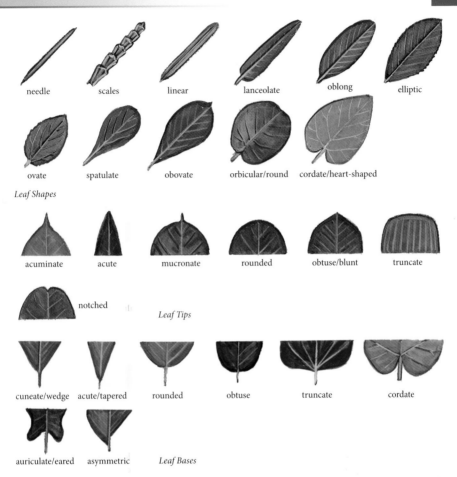

needle scales linear lanceolate oblong elliptic

ovate spatulate obovate orbicular/round cordate/heart-shaped

Leaf Shapes

acuminate acute mucronate rounded obtuse/blunt truncate

notched *Leaf Tips*

cuneate/wedge acute/tapered rounded obtuse truncate cordate

auriculate/eared asymmetric *Leaf Bases*

A compound leaf may be divided more than once; this is particularly common in pinnately compound leaves. If there is one more set of divisions—that is, the leaflets themselves are divided into leaflets—the leaf is *bipinnate*; if there is yet another division the leaf is *tripinnate*. In a bipinnate leaf, each divided section branching from the rachis has its own, secondary axis, called a *rachilla*, bearing leaflets; in this book we call the unit formed by the rachilla and its leaflets a *primary segment*. A tripinnate leaf has, in addition, secondary segments. Compound leaves often show pronounced responses to environmental conditions, with the leaflets orienting to the sun, folding together when it is hot and dry, or folding at night.

A compound leaf may resemble a spray of simple leaves: The presence of an axillary bud at the base of the petiole is a clue that a given stem is a twig with many small leaves rather than the rachis of a compound leaf. Buds do not occur in the axils of leaflets on a compound leaf.

SHAPES OF SIMPLE LEAVES Shapes of simple leaves range from the needlelike and scalelike leaves of many conifers to linear to circular blades. In addition, the shape of the leaf tip or apex and the leaf base can vary. Where water is sufficient, leaves may have considerable surface area to capture sunlight. In drier situations they may be needlelike, the reduced surface area helping to reduce evaporation and conserve water. The shape of the leaf blade helps with identification, although on any one tree, leaves in the sun may differ in shape and lobing from those in the shade, and leaves on rapidly growing shoots often are larger than those elsewhere.

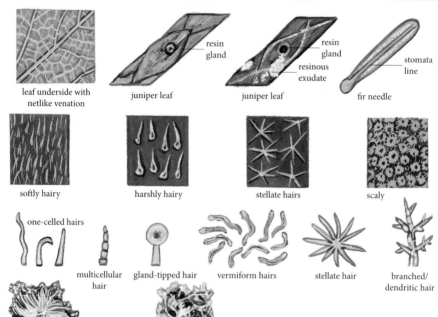

leaf underside with netlike venation   juniper leaf   resin gland   juniper leaf   resin gland   resinous exudate   fir needle   stomata line

softly hairy   harshly hairy   stellate hairs   scaly

one-celled hairs   multicellular hair   gland-tipped hair   vermiform hairs   stellate hair   branched/dendritic hair

peltate/shield-like hair   malpighian/T-shaped hair   wax scales

Leaf Surface Features

SURFACE FEATURES OF PLANT PARTS

It is often useful to examine features on the surfaces of leaves, twigs, and buds. Some features are visible, others can be detected by touch, and some can be seen only with a hand lens or other form of magnification.

STOMATA A leaf's surface is dotted with *stomata* (singular, *stoma*), microscopic pores through which carbon dioxide, oxygen, and water vapor move from the surrounding air to the interior of the leaf and vice versa; the *stomata* open or close to help control the flow of atmospheric gases and the moisture content of the leaf cells. In many conifers, the stomata form conspicuous whitish lines on the surface of the leaf, and the size, position, and number of these lines can be important features in identification.

THORNS, SPINES, AND PRICKLES Sharp-tipped thorns, spines, and prickles provide

protection to plants (plants with such protrusions are often described as "armed"). They are also useful in identification. *Thorns* are sharp-tipped twigs, sometimes very stout, occasionally branched. *Spines*, such as those in cacti or in many species of the bean family (Fabaceae), are modified leaves. *Prickles* are small, sharp-pointed growths from the surface tissue of the plant; the sharp barbs on the cones of some pines and the "thorns" on a rose are examples of prickles. *Bristles* (or awns) are minute hairlike extensions, such as those that tip the leaf lobes of some red oaks.

HAIRS, GLANDS, WAX, AND RESIN Leaves, twigs, fruits, and other plant parts may be *hairless* (*glabrous*) or *hairy* (*pubescent*). The hairs, which in plants are called *trichomes*, take many forms and colors, visible with magnification. Hairs may be unicellular or multicellular. Some have a sticky gland at the tip, while other glands lie directly on the leaf surface. *Vermiform* hairs are wormlike; *stellate* hairs are star-shaped; *dendritic* hairs branch like a tree; *peltate* hairs are somewhat shield-shaped with the attaching stalk at the center of the lower surface; and *malpighian* hairs are T-shaped.

When surfaces of leaves, twigs, or fruits are coated in a waxy substance they are described as *glaucous*; the wax, which imparts an often bluish hue, can be rubbed off, exposing the darker surface

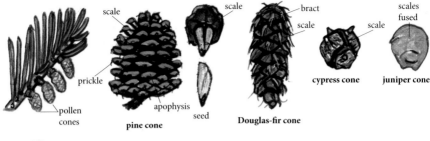

seeds

aril

yew ovulate structure

Gymnosperm Cones and Seeds

(as in a blueberry). Pale hairs and wax reflect light, reducing heating; wax is also impervious to water. Hairs, glands, and resins also help to protect plants from insect or large-animal herbivory. Some leaves are varnished with resin. The scalelike leaves of some conifers have a diagnostic gland that may or may not bear a drop of resin or whitish exudate and can be an important identification character.

TREE REPRODUCTION

Trees produce pollen, which bears the sperm, and ovules, which contain the egg and receive the sperm. The parts of the tree that produce these structures are often called male and female. In gymnosperms the ovules are borne in ovulate cones or occasionally develop singly at the end of a stalk; all gymnosperms covered in this book produce pollen in small, short-lived pollen cones. In angiosperms the reproductive structure is the flower; pollen is produced in the stamens, and the ovule(s) is contained in the pistil. Pollen is usually dispersed by wind, insects, or birds.

The basic flower is *bisexual*, containing both "male" stamens and a "female" pistil. In some species, stamens and pistils occur in different flowers, each sex separate and the flowers thus *unisexual*. Male unisexual flowers are described as *staminate*, female flowers as *pistillate*. Gymnosperms do not produce flowers; instead they have unisexual *pollen cones* (male) and *ovulate cones*, or *seed cones* (female).

Unisexual flowers or cones may be distributed in several ways. Species that have both male and female structures (whether bisexual flowers or both male and female unisexual cones or flowers) on the same individual are *monoecious* ("one house"). If the male and female reproductive structures occur on separate plants, each plant having only-male or only-female cones or flowers, the plants are *dioecious* ("two houses"). In some species, bisexual and unisexual flowers may be intermixed on the same plant.

GYMNOSPERM REPRODUCTIVE STRUCTURES Gymnosperms produce ovules that are not included in a vessel-like structure akin to the angiosperm pistil. Most gymnosperm species in this book are monoecious, each plant bearing both pollen cones and ovulate cones; a few are dioecious. Pollen cones in most of the plants covered here are small, fragile, and short-lived (a few trees retain pollen cones for a year or more after releasing the pollen). A pollen cone consists of a central axis and few to many scales, each of which has two to several sacs where pollen forms. When pollen is released, it is carried by wind to the ovules. For a brief period the ovules are exposed to the external environment, and pollen reaches the receptive ovule, delivering the sperm.

The mature ovule-bearing reproductive structures are highly varied in gymnosperms. Ginkgo produces two naked ovules at the end of a long stalk, usually only one maturing. The seed that develops has a fleshy outer coat and a hard inner coat. In *Taxus* and *Torreya*, the cone is reduced to a few tiny bracts, above which are one or two naked ovules, usually only one maturing. The hard external covering of the seed is partially or wholly surrounded by a fleshy or leathery *aril*.

Conifers (all other gymnosperms in this book) have ovules borne in well-defined cones with multiple woody or fleshy *scales*. On the upper side of each scale lies one to several ovules, from which the seeds develop. In many species the seeds are winged. After cones mature, which may take from one to three years, they may either disintegrate into their component scales, fall whole from the tree after seed dispersal, or remain on the tree either with or without seeds.

Ovulate cones differ from species to species and vary in persistence (lasting for a season or several years), providing many characters useful in identification. The cone has from 2 to more than 100 scales arranged around a central axis. The scales are separated from each other by a highly modified infertile leaf called a *bract*, which may or may not be visible on the surface of the cone. In some conifers, including the families Araucariaceae and Cupressaceae, the bracts and fertile scales are fused; in *Juniperus* species the fused scales form the fleshy or juicy "berry." In other groups, including the Pinaceae, the bracts and fertile scales are separate, and the bracts may be *exserted* from between the fertile scales and thus visible. The cones of most *Pinus* species take two years to mature; the intervening period of dormancy results in the formation of a thickening, called an *apophysis*, at the tip of each scale. Apophyses vary among species with regard to size, shape, color, and the presence or absence of a prickle at the extreme end; these characters are useful in identification.

ANGIOSPERM FLOWERS In their complexity, the flowers and fruits of angiosperm trees provide many characters useful in identification. A *complete flower* consists of four whorls of parts (beginning from the bottom, or outside): the *calyx*, *corolla*, *stamens*, and *pistil* or pistils. (Incomplete flowers lack one or more of these whorls of parts.) The calyx consists of *sepals*, usually flat green parts that protect the flower bud. The corolla consists of *petals*, often flat and colorful, which attract pollinators. Undifferentiated sepals and petals are often referred to as *tepals*. Stamens may be few or many, each consisting of a stalk (*filament*) with a pollen-bearing sac (*anther*) at its tip. The center of the flower may have one or more pistils, each consisting of an *ovary* that contains an *ovule* or several to many ovules. The ovary has one or more *styles*, each tipped by a pollen-receiving *stigma*. The pollen grain produces a tubular extension that grows through the style and places sperm at the opening of an ovule. Parts may be large, elaborate, and showy in flowers pollinated by insects or animals, or they may be tiny or even missing in flowers adapted for wind pollination. In trees, the tiny flowers are often unisexual.

Flowers that have the symmetry of a wheel when viewed from the top, their parts radiating equally in all directions, are *radially symmetric*. If the parts are oriented so that the flower can be divided only in one way to produce two equal halves, the flower is *bilaterally symmetric*. Any of the whorled parts of the flower (sepals, petals, stamens, pistils) may be fused to one another. This is particularly noticeable when the petals join to form a tube, funnel, bowl, or flask-shaped structure. Parts of adjacent series may also fuse together. For example, the bases of the sepals, petals, and stamens may all fuse into a cup that surrounds the ovary, forming a *hypanthium*, as in the rose family (Rosaceae).

Features of the pistil are important for plant identification. If all the flower parts attach at the base of the pistil, the ovary is said to be *superior*; if they attach at the top of the pistil, the ovary is *inferior*. The pistil may have one or several stigmas, and one to several chambers, both clues to the

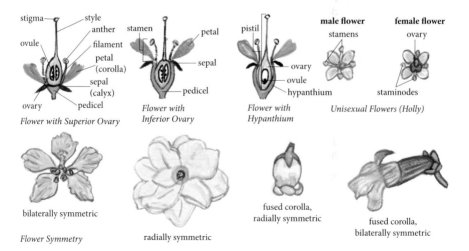

Flower with Superior Ovary

Flower with Inferior Ovary

Flower with Hypanthium

Unisexual Flowers (Holly)

bilaterally symmetric

radially symmetric

Flower Symmetry

fused corolla, radially symmetric

fused corolla, bilaterally symmetric

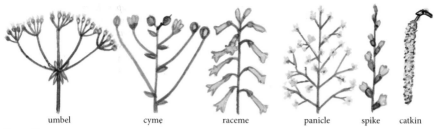

umbel   cyme   raceme   panicle   spike   catkin

Flower Clusters

number of carpels in the pistil (see "Gymnosperms and Angiosperms," pp. 7–9, for a discussion and illustration of the carpel). A *simple pistil* consists of a single carpel; it always has one chamber. A *compound pistil* consists of two or more fused carpels. If carpel walls remain in place, then the number of chambers suggests the number of carpels. If carpel walls have disappeared, the compound pistil may be one-chambered; the number of stigmas on the pistil usually indicates the number of carpels. These variations in simple and compound pistils result in the different types of fruits.

The positions of flowers, and the manner in which they are held, can be important in identification. Flowers may be *terminal* on the stem, growing from its tip, or they may arise from *axillary* buds, at the junction where a leaf meets the twig. They may be single or occur in large or small clusters or *inflorescences*, many of which have technical names. Large multibranched arrays are called *panicles*; tight, long, narrow arrays in which the flowers lack stalks are *spikes*; loose, narrow, elongate arrays with stalked flowers are *racemes*. *Catkins* are small, tightly packed clusters of highly reduced unisexual flowers.

ANGIOSPERM FRUITS The angiosperm fruit—the plant's seed-containing reproductive body—takes many forms and is so varied that a plethora of terms has been developed; we avoid the more technical ones as much as possible.

Many fruits are dry at maturity, and may or may not split open to release the seeds. A fruit that opens is said to be *dehiscent*; a fruit that does not is *indehiscent*. An indehiscent one-seeded fruit with a hard outer wall is a *nut*; an *achene* is also one-seeded, with a hard outer wall like a nut, but it is tiny. A hard, dry fruit with one or more wings, such as that of a maple, is a *samara*. A dry, more or less thin-walled, long and narrow, usually splitting fruit is often called a *pod*, a non-technical term that may refer to a follicle or a legume. The individual fruits of magnolia, which derive from a simple pistil, are dry, and split along one side, are *follicles*. A bean pod, also derived from a simple pistil and dry, splits along two sides and is technically a *legume*. A fruit that is dry and splits but is derived from a compound pistil is a *capsule*. Capsules may have one or several chambers.

There are also many kinds of fleshy fruits. The term *berry*, in its technical sense, refers to a fleshy

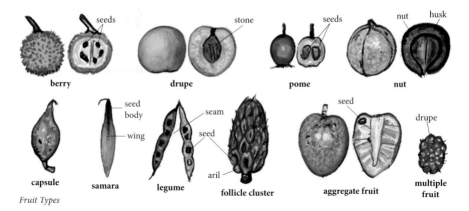

berry   drupe   pome   nut

seeds   stone   seeds   nut   husk

capsule   samara   legume   follicle cluster   aggregate fruit   multiple fruit

seed body   wing   seam   seed   aril   seed   drupe

Fruit Types

fruit with few to many seeds within. A *drupe* has an outer skin over a fleshy layer, and an innermost hard, bony layer (the "pit" or stone) that surrounds usually one seed; some drupes have several stones. The fruit of the apple is a *pome*, in which the hypanthium has become thick and fleshy and joined to the (inferior) ovary. Individual fruits of adjacent flowers may join together as a unit, as in the mulberry or fig; these are called *multiple fruits*. In an *aggregate fruit*, adjacent ovaries of a single flower, joined or not, form the single structure we call the fruit. A blackberry and a strawberry are examples.

■ FOREST STRUCTURE

The study of how trees are distributed on the landscape is part of forest ecology, a topic much too large to be covered in this book. There are, however, some ecological concepts that appear throughout this book in the discussions of habitat and plant associations. These include the physical structure of the forest, and also the way in which it is influenced by climate, soil composition, and topography. Other factors, such as fire and fire management practices, are also important.

The physical structure varies from forest to woodland to savanna. A forest occurs where the trees grow so closely together that they form a nearly continuous cover on the landscape. When the trees are separated by more space, so that their canopies cover less than half of the ground area, the area is called a woodland; usually woodland trees are shorter and smaller than the trees of a forest. When the trees are so widely distributed that they are isolated individuals on the landscape, covering only a small percentage of the ground area, the area is called a savanna.

Within each of these types, additional terms can be used to describe the composition of the vegetation. Forests and woodlands usually have several distinct layers in their vertical structure. The uppermost layer is the canopy, consisting of the crowns of the trees. If the crowns are dense and interlocked, blocking most of the sunlight from reaching the ground, the canopy is closed. If the crowns are not very dense or interwoven, and light reaches the forest floor, the canopy is open. The lower layer is the understory. If it is free from other vegetation or has only low herbaceous plants, the understory is open. Open understories devoid of vegetation occur in forests that shade the ground throughout the year. This is common in evergreen forests. When the canopy is open part of the year,

as in most hardwood forests, fast-growing herbaceous plants can take advantage of ample sunshine in the understory in spring before the trees leaf out and the canopy closes. Where there is plenty of water and sunlight the understory may be brushy, filled with shrubs and small trees, and in some highly productive forests these may make a third, intermediate layer of trees above the understory but below the canopy.

An assemblage of trees of a single species is a pure stand; a mixed stand contains appreciable numbers of two or more species. A mixed evergreen forest consists of a number of species of evergreen trees. Some forest types are named for their prominent tree species, such as piñon–juniper woodland and oak savanna.

Our habitat descriptions use several terms to describe climate: Arid, mesic, humid, and wet describe a range of increasing moisture availability; while arctic, alpine, boreal, montane, temperate, subtropical, and tropical describe increasing temperature, which may be due to either reduced latitude or reduced elevation. Ecologists have long remarked on this correspondence between latitude and elevation, whereby trees seen on mountaintops are often the same species (or at least the same genera) that can otherwise be found only far to the north. Climates that are highly seasonal, with hot summers and cold winters, are called continental because they are most commonly found in the interior of the continent; climates with cool summers and mild winters are called maritime, because they occur in areas downwind of oceans.

Some geographies have distinctive climate types. The climate in much of California, with its hot, dry summers and cool, damp winters, is called Mediterranean. Conversely, the perennially damp forests of the Pacific Northwest coast from northern California to southeastern Alaska are called temperate rain forests. Eastward from the Cascade–Sierra Nevada crest to the Great Plains, most western forests have low to moderate rainfall and strong temperature contrasts between summer and winter. Rainfall in this region may come from the northwest (primarily in winter), the southeast (primarily in summer), or the southwest (primarily from midsummer to mid-autumn). In the subarctic (from central Alberta north to the Arctic tree-line), precipitation occurs throughout the year, but cold and darkness cause the trees to enter dormancy from October to April, so the forests primarily benefit from spring and summer moisture and warmth.

Topography also affects the distribution of trees. In North America, mountain slopes facing south are warmer and drier than adjacent north-facing slopes, and the vegetation reflects this. Trees reach the limits of their tolerance to cold at timberline or treeline in the high mountains and in the far north, and in such severe environments they are often reduced in size, sometimes appearing stunted or as shrubs. The distribution of trees is also related to water availability. Wetland vegetation occurs where there is much water; the plants are shallowly rooted or have special adaptations to deal with saturated soils. Mesic vegetation occurs where plants are seldom limited by insufficient water, usually due to both ample rainfall and adequate soil water. Xeric (dry) forests and woodlands occur in semiarid climates or in places where the soil retains moisture poorly. Riparian forests or woodlands occur on the margins of water bodies, or sometimes along seasonal streams.

Chemistry of the soil is also important. Acid soils, often derived from igneous rock, may have different associations of trees than do basic soils, which are often derived from sedimentary dolomite, limestone, or ancient coral reefs, all high in carbonates. Habitats with basic soils are often referred to as "calcareous" in our descriptions. Some areas have rock types rich in heavy metals, such as serpentine, which is so nutrient-poor and chemically different from "normal" soils that very few plants can grow upon it.

■ LEAF KEYS

The two keys that follow are designed to help the user with leaf in hand locate a species match inside the book. The Key to the Gymnosperms by Leaf Type shows a representative leaf or twig for each type of gymnosperm likely to be encountered growing naturally in western North America. The Key to Selected Angiosperm Trees by Leaf Shape includes an array of angiosperm leaves grouped by leaf type, shape, proportions, arrangement on the twig, and details of the leaf margin. Each leaf shown represents its species, which is named in the caption, or its genus or occasionally a larger group of related species. Flip to the page noted, and compare your leaf in hand to the representative species and to its fellow genus and family members. The keys are not drawn to scale: Leaves that are very small may be adjacent to leaves that are very large; instead the keys emphasize length/width proportions, margins, lobing, and, in compound leaves, the nature of the leaflets.

KEY TO THE GYMNOSPERMS BY LEAF TYPE

LEAVES BROAD,   **LEAVES SCALELIKE**
FAN-SHAPED   **Irregularly Branching Twigs**

Ginkgo, p. 27   Junipers, pp. 40–48

Long, Ropy Twigs

sun foliage

Cypresses, pp. 32–38   Coast Redwood, p. 52   Giant Sequoia, p. 52   Norfolk Island Pine, p. 28

Twigs Forming Fans or Flattish Sprays

MacNab Cypress, p. 36   Alaska Yellow Cedar, p. 36   Incense Cedar, p. 30   Port Orford Cedar, p. 31   Western Redcedar, p. 50

LEAVES NEEDLELIKE
Needles 2-ranked, Falling with Branchlet   **Needles 2-ranked, Falling Singly**

deciduous   shade foliage

Ahuehuete, p. 50   Coast Redwood, p. 52   Bunya Pine, p. 28   Pacific Yew, p. 110   California Nutmeg, p. 110

Needles Solitary, Spirally Inserted

shade foliage

Firs, pp. 56–64   Western Hemlock, p. 108   Monkey-puzzle Tree, p. 28   Firs, pp. 56–64   Spruces, pp. 70–76

 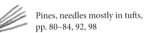

Douglas-firs, p. 106   Mountain Hemlock, p. 108   Cedars, pp. 65–66 evergreen   Tamarack and larches, pp. 66–68 deciduous

Needles in Clusters or Bundles

Bundles of 5

 Pines, needles in bottlebrush-like arrangement, pp. 78–80

 Pines, needles mostly in tufts, pp. 80–84, 92, 98

Bundles of 4   *Bundles of 3*   *Bundles of 2*   *1 Needle per Bundle*

Parry Piñon, p. 92

Pines, pp. 86, 90–98, 105   Pines, pp. 86, 88, 100–105   Singleleaf Piñon, p. 88

KEY TO SELECTED ANGIOSPERM TREES BY LEAF SHAPE
MISCELLANEOUS LEAVES
Leaves Absent or Obscure
Cacti

Other Leafless Trees

Engelmann
Pricklypear, p. 194

Saguaro, p. 182

Blue Palo
Verde, p. 240

Crucifixion Thorn
(*Canotia holacantha*),
p. 204

Spiny Allthorn,
p. 334

Crucifixion Thorn
(*Castela emoryi*),
p. 516

Leaves Scalelike

Leaves Strap-shaped or Daggerlike

Smoketree, p. 272

Five-stamen Tamarisk, p. 524

Joshua Tree, p. 122

Bigelow Beargrass, p. 120

Common Sotol, p. 119

SIMPLE LEAVES, MARGINS ENTIRE
Leaves Whorled

Leaves Opposite

Common Buttonbush,
p. 454

Berlandier Fiddlewood,
p. 534

Pomegranate, p. 386

Pacific Dogwood, p. 208

Ashy Silktassel, p. 322

Leaves Alternate
Narrow

Northern Catalpa, p. 174

Chamise, p. 403

Pygmy-cedar, p. 156

Desert Willow, p. 174

River Red Gum, p. 355

Parish's Goldenbush,
p. 154

Russian Olive, p. 213

Silverleaf Oak, p. 286

Blackwood
Acacia,
p. 246

California Bay, p. 338

Curlleaf Mountain
Mahogany,
p. 408

Victorian Box,
p. 380

Giant Golden
Chinquapin,
p. 276

Pacific Rhododendron,
p. 224

Emory Oak, p. 282

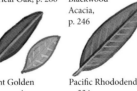

Bebb Willow, p. 498

Gum Bully, p. 514

Osage Orange, p. 348

Leaves Alternate (cont.)
Medium

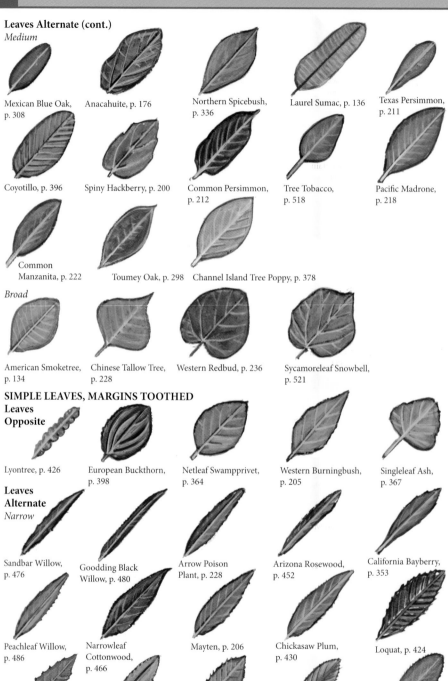

Mexican Blue Oak, p. 308

Anacahuite, p. 176

Northern Spicebush, p. 336

Laurel Sumac, p. 136

Texas Persimmon, p. 211

Coyotillo, p. 396

Spiny Hackberry, p. 200

Common Persimmon, p. 212

Tree Tobacco, p. 518

Pacific Madrone, p. 218

Common Manzanita, p. 222

Toumey Oak, p. 298

Channel Island Tree Poppy, p. 378

Broad

American Smoketree, p. 134

Chinese Tallow Tree, p. 228

Western Redbud, p. 236

Sycamoreleaf Snowbell, p. 521

SIMPLE LEAVES, MARGINS TOOTHED
Leaves Opposite

Lyontree, p. 426

European Buckthorn, p. 398

Netleaf Swampprivet, p. 364

Western Burningbush, p. 205

Singleleaf Ash, p. 367

Leaves Alternate
Narrow

Sandbar Willow, p. 476

Goodding Black Willow, p. 480

Arrow Poison Plant, p. 228

Arizona Rosewood, p. 452

California Bayberry, p. 353

Peachleaf Willow, p. 486

Narrowleaf Cottonwood, p. 466

Mayten, p. 206

Chickasaw Plum, p. 430

Loquat, p. 424

Tanbark Oak, p. 278

Mousehole Tree, p. 352

Toyon, p. 424

American Plum, p. 430

Summer Holly, p. 224

Leaves Alternate (cont.)
Medium

English Holly, p. 150

Cascara Buckthorn, p. 396

Black Cherry, p. 442

Birchleaf Buckthorn, p. 394

Pacific Madrone, p. 218

Western Crab Apple, p. 428

Alderleaf Mountain Mahogany, p. 408

Lemonade Sumac, p. 140

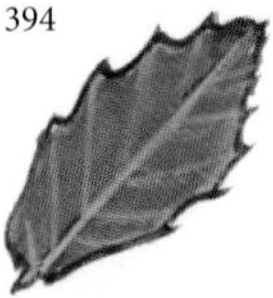

Arizona White Oak, p. 302

Siberian Elm, p. 532

Toumey Oak, p. 298

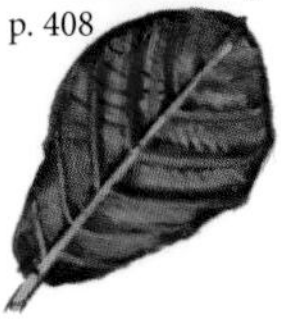

Netleaf Oak, p. 306

Cerro Hawthorn, p. 416

Balsam Poplar, p. 468

Broad

Interior Live Oak, p. 288

Chinquapin Oak, p. 308

Red Mulberry, p. 350

Feltleaf Ceanothus, p. 387

Utah Serviceberry, p. 406

Red Alder, p. 160

Water Birch, p. 164

American Basswood, p. 344

Black Hawthorn, p. 412

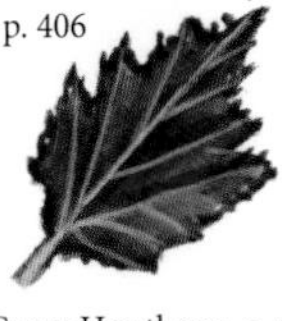

Gregg Hawthorn, p. 422

American Witch-hazel, p. 324

Hollyleaf Cherry, p. 436

Palmer Oak, p. 290

Plains/Rio Grande Cottonwood, p. 468

Fireberry Hawthorn, p. 416

SIMPLE LEAVES, MARGINS LOBED
Leaves Opposite, Palmately Lobed

Bigtooth Maple, p. 504

Bigleaf Maple, p. 504

Vine Maple, p. 501

California Flannelbush, p. 342

White Poplar, p. 465

Red Mulberry, p. 350

Chinese Parasoltree, p. 340

Edible Fig, p. 346

SIMPLE LEAVES, MARGINS LOBED (cont.)
Leaves Alternate, Palmately Lobed

California Sycamore, p. 382

Castor Bean, p. 228

Thurber's Cotton, p. 344

Leaves Alternate, Pinnately Lobed

Giant Tickseed, p. 154

Oneseed Hawthorn, p. 410

California Black Oak, p. 280

California Blue Oak, p. 312

Gambel Oak, p. 316

Post Oak, p. 318

Blackjack Oak, p. 284

Leaves Small, 3-lobed at Tip

Stansbury Cliffrose, p. 446

Sagebrush, p. 153

COMPOUND LEAVES
Leaves Palmlike

Canary Island Date Palm, p. 113

California Fan Palm, p. 116

Common Chastetree, p. 536

Ohio Buckeye, p. 510

Leaves Opposite, Palmately Compound or Trifoliolate

Lyontree, p. 426

Barreta, p. 458

Sierra Bladdernut, p. 520

Leaves Alternate, Palmately Compound or Trifoliolate

African Sumac, p. 148

Berlandier Jopoy, p. 458

Common Hoptree, p. 460

Leaves Opposite, Pinnately Compound

Leatherleaf Ash, p. 368

Lyontree, p. 426

Boxelder, p. 506

Oregon Ash, p. 374

Mountain Torchwood, p. 456

Leaves Alternate, Pinnately Compound
Terminal Leaflet Usually Absent

Blue Elderberry, p. 130

Guayacán, p. 538

Anacacho Orchid-tree, p. 232

Mount Atlas Mastic Tree, p. 136

Carob, p. 236

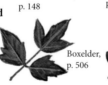

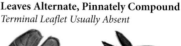

Terminal Leaflet Usually Absent (cont.)

Siberian Pea Tree,
p. 268

Western Soapberry,
p. 512

Black Walnut, p. 332

Terminal Leaflet Usually Present

Smooth Sumac,
p. 140

Littleleaf Sumac,
p. 142

Mexican Buckeye,
p. 510

Lime Pricklyash,
p. 462

Hercules' Club,
p. 460

Mescalbean, p. 268

Greene Mountain
Ash, p. 450

Goldenrain Tree,
p. 512

Ironwood, p. 272

Peppertree, p. 146

Silkoak, p. 385

Black Locust, p. 275

Tree-of-heaven, p. 516

Elephant Tree, p. 179

Leaves Alternate, Bipinnately or Tripinnately Compound

Jerusalem Thorn, p. 238

Foothill Palo Verde,
p. 240

Texas Ebony, p. 252

Catclaw Acacia, p. 262

Honey Mesquite,
p. 258

Jerusalem Thorn,
p. 238

Chinaberry-tree, p. 346

Japanese Angelica
Tree, p. 152

Honey Locust, p. 238

Pride-of-Barbados,
p. 234

Huisache, p. 266

Silktree, p. 250

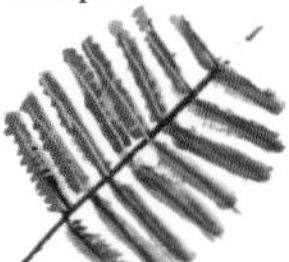

Black Wattle, p. 246

All gymnosperms are woody plants. Their seeds do not develop within a closed ovary, as those of the angiosperms do, but are exposed during fertilization and thereafter, in most cases, develop within a closed vegetative structure. Most gymnosperms contain aromatic resins in their wood, foliage, and reproductive structures. These resins serve several purposes, among them to discourage herbivory and fungal attack. Most species have tough evergreen foliage, simple or pinnate, with linear leaves or with broader leaves that have simple parallel venation.

Gymnosperms includes the conifers, ginkgo, cycads, and gnetophytes. No cycads are native to w. North America, but some are popular ornamental shrubs; the most common is the **Sago Palm** (cycads are often mistaken for palms), *Cycas revoluta*. There are 12 species of gnetophytes native to w. North America; all are shrubs in the genus *Ephedra*, sometimes called **Mormon-tea**, and are most common in the desert Southwest but encountered through most of the arid West. Species of *Ephedra* contain stimulant compounds and have a long history of medicinal use.

■ CONIFERS

The conifers are an ecologically and economically important group of about 650 species worldwide. They are usually classified into six families, of which the largest are the pine, podocarp, and cypress families, each with more than 130 species.

The araucaria, yew, and umbrella pine families are much smaller, totaling about 70 species. Of the families treated in this book, it appears that the pine family evolved first, then the araucarias, umbrella pine, cypresses, and yews.

Conifers are fundamentally distinguished from the flowering plants (all other trees in this book except the Ginkgo) by their reproductive structures, their wood, and their resins. Superficially, they are also generally distinguishable by their cones, growth form, and foliage. Their cones are generally spherical to cylindric, composed of few to many woody scales, but in junipers and the yew family the seeds are within fleshy green or red "berries." The conifer growth form generally features a single erect trunk, often with a uniform branching pattern. Their foliage (and often their wood) is aromatic with resins, is often in the shape of needles, and is usually evergreen (with a few exceptions in the pine and cypress families).

Worldwide, the conifers have great ecological importance, dominating forest landscapes throughout much of the temperate and most of the boreal climate zones. The pine and cypress families are very well represented in w. North America, where we also have 2 native yews. Most conifers are found in the mountains, but an immense woodland of junipers and scrubby pine (often called the piñon–juniper woodland) covers semiarid valleys and plains from Alta. south into Mexico, and locally, conifers are also an important component of wetland and riparian ecosystems.

Sago Palm

Mormon-tea

twig

GINKGOACEAE: GINKGO FAMILY

This family includes a single species, which now survives in the wild in only a small area in China. Ginkgo is a common ornamental in North America.

GINKGO *Ginkgo biloba* L.
A.K.A. MAIDENHAIR TREE

QUICK ID The fan-shaped leaves are unlike those of any other tree. The woody stubs covering the branches identify it in the winter.

Dioecious, deciduous tree, up to 30 m tall and usually with a single straight trunk to 1 m diam.; crown rounded or irregular. **BARK** Gray, with short, irregular furrows. **TWIG** Gray, bearing stubby, short woody shoots protruding up to 1 cm from the branch at regular intervals, each bearing a cluster of leaves and often a pollen cone or seed. **LEAF** Slightly leathery, fan-shaped, with a pattern of radiating veins (not seen in any other tree); blade 5–10 cm across, light green, turning golden and falling each winter. **POLLEN CONE** Borne on short shoots (woody stubs along the branch), catkin-like. **SEED** Naked, usually only 1 developing from a pair of ovules situated at the tip of a slender stalk borne on short shoots, appearing plum-like, ellipsoid, yellow to orange, about 2.5 cm long, the outer coating softening and giving off a foul odor when ripe.

HABITAT/RANGE Introduced. Native to China. A common ornamental in temperate climates.

Notes Millions of years ago members of the ginkgo family were common around the world, but they now occur in the wild only in sw. China. The name, meaning "silver seed," is of Chinese derivation. Various tissues of the plant are toxic, or are used medicinally, primarily in naturopathic and Chinese traditional medicine. Apart from being attractive landscape trees in general, Ginkgos are very resistant to air pollution, and are commonly planted in cities. Female plants are undesirable, owing to the unpleasant odor given off by the ripe seeds.

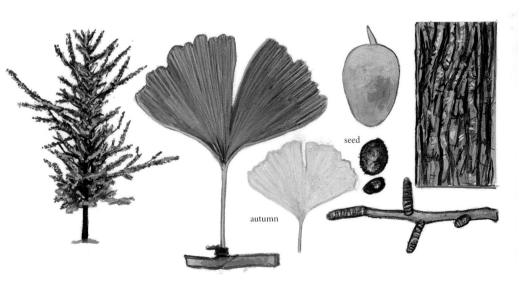

seed

autumn

Ginkgo

ARAUCARIACEAE: ARAUCARIA FAMILY

The Araucariaceae includes 3 genera and 40 species native to Southeast Asia, Australia, Oceania, and South America. Several species are ornamentals in North America.

■ *ARAUCARIA*: ARAUCARIAS

Araucaria, the principal genus of trees in the araucaria family, is native to the Southern Hemisphere and includes 19 species. These are tall trees with stiff branches emerging at nearly right angles from the stem, cloaked in a dense sheath of needle-shaped to triangular leaves. The 4 most common species in w. North America all have a single straight trunk covered in uniform whorls of branches arrayed perpendicular to the trunk, and can often reach 20 m tall and 60 cm diam. **BARK** Rough, dark gray, horizontally ridged. **LEAF** Evergreen, multi-veined, spirally arranged on twigs, branches, and even the trunk. **POLLEN CONE** The largest of any conifer. **SEED CONE** Dense and heavy, disintegrating before or soon after falling. The seeds are edible and very tasty, widely eaten within these species' native ranges.

   None of the species introduced in the West occurs in areas with temperatures colder than about –15° C and except in s. Calif. and the Central Valley, they are generally found only in coastal areas; only the Monkey-puzzle Tree extends north of Calif., into lower B.C. Araucarias are not known to have naturalized in the U.S., but the 4 species named here are popular ornamentals within their range.

BUNYA PINE *Araucaria bidwillii* Hook.

LEAF Flat, 2-ranked, spirally inserted on the branch, about 5 cm long, less than 1 cm wide at the base, stiff, with a sharp point. **CONES** Pollen cone 10–20 cm long; seed cone up to 30 cm long, weighing up to 5 kg.

MONKEY-PUZZLE TREE *Araucaria araucana* (Molina) K. Koch

LEAF Flat, triangular, spirally inserted on the branch, 3–5 cm long, 8–25 mm wide at the base, stiff, with a sharp point. **CONES** Pollen cone 10–20 cm long; seed cone up to 20 cm long.

COOK PINE *Araucaria columnaris* (J.R. Forst.) Hook.

LEAF Needlelike, blunt, 4–7 mm long, curved toward the branch, covering it on all surfaces. **CONES** Pollen cone 5–10 cm long; seed cone to 15 cm long.

NORFOLK ISLAND PINE *Araucaria heterophylla* (Salisb.) Franco

LEAF Scalelike, blunt, 4–7 mm long, curved toward the branch, covering it on all surfaces. **CONES** Pollen cone 3.5–5 cm long; seed cone up to 15 cm long.

Bunya
Pine

seed

leaves

cone

cone scale

Monkey-
puzzle
Tree

leaf

leaves

cone

seed

cone
scale

cone scale

seed

leaves

Cook Pine

cone

cone
scale

seed

Norfolk
Island
Pine

young
leaves

cone

cone

CUPRESSACEAE: CYPRESS FAMILY

The cypress family includes about 140 species divided into 28 genera, scattered across all continents except Antarctica, but most abundant and diverse in China and w. North America, where we have 8 native genera with 32 species. They occupy a great diversity of ecological conditions, but most can be recognized by the fibrous bark that peels off in long, thin strips, the small, usually round cones, and a fragrant, very rot-resistant wood. Many species in the family are widely planted as ornamental trees and shrubs.

Cypresses are trees or shrubs, monoecious or dioecious, deciduous or evergreen. **BARK** Usually reddish, brown, or gray, fibrous, often peeling in long strips but sometimes flaky. **LEAF** Generally of 2 types: simple scalelike leaves that cover the twig; or needlelike leaves that may either cover the twig, or be flattened, 2-ranked, and pinnately arranged. In all of our species only 1 type of leaf is predominant on mature trees. The twigs are shed, usually after 1–5 years, along with their attached leaves. **SEED CONE** Small and woody in most species, but the junipers produce small round, more or less fleshy cones with cone scales fused at maturity, the structure resembling a berry.

Many of the largest and oldest trees in the world belong to this family and live in w. North America. The **Umbrella Pine** (*Sciadopitys verticillata* [Thunb.] Siebold & Zucc.) was formerly assigned to the cypress family but is now the sole species in its own family, Sciadopityaceae. It is native to Japan but is planted as an ornamental in North America. It is usually seen as a small tree with soft, fibrous bark and fleshy, pliable needlelike leaves, 6–13 cm long, borne in whorls of 10–30 at nodes along the twig.

INCENSE CEDAR *Calocedrus decurrens* (Torr.) Florin
A.K.A. CALIFORNIA CEDAR, CEDRO DE INCIENSO

QUICK ID A large cypress with foliage held in vertical, planar sprays.

Tree, to 50 m tall, usually single-stemmed, to 1.5 m diam., often with a fluted trunk and a narrow, columnar crown. **BARK** Fibrous, red-brown to pale brown, becoming thick and fissured with age, often bearing char from past fires. **TWIG** Flattened, densely branched, arrayed in vertically oriented planar sprays. **LEAF** Scalelike, aromatic, shiny green, opposite in 4 ranks, 3–14 mm long, overlapping, with an acute (often long, slender) tip. **SEED CONE** Bilaterally symmetric, pale green, ripening reddish to golden brown, 14–25 mm long, oblong, comprised of 3 pairs of woody scales, the basal pair often reflexed. Up to 4 seeds per cone, in pairs, each with 2 unequal wings.

HABITAT/RANGE Native. Areas with dry summers and moist, snowy winters, usually in mixed conifer forests, often in much drier sites than other western "cedars," though growing best in riparian areas, 50–2,960 m; Ore. (south from Mount Hood), Nev. (Lake Tahoe area), and Calif. (widespread), extending into n. Baja California.

Notes Though the old-growth forests have been depleted, this remains an economically significant species because of its rapid growth and stable, aromatic, rot-resistant wood. The predominate

INCENSE CEDAR   PORT ORFORD CEDAR

open cone

seed

Incense Cedar

open cone seed

Umbrella
Pine

cone

Port Orford
Cedar

"cedar" throughout the Sierra Nevada, it is also a popular ornamental species from Calif. to B.C., widely planted in parks and gardens. The largest trees (heights to 69 m, trunk diam. to 450 cm) are found in montane and subalpine basins of the Klamath Mountains and Siskiyou Mountains.

PORT ORFORD CEDAR *Chamaecyparis lawsoniana* (A. Murray) Parl.
A.K.A. LAWSON CYPRESS

QUICK ID A large cedar of mixed conifer forest, bearing foliage in drooping, pinnate sprays with small round cones.

Tree, to 50 m tall, trunk to 2 m diam. **BARK** Furrowed, fibrous, reddish brown, turning gray and thickening with age, up to 20 cm thick on very old trees. **TWIG** Sprays predominantly pinnate. **LEAF** Scalelike, mostly 2–3 mm long, in alternate pairs, tip acute to acuminate, usually with an active gland. **SEED CONE** Round, 8–12 mm diam., purplish to reddish brown, not very resinous, composed of 8–10 woody scales. Seeds 2–4 per scale, each seed 2–5 mm diam., the wing about as wide as the body.

HABITAT/RANGE Native. Areas with a cool Mediterranean-type climate with summer fog, in mostly sandy and clay loam soils and rocky ridges, but also on serpentine (an extremely nutrient-poor soil rich in metals like manganese and chromium); usually in mixed stands with other conifers such as Incense Cedar, Douglas Fir, and White Fir; from Coos Bay in sw. Ore. to the Klamath River in nw. Calif. near the coast, and locally to 1,700 m in the Siskiyou Mountains and Mount Shasta area.

SIMILAR SPECIES Western Redcedar (*Thuja plicata*) bears a close resemblance, but has elongate cones comprised of several separating scales.

Notes Although this was formerly one of our largest native cypresses (stumps over 6 m across have been found), virtually all of the old-growth stands were logged during the 20th century. The few remaining stands, located in preserves, have suffered extensive mortality through infection by the introduced pathogen *Phytophthora*, varieties of which pose a serious threat to many of our native trees.

■ *CUPRESSUS*: CYPRESSES

The cypress (*ciprés* in Spanish, *cyprès* in French) genus contains 25 species occurring in temperate and subtropical regions of the Northern Hemisphere. In w. North America 1 species extends from Calif. to B.C. in temperate rain forest and subalpine areas. The other 10 species, found in lower Ariz., Calif., and s. Ore., are mostly in mountains or canyons, in areas with a semiarid or Mediterranean climate. Cypresses strongly resemble junipers, apart from the woody cones that, before opening, resemble a small soccer ball.

Our species are monoecious evergreen trees or large shrubs. **BARK** Fibrous or scaly. **TWIG** Round or 4-sided, spreading or in flattened sprays. **LEAF** Scalelike, bright green or glaucous, usually with a gland. **SEED CONE** Round or oblong, 8–40 mm diam., composed of 3–6 opposite pairs of thick woody scales, expanded and flattened at the tip. Seeds are 5–20 per scale, each with 2 narrow wings.

Most of our species look very similar and are most easily distinguished by their disjunct ranges and habitats. The **Mediterranean Cypress** (*C. sempervirens* L.) is a popular ornamental. It has smooth or furrowed bark and large seed cones, 25–40 mm diam. Many cultivars exist, among them the columnar Italian Cypress.

ARIZONA CYPRESS *Cupressus arizonica* Greene
A.K.A. ROUGHBARK CYPRESS, CIPRÉS DE ARIZONA

QUICK ID A southwestern cypress with leaves that lack conspicuous resin glands and cone scales bearing prominent central points.

Tree, up to 23 m tall, trunk over 1 m diam., with a conical to irregular crown. **BARK** Fibrous, smooth, becoming furrowed. **TWIG** Short, thick, 4-sided, spreading in all directions. **LEAF** Scalelike, 2 mm long, acuminate, sharp to the touch, with inconspicuous resin glands. **SEED CONE** Sessile or borne on a peduncle to 10 mm long, round, 2–3 cm diam., the scales with prominent central points.

HABITAT/RANGE Native. Semiarid woodlands and canyon riparian areas, often with Twoneedle Piñon or Alligator Juniper, 750–2,000 m; Mexico, and from Big Bend, Tex., to the Santa Catalina Mountains of s. Ariz.

SIMILAR SPECIES The closely related **Smooth Cypress** (*C. glabra* Sudw.) is distinguished from Arizona Cypress by its flaky reddish bark and leaves bearing prominent resin glands often marked by white drops of dried resin. It is found in similar habitat in Ariz. to the northwest of Arizona Cypress's range.

Notes Arizona Cypress can grow very large, up to 200 cm diam., in canyon riparian areas.

BAKER CYPRESS *Cupressus bakeri* Jeps.
A.K.A. MODOC CYPRESS

QUICK ID A large forest cypress with cones covered by resinous blisters; the only native cypress in its range.

Tree, to 30 m tall, usually with a single trunk, to 60 cm diam., and sparse, narrow crown. **BARK** Smooth at first, later building up in exfoliating layers. **TWIG** Branching at about a 45-degree angle, drooping slightly, 0.5–1.1 mm diam. **LEAF** Scalelike, initially 2 mm long, continuing to grow to as long as 10 mm, each with a conspicuous gland that produces drops of resin. **SEED CONE** Borne on a peduncle 10–25 mm long, round, 1–2 cm diam., silvery, the scales usually covered with resin blisters, each scale often with a prominent conical central point.

HABITAT/RANGE Native. Mixed evergreen forests, primarily growing in highly disjunct, isolated groves, 1,065–2,100 m; Plumas County, Calif., to Josephine County, Ore.

SIMILAR SPECIES MacNab Cypress, also found in n. Calif., has flattened sprays of foliage.

ARIZONA CYPRESS

BAKER CYPRESS

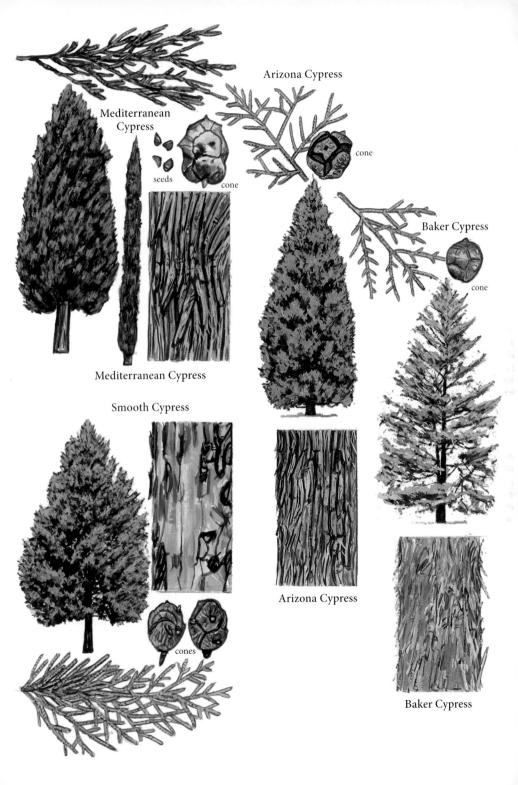

Arizona Cypress

Mediterranean Cypress

seeds

cone

cone

Baker Cypress

cone

Mediterranean Cypress

Smooth Cypress

Arizona Cypress

cones

Baker Cypress

TECATE CYPRESS *Cupressus forbesii* Jeps.

A.K.A. FORBES CYPRESS, CIPRÉS NEGRO

QUICK ID An often shrubby cypress that usually grows in chaparral and has patches of smooth, red bark.

Tree, to 10 m tall, often shrubby, with an open, rounded crown. **BARK** Fibrous, peeling off to leave a smooth, clear, light to dark red surface. **TWIG** Four-sided, 1–1.5 mm diam. **LEAF** Scalelike, 1.2 mm long, pointed, rounded or ridged on the back, light, rich green, with a usually inactive resin gland. **SEED CONE** Sessile or on a short peduncle, round, 2.5–3.5 cm diam., scales flat or with a low central hump, typically serotinous, sometimes becoming embedded in the growing branch.

HABITAT/RANGE Native. Chaparral, at 450–1,000 m; Orange County and San Diego County, Calif., and adjacent border country in Mexico.

Notes Many stands of this rare tree were ravaged by fire in the early 2000s, and it may need protection if it is to survive continued disturbance and habitat change. As with many other Calif. cypresses, Tecate Cypress both relies on fire for successful regeneration and is threatened by the destruction associated with severe fire. By disrupting the natural fire regime, humans threaten the species.

GOWEN CYPRESS *Cupressus goveniana* Gordon

QUICK ID A small-coned cypress of coastal Calif.; the only cypress in its very limited range.

Shrub or small tree, usually to 10 m tall but extremely variable in size and shape (cones have been found on trees from 0.2 m to 50 m tall). **BARK** Smooth or rough, fibrous. **TWIG** Four-sided, 1–1.5 mm diam., 8–30 mm long. **LEAF** Scalelike, light green, 1–2 mm long, pointed, closely appressed, gland inconspicuous or absent. **SEED CONE** Borne on a peduncle to

10 mm long, round, 1–2.5 cm diam., gray-brown, scales nearly flat at maturity.

HABITAT/RANGE Native. Within Monterey Pine and Knobcone Pine forests, especially on poor soils, 60–800 m, in a few small, isolated groves in Santa Cruz County and San Mateo County, coastal Calif.

Notes The very rare Santa Cruz Cypress (var. *abramsiana* [C.B. Wolf] Little) has smaller cones (13–20 mm long) than the typical variety. It is the only cypress that is federally protected as an endangered species.

MONTEREY CYPRESS *Cupressus macrocarpa* Hartw. ex Gordon

QUICK ID A large coastal cypress with a spreading, flattened crown.

Tree, usually to 20 m tall, often with multiple trunks, to 70 cm diam., and a sparse, broadly spreading crown. **BARK** Rough, fibrous, brown, fading to pale gray, in native habitat often bearing lichens or a conspicuous red algae. **TWIG** 8–15 mm long, 1.5–2 mm diam., spreading in all directions. **LEAF** Scalelike, bright green, 2 mm long, tightly appressed to the twig, some with an inconspicuous gland that appears as a small dark spot. **SEED CONE** Sessile or on a short peduncle, oblong, 2.5–4 cm long, green, maturing to gray-brown, the scales nearly flat at maturity.

HABITAT/RANGE Native. In 2 groves, where it grows alone (often just beyond the reach of the salt spray) or with Monterey Pine, in coastal sage scrub habitat, to 100 m, at Cypress Point and Point Lobos, Calif., near Monterey. A very popular ornamental on the West Coast north to Wash. and in other areas with moderate humidity and mild winters.

Notes The cones are often serotinous and may be opened by fire or sometimes by the heat on summer days. Due to fire suppression, young trees are rare, and conservation management is required if this species is to survive much longer in its native habitat.

Tecate Cypress

open cone

Gowan Cypress

cone

Monterey Cypress

closed cone

windswept tree

open cone

seedling

seed

LEYLAND CYPRESS *Cupressus ×*
leylandii A.B. Jacks. & Dallim.

Usually a tree. **BARK** Fibrous, gray. **TWIG** Flattened, forming flattened sprays. **LEAF** Scalelike, 1.5–2.5 mm long, lacking conspicuous glands; underside waxy, with white X-shaped marks of stomata. **SEED CONE** Many cultivars are sterile; seed cones, when present, are globose, 1.5–2 cm diam., slightly waxy, composed of 4 pairs of woody scales. *Notes* This plant, which arose in cultivation as a hybrid of Alaska Yellow Cedar (*C. nootkatensis* D. Don) and Monterey Cypress (*C. macrocarpa* Hartw.), is one of the most popular and diverse ornamental conifers, with dozens of named cultivars. There is great variability in its size and appearance.

MACNAB CYPRESS *Cupressus*
macnabiana A. Murray
A.K.A. SHASTA CYPRESS

QUICK ID A cypress of chaparral and woodland habitats that bears its foliage in flattened sprays.

Tree, to 12 m tall, trunk 40 cm diam., with a dense, broadly conical crown. **BARK** Rough, furrowed, fibrous. **TWIG** 3–10 mm long, 0.5–1 mm diam., borne in flattened, comblike sprays of 8–10 twigs. **LEAF** Scalelike, 1.5–10 mm long, not tightly appressed to the twig, with a conspicuous gland that produces drops of resin. **SEED CONE** Sessile or on a short peduncle, round, 1.5–2.5 cm diam., brown or gray, scales with prominent conical central points.

HABITAT/RANGE Native. Chaparral and foothill woodland, often on serpentine-derived soils, 300–850 m; Calif.

Notes In some places this species hybridizes with Sargent Cypress. Their offspring are the only known natural hybrids between cypress species.

ALASKA YELLOW CEDAR *Cupressus*
nootkatensis D. Don
A.K.A. NOOTKA CYPRESS

QUICK ID A large temperate rain-forest cypress with drooping fans of foliage, ash-gray bark, and small cones.

Tree, to 40 m or dwarfed at high elevations; trunk to 2 m diam.; usually with a single trunk and an open, columnar crown. **BARK** Initially smooth and reddish brown, becoming fissured and ash gray. **TWIG** In drooping pinnate sprays 15–30 cm long. **LEAF** Scalelike, usually overlapping, 1.5–2.5 mm long, stout, tip rounded to acuminate, glands usually absent (circular when present). **SEED CONE** Sessile or borne on short peduncles, round, 8–12 mm diam., dark reddish brown, composed of 4–6 woody scales. Seeds 2–4 per scale, 2–5 mm long, wing equal to or broader than body.

HABITAT/RANGE Native. Usually found on moderately wet sites such as avalanche chutes, snowy timberlines, and bog–forest transition areas; usually in mixed conifer forests (often with Mountain Hemlock), but occasionally in pure stands, 0–2,100 m (sea-level in Alaska, subalpine in Ore. and Calif.); Pacific Coast from s. Alaska to extreme nw. Calif., in areas experiencing damp winters with heavy snowfall; locally found farther inland, with disjunct inland populations in B.C. and Ore.

Notes This species was long thought to be related to the Port Orford Cedar (*Chamaecyparis lawsoniana*) and was placed with it in the genus *Chamaecyparis*, but molecular DNA analysis has shown that it is indeed a true New World cypress. The severely drooping foliage sprays shed snow very easily. This was a very valuable timber tree, but now that almost all old-growth stands have been either logged or protected, its primary significance is ecological, as a locally important forest-dominant species.

MACNAB CYPRESS

ALASKA YELLOW CEDAR

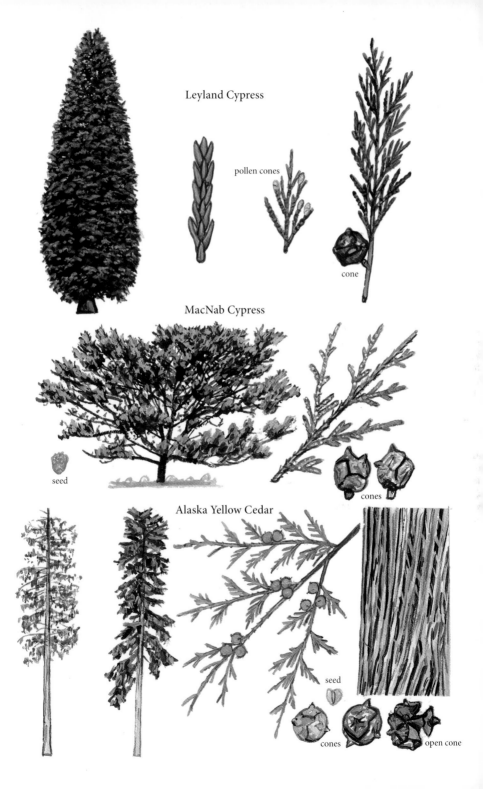

Leyland Cypress

pollen cones

cone

MacNab Cypress

seed

cones

Alaska Yellow Cedar

seed

cones

open cone

PIUTE CYPRESS *Cupressus nevadensis*
Abrams

QUICK ID A small cypress that grows in chaparral and has leaves bearing a conspicuous resin gland.

Tree, to 10 m tall, with a straight trunk, to 60–80 cm diam., and pyramidal crown. **BARK** Red-brown, exfoliating, becoming fibrous. **TWIG** About 20 mm long, 1–1.5 mm diam., 4-sided. **LEAF** Scalelike, glaucous, 2 mm long, pointed, with a conspicuous resin gland. **SEED CONE** Ovoid to globose, 2–3 cm long, borne on a peduncle 10–15 mm long, usually in aggregations of 15–25 cones, remaining closed for several years.

HABITAT/RANGE Native. Sparse desert woodland, at 1,200–1,800 m., with California Juniper, Gray Pine, and Singleleaf Piñon; found only in Kern County, Calif.

Notes The largest stand of this rare tree is preserved as a natural area on the north side of Bald Eagle Peak in the Piute Mountains.

SARGENT CYPRESS *Cupressus sargentii*
Jeps.

QUICK ID The only native cypress in most of its range; in the Clear Lake area, MacNab Cypress differs in having flattened sprays of foliage.

Shrub or small tree, to 10 m tall, trunk to 30 cm diam. **BARK** Rough, furrowed, fibrous. **TWIG** 2–2.5 mm diam., up to 10 mm long, 4-sided or round. **LEAF** Scalelike, dull green to glaucous, blunt, 2 mm long, usually with an inconspicuous gland. **SEED CONE** Borne on a peduncle to 10 mm long, round, 2–2.5 cm diam., brown or gray, scales with scattered resin blisters and a variably sized central point.

HABITAT/RANGE Native. Chaparral, pine–oak woodland, and lower montane forests, often on serpentine-derived soils, 200–1,100 m; Coast Ranges from Mendocino County south to Santa Barbara County, Calif. These sites have a Mediterranean (maritime, winter-wet) climate with about 60 cm annual precipitation.

Notes Like most Calif. cypresses, the Sargent Cypress has serotinous cones that can be opened by the heat of a fire. Such a blaze usually kills the tree, but the abundant seed crop then regenerates the forest.

CUYAMACA CYPRESS *Cupressus stephensonii* C.B. Wolf

QUICK ID The only cypress occurring within its very limited range.

Tree, to 16 m tall, with a straight central trunk, to 70 cm diam. **BARK** Thin, cherry red, smooth, exfoliating. **TWIG** 10 mm long, 1.5–2 mm diam., 4-sided. **LEAF** Scalelike, continuing to grow for several years, ultimately 4 mm by 10 mm with a free tip 2–3 mm long, pointed, with a resin gland at the base of the free tip. **SEED CONE** Sessile or borne on short peduncles, 20–30 mm diam., scales with a tall conical central point 3–4 mm tall; often serotinous.

HABITAT/RANGE Native. In small riparian groves amid chaparral, at approximately 1,500 m; only on the southwestern side of Cuyamaca Peak, San Diego County, Calif.

Notes The only known stands of this rare tree were heavily burned in 2003, and now only a few mature trees survive. It may require protection in order to assure its continued survival in its native habitat.

PIUTE CYPRESS   SARGENT CYPRESS

Piute Cypress

cones

glands

Sargent Cypress

cone

Cuyamaca Cypress

closed cone

open cone

■ *JUNIPERUS*: JUNIPERS

Worldwide, the juniper (*enebro* or *táscate* in Spanish, *genévrier* in French) genus includes about 50 species of trees and shrubs that dominate vast areas of semiarid woodland in Europe, Asia, Africa, and North America. They have the widest elevation range of any conifer genus, occurring from sea-level to over 4,800 m (in the Himalayas). Fifteen species are native to w. North America in highly varied habitats.

Monoecious or dioecious, evergreen shrubs and trees, varying from less than 1 m tall to 30 m tall and 250 cm diam. **BARK** Fibrous, gray to red. **TWIG** 0.6 to 2.5 mm diam., erect to drooping, bearing leaves in alternating pairs or whorls of 3. **LEAF** Most seedlings bear sharp needles up to 10 mm long, jutting out from the twig. All of our species except Common Juniper, when they grow to sapling size lose most or all of their needle leaves and grow leaves shaped like small scales, 1–3 mm long and about as wide, that cover the twig. Important characteristics of these scale leaves include their size relative to twig thickness, whether or not they overlap, the presence of a visible gland or a keel on the leaf, and whether it produces a resinous secretion. **SEED CONE** Resembles a small, hard berry, up to 10 mm diam., usually green when immature and from light blue to reddish or black, sometimes with a glaucous bloom, when mature, containing 1–3 seeds. Seeds mature in 3–18 months.

Because they come wrapped in a berrylike cone, the seeds of junipers are distributed across the landscape by birds, instead of by the wind, as in all other trees of the cypress family. Two western junipers, **Common Juniper** (*Juniperus communis* L.) and Creeping Juniper (*J. horizontalis* Moench), grow as low, mat-forming shrubs, seldom more than 1 m tall. Common Juniper is widespread in mountains and has only needlelike leaves. Creeping Juniper occurs in mountains and woodlands of the Rockies north from Wyo. and in boreal w. Canada, and has scalelike leaves.

MOUNTAIN CEDAR *Juniperus ashei* J. Buchholz
A.K.A. ASHE JUNIPER, ENEBRO DE MONTE

QUICK ID A juniper of c. Tex. with large, dark blue seed cones, and a raised gland on the needlelike leaves.

Dioecious shrub or small tree to 15 m tall, usually with a single short trunk, 30–50 cm diam., and an open, rounded or irregular crown. **BARK** Pink, turning gray and flaky, later brown and fibrous, finally turning gray and peeling in thin strips. **TWIG** Stiff, 1–1.3 mm diam. **LEAF** Mostly scalelike, but some needlelike. Scalelike leaves in alternating pairs, keeled, with 2 bands of stomata. Needlelike leaves bear a raised gland that resembles a small pimple, without visible resin. **SEED CONE** 6–10 mm diam., pink, maturing dark blue, usually glaucous, resinous, with 1 or 2 seeds.

HABITAT/RANGE Native. Open woodland with various types of oak and occasionally piñon pine, 150–1,550 m; primarily in Tex. hill country, with small populations in Mo., Ark., Okla., and nw. Mexico.

Notes Some authorities recognize 2 varieties. The cone of var. *ashei*, found in Mo., Ark, Okla., and in Tex. east of the Pecos River, is 9–10 mm diam. and contains 1 seed; var. *ovata* R.P. Adams, which occurs in Coahuila and in Tex. west of the Pecos, has cones mostly 6 mm diam. bearing 2 seeds.

CALIFORNIA JUNIPER *Juniperus californica* Carrière
A.K.A. CALIFORNIA WHITE CEDAR, HUATA, CEDRO

QUICK ID An often shrubby juniper, mainly of California, with mostly 1-seeded cones.

Common Juniper

cone

leaves

cone

MOUNTAIN CEDAR

CALIFORNIA JUNIPER

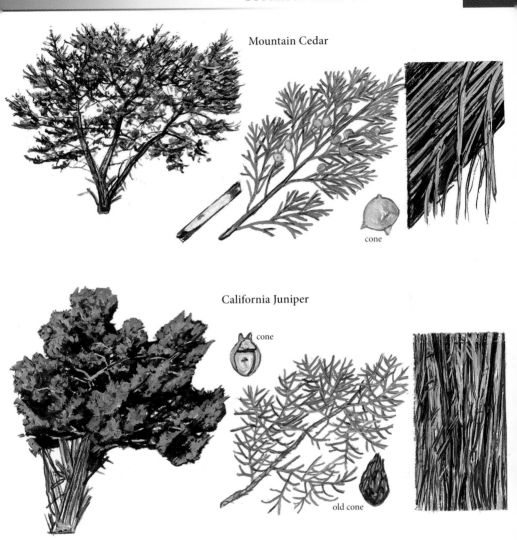

Mountain Cedar

cone

California Juniper

cone

old cone

Dioecious shrub or tree to 8 m tall, trunk to 50 cm diam., usually multistemmed, with a rounded crown. **BARK** At first smooth, brown to gray, later gray and exfoliating in thin strips. **TWIG** Erect, round, about as wide as the length of the scalelike leaves. **LEAF** Primarily scalelike, 1–2 mm long, light green with a conspicuous gland, not or slightly overlapping, closely appressed to the branchlet. **SEED CONE** Matures in 1 year, round, 8–11 mm diam., glaucous, bluish brown, fibrous, mostly with a single seed 5–7 mm long.

HABITAT/RANGE Native. Dry, rocky slopes and flats, 270–1,600 m; Nev., Calif., Ariz.

Notes Often grows with Singleleaf Piñon in woodlands and with Joshua Tree in drier areas; as such, it is the most drought-tolerant juniper in the region. Although it is usually little more than a large shrub, California Juniper is often the largest woody plant on the landscape, providing cover and food for songbirds and small mammals.

ALLIGATOR JUNIPER *Juniperus deppeana* Steud.
A.K.A. MOUNTAIN CEDAR, CEDRO, TÁSCATE

QUICK ID A juniper of oak–pine woodlands with bark broken up into rectangular plates.

Dioecious tree up to 30 m tall, trunk to 2 m diam., usually single-stemmed with a rounded crown. **BARK** Brown, smooth at first, on larger branches and trunk exfoliating in conspicuous rectangular plates. **TWIG** Erect, 3- to 4-sided in cross section, about ⅔ as wide as the length of the scalelike leaves. **LEAF** Scalelike, keeled, 1–2 mm long, not overlapping, tip acute, appressed to the branchlet, sometimes glaucous, bearing a single conspicuous gland. **SEED CONE** Matures in 2 years, of 2 distinct sizes, round, 8–15 mm diam., variably glaucous, reddish brown, fibrous, with 2–7 seeds, each 6–9 mm long.

HABITAT/RANGE Native. Pine forest and pine–oak woodlands, 1,500–2,900 m; Ariz., N.M., and Tex., and south far into Mexico.

Notes The common name comes from the bark, which resembles the skin on an alligator's back and is unlike that of any of our other junipers. This is another juniper that can resprout after it has been cut.

DROOPING JUNIPER *Juniperus flaccida* Schltdl.
A.K.A. CEDRO LISO, TÁSCATE

QUICK ID A juniper with drooping branchlets, found only in the Chisos Mountains of w. Tex.

Dioecious tree or shrub, up to 12 m tall, trunks usually forking 1–2 m above the base, crown globose, comprised of drooping branches and twigs (this is the only juniper in our area to show this character). **BARK** Red-brown to gray, smooth at first, later exfoliating in broad, interlaced fibrous strips. **TWIG** Somewhat droopy, 3- to 4-sided in cross section, ⅔ (or less) as thick as the length of the scalelike leaves. **LEAF** Scalelike, 1.5–2 mm long, overlapping by ⅕–¼ their length, with a conspicuous gland. **SEED CONE** Matures in 1 year, smooth, round, 9–20 mm diam., pale to purplish brown, glaucous, woody, usually with 6–10 seeds, each 5–6 mm long.

HABITAT/RANGE Native. From the Chisos Mountains, Tex., far into Mexico, 1,830–2,440 m.

SIMILAR SPECIES Rocky Mountain Juniper also has drooping twigs, but it occurs in much colder climates and lacks Drooping Juniper's distinctive overall "weeping" growth habit.

Notes The fragrant decay-resistant wood is preferred for fence posts and, historically, mine timbers.

ONESEED JUNIPER *Juniperus monosperma* (Engelm.) Sarg.
A.K.A. CHERRYSTONE JUNIPER, SABINA

QUICK ID An often shrubby juniper of piñon–juniper woodlands with small, mostly 1-seeded cones.

Dioecious shrub or tree, commonly to 7 m tall, 30 cm diam., usually branching near the base; crown round, often flattened. **BARK** Brown to gray, first smooth, later exfoliating in flakes or thin strips. **TWIG** Erect, 4- to 6-sided, about ⅔ as thick as the length of the scalelike leaves. **LEAF** Scalelike, keeled, green to dark green, 1–3 mm long, not overlapping or overlapping by up to ¼ their length, tip acute to acuminate, each leaf with a conspicuous gland. **SEED CONE** Matures in 1 year, round to ovoid, 6–8 mm diam., reddish to brownish blue, glaucous, fleshy and resinous, usually with 1 seed, 4–5 mm long.

HABITAT/RANGE Native. Semi-arid areas, usually on rocky soils, often with Utah Juniper or Rocky Mountain Juniper, 1,000–2,300 m; Ariz., Colo., N.M., Okla., Tex., far into Mexico.

Notes This shrubby and abundant little tree provides habitat for desert wildlife, and was once an important local source of firewood and fence posts.

ALLIGATOR JUNIPER

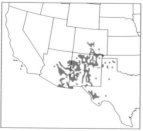

ONESEED JUNIPER

Alligator Juniper

seeds

cone

Drooping Juniper

cone

Oneseed Juniper

cone

REDBERRY JUNIPER *Juniperus coahuilensis* (Martinez) Gaussen ex R.P. Adams
A.K.A. ROSEBERRY JUNIPER, TÁSCATE

QUICK ID A grassland juniper with fleshy glaucous, orange or red cones that resprout after cutting or fire.

Dioecious shrub or tree up to 8 m tall, branched at the base or with a single stem up to 1 m diam.; crown round to irregular. **BARK** Brown to gray, first smooth, on trunk and larger branches exfoliating in long, ragged strips, or occasionally in flakes. **TWIG** Erect, 3- or 4-sided in cross section, about ⅔ as thick as the length of the scalelike leaves. **LEAF** Green to light green, 1–3 mm long, tip acute, not overlapping or overlapping by up to ¼ of their length, with conspicuous glands, at least ¼ of which show a white crystalline exudate. **SEED CONE** Matures in 1 year, round to ovoid, 6–7 mm diam., glaucous, yellow-orange to dark red, fleshy and somewhat sweet, usually with 1 seed, 4–5 mm long.

HABITAT/RANGE Native. On grasslands and nearby rocky slopes, 980–2,200 m; Ariz., N.M., Tex., n. Mexico.

Notes In Arizona it sometimes occurs with Utah Juniper, cacti, or yuccas, but commonly it is the only woody plant in a grassland, which is an unusual setting for a conifer. Its persistence in grasslands may be due to its unusual ability to resprout from cut or fire-killed stumps. Some scientists assign the trees of Ariz. and sw. N.M. to a different species, Arizona Juniper (*Juniperus arizonica* [R.P. Adams] R.P. Adams), which differs in having slightly smaller glands on the needlelike leaves.

WESTERN JUNIPER *Juniperus occidentalis* Hook.
A.K.A. SIERRA JUNIPER

QUICK ID A juniper of mountains or cool temperate deserts that has scalelike leaves with glands that often produce a clear exudate, and oblong blue cones.

Monoecious or dioecious tree, 10–30 m tall, usually with a single trunk up to 2.5 m diam., and thick, spreading branches with the foliage forming dense, rounded tufts at the ends of the branches; crown pyramidal in young trees, becoming irregular with age. **BARK** At first smooth, pink-brown, with age becoming gray and flaky, then fibrous, red-brown to brown, and exfoliating in thin strips. **TWIG** Numerous, stout, 3- or 4-sided in cross section, 1.2–2 mm diam. **LEAF** Primarily scalelike, 2–3 mm long, dark green, with conspicuous oval glands that often show a droplet of exudate; in alternate whorls of 3 or 4, not overlapping. **SEED CONE** Matures in 2 years, initially 2 mm diam. with 4–6 spreading bracts, at maturity glaucous, purple-red to blue or purple, often oblong, 6–10 mm long, 5–8 mm diam., fleshy or pulpy, more or less resinous, falling soon after ripe. Seeds mostly 2 per cone, ovoid, 5–7 mm long, 4–5 mm diam., yellow-brown.

HABITAT/RANGE Native. Widespread in cool temperate semiarid areas, 185–3,050 m, Wash., Ore., Idaho, Nev., Calif.; prevalent in the Sierra Nevada.

Notes There are 2 subspecies: the northern subspecies (subsp. *occidentalis*), which extends south to n. Calif. and nw. Nev.; and the Sierra Juniper (subsp. *australis* Vasek), of the Sierra Nevada, found only in Calif. and extreme w. Nev. The northern subspecies mostly has leaves in whorls of 3 and is variably monoecious or dioecious; the Sierra Juniper has alternating leaves and is mostly dioecious. Western Juniper is one of the longest-living trees in the West, reaching ages of up to 1,600 years in the northern subspecies and up to 2,675 years in the Sierra Juniper. Many thousands of these ancient trees have been destroyed, though, to allow for more cattle grazing on public lands.

REDBERRY JUNIPER   WESTERN JUNIPER

Redberry Juniper

cone

seed

Western Juniper

juvenile leaves

cone

UTAH JUNIPER *Juniperus osteosperma*
(Torr.) Little
A.K.A. DESERT CEDAR

QUICK ID Our only consistently monoecious juniper, with 2-seeded cones; scalelike leaf glands are absent or very inconspicuous.

Monoecious shrub or small tree to 12 m tall, 80 cm diam., usually multistemmed, with an irregular or rounded crown. **BARK** At first smooth, with age exfoliating in thin gray-brown strips. **TWIG** Stiff, 3- or 4-sided in cross section, about as thick as the length of the scalelike leaves. **LEAF** Scalelike, keeled, 1–2 mm long, light yellow-green, without conspicuous glands, not or barely overlapping, appressed to the branchlet. **SEED CONE** Matures in 1–2 years, round, usually 8–9 mm diam., glaucous, bluish brown, fibrous, mostly with 1 seed 4–5 mm long.

HABITAT/RANGE Native. Dry, rocky soils and slopes, 1,300–2,600 m; from s. Calif. north to Idaho, east to Wyo., and south to N.M.

SIMILAR SPECIES Rocky Mountain Juniper has a similar distribution but generally occurs at higher elevations; it is dioecious, is usually single-stemmed, has darker green foliage, and its terminal stems tend to droop.

Notes This species is the dominant juniper of Utah, often forming vast stands, and commonly grows with Singleleaf Piñon. It is closely related to Western Juniper, and hybrids have been reported. The brittle wood of Utah Juniper is not rot-resistant and is rarely used except as firewood.

PINCHOT JUNIPER *Juniperus pinchotii*
Sudw.
A.K.A. REDBERRY JUNIPER, PINCHOT'S JUNIPER

QUICK ID A juniper that bears juicy copper-colored cones, and that will resprout after cutting or fire.

Dioecious shrub or small tree to 6 m tall, usually with multiple stems, each usually to about 20 cm diam., and an irregular crown. **BARK** At first smooth, becoming flaky, and then fibrous and pale gray, exfoliating in strips. **TWIG** Stiff, about 1 mm diam., erect, 3- or 4-sided in cross section. **LEAF** Both needlelike and scalelike, but scalelike leaves predominate; they are yellow-green, 1–2 mm long, not overlapping or overlapping only slightly, and have an acute tip; many bear ruptured glands that emit an aromatic white exudate. **SEED CONE** Matures in 1 year, 6–8 mm diam., copper to copper-red, juicy, sweet (not resinous), mostly with a single seed, 4–5 mm diam.

HABITAT/RANGE Native. On gravelly limestone and gypsum soils, 300–1,000 m; Okla., Tex., N.M., to Nuevo León, Mexico.

Notes Pinchot Juniper commonly occurs in association with Honey Mesquite or any of several shrubby oaks. The seeds can survive ground fire, and the plants can resprout after cutting or fire. It does not compete effectively with bunchgrasses, though, and frequent fire favors development of grassland, while fire suppression leads to development of juniper woodland. Cattle grazing, which reduces competition from bunchgrasses, also favors juniper development.

UTAH JUNIPER

PINCHOT JUNIPER

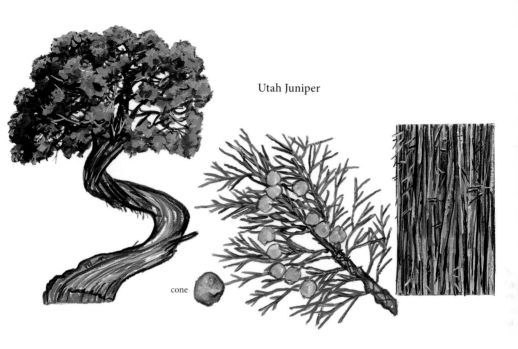

Utah Juniper

cone

Pinchot Juniper

cone

ROCKY MOUNTAIN JUNIPER
Juniperus scopulorum Sarg.
A.K.A. CEDRO ROJO, GENÉVRIER DES MONTAGNES
ROCHEUSES

QUICK ID A widely distributed juniper with 4-sided twigs bearing very small scalelike leaves that have a conspicuous gland, and glaucous blue cones.

Dioecious tree, to 15 m tall, with 1 to several short trunks, to 1 m diam., and a conical to rounded or irregular crown. **BARK** Red-brown to dark brown, weathering gray, peeling in long strips. **TWIG** Spreading, erect to drooping, 4-sided, 0.8–1.2 mm diam. **LEAF** Almost all scalelike, sometimes keeled, 1–2 mm long, not or barely overlapping with a conspicuous large gland that often bears a droplet of clear or whitish exudate. **SEED CONE** Solitary at twig tips, glaucous blue at maturity, 6–8 mm diam., mostly with 2 seeds (occasionally 1), each 4–5 mm long.

HABITAT/RANGE Native. Mostly on rocky soils in cool temperate semiarid areas, 200–2,700 m; B.C. and all western states except Calif.; also nw. Mexico.

SIMILAR SPECIES In places on the Great Plains, Rocky Mountain Juniper hybridizes with Eastern Redcedar, a widespread eastern species that enters the West in all Great Plains states from S.D. to Tex. Eastern Redcedar is similar, but its cones have 1 or 2 seeds that are 1.5–4 mm diam., and its scalelike leaves overlap by more than ¼ of their length. Hybrids appear intermediate between the 2 species. **Seaside Juniper** (*J. maritima* R.P. Adams) occurs in coastal Wash. and B.C. It is extremely similar to Rocky Mountain Juniper, except the seeds are usually partially exserted from mature cones, and the trees have upswept branches and a uniform dark green color.

Notes At its lower-elevation limits, Rocky Mountain Juniper occurs with Utah Juniper and Single-leaf Piñon, but it mostly occurs in montane forest with Ponderosa Pine, Douglas-fir, and White Fir. It cannot outcompete these larger trees on good sites, but on dry and rocky sites it can grow well and attain great age.

EASTERN REDCEDAR *Juniperus virginiana* L.
A.K.A. PENCIL CEDAR, SOUTHERN JUNIPER

QUICK ID The Great Plains distribution and the dark blue, glaucous cones containing 1 or 2 seeds, 1.5–4 mm long, generally distinguish this species from other native western junipers.

Dioecious tree to 30 m tall, with usually 1 trunk, to 100 cm diam., and a conical to globular crown. **BARK** Smooth when young, becoming fibrous and brown with increasing age, peeling in thin strips. **TWIG** Generally erect but sometimes lax, 3- or 4-sided, 0.6–2.0 mm diam. **LEAF** Primarily scalelike, 1–3 mm long, overlapping by more than ¼ their length, with a conspicuous gland that does not show a resinous exudate; tip obtuse to acute. Needlelike leaves, 3–6 mm long, are mostly borne on young plants or on shaded foliage. **SEED CONE** 3–6 mm diam., green, maturing dark blue with a glaucous bloom, containing 1 or 2 seeds, each 1.5–4 mm long.

HABITAT/RANGE Native. Often grows on calcareous soils, typically in o pen areas and woodlands, and less commonly in forest interior settings, 0–1,070 m; widespread in the East, entering the West from S.D. to Tex.

ROCKY MOUNTAIN JUNIPER   SEASIDE JUNIPER   EASTERN REDCEDAR

cone

Rocky Mountain Juniper

Eastern Redcedar

cone

juvenile leaves

WESTERN REDCEDAR *Thuja plicata*
Donn ex D. Don
A.K.A. GIANT ARBORVITAE

QUICK ID A native cypress with fibrous reddish bark, foliage in flattened, pinnate sprays, and a bilaterally symmetric cone.

Tree to 50 m tall, trunk to 2 m diam., often buttressed at the base, with a conical to irregular crown; old specimens frequently have many leaders and many dead spike tops. **BARK** Red-brown, graying with age, 10–25 mm thick, fibrous, with shallow longitudinal fissures, easily peeled. **TWIG** Pendent, forming flattened or slightly concave, pinnate sprays. **LEAF** Scalelike, opposite in 4 ranks, green, 1–6 mm long (shortest leaves at the tips of shoots, longest leaves at the base of shoots), tip acute, stomata in an irregular patch. **SEED CONE** Borne in a central region of foliage sprays, bilaterally symmetric, composed of 4 pairs of woody scales, 10–12 mm long and about ½ as wide when dry and fully opened. Seeds 8–14 per cone, 4–7.5 mm long (including wings), reddish brown.

HABITAT/RANGE Native. Found on various soils in mixed forests with conifers such as Douglas-fir and Western Hemlock, 0–2,000 m; Coast Ranges and Cascade Range from se. Alaska to nw. Calif., and Rocky Mountains from B.C. and Alta. to Idaho and Mont.

Notes This species was enormously important to Northwest Coast Indian tribes, who used it for their canoes, houses, totem poles, and dozens of other cultural implements; even clothing was woven from the bark, and medicines made from the resinous parts. It remains a mainstay of their cultural traditions but is also an economically important timber species, the source of most of the "cedar" sold in w. North America. It is extremely resistant to windthrow and can grow in swampy areas where a high water table limits rooting depth.

AHUEHUETE *Taxodium distichum* var. *mucronatum* (Ten.) A. Henry
A.K.A. MONTEZUMA BALDCYPRESS

QUICK ID The feather-like leafy shoots distinguish this tree in its range; only Coast Redwood has similar leaves.

Monoecious, deciduous or semi-deciduous tree, to 40 m tall, trunk to 3 m diam. It usually has a single straight trunk with a broad base, often surrounded by brown woody "knees" projecting up to 1 m from the ground nearby, and forms a pyramidal crown that flattens in old trees. **BARK** Light brown, turning gray, exfoliating in long, thin strips. **TWIG** Slender, green to light brown, each year's growth consisting of a single long shoot with multiple lateral short shoots. **LEAF** Linear, 2-ranked, in feather-like shoots, with 40–80 leaves in each "feather." Each leaf 7–10 mm long, acute, with stomata on both surfaces. **SEED CONE** Round, 1.4–2.5 cm diam., green and fleshy when young, at maturity brown and woody, with 5–10 seed scales.

HABITAT/RANGE Native. In low-lying, usually swampy areas, up to 100 m, along the lower Rio Grande valley (Cameron County, Hidalgo County, and Starr County) in s. Tex. and far into Mexico.

Notes The closely related Baldcypress (*Taxodium distichum* var. *distichum* [L.] Rich.) occurs in the East, reaching c. Tex. at the eastern extremity of the area covered by this book. It differs primarily in having stomata mostly on the lower side of the leaf, instead of about equally distributed on both lower and upper sides. These two trees were formerly regarded as distinct species, but both genetic and morphological evidence shows them to be nearly indistinguishable.

WESTERN REDCEDAR

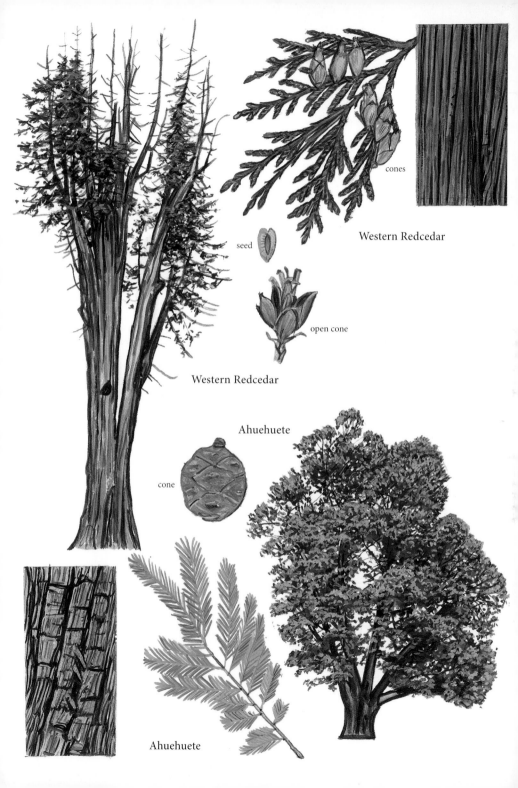

cones

Western Redcedar

seed

open cone

Western Redcedar

Ahuehuete

cone

Ahuehuete

COAST REDWOOD *Sequoia sempervirens* (D. Don) Endl.

QUICK ID A giant cypress-like tree with red bark and leaves arranged feather-like along the twig.

Tree to 115 m tall, trunk to 7.2 m diam., with a buttressed, swollen base and often bearing large rounded swellings (burls). Crown at first conical, but with age most trees develop multiple crowns; branching is irregular and open. **BARK** Red-brown, to 30 cm thick, tough and fibrous, deeply furrowed. **LEAF** Of 2 very different types: those from the upper crown scalelike, appressed to the twig, 2–10 mm long, with stomata on both surfaces; those borne in the shade linear, 2-ranked, arranged feather-like along the shoot, with 30–50 leaves in each "feather." Each leaf 1–20 mm long, acute, with stomata on the lower surface. **SEED CONE** Pendent, at the end of twigs, 12–35 mm long, elliptical, reddish brown, with many flat, short-pointed scales. Seeds 2–5 per scale, light brown, 2-winged, flattened, 3–6 mm broad.

HABITAT/RANGE Native. Confined to coastal areas experiencing a great deal of fog, 0–300 m; sw. Ore., nw. Calif.

Notes Coast Redwood grows mostly in alluvial soils, where it forms pure stands or occurs with Douglas-fir, Port Orford Cedar, or other local conifers, with a hardwood understory of trees such as Tanbark Oak and Golden Chinkapin. Coast Redwood is an important timber tree; its decay-resistant wood is valued for exterior uses, and stumps are often salvaged for their beautifully figured wood. This is one of the most extraordinary of all trees. It has 6 sets of chromosomes, 3 times as many as almost all other conifers. It commonly sprouts from the stump of a burned or cut tree. It is the tallest tree on Earth, and until 1945 was also the largest (logging eliminated the largest trees ever recorded). Redwood forests have more biomass per unit area than any other ecosystem in the world. Redwoods played a major role in the history of the American conservation movement and remain, to millions of people, the most spiritually inspiring of all trees. All old-growth groves are now protected in public and private preserves.

GIANT SEQUOIA *Sequoiadendron giganteum* (Lindl.) J. Buchholz
A.K.A. SIERRA REDWOOD, WELLINGTONIA, BIG TREE

QUICK ID The scalelike leaves are longer and larger than those in other species of the cypress family, but sequoias can usually be picked out from a distance by their great size and, in younger trees, the uniform conical crown.

Tree to 95 m tall, trunk to 8.25 m diam.; crown conical when young, becoming columnar and somewhat irregular with age. **BARK** Red-brown, up to 60 cm thick (the thickest of any tree), fibrous, ridged and furrowed. **TWIG** Covered by leaves, stiff, 2–5 mm diam. **LEAF** Scalelike, 8–15 mm long, mostly appressed to the shoot, with stomata on both surfaces. **SEED CONE** Solitary or in pairs, borne at the tips of twigs, oval, 4–9 cm long, with 25–45 thick woody scales; matures and opens usually in 2 years but sometimes remains green and closed for many years. Seeds 3–9 per scale, lens-shaped, 2-winged, 3–6 mm diam.

HABITAT/RANGE Native. In isolated groves, among mixed coniferous forests, 900–2,700 m; Calif., west of the Sierra Nevada crest. Naturalized in the San Gabriel Mountains and San Jacinto Mountains. Widely planted from s. Calif. north through sw. B.C.

Notes This is the largest tree in the world and the third longest living (3,266 years). Almost as soon as the trees were described, people began to log them, though the low-quality wood was primarily used to make matchsticks. The species is highly adapted to fire, and in areas that have experienced fire suppression, White Fir is commonly a major component of the understory. Giant Sequoia is also an extremely popular ornamental, widely planted in parks around the world.

COAST REDWOOD

GIANT SEQUOIA

Coast Redwood

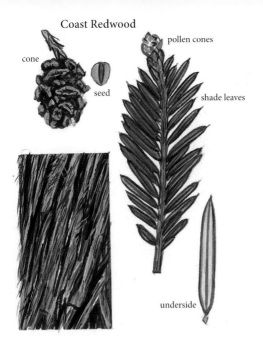

cone

seed

pollen cones

shade leaves

underside

Giant Sequoia
full tree shown on p. 54

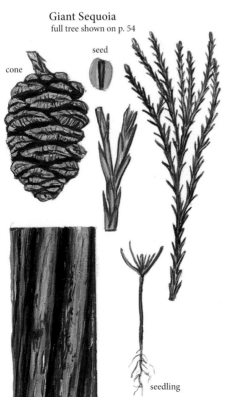

cone

seed

seedling

Coast
Redwood

THE BIGGEST TREES

California contains the tallest and largest trees in the world, and both are remarkable for the way they have transformed the relationship between humans and their natural environment. The largest trees now alive are the Giant Sequoias, which reach heights of 95 m, a trunk diameter of 825 cm, and an age of 3,266 years; one of the largest ones was recently estimated to bear 2.8 billion leaves. The Coast Redwoods grow even taller, to almost 116 m, and although the largest tree now has a trunk diameter of "only" 722 cm, there are reliable records of Coast Redwoods that, when logged, were larger than any Giant Sequoia now living.

The stature of these trees is awe-inspiring, and no one who has walked in one of these forests remains unmoved by the experience. One of the finest and largest of all the Giant Sequoia stands, the Converse Basin grove, was almost entirely logged in the mid-1800s. The American conservationist John Muir led a public outcry at this destruction, which culminated on September 26, 1890, with the designation of Sequoia National Park, the second national park (after Yellowstone) to be set aside in the U.S. All the Giant Sequoia groves are now fully protected in national parks and monuments. Similarly, the uproar created by destructive logging in the Coast Redwood forests, which eliminated over 90 percent of the largest trees, led to a proposal in 1852 that all these trees be placed under public protection. That effort failed, but public and private efforts beginning very early in the 20th century, and continuing almost to the 21st, have resulted in the protection of all old forests of this species. Much of this protection came from donations by millions of private individuals, which enabled the purchase and protection of most of the surviving groves. Many trees are loved, but few species can show such clear evidence of human devotion to their protection.

Giant Sequoia
General Sherman Tree

PINACEAE: PINE FAMILY

Pinaceae is the largest conifer family, with about 235 species in 11 genera; 47 species in 5 genera are native to w. North America. Species in our region are all monoecious trees; most are 10–30 m tall, with a single trunk 30–60 cm diam., but trees of the coastal forests from Calif. to B.C. can be up to 100 m tall and 540 cm diam., while many species grow at the alpine timberline as shrubby or mat-forming krummholz trees.

BARK/TWIG Highly variable. The branching pattern is very regular in fir (*Abies*), with a single terminal and 2 lateral shoots produced each year at the tip of most active branches. This geometric regularity of form is only a little less common in spruce (*Picea*) and larch (*Larix*), is rather unusual in pine (*Pinus*), and is not found in hemlock (*Tsuga*). **LEAF** Simple needle, shed singly, or in bundles of 2–5 needles in pines. **SEED CONE** Usually woody, comprised of many scales, maturing in 2–3 years in pines, in 1 year in other genera, then opening and shedding seeds upon maturity. In some species cones are serotinous, remaining closed usually until opened by the heat of a fire. Seeds are winged and dispersed by wind, except in a few pines that have seeds adapted for dispersal by birds and retain only a vestigial wing.

In w. North America, Pinaceae species occur in a great variety of forest and woodland habitats, ranging from hot semideserts through a wide array of pine-family-dominated closed-canopy forests, up to cold windswept timberline environments where many species cannot maintain erect growth but become shrubs that can shelter beneath the winter snows. Most species in the family, but especially the pines, are adapted to disturbance in the form of fire, and many species cannot persist on the landscape without it. Among gymnosperms, only the ginkgo family is thought to be older. Worldwide, species of the pine family are more widely distributed, ecologically important, and economically valuable than those of any other tree family.

■ *ABIES*: FIRS

There are more than 50 species of firs, distributed through much of the Northern Hemisphere; 8 native species occur in the w. U.S. Fir species occur in all states and provinces west of the Great Plains, primarily in mountains. Most live in regions that have snow cover for many months each year. Firs in general have a low tolerance for fire and a high tolerance for shade. They can be distinguished from other Pinaceae genera by the often spire-shaped crown, resin blisters on the bark, and the erect (rather than pendent) cones located near the top of the tree, disintegrating when ripe and leaving a woody spike.

Single-trunked evergreen trees, with a conical crown, often flattening in old trees. Branching is regular; a whorl of branches is usually produced every year. **BARK** Smooth and thin on young trees, bearing resin blisters; in age often thick and furrowed or flaky. **LEAF** Simple needle with 2 white bands of stomata on the lower surface; spirally arranged on the twig but often appearing 2-ranked as an adaptation to low light conditions in the understory; foliage formed in full sun is often thicker and stiffer than foliage formed in the shade. Needles usually persist for 5 or more years, leaving a smooth scar on the twig after falling. All *Abies* have 2 stomatal bands on the lower surface; the presence or absence of stomata on the upper surface is a useful character for identification. **POLLEN CONE** Borne along the length of the current year's twig, pendent. **SEED CONE** Borne erect on year-old twigs, usually in the upper crown, ovoid to cylindric, resinous, maturing in 1 season, falling apart on maturity, the cone axis persisting as an erect spike on the branch after the scales fall away. Seeds 2 per scale, winged.

BRISTLECONE FIR *Abies bracteata* (D. Don) Poit.

A.K.A. SANTA LUCIA FIR

QUICKID The only fir in its very limited range, Bristlecone has long needles and unmistakable cones with long bracts extending from the scales.

Tree to 30 m tall, trunk to 1 m diam., with a spire-like crown. **BARK** Light red-brown, thin, smooth, with age becoming dark gray, fissured, and scaly. **TWIG** Smooth to pubescent, shiny, light green to brown. **LEAF** Needle, 3.5–5.5 cm long, 2.5–3 mm wide, flattened, stiff, sharp-pointed. **SEED CONE** 7–10 cm long, 4–5.5 cm wide, ovoid, resinous, violet-brown to purple-brown; scales about 1.5–2 cm long, 2–2.5 cm wide, bracts exserted 4–5 cm beyond the scales. Seeds shiny, red-brown, 5 mm long, with a wing 8–11 mm long.

HABITAT/RANGE Native. Moist canyon bottoms and rocky slopes where fuel accumulations do not permit fire, 180–1,570 m; only in the coastal Santa Lucia Mountains, Calif.

Notes One of the rarest firs in the world, the Bristlecone may be more numerous in cultivation than in the wild. In its native habitat, common associates are Coulter Pine, Ponderosa Pine, Douglas-fir, and Canyon Live Oak.

PACIFIC SILVER FIR *Abies amabilis*

Douglas ex J. Forbes

A.K.A. AMABILIS FIR

QUICKID A highly shade-tolerant fir with dark green foliage, very pale gray bark, and large cones.

Tree to 75 m tall, with a single straight trunk, to 2.5 m diam., and cylindric crown, forming krummholz at the timberline. **BARK** Light gray, smooth but for resin blisters, with age breaking into scaly reddish-gray plates. **TWIG** Tan, pubescent. **LEAF** Needle, 1–2.5 cm long, 1–3 mm wide, grooved and shiny, dark green above, whitish below, notched at the tip; spreading in 2 rows, overlapping above, curved upward on sun foliage. **SEED CONE** Erect, 8–10 cm long, 3.5–5 cm wide, ovoid-cylindric, resinous, finely pubescent, purple-gray, turning brown; scales 2 cm long and wide, bracts hidden, purplish, about 1 cm long. Seeds tan, 10–12 mm long, 4 mm wide, wing about as long as body.

HABITAT/RANGE Native. Prefers deep, well-drained soils in cool, moist coastal forests, from sea-level (in the north) to the timberline, 0–2,300 m; se. Alaska, B.C., Wash., Ore., Calif.

Notes In Pacific Silver Fir's habitat, the climate is maritime, with long, snowy winters. Fire is rare, typically occurring at intervals of centuries, and Pacific Silver Fir is extremely intolerant of fire. However, it is among the most shade-tolerant of all our native conifers, often growing in forest understories much too dark for any other firs. Especially in patchy stands or near the alpine timberline, though, it often grows with a wide variety of other conifers, including Subalpine Fir, Red Fir, Grand Fir, Noble Fir, Sitka Spruce, Douglas-fir, Western Hemlock, Mountain Hemlock, and Alaska Yellow Cedar. This is probably the most long-lived of all firs, with maximum ages surpassing 800 years. Small trees in the shady forest understory are often more than a century old, and their needles can persist for more than 50 years—longer than those of any other conifer.

BRISTLECONE FIR

PACIFIC SILVER FIR

Bristlecone Fir

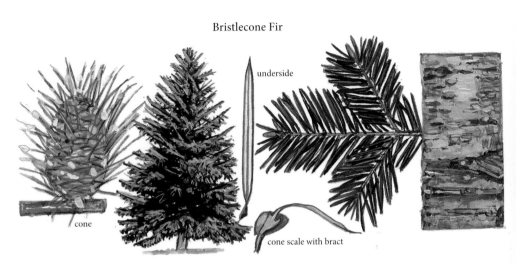

underside

cone

cone scale with bract

Pacific Silver Fir

underside

underside

cone

BALSAM FIR *Abies balsamea* (L.) Mill.
A.K.A. CANADA BALSAM, SAPIN BAUMIER

QUICK ID A common fir with gray bark, glaucous foliage, and bluish cones, found in boreal forest uplands at elevations below 600 m.

Tree to 25 m tall, trunk to 1 m diam., with a conical crown; forms krummholz at the timberline. **BARK** Gray, splitting into shallow blocks with age. **TWIG** Yellowish green, smooth, with sparse, short gray hairs. **LEAF** Needle, 1.5–2.5 cm long, 2 mm wide, the tip varying from notched to pointed, dark green, stomata mostly on the lower surface, in 4–8 rows in each of 2 greenish-white stomatal bands. **SEED CONE** Ellipsoid, 4–7 cm long, 2–3 cm wide when mature, blue-gray, turning brown; scales about 10 mm wide and 15 mm long, with bracts hidden under the scales or just the tips sticking out. Seeds brown, 3–6 mm long, with a wing about twice as long as the seed.

HABITAT/RANGE Native. In the West restricted to the boreal forests of Alta., Sask., and Man., 250–600 m; range extends east in forests through much of e. Canada and from Minn. to Maine, south to Pa. and Va.

Notes Balsam Fir is usually found in mixed conifer forests with Black Spruce, White Spruce, and Jack Pine; it also grows with Balsam Poplar and birches. Trees in w. Alta. are hybrids with Subalpine Fir; the 2 species are extremely similar, and some botanists regard Subalpine Fir as a subspecies of Balsam Fir. The timber of Balsam Fir is exploited for pulp, and the tree is also the source of a resin called Canada balsam that was formerly widely used in medicine, optics, and microscopy but has now largely been replaced by synthetics. It is highly shade-tolerant, is not fire-tolerant, and is usually short-lived; the oldest tree recorded was fewer than 250 years old.

SUBALPINE FIR *Abies lasiocarpa* (Hook.) Nutt.
A.K.A. ROCKY MOUNTAIN FIR

QUICK ID A common fir with gray bark, glaucous foliage, and bluish cones, usually found in the mountains.

Tree to 50 m tall, with a single round trunk, to 2 m diam.; commonly forms krummholz at the timberline. Crown spire-like, becoming somewhat flattened and irregular in old trees. **BARK** Gray, thin, smooth, with resin blisters in young trees, becoming furrowed and scaly with age; "corkbark" fir (var. *arizonica*) of Ariz., Colo., and N.M. has a thickened corky bark. **TWIG** Stout, stiff, green-gray to light brown, with a sparse brown pubescence. **LEAF** Needle, 11–31 cm long, 1.25–2 mm wide, flexible, flat in cross section, upper surface grooved, light green to blue-green, with numerous stomata toward the tips of sun foliage. **SEED CONE** 5–12 cm long, 2–4 cm wide, cylindric with a rounded tip, resinous, blue-gray, turning brown; scales about 15 mm wide and 25 mm long, bracts not visible. Seeds brown, 5–7 mm long, 2–3 mm wide, with a light brown wing about 1.5 times as long as the seed.

HABITAT/RANGE Native. Usually at relatively high elevation from forest interiors to alpine timberlines, 0–3,700 m; from se. Alaska east to Alta. and south to n. Calif., c. Nev., c. Ariz., and c. N.M.

Notes Subalpine Fir has one of the widest elevation ranges of any conifer, from sea-level in Alaska to 3,700 m in southern mountains, and consequently grows with a very wide variety of other trees; it forms a major, widespread forest type with Engelmann Spruce. Subalpine Fir commonly reproduces asexually via layering, which occurs when a branch comes in contact with the soil and produces roots; the branch then starts erect growth and eventually functions as a separate tree. Asexual reproduction allows this species to persist a very long time in cold, high-mountain environments that are usually hostile to seedling establishment. Like most firs it can grow quickly but has low resistance to decay or to fire, and is usually not long-lived, though a few specimens more than 450 years old have been found.

BALSAM FIR

SUBALPINE FIR

cone

underside

Balsam Fir

twig

seed

Subalpine Fir

disintegrating cone

underside

shade leaves

WHITE FIR *Abies concolor* (Gordon & Glendinning) Hildebrand
A.K.A. ABETO DEL COLORADO

QUICK ID Green cones and relatively long needles distinguish White Fir from other firs in its range.

Tree to 60 m tall, trunk to 1.9 m diam., with a spire-like crown that becomes more cylindric with age. **BARK** Gray, thin, smooth, thickening with age and breaking into deep longitudinal furrows, often revealing the yellowish inner bark, variably corky. **TWIG** Mostly opposite, glabrous or with yellowish pubescence. **LEAF** Needle, 1.5–6 cm long, 2–3 mm wide, flexible, flattened, upper surface sometimes grooved, lower surface with 2 parallel bands of stomata; apex usually rounded; mostly 2-ranked. **SEED CONE** 7–12 cm long, 3–4.5 cm wide, cylindric with a rounded tip, olive green, turning yellow-brown then darker brown; scales 2.5–3 cm long, 2.8–3.8 cm wide, pubescent, bracts not showing. Seeds tan or dull brown, 8–12 mm long, 3 mm wide, with a tan or brown wing about twice as long as the seed body.

HABITAT/RANGE Native. Grows predominately in areas where a large fraction of annual precipitation falls as snow, typically on drier sites than other firs, usually with various species of pine, 900–3,400 m; Ore. to Calif., se. Idaho, Nev., and Colo. to Ariz. and N.M., also in n. Baja California and Sonora, Mexico.

Notes In most of its range, White Fir is the dominant shade-tolerant species and has become a substantial fire hazard as human-caused fire suppression has allowed it to achieve very high stem densities in what were formerly open stands of mixed conifer or pine forest. Where their ranges overlap, White Fir forms hybrids with Grand Fir, but White Fir mostly occurs on slightly warmer, drier sites. Most White Firs

have glaucous needles, but trees of Calif. have green needles; some botanists assign these to a separate variety, California White Fir (*Abies concolor* var. *lowiana* [Gordon] Lemmon).

GRAND FIR *Abies grandis* (Douglas ex D. Don) Lindl.

QUICK ID A green-coned fir with non-glaucous needles that are notched at the tip.

Tree to 75 m tall, trunk to 1.5 m diam., with a conical crown that becomes rounded with age. **BARK** Gray, thin, with age thickening and turning brown, forming long furrows that often reveal a reddish inner bark. **TWIG** Mostly opposite, light brown, pubescent. **LEAF** Needle, 2–6 cm long, l.5–2.5 mm wide, flexible, notched at the tip, in cross section flat with a midline groove on the upper surface; 2 whitish stomatal bands on the lower surface, few or no stomata on the upper surface; odor pungent. Strong variation between 2-ranked shade foliage and spirally arranged sun foliage. **SEED CONE** 6–7 cm long, 3–3.5 cm wide, cylindric with a rounded tip, usually green; scales 2–2.5 cm long and wide, densely pubescent, bracts hidden. Seeds tan, 6–8 mm long, 3–4 mm wide, with a tan wing about 1.5 times as long as the seed body.

HABITAT/RANGE Native. Montane and riparian forests, 0–1,830 m; B.C., Idaho, Mont., Wash., Ore., Calif.

Notes East of the Cascade crest, Grand Fir is usually the most shade-tolerant tree in the forest, often in riparian areas dominated by a wide variety of conifers. West of the crest, it is most common in moist, productive, young to mature upland forests as a codominant with other conifers, or with Black Cottonwood, Oregon Ash, Red Alder, or Bigleaf Maple. Although it can grow very large, Grand Fir is a relatively short-lived species (rarely surpassing 400 years) and thus is rare in old-growth forests west of the Cascade crest. It is common in the coastal zone, often providing perch or nest sites for Bald Eagles (*Haliaeetus leucocephalus*).

WHITE FIR

GRAND FIR

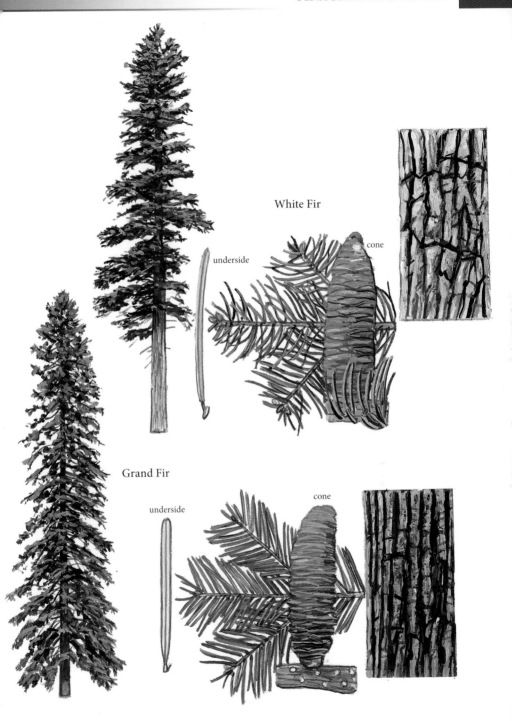

White Fir

underside

cone

Grand Fir

underside

cone

RED FIR *Abies magnifica* A. Murray
A.K.A. SILVERTIP FIR

QUICK ID A large-coned fir of montane forests with no groove on the upper surface of the leaf.

Tree to 57 m tall, trunk to 2.5 m diam., with a narrow conical crown that becomes columnar with age; forms krummholz at the timberline. **BARK** Grayish, thin, thickening with age and becoming deeply furrowed between broad reddish plates. **TWIG** Opposite to whorled, pale yellow to tan, reddish-pubescent for the first 1–2 years. **LEAF** Needle, 2–3.7 cm long, 2 mm wide, flexible, tip rounded or pointed, the basal portion often appressed to the twig for 2–3 mm (best seen on the lower surface of the twig), flattened on shade foliage, 3- or 4-sided on sun foliage; 2 whitish stomatal bands on the lower surface and 1 stomatal band on the glaucous upper surface; mostly spirally arranged. **SEED CONE** 15–20 cm long, 7–10 cm wide, ellipsoid, purple, turning brown; scales 3 cm long, 4 cm wide, pubescent, bracts may or may not be visible on the closed cone. Seeds dark reddish brown, 15 mm long, 6 mm wide, with a reddish wing about as long as the seed body.

HABITAT/RANGE Native. Cool, moist montane mixed-conifer forests, usually 1,400–1,830 m (though as high as 2,700 m); Ore., Calif., extreme w. Nev. Sometimes occurs at the timberline, especially in s. Sierra Nevada.

Notes This is one of the largest and longest-lived firs, with recorded ages of up to 665 years and trunk diameters up to 295 cm. In trees of var. *critchfiedii* Lanner, of the southern Sierra Nevada, the cones have exserted bracts. In coastal Calif. and the southern Cascades, Red Fir occurs with and hybridizes with the very similar Noble Fir; these trees are often called Shasta Red Fir (*Abies × shastensis* Lemmon). Red Fir and Noble Fir are the only North American firs that are economically important timber species.

NOBLE FIR *Abies procera* Rehder

QUICK ID A large fir with large cones and blue-green foliage; the lower part of the needle is appressed to the twig and its lower surface has a raised midrib.

Tree to 80 m tall, trunk to 2.75 m diam., with a spire-like crown that becomes columnar with age. **BARK** Grayish brown, with age becoming thick and deeply furrowed, with reddish-brown plates. **TWIG** Red-brown, finely pubescent. **LEAF** Needle, 1–3 cm long, 1.5–2 mm wide, flexible, tip rounded to notched, basal portion often appressed to the twig for 2–3 mm (best seen on the lower surface of the twig); flattened, with a prominent raised midrib on the lower surface, or 4-sided in cross section on sun foliage; lower surface with 2 stomatal bands; upper surface blue-green with 0–2 stomatal bands. **SEED CONE** 10–15 cm long, 5–6.5 cm wide, ellipsoid; green, red, or purple, at maturity brown; scales 2.5 cm long, 3 cm wide, pubescent; pale green bracts are visible on the closed cone, emerging from between scales and bent downward. Seeds reddish brown, 12 mm long, 6 mm wide, with a pale brown wing slightly longer than the seed body.

HABITAT/RANGE Native. Montane mixed-conifer forests, very commonly with Douglas-fir or Western Hemlock, usually on upland sites in rugged mountains, 60–2,700 m; Wash., Ore., n. Calif.

Notes Noble Fir is less shade-tolerant than any other North American fir. Because of its exceptional resistance to wind breakage it is more competitive at higher elevations. This is the largest of all firs, with trunk diam. to 275 cm and height to 80 m. Noble Fir and Red Fir produce the best timber of any North American fir; due to its exceptional strength, Noble Fir was once widely used for airplanes and ladders.

RED FIR

NOBLE FIR

Red Fir

cone

underside

Noble Fir

cone

cone scale

underside

Ornamental Firs

Non-native firs are not especially common in w. North America, perhaps because many of our natives are among the most popular ornamental species. Gardens of Europe are filled with fine White Firs, Red Firs, Grand Firs, and Noble Firs, including many cultivars. However, it is not unusual to see several Eurasian species in our gardens or parks. The 3 trees described below are commonly 15 m tall and 50 cm diam., occasionally much larger. All have smooth gray bark that becomes darker, scaly, and fissured with age.

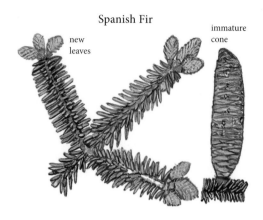

Spanish Fir

new leaves

immature cone

SPANISH FIR *Abies pinsapo* Boiss.

Tree with a pyramidal crown that becomes broader and flat with age. **TWIG** Red-brown, very stiff. **LEAF** Needle, 6–20 mm long, stiff, blunt, surrounding the twig and bent up to a point skyward. **SEED CONE** Borne on sunny branches throughout the crown, cylindric, 9–16 cm long, 3–5 cm wide; the bracts are hidden. **HABITAT/RANGE** Introduced from Spain and Morocco; cultivated in warm climates.

immature cones   Korean Fir

cone

cone

pollen cones

KOREAN FIR *Abies koreana* E.H. Wilson

Tree with a pyramidal crown. **TWIG** Yellowish green, shallowly grooved. **LEAF** Needle, 1–2 cm long, 2 mm wide. **SEED CONE** Ellipsoid, 4–7 cm long, blue, maturing purple-brown, with very conspicuous bracts that are bent downward; considered the loveliest of all fir cones. **HABITAT/RANGE** Introduced from Korea; cultivated, popular in the cool, wet Pacific Northwest.

CAUCASIAN FIR *Abies nordmanniana* (Steven) Spach

Tree with a pyramidal crown; grows quickly to a large size. **TWIG** Olive brown, ridged, grooved. **LEAF** Needle, 2–3 cm long, 1.5–2.5 mm wide. **SEED CONE** Cylindric, 12–16 cm long, often crowded together, with visible bracts that are bent downward. **HABITAT/RANGE** Introduced from the Caucasus region of Asia; cultivated, tolerant of cold winters.

Caucasian Fir

cone

pollen cones   immature cone

■ *CEDRUS*: CEDARS

The 2 species of cedars, native to mountains south and east of the Mediterranean and to the w. Himalayas, are very similar in appearance. The needles of cedars grow in tufts from stubby "short shoots" that are seen only on cedars and larches; cedars are evergreen (larches are deciduous), with darker green or highly glaucous foliage.

Evergreen trees to 30 m tall and 100 cm diam.; crown conical. **BARK** Dark gray-brown, fissured or breaking up into irregular blocks. **TWIG** Two types: long shoots that elongate and form twigs, and short shoots that appear as stubs on the sides of the long shoots and produce leaves. **LEAF** Needle, pliable, 5–40 mm long, in tufts of 15–45 at ends of short shoots. **POLLEN CONE** 3–8 cm long, abundant, producing clouds of pollen when ripe. **SEED CONE** Ovoid, 5–12.5 cm long, brown when ripe, disintegrating completely while on the tree, shedding seeds 10–15 mm long, with an attached wing 10–20 mm long.

Both cedars are popular ornamentals. While they are lovely landscaping trees, the full-size cultivars can grow very large, so they are best reserved for parks rather than streets or gardens. Cedar of Lebanon is available in a wide array of strangely shaped cultivars.

DEODAR CEDAR *Cedrus deodara* (Lamb.) G. Don

TWIG First-year twig densely pubescent. **LEAF** More than 2.5 cm long, not or very slightly glaucous. **POLLEN CONE** More than 5 cm long, maturing and spreading pollen in autumn. **SEED CONE** Matures in autumn, disintegrating in early winter. **HABITAT/RANGE** Introduced, native to the Himalayas; cold-tolerant to USDA Zone 6, very widely planted in the wet Pacific Northwest.

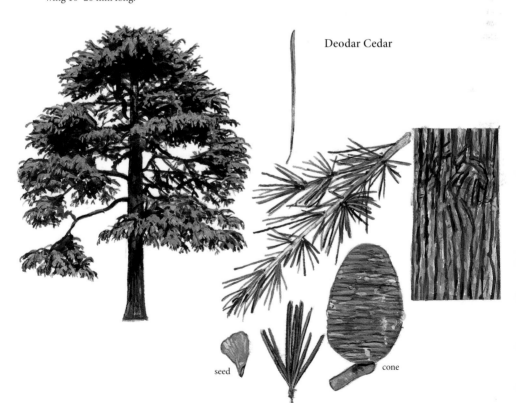

Deodar Cedar

seed

cone

CEDAR OF LEBANON *Cedrus libani*
A. Rich.

TWIG First-year twig hairless or nearly so. **LEAF** Usually less than 2.5 cm long, weakly to strongly glaucous, depending on the cultivar. **POLLEN CONE** Less than 5 cm long, maturing and spreading pollen in summer. **SEED CONE** Matures in late summer–autumn, disintegrating through winter. **HABITAT/RANGE** Introduced, native to the Mediterranean from Morocco to Lebanon; widely planted in w. North America in the warmer areas (Pacific Coast from Wash. to Calif. and s. Nev., Ariz., and N.M.).

■ *LARIX*: LARCHES

Larches occur in mountains and at high latitudes; the northernmost trees in the world are larches. The 3 native species of w. North America extend from the arctic tree line south through mountains of Ore., Idaho, and Mont.

Deciduous trees with needles in tufts on short, stubby shoots and sparse, open crowns. **BARK** Silver-gray to gray-brown on young trees, becoming reddish brown to brown, thickened and furrowed with age. **TWIG** Long shoots (several cm long) initiate or elongate branches; short shoots (several mm long), prominent on twigs 2 years or more old, bear leaves and cones. **LEAF** Needle, in tufts of 10–60 on short shoots or borne singly on 1st-year long shoots. **SEED CONE** Erect, ellipsoid to ovoid, initially brilliant red or violet, turning green and then brown with age; scales thin, tough and leathery, with visible or hidden bracts. Seeds winged. Cones mature and shed seeds in 1 season but persist on the twig for several years after seed-release.

As deciduous conifers, larches are an anomaly. Compared to evergreen conifers, they use less energy to create their foliage and are highly efficient in their use of nutrients. They live in climates where photosynthesis is impossible in winter owing to low temperatures, which negates what is otherwise one of the principal competitive advantages of evergreens—they can photosynthesize year-round.

Many larches are popular ornamentals, valued mostly for their golden autumn foliage. The most common ornamental larch in w. North America is the **European Larch** (*Larix decidua* Mill.).

TAMARACK *Larix laricina* (Du Roi)
K. Koch
A.K.A. AMERICAN LARCH, MÉLÈZE LARICIN

QUICK ID A deciduous conifer with needles in tufts on short shoots and very small seed cones, boreal to polar in distribution.

Deciduous tree to 30 m tall, trunk 80 cm diam., with an open, ovoid or conical crown. **BARK** Gray, smooth, becoming reddish brown and scaly, weathering to gray. **TWIG** Slender, flexible, orange-brown, hairless. **LEAF** Needle, 2–3 cm long, 0.5 mm thick, in tufts of 15–25 on short shoots, very flexible; light green at first, darker in summer, turning yellow and falling in autumn. **POLLEN CONE** Spherical, 3–4 mm diam., on short shoots. **SEED CONE** 1–2 cm long, globose or ovoid, usually red at first, maturing yellow-brown, borne upright on short shoots, usually on a curved stalk 2–5 mm long; comprised of 10–30 scales. Seeds 2–3 mm long with a wing 4–6 mm long.

HABITAT/RANGE Native. Mostly on acid soils with other northern conifers, especially Black Spruce; reaching to the Arctic timberline, it is abundant on well-drained uplands and in muskeg, and often forms pure stands, 0–1,220 m. This is one of the most widely distributed conifers in the world, common from Alaska to Nfld.

SIMILAR SPECIES The widely planted European Larch differs from Tamarack primarily in having much larger cones, usually 4–5 cm long.

TAMARACK

Cedar of Lebanon

pollen cone

cone scale

cone

seeds

European Larch

cones

autumn

Tamarack

cones

winter twig

cone

seed

winter

emerging leaves
and cones

SUBALPINE LARCH *Larix lyallii* Parl.
A.K.A. ALPINE LARCH

QUICK ID A larch that occurs near the alpine timberline in temperate zone mountains.

Deciduous tree to 25 m tall, trunk to 1.2 m diam.; crown sparse, conical to irregular; sometimes forms krummholz at the timberline. **BARK** Thin, smooth, yellowish gray when young; becoming furrowed and flaking into red- to purple-brown scales with age. **TWIG** Covered with dense whitish hairs that remain for 2–3 years. **LEAF** Needlelike, 2–3.5 cm long, 0.4–0.6 mm thick, in tufts of 30–40 on short shoots; light green, turning golden yellow in autumn. **SEED CONE** 2.5–4 cm long, 1–2 cm wide, ellipsoid, red when young, turning brown with age, borne upright on curved stalks; scales 45–55, lower surface densely hairy at maturity, bracts extending up to 6 mm beyond the scales on closed or open cones. Seeds yellow to purple, 3 mm long, with a wing 6 mm long.

HABITAT/RANGE Native. Locally common on exposed northern subalpine slopes to the timberline, often with very rocky soils; 1,800–2,400 m; B.C., Alta, Wash., Idaho, and Mont.

Notes Alpine Larch has very low tolerance for either shade or fire, and typically forms open stands on sites with very little understory vegetation. Being deciduous, it is resistant to winter desiccation, which allows it to reach timberline elevations that may be far above the reach of other conifers and to retain an erect growth form on those sites. Although usually forming pure stands, it sometimes occurs with Subalpine Fir, Engelmann Spruce, Whitebark Pine, and even Mountain Hemlock. Its fall coloration is extraordinarily beautiful, comparable to the finest Rocky Mountain aspen groves. Living only in high mountains, Alpine Larch has been used little by humans, but the rings of this very long-lived species (recorded age to 1,011 years) have been examined in studies of past climates and various ecological problems.

WESTERN LARCH *Larix occidentalis* Nutt.
A.K.A. WESTERN TAMARACK

QUICK ID A larch of the montane forests with mostly smooth, hairless twigs bearing tufts of 15–30 needles; mature cones reach 4 cm long.

Deciduous tree, to 50 m tall, with a long, clear trunk to 2 m diam.; crown short, conical, becoming columnar with age. **BARK** Thin and scaly when young, becoming thick, plated, deeply furrowed, and reddish brown when older. **TWIG** Orange-brown, initially pubescent, becoming glabrous during the 1st year. **LEAF** Needle, 2–5 cm long, 0.4–0.6 mm thick, soft, pale green, turning bright yellow in autumn, mostly on short shoots, in tufts of 15–30. **SEED CONE** 2–4 cm long, 1.3–1.6 cm wide, ovoid, on a curved stalk 2.5–4.5 mm long; 45–55 pubescent scales, bracts visible on closed or open cones. Seeds reddish brown, 3 mm long, with a wing 6 mm long.

HABITAT/RANGE Native. Usually in mountain valleys and lower slopes on well-drained soils, 500–2,135 m; Mont., Idaho, Wash., Ore.

Notes Western Larch occurs often in pure stands or mixed with Douglas-fir or Ponderosa Pine. It is very shade-intolerant and regenerates well after fire, so human fire-suppression activities have limited its range, and fuel control with prescribed fire is critical to saving the few remaining old-growth stands. Due to its exceptionally strong, straight-grained wood, Western Larch is one of the most valued timber trees in its range; its resins also have specialty uses. It is by far the biggest larch, reaching a diam. of 221 cm and a height of 58.5 m; ages to 920 years have been reported.

SUBALPINE LARCH   WESTERN LARCH

Subalpine Larch

cones

seed

cone

Western Larch

cone

cone

young cone

winter twig

pollen cone

cone

seed

■ *PICEA*: SPRUCES

The spruce genus contains 33 species and occurs throughout the Northern Hemisphere, mostly in mountains and at high latitudes. In w. North America, it is confined to the boreal forest, mountains, and coastal areas, south to n. Calif., the Rocky Mountains, and into the mountains of Mexico. They are conifers with sharp, bottlebrush-like needles and abundant fallen cones with flexible scales and no visible bracts.

Evergreen trees; crown conical to columnar, usually with a single erect leader; branches mostly in whorls. Stiff, bottlebrush-like needles and abundant fallen cones with flexible scales and no visible bracts distinguish spruces from other genera in the pine family. **BARK** Gray to red-brown, thin and scaly, sometimes with resin blisters, thickening with age. **TWIG** Rough, with peg-like persistent leaf bases. **LEAF** Needle, 4-angled in cross section, stiff, usually sharp-pointed, sometimes blunt, with stomata on all surfaces. Spirally arranged on twigs, persisting for up to 10 years. **POLLEN CONE** Single or in groups, borne along the length of the current year's twig, pendent, oblong, yellow to purple. **SEED CONE** Borne mostly pendent from upper branches, ovoid to cylindric, green to purple, maturing pale to dark brown; scales flexible, bracts not visible. Seeds winged. Cones usually shed at maturity.

Recent studies suggest that the spruces evolved in w. North America about 65 million years ago, and Brewer Spruce is the most primitive surviving member of the genus.

BREWER SPRUCE *Picea breweriana*
S. Watson
A.K.A. WEEPING SPRUCE

QUICK ID In its limited range, the drooping foliage and blunt-tipped needles of Brewer Spruce set it apart from Sitka Spruce.

Tree to 40 m tall, trunk to 1.5 m diam., with a conical to cylindric crown of drooping branches. **BARK** Scaly, gray to brown. **TWIG** Long, drooping (except in saplings), slender, gray-brown, finely pubescent. **LEAF** Needle, 1.5–3 cm long, blunt-tipped, flattened or broadly triangular in cross section, dark green, with whitish bands of stomata. **SEED CONE** 7–12 cm long, cylindric, dark red-purple, ripening brown; scales stiff, fan-shaped, with a slightly wavy margin. Seeds black, 3–4 mm long, with a pale brown wing 12–18 mm long.

HABITAT/RANGE Native. Montane to subalpine forests of the Siskiyou Mountains, 530–2,300 m; sw. Ore., nw. Calif.

Notes The slow growth and drooping habit make this a moderately popular ornamental tree. In its native range it often grows on severely infertile soils derived from ultra-basic rocks, or as a co-dominant or subdominant tree in the company of other conifers, compared to most of which it is intolerant of fire.

ENGELMANN SPRUCE *Picea engelmannii* Parry ex Engelm.

QUICK ID A large, often blue spruce of western mountains with cones less than 7 cm long.

Tree to 67 m tall, trunk to 2.2 m diam., with a conical to columnar crown; often forms krummholz at the timberline. **BARK** Scaly, gray to reddish brown. **TWIG** Stiff, not drooping, yellow-brown, usually finely hairy. **LEAF** Needle, 1.6–3 cm long, 4-angled in cross section, stiff, sharp, blue-green, with stomata on all surfaces. **SEED CONE** 3–7 cm long, ellipsoid to cylindric, violet or deep purple, ripening to buff-brown; scales with irregularly toothed margins. Seeds 2–3 mm long, with a wing 10–12 mm long.

BREWER SPRUCE

ENGELMANN SPRUCE

cone

Engelmann Spruce

cone scale

cone

Brewer Spruce

HABITAT/RANGE Native. Cold, dry to mesic mountains, 520–3,650 m; w. U.S., B.C., Alta.

SIMILAR SPECIES Glaucous forms of Engelmann Spruce closely resemble Blue Spruce, which has larger cones and stiffer needles directed forward along the shoot, and are often sold as Blue Spruce by nurseries. See White Spruce for remarks on hybrids with Engelmann Spruce.

Notes The species' extremely broad range reflects its ability to dominate riparian forests at low foothill elevations while also succeeding at elevations above the timberline on the highest peaks. At intermediate elevations Engelmann Spruce dominates both upland and riparian forests, often in the company of Subalpine Fir, Lodgepole Pine, or Quaking Aspen. Engelmann Spruce is less shade-tolerant but more long-lived than its associate Subalpine Fir, which is a good example of how different traits can allow dissimilar species to compete effectively for the same habitat. Engelmann Spruce regenerates readily after fire, which often afflicts stands that have recently experienced extensive kill due to bark beetles or Western Spruce Budworm (*Choristoneura occidentalis*).

WHITE SPRUCE *Picea glauca* (Moench) Voss
A.K.A. SKUNK SPRUCE, ÉPINETTE BLANCHE

QUICK ID A spruce with sharp-pointed, waxy blue-green needles and cones to 6 cm long.

Tree to 30 m tall, trunk to 1 m diam., with rows of horizontal branches forming a conical crown. **BARK** Gray-brown, reddish in fissures, flaky. **TWIG** Pinkish brown, hairless, slender. **LEAF** Needle, 12–19 mm long, stiff, waxy, blue-green, sharp-pointed, giving off a skunky odor when crushed. **SEED CONE** Solitary, hanging near the ends of twigs, 3–6 cm long, long-ellipsoid, green or violet, ripening light brown; scales thin, flexible, with a rounded, untoothed upper margin. Seeds 2–4 mm long, with a wing 5–8 mm long.

HABITAT/RANGE Native. Abundant in the boreal forest throughout North America; in the West, it grows from near sea-level to 1,500 m; Alaska and Canada, extending south into Mont., with an outlying population in the Black Hills of S.D.

SIMILAR SPECIES Where the 2 species co-occur, White Spruce and Engelmann Spruce readily hybridize to form Alberta Spruce (*Picea × albertiana* Sargent), which is widespread in c. B.C. and Alta. The hybrid trees have hairless shoots and slightly longer needles than White Spruce.

Notes White Spruce is usually found on upland sites in pure stands or with Tamarack, Jack Pine, Red Pine, Balsam Fir, Black Spruce, Paper Birch, Quaking Aspen, or Balsam Poplar. Stands are subject to replacement by fire, and the species is also subject to a wide variety of insect pests. Native peoples used White Spruce extensively, including for medicine, food, structures, implements, and spiritual purposes. Today, this is the most economically important timber tree in the boreal forest, its wood used in musical instruments and for construction. Within its range, it is also a popular ornamental tree. Trees up to 688 years old have been found. It is the provincial tree of Man. and the state tree of S.D.

BLACK SPRUCE *Picea mariana* (Mill.) Britton, Sterns, & Poggenb.
A.K.A. BOG SPRUCE, ÉPINETTE NOIRE

QUICK ID A small northern spruce with short, blunt needles and very small cones.

Tree to 15 m tall, trunk to 25 cm diam., with a spire-like crown often topped by a "knot" of dense branches; forms krummholz at the timberline. **BARK** Gray-brown, thin, and scaly. **TWIG** Yellow-brown, with a dense covering of short hairs. **LEAF** Needle, 0.8–1.5 cm long, rigid, blue-green, with wax that tends to wear away with time, usually blunt-tipped. **SEED CONE** 1.5–3 cm long, short-ovoid to ovoid, dark purple, ripening red-brown; scales thin, woody, brittle, with a minutely toothed upper margin. Seeds 2–3 mm long, with a wing 2–5 mm long. Cones often serotinous.

HABITAT/RANGE Native. Bogs and other wet areas throughout the boreal forest in Alaska and Canada, north to the Arctic timberline and from lowland forest to the alpine zone, 0–1,600 m.

Notes This little spruce is abundant in pure stands on the wettest sites, frequently covering bogs and other peatlands with a nearly continuous forest and an understory dominated by various mosses and lichens. It also grows with a variety of other trees, especially Tamarack, White Spruce, and Paper Birch, on slightly better sites. Extremely well adapted to fire, it is easily killed by a burn but in the aftermath spreads its seeds widely over the fresh seedbed. In consequence, it is one of the most common trees in the northern forest, often forming nearly pure stands that cover very large areas. Exploited mainly for pulp (it is also a major source of wood for chopsticks), this is an economically important timber tree in the boreal forest.

WHITE SPRUCE

BLACK SPRUCE

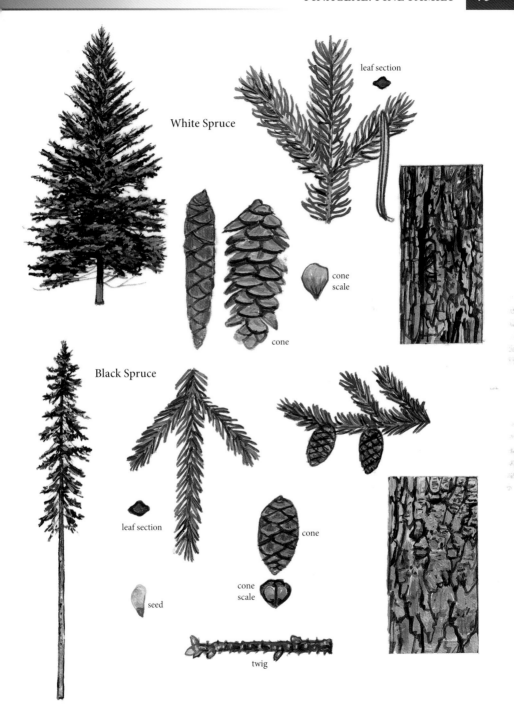

White Spruce

leaf section

cone scale

cone

Black Spruce

leaf section

cone

cone scale

seed

twig

BLUE SPRUCE *Picea pungens* Engelm.
A.K.A. COLORADO BLUE SPRUCE

QUICK ID A spruce with cones mostly longer than 7 cm and very stiff, sharp needles that are often not blue.

Tree to 50 m tall, trunk to 1.5 m diam., with a broadly conical crown of slightly drooping branches. **BARK** Gray to brown, scaly. **TWIG** Stout, not drooping, yellow-brown, hairless. **LEAF** Needle, 1.6–3 cm long, 4-angled in cross section, stiff, sharp-tipped, dark green to blue-green, with stomata on all surfaces, directed forward along the shoot. **SEED CONE** Ellipsoid to cylindric, 6–11 cm long, green or violet, ripening pale brown; scales stiff, with an irregular margin. Seeds 3 mm long, with a wing 6–9 mm long.

HABITAT/RANGE Native. Mostly in lower montane forests near wet meadows, and in riparian areas, 1,800–3,000 m, Rocky Mountains, Utah plateaus, and other high country from extreme e. Idaho to n. N.M., with some isolated populations in sc. Mont.

SIMILAR SPECIES Engelmann Spruce has smaller cones and slightly less stiff needles.

Notes Due to its preference for moist sites and its wide elevation range, Blue Spruce occurs with a great variety of other trees, but Fremont Cottonwood and Quaking Aspen are particularly common associates. Although ornamental trees can be very blue, both this species and Engelmann Spruce can range from dark green to pale blue. The blue color derives from a coat of wax on the needles, which reduces moisture loss. Stomata, tiny pores in the leaf epidermis, are a principal channel for water loss by evaporation. A tree with much wax and many stomata can have the same water balance as a tree with little wax and few stomata, so

green and blue trees may grow side by side with equal success. This contrast can be seen in many conifers.

SITKA SPRUCE *Picea sitchensis* (Bong.) Carrière
A.K.A. COASTAL SPRUCE

QUICK ID A very large coastal spruce with piercingly sharp needles.

Tree to 96 m tall, trunk to 5.4 m diam., with a straight trunk rising from a buttressed base and an open, conical crown. **BARK** Gray, smooth, thin, with age darkening to brown or black and becoming scaly. **TWIG** Not or slightly drooping, stout, pinkish brown, hairless. **LEAF** Needle, 1.5–2.5 cm long, flattened or broadly triangular in cross section, stiff, sharp (painful when twig is grasped), dark green to yellow-green, with whitish stomatal bands on lower surface. **SEED CONE** 5–9 cm long, cylindric, short-stalked, hanging from the ends of twigs, green or reddish, ripening to light brown, opening at maturity and falling soon after; cone scales thin and flexible, with an irregular margin. Seeds 3 mm long, black, with a light brown wing 7–9 mm long.

HABITAT/RANGE Native. Typically found in areas with high rainfall and a cool climate, never more than 200 km from the sea and usually much closer, from sea-level to 1,000 m, along the nw. coast of North America from Kodiak Island in the w. Gulf of Alaska to Mendocino County, Calif.

Notes Stands are usually regenerated after severe windthrow (rather than fire). Sitka Spruce is very often found growing with Western Hemlock, Western Redcedar, Red Alder, or Bigleaf Maple. The largest of all spruces, it is also the dominant species of the coastal moist conifer

BLUE SPRUCE

SITKA SPRUCE

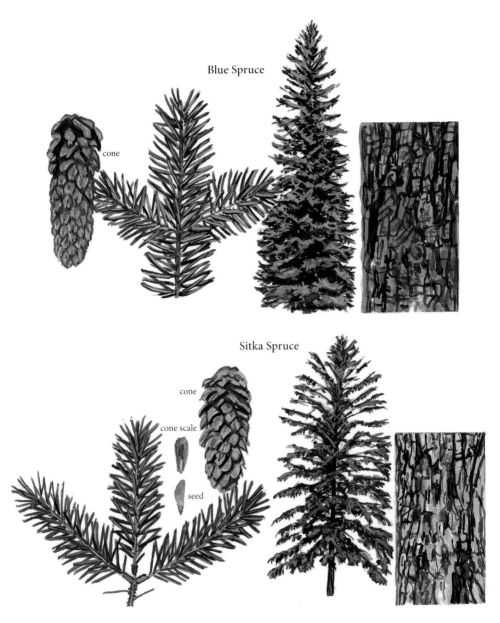

Blue Spruce

cone

Sitka Spruce

cone

cone scale

seed

forest. Formerly it was an important tree for native peoples; for instance, the young shoots are a rich source of vitamin C. Nowadays it is an important timber tree here and abroad; plantations have made it the most common tree in Scotland.

Sitka Spruce has a light, strong, straight-grained wood that, among many other things, is the preferred wood for the sounding boards of many fine stringed instruments, and was formerly preferred for use in aircraft.

Ornamental Spruces

There are relatively few non-native spruces in w. North America, partly because our natives are very popular ornamentals. Spruces in general do not do well in warm climates. These 3 species are among the few introduced here from other parts of the world.

NORWAY SPRUCE *Picea abies* (L.) Karst.

Typically a tree to 40 m tall, trunk to 1.5 m diam., with a conical crown. **BARK** Orange-brown, finely flaky, becoming gray-brown and scaly on old trees. **TWIG** Drooping, orange-brown. **LEAF** Needle, 10–25 mm long, stiff and blunt, spirally inserted and surrounding the twig. **SEED CONE** Very large for a spruce, 12–16 cm long. **HABITAT/ RANGE** Introduced from Europe and w. Siberia; not naturalized in w. North America. Tolerates extremely low temperatures (to –40°C/F) and is a popular ornamental in cold climates.

ORIENTAL SPRUCE *Picea orientalis* (L.) Link

Commonly a large tree with a conical to spire-like crown. **LEAF** Needle, soft, glossy green, extremely short, less than 10 mm long. **SEED CONE** 5–9 cm long. **HABITAT/RANGE** Introduced from mountains around the eastern end of the Black Sea; not naturalized in North America. Not quite as cold-tolerant as Norway Spruce, but does well in areas that experience winter temperatures well below freezing.

SERBIAN SPRUCE *Picea omorika* (Pančić) Purk.

Tree to 40 m tall, trunk to 1 m diam., with a tall, narrow crown of pendulous branches that reach nearly to the ground. **TWIG** Orange-brown, short, slender, and flexible. **LEAF** Needle, 10–20 mm long and 1.5–2.2 mm wide, nearly 2-ranked, at least on the lower branches; upper surface dark green; lower surface pale, with 2 stomatal lines. **SEED CONE** 4–6.5 cm long. **HABITAT/RANGE** Introduced from Serbia and Bosnia; not naturalized in North America. Tolerant of poor soils and polluted air, it is well suited to urban areas with subzero winter temperatures.

Norway Spruce

cone

Oriental Spruce

immature cones

pollen cones

fertile cone

cone

Serbian Spruce

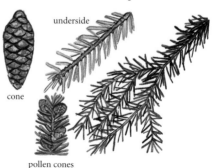

underside

cone

pollen cones

■ *PINUS*: PINES

Pinus is the most economically important tree genus in the world. Pines have fed, sheltered, and kept humans warm since before the dawn of history, and they continue to be the mainstay of timber production in North America. They are thought to have separated from the rest of the pine family about 125 million years ago. "Pine" is the popular name for conifers; a great many trees not in *Pinus* are frequently called "pines."

True pines are distinguished from other Pinaceae genera by their needle-shaped leaves occurring in bundles of 2–5. *Pinus* species occur throughout the Northern Hemisphere and are the most widely planted trees in the Southern Hemisphere. They occur throughout w. North America, which (including w. Mexico) supports the greatest diversity of pines in the world.

Evergreen trees; crown variable, usually rounded or irregular, with spreading, ascending branches; foliage is often borne in rounded clumps near the branch ends or is in a bottlebrush arrangement on branches. **BARK** Scaly, or with layered plates separated by furrows. **TWIG** Slender to stout, pliable to stiff, smooth in soft pines, scaly in hard pines (see discussion below). **LEAF** On mature plants, leaves needle-shaped, typically 2–5 (1 in 1 species) bound together in a bundle clasped at the base in a papery sheath that usually wears shorter with age and may fall off completely. **POLLEN CONE** Small, numerous, cylindric to conical, in a dense cluster around the base of the current year's growth. **SEED CONE** Solitary to few, scales numerous. In most species, cones take 2 growing seasons to mature, so they have secondary growth in the form of a thickened "wart" called an apophysis near the tip of each cone scale. Two winged seeds form at the base of each cone scale; wing vestigial in some species. Cones are sometimes serotinous, not opening upon maturity but much later, usually in response to fire.

Plants with bundles of 2 or 3 needles bound in a durable sheath and stiff woody cone scales are called hard pines, while those with 1, 2, 4 or 5 needles, bound in a weak sheath that is soon lost, and pliable cone scales are called soft or white pines; the latter group includes the piñons, also called pinyons. In this book the pines are presented in a sequence that keeps related species together, first the soft and then the hard pines.

PINE ECOLOGY

Pines show an ecological breadth not seen in any other conifer group. They grow from the Equator to both the Arctic and alpine timberlines, and from bogs to semideserts. They owe this success to a number of adaptations that, although not exclusive to pines, are exceptionally well developed and widely expressed in this group. Most conspicuous are their adaptations to fire and to seed dispersal by birds.

Most pines are fire-adapted, meaning that the recurrence of fire permits pines to maintain a dominant role in forest ecosystems that would otherwise, over time, lead to dominance by non-pines (usually, hardwoods or more shade-tolerant conifers). There are 2 main forms of fire adaptation. In one (Ponderosa Pine and Apache Pine are good examples), mature trees can withstand frequent low-intensity fires and shed their needles abundantly; the forest floor, covered with tinder, will then burn in response to any ignition source, usually a lightning strike. One study of Ponderosa Pines in the Gila Mountains of New Mexico found that in prehistoric times, the forest burned an average of once every 2–3 years. In the other form of adaptation (Lodgepole Pine and Knobcone Pine are good examples), the trees grow thick and fast, producing high fuel accumulations that, when ignited, result in a high-intensity fire that destroys the stand. These species generally have serotinous cones, which are opened by the heat of a fire and spread a fresh seed crop over the newly burned ground, thereby ensuring that a new generation of pines springs up after a fire. Fire history studies suggest that such fires usually occur at intervals of decades to centuries.

A minority of pines are not fire-adapted, and these mostly grow on inhospitable sites such as rocky mountainsides or nutrient-poor soils. Many of these species produce large, nutritious seeds that are gathered and cached by birds, chiefly of the jay family. One example is Whitebark Pine, which produces wingless seeds inside a cone that does not open; this tree is entirely dependent upon birds to gather and plant its seeds. The birds do not cache the seeds on barren rock, but bury them in isolated pockets of soil in the high mountains, thereby helping to ensure that seeds not eaten will find fertile ground for growth.

GREAT BASIN BRISTLECONE PINE *Pinus longaeva* D.K. Bailey

QUICK ID The only 5-needle pine in its range with stiff needles and bottlebrush-shaped branchlets.

Tree to 16 m tall, trunk to 3.6 m diam., with a conical crown that becomes irregular; sometimes forms krummholz at the alpine timberline. **BARK** Red-brown, scaly, longitudinally fissured. **TWIG** Pale red-brown, aging gray to yellow-gray, young branches resembling long bottlebrushes because of persistent leaves with closely spaced needle whorls. **LEAF** Needle, 1.5–3.5 cm long, 0.8–1 mm thick, curved, stiff, deep yellow-green, in tight bundles of 5, persisting up to 43 years. **POLLEN CONE** Cylindric, 7–10 mm long, purple-red. **SEED CONE** Spreading, symmetric, blunt-conical, 6–9.5 cm long, purple, aging red-brown; scales with apophyses thickened, sharply keeled, bearing a slender but stiff prickle 1–6 mm long. Cones shed seeds and fall soon after maturity. Seeds ovoid, mottled brown, 5–8 mm long, with a wing 10–12 mm long.

HABITAT/RANGE Native. Usually alone in open woodland on extremely thin, rocky soils, but sometimes forming closed forest (sometimes with Singleleaf Piñon or White Fir); it does best on limestone-, dolomite-, or marble-derived soils; 1,700–3,400 m, Calif., Nev., Utah.

Notes These trees grow at remarkably high elevations, in some cases appearing only at elevations higher than all other trees. This pine of the desert mountains is widely known as the longest-lived tree in the world; hundreds of individual trees are known to exceed ages of 3,000 years, and the oldest tree known is more than 5,000 years old. Researchers studying bristlecone pine DNA have

learned that the trees have unique adaptations to long life, but they also live in a very cold, dry environment that does not support the pests and diseases that afflict trees on warmer, wetter sites, and they live in forests that are essentially fireproof because the trees are widely spaced and there is no undergrowth. Traditionally the main hazard to bristlecones was lightning strikes, which can kill individual trees, but now whole stands are threatened by climate change, which is forcing them to migrate upward to cooler elevations. For a tree that grows on mountaintops, a warming climate is a death sentence.

ROCKY MOUNTAIN BRISTLECONE PINE *Pinus aristata* Engelm.

QUICK ID A 5-needle pine, usually near the timberline, with "bottlebrush" foliage that bears whitish scales resembling dandruff.

Tree to 15 m tall, trunk to 1 m diam., with a pyramidal crown, but near the timberline often contorted, crown irregular. **BARK** Pale gray, smooth, maturing dark gray to red-brown, irregularly ridged, shallowly fissured. **TWIG** Pale red-brown, with foliage borne in closely spaced whorls. **LEAF** Needle, 3–4 cm long, 0.8–1 mm thick, curved, stiff, bearing occasional scales of dried white resin and with a narrow groove on the lower surface; in tight bundles of 5. **POLLEN CONE** Borne in tight clusters at ends of branchlets, about 10 mm long, bright yellow at maturity. **SEED CONE** Tapering ovoid, 6–11 cm long, purple to brown, stalkless, each scale bearing a brittle prickle 4–10 mm long. Cones fall soon after maturity. Seeds 5–6 mm long, with a wing 10–13 mm long.

HABITAT/RANGE Native. Mountains, 2,300–3,650 m; Colo., N.M., Ariz. (San Francisco Peaks).

GREAT BASIN BRISTLECONE PINE

ROCKY MOUNTAIN BRISTLECONE PINE

Great Basin Bristlecone Pine

cone

5

Rocky Mountain Bristlecone Pine

cone

5

Notes This bristlecone often forms woodlands of ancient gnarled trees on high mountains, but it also has another role, coming in soon after forest fires to form montane forests. Rocky Mountain Bristlecone Pine, Great Basin Bristlecone Pine, and Foxtail Pine have changed little in the past 65 million years, which makes them the "living fossils" of the pine world. Members of all 3 species are also among the oldest trees in the world.

FOXTAIL PINE *Pinus balfouriana* Grev. & Balf.

QUICK ID A 5-needle pine of Calif. with fairly short needles borne in a tight "foxtail."

Tree to 22 m tall, trunk to 2.6 m diam., often with a contorted trunk and irregular crown. **BARK** Red-brown, shallowly fissured into irregular plates. **TWIG** Gray, rough with the bases of fallen needles; leaves are borne in closely spaced whorls or "foxtails." **LEAF** Needle, 1.5–4 cm long, 1–1.4 mm thick, curved, stiff, in tight bundles of 5, persisting for many years. **POLLEN CONE** In tight clusters near the branchlet ends, 6–10 mm, green, maturing yellow. **SEED CONE** Tapering ovoid, 6–9 cm long, stalkless, often resinous, lacking the prominent prickle of the bristlecone pines. Cones fall soon after maturity. Seeds to 10 mm long, with a wing 10–12 mm long.

HABITAT/RANGE Native. There are 2 subspecies: Subsp. *balfouriana* grows in open- to closed-canopy, pure to mixed stands, at 1,525–1,830 m, in the inner Coast Ranges in n. Calif.; subsp. *austrina* R. Mastrogiuseppe & J. Mastrogiuseppe occurs only in pure or nearly pure stands, at 2,750–3,650 m, in the s. Sierra Nevada, Calif., almost entirely within Sequoia National Park.

Notes Although it often grows near the timberline, higher than any other tree in its range, Foxtail Pine almost never forms a krummholz.

WHITEBARK PINE *Pinus albicaulis* Engelm.

QUICK ID A 5-needle pine of the high mountains with needles in open clusters, very pale bark that becomes scaly with age, and dark, glossy cones that do not open.

Tree to 21 m tall, trunk straight to contorted, to 1.5 m diam.; crown conical, becoming very rounded or irregular, often forming alpine krummholz. **BARK** Smooth, purplish to pale gray, in age pale to medium gray, scaly. **TWIG** Slender, pale red-brown, minutely hairy, bearing needles in whorls along their length. **LEAF** Needle, 3–7 cm long, 1–1.5 mm thick, mostly curved, deep yellow-green, in open bundles of 5, persisting 5–8 years. **POLLEN CONE** Borne in tight clusters near the ends of branchlets, 10–15 mm long, bright red, ripening yellow. **SEED CONE** Broadly ovoid, 4–8 cm long, not opening at maturity, seldom seen because nearly always harvested by birds or squirrels. Seeds 7–11 mm long, brown, wingless.

HABITAT/RANGE Native. On sandy soils, usually in pure stands but often in mixed stands with other conifers, at montane to timberline elevations, 1,300–3,700 m; c. Alta. to s. Calif.

Notes Whitebark Pine is often early successional, establishing in meadows after fire and later giving way to more shade-tolerant but less drought-tolerant conifers. This species has been very much depleted by white pine blister rust, an introduced disease caused by the fungus *Cronartium ribicola*, and mountains throughout its range are filled with "ghost forests" of bleached snags killed in recent decades. It is one of the most ecologically interesting pines, because its nutritious seeds are dispersed only by animals, primarily by Clark's Nutcracker (*Nucifraga columbiana*), though many other animals, from insects to Grizzly Bears (*Ursos arctos horribilis*), also partake of this oil-rich food source. The loss of Whitebark Pine forests has contributed to the decline of these other species, and the Whitebark is proposed for listing as an endangered species.

FOXTAIL PINE

WHITEBARK PINE

Foxtail Pine

5

cone

Whitebark Pine

cone

5

LIMBER PINE *Pinus flexilis* E. James

QUICK ID A 5-needle pine of the high mountains with needles in open clusters, fissured red-brown bark, and dark tan cones that open wide and often litter the ground beneath it.

Tree 12–26 m tall, trunk to 60–200 cm diam., straight to contorted, with the crown pyramidal to irregular; often forming krummholz near the timberline. **BARK** Light gray, nearly smooth, becoming reddish brown with age, forming scaly plates and ridges. **TWIG** Pale red-brown, aging gray, tough and flexible, smooth. **LEAF** Needle, 3–7 cm long, 1–1.5 mm thick, curved, pliable, dark green, spreading, in bundles of 5. **POLLEN CONE** About 15 mm long, pale red, ripening yellow. **SEED CONE** Tapering ovoid, 7–15 cm long, green, maturing yellow-brown, short-stalked; scales broad, leathery, often resinous. Cones fall soon after maturity. Seeds 10–15 mm long, brown, wingless or nearly so.

HABITAT/RANGE Native. Usually on dry, rocky slopes and ridges of high mountains up to the timberline, 1,000–3,700 m; through most of the Rocky Mountains and west to s. Calif.

SIMILAR SPECIES Whitebark Pine closely resembles Limber Pine; where the two species overlap, Limber Pine generally has a less-rounded crown and grows on steeper, rockier sites.

Notes Limber Pine grows in pure stands or mixed with other high-mountain conifers. This is one of the longest-lived trees, reaching ages of more than 2,200 years. Like Whitebark Pine, it has large, nutritious seeds distributed mostly by birds; like the bristlecone pines, it lives alone on high, dry mountains; and like the piñon pines, it forms extensive arid woodlands with scrubby junipers.

SUGAR PINE *Pinus lambertiana* Douglas
A.K.A. PINO DE AZUCAR

QUICK ID A very large 5-needle pine with extraordinarily large, but not heavy, cones.

Tree to 81 m tall, trunk to 3.5 m diam., usually with a single, unusually round and straight trunk and an open crown of very long, horizontal branches, often with cones at the tips. **BARK** Cinnamon brown to gray-brown, deeply furrowed into long, scaly plates. **TWIG** Gray-green to red-tan, aging gray. **LEAF** Needle, 5–10 cm long, 1–1.5 mm thick, pointed, straight, slightly twisted, flexible, all surfaces bearing whitish stomatal lines; spreading in bundles of 5. **POLLEN CONE** Cylindric, to 15 mm long, yellow. **SEED CONE** Hanging (often from the ends of branches), pointed-cylindric, 25–50 cm long, shiny yellow-brown, on stalks 6–15 cm long, falling soon after maturity. Seeds 1–2 cm long, with a broad wing 2–3 cm long.

HABITAT/RANGE Native. In mountains, usually as a canopy-emergent tree in montane mixed conifer forests, but sometimes up to the timberline, 300–3,200 m (elevations generally increasing from north to south); c. Ore. to n. Baja California.

Notes Sugar Pine is resistant to fire of moderate severity but is not especially drought-tolerant. Although much larger trees than any now living were logged historically, it is still the largest pine in the world and has some of the longest branches and among the longest cones of any pine. It was formerly an important and valuable timber tree, but the best groves were cut in the 19th century; many San Francisco mansions were framed and finished in its lumber. The common name comes from a resin that exudes from the sapwood and which, when heated to caramelize the sugars, becomes very sweet.

LIMBER PINE

SUGAR PINE

Limber Pine

seed

5

cones

5

Sugar Pine

cone

WESTERN WHITE PINE *Pinus monticola* Douglas ex D. Don
A.K.A. IDAHO PINE

QUICK ID A 5-needle forest pine with cones of distinctive size and, on large trees, an unusual hexagonal bark pattern.

Tree to 70 m tall, usually with a single straight trunk, to 2 m diam.; crown conical, becoming columnar. **BARK** First gray and thin, smooth, eventually becoming furrowed and forming distinctive red-brown subhexagonal scaly plates. **TWIG** Smooth, slender, pale red-brown, slightly glandular. **LEAF** Needle, 4–10 cm long, 0.7–1 mm thick, straight, slightly twisted, pliable, stomatal lines visible on 2 surfaces only; spreading, in bundles of 5. **POLLEN CONE** Ellipsoid, 10–15 mm, yellow. **SEED CONE** In groups of 1–4 cones, pointed-cylindric, 10–25 cm long, creamy brown, resinous, hanging from stalks up to 2 cm long, falling soon after maturity. Seeds red-brown, 5–7 mm long, with a wing 20–25 mm long.

HABITAT/RANGE Native. Occurs in lowland fog forests or on moist mountain soils, occasionally in forested bogs, often in montane valley or lower slope forests, occasionally in the subalpine zone or even at the timberline, sea-level to 3,000 m; B.C. and Alta. south to Calif., w. Nev., Idaho, w. Mont.

Notes Western White Pine usually grows in mixed conifer forests with a wide range of associated species but occasionally in pure stands. This close relative of the Eastern White Pine is the largest pine throughout most of its range (exceeded primarily by Sugar Pine) and reaches ages of more than 600 years. Throughout its range north of Calif. it has been much reduced in abundance by logging and by the white pine blister rust, an introduced

disease caused by the fungus *Cronartium ribicola* that also afflicts most other 5-needle pines in w. North America. As a result, this tree is neither economically nor ecologically as important as it once was.

SOUTHWESTERN WHITE PINE *Pinus reflexa* (Engelm.) Engelm.

QUICK ID A montane 5-needle pine with long, slender cones.

Tree to 34 m tall, slender, usually with a single straight trunk, to 1.5 m diam.; crown conical, becoming columnar. **BARK** Smooth and gray on young trees, aging dark gray-brown, broken into rough polygonal plates. **TWIG** Slender, smooth, pale red-brown, sometimes glaucous. **LEAF** Needle, 4–10 cm long, 0.6–1 mm thick, straight, slightly twisted, pliable, stomata on 2 of the 3 surfaces; spreading, in bundles of 5. **POLLEN CONE** Cylindric, 6–10 mm long, pale yellow-brown. **SEED CONE** Pointed-cylindric, 15–25 cm long, light yellow-brown, hanging from a stalk to 6 cm long, falling soon after maturity. Seeds 10–13 mm long with only a vestigial wing.

HABITAT/RANGE Native. Dry montane slopes in isolated mountain ranges, often scattered within mixed conifer forest, 1,900–3,000 m; s. Ariz., N.M., w. Tex.

Notes Southwestern White Pine is an intermediate species that shows features of both Limber Pine and Mexican White Pine (*Pinus strobiformis* Engelm.), a species of Mexico. This tree is susceptible to white pine blister rust, a disease caused by the fungus *Cronartium ribicola.*

WESTERN WHITE PINE

SOUTHWESTERN WHITE PINE

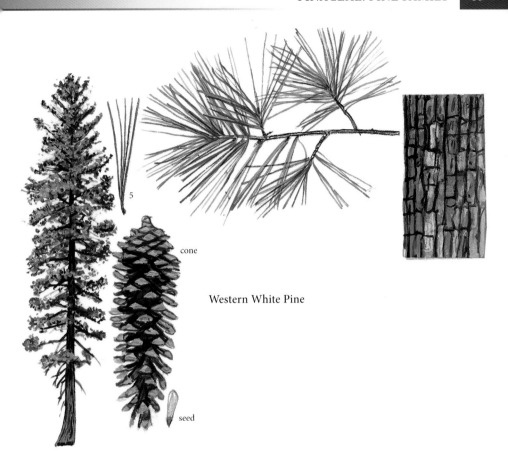

5

cone

Western White Pine

seed

Southwestern White Pine

cone

cone

5

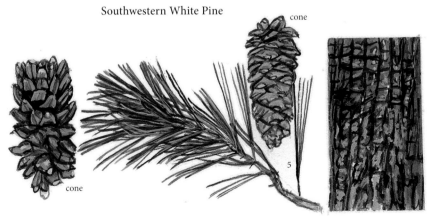

TEXAS PIÑON   *Pinus remota* (Little) D.K. Bailey & Hawksw.

A.K.A. PAPER-SHELL PIÑON

QUICK ID A 2-needled piñon with very thin-shelled seeds, found only on the Edwards Plateau and Big Bend region, Tex.

Tree or shrub to 9 m tall, usually with contorted, forking trunks, to 40 cm diam., . **BARK** Gray, thin, smooth, soon becoming flaky, later darker, thick, and rough. **TWIG** Stout, rough with the bases of fallen leaf bundles. **LEAF** Needle, 3–4.5 cm long, 0.8–1.1 mm thick, curved, stiff, pointed, stomatal lines on all leaf faces; spreading, in bundles of 2 (less often 3). **POLLEN CONE** Numerous near the ends of new shoots, ovoid, 4–5 mm long. **SEED CONE** Solitary or in pairs, globose before opening, then flattened-ellipsoid, dull brown at maturity, 2.5–4 cm long, 3–6 cm wide when opening, falling soon after maturity. Seeds very thin-shelled, wingless, each 12–16 mm long, 8–10 mm wide.

HABITAT/RANGE Native. Desert, 450–1,850 m; Tex., on the Edwards Plateau and in the extreme west along the Rio Grande and into Mexico.

Notes Texas Piñon grows at a lower elevation than any other piñon. A species of the Chihuahuan Desert, it typically grows with Mountain Cedar, Oneseed Juniper, or shrub oaks. Like those of all other piñons, its seeds are edible and very tasty.

TWONEEDLE PIÑON   *Pinus edulis* Engelm.

A.K.A. COLORADO PIÑON, PIÑON

QUICK ID Needles in bundles of 2; small, wide-opening cones with wingless seeds; and semi-arid woodland habitat.

Tree to 21 m tall, trunk to 60 cm diam., usually with a dense, rounded crown and branches down to the base of the trunk. **BARK** Red-brown, shallowly furrowed between scaly ridges. **TWIG** Tan to reddish brown, aging gray, smooth. **LEAF** Needle, 20–40 mm long, 1–1.5 mm thick, curved, blue-green, in bundles of 2 (sometimes 1 or 3). **POLLEN CONE** Ellipsoid, 7 mm long, yellow to red-brown. **SEED CONE** Ovoid before opening, globose when open, 3.5–5 cm long, pale yellow, resinous, nearly sessile to short-stalked, falling soon after maturity. Seeds brown, 10–15 mm long, wingless.

HABITAT/RANGE Native. Semiarid, mostly mountainous regions, 1,500–2,700 m; from s. Wyo. to Chihuahua, Mexico. Occupies relatively cool habitats with 250–560 mm of precipitation and annual average temperatures of 4–16°C; it commonly grows with Utah Juniper.

Notes The piñon–juniper woodland is one of the principal forest types of w. North America. Most such woodlands are dominated by 1 or 2 species of pine and another 1 or 2 species of juniper. The principal pines involved are Twoneedle Piñon, Singleleaf Piñon, and Mexican Piñon. The piñon–juniper woodland is of great ecological importance, because the dominant trees create a structure that produces habitat diversity, retains snow cover and

FORESTS AND CLIMATE CHANGE

Global climate is changing, and so are the world's forests. Climate changes being recorded in w. North America include seasonal changes in temperature and changes in the type (rain or snow), amount, and timing of precipitation. These changes produce direct physiological effects, such as drought mortality, as well as indirect effects such as changes in fire frequency and in the frequency of attack by pests (primarily insects) and pathogens (primarily fungal diseases).

One example of an effect related to climate change is the extensive tree death caused by Mountain Pine Beetle (*Dendroctonus ponderosae*) and its relatives, including Douglas-fir Beetle (*D. pseudotsugae*), in recent years. Pine beetles are normally "pitched out" by vigorous sap flow in healthy trees, but can become epidemic in a forest stressed by drought. Millions of hectares of western forests have been killed by such outbreaks. The epidemics have become larger and more persistent due to reduced frequency of very cold winters, which can kill the beetles. The problem has also been made worse by human forest management. In areas where multi-age forests have been replaced with single-species stands of uniform-size trees, we have created ideal breeding grounds for pine beetles.

There has also been a widespread increase in the size and severity of forest fires compared to historical conditions. There are several causes for this change: increased drought severity places the forests at greater risk; large areas of trees killed by pests create a large stock of standing dead fuel for fires; and a legacy of fire suppression by humans in naturally fire-adapted systems has also increased fuel loads, which means that when fires do occur, they are much more severe and destructive than they used to be. These examples show that the effects of climate change are often complex, involving interactions with forest ecosystems and the history of human activity in the forest.

Texas Piñon

open cone

cone

3

2

Twoneedle Piñon

2

cone

seed

open cone

enhances soil moisture, and provides an important food source (pine nuts and juniper berries) for many species of birds, mammals, and insects. All of the piñon pines have a symbiotic relationship with the birds (members of the jay family) that gather, cache, and eat their seeds, and upon which the trees are completely dependent for seed dissemination. A cottage industry that involves gathering piñon "nuts" and selling them along roadsides is common in the Southwest.

TEXAS PIÑON

TWONEEDLE PIÑON

SINGLELEAF PIÑON   *Pinus monophylla*
Torr. & Frém.

A.K.A. PINO MONOAGUJA

QUICK ID The only pine in the world that typically bears its needles solitary, rather than in bundles of 2 or more.

Tree 5–14 m tall, trunk to 50 cm diam., much branched, with a dense, usually rounded crown. **BARK** Red-brown, scaly, irregularly furrowed. **TWIG** Stout, orange-brown, aging gray, smooth or with sparse, fine hairs. **LEAF** Needle, 2–6 cm long, 1.3–2 mm thick, curved, gray-green, single or rarely in bundles of 2. **POLLEN CONE** Ellipsoid, 10 mm long, yellow. **SEED CONE** Ovoid before opening, globose when open, 4–6 cm long, pale yellow-brown, opening and falling soon after maturity. Seeds brown, 15–20 mm long, wingless.

HABITAT/RANGE Native. Semiarid regions, usually on dry, gravelly slopes or in canyons, 1,000–2,300 m; through most of the Great Basin to n. Baja California.

Notes Where found, this piñon is generally the predominant tree species, dominating large areas throughout isolated mountain ranges of the Great Basin, usually in piñon–juniper woodlands. At high elevations it commonly occurs with Great Basin Bristlecone Pine. In some areas it occurs with Twoneedle Piñon or Parry Piñon, and it hybridizes naturally (with both species); most hybrids bear needles in bundles of 2. The single needles are derived from a fusion of 5 needles, which you can see if you cut a cross section and examine it with a hand lens or microscope. As with the other piñon pines, the seeds are edible and have long been an important oil and protein source for Native Americans living within the species' range.

BORDER PIÑON   *Pinus discolor* D.K.
Bailey & Hawksw.

Very similar to Mexican Piñon but has very pliable needles that are bicolored, with the lower surface glaucous and the upper surface dark green. **HABITAT/RANGE** Native. N. Mexico, crossing the U.S.–Mexico border in se. Ariz. and sw. N.M.

MEXICAN PIÑON   *Pinus cembroides*
Zucc.

A.K.A. PIÑONERO

QUICK ID A shrubby tree of piñon–juniper and lower mixed conifer woodlands, with small, wide-opening cones and needles in bundles of 3.

Shrub or tree to 15 m tall, trunk to 30 cm diam., much branched, with a rounded crown. **BARK** Red-brown to dark brown, shallowly furrowed, with broad, scaly ridges. **TWIG** Red-brown, aging gray, smooth. **LEAF** Needle, 2–6 cm long, 0.6–1 mm thick, curved, stiff, blue- to gray-green, primarily in bundles of 3. **POLLEN CONE** Ellipsoid, 10 mm long, yellow. **SEED CONE** Ovoid before opening, flattened ovoid when open, 1–3.5 cm long, pale yellow or reddish brown, resinous, falling soon after maturity. Seeds brown, 12–15 mm long, wingless, edible.

HABITAT/RANGE Native. Piñon–juniper woodland, where soils are generally thin and rocky, climate is dry, and frosts uncommon, 700–2,400 m; se. Ariz., sw. N.M., and w. Texas, far south into Mexico.

Notes Mexican Piñon typically grows with various junipers, oaks, yuccas, and cacti. As with all other piñons, the edible seeds are gathered and cached by jays, and this is how the tree is spread across the landscape.

SINGLELEAF PIÑON

MEXICAN PIÑON

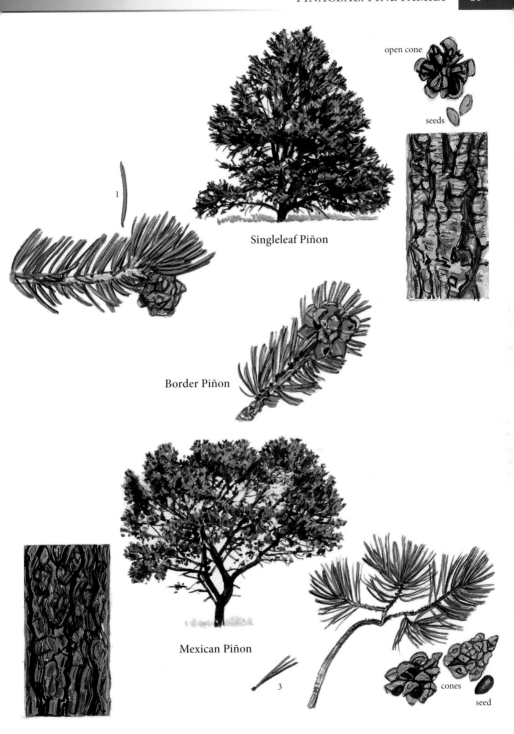

open cone

seeds

1

Singleleaf Piñon

Border Piñon

Mexican Piñon

3

cones

seed

PARRY PIÑON   *Pinus quadrifolia* Parl. ex Sudw.
A.K.A. FOUR-NEEDLE PIÑON, PINO CUATRO HOJAS

QUICK ID A shrubby tree of semiarid woodlands, with small, wide-opening cones and needles in bundles of 4 or 5.

Tree 5–15 m tall, with a fairly straight single trunk, to 50 cm diam., and a much-branched, irregularly rounded crown. **BARK** At first light gray and smooth, with age becoming red-brown, thick, scaly, longitudinally and horizontally furrowed. **TWIG** Slender, pale orange-brown, aging gray-brown. **LEAF** Needle, 1.5–6 cm long, 1–1.7 mm thick, slightly curved, stiff, sharp, green to blue-green, in bundles of 4 or 5, sometimes appearing single (roll between the fingers to separate). **POLLEN CONE** Ovoid, 10 mm long, yellow. **SEED CONE** Ovoid, 4–10 cm long, opening wide, pale yellow-brown, falling soon after maturity. Seeds 14–17 mm long, wingless, edible.

HABITAT/RANGE Native. Widespread in semiarid to arid foothills and mesas, 1,100–2,000 m; s. Calif. and adjacent Baja California.

Notes This was first described as a 4-needle pine, but 5-needle trees are much more common. Rainfall is less than 500 mm per year in its habitat. On relatively moist sites it may occur as an understory tree in Jeffrey Pine woodlands; on drier sites it becomes the dominant tree in extensive woodlands with California Juniper and sometimes Singleleaf Piñon; it is also a component of chaparral. Where Parry Piñon occurs with Singleleaf Piñon, the 2 commonly hybridize, producing trees that have intermediate characters, such as needles in bundles of 2 or 3.

PONDEROSA PINE   *Pinus ponderosa* Douglas ex C. Lawson
A.K.A. YELLOW PINE

QUICK ID A mountain pine with long needles in bundles of 3 and conical-ovoid cones.

Tree to 72 m tall, trunk to 2.5 m diam., usually with a straight bole and rounded crown. **BARK** Yellow- to red-brown, deeply furrowed into scaly polygonal plates; scales resemble jigsaw-puzzle pieces. **TWIG** Stout, orange-brown to dark gray, rough. **LEAF** Needle, 7–25 cm long, 1.2–2 mm thick, flexible, slightly twisted, yellow-green to dark green, spreading to erect, in tufts at the branchlet tips in bundles of 3, held in a persistent basal sheath 1.5–3 cm long. **POLLEN CONE** Cylindric, 1.5–3.5 cm long, yellow or red. **SEED CONE** Solitary or in pairs, axis straight or slightly curved, conical-ovoid before opening, broadly ovoid when open, 5–15 cm long, reddish brown, stalkless, the scales with or without a sharp prickle; falling within a year of maturity. Seeds 4–9 mm long, with a wing 15–25 mm long.

HABITAT/RANGE Native. Mostly in mountains, in pure stands or mixed conifer forests, 0–3,000 m; all western states and provinces from sc. B.C. to the Chisos Mountains of w. Tex.

SIMILAR SPECIES Ponderosa Pine shows great variation in size and appearance across its vast range, and some authorities recognize as many as 4 different subspecies. In the range of the very similar Jeffrey Pine, a Jeffrey cone feels smooth while a Ponderosa cone has sharp prickles. In s. Ariz., where Ponderosa Pine hybridizes with Arizona Pine, the Ponderosa cone has sharp, outcurved prickles, while the Arizona cone has incurved prickles. In the Pacific Northwest and the n. Rockies, Ponderosa Pine cones mostly have small outcurved prickles. Some authorities recognize a rare variety found in w. Nev. and n. Calif. as

PARRY PIÑON

PONDEROSA PINE

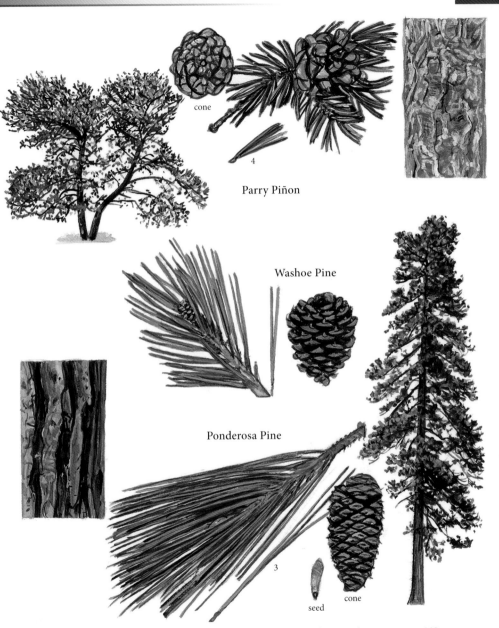

cone

4

Parry Piñon

Washoe Pine

Ponderosa Pine

3

seed

cone

Washoe Pine (*Pinus washoensis* H. Mason & Stockw.); it has short leaves (7–10 cm long) and mostly small cones with many scales.

Notes The most common pine of the w. U.S., Ponderosa Pine is superbly adapted throughout its range to frequent, low-intensity wildfire; most healthy stands experience ground fires at intervals that average between 2 and 20 years, and nearly all successful reproduction occurs in the aftermath of such fires.

ARIZONA PINE *Pinus arizonica* Engelm.
A.K.A. PINO DE ARIZONA

QUICK ID A Ponderosa-like pine of s. Ariz. and N.M., with 3–5 needles per bundle and cones that bear a recurved prickle and thus do not feel sharp.

Tree to 35 m tall, usually with a straight trunk, to 1.2 m diam., and open, round-topped crown. **BARK** At first dark brown, rough and scaly, with age becoming thick, deeply furrowed, and divided into large irregular plates of cinnamon-brown scales. **TWIG** Stout, rough, orange-brown, turning dark gray-brown. **LEAF** Needle, 10–20 cm long, 1–1.5 mm thick, slightly twisted, dark green, tufted at the ends of the branches, in bundles of 3–5 held in a persistent sheath up to 30 mm long. **POLLEN CONE** Clustered at the ends of new shoots, 15–20 mm long, yellow-brown. **SEED CONE** In clusters of 1–3 on short, stout stalks, ovoid, 5–7 cm long, light red-brown, the scales with slender, recurved spines; generally falls within a year after maturity. Seeds 4–6 mm long, with a wing 12–15 mm long.

HABITAT/RANGE Native. On various substrates, mostly in moderately dry forest, 2,000–2,700 m; se. Ariz., sw. N.M., and deep into Mexico.

Notes Arizona Pine is a common and widespread Mexican pine that grows locally in the U.S. and is commonly found with various oaks, pines, and junipers. It grows and sometimes hybridizes with Ponderosa Pine. Like the Ponderosa, it is well adapted to frequent, low-intensity fire and is often harvested for timber.

APACHE PINE *Pinus engelmannii* Carrière
A.K.A. PINO APACHE

QUICK ID A 3-needle pine with solitary asymmetric cones, and longer needles than any other western pine.

Tree to 35 m tall, with a straight trunk, to 60 cm diam., and a sparse, irregularly rounded crown. **BARK** Dark brown, deeply furrowed into narrow, scaly plates. **TWIG** Rough, stout, pale gray-brown, aging darker brown. **LEAF** Needle, 25–45 cm long, 2 mm thick, often drooping, dull green, borne at branch tips in bundles of 3, held in a persistent sheath 3–4 cm long. **POLLEN CONE** 25 mm long, yellow to yellow-brown. **SEED CONE** Solitary at twig ends, axis often curved, ovoid, 11–14 cm long, light, dull brown, very short-stalked, the scales bearing an outcurved claw; falls soon after maturity. Seeds 8–9 mm long, with a wing 20 mm long.

HABITAT/RANGE Native. High, dry mountains, commonly with oaks and other pines, 1,500–2,500 m; se. Ariz., sw. N.M., and nw. Mexico.

Notes Apache Pine strongly resembles Longleaf Pine of the e. U.S.; both species have very long needles, are highly fire-adapted, and have fire-tolerant "grass stage" seedlings that for several years resemble clumps of bunchgrass and can usually survive low-severity ground fires.

ARIZONA PINE

APACHE PINE

Arizona Pine

3/5

cones

Apache Pine

cone

3

pollen cones

JEFFREY PINE *Pinus jeffreyi* Balf.
A.K.A. BULL PINE, PINO DE JEFFREY

QUICK ID A pine very like Ponderosa Pine but with recurved prickles on the cone scales, so the cone feels smooth to the touch.

Tree to 61 m tall, usually with a straight trunk, to 2.5 m diam., and conical to columnar crown. **BARK** Yellowish to reddish brown, deeply furrowed into polygonal scaly plates. **TWIG** Stout, rough, purple-brown. **LEAF** Needle, 12–22 cm long, 1.5–2 mm thick, slightly twisted, gray- to yellow-green; spreading, in bundles of 3 held in a persistent sheath 1.5–2.5 cm long. **POLLEN CONE** Cylindric, 20–35 mm long, yellow. **SEED CONE** Borne near the twig ends, axis slightly curved, ellipsoid to ovoid, 15–30 cm long, light red-brown, nearly stalkless; scales bearing a short, slender, recurved prickle; falls soon after maturity. Seeds to 10 mm long, with a wing up to 25 mm long.

HABITAT/RANGE Native. Mountains, 2,000–3,100 m; Ore. south into n. Baja California, very common in Sierra Nevada. Also often found on serpentine and other nutrient-poor soils, especially in the Klamath and Siskiyou mountains, where it grows slowly but competes with other trees.

SIMILAR SPECIES This species occurs with and closely resembles Ponderosa Pine, but typically occurs at somewhat greater elevations, has darker and longer foliage, has more nearly ellipsoidal cones with more scales per cm of cone length, and the scales have a recurved prickle, while Ponderosa cones feel sharp-prickled.

Notes The sap is extremely flammable; historically, efforts to extract turpentine from this species often led to explosions. The flammable constituent, heptane, later became the standard for the octane scale used to rate gasolines.

COULTER PINE *Pinus coulteri* D. Don
A.K.A. PINO DE COULTER

QUICK ID A 3-needle pine resembling Ponderosa Pine but with very large, heavy, dangerous-looking cones.

Tree to 25 m tall, usually with a straight trunk, to 1.4 m diam., and an open, columnar crown. **BARK** Dark gray-brown to near black, deeply furrowed, with scaly, rounded ridges. **TWIG** Rough, thinner than usual for large hard pines, violet-brown, aging gray-brown. **LEAF** Needle, 15–30 cm long, 2 mm thick, twisted, gray-green, slightly spreading, not drooping, in bundles of 3 held in a persistent sheath 2–4 cm long. **POLLEN CONE** To 25 mm long, light purplish brown. **SEED CONE** Ovoid-ellipsoid, 20–35 cm long, pale yellow-brown, resinous, massive, heavy, drooping, on a stalk to 3 cm long; scales tipped with long, upcurved claws 2.5–3 cm long; most cones fall soon after maturity. Seeds 15–22 mm long, with a wing 25 mm long.

HABITAT/RANGE Native. Usually in chaparral, oak–pine woodland, or montane forest, often on steep south-facing slopes, 300–2,100 m; Calif., n. Baja California.

Notes Coulter Pine's typical associates include Canyon Live Oak, Blue Oak, Gray Pine, Jeffrey Pine, Douglas-fir, and White Fir; locally it grows with Coast Redwood. The species is more fire-tolerant than most pines, and some populations, especially in chaparral and oak woodland, bear serotinous cones. Coulter Pine's cones are the largest and heaviest of any pine, with recorded examples up to 50 cm long and weighing up to 3.6 kg. The large, nutritious seeds are an important food source for squirrels, woodpeckers, and other wildlife. Trees grow quickly and are handsome, so are popular ornamentals; the largest known specimen is an ornamental in New Zealand.

JEFFREY PINE

COULTER PINE

3

cone

Jeffrey Pine

3

cone

Coulter Pine

seeds

CHIHUAHUA PINE *Pinus leiophylla* var. *chihuahuana* (Engelm.) Shaw

A.K.A. OCOTE CHINO, PINO REAL

QUICK ID A 2- or 3-needle hard pine with a needle sheath that soon falls away, and abundant small cones.

Tree to 26 m tall, trunk to 1 m diam., slender, often forked higher up; crown conical, becoming rounded. **BARK** Brown to red-brown, narrowly furrowed, cross-checked into long, irregularly and narrowly rectangular, flat, scaly ridges. **TWIG** Slender, orange-brown or glaucous, aging red-brown. **LEAF** Needle, 6–12 cm long, 0.8–1.3 mm thick, gray-green; spreading, in bundles of 2 or 3 held in a sheath 1.5 cm long that soon falls away. **POLLEN CONE** Ellipsoid, 10–15 mm long, brown or yellow. **SEED CONE** Paired or solitary, broadly ovoid, 3.5–5 cm long, on a stalk to 1.5 cm long, brown, aging gray, and remaining on the tree for some years. Seeds 2 mm long, with a wing to 10 mm long.

HABITAT/RANGE Native. Mountains, commonly with junipers, piñon pines, Apache Pine, and Arizona Pine, 1,500–2,700 m; Mexico, Ariz., N.M.

Notes This and Torrey Pine are our only native pines that take 3 years to mature their cones. This is the only hard pine in which the needle sheath is not persistent, and one of the few pines that can resprout from a cut stump.

GRAY PINE *Pinus sabiniana* Douglas ex D. Don

A.K.A. FOOTHILLS PINE, DIGGER PINE

QUICK ID A pine with grayish foliage, an open crown, and large, heavy cones, commonly found in chaparral or oak woodland.

Tree to 25 m tall, trunk to 1.2 m diam., often with a forked trunk and sparse conical to irregular crown. **BARK** Deeply furrowed, scaly, dark brown but orangish at the bottom of the furrows. **TWIG** Of varying thickness, rough, pale purple-brown, graying with age. **LEAF** Needle, 15–32 cm long, 1.5 mm thick, slightly twisted, pale blue-green, mostly in bundles of 3, held in a persistent basal sheath to 2.4 cm long. **POLLEN CONE** Ellipsoid, 10–15 mm long, yellow. **SEED CONE** Ovoid or blunt-ellipsoid, 15–25 cm long, dull brown, resinous, massive, heavy, hanging from a stalk up to 5 cm long; scales long, thick, bearing at the tips upcurved claws to 2 cm long; cones fall soon after maturity. Seeds thick-walled, 20 mm long, with a wing to 10 mm long.

HABITAT/RANGE Native. Dry foothills, usually in woodlands with California Blue Oak or Canyon Live Oak, sometimes on serpentine soils, 300–900 m; Calif., sw. Ore.

Notes Gray Pine is moderately fire-adapted; its short life span and prolific cone production are typical for pines, which are usually killed by fire but shed seeds that quickly reestablish the forest. The name Digger Pine is common in older books and internationally but is now regarded as disrespectful of the Native Americans who formerly gathered the seeds of this pine. The seeds, which have vestigial wings, are distributed primarily by Steller's Jays (*Cyanocitta stelleri*) and Western Scrub-jays (*Aphelocoma californica*), which gather them and bury them in caches, much as squirrels bury nuts.

TORREY PINE *Pinus torreyana* Parry ex Carrière

A.K.A. SOLEDAD PINE, DEL MAR PINE

QUICK ID A round-crowned pine with needles in bundles of 5 and large, heavy cones.

Tree to 30 m tall, trunk to 1 m diam. (sometimes larger in cultivation), in nature mostly crooked and leaning but in cultivation tall and straight; crown rounded to irregular. **BARK** Reddish brown, deeply furrowed, with scaly ridges. **TWIG** Stout (1–2 cm thick), green, aging deep gray-brown, rough. **LEAF** Needle, 20–30 cm long, 2 mm thick, straight or curved, slightly twisted, pointed,

CHIHUAHUA PINE

GRAY PINE

2/3

cone

Chihuahua Pine

cone

3

Gray Pine

TORREY PINE *continued*

dark green, all surfaces with fine stomatal lines; clustered near branch tips, spreading, in bundles of 5 held in a sheath to 2 cm long that is shed early. **POLLEN CONE** Ovoid, 20–30 mm long, yellow. **SEED CONE** Lateral, ovoid, 10–15 cm long, massive and heavy, yellow- to red-brown, lustrous; scales with thick apophyses; most cones fall after maturity, but some remain on the tree for years. Seeds ovoid, brown, 16–24 mm long, with a wing up to 15 mm long.

HABITAT/RANGE Native. Calif., on the coast at Torrey Pines State Natural Reserve in San Diego County and at the eastern end of Santa Rosa Island, 0–200 m. Also a common ornamental in s. Calif.

Notes Its very small native distribution makes this the rarest North American pine.

BISHOP PINE *Pinus muricata* D. Don
A.K.A. PINO OBISPO

QUICK ID A closed-cone pine with needles in bundles of 2, native to Calif.

Tree to 24 m tall, trunk to 90 cm diam., straight to contorted, crown rounded, flattened, or irregular. **BARK** Dark gray, deeply furrowed into long ridges, scaly. **TWIG** Slender to stout, orange-brown, aging darker brown, rough. **LEAF** Needle, 8–15 cm long, 1.5 mm thick, curved, slightly twisted, tip pointed, dark yellow-green, glaucous in northern populations, all surfaces with stomatal lines; spreading, in bundles of 2 held in a persistent sheath to 1.5 cm long. **POLLEN CONE** Ellipsoid, to 5 mm long, orange. **SEED CONE** Mostly in whorls of 1–5 cones, axis curved, long-ovoid before opening, ovoid when open, 4–9 cm long, glossy brown; scales with apophyses thick, each scale tipped by a stout, curved claw; cones serotinous, persisting for decades (longer than any other pine). Seeds ellipsoid, dark brown, 6–7 mm long, with a wing 15–20 mm long.

HABITAT/RANGE Native. Dry ridges, coastal wind-shaped forests, often in or around bogs or in other nutrient-poor soils, 0–300 m; scattered locations along the entire Calif. coast and offshore on Santa Cruz Island and Santa Rosa Island, and in n. Baja California.

Notes Like its close relatives Monterey Pine and Knobcone Pine, this pine has a limited distribution in Calif. and is highly adapted to fire, which it requires to open its cones so they may shed their seeds.

KNOBCONE PINE *Pinus attenuata*
Lemmon
A.K.A. PINO DE ELDORADO

QUICK ID A closed-cone pine with needles in bundles of 3, with a more interior and drier distribution compared to Monterey Pine.

Tree to 35 m tall, trunk to 90 cm diam., or on very poor sites a shrub; crown usually conical. **BARK** Purple-brown to dark brown, smooth, becoming narrowly fissured between scaly plates. **TWIG** Slender, red-brown. **LEAF** Needle, 9–15 cm long, 1.3–1.8 mm thick, straight or slightly curved, twisted, pointed, yellow-green, all surfaces with fine stomatal lines; spreading, in bundles of 3 held in a persistent sheath 1.5–2 cm long. **POLLEN CONE** Cylindric, 10–15 mm long, orange-brown. **SEED CONE** Abundant, in whorls of 1–5 cones, heavy, axis strongly curved, conical, 8–16 cm long, yellow-brown or pale brown; scales swollen (knobby), with a low, sharp, upcurved point; cones serotinous, sometimes remaining closed for 20 years or more. Seeds compressed-ovoid, black, 6–7 mm long, with a narrow wing 15–20 mm long.

HABITAT/RANGE Native. Mainly on dry slopes and foothills, coastal and interior mountains 400–1,700 m; sw. Ore., Calif., n. Baja California.

Notes This short-lived little tree is superbly adapted to frequently burned sites with poor soils, where it can outcompete all other trees, maintaining dominance by soon regenerating after a fire.

KNOBCONE PINE

Torrey Pine

cone

5

Bishop Pine

cone

2

Knobcone Pine

cones

cone

3

MONTEREY PINE *Pinus radiata* D. Don
A.K.A. RADIATA PINE

QUICK ID A closed-cone pine with needles in bundles of 3, native to a small stretch of coastal Calif.

Tree to 38 m tall, trunk to 2 m diam., contorted to straight, with a broadly conical crown. **BARK** Scaly, gray to reddish brown, with deep longitudinal furrows. **TWIG** Slender, red-brown, sometimes glaucous, turning gray with age. **LEAF** Needle, 9–15 cm long, 1.3–1.8 mm thick, straight, pointed, slightly twisted, deep yellow-green, all surfaces with stomatal lines; spreading, in bundles of 3 held in a persistent sheath 1.5–2 cm long. **POLLEN CONE** Cylindric, 10–15 mm long, orange-brown. **SEED CONE** Numerous, solitary or in whorls of up to 5, axis strongly curved, ovoid before opening, broad-ovoid when open, 7–15 cm long, yellow-brown, lustrous, scales rigid, occasionally with a slender, fragile prickle; mostly serotinous, persisting many years. Seeds dark brown, 6 mm long, with a wing 20–30 mm long.

HABITAT/RANGE Native. The U.S. population occurs naturally at only 3 localities in a fog belt on the coast of c. Calif., 30–400 m. Ornamental specimens north to coastal Ore. show signs of naturalizing.

Notes The 3 surviving native stands of Monterey Pine are infected and under threat of extinction from pitch canker, a disease caused by the fungus *Fusarium circinatum*, which is native to the se. U.S. and in 1986 was found to have been introduced to Calif. When trees begin to die of the disease, they attract bark beetles, which provide a pathway for infection of other trees. Meanwhile, Monterey Pine has been introduced as a timber tree in vast areas of New Zealand (where the largest and tallest specimens are found), Australia, Chile, sw. Europe, and South Africa. These overseas plantations have been selectively bred and bear increasingly little resemblance to the native trees; they could be called a domesticated pine.

LODGEPOLE PINE *Pinus contorta*
Douglas

QUICK ID A 2-needle pine with small woody cones.

Tree or shrub, to 50 m tall, trunk to 90 cm diam., straight to contorted, with a variably conical-

cylindric crown. **BARK** Gray- or red-brown, plated to furrowed. **TWIG** Slender, rough, orange to red-brown, aging darker brown. **LEAF** Needle, 2–8 cm long, 0.7–2 mm thick, twisted, blunt to sharp, yellow-green to dark green, all surfaces with fine stomatal lines; spreading, persisting 3–8 years, in bundles of 2 held in a persistent sheath 3–6 mm long. **POLLEN CONE** Ovoid, 5–15 mm long, red to yellow. **SEED CONE** Axis usually curved, conical to ovoid when closed, globose when open, 3–6 cm long, pale to reddish brown, lustrous, variably serotinous, variably persistent. Seeds obovoid, black, 5 mm long, with a wing 10–14 mm long.

HABITAT/RANGE Native. Found in a greater variety of habitats than any other conifer, at 0–3,900 m, in most of w. North America. There are 3 subspecies, each in a different habitat: Shore Pine (subsp. *contorta*) grows as a typically short, contorted tree on exposed coastal headlands, in bogs, and as an early-successional species in fire-maintained prairies from se. Alaska to n. Calif.; Sierra Lodgepole (subsp. *murrayana* [Balf.] Engelm.) grows as a large tree within mixed conifer forest from montane to timberline settings from s. Ore. to n. Baja California; Rocky Mountain Lodgepole (subsp. *latifolia* [Engelm. ex S. Wats.] Critchfield) forms vast, single-species stands that regenerate after fire, at montane to alpine elevations from Y.T. to Colo.

Notes The Lodgepole Pine is a close relative of Jack Pine, and Rocky Mountain Lodgepole has a similar ecology. Both species are shade-intolerant but regenerate after fire, their cones opened by its heat. They both form dense, continuous stands that are vulnerable to death by insect attack, which is generally followed within a few years by another fire. Thus, although individual trees usually do not live long or grow large, each species perpetuates itself on the landscape indefinitely, effectively competing against other forest trees.

LODGEPOLE PINE

Monterey Pine

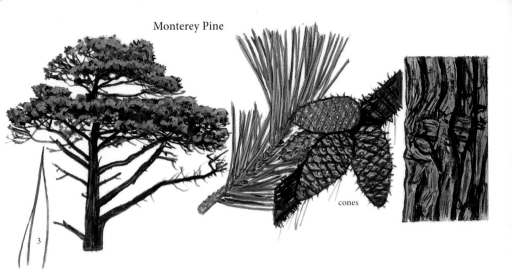

cones

3

Lodgepole Pine

2

cone

seeds

JACK PINE *Pinus banksiana* Lamb.
A.K.A. BLACKJACK PINE, PIN GRIS

QUICK ID A 2-needle pine of Canada with small cones borne in whorls on the twigs.

Tree to 27 m tall, trunk to 60 cm diam., but often small and spindly. **BARK** Scaly, orange-brown. **TWIG** Slender, reddish when young, gray-brown and rough with age. **LEAF** Needle, 2–5 cm long, 1–1.5 mm thick, twisted, yellow-green, in bundles of 2 held in a sheath 3–6 mm long. **POLLEN CONE** 10–15 mm long, yellow to orange-brown, in small clusters. **SEED CONE** In whorls of 1–4 at intervals on twigs, axis curved, conical when closed, ovoid when open, pointing forward along branch, 3–5.5 cm long, light brown, sessile or short-stalked; scales thickened at the tip, with an easily broken prickle; cones shed seeds soon after maturity or are serotinous; variably persistent.

HABITAT/RANGE Native. Often on thin, poor or dry sandy soils, primarily in boreal forest, extending north to the Arctic timberline, 0–800 m; from Y.T. east to Man. and onward to the shores of the Atlantic Ocean.

SIMILAR SPECIES Resembles Lodgepole Pine but has very small cones and a more easterly range.

Notes Jack Pine is the most widespread Canadian pine; it often grows with Paper Birch, Quaking Aspen, or Black Spruce. Jack Pine rarely reaches 150 years of age, and the oldest tree known was less than 250 years old. It is superbly adapted to fire; its cones open and shed seeds soon after a burn, and the young trees produce cones at an early age.

SCOTS PINE *Pinus sylvestris* L.
A.K.A. SCOTCH PINE

QUICK ID An ornamental pine with orange-red bark and fairly short glaucous needles; the only 2-needled hard pine with blue-green or gray-green leaves.

Tree to 25 m tall, with a straight trunk, to 70 cm diam., and highly variable crown. **BARK** Thin, flaking, and orange-red, with age growing thick, scaly-plated, and gray-brown. **TWIG** Slender, green at first, becoming gray-buff by the end of the first summer. **LEAF** Needle, 4–6 cm long (longest on vigorous young trees, shorter on old trees), 1.5–2 mm thick, always glaucous, blue-green to gray-green, in bundles of 2 held in a sheath 5–8 mm long. **POLLEN CONE** 8–12 mm long, yellow or pink. **SEED CONE** Conical to ovoid, 3–6 cm long, gray-buff to gray-green; scales with a very small prickle; cones fall soon after maturity.

HABITAT/RANGE Introduced, with the largest natural distribution of any pine in the world, from Scotland to Siberia. A very popular ornamental throughout the cool-temperate states and provinces; in the West, naturalized in B.C., Alta., Man.

SIMILAR SPECIES The popular dwarf ornamental Mugo Pine closely resembles Scots Pine but usually has gray bark and smaller cones; its foliage, usually dark green, is not glaucous.

JACK PINE

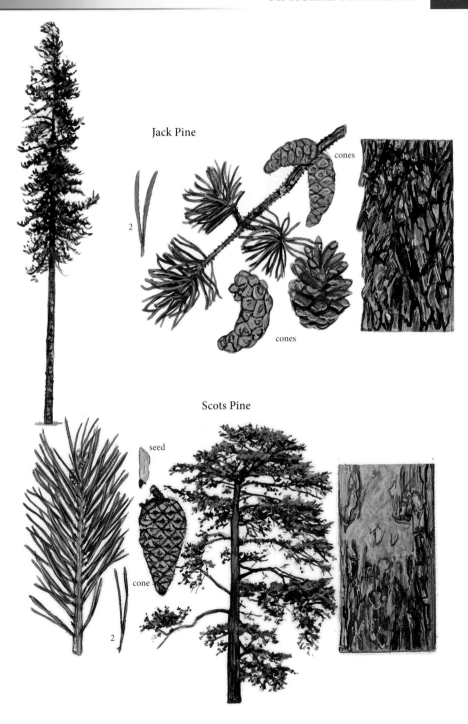

Jack Pine

2

cones

cones

Scots Pine

seed

cone

2

Ornamental Pines

Many ornamental pines are commonly grown in w. North America, some more common than others. Mugo Pine and Austrian Pine are the most cold-tolerant of these 5 species.

AUSTRIAN PINE *Pinus nigra* J.F. Arnold

LEAF This pine is distinctive for its thick, stiff, dark green needle, 8–15 cm long, 1.5–2 mm thick, in bundles of 2. **SEED CONE** Conical with a curved axis, 5–10 cm long, borne in whorls near branch ends, falling soon after opening. **HABITAT/RANGE** Introduced from Europe; a popular ornamental in B.C., Wash., Ore., and many interior locations.

JAPANESE RED PINE *Pinus densiflora* Siebold & Zucc.

BARK Distinctive reddish plates. **LEAF** Similar to that of Austrian Pine. Needle, 8–12 cm long, 0.7–1.2 mm thick, in bundles of 2. **SEED CONE** Ovoid, 4–7 cm long, retained on the tree for several years after opening. **HABITAT/RANGE** Introduced from Asia; popular from coastal B.C. south into n. Calif.

STONE PINE *Pinus pinea* L.

Distinctive dense, dome-shaped crown. **BARK** Thick, plated, deeply fissured. **LEAF** Needle, 10–18 cm long, about 1.5 mm thick, in bundles of 2; often also bears pale blue-green juvenile foliage less than 4 cm long. **SEED CONE** Ovoid, 8–12 cm long, with very thick woody scales; take 3 full years to develop, falling after maturity. **HABITAT/RANGE** Introduced from Mediterranean region; grown mostly from Central Valley, Calif., southward and in s. Ariz. *Notes* The source of *pignoli*, the pine nuts popular in Italian cooking.

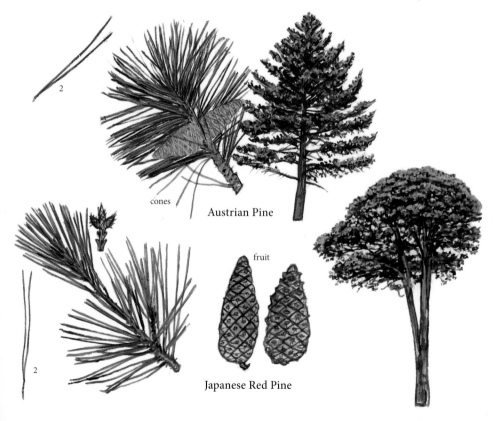

2

cones
Austrian Pine

fruit

2

Japanese Red Pine

cone

seeds

2

Stone Pine

cone

3

Canary Island Pine

Canary Island Pine

seed

pollen cones

2

cone

Mugo Pine

cone

cone

CANARY ISLAND PINE *Pinus canariensis* C. Sm. ex Buch

Crown of long, stout branchlets tipped with ball-shaped tufts of foliage. **LEAF** Needle, 15–28 cm long, pliable, in bundles of 3. Frequently sprouts pale blue-green juvenile needles from the trunk. **SEED CONE** Axis slightly curved, ovoid, hard, heavy, 10–20 cm long, falling after maturity. **HABITAT/RANGE** Introduced from the Canary Islands; the least cold-tolerant of these 4 species, but a very popular ornamental where it can be grown, mainly in Calif. south from Sacramento.

MUGO PINE *Pinus mugo* Turra

Shrub or (rarely) small tree. **LEAF** Needle, 2.3–7.5 cm long, in bundles of 2, light to dark green, not glaucous. **SEED CONE** Sessile, symmetric, 2–5 cm long, globose when open. **HABITAT/RANGE** Introduced from Europe; this is one of the few trees of the high mountains (in its native range it occurs in the Alps and Carpathians) that thrives and remains small when planted at low elevations.

■ *PSEUDOTSUGA:* DOUGLAS-FIRS

A genus of 7 species of East Asia and w. North America; all are predominately forest trees of the mountains, but they may occur in woodlands, near the timberline, or (rarely) in rocky arid woodlands. The cones, with prominently 3-pointed bracts extending from between the scales, are unique; some fir cones are similar, but they disintegrate before falling from the tree.

Evergreen trees with single trunks and pyramidal crowns that often become irregular with age. **BARK** Reddish brown to black, thick, furrowed. **TWIG** Slender. **LEAF** Needle, 15–45 mm long, with 2 whitish stomatal bands on the lower side, spirally arranged on the twig. **SEED CONE** Borne at the tips of year-old twigs, maturing in 1 year, long-ovoid, with numerous seed scales interleaved with conspicuous 3-pointed bracts, the cones falling soon after seed dispersal. Seeds 2 per scale, winged.

Within the pine family, the Douglas-firs are most closely related to the larches (*Larix*); the 2 genera diverged from the rest of the family about 135 million years ago and from each other about 70 million years ago.

DOUGLAS-FIR *Pseudotsuga menziesii*
(Mirb.) Franco
A.K.A. Douglas Spruce, Douglasia Verde

QUICK ID Cones less than 10 cm long with projecting 3-pointed bracts distinguish Douglas-fir from all other conifers.

Tree to 100 m tall, usually with a single trunk, to 4.4 m diam., and a conical crown that becomes flattened or irregular with age. **BARK** Reddish brown to black, plated, usually hard and deeply furrowed, but sometimes soft, smooth, and flaky. **TWIG** Slender, finely hairy. **LEAF** Needle, 15–30 mm long, 1–1.5mm wide, various shades but usually dark green or blue-green, spirally arranged along the length of the twig. **SEED CONE** Long-ovoid, 4–10 cm long, 3-pointed bracts exserted from between scales, bracts variously appressed to reflexed. Seeds 5–6 mm long, with a wing 6–8 mm long.

HABITAT/RANGE Native. From central B.C. south into Mexico, in all states and provinces west from the Rocky Mountains, at elevations ranging from sea-level in the north to about 2,800 m in s. Ariz. and N.M. With this enormous range, it occurs in a very wide range of habitats, from riparian areas in the desert to coastal rain forests and alpine timberlines.

Notes There are 2 varieties: The coastal variety (var. *menziesii*) is as described above and usually has cones with appressed bracts; the interior variety (var. *glauca* [Mayr] Franco) is usually a smaller tree, seldom above 30 m tall and 100 cm diam., with furrowed black bark and cones with reflexed bracts. The coastal variety is found from the coast inland to the e. Cascades and Sierra Nevada, where it gradationally transitions to the interior variety. Douglas-fir is one of the world's most important timber trees, the mainstay of timber production in the Pacific Northwest and now also planted in many other countries, including New Zealand and Germany. On good sites it can quickly grow to very large sizes (1 specimen is the largest tree in the pine family), and it produces an extremely strong, durable timber ideally suited for construction use. Ecologically, it is as important as Ponderosa Pine, acting as the dominant tree species in forests that cover nearly 1.3 million square kilometers in North America.

BIGCONE DOUGLAS-FIR *Pseudotsuga macrocarpa* (Vasey) Mayr
A.K.A. Bigcone Spruce, Desert Fir

QUICK ID A tree of s. Calif. mountains, very like Douglas-fir but with much larger cones.

Tree to 30 m tall, trunk to 1 m diam., with a conical crown that commonly becomes irregular with age. **BARK** Rough, dark gray, furrowed. **TWIG** Slender, finely hairy. **LEAF** Needle, 25–45 mm long, 1–1.5 mm wide, bluish green, with a pointed but

DOUGLAS-FIR

BIGCONE DOUGLAS-FIR

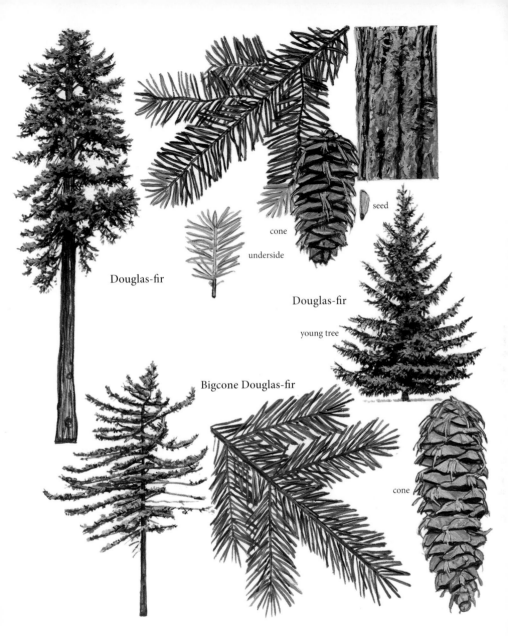

Douglas-fir

Douglas-fir
young tree

Bigcone Douglas-fir

cone

underside

cone

seed

not sharp tip. **SEED CONE** Long-ovoid, 9–20 cm long, 4–7 cm wide when open, the 3-pointed bracts usually exserted from between the scales. Seeds 9–12 mm long including the wing.

HABITAT/RANGE Native. Usually on mountain slopes, cliffs, and canyons, in chaparral and mixed conifer forests, 200–2,400 m; sw. Calif.

Notes Bigcone Douglas-fir's common associates are chaparral shrubs, Coulter Pine, Incense Cedar, and Canyon Live Oak, or in riparian settings Bigleaf Maple and Black Cottonwood. It does not occur with Douglas-fir. Tolerant of fire, it will often survive a blaze intense enough to kill all living foliage, and will sprout vigorously from branches and bole after a burn.

■ *TSUGA*: HEMLOCKS

There are 7 hemlock species found in e. and w. North America and East Asia; 2 species occur in w. North America. Hemlocks are monoecious evergreen trees, usually with a straight, single trunk; the crown is topped by a single drooping leader. They are broadly similar to spruce or fir, but branchlets are produced throughout the growing season, the leader droops, and trees have short, blunt needles, and very small cones. **BARK** Rough, scaly, fissured. **LEAF** Needle, spirally arranged on twigs but usually appearing 2-ranked, flattened, upper surface shiny, stomata in 2 whitish bands on the lower surface. **POLLEN CONE** Solitary, subglobular. **SEED CONE** Solitary, erect at pollination but soon becoming pendulous, bracts hidden within the seed scales.

Both of our native hemlock species grow in moist forest on good soils or up into the subalpine parkland, usually as codominants with a variety of other conifers. They are shade-tolerant trees, able to establish under a forest canopy and slowly grow to become canopy-dominant trees. The genus name, *Tsuga*, is the common Japanese name for hemlock, and is also the common name in most countries where there are no native hemlocks.

WESTERN HEMLOCK *Tsuga heterophylla* (Raf.) Sarg.

QUICK ID A conifer similar to a spruce or fir but with 2-ranked leaves less than 20 mm long and cones less than 2.5 cm long.

Tree to 75 m tall, trunk to 2 m diam., with a conical to columnar crown topped with a drooping leader. **BARK** Gray-brown, scaly, and moderately fissured. **TWIG** Yellow-brown, finely hairy, 0.7–2 mm thick; produces multiple lateral twigs over the course of a growing season. **LEAF** Needle, 10–20 mm long, flattened, thin, very flexible, mostly blunt-tipped; upper surface shiny, dark green; lower surface pale green with 2 broad whitish stomatal bands; appears roughly 2-ranked but with scattered leaves pointing varying degrees upward or downward. **SEED CONE** Ellipsoid or ovoid, 1.5–2.5 cm long, brown, composed of about 25 ovate scales each 8–15 mm long and 6–10 mm wide.

HABITAT/RANGE Native. Coastal to mid-montane forests, usually as a codominant with other conifers, particularly Douglas-fir, Sitka Spruce, and Western Redcedar, 0–1,830 m; Alta. to Calif.

Notes Due to its high shade tolerance and ability to take root on downed wood (traits that it shares with Sitka Spruce), Western Hemlock can persist for millennia, even in forests that do not experience fire. The oldest known tree, 1,238 years, was found in an ancient forest that has not known fire for at least several thousand years. The tallest known tree, 83 m, is growing next to an even taller Coast Redwood. The bark has a high tannin content, and native peoples used it as a tanning agent, pigment, and cleansing solution. They used the branches for bedding and the pitch and inner bark for medicinal purposes. Today, the tree is the most economically important timber species among the hemlocks.

MOUNTAIN HEMLOCK *Tsuga mertensiana* (Bong.) Carrière

QUICK ID Short needles lacking conspicuous stomatal bands and long-ellipsoid cones of stiff, fan-shaped scales identify this species.

Tree to 40 m tall, trunk to 1.5 m diam.; crown conical. **BARK** Charcoal gray to reddish brown, scaly and deeply fissured. **TWIG** Yellow-brown, densely hairy. **LEAF** Needle, 10–25 mm long, thickened

WESTERN HEMLOCK

MOUNTAIN HEMLOCK

Western Hemlock

cone

Mountain Hemlock

cone

centrally along the midline, somewhat rounded in cross section, glaucous, with inconspicuous stomatal bands; mostly spreading in all directions from the twig. **SEED CONE** Ellipsoid, 3–6 cm long; purple, ripening brown; comprised of many fan-shaped scales.

HABITAT/RANGE Native. Upper subalpine forest or in the subalpine parkland, often in pure stands, or with other subalpine conifers; in its lower elevational range it overlaps with the Western Hemlock; 0–3,050 m, with elevations increasing at lower latitudes; Alaska to Calif.

Notes Mountain Hemlock is most abundant in areas with an average annual temperature of about 4°C, and with more than 100 cm annual precipitation. It commonly forms tree clumps in the subalpine parkland. Most such sites experience very heavy winter snowfall. The trees can establish on sites with locally reduced snow, often during a spell of dry years. Once established, blackbody radiation from the trees causes the snow to melt earlier around them, so there is a longer growing season, and hence new seedlings tend to establish very close to existing trees. Over time, this process leads to the formation of tree clumps.

TAXACEAE: YEW FAMILY

A family of 6 genera and 28 species, found throughout much of the Northern Hemisphere and farther south in Indonesia, with 2 genera and 2 species occurring in w. North America, locally distributed from Alta. to Calif.

Dioecious or monoecious evergreen trees and shrubs, often multistemmed. **BARK** Scaly or fissured, usually reddish. **LEAF** Needle, alternate, appearing 2-ranked; crushed leaves do not smell resinous (unlike those of other conifers). **SEED** Naked, at the end of a short stalk, partially or completely covered by a fleshy aril, resembling small green or red berries, usually only 1 ovule of 2 developing. The seeds are mostly dispersed by birds.

CALIFORNIA NUTMEG *Torreya californica* Torr.
A.K.A. CALIFORNIA TORREYA

QUICK ID A small Yew-like tree with very sharply pointed leaves and a cone that resembles a small lime.

Tree to 40 m tall, trunk to 2 m diam., but usually much smaller, with a conical to irregular crown. **BARK** Gray-brown, coarsely scaly, with lateral and longitudinal furrows. **TWIG** At first green, clad in green leaves; in its 2nd year red-brown, thereafter developing bark. **LEAF** Needle, 3–8 cm long, 1–2 mm wide, very sharply pointed, the lower surface with 2 pale stomatal bands, 2-ranked; has a strong nonresinous odor when crushed. **SEED CONE** Short-ellipsoid, 2.5–3.5 cm long, green, the leathery aril completely covering the seed.

HABITAT/RANGE Native. Uncommon, in riparian areas and on mountain slopes, 0–2,000 m; Coast Range and Sierra Nevada, Ore. and Calif.

Notes California Nutmeg frequently grows with Canyon Live Oak or California Bay. Native Americans used the wood to make bows and the roots to make baskets, and ate the seeds.

PACIFIC YEW *Taxus brevifolia* Nutt.
A.K.A. WESTERN YEW

QUICK ID A conifer with 2-ranked green needles, scaly reddish bark, and red "berries" instead of cones.

Dioecious shrubs or small trees to 25 m tall, trunk to 1.4 m diam., but usually found as small understory trees with open, irregular crowns. **BARK** Reddish brown, smooth to coarsely scaly. **TWIG** Green, entirely covered by leaf bases; in later years turning red-brown. **LEAF** 8–35 mm long, 1–3 mm wide, linear, pointed but not sharp, flexible, often curved, green, often with a bronze tint, stomata in 2 yellow-green bands on the lower surface, 2-ranked. **SEED CONE** Berrylike, with a fleshy red aril, 10 mm diam., covering all but the tip of a seed 6 mm diam.

HABITAT/RANGE Native. Locally common in open to dense forests, along streams, moist flats, slopes, deep ravines, and coves, 0–2,200 m; from sc. B.C. and Alta. south to the c. Sierra Nevada.

Notes In most of its range, Pacific Yew grows as a tree beneath a closed forest canopy in old forests dominated by large conifers, but on open sites

CALIFORNIA NUTMEG

PACIFIC YEW

California Nutmeg

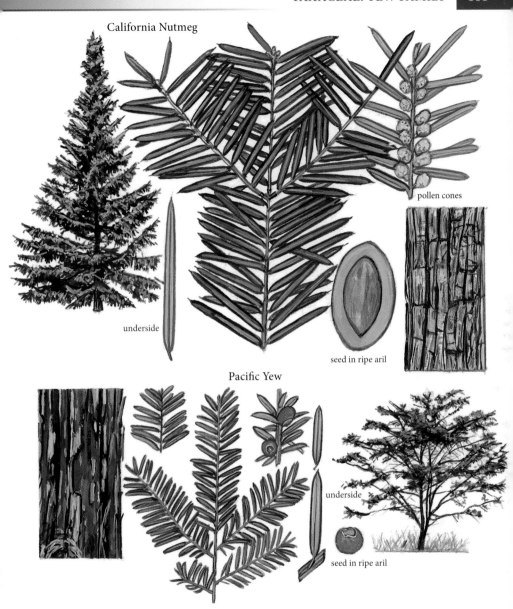

pollen cones

underside

seed in ripe aril

Pacific Yew

underside

seed in ripe aril

such as rocky mountainsides it forms a spreading shrub that may cover many square meters. Native peoples living within its range considered the wood very valuable, using it for weapons and implements that require strength and toughness. Nearly every tribe that could collect or trade for it used it to make bows. Yew also has had many medicinal uses, including wound treatment and applications of a magical nature, such as using the tree to impart strength. Many yew populations were decimated in the 1990s when it was found that the plants contain paclitaxel (taxol), which is effective against uterine cancer. Today, however, taxol is derived from other sources.

Angiosperms, the flowering plants, may be herbaceous or woody, large or small, with large showy flowers or tiny flowers that escape notice. Found almost throughout the world, they are absent from only the harshest environments. There are 250,000–400,000 species of angiosperms.

MONOCOTS

Monocotyledons (monocots for short) are a large group of the flowering plants (angiosperms) that includes the palms, agaves and yuccas, grasses, orchids, sedges, rushes, and lilies. Most monocots have parallel leaf veins (as opposed to the netlike venation of the other major assemblage, the dicotyledons, or dicots) and the flower parts, such as sepals, petals, and stamens, are usually in multiples of 3 (rather than 4 or 5).

ARECACEAE: PALM FAMILY

The palms compose a family of tropical shrubs and trees with about 190 genera and 2,500 species. Of the 29 species that occur in the U.S. north of Mexico, 6 are trees in the West, and of these only 2 are native.

Palms are evergreen trees or shrubs, or rarely vinelike. The distinctive structure makes them immediately recognizable. Palms grow upward from a single large meristem at the tip of the trunk, which progressively adds to the stem as it produces massive evergreen leaves arranged in a tight spiral, producing a rosette. If the tip is seriously damaged or is removed, the tree will die. **TRUNK** Though palms are "woody," the wood is very fibrous, and the food-conducting cells (phloem) and water-conducting cells (xylem) within their trunks are more or less intermixed (rather than separated, with the xylem internal to the phloem, as in woody dicots). The surface of the trunk is composed of living tissue that does not flake off like the bark of dicot trees; hence, external injuries to a palm's trunk do not disappear. Palms also do not produce twigs, and branching is rare. The trunks of some palms are covered with the remains of old leaf scars or leaf bases, the latter sometimes referred to as "boots." **LEAF** Pinnate, palmate, or in some cases appearing palmate but with a very short midrib extending beyond the tip of the petiole (costapalmate); the petiole sometimes bears conspicuous piercing spines. **FLOWER** Bisexual or unisexual; when the latter, may be on the same or separate plants. Flowers are borne in clusters that arise from leaf axils within or below the crown. Sepals and petals number 3 each, stamens usually 6; the ovary is usually superior and most often 3-chambered. **FRUIT** Usually a drupe or drupelike.

Palms are popular as ornamentals in the warmer parts of the U.S. In their native areas they are sources of food, such as coconuts and dates, beverages, structural materials and thatching, fertilizers, clothing, furniture, oil for the food industry, and an assortment of household items. The low cost and high yield of palm oil has resulted in the removal of immense areas of forest in Southeast Asia, replaced by palm monoculture.

■ *PHOENIX*: DATE PALMS

A genus of about 137 species native to warm areas of the Eastern Hemisphere; 3 introduced, used horticulturally, and more or less naturalized in the U.S., 2 of these in the West.

Date palms are characterized by pinnate leaves with armed petioles and fleshy, drupelike fruits. **FLOWERS** Unisexual, in multibranched clusters, male and female on separate plants. In commercial orchards, which are mostly female trees, flowers are pollinated by hand or mechanically to insure good fruit production.

CANARY ISLAND DATE PALM *Phoenix canariensis* Chabaud

Evergreen tree, 15–27 m tall; erect, single trunk, 55–90 cm diam., without new shoots at base. Crown rounded, dense, with 50–200 overlapping, drooping fronds. **TRUNK SURFACE** Light brown, with stout, closely set rings of horizontally elongate, diamond-shaped leaf bases. **LEAF** Pinnate, 3–6 m long, V-shaped in cross section. Blade segments stiff, dark green, the lowermost modified into long orange spines. **FLOWER** Inflorescence tinted orange, arising within the crown; Oct.–Apr. **FRUIT** Drupelike, ellipsoid, about 2.5 cm long, 1 cm diam., pulp thin; green at first, maturing to reddish purple or orange. **HABITAT/RANGE** Introduced from the Canary Islands; commonly cultivated in warm regions, sparingly naturalized near developed areas in c. and s. Calif., 0–1,000 m.

Canary Island Date Palm

fruit

fruit

DATE PALM *Phoenix dactylifera* L.

Evergreen tree, 15–25 m tall; erect, often with several trunks, 30–50 cm diam. Crown rounded, with 20–40 fronds. **TRUNK SURFACE** Brownish, with closely set rings of leaf bases. **LEAF** Pinnate, 3–5 m long. Blade segments stiff, gray-green, the lowermost forming pale brown spines. **FLOWER** In more or less orange clusters, arising within the crown; Oct.–Apr. **FRUIT** Drupelike, ellipsoid, 2.5–7 cm long, 2–3 cm diam., maturing to yellow or red and finally brown. **HABITAT/RANGE** Introduced from North Africa; occasional waif in s. Calif., 0–300 m. *Notes* Source of the commercial date.

RIO GRANDE PALMETTO *Sabal mexicana* Mart.
A.K.A. MEXICAN PALMETTO

QUICK ID This palm of s. Tex. is distinguished by the combination of its subpalmate, V-angled leaves and drupes 15–19 mm diam.

Evergreen tree, 12–15 m tall; single erect, stout trunk, 20–35 cm diam.; crown rounded, with 10–30 leaves, leaf tips drooping. **TRUNK SURFACE** Brown or grayish brown, horizontally ribbed, sometimes roughened with the remains of old leaves. **LEAF** Subpalmate; blade circular in outline, 1.5–1.8 m broad, about as long; petiole 0.9–1.2 m long, lacking spines. Blade segments numerous, closely set, oriented in a V-pattern from a short axis extending from the petiole; upper surface lustrous green, lower surface gray-green; segments

80–145 cm long, tapering to a divided tip, margins often bearing threadlike fibers. **FLOWER** Bisexual, small, creamy white, many, in a much-branched, arching cluster 1.2–1.8 m long; Mar.–Jun. **FRUIT** Nearly round black drupe, about 1.5–2 cm diam.

HABITAT/RANGE Native; floodplains, riverbanks, wet areas, 0–50 m; s. Tex., south to Central America; apparently introduced in e. Tex.

Notes *Sabal*, a genus occurring widely in the Americas, contains about 16 species; only this one enters the West.

QUEEN PALM *Syagrus romanzoffiana* (Cham.) Glassman
A.K.A. COCOS PALM

Evergreen tree, to 15 m tall, with a single, slender trunk. **TRUNK SURFACE** Grayish, faintly ringed by leaf scars. **LEAF** Plumelike, large, arching, pinnate, 5 m long, unarmed, with ribbonlike, dark green leathery segments 60–90 cm long in multiple planes. **FLOWER** Unisexual, tiny, whitish, tightly packed on close, ropelike, drooping branches, the entire branching cluster 1–1.5 m long, on a stalk as long; bracts large, boat-shaped. Year-round. **FRUIT** Smooth, ovoid yellow- to orange-brown drupe, 3–3.5 cm long, aggregated in massive hanging clusters. **HABITAT/RANGE** Introduced from South America; near irrigation and along streams, 0–200 m, Calif.; also Fla.

RIO GRANDE PALMETTO

Date Palm

fruit

dried fruit

seed

fruit section

Rio Grande Palmetto

old tree

young tree

fruit

fruit

old leaf bases

Queen Palm

fruit cluster

fruit

seed

■ *WASHINGTONIA*: FAN PALMS

The 2 species of fan palms are native to the U.S. Southwest and Mexico. **TRUNK** Solitary, erect, partly or completely covered with a "skirt" of old leaves and leaf bases. **LEAF** Blade with a more or less palmate arrangement of segments, resembling a fan, the segment margins fibrous. Petiole split at the base and armed with teeth along the margins. **FLOWER** Bisexual. **FRUIT** Small blackish drupe.

CALIFORNIA FAN PALM *Washingtonia filifera* Wendl.
A.K.A. DESERT PALM, CALIFORNIA WASHINGTONIA

QUICK ID A single massive trunk with a crown of palmate leaves identifies this species in its native habitat.

Evergreen tree to 25 m tall. Massive trunk, 60–100 cm diam., not markedly flared at the base; crown of fan-shaped leaves clustered in a tight spiral at the top, dead and dried leaves hanging below it sheathing the trunk. **TRUNK SURFACE** Grayish, with gray-brown or red-brown rings intersected by small vertical fissures. **LEAF** Subpalmate; blade 1–2 m long; petiole 1–2 m long, 5 cm broad, split at base, 2-edged, the edges cartilaginous and orange and, at least on the lower half, bearing large hooked spines of varying sizes. Blade pleated, palmately cut from the tip to about halfway to the base, forming about 50 folded, coarse, leathery ribbons with shredding fibrous edges, their tips split in 2. Living leaves gray-green; new leaves erect, older leaves spreading. **FLOWER** Slightly fragrant, cream-white, 8 mm long, numerous; produced in a massive cluster 1.5–4 m long, spreading and arching beyond the leaves; May–Jun. **FRUIT** Egg-shaped black drupe,

8 mm diam., at first thinly fleshy, becoming hard and dry, with 1 brown seed; fruits numerous, crowded, in a huge hanging cluster.

HABITAT/RANGE Native. Seeps and springs on desert flats and in canyons, 100–1,200 m; s. Calif., sw. Ariz., nw. Mexico. Widely planted as an ornamental in warm regions; apparently naturalized in Fla., Nev.

SIMILAR SPECIES Mexican Fan Palm is also commonly planted as an ornamental; its trunk reaches less than 80 cm diam. and is widely flared at the base, and below its shag of dead leaves the bases of even older leaves form a crisscross pattern on the trunk. The 2 species may intergrade, particularly in hybridized cultivated plants.

Notes This is the only native palm west of Tex. and is the largest native palm in the U.S. Trees are tightly associated with permanent ground water, occurring in scattered groves in the Colorado Desert, and may live for 200 years. The long-persistent dead leaves cloaking the trunk have inspired the names Petticoat Palm, Overcoat Palm, and Hula Palm, in an allusion to the "grass skirt." Though small, the fruits are edible, and the tree has been called "Wild Date." Trees have provided shelter, thatching, cordage, and food for indigenous people. In cultivated plants, the dead leaves are usually removed for appearance, fire safety, and to reduce habitat for vermin.

MEXICAN FAN PALM *Washingtonia robusta* H. Wendl.
A.K.A. WASHINGTON FAN PALM

Evergreen tree, 21–30 m tall, with a single slender trunk to about 80 cm diam., flared at the base. **TRUNK SURFACE** Usually crisscrossed with old leaf bases. **LEAF** Subpalmate, blade 90–120 cm broad; petiole to about 1.2 m long, armed with slightly recurved reddish spines, the tip extending into the leaf blade and giving rise to closely set segments. Blade bright green; segments 45–60 cm long, drooping at the tip, margins with thread-like fibers. **FLOWER** Yellowish white, many, in a much-branched, arching cluster extending beyond the leaves. Apr.–Jun. **FRUIT** Ellipsoid black drupe, about 6 mm diam. **HABITAT/RANGE** Introduced from nw. Mexico; widely planted ornamental in the Southwest, weakly naturalizing in disturbed areas, along washes, s. Calif., 0–500 m.

CALIFORNIA FAN PALM

California Fan Palm

dead
leaves

fruit

petiole

Mexican Fan Palm

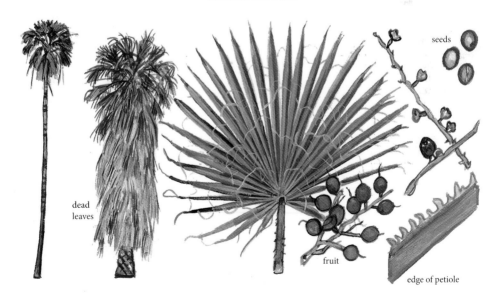

seeds

dead
leaves

fruit

edge of petiole

ASPARAGACEAE: ASPARAGUS FAMILY

The circumscription of families in this group of plants has been controversial for many decades, and a number are now placed in a broadly expanded, inclusive Asparagaceae. When the family Agavaceae is recognized as distinct, *Agave* and *Yucca* are at the core of that family; there is less agreement on our other 3 similar arborescent genera, *Cordyline, Dasylirion*, and *Nolina*. Earlier data suggested that these 3 genera be placed in 2 families, the first in Laxmanniaceae, the other 2 in the Nolinaceae. Even earlier, all these genera and many others were placed in a broadly construed family, Liliaceae. Molecular data has helped researchers to sort these genera into groups of relatives and absorb them into the large and variable Asparagaceae, a family distributed nearly worldwide and consisting of about 2,500 species comprising 150 genera. In the U.S. there are approximately 25 genera, 22 native and 3 introduced, with about 150 species. They are a diverse group in the West, and a number of arborescent species are common in arid regions of the Southwest.

The asparagus family contains a diverse assemblage of usually terrestrial perennial plants, often with leaves in a rosette, from which arises a long, central flower stalk. A few species are epiphytes, anchoring on limbs of trees. Plants are evergreen, and their leaves are replaced annually as new leaves appear before the old ones die, or the leaves persist for many years, as in the species described here. Stems may be subterranean or above ground. The plants described in this book are all long-lived perennials that have well-defined trunks and that bloom year after year. (There are species in other, closely related genera, such as many of the so-called "century plants" of the genus *Agave*, that may live a long time, bloom once, producing thousands of seeds, and then die, but that have no trunk.) **LEAF** Our species have simple, mostly lanceolate or strap-shaped leaves arranged in a rosette. **FLOWER** Inflorescences are terminal or axillary spikes or panicles, sometimes huge. Flowers are bisexual, with 6 petal-like tepals, usually 6 stamens, and a usually 3-chambered superior or inferior ovary. **FRUIT** The ovary develops into a berry or a capsule; fruits may be dehiscent or indehiscent.

Agaves and yuccas contain steroidal sapogenins, chemical compounds used in folk medicine and as a soap. Leaves provide fibers for rope, blankets, mats, baskets, and hats. The roasted stems ("hearts") of *Agave* may be fermented into intoxicating beverages, and distilled into popular liquors such as tequila and mescal. Many species are popular ornamentals in water-conserving xeriscapes.

NEW ZEALAND CABBAGE TREE
Cordyline australis (G. Forst.) Endl.
A.K.A. TORBAY PALM, GIANT DRACAENA

Open evergreen tree to 20 m tall (in native habitat); crown round, with branches stout and somewhat contorted, and strap-shaped leaves clustered at their ends. **LEAF** Flexible, erect, then drooping, tapering to a pointed tip; 40–100 cm long, 3–7 cm broad. **FLOWER** 5–7 mm diam., white, sweetly fragrant, in dense panicles 60–100 cm long; panicle branches erect, slender, many-flowered. **FRUIT** Bluish or bluish-white berry, 5–7 mm diam. **HABITAT/RANGE** Native to New Zealand; introduced as an ornamental in Calif., established and spreading as an understory plant in cool areas in at least 2 places on the n. Calif. coast, 0–50 m (perhaps to 700 m).

leaf

flowers

flowers

New Zealand Cabbage Tree

Common Sotol

leaf

old tree

flower cluster

flower spikes

flower

leaf

fruit

leaf

COMMON SOTOL *Dasylirion wheeleri*
S. Watson ex Roth.
A.K.A. DESERT SPOON

QUICK ID Common Sotol is distinguished by its dense rosettes of numerous narrow, strap-shaped leaves with hooked spines on the margins.

Evergreen tree to 2 m tall. Trunk 40 cm diam., clothed in old leaves; crown round, 1–1.5 m across, formed by hundreds of leaves. **LEAF** Flexible, strap-shaped, bluish green, hairless, 90–120 cm long, 1–3 cm broad; margins with forward-hooked golden to brownish spines 3 mm long. **FLOWER** Unisexual, male and female on separate plants; hundreds borne on short spikes

tightly arrayed in a dense columnar cluster, 1.5–5 m tall, 15–30 cm broad, arising from the axils of large triangular bracts; each flower tiny, with 6 finely toothed, ovate greenish or purplish-tinged tepals, about 2 mm long; ovary superior. **FRUIT** Three-winged, pale tan capsule, rounded in outline, notched at the top, 4–9 mm long, containing 1 seed.

HABITAT/RANGE Native; on rocky, open slopes, 1,200–1,900 m; se. Ariz. to western tip of Tex., n. Mexico.

Notes There are 17 species of sotol, 3 of which occur north of the U.S.–Mexico border. Common Sotol often has a pronounced trunk. In Mexico, a tequila-like liquor, *sotol*, is distilled from the juice of the roasted plant base.

COMMON SOTOL

◾ *NOLINA*: BEARGRASSES

About 30 species of beargrasses (a.k.a. sacahuista) occur from the s. U.S. to nc. Mexico, 14 of which range north of the border. The 4 or so that are tree-like are common and conspicuous components of the vegetation of deserts and arid grasslands to pine scrub and piñon–juniper woodland, from sea-level to moderate elevations. These rosette-forming plants have many flexible strap-shaped leaves aggregated in a dense, rounded clump that usually sits flush with the ground surface. In arborescent species the trunk is clothed with old, dried leaf bases.

LEAF Simple, long, expanded into a broad base and tapering to a fine-pointed tip. Margins entire or with minute, closely set teeth; sometimes margins shred into tough fibers. **FLOWER** Tiny, radially symmetric, borne in a dense branched columnar or narrowly ovoid inflorescence. Functionally unisexual, bearing either vestigial stamens or pistils, sexes on same plant. Tepals 6, separate, cream or white; stamens 6; ovary superior. **FRUIT** Small 3-chambered, stiffly papery capsule, each chamber with 1–3 brown to black seeds.

Species of *Nolina* are variable and in the Southwest are often difficult to identify. Leaves are used by rural people in Mexico to weave mats and coarse baskets and are used in thatching. Fibers from the leaves are used in fine basketry. Young inflorescences are eaten by sheep and goats, which may account for the scarcity of some species in some areas.

BIGELOW BEARGRASS *Nolina bigelovii* (Torr.) S. Watson
A.K.A. BIGELOW NOLINA

QUICKID This beargrass has numerous strap-shaped leaves 1–5 cm wide with pale brown fibers curling from the untoothed margins; the bracts on the flower stalk are deciduous.

One to several trunks, 1–2.5 m tall. **LEAF** Flat, 50–150 cm long, 1–5 cm broad; margins lack fine teeth and shred into pale brown fibers. **FLOWER** In panicles 70–130 m tall, 15–45 cm broad (occasionally to 110 cm); bracts deciduous; tepals 2–4 mm long; Apr.–May. **FRUIT** Capsule 8–12 mm long, equally wide, notched at the base and tip.

HABITAT/RANGE Native; rocky areas in deserts, 300–1,500 m; s. Calif., w. Ariz.

CHAPARRAL BEARGRASS *Nolina cismontana* Dice
A.K.A. CHAPARRAL NOLINA

QUICKID Numerous strap-shaped leaves 1–3 cm wide, with fine teeth on the margins and no curling fibers, help distinguish Chaparral Beargrass. The flower stalk is 1.5–3.5 cm diam. at the base, its bracts persistent.

One to several trunks, usually only to 40 cm tall, sometimes to 1.5 m. **LEAF** Flat; margins with close, minute teeth, not shredding; blade 50–140 cm long, 1–3 cm broad. **FLOWER** In panicles to 90–180 cm tall, 10–40 cm wide; stalk at base 14–35 mm diam.; bracts persistent; tepals 2–5 mm long; Apr.–Jun. **FRUIT** Capsule 8–11 mm long, equally wide, notched at the tip and base.

HABITAT/RANGE Native; dry slopes in brush, 200–1,300 m; s. Calif.

SIMILAR SPECIES Easily confused with Giant Nolina, which usually has a taller trunk, often wider leaves, and a flower stalk that is broader at the base.

BEARGRASS *Nolina erumpens* (Torr.) S. Watson
A.K.A. MESA SACAHUISTA

QUICKID This nolina also has numerous strap-shaped leaves 1–2 cm wide, with fine teeth on the margins and no curling fibers, but the leaves are convex on top. Bracts on the flower stalk are deciduous.

Usually without a trunk, occasionally with 1 to several trunks, 1–2.5 m tall. **LEAF** Convex above, midrib strongly raised below; margins with close, minute teeth, not shredding; blade 60–200 cm long, 1–2 cm broad. **FLOWER** In panicles to 120 cm tall and 40 cm wide; bracts deciduous; tepals 4 mm long; May–Jul. **FRUIT** Capsule 2.5–4.5 mm long, 3.5–5.5 mm wide, indistinctly notched at the tip.

HABITAT/RANGE Native; arid limestone slopes and flats in brush, 900–2,300 m; w. Tex., n. Mexico.

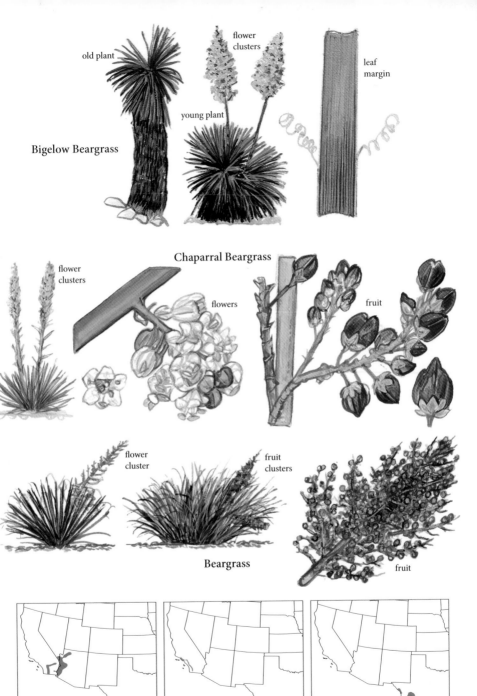

old plant

young plant

flower clusters

leaf margin

Bigelow Beargrass

flower clusters

Chaparral Beargrass

flowers

fruit

flower cluster

fruit clusters

Beargrass

fruit

BIGELOW BEARGRASS

CHAPARRAL BEARGRASS

BEARGRASS

GIANT NOLINA *Nolina parryi* S. Watson
A.K.A. PARRY NOLINA

QUICK ID Overall this species is larger than other nolinas. It has numerous strap-shaped leaves 2–4 cm wide, with fine teeth on the margins and no curling fibers. Its flower stalk is 2.5–9 cm diam. at the base, the bracts persistent.

One to several trunks, 0.5–2.1 m tall. **LEAF** Flat; margins with close, minute teeth, not shredding; blade 50–140 cm long, 2–4 cm broad. **FLOWER** In panicles 90–180 cm tall, 20–130 cm wide; stalk at the base 26–90 mm diam.; bracts persistent; tepals 2–5 mm long; Apr.–Jun. **FRUIT** Capsule 9–13 mm long, about as wide, notched at the base and tip.

HABITAT/RANGE Native; rocky areas in deserts and piñon–juniper woodland, 900–2,100 m; s. Calif.

SIMILAR SPECIES Easily confused with Chaparral Beargrass.

■ *YUCCA*: YUCCAS

There are about 40 species of *Yucca*; they range from the s. U.S. to Central America. North of the U.S.–Mexico border are 28 species, a few of which are treelike. They occur from sea-level to moderate elevations, mostly in arid situations.

Yuccas (a.k.a. Spanish bayonets, palmillas) are evergreen plants of arid lands, easily recognized by their usually branched habit, the commonly stiff, pointed leaves in tight spirals, forming rosettes, and their large clusters of bell-shaped creamy-white flowers. Unlike the similar, but never treelike, century plants (*Agave*), yuccas bloom year after year. **BARK** For a number of years after leaves die, they will clothe the trunk; eventually they drop, exposing a thin, rind-like grayish bark. **LEAF** Simple, long, slender, ending in a sharp spine, hairless,

more or less concave on the upper surface, margins sometimes with minute teeth, often shredding into coarse fibers. **FLOWER** Inflorescence a large ovoid panicle-like cluster of showy, bisexual, radially symmetric waxy flowers; 6 tepals, separate or joined at base, 6 stamens, and a superior, 6-sided, 3-chambered ovary. **FRUIT** Stiffly woody-papery capsule, or fleshy squash-like berry that very slowly dries and is indehiscent. In each of the fruit's 3 chambers are many flat black seeds, tightly stacked. Typically about half the seeds are consumed by moth larvae.

Each yucca species relies on a single species of moth (genera *Parategiticula* and *Tegiticula*) for cross-pollination and seed production. The moth carries pollen from one plant to another, packing it into a receptacle on the stigma. It then lays eggs on the developing ovary, and the larvae feed upon some but not all of the seeds. The emergence of adult moths from pupae in the soil must be timed to correspond to the flowering of the yuccas. Synchronization is frequently poor, and in some dry years yuccas flower poorly. As "insurance" to perpetuate the symbiosis, not all pupae break dormancy in any one year, and yuccas flower to greater or lesser extent year after year.

Yucca flowers are an edible delicacy, and their consumption contributes to reduced seed production in some populations in rural Mexico. The leaves have been used to make sandals, coarse rope, and baskets. An extract from the subterranean stem of some species has detergent qualities and may be used as soap or shampoo.

JOSHUA TREE *Yucca brevifolia* Engelm.
ex S. Watson

QUICK ID This unmistakable, bizarre, irregularly branched desert tree has a more or less round crown bearing thick, stubby branches tipped by dense rosettes of short daggerlike leaves.

Small, stout, stubby-branched tree to 15 m tall; trunk short, stout, to 1 m diam. Crown columnar when young, in older plants becoming open, ragged, rounded. Branches spread in all directions, the longer ones hanging. **LEAF** Clustered near the ends of branches; stiff, daggerlike, tapering from a broad base to a narrow, dark, sharply pointed tip, dark or bluish green;

GIANT NOLINA

JOSHUA TREE

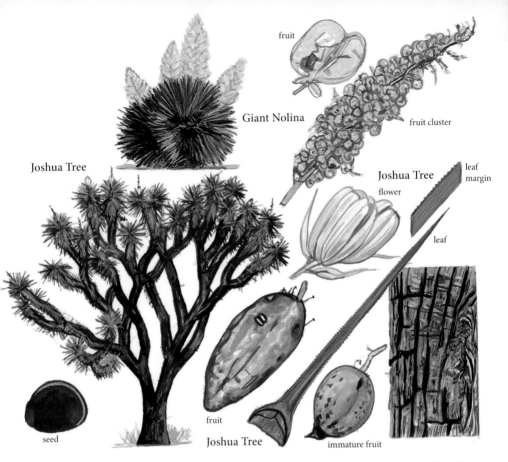

Giant Nolina

fruit

fruit cluster

Joshua Tree

Joshua Tree
flower

leaf margin

leaf

fruit

seed

Joshua Tree

immature fruit

margins whitish or yellowish, minutely toothed. Blade 12–35 cm long, 7–15 mm broad. **FLOWER** Ellipsoid or globose, densely packed in erect, round or ovoid panicle-like clusters, 30–55 cm long, 30–38 cm wide, borne at the ends of branches. Tepals slightly united at the base, lanceolate or oblong, 2.5–7 cm long. Feb.–Apr. **FRUIT** Ellipsoid berry, 6–8.5 cm long, 4–6 cm wide; at first green, often blushed reddish, becoming tan, dry, and spongy when fully mature.

HABITAT/RANGE Native. Arid mesas and slopes, 400–1,800 m; largely confined to the Mojave Desert of s. Calif., s. Nev., sw. Utah, and w. Ariz.

SIMILAR SPECIES Most other treelike yuccas are more easterly in distribution and have longer and often broader leaves. Thompson Yucca has leaves similar in size to Joshua Tree, but it has dehiscent fruits, its flower clusters are longer on average, and it is restricted to sw. Tex. and adjacent Mexico.

Notes This odd-looking tree is reputed to have been named by Mormon settlers, who saw in it the biblical Joshua, raising his arms in praise to God. The tree provides nesting sites for many birds, among them Gila Woodpecker (*Melanerpes uropygialis*), Red-shafted Flicker (*Colaptes auratus cafer*), and a number of owls. In pioneer days, stems were used for fence posts and fuel in mines. Trees grow rapidly, about 8 cm per year, until about 10 years old, at which time growth slows to about 3.5 cm per year. The wood, uniformly fibrous like that of a palm, has no growth rings, so trees cannot be accurately aged; the oldest are believed to be about 1,000 years old. The future of Joshua Tree is uncertain. Introduced grasses on the desert in wet years produce sufficient fuel to sustain tree-killing wildfires, a new evolutionary force in the Mojave Desert. Climate change is also likely to affect the species, and the ability of the tree to migrate is uncertain. In the Pleistocene, the giant Shasta Ground Sloth (*Nothrotheriops shastensis*) fed upon the tree's fruits and perhaps distributed seeds in its dung.

SOAPTREE YUCCA *Yucca elata* Engelm.
A.K.A. SOAPWEED YUCCA, PALMELLA

QUICK ID A yucca with stems usually un-branched, often in clusters, topped with a ro-sette of flexible gray-green leaves, each up to 1.3 cm wide, with fibers on their margins. Flow-ers are 3–5 cm long and capsules 4–8 cm long.

When arborescent, to 4.5 m tall, sometimes taller, with many narrow leaves in dense clusters near the ends of stems. Trunks 1 to several in a clus-ter, usually clothed with old leaves until very tall; when branched, the branches short and stout. **LEAF** Fairly flexible, almost linear, widest near the mid-dle, tapering to a short spine at the tip, pale bluish green; margins whitish, lacking teeth, with sparse, curling white fibers along their length. Blade 25–95 cm long, 3–13 mm broad. **FLOWER** Ovoid, erect or spreading, 3–6 cm long, in erect, open panicle-like clusters, 70–150 cm long, ⅓ as wide; May–Jun. **FRUIT** Three-lobed, ovoid-cylindric cap-sule, 4–8 cm long, sometimes slightly constricted around the middle, tan and woody-papery at ma-turity, splitting open at the tip.

HABITAT/RANGE Native. Arid grasslands and flats, 300–1,900 m; c. Ariz. to w. Tex. and n. Mexico.

Notes Soaptree Yucca is a common ornamental in southwestern xeriscapes. A soap, locally popular as a shampoo, is made from the rhizome. Plants from c. Ariz. have capsules only 4–4.5 cm long and com-prise var. *verdiensis* (McKelvey) Reveal; var. *elata* occurs across the rest of the range.

SPANISH DAGGER *Yucca faxoniana* Sarg.
A.K.A. FAXON YUCCA, EVE'S NEEDLE

QUICK ID This yucca is a solitary, massive plant with a crown of stiff, daggerlike, dark yellow-ish-green leaves up to about 1 m long, the mar-gins with curling fibers. The flowers have tepals united basally, and fruits are fleshy.

Massive plant to 7 m tall, crown usually a single rosette of dense leaves, or in older plants bearing short branches tipped by rosettes. Trunk usu-ally single, to 60 cm diam., clothed with old leaves above, usually bare below. **LEAF** Stiff, tapering and daggerlike, flat or concave, pale bluish green; mar-gins lack teeth, with curling brownish fibers along their length. Blade 40–115 cm long, 3–8.5 cm broad. **FLOWER** Pendent, bell-shaped, 4–11 cm long, in erect, densely ovoid panicle-like clusters, 0.5–2.5 m long. Tepals basally united, forming a cuplike base 1–32 mm long; pistil 3–8 cm long. Mar.–May. **FRUIT** Fleshy, usually succulent, cylin-dric berry, pendent, green to tan, 4–14 cm long; dry and spongy when mature.

HABITAT/RANGE Native. Rocky slopes and flats, 800–1,200 m; se. N.M. to w. Tex. and nc. Mexico.

SIMILAR SPECIES Also called Spanish Dagger, *Y. treculeana* is similar, but its tepals are not joined at the base, and its pistil is only 1.5–3.5 cm long.

Notes This is a popular ornamental in the Southwest.

SOAPTREE YUCCA

SPANISH DAGGER

Soaptree Yucca

flower cluster

flowers

leaf

old plants

young plant

fruit

Spanish Dagger

old plants

flower cluster

leaf

leaf margin

young plant

fruit

SIERRA MADRE YUCCA *Yucca madrensis* Gentry

QUICK ID Long, straight, daggerlike leaves that are stiff but flexible, 3–5 cm broad, and with margins that lack teeth and usually lack fibers, help to distinguish this yucca from others. Its flowers are 3.5 cm long, and the fruit is fleshy and indehiscent.

Small tree to 3 m tall, stems usually unbranched. **LEAF** Stiffly flexible, long-tapering, flat to concave, bluish green to yellow-green; margins without teeth and usually without fibers; blade 40–80 cm long, 3–5 cm broad. **FLOWER** Pendent, ovoid, 3.5 cm long, in more or less open, elongate panicle-like clusters to 80 cm long; Jul.–Sep. **FRUIT** Pendent, fleshy, long-ovoid berry, 6–13 cm long, tan, dry and spongy when mature.

HABITAT/RANGE Native; pine–oak woodlands, 1,400–1,600 m; se. Ariz., nw. Mexico.

Notes This and similar plants to the north and east have been classified as Hoary or Mountain Yucca (*Y. schottii* Engelm.), which is suspected of being a hybrid complex involving *Y. baccata* (Banana Yucca, Dátil), a smaller more shrublike yucca, and *Y. elata*, and *Y. madrensis*.

BEAKED YUCCA *Yucca rostrata* Engelm. ex Trel.

QUICK ID The crown of this stout yucca is made up of more than 100 stiff, but flexible, smooth leaves with thin, minutely toothed, translucent yellowish margins. The capsule is erect, dehiscent at the tip.

Stout plant, 2.5–3.5 m tall (without inflorescence), sometimes with up to 3 short branches. **LEAF** Stiffly flexible, more or less linear but widest well above the middle, flat to concave, bluish green to yellow-green, smooth; margins minutely toothed, lemon yellow, thin, and translucent. Blade 25–60 cm long, 12–17 mm broad. **FLOWER** Pendent, globose to bell-shaped, 4–5 cm long, in dense, ovoid panicle-like clusters, 30–100 cm long; Apr.–May. **FRUIT** Erect, ovoid capsule, 4–7 cm long, dehiscent at the tip.

HABITAT/RANGE Native; rocky slopes and canyons, 700 m; sw. Tex., n. Mexico.

SIMILAR SPECIES Thompson Yucca is similar, but is smaller on average and has rough-feeling, narrower leaves.

SIERRA MADRE YUCCA

BEAKED YUCCA

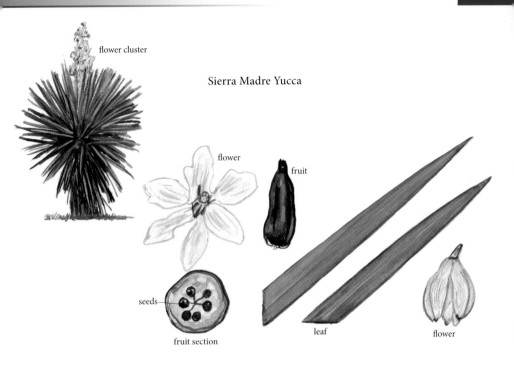

flower cluster

Sierra Madre Yucca

flower

fruit

seeds

fruit section

leaf

flower

Beaked Yucca

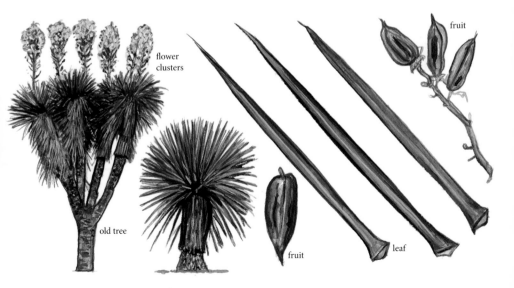

flower clusters

fruit

old tree

fruit

leaf

MOJAVE YUCCA *Yucca schidigera* Roezl ex Ortgies

QUICKID Forms colonies of stems that appear shaggy and unkempt, covered by weathered old leaves.

Colony-forming plants, to 5 m tall, with a few to perhaps a dozen stems clumped together, each sheathed by old leaves. **LEAF** Thick and stiff, sword-shaped, concave, yellowish green; margins reddish brown, lacking teeth, shredding into coarse fibers along their length. Blade 30–130 cm long, 3–5 cm broad. **FLOWER** Pendent, globose, 3–7.5 cm long, with style 1–2 mm long; in erect, dense, obovoid or ellipsoid panicle-like cluster, more or less flattened across the top, 30–60 cm long; Mar.–May. **FRUIT** Ovoid berry, 5–12 cm long, fleshy, succulent and green, maturing to tan, spongy, and dry.

HABITAT/RANGE Native. Rocky slopes, outwash fans, flats, in deserts and chaparral, 300–1,200 m; s. Calif., s. Nev., w. Ariz., nw. Mexico.

SIMILAR SPECIES Spanish Dagger (*Y. treculeana*) resembles Mojave Yucca, but has less of a tendency to form colonies, and its flower has a style 2–8 mm long.

Notes This is a common yucca of the Mojave Desert, often used in xeriscaping. Native Americans made use of the plant for many purposes.

THOMPSON YUCCA *Yucca thompsoniana* Trel.
A.K.A. BAYONETTA

QUICKID Less than 3 m tall. The leaves are 20–45 cm long and up to 12 mm wide, their surfaces rough like shark's skin, and the margins yellowish to reddish and minutely toothed.

Small tree to 3 m tall, trunks usually unbranched, sometimes in colonies. **LEAF** Stiffly flexible, more or less linear, widest at or above the middle, flat to concave, rough (like shark's skin), bluish green to yellow-green; margins minutely toothed, yellow or orange-red, hard and somewhat thick. Blade 20–45 cm long, 7–12 mm broad. **FLOWER** Pendent, globose or bell-shaped, 3.5–6.5 cm long, in dense, ovoid-elongate, panicle-like clusters, 50–80 cm long, the tip often elongate and unbranched; Apr.–May. **FRUIT** Erect, ovoid capsule, 3.5–7 cm long, dehiscent at the tip.

HABITAT/RANGE Native; rocky slopes, 200–1,400 m; sw. Tex., n. Mexico.

Notes This species may be a northern variant of Beaked Yucca.

SPANISH DAGGER *Yucca treculeana* Carrière
A.K.A. PALMA PITA, DON QUIXOTE'S LACE

QUICKID Plants are often colonial, to 7 m tall, with stiff, daggerlike, deeply concave, slightly roughened leaves, their margins shredding into more or less straight, coarse fibers. Fruits are fleshy and indehiscent.

Tree to 7 m tall, stem single or in small colonies, usually sheathed by old leaves. **LEAF** Thick, stiff, sword-shaped, concave, yellowish green to bluish green; margins light brown, lacking teeth, shredding into sparse, more or less straight, coarse fibers. Blade 40–130 cm long, 2–7 cm broad, the surface slightly rough (like shark's skin). **FLOWER** Pendent, globose, 3–8 cm long, with style 2–8 mm long; in erect, dense panicle-like clusters barely exceeding the leaves, 0.5–2 m long; Feb.–Apr. **FRUIT** Ovoid to ovoid-cylindric berry, 4–19 cm long, fleshy and succulent when green, spongy when dry.

MOJAVE YUCCA

THOMPSON YUCCA

SPANISH DAGGER

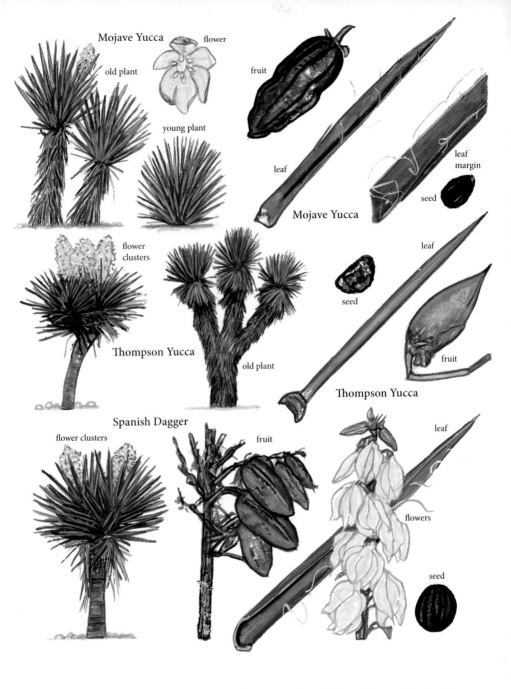

Mojave Yucca

flower

old plant

young plant

fruit

leaf

Mojave Yucca

leaf
margin

seed

flower
clusters

leaf

seed

Thompson Yucca

old plant

fruit

Thompson Yucca

Spanish Dagger

flower clusters

fruit

leaf

flowers

seed

HABITAT/RANGE Native. Rocky slopes, outwash fans in deserts, arid grassland, or brush, 0–1,600 m; s. N.M. to s. Tex. and n. Mexico.

Notes This variable species now includes what was once known as the Torrey Yucca (*Y. torreyi* Shafer), said to have more fibers on the leaf margins and a broader ovary; the 2 phases intergrade.

DICOTS

Dicotyledons (dicots for short) are a very large assemblage of the flowering plants (angiosperms). Dicots usually lack the parallel leaf veins seen in the monocots (the other major group), displaying instead netlike venation, and the flower parts (sepals, petals, stamens, etc.) are usually in multiples of 4 or 5.

ADOXACEAE: MOSCHATEL FAMILY

The moschatel family includes 4 or 5 genera and 220–245 species, distributed mostly in temperate and tropical montane zones, primarily in the Northern Hemisphere. There are 11 species in the West, several of which are herbs or shrubs. Some members of the family—including all of those treated here—have been included within the Caprifoliaceae, which is distinguished from traditional Adoxaceae by its bilateral flowers and elongate style.

Species of the modern, reconstrued Adoxaceae are mostly shrubs or small trees, less frequently vines and herbs. **LEAF** Opposite, either simple or compound. **FLOWER** Bisexual, radially symmetric, usually small and borne in showy, often flat-topped or convex clusters. **FRUIT** Berrylike drupes with 1–5 stones, the stones compressed and single-seeded, developed from an inferior ovary. The fleshy fruits are attractive to wildlife, and the seeds are usually dispersed by birds.

■ *SAMBUCUS:* ELDERBERRIES

A genus of about 10 species distributed in temperate and subtropical regions. The variable North American populations, once considered to be numerous species, have been reduced to 2 species, both widespread in the West.

Deciduous shrubs, small trees, or herbs; shrubby or treelike species usually have very soft wood and conspicuous pith; branches usually have raised, elongate lenticels. **LEAF** Opposite, compound, usually pinnate, sometimes the lower leaflets also divided and the leaves then partly bipinnate; leaflets large, lanceolate or ovate, often asymmetric at the base; margins distinctly toothed. **FLOWER** Small, white, petals 3–5, stamens 5. **FRUIT** Round, lustrous red or black berrylike drupe, often glaucous, with 3–5 stones.

Stout, pithy twigs that lack a central end bud, and very different flowers and fruit, distinguish *Sambucus* from ashes (*Fraxinus*, Oleaceae) and Boxelder (*Acer negundo*, Sapindaceae), which also have opposite, pinnately compound leaves.

BLUE ELDERBERRY *Sambucus nigra* L. subsp. *caerulea* (Raf.) R. Bolli

QUICK ID Opposite, pinnately compound leaves (unusual in the West); large, flat or convex clusters of small white flowers; and round black berries covered in a pale waxy bloom help identify the species.

Deciduous fast-growing shrub or small tree to about 12 m tall, with 1 to several trunks up to 40 cm diam.; branches stout and spreading, forming a broad, round-topped crown. **BARK** Bright brown to silvery gray, smooth when young, becoming rough and irregularly fissured with age. **TWIG** Stout, brownish or greenish, covered with a waxy bloom when young, the elongate lenticels conspicuous; pith thick, white in the 1st year, creamy, spotted, or light brown later. **LEAF** Opposite, usually pinnately compound, sometimes bipinnate, 15–50 cm long, petiole 3–10 cm long; fleshy or somewhat leathery. Leaflets 5–11, lanceolate to ovate, tapering to a slender point, usually almost hairless when mature (in some populations pubescent to velvety); margin coarsely toothed;

BLUE ELDERBERRY

Blue Elderberry

fruit

flowers

flower

twig

leaflet blade 3–15 cm long, 1–6 cm broad; stalk 5–50 mm long. Upper surface yellowish or dark green; lower surface grayish green. **FLOWER** White, 3–7 mm diam., petals 5, spreading; stamens 5; pistil 1; hundreds of flowers in a large, showy, flat or convex terminal cluster to about 30 cm across, mostly lacking a central axis beyond the 4 or 5 principal branches. Apr.–Aug. **FRUIT** Globose, juicy, berry-like drupe with 3–5 stones, 4–6 mm diam., covered with a pale blue waxy bloom that is easily rubbed off to reveal a shiny black surface.

HABITAT/RANGE Native. Moist places in canyons and on slopes, 0–2,700 m; scattered throughout the mountainous West from s. B.C. to nw. Mexico.

SIMILAR SPECIES The other North American subspecies, subsp. *canadensis* (L.) R. Bolli, spreads by underground runners and lacks the waxy bloom on twigs and berries; widespread in the East, it barely enters the West on the Great Plains and in Tex. Red Elderberry is distinguished from Blue Elderberry by its shiny red or purplish-black fruit, orange-brown twig pith, and the more or less conical flower cluster with a central axis.

Notes Foliage and twigs give off a rank odor when crushed. The fruits are used to make jams, jellies, pies, and wine.

RED ELDERBERRY *Sambucus racemosa* L.

QUICKID The opposite compound leaves, often conical cluster of small white flowers, and usually red berries distinguish this shrub or tree.

Deciduous, fast-growing shrub or small tree, 2.5–6 m tall. Trunks usually several, rarely more than 15 cm diam., often arching. **BARK** Gray to reddish brown, with prominent lens-shaped lenticels. **TWIG** Stout, soft, with a large, spongy pith that turns orange-brown by the 3rd year. **LEAF** Opposite, pinnately compound, 15–30 cm long, petiole 5–8 cm long. Leaflets 5–7, lanceolate to elliptic, tapered to a slender tip; margins toothed; leaflet blade 6–16 cm long, 2–4 cm broad; stalk 0–5 mm long. Upper surface lustrous, dark or medium green, hairless; lower surface paler. **FLOWER** White, petals often drooping; hundreds of flowers borne in a strongly convex or conical cluster about 10 cm across, a central axis usually present above the lowermost branches. Apr.–Aug. **FRUIT** Shiny, several-stoned red or purple-black berrylike drupe, 4–6 mm diam.

HABITAT/RANGE Native. Moist to wet woodlands and wetland margins; throughout the Northern Hemisphere, in our region extending from coastal Alaska to Calif., Ariz., and N.M.

SIMILAR SPECIES Blue Elderberry can be distinguished by its glaucous blue fruit, white pith in young twigs, and the flatter flower cluster. Red-fruited sumacs (*Rhus*, Anacariaceae) have alternate leaves.

■ *VIBURNUM*: VIBURNUMS

A genus of 175–200 species distributed in north temperate and tropical montane zones; 26 occur in North America, 2 of which barely enter the West.

Deciduous or evergreen trees or shrubs. **LEAF** Opposite, simple; margins often toothed. **FLOWER** Small, white or creamy (rarely pinkish); petals and stamens 5, the 3 stigmas usually sessile at the summit of the ovary; usually borne in a showy, flat-topped cluster. **FRUIT** Dark blue to black, coppery, or red 1-seeded drupe with a flattened stone.

Many species and horticultural forms are cultivated for their bright flowers and colorful fruits. Dogwoods (*Cornus*, Cornaceae) also have opposite leaves, but with margins entire and paired, prominent arching parallel veins, and the flowers have 4 petals.

NANNYBERRY *Viburnum lentago* L.
A.K.A. SHEEPBERRY

QUICKID This shrub or small tree has simple, opposite, finely toothed leaves; tiny creamy-white flowers; and bluish-black drupes in flat-topped clusters.

Deciduous shrub or tree, 5–10 m tall. Crown rounded, irregular, open, with few arching, crooked branches. **TWIG** Ultimately hairless. **LEAF** Opposite, simple, ovate, elliptic, or nearly round; tip abruptly long-pointed; margins finely toothed. Upper surface lustrous; lower surface paler, with tiny dark dots. Blade 5–10 cm long; petiole often winged. **FLOWER** Creamy white, in showy, flat-topped clusters, 5–10 cm wide; May–Jun. **FRUIT** Ellipsoid bluish-black drupe, 8–15 mm long.

HABITAT/RANGE Native; moist places, 0–800 m; Mont. to Colo., eastward in Canada and the U.S.

SIMILAR SPECIES Rusty Blackhaw (*V. rufidulum* Raf.) has rusty-hairy twigs and oval or broadly elliptic, finely toothed leaves, and flat-topped clusters of creamy-white flowers in Mar.–May; it barely enters c. Tex. from se. U.S.

RED ELDERBERRY

NANNYBERRY

RUSTY BLACKHAW

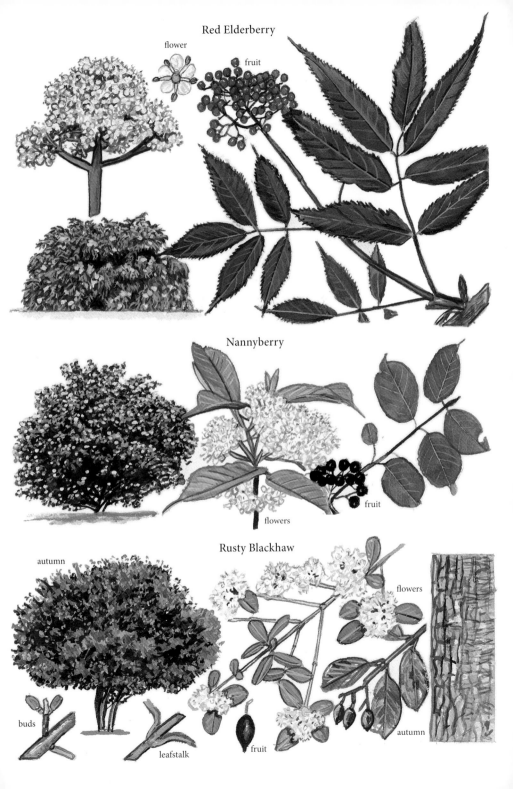

Red Elderberry

flower

fruit

Nannyberry

flowers

fruit

Rusty Blackhaw

autumn

flowers

buds

leafstalk

fruit

autumn

ANACARDIACEAE: CASHEW FAMILY

The cashew family includes about 600 species, ranging from subshrubs to trees, distributed worldwide in warm temperate to tropical regions. Approximately 10 genera and 30 species are native to or naturalized in the U.S. Tubular resin ducts occur in the twigs, bark, in the larger veins of the leaves, and often also in the flowers and fruits. This resin imparts a spicy odor ranging from pleasant to obnoxious; in sensitive individuals it may also cause contact dermatitis when the plant is touched or result in severe irritation of mucous membranes or even anaphylaxis when ingested.

Evergreen or deciduous shrubs and trees. **LEAF** Alternate, pinnately compound or simple by reduction and therefore unifoliolate, thin and flexible or thick and leathery. In pinnately compound leaves the rachis is often winged. **FLOWER** Usually small, whitish to greenish, radially symmetric, unisexual and borne on separate plants, or unisexual with bisexual flowers intermixed (plants then polygamodioecious). Each flower usually has 5 separate petals and sepals, and 5–10 stamens and/or a single ovary with 1–3 styles. At the base of the flower is a small, thick disk. Flowers occur in small to large, sometimes extensively branched clusters. **FRUIT** Usually a small to large drupe with resinous flesh.

Economically important fruits and nuts come from the family, among them mango (*Mangifera*), pistachio (*Pistacia*), and cashew (*Anacardium*). Several species have become aggressive, troublesome weeds that displace other vegetation. Poison Oak, Poison Ivy, and Poison Sumac (*Toxicodendron*) are widespread creeping to treelike members of the family, appreciated for their brilliant color in the fall but notorious for causing contact dermatitis in susceptible people.

AMERICAN SMOKETREE *Cotinus obovatus* Raf.
A.K.A. CHITTAM-WOOD

QUICK ID Easily identified by the distinctive alternate, broadly elliptic or obovate leaves, the plumelike flowering/fruiting clusters, and the very hairy purplish individual flower stalks.

Deciduous large shrub or small tree, to 30 m tall, usually with multiple trunks or with a dominant trunk to 50 cm diam. **BARK** Scaly, strongly aromatic when crushed. **LEAF** Alternate, unifoliolate, thin, obovate to broadly elliptic-obovate, tapered at the base, more or less rounded at the tip; margins entire. Upper surface dark green, hairless; lower surface paler, with silky hairs at first, becoming sparsely hairy at maturity. Blade 10–17 cm long, 5–9 cm broad; petiole 1.5–6 cm long. Autumn foliage brilliant orange or scarlet. **FLOWER** Unisexual (rarely bisexual), yellowish white or greenish white, 3 mm diam., numerous, in lax terminal panicles to about 15 cm long; individual flower stalks very hairy, purplish. Apr.–May. **FRUIT** Dry, 1-seeded, flattened, kidney-shaped or oblique drupe, 3–6 mm long, sparingly produced; fruiting panicles to 30 cm long, usually mostly empty of fruits.

HABITAT/RANGE Native. Dry, open woods, usually on limestone, 200–1,000 m; scattered, c. Tex. to s. Mo. and ne. Ala.

SIMILAR SPECIES The introduced **European Smoketree** or **Wig Tree** (*C. coggygria* Scop.) is

AMERICAN SMOKETREE

American Smoketree

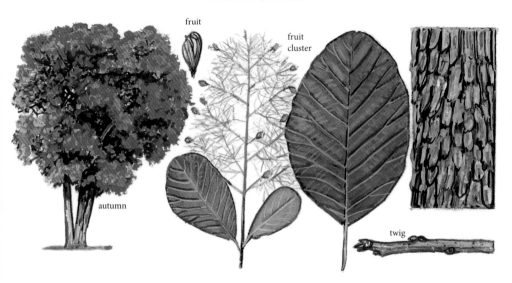

European Smoketree

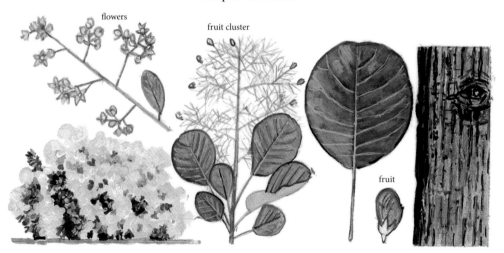

cultivated, perhaps sometimes a waif in the West; its leaves are hairless on the underside.

Notes *Cotinus* is a genus of 5 species of shrubs or trees from Eurasia and North America that have deciduous, alternate, unifoliolate leaves, yellow wood, pungent sap, and hairy inflorescences often nearly devoid of fruit.

LAUREL SUMAC *Malosma laurina*
(Nutt.) Abrams
A.K.A. LENTISCO

QUICK ID The evergreen, shiny, leathery, up-folded unifoliolate leaves, in combination with the slender inflorescence branches and small hairless fruits, distinguish this sumac from other species in its region.

Evergreen dense, rounded large shrub or small tree, 2–5 m tall. **BARK** Smooth, brown or reddish brown when young, grayish when mature. **TWIG** Stout, reddish, and finely pubescent. **LEAF** Alternate, unifoliolate, leathery, elliptic to lanceolate, folded upward along the midrib, abruptly pointed at the tip; margins entire. Dark green, shiny, nearly hairless above; paler below. Blade 4.5–10 cm long, 2–4 cm broad; petiole 3–6 mm long, pinkish. **FLOWER** Bisexual and unisexual, pinkish to whitish, tiny, petals 5, borne in dense slender-branched, nearly hairless, conical clusters, to 15 cm long, at the ends of twigs. **FRUIT** Ovoid, hairless drupe, reddish when young, apparently whitish when fully mature, 2–3 mm diam.

HABITAT/RANGE Native. Brushy foothills and flats, 0–1,000 m; s. Calif., nw. Baja Calif.

SIMILAR SPECIES Sugar Sumac also has upward-folded leathery leaves, but its petioles are 10–30 mm long, and its drupe is reddish, larger, and sticky-hairy.

Notes A bitter almond odor emanates from this plant when in bloom; the name of this one-species genus comes from the Greek for "strong odor." Laurel Sumac has leaves reminiscent of true laurels (Lauraceae), but is not at all closely related. It is often included in the genus *Rhus*. The plants make fine ornamentals and hedges in frost-free areas. Birds relish the mature fruits.

LAUREL SUMAC

■ *PISTACIA*: PISTACHIOS

There are about 11 species of *Pistacia*, most from the Mediterranean region, a few from warm parts of North America. They are mostly woodland plants growing at low to moderate elevations.

Deciduous or semievergreen shrubs or small to medium trees, often with dense crowns, irregular when young, but nearly round and even when older. **LEAF** Alternate, pinnately compound, with or without a terminal leaflet; leaflet margins entire or toothed. The rachis is flattened and more or less winged along the 2 sides. In autumn, leaves may turn brilliant yellow or red. **FLOWER** Unisexual, male and female flowers on separate plants, tiny, without petals or sepals, male flowers have 4–7 stamens, female flowers have a single ovary with 3 styles; borne in dense or open-branched clusters in the axils of leaves or at branch tips. **FRUIT** Thinly fleshy drupe, often quickly drying, spheric to obovoid to more or less lens-shaped.

The edible pistachio nut comes from the Common Pistachio (*P. vera* L.), native to parts of Asia. Pistachios tolerate poor soils and flourish in areas with hot, dry summers and mild winters, conditions found in parts of the sw. U.S., where they are commercially grown. The genus and vernacular names derive from the Persian word *pistah*, referring to the nut. Because of their hardiness, attractive shape, dense foliage, and fall coloration, several species are popular ornamentals.

MOUNT ATLAS MASTIC TREE
Pistacia atlantica Desf.
A.K.A. MOUNT ATLAS PISTACHE

QUICK ID The pinnately compound leaves with 5–11 thickish leaflets, including a terminal leaflet, and a winged rachis, distinguish this tree.

Deciduous or semievergreen (in warm areas) tree to 20 m tall. Trunk stout; dense round crown of spreading and erect branches. **BARK** Light grayish brown, vertically fissured and cross-checked. **LEAF** Alternate, pinnately compound, to 20 cm long, rachis flattened and slightly winged. Leaflets 5–11, somewhat thick, lanceolate or oblong; margins entire; leaflet blade about 5 cm long. Dark green and shiny above, with a bluish-gray tint; paler beneath. **FLOWER** Tiny, greenish white, soon falling; Feb.–May. **FRUIT** Obovoid drupe, 6–8 mm long, thinly fleshy, dry at maturity, pinkish to reddish early, ripening to bluish.

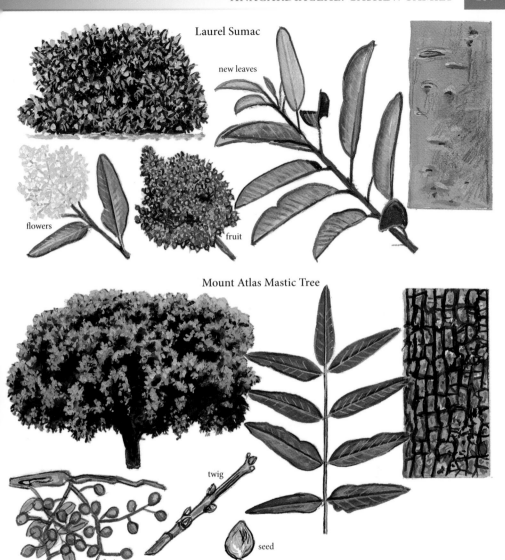

Laurel Sumac

new leaves

flowers

fruit

Mount Atlas Mastic Tree

twig

seed

fruit

HABITAT/RANGE Introduced from the Mediterranean region; in disturbed areas and open woodlands, mostly below 100 m, but up to 800 m in Utah; locally naturalized in c. and s. Calif., sw. Utah, and perhaps Tex.

SIMILAR SPECIES Chinese Pistache, also widely cultivated and sometimes escaping, has larger leaflets, the terminal leaflet often absent.

Notes Mount Atlas Mastic Tree is a hardy, easily grown ornamental commonly used in landscaping in the West and may be invasive in mild climates. It is also used as rootstock for the commercial Common Pistachio (*P. vera* L.). In its native area the fruit is eaten, tannins were extracted from leaf galls for tanning, and resins from the tree were used medicinally.

CHINESE PISTACHE *Pistacia chinensis* Bunge

Deciduous, drought-tolerant tree, 7–12 m tall, with a rounded crown. **LEAF** Pinnately compound, 10–12 leaflets 5–9 cm long, terminal leaflet usually lacking. **FRUIT** Small, laterally compressed red drupe, 5 mm diam.

HABITAT/RANGE Introduced from China; used ornamentally in the s. U.S., occasionally a waif or may naturalize in c. Tex.

Notes Planted primarily for its easy cultivation, dense shade, and stunning red and orange autumn foliage. Seeds are used in China for the production of biodiesel.

AMERICAN PISTACHIO *Pistacia mexicana* Kunth
A.K.A. MEXICAN PISTACHIO, TEXAS PISTACHE, WILD PISTACHIO, LENTISCO

QUICK ID This Texas tree is recognized by its **pinnately compound leaves with 9–21 leaflets (terminal leaf present), the rachis slightly winged, and tiny flowers without petals.**

Evergreen or late-deciduous shrub or small multi-trunked tree, 4–10 m tall, 20–35 cm diam. **BARK** Gray-brown, at first smooth, then vertically fissured. **LEAF** Alternate, pinnately compound, 5–10 cm long. Leaflets 9–21, flexible, lanceolate to broadly rounded, sometimes curved; margins entire, sometimes slightly and irregularly rolled downward; leaflet blade 8–20 mm long, 7–9 mm broad. Dark green and slightly hairy above; paler beneath. **FLOWER** Unisexual, male and female flowers on separate trees, tiny, reddish orange, lacking petals and sepals; flowers mostly just before new leaves in spring but sporadically throughout

AMERICAN PISTACHIO

the year. **FRUIT** More or less lens-shaped drupe, 6–8 mm long, thinly fleshy, dry at maturity, at first reddish, drying blackish.

HABITAT/RANGE Native. Rocky limestone banks, bluffs, and ravines, mostly 200–300 m; sc. Tex., mostly near the Rio Grande, south to Guatemala.

SIMILAR SPECIES The related sumacs (*Rhus*) are similar, but unlike pistachios they have flowers with petals and sepals, and the leaflets are often larger and more leathery or pubescent.

Notes This uncommon species is more treelike in the southern parts of its range. In many areas it is declining due to habitat loss. Goats will browse the foliage. Thriving in sunshine and producing rich, dark red new leaves in the spring, the plant has potential for ornamental use.

■ *RHUS*: SUMACS

There are 30 to 250 species of *Rhus* worldwide, depending on which classification is followed. The present tendency, followed here, is to cleave the very large genus into smaller units as molecular genetic studies reveal relationships. In the West about 12 species occur from protected slopes in the deserts to grasslands and open woodlands, from sea-level to moderate elevations.

Deciduous or evergreen shrubs or small trees widely distributed in the U.S., the deciduous species providing rich red-orange to purplish foliage in the fall. **LEAF** Alternate, compound or simple by reduction and therefore unifoliolate, with entire or toothed margins; the rachis of compound leaves often slightly to conspicuously winged along the edges. **FLOWER** Unisexual, male and female flowers on separate trees, sometimes with bisexual flowers among the unisexual flowers, produced in terminal or axillary clusters; small, radial, with 5 separate sepals, 5 separate whitish or pinkish petals, 5 stamens, and a 1-chambered, 1-ovuled ovary topped by 3 styles. **FRUIT** Small, hairy or hairless, often reddish drupe, the solitary seed on a small stalk arising at the base of the ovary.

None of the species in the genus as it is presented here produces irritating oils similar to those of Poison Oak, Poison Sumac, or Poison Ivy, all once included in *Rhus* but now in the genus *Toxicodendron*. *Rhus* species are used as ornamentals

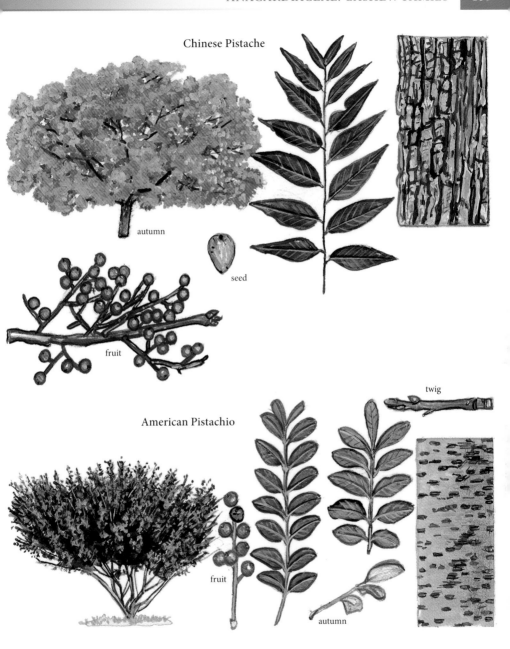

Chinese Pistache

autumn

seed

fruit

twig

American Pistachio

fruit

autumn

for their lustrous evergreen foliage or colorful autumn foliage and their showy clusters of bright reddish fruits. They have little other economic use. Birds feed upon the berries. Western species with unifoliolate leaves occasionally have a few compound or partially compound leaves, suggesting that though they appear to be simple leaves, they evolved by reduction from compound leaves.

SMOOTH SUMAC *Rhus glabra* L.

QUICK ID A sumac easily distinguished by its hairless whitish twigs and hairless leaves with an unwinged rachis.

Deciduous, usually a shrub under 3 m tall in the West, occasionally treelike, often sprouting from the roots and creating dense colonies. **TWIG** With a whitish bloom and numerous raised lenticels, exuding a milky sap when crushed. **LEAF** Alternate, pinnately compound, 30–90 cm long, rachis not winged. Leaflets 9–31, lanceolate; margins coarsely toothed; leaflet blade 5–15 cm long, 1–4 cm broad. Upper surface bright green, hairless; lower surface grayish, hairless. Turns brilliant red in autumn. **FLOWER** Greenish white or yellowish green, 6 mm diam., borne in a cone-shaped panicle 10–15 cm long; Apr.–Aug. **FRUIT** Rounded, thickly hairy reddish drupe, 3–4 mm diam., in narrow, conical terminal clusters.

HABITAT/RANGE Native; common in disturbed areas sporadically across the West, 300–2,400 m; in the East, more common, larger, and at lower elevations.

LEMONADE SUMAC *Rhus integrifolia*
(Nutt.) W.H. Brewer & S. Watson
A.K.A. LEMONADE-BUSH, LEMONADE-BERRY, MAHOGANY SUMAC

QUICK ID An evergreen sumac with dense foliage, the unifoliolate leaves flat or convex, leathery, sometimes toothed; and the whitish or pink flowers and reddish fruits in dense terminal clusters.

Evergreen thicket-forming shrub, especially on sea bluffs, usually 3–4 m tall; or small tree in canyons, to 8 m tall. Trunk short, low-branched, 8–20 cm diam.; crown dense, round, the branches wide-spreading. **BARK** Smooth and gray when young, often with a subtle reddish hue; fissured when older, reddish in the fissures. **TWIG** Stout, reddish, finely hairy. **LEAF** Alternate, usually unifoliolate, sometimes divided into 3 leaflets, or sometimes with 1 or 2 lateral lobes at the base; stiff and leathery, the blade in unifoliolate leaves oblong-ovate, elliptic, or nearly circular, flat or occasionally convex; margin entire or irregularly and sharply low-toothed. Upper surface dark yellow-green above and lustrous when older; lower surface paler, with conspicuous veins. Blade 2.5–5.5 cm long, 2–3 cm broad; petiole 3–6 mm long. **FLOWER** Bisexual and unisexual intermixed, 6 mm diam., whitish to pink, sepals and petals hairy on margins, densely arranged in branched, downy, pale gray terminal clusters 2.5–8 cm long. Feb.–May, sometimes later. **FRUIT** Egg-shaped to lens-shaped drupe, 7–10 mm long, at first green, then yellowish, maturing dark red, sticky-hairy and covered with a waxy secretion, tightly aggregated in clusters.

HABITAT/RANGE Native. In chaparral and coastal sage in dry canyons, slopes, and ocean bluffs, 0–900 m; s. Calif. and n. Baja Calif.

SIMILAR SPECIES Sugar Sumac has folded unifoliolate leaves with the margins entire.

Notes Lemonade Sumac is so named because a tart, cooling drink can be made by steeping the ripe berries. Mature berries were also ground and added to soups by Native Americans. A warning: Some individuals are allergic to all parts of the plant when ingested. The plants are used as ornamentals and for slope stabilization in Calif.

SMOOTH SUMAC

LEMONADE SUMAC

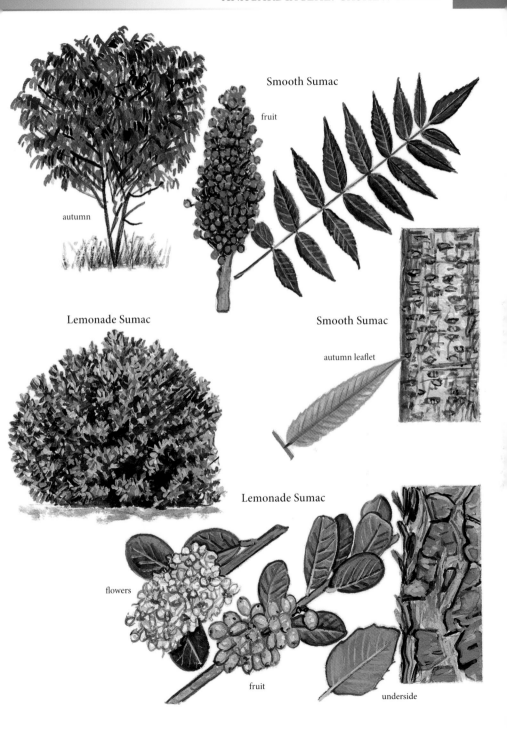

Smooth Sumac

fruit

autumn

Lemonade Sumac

Smooth Sumac

autumn leaflet

Lemonade Sumac

flowers

fruit

underside

KEARNEY SUMAC *Rhus kearneyi* F.A. Barkley

QUICK ID A desert shrub or tree identified by its unifoliolate leaves (occasionally with 3 leaflets), the upper margins often rolled under, the veins pale green to whitish, and whitish flowers in dense branched clusters.

Dense evergreen shrub or tree, to 5 m tall. **LEAF** Unifoliolate (sometimes with 1 or 2 lobes), or with 3 leaflets; leathery, oblong to ovate; margins usually entire, often rolling under near the tip. Upper surface dark green, lustrous, with pale veins. Blade 2.5–8.5 cm long; petiole short, pinkish. **FLOWER** Small, whitish or pink, in terminal clusters 5–8 cm long. Mar.–Apr. **FRUIT** Oblong slightly flattened, hairy reddish drupe, 8–10 mm long.

HABITAT/RANGE Native; rocky slopes and cliffs where shaded, 300–450 m; sw. Ariz. to c. Baja Calif.

LITTLELEAF SUMAC *Rhus microphylla* Engelm.

QUICK ID This common dryland species has small, hairy, pinnately compound leaves with a winged rachis, and small whitish flowers that appear before the leaves.

Deciduous large shrub, or rarely a small tree to 5 m tall with a dense, intricately branched, spreading crown. **TWIG** Stiff, almost spine-tipped, crooked, finely hairy at first. **LEAF** Pinnately compound, 1–3 cm long; petiole 1–3 mm long, rachis winged. Leaflets 5–9, terminal leaflet present; leaflet blade oblong, elliptic, ovate, or obovate, 3–15 mm long, hairy, margins entire. **FLOWER** Small, whitish, in dense clusters on stiff spikes. Mar.–May, before leaves appear. **FRUIT** Glandular hairy, ovoid to nearly globose reddish-orange drupe, 5 mm diam.

HABITAT/RANGE Native; slopes, washes, plains, often in thickets, 200–1,800 m; se Ariz. to n. and c. Tex., sw. Okla., south to Mexico.

PRAIRIE SUMAC *Rhus lanceolata* (A. Gray) Britton
A.K.A. TEXAS SUMAC, PRAIRIE FLAMELEAF SUMAC

QUICK ID This deciduous sumac has large, pinnately compound leaves bearing 9–21 forward-curved leaflets with few or no marginal teeth; a terminal leaflet is present. The fruits are small, red, and hairy, and borne in dense clusters.

Deciduous, often thicket-forming shrub or small tree to 10 m tall. Trunk, 20 cm diam., short, branching near the ground; crown of slender, spreading to upright branches. **BARK** Greenish to reddish, dotted with many pale lenticels, ultimately dull or dark brown and scaly on older branches and trunk. **TWIG** Slender, greenish to reddish when young. **LEAF** Alternate, pinnately compound, 12–24 cm long; petiole 25–35 mm long; rachis winged, to 3.5 mm wide, often only obscurely winged on lower segments. Leaflets 9–21 (terminal leaflet present), flexible, sessile or short-stalked, linear to lanceolate, tapering to a narrowly pointed tip, those near base broader and variably sickle-shaped; margins entire or with a few sharp teeth; leaflet blade 2.5–7.5 cm long, 6–12 mm broad. Upper surface dark green and shiny; lower surface paler and slightly hairy. **FLOWER** Bisexual and unisexual flowers intermixed; tiny, whitish, in dense branched, conical terminal clusters. Jul.–Aug. **FRUIT** Rounded or somewhat flattened, dark red drupe, 3–4 mm diam., thinly fleshy, glandular hairy, in clusters.

HABITAT/RANGE Native. Calcareous, dry, rocky soils, hillsides, forest edges, along highways, 0–1,300 m; from s. N.M. to sc. Okla., south through Tex. to ne. Mexico.

Kearney Sumac

underside

fruit

fruit

Littleleaf Sumac

fruit

fruit

Prairie Sumac

autumn

fruit

SIMILAR SPECIES Smooth Sumac, which is widespread across the country, has no wings on the leaf rachis, and its leaflet margins are mostly sharply toothed. Winged Sumac (*Rhus copallinum* L.), which barely enters the West in c. Tex., has wings more than 4 mm wide on the rachis of at least some leaves, and has 9–23 leaflets that are ovate-lanceolate, scarcely curved, and 2–4 times as long as wide.

Notes Prairie Sumac is common in the Edwards Plateau of c. Tex. The leaves turn rich reddish purple or red-orange in autumn, and the red berries may persist until well after leaf-fall. Wildlife find shelter in the thickets, and birds relish the berries. A black dye and a tart beverage may be made from the fruits. Plants may be planted in erosion-control projects.

SUGAR SUMAC *Rhus ovata* (Nutt.) S. Watson
A.K.A. SUGAR BUSH, CHAPARRAL SUMAC, MOUNTAIN LAUREL

QUICK ID This common evergreen sumac has shiny, leathery, entire, upfolded unifoliolate leaves on rather long petioles. Flowers are whitish or pink, producing reddish fruits in dense terminal clusters.

Evergreen shrub or small tree to 8 m tall. Trunk, 8–20 cm diam., short, low-branched; crown dense, round or somewhat irregular. **BARK** Smooth and grayish brown when young, becoming crosschecked and shaggy when older. **TWIG** Stout, reddish, hairless, spreading or ascending. **LEAF** Alternate, usually unifoliolate (rarely divided into 3 leaflets), stiff and leathery, ovate, usually folded upward along the midrib; margins entire. Upper surface shiny, dark yellow-green; lower surface a little paler, smooth; petiole reddish. Blade 4–8.5 cm long, 2–5 cm wide; petiole 10–30 mm long. **FLOWER** Bisexual and unisexual flowers intermixed; white or pinkish, about 1 cm diam., sepals and petals hairy on the margins, densely arranged in finger-like spikes in finely hairy or hairless, branched terminal clusters about 5 cm long. Mar.–May. **FRUIT** Flattened, egg-shaped drupe, 6–8 mm long, reddish when mature, sticky-hairy and covered with a waxy secretion; tightly aggregated in clusters.

HABITAT/RANGE Native. Dry rocky slopes and canyons in chaparral and other shrubby vegetation, mostly away from the coast, 0–1,300 m; s. Calif., c. Ariz., n. Baja Calif.

SIMILAR SPECIES Lemonade Sumac, with which this species hybridizes, has flat or convex unifoliolate leaves with the margins entire or toothed. Laurel Sumac has leaves with much shorter petioles.

Notes Sugar Sumac is pest-free and makes a fine ornamental, with its shiny evergreen foliage and clusters of flowers and reddish fruits. Several should be planted together to ensure good pollination and displays of fruit.

EVERGREEN SUMAC *Rhus virens* Lindh. ex A. Gray
A.K.A. TOBACCO SUMAC, LENTISCO

QUICK ID Leathery leaves with only 3–9 leaflets, hairless or nearly so, and small, hairy red fruits in dense clusters distinguish Evergreen Sumac from other pinnate-leaved species in the West.

Evergreen shrub or small tree to 5 m tall. Trunk to 15 cm diam., short, branching near the ground; open, irregular or round crown. **BARK** Gray to brown, smooth on branches, breaking into thin, small flakes on the trunk. **TWIG** Greenish brown or maroon-brown, at first finely hairy but often becoming hairless. **LEAF** Alternate, pinnately compound, leathery, 2–14 cm long; petiole 3–15 mm long. Leaflets 3–9, short-stalked, terminal leaflet present; ovate to ovate-lanceolate or roughly diamond-shaped, tapering to a narrowly pointed tip; margins entire, rolled under; leaflet blade 2.5–5 cm long, 1–2.5 mm broad. Upper surface dark green, shiny, and lightly hairy or hairless; lower surface paler and hairless to velvety. **FLOWER** Bisexual and unisexual flowers mixed; tiny, creamy white, in dense, branched, cone-shaped clusters 4–5 cm long, at branch tips. Jul.–Aug. **FRUIT** Rounded or somewhat flattened reddish or brownish drupe, 6–7 mm diam., thinly fleshy, glandular hairy, in clusters.

HABITAT/RANGE Native. Gullies, rocky hillsides, bluffs, cliffs, often on limestone, 600–2,500 m; from se. Ariz. to ec. Tex., south into Mexico.

SUGAR SUMAC

EVERGREEN SUMAC

Sugar Sumac

opening flowers

fruit

underside

fruit

Evergreen Sumac

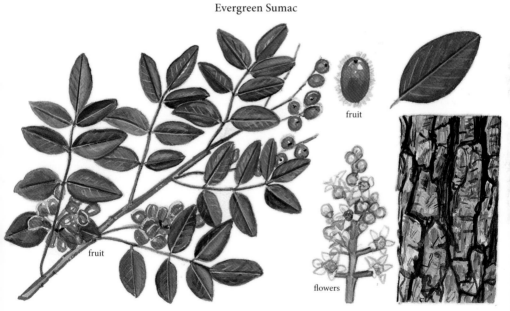

fruit

fruit

flowers

SIMILAR SPECIES Smooth Sumac and Winged Sumac are both deciduous and have more numerous, thinner, and more flexible leaflets; the latter has a winged rachis.

Notes There are 2 varieties of *R. virens*, often treated as separate, closely related species. The var. *virens* has 5–9 leaflets that are velvety-hairy and soft

to the touch beneath; it occurs from se. N.M. to ec. Tex. The var. *choriophylla* (Woot. & Standl.) L. Benson, known as Toughleaf Sumac, Mearns Sumac, or New Mexico Evergreen Sumac, usually has 3–5 leaflets that are hairless or almost so beneath; it occurs in se. Ariz., sc. N.M., and the western tip of Tex. Native Americans smoked a mixture of leaves of var. *virens* and tobacco (*Nicotiana*).

■ *SCHINUS*: PEPPERTREES

There are nearly 30 species of peppertrees, all native to areas of tropical America with moderate climates. Several have been introduced to the warmer parts of the U.S. as ornamentals and have naturalized or become seriously invasive and problematic weeds. Peppertrees are evergreen shrubs or trees with resin ducts in the twigs. The sap in these ducts, and the leaves and fruits when crushed, emit a range of odors from turpentine-like to sweetly and spicily resinous.

LEAF Alternate, pinnately compound with a terminal leaflet and a rachis usually winged along the edges, or simple by reduction and therefore unifoliolate. **FLOWER** Unisexual, or unisexual and bisexual intermixed, male and female on separate plants, tiny, usually greenish cream, usually many in a cluster; sepals and petals 4 or 5, stamens 8–10 (those opposite the petals much shorter than others), single ovary with 3 styles, the ovary surrounded by a thickened disk. **FRUIT** Small drupe with parchment-textured skin, thin and often sticky and aromatic flesh, and a large stone that is spicily pungent when crushed.

Species of peppertrees are cultivated for shade and their colorful fruits, and indigenous peoples have used extracts from the plants medicinally. Several species cause contact dermatitis and respiratory problems.

CHILEAN PEPPERTREE *Schinus polygamus* (Cav.) Cabrera
A.K.A. PERUVIAN PEPPERTREE, HARDEE PEPPERTREE

Evergreen shrub or tree to 9 m tall, with a dense, rounded crown. **TWIG** Spine-tipped. **LEAF** In short shoots; unifoliolate, leathery, narrow, acute at the tip, usually hairless; blade 2.5–6 cm long. **FLOWER** 4–5 mm diam., borne in dense clusters about 2.5 cm long along branches; petals pale yellowgreen, sepals sparsely hairy on back. May–Sep. **FRUIT** Drupe round, shiny, 3–5 mm diam., purplish to blackish. **HABITAT/RANGE** Native to w. South America; naturalized in s. Calif., abandoned field, slopes, brush, 0–1,000 m, potentially invasive. **SIMILAR SPECIES** Longleaf Peppertree (*S. longifolius* [Lindl.] Speg.) is similar, but the leaf tip is broadly angled, the sepals hairless on the back, and the fruit lavender in color. Introduced from ec. South America, it is cultivated in Calif. and Tex.; erroneously reported as naturalized in Tex.

PEPPERTREE *Schinus molle* L.
A.K.A. PERUVIAN PEPPERTREE, FALSE PEPPER, PIRUL

QUICK ID Drooping, pinnately compound leaves with numerous narrow leaflets that are aromatic when crushed characterize this species.

Evergreen shrub or tree to 15 m tall, with 1 to few trunks up to 1 m diam. Crown open, round, with drooping twigs and leaves. **BARK** When mature, tannish gray, rough, with shallow fissures, twisted ridges, and long, flaking scales. **LEAF** Alternate, pinnately compound, blade narrowly ovate in outline, 8–25 cm long, petiole 2–3 cm long. Leaflets 19–41, terminal leaflet present; narrowly lanceolate, often curved at the tip, margins entire or obscurely finely toothed; leaflet blade 1–6 cm long, 4–8 mm wide. Upper surface green, hairless or finely hairy; lower surface paler. Spicily aromatic when crushed. **FLOWER** Tiny, white to cream, in open, branched, drooping clusters 8–15 cm long. Feb.–Jul. **FRUIT** Globose, lustrous lavender-pink drupe, 6–8 mm diam., thinly fleshy, with a parchment-like skin, the flesh spicily sweet; the drooping fruit clusters persist for much of the year.

HABITAT/RANGE Introduced from w. South America; naturalized in waste places in Calif., possibly also Ariz. and s. Tex., 0–700 m.

Notes Cultivated as a hardy ornamental, the species is often invasive. The fruit has been added to pepper (genus *Piper*, family Piperaceae) mixes for complexity in taste and color. Children suffer gastric distress upon eating the fruit. Leaflets, floated on still water, will jerk and wiggle because of discharge of oil.

BRAZILIAN PEPPERTREE *Schinus terebinthifolius* Raddi

Evergreen shrub or tree to 8 m tall; crown broad. **LEAF** Alternate, pinnately compound, 3–10 cm long, petiole 1–4 cm long, rachis narrowly winged. Leaflets 5–9 (rarely 11), leathery, lanceolate or narrowly elliptic; margins bluntly toothed (rarely entire). Leaflet blade 2–8 cm long, 1.5–2 cm broad; upper surface dark, lustrous green, finely hairy; lower surface dull, light green. Has turpentine aroma when bruised. **FLOWER** Tiny, white, in panicles 3–8 cm long in axils of upper leaves, yearround. **FRUIT** Globose, hairless red drupe, 6–8 mm diam. **HABITAT/RANGE** Introduced from South America for ornamental use; invasive in disturbed sites in s. Calif. and along the Gulf coast.

Chilean Peppertree

flowers

fruit

seed

Peppertree

fruit

flower

flowers

seed

Brazilian Peppertree

fruit

seed

AFRICAN SUMAC *Searsia lancea* (L.f.)
F.A. Barkley
A.K.A. KAREE

Lacy, weeping, small evergreen tree, 2–5 m tall, with 1 or several trunks. **LEAF** Alternate, pinnately compound, divided into 3 shiny, dark green leathery leaflets, each 2.5–12 cm long, narrowly lanceolate, margins entire or toothed. **FLOWER** Tiny, whitish to cream, borne in branched clusters 2–9 cm long. Feb.–May. **FRUIT** Yellowish, tan, or reddish, usually hairless drupe, 5–8 mm diam. **HABITAT/ RANGE** Introduced from s. Africa; a popular ornamental in s. Calif. and s. Ariz., naturalized in disturbed places, shrublands, woodlands, and on alluvial fans below 700 m. *Notes Searsia* is a genus of about 120 species mostly from Africa and Asia. African Sumac is often included in the genus *Rhus*.

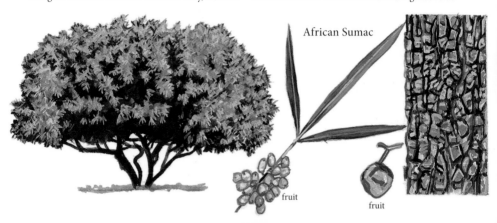

African Sumac

fruit

fruit

APOCYNACEAE: OLEANDER FAMILY

The oleander family includes about 355 genera and 3,700 species of trees, shrubs, vines, and herbs. The woody members of the family are distributed primarily in the tropics and subtropics, the herbs primarily in temperate zones. It occurs through the United States at low and moderate elevations.

Common Oleander

flowers

COMMON OLEANDER *Nerium oleander* L.

Evergreen, robust, essentially hairless, many-stemmed shrub, or sometimes a small tree to 5 m tall. **LEAF** Commonly in whorls of 3 or 4, sometimes opposite, simple, lanceolate, 6–20 cm long, more or less leathery. **FLOWER** Five-lobed, funnel-shaped pink, rose, white, cream, or salmon corolla with 5 scales or a fringe at the mouth of the tube; stamens 5; ovary superior; May–Sep. **FRUIT** Slender, cylindric capsule, 8–20 cm long, pointed at both ends, splitting along the seams, woody when mature. **HABITAT/RANGE** Introduced from Eurasia; commonly planted along highways and in gardens, and persisting around old dwellings and in plant dumps, rarely establishing from seed in the wild, 0–1,300 m; s. U.S. *Notes* The tree in the illustration has been horticulturally formed. All parts of the plant are toxic.

AQUIFOLIACEAE: HOLLY FAMILY

The nearly 400 species of hollies are distributed almost worldwide. As currently circumscribed, Aquifoliaceae includes only the holly genus, *Ilex*.

■ *ILEX*: HOLLIES

Nineteen hollies are native to the U.S., and at least 4 commonly cultivated non-native species have also naturalized to some degree. Two native species barely cross into c. Tex. from the East, and 1 naturalized species is found on the West Coast. In the U.S., hollies mostly occur at low elevations in cooler, moist climates.

Deciduous or evergreen trees and shrubs. **BARK** Gray, often mottled, usually smooth. **TWIG** Usually gray or brown, often bearing circular or elongate lenticels. **LEAF** Alternate (often closely clustered at the tips of short shoots in deciduous species, appearing whorled), simple; margins usually toothed, rarely entire, teeth sometimes spine-tipped. **FLOWER** Functionally unisexual, male and female flowers on separate trees, greenish white, yellowish white or creamy white. Petals average about 5 mm wide at bloom time in most species; petal number varies within a plant, and varies by species, some species having 3–5 petals, others mostly 5–9 petals. Male flowers usually have conspicuous stamens with pollen-filled anthers surrounding a shriveled or diminutive ovary. Female flowers usually have a plump, superior ovary, with no or almost no style; the small stigma sits directly on the ovary. Surrounding the ovary are several staminodes. **FRUIT** Round, multi-stoned red, yellow, orange, or black drupe, often called a "berry" in common usage.

Several species of hollies are cultivated for their cheery "berries" and attractive foliage. The highly caffeinated Paraguayan beverage *mate* is brewed from *Ilex paraguariensis* A. St.-Hil. Native Americans also brewed Yaupon leaves to make a stimulating drink. The pale, almost white wood is valued for quality inlay work.

AMERICAN HOLLY *Ilex opaca* Aiton

Evergreen tree to 20 m tall. **LEAF** Semi-lustrous, dark green (paler and duller below), oblong or elliptical, the apex spine-tipped; margins usually rolled downward and bearing relatively large spine-tipped teeth. **FLOWER** Male flowers mainly in clusters in the leaf axils; female flowers mostly between the leaves along developing stems. **HABITAT/RANGE** Native to e. and se. U.S. Cultivated in the West, occasionally escaped in Wash.

fruit

American Holly

ENGLISH HOLLY *Ilex aquifolium* L.

QUICK ID This tree is recognized by its lustrous, dark green leaves more than 4 cm long, with spiny, wavy margins.

Evergreen shrub or small tree, 6–10 m tall (sometimes to 25 m), usually to about 40 cm diam. Trunk erect; crown more or less pyramidal or oval, with stiff, laterally spreading branches. **BARK** Gray, smooth when young, becoming horizontally wrinkled when older, with shallow furrows. **TWIG** Greenish or purplish. **LEAF** Alternate, simple, stiff, usually oval or elliptic; margins wavy, spiny-toothed but sometimes nearly entire in older trees. Upper surface lustrous, dark green; lower surface paler. Blade 2–8 cm long, 2–6 cm broad; petiole to about 5 mm long. **FLOWER** Creamy white, petals 4, the female flowers borne in umbel-like clusters of 1–8 or in short spurs. May–Jun. **FRUIT** Drupe round, reddish, 6–10 mm diam., with 2–4 stones.

HABITAT/RANGE Introduced   from   Europe. Cool, wooded areas, 0–200 m; sw. B.C. to n. Calif., and e. U.S. and adjacent Canada.

SIMILAR SPECIES Two other hollies are rarely found in the wild in Wash.: American Holly (*I. opaca* Aiton), an eastern native, has similarly large, spiny leaves, but the leaves are comparatively dull on top, and the female flowers are borne mostly singly, scattered on the twig. Japanese or Box-leaf Holly (*I. crenata* Thunb.) has minutely toothed but not spiny leaves less than 3 cm long and black drupes.

Notes This holly, widely planted as an ornamental, has naturalized widely west of the Cascade Mountains, showing tendencies to be invasive. Various birds spread the seeds. Cut twigs with the green leaves and red "berries" are popular Christmas decorations.

DECIDUOUS HOLLY *Ilex decidua* Walter
A.K.A. POSSUMHAW HOLLY, WINTERBERRY

QUICK ID This deciduous holly may be recognized by its bluntly toothed, spatulate leaves and reddish "berries" on short fruit stalks.

Deciduous shrub or small tree, to 10 m tall. **LEAF** Alternate, but often in closely set clusters on short shoots; usually spatulate or obovate, wider toward the usually notched tip, with a long-tapering base; margins scalloped or bluntly toothed, each tooth tipped with a tiny gland. Upper surface dark green, hairless or nearly so; lower surface moderately to densely hairy, at least on the midvein; petiole usually hairy on the upper side. Blade 1–8 cm long. **FLOWER** Greenish white, petals 4–6, usually 5. Mar.–May. **FRUIT** Drupe red, orange, or yellow, 4–9 mm diam., 4-stoned, on a stalk up to 1 cm long.

HABITAT/RANGE Native; usually in moist areas, 0–350 m; e. U.S., barely entering sc. Tex.

YAUPON *Ilex vomitoria* Aiton

QUICK ID This evergreen thicket-forming holly is recognized by its small, bluntly toothed leaves and bright, lustrous red "berries."

Evergreen shrub forming dense thickets, sometimes a tree to 10 m tall. **LEAF** Stiff, narrowly oval or elliptic; margins bluntly toothed. Upper surface lustrous, dark green, hairless when mature; lower surface paler, dull green, usually hairless. Blade 5–30 mm long, 5–25 mm broad. **FLOWER** White to yellowish, petals 4. Apr.–May. **FRUIT** Drupe bright red, 4–8 mm diam., 4-stoned, on a stalk up to 4 mm long.

HABITAT/RANGE Native; low, open woods, 0–500 m; e. U.S., barely entering our range in sc. Tex.

ENGLISH HOLLY   DECIDUOUS HOLLY   YAUPON

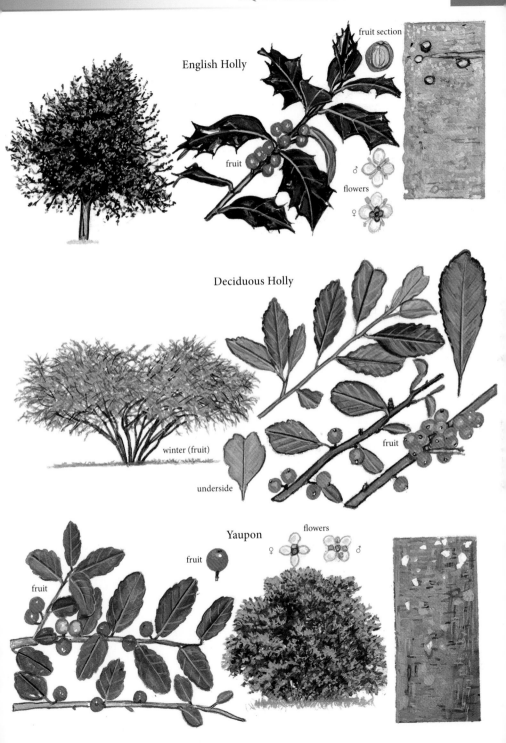

English Holly

fruit section

fruit

♂
flowers
♀

Deciduous Holly

winter (fruit)

underside

fruit

Yaupon

flowers

fruit

♀   ♂

fruit

fruit

ARALIACEAE: GINSENG FAMILY

The ginseng family has about 43 genera and 1,450 species found mostly in the tropics and subtropics. Most species have ethereal oils and resins in their tissues, making them aromatic when crushed. Ginseng (*Panax* spp.) and Wild Sarsaparilla (*Aralia nudicaulis* L.) are used medicinally, and English Ivy (*Hedera helix* L.) and various treelike aralias are popular ornamentals. One such introduced ornamental, Japanese Angelica Tree, is the only treelike member of the family in the West.

JAPANESE ANGELICA TREE *Aralia elata* (Miq.) Seem.

Deciduous large shrub or small tree to 15 m tall; 1 to several trunks, spiny gray, to 15 cm diam., with few or no branches. **LEAF** Alternate, bipinnately compound, spreading, arching, large, 40–150 cm long and nearly as broad; 3–5 pairs of primary segments, each with 5–15 gracefully drooping leaflets, 6–12 cm long, ovate, tapered to a fine point, margins toothed. **FLOWER** Tiny, greenish white, borne in small umbels at the ends of a many-branched terminal inflorescence 20–55 cm tall, 35–100 cm wide; sepals, petals, and stamens 5. Jul.–Aug. **FRUIT** Dark reddish-purple to nearly black, berry-like drupe, 4–5 mm diam., with several flattened, seedlike stones. **HABITAT/ RANGE** Introduced from e. Asia; naturalized in open brushy areas, 0–150 m; w. Wash., ne. U.S. Potentially invasive.

ASTERACEAE: ASTER FAMILY

The aster family is among the largest families of flowering plants, containing about 1,500 genera and 23,000 species distributed nearly worldwide. Nearly 420 genera and about 2,400 species occur in North America north of Mexico. An older, conserved family name, Compositae, is often still used. That name reflects the composite structure of the usually densely compact, highly organized, multiflowered inflorescence that to the layperson resembles a single flower.

Most species of Asteraceae are herbaceous, a smaller number are woody shrubs, and even fewer are small trees. **LEAF** Alternate, simple to compound. **FLOWER** The typical inflorescence, often called a "flower head," includes a central collection of tightly packed disk flowers, often surrounded by few to many petal-like ray or ligulate (strap-shaped) flowers, all subtended by a cuplike whorl of bracts called an involucre. The structure of the "head" varies among species, with some species having only ligulate flowers, others having only disk flowers, and many having both types. **FRUIT** Referred to colloquially as a seed, and sometimes botanically as an achene, but because the ovary is inferior it is technically a cypsela (for simplicity, we use "seedlike fruit").

The family is best known to plant lovers for its numerous herbaceous wildflowers, usually considered too difficult to identify, though with a little practice they are not. Sunflower seeds, safflower oil, artichokes, lettuce, and numerous ornamentals (such as chrysanthemums, marigolds, daisies, gaillardias, and bachelor's buttons) come from this large family. A number of serious and unloved weeds belong to the family, the most notorious perhaps being many kinds of thistles.

Japanese Angelica Tree

fruit

leaflet

twig

Sagebrush

flower cluster

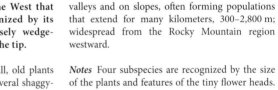

leaf

SAGEBRUSH *Artemisia tridentata* Nutt.
A.K.A. BIG SAGE, COMMON SAGEBRUSH

QUICK ID Sagebrush, forming extensive expanses of gray in arid areas of the West that have cold winters, may be recognized by its large stature and narrow, inversely wedge-shaped gray leaves with 3 teeth at the tip.

Evergreen, usually a shrub 1–2 m tall, old plants rarely small trees to 3 m tall, with several shaggy-barked brownish-gray trunks to 15 cm diam. **LEAF** Alternate, simple; sessile and very narrowly wedge-shaped, the broad tip divided into 3 blunt teeth that may extend up to ⅓ the length of the blade. Densely hairy, grayish green. Blade 5–35 mm long. **FLOWER** Heads 1–2 mm long, rayless, many in erect branched clusters, the tiny yellowish flowers inconspicuous; Jul.–Oct. **FRUIT**

SAGEBRUSH

Seedlike, 1–2 mm long, hairy or not, with a crown of scales at the top.

HABITAT/RANGE Native. Very common in dry valleys and on slopes, often forming populations that extend for many kilometers, 300–2,800 m; widespread from the Rocky Mountain region westward.

Notes Four subspecies are recognized by the size of the plants and features of the tiny flower heads. There are as many as 500 species of *Artemisia*, mostly in drier parts of the Northern Hemisphere, but some species occur in South America and Africa. Of the approximately 50 in the U.S., only Sagebrush is ever treelike. The iconic shrub of the Great Basin, it often fills the air with its spicy, resinous odor, reminiscent of true sage (*Salvia*, Lamiaceae).

PARISH'S GOLDENBUSH *Ericameria parishii* (Greene) H.M. Hall
A.K.A. PARISH'S RABBITBRUSH

QUICKID Minutely gland-dotted narrow leaves and small heads of golden-yellow flowers help distinguish this large shrub or small tree.

Evergreen, sometimes arborescent, to 5 m tall, with many twigs in dense broomlike clusters. **LEAF** Alternate, simple, oblong to oblanceolate, nearly stalkless, mostly hairless, gland-dotted, the midrib conspicuously raised below; blade 2.5–7 cm long, 3–12 mm broad. **FLOWER** Heads narrow, about 6 mm long, rayless, golden yellow, in dense, round clusters to 9 cm wide; bracts at base of each head with brownish midribs. Jul.–Oct. **FRUIT** Seedlike, narrow, 2–3 mm long, often silver-hairy, topped by many fine, dingy to brownish bristles.

HABITAT/RANGE Native. Chaparral and open woods, 400–2,200 m; coastal mountain ranges of s. Calif.

Notes The 36 species of goldenbush are all evergreen resinous shrubs, restricted to dry areas in warmer parts of w. North America.

SCALEBROOM *Lepidospartum squamatum* A. Gray

QUICKID This grayish-green broomlike shrub or small tree has small yellow flowers in heads and very short leaves that are strongly ascending or appressed to the branches.

Evergreen shrub or rarely a small tree, to 2.5 m tall, with several trunks and rigid, erect grayish-green branches. **LEAF** Obovate, 5–12 mm long, sparse and ascending on branches, on flowering stems denser, shorter, and appressed. **FLOWER** Tiny, yellow, in narrow rayless heads, 4–7 mm long, with 12–23 bracts, the few long inner bracts surrounded by very short outer ones; Jun.–Dec. **FRUIT** Seedlike, 3–5 mm long, body hairless, crowned by many straight white or very pale tan hairs up to 8 mm long.

HABITAT/RANGE Native; sandy washes and gravelly places, 30–1,600 m; s. Calif. to Baja Calif.

Notes There are 2 other species of *Lepidospartum*, both shrubs, in the sw. U.S. and adjacent Mexico.

GIANT TICKSEED *Leptosyne gigantea* Kellogg

QUICKID This coastal species is distinguished by its naked gray trunks crowned by a cluster of pinnately lobed leaves with hair-fine lobes, above which bob brilliant yellow flowers.

Bizarre-looking deciduous shrub or tree with 1 to several bare brownish-gray trunks and a few or no branches. **LEAF** Technically alternate but grouped in shaggy hanging clusters at the tips of otherwise naked branches, appearing in winter, withering and dropping in summer; succulent, pinnately lobed, the lobes hairlike, usually up to 3.5 cm long. Blade up to 25 cm long. **FLOWER** Pale yellow daisy-like heads about 8 cm across from ray tip to ray tip, borne 1–12 per stem at the ends of stalks 4–18 cm long; each head with 10–16 rays 2–3.5 cm long. Mar.–May. **FRUIT** Seedlike, brown, more or less flat, hairless, 5–7 mm long, with 2 narrow, pale, untoothed wings.

HABITAT/RANGE Native. Coastal bluffs and dunes, 0–200 m; s. Calif., n. Baja Calif.

Notes The 8 species of *Leptosyne*, all from sw. North America, were traditionally placed in the genus *Coreopsis*. The seed of some species resembles a tick.

PARISH'S GOLDENBUSH

SCALEBROOM

GIANT TICKSEED

flower buds

leaf

flowers

Parish's Goldenbush

Scalebroom

flower head

flowers

leaves scalelike

Giant Tickseed

flowers

flower

maturing seed heads

leaves

flower head section

PYGMY-CEDAR *Peucephyllum schottii*
A. Gray

QUICK ID Short, dense, linear, bright green leaves and cylindric, rayless heads distinguish this species, which frequents hot rocky desert areas.

Evergreen shrub, or rarely a small tree, 1–3 m tall. **LEAF** Alternate, sessile, bright green, gland-dotted, very narrowly linear, usually 5–25 mm long, rarely with 1 or 2 small, narrow lobes. **FLOWER** Tiny, numerous, yellow, in rayless cylindric heads 1–1.5 cm long, bracts surrounding heads very narrow, all about the same length, gland-dotted; Mar.–May. **FRUIT** Seedlike, very narrow, 3–4 mm long, minutely hairy, topped by numerous straight white hairs slightly longer than the fruit.

HABITAT/RANGE Native; dry canyons and slopes, −50–1,400 m; sw. Utah, s. Nev., w. Ariz., and s. Calif. to Baja Calif.

Notes There is only 1 species of *Peucephyllum*; the name pygmy-cedar comes from the balsam-like odor and linear evergreen leaves.

PYGMY-CEDAR

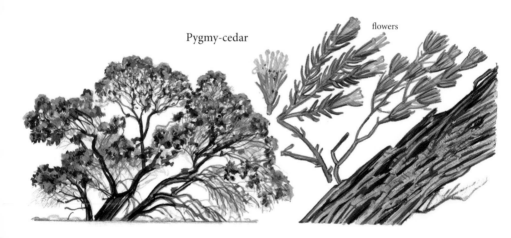

Pygmy-cedar

flowers

BETULACEAE: BIRCH FAMILY

This relatively small but well-known family includes 6 genera and 125–157 species, distributed primarily in cool temperate zones of the Northern Hemisphere. Five genera and 35 species occur in North America, 31 native, 4 introduced. Taxonomically, the family is divided into 2 subfamilies: Betuloideae, which includes the North American alders (*Alnus*) and birches (*Betula*); and Coryloideae, with hornbeams (*Carpinus*), hazels (*Corylus*), and hophornbeams (*Ostrya*).

All members of the family are deciduous woody shrubs or trees. **BARK** Variable, but usually distinctive within species; may be smooth, thin, and peeling in large or small sheets, flaking in platelets or large plates, or thick, with longitudinal ridges and fissures, varying whitish to brown or bluish gray. **TWIG** Buds lateral, or near or at twig tips, the scales meeting at the edges (valvate) like a clamshell or with the edges overlapping. **LEAF** Alternate, simple, with margins usually double-toothed, occasionally lobed, sometimes nearly entire. **FLOWER** Tiny, unisexual, sepals and petals very small, the sexes borne on the same tree in small, compact elongate clusters (catkins); within a catkin, groups of 2 or 3 flowers are subtended by small bracts. Male flowers have 1–6 (usually 2–4) stamens and are usually produced in slender, cylindric, often conspicuously dangling catkins. Female flowers typically have a single pistil and an inferior ovary with 2 or 3 chambers, and are usually borne in shorter dangling or erect catkins, or in tiny clusters. Most species flower in the spring, with or prior to leaf emergence, and are wind-pollinated. **FRUITS** Tiny samaras, nutlets (achenes), or nuts.

The family is ancient, traceable to the upper Cretaceous (100–70 million years ago). It is commercially important for filberts and hazelnuts (*Corylus*), the production of timber and wood pulp (*Betula, Alnus*), land reclamation (*Alnus*), and ornamental uses (*Betula, Corylus, Carpinus, Ostrya*). Fruits are dispersed by wind, water, or rodents and other small mammals, and the catkins are consumed by birds.

■ *ALNUS*: ALDERS

A genus of about 25 species, 8 in North America, of which 3 are introduced; 5 native tree species occur in the West.

Deciduous shrubs or small trees, usually with several trunks; winter buds usually occur on a short stalk. **BARK** Often waxy gray at first, usually with conspicuous horizontal orange or reddish-brown lenticels, remaining smooth or splitting with age to reveal reddish-brown inner bark. **TWIG** Green, brown, or purplish, 2-ranked or diffusely spreading, hairy or not. Bud usually stalked (sessile in some species), lateral or near the twig tip. **LEAF** Alternate, simple, thin or leathery; margins finely or coarsely toothed. **FLOWER** Male and female flowers are borne in separate inflorescences on the same plant. Male flowers usually in conspicuous, slender, dangling catkins; stamens usually 2 or 3 per flower, filaments not divided below anthers (as they are in birches). Female flowers usually 2 per scale in short catkins that become woody and persistent; scales with 5 lobes. **FRUIT** Numerous tiny samaras develop in the woody conelike fruiting female catkin.

Some North American species have been used medicinally by Native Americans, others for wetland reclamation. Through interaction with bacteria, the roots fix atmospheric nitrogen, enriching the soil, helping to make nitrogen available to other plants. The small ovoid brown or blackish woody conelike female catkins distinguish alders from other trees in the West.

MOUNTAIN ALDER *Alnus incana* (L.) Moench.
A.K.A. SPECKLED ALDER

QUICK ID Ovate or elliptic leaves with flat, coarsely double-toothed margins distinguish this alder from others in most of its range.

Deciduous shrub or tree to 12 m tall, with multiple or a single erect trunk to 15 cm diam.; crown open, spreading. **BARK** Reddish brown, light or dark gray, or dark brown; smooth, with prominent whitish lenticels. **LEAF** Alternate, simple, thin or thick; ovate or elliptic, base wedge-shaped to narrowly rounded; tip varying from bluntly pointed to tapered to a narrow point; margins coarsely double-toothed, the teeth acutely pointed or secondary teeth blunt. Upper surface hairless or sparsely hairy; lower surface often whitish, hairy or not. Blade 5–10 cm long, to about 5 cm broad; petiole 5–25 mm long. **FLOWER** Male catkins 2–10 cm long, dangling in clusters of 2–5; female catkins erect, in clusters of 2–6. Mar.–May, prior to leaf emergence. **FRUIT** Conelike fruiting structure 1–2 cm long, about 1 cm diam., with thick, blunt 3-lobed, dark brown scales, releasing tiny elliptic or obovate winged samaras.

HABITAT/RANGE Native. Wet or moist areas, often somewhat weedy and forming dense thickets, 0–3,000 m; Alaska to e. Canada, south to the n. U.S.

MOUNTAIN ALDER *continued*

SIMILAR SPECIES Arizona Alder has similar but proportionately narrower leaves, and grows mostly south of the range of Mountain Alder in the mountains of Ariz. and N.M.

Notes There are 2 intergrading subspecies of *A. incana*, which geographically overlap in w. Canada. Of the 2, subsp. *tenuifolia* (Nutt.) Breitung (called Mountain Alder or Thin-leaf Alder) is the more westerly, occurring from Alaska south to Calif., ne. Ariz., and nw. N.M. It is a shrub or tree to 12 m tall, the bark light gray to dark brown with nearly round to elliptic lenticels. The slender twigs are light red-brown or tan, sticky when young, and the sharp-pointed purplish buds 12–14 mm long and 2-ranked along the twigs. It has thin, papery leaves with blunt secondary teeth, staminate (male) catkins in clusters of 3–5 and pistillate (female) catkins in clusters of 2–5. The much shrubbier **Speckled Alder** (subsp. *rugosa* [Du Roi] R.T. Clausen, a.k.a. Swamp Alder) is primarily northeastern, entering the West in Sask. and Man., and perhaps extending farther west. It is up to 9 m tall, the bark dark grayish to reddish brown with notably horizontal lenticels. Its blunt red-brown buds are 3-ranked along the red-brown twigs. It has thick leaves with sharp teeth, staminate catkins in clusters of 2–4, and pistillate catkins in clusters of 2–6.

MOUNTAIN ALDER

SPECKLED ALDER

ARIZONA ALDER *Alnus oblongifolia* Torr.

A.K.A. NEW MEXICAN ALDER, MEXICAN ALDER, ALISO

QUICK ID The narrowly ovate, double-toothed leaves with finely tapered points on the teeth distinguish this species.

Deciduous fast-growing large shrub or moderate tree, usually less than 10 m tall, sometimes to 30 m; 1 to several straight trunks, 8–80 cm diam., with an open, spreading, rounded crown. **BARK** Grayish, tinged with brown or red-brown, becoming cracked and checkered into shallow vertical plates when older. **TWIG** Green and hairy when young, becoming gray, reddish brown, or orange-red and hairless when older. Terminal bud about 4–8 mm long, narrowly egg-shaped, dull red, downy, moderately resin-coated, the edges of the 2 scales barely meeting; on a stalk 1.5–4 mm long. **LEAF** Alternate, simple, more or less leathery, narrowly ovate to elliptic, usually broadest in the lower ½; base wedge-shaped to rounded; tip pointed; margins flat, coarsely double-toothed, the major teeth acute, gradually tapered to a fine point. Upper surface dark yellowish green; lower surface paler and hairless to finely hairy, often with brown tufts of hairs in the vein axils. Blade 4–9 cm long, 3–6 cm broad; petiole 1–2 cm long. **FLOWER** Male catkins 4–10 cm long; female catkins egg-shaped, about 12 mm long. Mar.–Jun., before the leaves emerge. **FRUIT** Conelike fruiting structure 13–25 mm long, with hard blackish scales, releasing tiny flat, elliptic to obovate samaras with wings narrower than the body.

HABITAT/RANGE Native. Mountain streams and seeps, 1,200–2,300 m; Ariz., N.M., nw. Mexico.

SIMILAR SPECIES The more westerly Red Alder also has double-toothed leaves, but its leaf margins are rolled under.

ARIZONA ALDER

Mountain Alder

fruit catkin

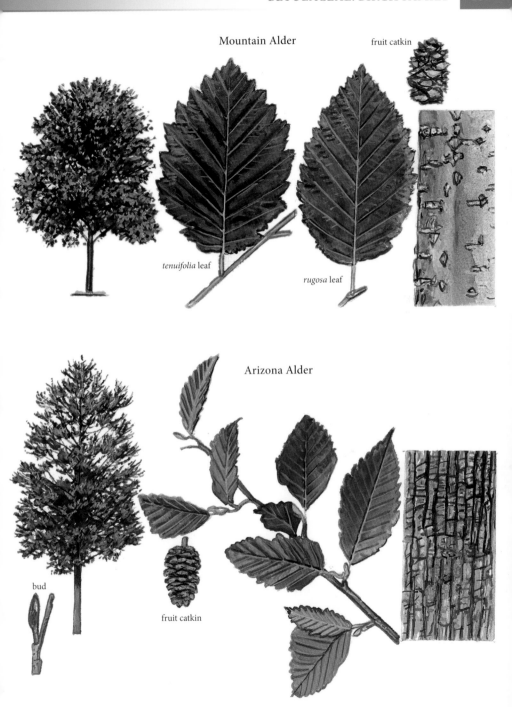

tenuifolia leaf

rugosa leaf

Arizona Alder

bud

fruit catkin

WHITE ALDER *Alnus rhombifolia* Nutt.
A.K.A. WESTERN ALDER, CALIFORNIA ALDER

QUICK ID This alder has flat leaf margins bearing fairly uniform fine teeth.

Deciduous fast-growing tree to 30 m tall; usually with a single straight trunk, 20–90 cm diam., often free of branches for ½ its height; crown wide, open, rounded, upper branches erect, lower branches spreading or drooping near the tips. BARK Thin, to about 2.5 cm thick on older trees, smooth and gray when young, often mottled with white, becoming brownish and broken into irregular plates and ridges when older, and the surface breaking into scales. TWIG At first green and hairy, becoming dark orange-red and hairless, the lenticels small and scattered. Terminal bud about 1 cm long, slender, tapered to the tip, dark red, covered with short hairs, moderately to heavily resin-coated, the edges of the 2 scales barely meeting; on a stalk 3–5 mm long. LEAF Alternate, simple, more or less thick, ovate to elliptic, the tip angled to rounded, base wedge-shaped to rounded; margins flat, finely toothed. Upper surface dark green and dull to slightly lustrous, the major veins not indented; lower surface paler and finely hairy. Blade 4–9 cm long, 2–5 cm broad; petiole 1–2 cm long. FLOWER Male catkins 3–10 cm long, in 1 or more clusters of 3–7; female catkins egg-shaped, 1–2 cm long, on stalks 1–10 mm long. Jan.–Apr., before the leaves emerge. FRUIT Conelike fruiting structure 15–20 mm long, with thin scales lobed at the tip, releasing tiny flat, broadly elliptic samaras with a thin wing narrower than the body.

HABITAT/RANGE Native. Rocky or gravelly soils in canyons, along streams, and on bottomlands, 100–2,400 m; sw. B.C. to s. Calif., east to w. Idaho.

SIMILAR SPECIES Red Alder has leaf margins that are rolled under and double-toothed, with larger and smaller teeth. Italian Alder (*A. cordata* [Loisel.]

Duby), introduced as an ornamental and escaped in at least 1 site in n. Calif., has leaves that are shiny on the upper surface, in general heart-shaped in outline, broader near the base, with the base indented or truncate at the attachment of the petiole.

Notes White Alder is the common alder found away from the coast in Calif.

RED ALDER *Alnus rubra* Bong.
A.K.A. OREGON ALDER, WESTERN ALDER

QUICK ID The double-toothed, rolled-under leaf margins distinguish this from other alders.

Deciduous fast-growing tree to 40 m tall; usually with a single straight trunk to 1 m diam., continuing as an axis to the top of the crown and often free of branches in the lower ½; crown wide, open, rounded, upper branches erect, lower branches spreading or drooping near the tips. BARK Smooth and pale gray when young, often mottled when older and sometimes roughened with wartlike swellings, broken into irregular plates and ridges near the base. TWIG Young twig at first light green and hairy, becoming purplish brown and hairless, dotted with numerous pale lenticels, later gray. Terminal bud about 6–10 mm long, tapered to the tip, dark red, covered with short hairs, usually heavily resin-coated, with 2 or 3 scales, the outer 2 with their edges barely meeting; on a stalk 2–8 mm long. LEAF Alternate, simple, fairly thick, ovate to widest at the middle and tapered to both ends, the tip pointed to rounded, the base broadly wedge-shaped to rounded; margins rolled under, with large teeth at ends of veins, these teeth bearing smaller, short-pointed teeth. Upper surface dull, dark green, the major veins indented; lower surface paler and usually rusty-hairy. Blade 6–16 cm long, 3–11 cm broad; petiole 1–3 cm long. FLOWER Male catkins 3–15 cm long, in 1 or more clusters of 2–6; female catkins egg-shaped, 1–2 cm long, on stalks 1–10 mm long. Feb.–May, before the leaves emerge. FRUIT Conelike fruiting structure 15–25 mm long, with thick, blunt scales, releasing tiny flat, broadly elliptic samaras with a wing ⅕–½ as wide as the body.

HABITAT/RANGE Native. Moist slopes, streamsides, floodplains, 0–300 m; s. Alaska to c. coastal Calif.

WHITE ALDER

RED ALDER

White Alder

fruit catkin

bud

immature
fruit catkin

twig

Red Alder   underside ♀ catkins

♂ catkin

bud

fruit
catkin

SIMILAR SPECIES White Alder, found slightly inland from Red Alder, has flat and finely toothed margins on its leaves.

Notes The underbark of Red Alder soon turns orange-red when exposed, as does the wood. This is the largest alder north of Mexico. The seeds are light, borne upon the wind; in recently burned or logged areas, this tree and White Alder, intolerant of shade, soon establish dense populations in the early stages of ecological succession. It is used for interior structure in cabinets, as veneer, as fuel, and as a delicate smoking wood for fish. Various parts of the plant were used medicinally by Native Americans to treat many afflictions.

SITKA ALDER *Alnus viridis* (Vill.) DC. subsp. *sinuata* (Regel) Á. Löve & D. Löve)
A.K.A. MOUNTAIN ALDER

QUICK ID Stalkless, or nearly stalkless, sharply pointed winter buds help to distinguish this species, as do the long-pointed, gland-tipped teeth of 2 sizes on the leaf margin.

Deciduous shrub or small tree 5–15 m tall; trunk 10–20 cm diam. TWIG Young twig gland-dotted, sweet-scented. Winter bud 12–14 mm long, purplish brown, curved, sharp-pointed, covered by 4–6 overlapping scales, stalkless or nearly so, usually 2-ranked on twigs. LEAF Alternate, simple, thin, ovate, yellowish green and shiny above, 4–12 cm long; margins flat, sharply and coarsely double-toothed, the teeth long-pointed, gland-tipped (no teeth near petiole). FLOWER Male catkins 7–13 cm long; female catkins egg-shaped, 1–2 cm long, on thin stalks 1–3 cm long; Mar.–Jun., as the leaves emerge.

HABITAT/RANGE Native. Gravelly, moist, open areas, 0–2,500 m; s. Alaska to Idaho and nw. Wyo.

Notes Several other, shrubby varieties of *A. viridis* are found across n. North America.

■ *BETULA*: BIRCHES

A genus of about 35 species. Eighteen occur in North America; of these, 9 occur in the West, where 6 are trees.

Deciduous trees or shrubs, often with several trunks. BARK Dark brown to silvery white, usually smooth, often peeling into thin, large or small sheets; typically with conspicuous horizontal lenticels. LEAF Alternate, simple, usually ovate or triangular, varying to elliptic or nearly rounded; margins toothed or double-toothed (especially in

tree forms); petioles ¼–½ length of blade. FLOWER Male and female flowers borne in separate catkins on the same plant; male catkins slender, dangling, usually terminal on the branch, stamens usually 2 or 3 per flower, the filament divided below the anther; female catkins inconspicuous at flowering, mostly borne at the base of male catkins. FRUIT Female fruiting catkins conspicuous, erect or pendent, cylindric, become leathery at maturity, a tiny 2-winged, seedlike samara (the actual fruit) nestled in the axil of each of the many catkin scales. Scales each with a 3-lobed tip, scales and samaras progressively falling away, leaving the central axis of the catkin attached to the twig

The leaves of birches typically are yellow in autumn. Certain identification of birch species requires attention to characteristics of bark, leaves, and often the shape and nature of the lobes of the catkin scales.

KENAI BIRCH *Betula kenaica* W.H. Evans
A.K.A. KENAI PAPER BIRCH, RED BIRCH

QUICK ID The sharply toothed, ovate or triangular leaves; peeling, often dark bark; and scales of the fruiting catkin with equal-length lobes together distinguish this birch.

Deciduous tree 6–25 m tall; trunk 10–45 cm diam. BARK Dark reddish brown or brown, occasionally pinkish or grayish white, peeling in papery sheets. TWIG Reddish brown, somewhat hairy, often with scattered resinous glands, becoming very dark and hairless. LEAF Alternate, simple, thick, ovate to nearly triangular, with 2–6 pairs of lateral veins; tip forming a narrow angle; margins sharply toothed. Upper surface dull, dark green; lower surface pale yellow-green, gland-dotted, hairy especially along the veins. Blade 4–7.5 cm long; 2.5–4.5 cm broad. FLOWER Male catkins 2.5 cm long, dark brown; female catkins

SITKA ALDER

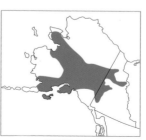

KENAI BIRCH

Sitka Alder

fruit catkins

spring

immature fruit catkins

Kenai Birch

underside

catkin scale

samara

cylindric, 2–5 cm long, erect or spreading on stout stalks; lobes of catkin scales about equal length, strongly diverging. Apr.–Jun. **FRUIT** Tiny samara with wings narrower to broader than the body, broadest near the middle, not extending beyond the tip of the seedlike body.

HABITAT/RANGE Native. Disturbed areas, 0–650 m; Alaska, w. Y.T.

SIMILAR SPECIES Paper Birch usually has larger leaves with 6–9 pairs of veins. Water Birch has bark that does not readily peel, and the central lobe of the catkin scale is much shorter than the lateral lobes.

Notes Kenai Birch is shade-intolerant; it soon establishes in cleared areas and is succeeded by different trees.

RESIN BIRCH *Betula neoalaskana* Sarg.
A.K.A. ALASKA BIRCH, ALASKA WHITE BIRCH, ALASKA PAPER BIRCH

QUICKID This birch has pale bark, sharply double-toothed, long-pointed leaves, and twigs densely covered with resin glands.

Deciduous tree 6–15 m tall; trunk usually 10–40 cm diam. **BARK** Young bark dark reddish brown, later pinkish white to light reddish, or white in c. Alaska, peeling in papery sheets. **TWIG** Bright reddish brown, hairless, abundantly covered with resin glands. **LEAF** Alternate, simple, oval to nearly triangular, with 5–18 pairs of lateral veins; tip long-tapered to a fine point; margins sharply double-toothed. Upper surface shiny, dark green; lower surface pale yellow-green, gland-dotted, and hairy especially along the veins. Blade 3–8 cm long; 2–6 cm broad. **FLOWER** Male catkins 2.5–4 cm long, greenish brown; female catkins cylindric, 1–3.5 cm long, drooping or spreading; lobes of catkin scales about equal length or central lobe shorter, lateral lobes spreading or curved slightly backward. Apr.–Jun. **FRUIT** Tiny samara with wings broader than the body, broadest near the tip, extending beyond the tip of the seedlike body.

HABITAT/RANGE Native. Poorly drained sites, bog margins, often with Black Spruce, 100–1,200 m; c. Alaska to sc. Canada.

SIMILAR SPECIES Paper Birch leaves have a shorter point at the tip, and the lobes of the catkin bracts are about equal in length, but the lateral lobes are broader.

Notes This birch is more closely related to Asian species than to Paper Birch of North America, with which it was sometimes merged.

WATER BIRCH *Betula occidentalis* Hook.
A.K.A. WESTERN BIRCH, RIVER BIRCH, RED BIRCH, BROWN BIRCH, BLACK BIRCH

QUICKID Non-peeling purplish or brownish bark, small leaves with 4 or 5 pairs of veins, and reddish-warty twigs help identify this birch.

Deciduous shrubby or small tree, usually to about 12 m tall; trunk mostly 10–20(–35) cm diam.; variable, sometimes forming a clump of dozens of trunks, or other times a moderate tree to 35 m tall with a trunk diam. to 1 m. Crown narrowly oval, upright, the branches ascending, drooping at the tip. **BARK** Alternate, simple, thin, smooth, with pale horizontal lenticels; loosening, curling, but not peeling in big patches, exposing light orange underbark; mature bark dark to blackish on young branches and stems, dark reddish brown to bronze or purplish on larger branches and trunk. **TWIG** At first green or light yellowish brown, minutely downy, and densely gland-dotted; later reddish brown, finally gray-brown. Winter bud bright orange-brown or greenish brown. **LEAF** Thin, pendulous, ovate to nearly diamond-shaped, the tip forming a sharp or blunt angle, usually with 4 or 5 pairs of yellowish lateral veins, the veins ending in a large tooth, with 3–4 smaller teeth between (margins thus coarsely double-toothed). Upper surface deep green, often lustrous, resinous when young; lower surface paler, dotted with dark glands, hairy or not. Blade 4–6 cm long; 1–4.5 cm broad; petiole 5–20 mm long, hairy. **FLOWER** Male catkins 6 cm long, pendent female catkins about 2 cm long, cylindric, the central lobe of the catkin scales narrower and longer than the lateral lobes. Flowers generally in late spring before or with the leaves, but Feb.–Aug. across the species' wide range. **FRUIT** Catkins 2–4 cm long in fruit; tiny samara with wings broader than the body, broadest near the tip, extending beyond the tip of the seedlike body.

RESIN BIRCH

WATER BIRCH

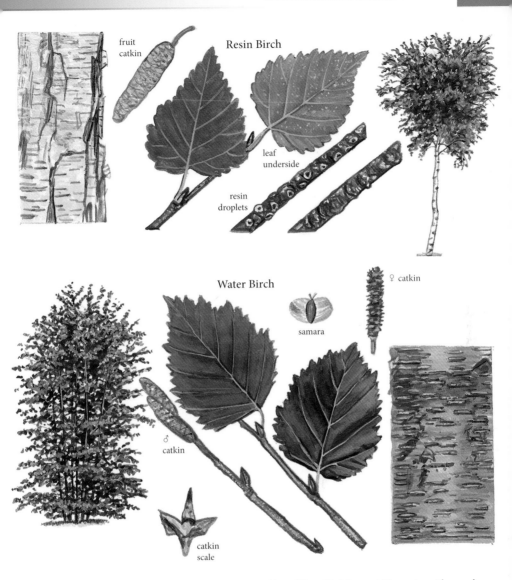

fruit
catkin

Resin Birch

leaf
underside

resin
droplets

♀ catkin

Water Birch

samara

♂
catkin

catkin
scale

HABITAT/RANGE Native. Moist or wet areas, commonly with poplars, willows, and alders, 100–3,000 m; Alaska east to Hudson Bay, south to Calif., n. Ariz., n. N.M., w. S.D., e. N.D.

SIMILAR SPECIES Paper Birch usually has larger leaves with 6–9 veins and peeling, brilliant white bark. Kenai Birch has peeling brownish to whitish bark, and scales of the female catkin with the central lobe as about as long as the lateral lobes.

Notes Water Birch is a variable species with regard to its habit. In the Rocky Mountain region it is a common streamside tree or shrub, valuable for bank stabilization and wildlife habitat. Along rivers in s. B.C. it is a large tree, reputed to be the tallest birch in the world. The wood is used for fuel.

PAPER BIRCH *Betula papyrifera* Marshall
A.K.A. CANOE BIRCH, WHITE BIRCH

QUICK ID This tree is easily recognized by the combination of creamy-white papery bark that exfoliates in thin, curly sheets, orange inner bark, and double-toothed leaves.

Deciduous fast-growing, shade-tolerant tree, usually 15–22 m tall, potentially to 30 m tall; trunk erect, usually 1, sometimes more, 30–60 cm diam. Crown of young trees compact, pyramidal or oval, with many slender branches; crown of mature trees broad and spreading with few large branches. **BARK** Smooth, reddish brown on young trunks, becoming creamy white, exfoliating in thin, curly plates to reveal orange inner bark; eventually crusty and dark brown or nearly black at the base of the trunk. **TWIG** Slender and dull red at first, becoming lustrous orange-brown; slightly or moderately hairy. **LEAF** Alternate, but sometimes closely set in groups of 3 at the tips of short shoots of older branches; simple, thick, stiff, ovate, lightly or densely hairy beneath, especially along the veins and in vein axils, with a rounded or flattened base, the tip abruptly short-tapered, the lateral veins 9 or fewer pairs; margins double-toothed. Upper surface dark green; lower surface paler, sparsely to moderately hairy, covered with numerous resinous glands. Blade 5–10 cm long, 3–7 cm broad; petiole 1.5–2.5 cm long, stout, hairy or not. **FLOWER** Male catkins 7–10 cm long, slender, pendent, brownish; female catkins 3–4 cm long, slender, pendent, greenish, the catkin scales with widely diverging lobes, the central lobe narrow, the lateral lobes about as long but much broader. Mar.–Jun. **FRUIT** Catkins 3–4 cm long in fruit; tiny samara with wings as broad as or slightly broader than the seedlike body, extending slightly beyond the tip.

HABITAT/RANGE Native. Upland forest, cutover or burned-over woodlands, lake and stream

margins, swamps; tolerant of a wide range of soils and moisture regimes, varying from acidic to basic, 300–900 m; across North America from Y.T., B.C., and Wash. to Nfld., ne. U.S. as far south as Colo. and Va.

SIMILAR SPECIES Both Kenai Birch and Resin Birch may have pale, peeling bark; they differ in having leaves that are hairless beneath or slightly hairy along the veins. The largest leaf blades of Kenai Birch are usually less than 5 cm long. Resin Birch leaves often have more pairs of veins.

Notes This is the birch used by Native Americans for the fabrication of the birch-bark canoe; the bark is high in oil content and is waterproof. Because of its durability and water-resistance, it was also used as sheeting under sod on cabin roofs. Locally, the wood is used for fuel, mine props, and lumber. Because of its attractive bark, the species is a popular ornamental in cooler climates.

EUROPEAN WHITE BIRCH *Betula pendula* Roth
A.K.A. WEEPING BIRCH, SILVER BIRCH

QUICK ID The silvery-white bark that exfoliates in long horizontal strands and leaf blades that are sparsely hairy or hairless beneath help to distinguish the birch.

Deciduous tree to about 25 m tall, usually with multiple erect trunks; crown broad, spreading, with pendulous branches. **BARK** Smooth, silvery or creamy white, exfoliating in long horizontal strands. **TWIG** Reddish purple, hairless, with numerous resinous glands. **LEAF** Alternate, simple, ovate or triangular, with 5–8 pairs of lateral veins; base broadly wedge-shaped, rarely squared-off; tip pointed; margins coarsely double-toothed. Upper surface dark green; lower surface paler, sparsely hairy or hairless, covered with numerous resinous glands. Blade 3–7 cm long, 2.5–5 cm broad; petiole 2–3 cm long. **FLOWER** Male catkins slender, 4–9 cm long, in groups of 2–4; female catkins pendulous, 2–4 cm long, catkin scales with the central lobe very short and bluntly pointed, the lateral lobes longer and rounded. Apr.–Jun. **FRUIT** Tiny winged samara, the wings much broader than the seedlike body.

HABITAT/RANGE Introduced from Europe; established in ne. U.S., naturalized in B.C. and Wash.; roadsides, bog margins, disturbed sites, 0–350 m.

PAPER BIRCH

Paper Birch

spring

samara

catkin scale

catkin scale

autumn

fruit catkin

♀ catkin

♂ catkin

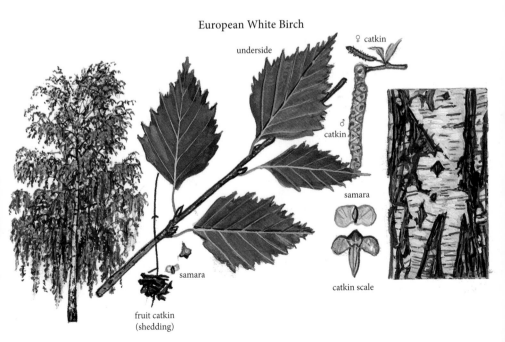

European White Birch

underside

♀ catkin

♂ catkin

samara

catkin scale

samara

fruit catkin
(shedding)

DOWNY BIRCH *Betula pubescens* Ehrh.

Deciduous shrub or tree to 20 m tall. Usually a single trunk, to 70 cm diam.; crown narrow, with ascending-spreading, not drooping, branches. **BARK** Smooth, dull grayish white, with dark horizontal lenticels. **TWIG** Gray-brown, hairy, with fine, short, stiff hairs, usually also with resinous glands. **LEAF** Alternate, simple, ovate; base rounded, flattened, or wedge-shaped; tip acutely pointed; margins finely or coarsely toothed. Lower surface hairy, at least along the major veins. Blade 3–6 cm long, 2–6 cm broad; petiole 1–2.5 cm long, hairy. **FLOWER** Female catkins 2.5–3 cm long; scale lobes divergent. Apr.–Jun. **FRUIT** Tiny samara with wings slightly broader than the seedlike body. **HABITAT/RANGE** Introduced from Europe; sporadically established in B.C. and Wash., perhaps in Rocky Mountain states, naturalized in ne. U.S.; moist roadsides, abandoned plantings, 0–200 m. *Notes* This is the only tree native to Iceland and Greenland.

■ *CORYLUS*: HAZELS

There are about 15 species of hazels from temperate areas in the Northern Hemisphere, 3 in North America. Of the 2 species that occur in the West, one is introduced.

Deciduous shrubs or small trees. **LEAF** Alternate, simple, with toothed margins. **FLOWER** Tiny, unisexual, with both sexes on the same tree. Male with 4 stamens divided to form 8 half stamens, aggregated 3 per scale in pendulous catkins on the previous year's twigs, catkins expanding with leaves in early spring; female flowers in clusters near ends of twigs, surrounded by an involucre. **FRUIT** Nearly globose nut developing within the base of the involucre (commonly called the husk). Hazelnuts are edible.

EUROPEAN HAZEL *Corylus avellana* L.
A.K.A. HAZELNUT, EUROPEAN FILBERT

Deciduous small tree or large shrub, usually 3–8 m tall, the crown spreading. **LEAF** Alternate, simple, thin, broadly ovate to elliptic, the tip tapered to a narrow point, the margins doubly, sharply toothed; surfaces bristly-glandular hairy; blade 5–12 cm long, 4–12 cm broad. **FLOWER** Male catkins 3–6 cm long, usually in groups of 2–4; female catkins small, with 1–4 flowers. Jan.–Mar. **FRUIT** Globose or ovoid brown nut, 1.5–2 cm long, enclosed in a toothed involucre about as long as

the nut; in clusters of 1–4. **HABITAT/RANGE** Introduced from Eurasia; established in disturbed areas, 0–120 m, w. Wash., w. Ore., also ne. U.S. *Notes* This is the filbert or hazelnut of commerce.

BEAKED HAZELNUT *Corylus cornuta* Marshall

QUICK ID A shrub or small tree distinguished by a soft, bristly, tubular involucre (husk) surrounding the fruit, and a softly hairy or hairless petiole.

Deciduous shrub to 6 m tall, occasionally a small tree to 15 m tall, usually with several erect-ascending trunks; branched near the base. **BARK** Gray-brown, smooth. **TWIG** Slender, light brown, usually zigzag, hairless or sparsely hairy. **LEAF** Alternate, simple, ovate, oval, or narrowly elliptic; margins coarsely and irregularly double-toothed. Upper surface dark green, finely hairy; lower surface paler, hairy on the veins or hairless. Blade 5–12 cm long, 3–9 cm broad; petiole 5–10 mm long, hairless or moderately hairy. **FLOWER** Male catkins 4–6 cm long, in clusters of 2 or 3 on short shoots. Female flowers hidden in the ovoid base of the involucre, only the red styles protruding. Jan.–Mar. **FRUIT** Globose nut, 12 mm diam., a tiny, sharp beak at tip; nuts in clusters of 2–6, concealed in bristly-hairy bracts joined into a tube 2–4 times length of nut.

HABITAT/RANGE Native. Roadsides, disturbed sites, thickets, 100–2,500 m; across Canada, south to Calif., Colo., se. U.S.

Notes Two subspecies: Subsp. *californica* (A. DC.) E. Murray is often treelike, usually with glandular hairs on twigs and petioles; sw. B.C. to c. Calif., 1,000–2,500 m. Subsp. *cornuta* is shrubby, lacks glandular hairs; B.C. and e. Wash. to East Coast, 100–500 m.

BEAKED HAZELNUT

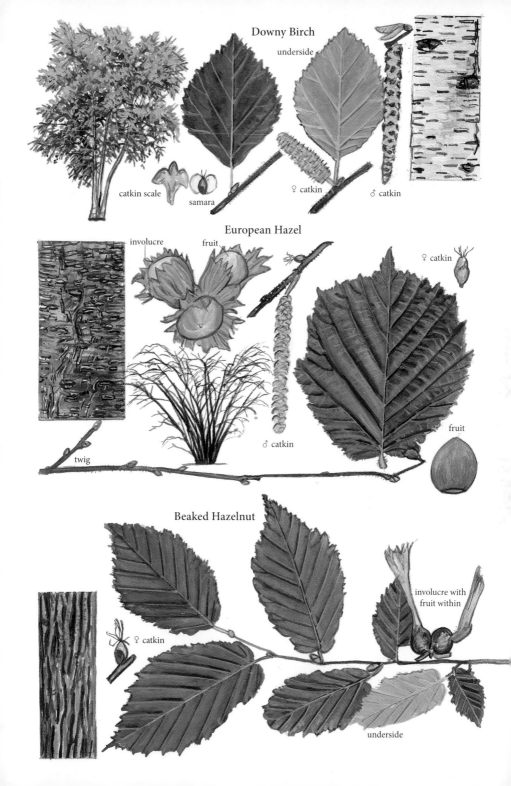

Downy Birch

underside

catkin scale

samara

♀ catkin

♂ catkin

European Hazel

involucre

fruit

♀ catkin

♂ catkin

fruit

twig

Beaked Hazelnut

♀ catkin

involucre with fruit within

underside

■ *OSTRYA*: HOPHORNBEAMS

The hophornbeams comprise a small genus of 5 species in temperate areas of the Northern Hemisphere, three of which occur in the West. Deciduous shrubs or small trees with conspicuously 2-ranked branchlets, twigs, and leaves. **LEAF** Alternate, simple, margins toothed, borne on long and short shoots. **FLOWER** Tiny, borne in thin, papery bracts, unisexual, the sexes on the same tree. Male flowers, each usually with 3 stamens, occur 3 per bract, all crowded together into pendulous catkins at the ends of branches. Female flowers occur 2 per bract, these and accessory bracts conspicuous and papery, united and bladderlike when mature, gathered into a soft, conelike catkin resembling the fruiting structure of hops. **FRUIT** Small, longitudinally striped nutlet, enclosed in an inflated bladderlike complex of bracts that is deciduous with the nutlet.

Hophornbeams presently have little economic value. At one time, because of its hardness, the wood was used to make sleigh runners, wheel rims, propellers, and hand tools.

BIG BEND HOPHORNBEAM *Ostrya chisosensis* Correll
A.K.A. CHISOS HOPHORNBEAM

QUICKID This is the only hophornbeam in the Chisos Mountains, the hop-like fruiting structures distinguishing it from other trees there.

Deciduous small tree up to 14 m tall, with an open cylindric crown. Lacks stalked glands on the twigs and leaves. **LEAF** Alternate, simple, thin, broadly elliptic to elliptic-lanceolate, the tip blunt or sharp-angled, margins finely double-toothed. Blade 3.5–5 cm long, 2–3 cm broad. **FLOWER** Male catkins 3.5–5 cm long; female catkins 8–15 mm long. May–Jun. **FRUIT** Fruiting catkin pendulous, 2–4 cm long, 1.5–2.5 cm wide.

HABITAT/RANGE Native. Wooded canyons, 1,500–2,300 m; Chisos Mountains, Tex.

SIMILAR SPECIES Resembles Eastern Hophornbeam, but the leaf tip is more bluntly pointed; sometimes considered a subspecies of that species.

WESTERN HOPHORNBEAM *Ostrya knowltonii* Coville
A.K.A. KNOWLTON HOPHORNBEAM, WOOLLY HOPHORNBEAM

QUICKID The small leaves with stalked glands and double-toothed margins and the hanging hoplike fruit clusters distinguish this tree.

Small deciduous tree to 12 m tall, 15–45 cm diam. **BARK** Light brownish or reddish gray, shallowly furrowed and breaking into narrow vertical scales or ragged short strips. **TWIG** Dark green to reddish brown or gray, lightly hairy and with stalked glands, later becoming nearly hairless and lustrous. **LEAF** Alternate, simple, thin, broadly ovate to elliptic, tip rounded or forming a narrow angle, base rounded or slightly heart-shaped, sometimes somewhat asymmetric; margins irregularly and sharply double-toothed. Upper surface dark yellowish green, washboard-like from the impression of the veins, hairless or lightly hairy; lower surface paler, hairy, and with stalked glands, especially along the raised veins and on the petiole. Blade 2.5–6.5 cm long; 1.5–5 cm broad; petiole 3–6 mm long. **FLOWER** Male catkins 2–3 cm long, the bracts broad, rounded, with a minute point at tip; female catkins 6–10 mm long. Mar.–May, the flowers expanding with the leaves. **FRUIT** Fruiting catkins pendulous, egg-shaped, lightly hairy, 2.5–4 cm long, on a stalk 2 cm long; the nut-bearing saclike bracts 10–25 mm long, loosely overlapping, greenish white to brownish; nut tan, 6 mm long, ovoid, flattened, ribbed.

BIG BEND HOPHORNBEAM

WESTERN HOPHORNBEAM

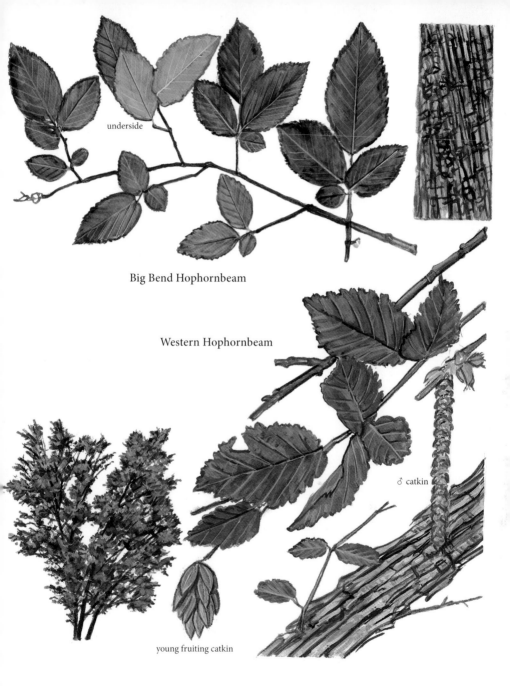

underside

Big Bend Hophornbeam

Western Hophornbeam

♂ catkin

young fruiting catkin

HABITAT/RANGE Native. Uncommon and widely scattered in wooded canyons, near seeps, along streams, 1,100–2,400 m; se. Utah, n. Ariz., sc. N.M., w. Tex., n. Mexico.

SIMILAR SPECIES Big Bend Hophornbeam and Eastern Hophornbeam lack the stalked glands on the twigs and leaves.

EASTERN HOPHORNBEAM *Ostrya virginiana* (Mill.). K. Koch
A.K.A. IRONWOOD

QUICK ID Easily recognized by the combination of double-toothed leaves, shredding bark, and the hop-like fruiting catkin.

Deciduous tree to 22 m tall, with a trunk to 90 cm diam. **BARK** Grayish brown or steely gray, shredding into often ragged, narrow, vertical strips. **LEAF** Unevenly double-toothed; tip abruptly tapered to a narrow point; blade 5–13 cm long; petioles usually lack stipitate glands. **FRUIT** Fruiting catkin 3.5–6.5 cm long.

HABITAT/RANGE Native. Widespread in eastern forests in well-drained woods and on moist slopes, barely entering the West, at about 500–1,500 m; Nebr., the Dakotas, ne. Wyo.

EASTERN HOPHORNBEAM

BIGNONIACEAE: BIGNONIA FAMILY

The bignonia family includes 104–110 genera and 800–860 species of trees, shrubs, and woody vines distributed mainly in the tropics and subtropics. As many as 16 species in 13 genera occur in North America, 6 native, 10 introduced.

Evergreen or deciduous trees and shrubs. **LEAF** Usually opposite and compound. **FLOWER** Bisexual, large and brightly colored, bilateral, the calyx and corolla with 5 sepals and 5 petals, respectively. There are usually 4 fertile stamens and 1 sterile stamen. The ovary is superior, usually with 2 chambers, and with a 2-lobed stigma. **FRUIT** A capsule, sometimes long and beanlike, or occasionally a berry or indehiscent pod. Seeds are often flat, with a ragged wing extending from the edges.

Numerous species are grown as ornamentals in warm regions. Yellow Trumpetbush (*Tecoma stans* [L.] Juss. ex Kunth), with large, brilliant yellow flowers, is a native shrub in the Southwest that becomes a small tree in frost-free areas. Black Poui (*Jacaranda mimosifolia* D. Don) is a South American tree grown for its bright blue-purple flowers, common in s. Calif.

■ *CATALPA*: CATALPAS

A genus of 12 species distributed in North America, the Greater Antilles, and East Asia. Two species are native to e. North America, both of which are grown as ornamentals in the West, occasionally escaping and weakly naturalized.

Deciduous fast-growing trees, usually with a single erect trunk. **LEAF** Opposite or whorled, simple, heart-shaped, with 5 veins arising from the base of the blade; margins entire. **FLOWER** In racemes or panicles at the branch tips, bilateral, roughly bell-shaped, the petals fused, crinkled on margins, forming a 2-lobed upper lip and a 3-lobed lower lip, usually white or pale yellow with purple spotting in the throat or lower lip. Fertile stamens 2.

Ovary superior, long and narrow. **FRUIT** Narrow, long capsule splitting on 1 side, exposing numerous seeds, each with a fringed wing on each end.

SOUTHERN CATALPA *Catalpa bignonioides* Walter

Deciduous tree, usually to about 15 m tall. **LEAF** Opposite or whorled, base heart-shaped, tip abruptly tapered to a point; upper surface hairless, lower surface paler, hairy. Margins entire or with 1 or 2 small, broadly pointed lobes. Blade 10–30 cm long, 8–18 cm broad; petiole 7–29 cm long. Leaves have an unpleasant odor when crushed. **FLOWER** 4–5 cm long, 3–5 cm diam., white with

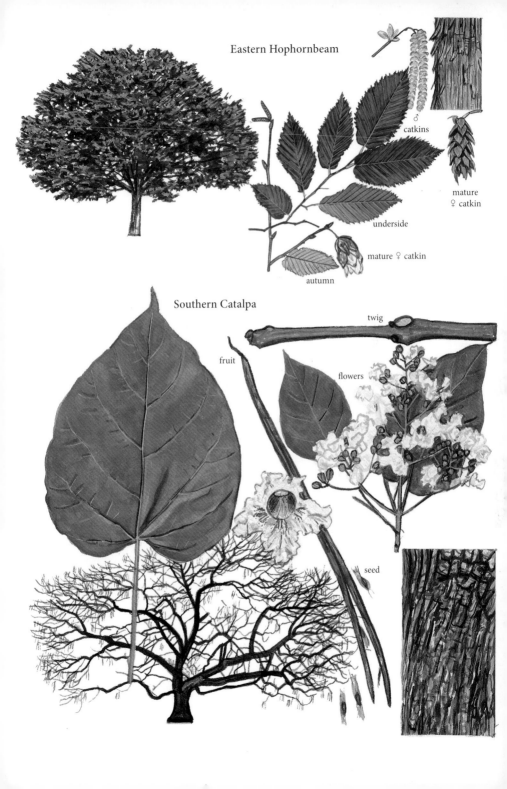

Eastern Hophornbeam

♂ catkins

mature
♀ catkin

underside

mature ♀ catkin

autumn

Southern Catalpa

twig

fruit

flowers

seed

SOUTHERN CATALPA *continued*

conspicuous yellow and purple spots; many in pyramidal clusters. Mar.–Jul. **FRUIT** Slender capsule, 10–40 cm long, about 1 cm diam. **HABITAT/ RANGE** Introduced from se. U.S. Stream banks and disturbed areas, 0–1,500 m,; c. and s. Calif., occasionally escaped or persisting in old plantings elsewhere in the West.

NORTHERN CATALPA *Catalpa speciosa*
Warder ex Engelm.

QUICK ID This attractive tree has large heart-shaped, non-malodorous leaves; bell-shaped, pale bilateral flowers with fringed margins; and long capsules at least 1.5 cm wide.

Deciduous tree, usually to about 30 m tall. Trunk usually single, erect, to 1 m diam., the crown narrow, rounded. **BARK** Dark gray, brown, or reddish brown, fissured, and scaly. **LEAF** Opposite, simple, moderately thick to nearly leathery, heart-shaped or rounded at the base, tip gradually tapering to a narrow point; margins entire or with a broadly pointed lobe. Upper surface dark green, hairless; lower surface paler, hairy. Blade 10–30 cm long, 8–18 cm broad; petiole 10–16 cm long. **FLOWER** 4–5 cm long, 6–7 cm diam., white with conspicuous yellow stripes and purple spots; few to several in pyramidal clusters. Mar.–Jul. **FRUIT** Slender capsule 25–60 cm long, 1.5–2 cm diam.

HABITAT/RANGE Introduced from e. U.S.; stream banks and disturbed areas in c. Calif., 0–1,500 m, occasionally escaped and persisting in old plantings elsewhere in the West.

SIMILAR SPECIES Southern Catalpa has smaller flowers with more per cluster, narrower fruit pods, and malodorous crushed leaves.

DESERT WILLOW *Chilopsis linearis*
(Cav.) Sweet
A.K.A. MIMBRE

QUICK ID Narrow leaves and showy, snapdragon-like white to rose-colored flowers distinguish this species.

Deciduous shrub or tree to 12 m tall, with 1 to few often leaning, twisted trunks 10–40 cm diam., and an open irregular crown. **BARK** On young branches gray-brown, smooth; on older trunks dark brown or black, deeply and irregularly fissured, the broad ridges with small scales. **TWIG** Slender, flexible, at first green and lightly hairy, later gray to red-brown and hairless. **LEAF** Alternate, or near the base of the twig often opposite; simple, linear-lanceolate, long-tapered at both ends; margins entire. Green and lustrous on both surfaces, sometimes lightly hairy. Blade 10–25 cm long, 4–6 mm broad; petiole absent or very short, base of blade continuous with petiole and forming a wing. **FLOWER** Bisexual, bilateral, showy, in loose conical clusters to 30 cm long. Calyx swollen, 2-lipped; corolla 2–5 cm long, the tube flared into a 2-lobed upper lip, and a 3-lobed lower lip, white or shades of pink, rose, or magenta, lined in the throat with maroon, yellow on ridges in the tube and at the base of the lower lip; lobes of lip broad, round, crinkled, and with ragged margins. Fertile stamens 2 long, 2 short, a 5th sterile, shorter. Ovary slender, superior, the 2-lobed stigma closing when touched. Apr.–Sep., flowering most profusely May–Jun. **FRUIT** Persistent narrow, cylindric, pendulous brownish capsule, tapered at both ends, 15–35 cm long, splitting in 2 parts to release flat seeds that have 2 fringed white wings.

HABITAT/RANGE Native. Washes in arid areas, 400–1,600 m; s. Calif. to Tex., n. Mexico. Widely introduced as an ornamental in warm regions and perhaps escaping from cultivation on the s. Great Plains, where it is widespread.

NORTHERN CATALPA

DESERT WILLOW

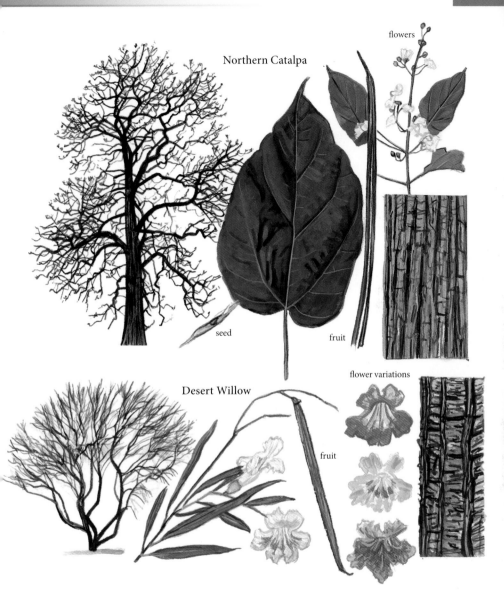

flowers

Northern Catalpa

seed

fruit

flower variations

Desert Willow

fruit

SIMILAR SPECIES Willows (*Salix*, Salicaceae) are similar, but have toothed margins on the leaves and tiny flowers borne in catkins.

Notes The single species of *Chilopsis* is a shrub or tree, vegetatively resembling a true willow but not at all closely related. There are 2 subspecies. Subsp. *linearis*, with straight, ascending or spreading leaves, occurs from c. N.M. to Tex. Subsp. *arcuata* (Fosberg) Henrickson, with curved, scythe-shaped, drooping leaves, occurs from c. N.M. to s. Calif. Desert Willow is one of the parents in the intergeneric hybrid ornamental tree Chitalpa (× *Chitalpa tashkentensis* Ellis & Wisura); the other parent is Southern Catalpa (*Catalpa bignonioides*).

BORAGINACEAE: BORAGE FAMILY

A worldwide family of about 150 genera and 2,750 species of herbs, shrubs, and trees distributed in temperate and tropical regions, with the greatest concentration of species in the Mediterranean area.
LEAF Alternate, simple. **FLOWER** Usually bisexual or functionally unisexual. Sepals 5, joined; petals 5, fused to form a tube, widely flared at the top; stamens 5, usually included in the tube; ovary superior, basically 2-chambered, but by division often 4-chambered. Flowers in full bloom are held at the top of a coil, though this is not so evident in our woody species. **FRUIT** In woody species, often a drupe or drupelike, sometimes a nut.

The borage family produces some bedding plants and ornamental shrubs. Plants produce dyes, edible fruit, and valuable hardwoods used in tropical furniture, cabinetry, and novelty items.

ANACAHUITE *Cordia boissieri* A. DC.
A.K.A. TEXAS OLIVE, TEXAS WILD OLIVE, WHITE GEIGER, MEXICAN OLIVE, WHITE CORDIA

QUICK ID This shrub or tree of s. Tex. has leaves that are harshly hairy above and pale and velvety beneath, and 5-lobed white flowers, 1.5–6 cm diam., borne in clusters.

Evergreen (deciduous in cold winters) shrub or small tree to 8 m tall, with 1 or few trunks to 20 cm diam. **BARK** Thick, gray, and ridged when mature. **TWIG** Twigs and buds woolly. **LEAF** Alternate, simple, leathery, ovate or lanceolate-ovate; margins entire, sometimes slightly wavy. Upper surface grayish green and stiffly hairy; lower surface pale, velvety. Blade 9–20 cm long, 5–15 cm broad; petiole to 4 cm. **FLOWER** Bisexual, showy, 6–8 in clusters aggregated into a large branched, round-topped cluster. White with a yellow throat, trumpet-shaped, 3.5–4.5 cm long, 1.5–6 cm diam.; corolla with 5 round, shallow, crepe-like, crinkled lobes, the edges minutely fringed. Style shallowly cleft into 4 lobes. Flowers mostly in Apr.–Jun., but some throughout the year. **FRUIT** Ovoid, shiny drupe, 1.5–4 cm long, about ½ clasped in the 5-toothed calyx; at first whitish or yellow-green, at maturity reddish brown, with a single large stone.

HABITAT/RANGE Native. Thickets, fencerows, stream banks, 0–100 m; s. Tex. to ne. Mexico.

SIMILAR SPECIES Anacua (*Ehretia anacua*) has flowers only 6 mm diam. and small round yellow-orange fruits.

Notes Cordia is a genus of about 325 species of showy trees and shrubs, mostly of the American tropics, five of which occur in the s. U.S. Anacahuite's flowers are heterostylic; that is, some plants have flowers with short styles and others with long ones, to encourage outbreeding. Fruits are eaten by Collared Peccaries (*Pecari tajacu*). The tree is often planted in warm climates for its showy flowers.

ANACUA *Ehretia anacua* (Terán & Berland.) I.M. Johnst.
A.K.A. SANDPAPER TREE, SUGARBERRY, KNOCKAWAY, MANZANITA

QUICK ID Oval sandpapery, leathery leaves, nearly hairless beneath, and small white 5-lobed flowers in clusters distinguish this shrub or tree of c. and s. Tex.

Evergreen (partially deciduous in cold winters) shrub or tree to 15 m tall; trunks 10–30 cm diam., often several, surrounded by suckers, and a compact round crown. **BARK** Thick, gray to reddish brown, furrowed, the narrow ridges becoming scaly. **TWIG** Slender, crooked, hairless at maturity; buds hairless. **LEAF** Alternate, simple, leathery, oval, with a rounded tip ending in a small point; margins entire or with a few teeth above the middle; 5 or 6 pairs of veins indented above, raised below. Upper surface dull, dark green and stiffly hairy; lower surface paler and thinly velvety or nearly hairless. Blade 2.5–8 cm long, 2–4 cm broad; petiole short. **FLOWER** Bisexual, fragrant, in branched clusters 2.5–8 cm long. White, bell-shaped, 9 mm long,

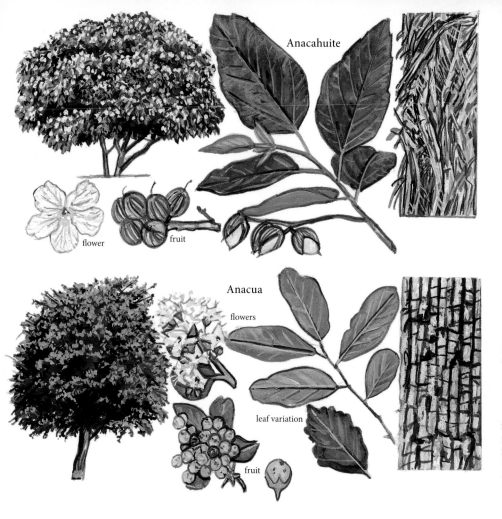

Anacahuite

flower

fruit

Anacua

flowers

leaf variation

fruit

about 6 mm wide; corolla with 5 round lobes, the edges rolled under. Style shallowly cleft or 2-lobed. Mar.–Apr. **FRUIT** Round, shiny drupe, 5–8 mm wide, yellowish orange when mature; each of the 2 hemispheric stones with 2 seeds.

HABITAT/RANGE Native. Well-drained soil, on slopes and in valleys, 0–1,000 m; c. Texas to ne. Mexico.

SIMILAR SPECIES Anacahuite (*Cordia boissieri*) has larger flowers, 35–45 mm long, and an ovoid reddish-brown fruit.

Notes This is the only species of *Ehretia*, a tropical genus of about 75 species, to occur in the U.S. Anacua's berries are edible and are relished by birds. The small metallic Texas Tortoise Beetle (*Coptocycla texana*) feeds on only this species.

ANACAHUITE

ANACUA

BUDDLEJACEAE: BUDDLEJA FAMILY

Buddlejaceae (sometimes spelled Buddleiaceae) is a warm-region family of about 9 genera and 150 species of shrubs or trees; it is often considered part of the warm temperate to tropical logania family (Loganiaceae), from which curare and strychnine are derived. This family, also of warm temperate and tropical regions, has 2 native shrubby or treelike genera in the U.S. north of Mexico. Our single treelike representative is an introduced species of *Buddleja*; there are also several native shrubby *Buddleja* in the West.

FALSE OLIVE *Buddleja saligna* Willd.
A.K.A. SQUARESTEM BUTTERFLYBUSH

Evergreen or deciduous shrub or tree to 7 m tall, with white-velvety 4-angled twigs. **LEAF** Opposite, linear-oblong, 1.5–10 cm long, olive green and hairless above, whitish beneath with star-shaped scales. **FLOWER** In clusters about 5 cm wide and 12 cm long. Corolla radially symmetric, with a tubular base 2 mm long and 4-spreading lobes 1 mm long, cream, often orange or reddish in the center. Four stamens protrude from the tube. Sep.–Oct. **FRUIT** Hairy, ovoid, 2-chambered capsule, 2 mm long. **HABITAT/RANGE** Introduced from s. Africa; disturbed areas and chaparral, 200–700 m, Santa Monica Mountains, Calif.

BURSERACEAE: TORCHWOOD FAMILY

This small primarily tropical family of trees and shrubs has about 17 genera and 500 species. Species are found from deserts to broadleaf forests and from sea-level to moderate elevations; all are frost-sensitive. Only the genus *Bursera* occurs naturally north of Mexico. Most species are highly aromatic, the leaves and bark containing abundant resins. (The aromatic substances frankincense and myrrh come from Old World genera closely related to *Bursera*.)

LEAF Usually alternate and 1–3 times pinnately compound, or simple by reduction and therefore unifoliolate. **FLOWER** Small, mostly borne singly or in open, loose branching clusters. Flowers are radial and unisexual or bisexual; when unisexual, plants are predominantly either male or female (dioecious). Sepals and petals are mostly separate, 3–5 each (petals occasionally absent). Stamens are usually equal to, or double the number of, the petals. **FRUIT** The superior ovary develops into a drupelike fruit with 1 to several 1-seeded stones, or 1 stone containing all the seeds.

■ *BURSERA*: BURSERAS

There are 50–100 species of *Bursera*, all from tropical or hot areas in the Americas, occurring from sea-level to moderate elevations. All are aromatic trees and shrubs. Three species barely enter warmer parts of the U.S.; 2 species contribute to the tree diversity of the arid Southwest. In the West, species are restricted to low, hot deserts.

BARK Commonly reddish to grayish or nearly white, smooth, and often peeling. **LEAF** Alternate, 1–3 times pinnately compound; in some species the first leaves on the twigs may be unifoliolate. **FLOWER** Unisexual or bisexual, single or in open, branched clusters, small, radial, with 3–5 separate sepals and 3–5 separate petals; stamens twice as many as petals, or reduced to only 5. **FRUIT** Small 1-seeded drupe, fleshy to leathery, and dehiscent along 2 or 3 seams, the sides then falling away, exposing a brightly colored fleshy layer (aril) that covers the comparatively large seed.

The wood of burseras is soft and easy to carve, employed by indigenous people for masks, bowls, and utensils.

flowers   False Olive

stem section

Elephant Tree

flower

fruit

fruit

ELEPHANT TREE *Bursera microphylla*
A. Gray

QUICK ID This small aromatic desert tree has a swollen pale trunk and small pinnate leaves.

Deciduous contorted shrub or small tree 2–5 m tall; trunk swollen, short, 20–70 cm diam. **BARK** Reddish on twigs, when older whitish and peeling in small patches, exposing greenish inner bark. **TWIG** Flexible, with short spur branches. **LEAF** Alternate or clustered on spur branches, pinnately compound, narrow, 1.5–8 cm long, dark green, with a resinous odor; rachis winged.

Leaflets 9–33, margins entire, somewhat succulent, 5–10 mm long, 1–2 mm broad. **FLOWER** Mostly unisexual, borne on spur branches. Petals white to cream, 4 mm long. Jun.–Jul. **FRUIT** Ellipsoid, 3-angled, dull reddish or purplish drupe, 7–8 mm long; leathery, splitting along angles, exposing a bright red fleshy layer covering 1 yellowish seed.

HABITAT/RANGE Native. Rocky desert slopes, 300–750 m; s. Calif., sw. Ariz., nw. Mexico.

Notes The pale branches taper, resembling an elephant's trunk. The highly aromatic sap, released under pressure when the surface is broken, serves to deter herbivores.

ELEPHANT TREE

FRAGRANT ELEPHANT TREE *Bursera fagaroides* (Kunth) Engl.

QUICK ID The short, thick trunk and pinnately compound, bright green leaves with a citrusy odor identify this tree of sc. Ariz.

Similar habit to Elephant Tree. **LEAF** Alternate, compound, up to 10 cm long; leaflets usually 5–11, lanceolate, 1–3 cm long, up to 5 cm long in the south of the range, more or less succulent, emitting a sweet citrus odor when crushed; margins entire or finely and irregularly toothed.

HABITAT/RANGE Native. On limestone cliffs, 1,200 m; rare in Baboquivari Mountains, Ariz., common in Mexico.

FRAGRANT ELEPHANT TREE

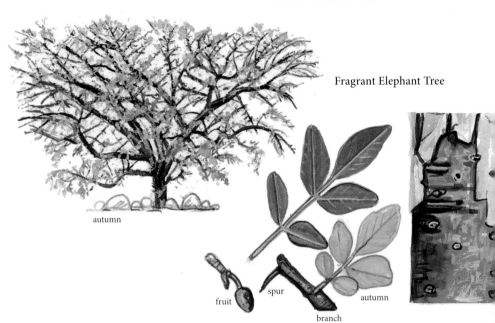

Fragrant Elephant Tree

autumn

fruit

spur

branch

autumn

CACTACEAE: CACTUS FAMILY

The cactus family comprises about 125–130 genera and about 1,800 species of succulents, originally only from the Western Hemisphere except for a single epiphytic species that probably arrived in wc. Africa prior to European expansion into the New World. North of the Mexican border there are 34 genera and 189 species, a few extending to Canada.

Cacti are water-conserving plants and are common in the warm, arid climate of the American West; few are cold-tolerant. The chollas (*Cylindropuntia*) form the largest genus of shrubby or treelike cacti in the West. Though succulent and unusual in appearance, larger cacti are woody within and have a single trunk with branches, meeting the definition of a tree. There are about 22 such species in the West.

FLOWER Bisexual and radial. Sepal- and petal-like parts are many; they intergrade and are called sepaloids and petaloids, respectively. These are joined to the top of a short or long floral tube that attaches to the top of the ovary. The inner petaloids usually are brightly colored and the largest in the series. Stamens too are numerous, sometimes thousands. The ovary is inferior, usually comparatively large, with few to many stigmas. **FRUIT** Dry or fleshy and usually indehiscent (not splitting open), and contains few to many seeds. Some species are genetically sterile, producing no seeds, reproducing only by the rooting of detached stems or fruits that drop on the ground. The capacity for vegetative reproduction allows many species to be easily propagated in cultivation.

LEAF/AREOLE The family is distinctive in its succulence and absence of leaves, and in its adaptations to heat and aridity. *Pereskia*, a shrubby cactus from Central and n. South America, has obvious flat green leaves and woody stems. From such plants modern cacti evolved. Vestigial leaves may be seen readily on young stem segments of *Cylindropuntia* and *Opuntia*, but they soon wither and drop. Also characteristic of cacti is the areole, a cluster of spines arising closely together, often in and around a tiny woolly patch. Each areole is a modified branch that grows no further; the spines it bears are modified leaves. An areole forms in a leaf axil (or at the vestiges of an axil in truly leafless cacti); areoles are arranged spirally (leaves are fundamentally alternate) around the stem, the spiral often obscured by the rows of areoles arrayed along ribs of the stem. Spines afford protection from animals, and their density and paleness also reflect heat and give some shading. In *Opuntia*, *Cylindropuntia*, and related genera, dense clusters of tiny, sharp, barbed, easily detached, stiff bristles, called glochids, are tightly packed at the base of the spine cluster. Glochids are probably derived from hairs.

As is the case for all succulents, cacti exhibit a special kind of photosynthesis (the production of sugar using the sun's energy and carbon dioxide). The epidermis (or "skin") covering green tissue in plants is perforated by tiny pores called stomata; in most plants these are in the leaves, but in cacti they are in the stems. Stomata open and close, depending on water pressure within the cells (guard cells) around the opening. As carbon dioxide enters the plant, water exits—a liability in arid lands. Cacti open stomata at night, when it is cooler, resulting in less water loss, allowing entrance of carbon dioxide, which is then stored chemically. In early morning, stomata close, conserving water, and the carbon dioxide is released within the cells for the construction of sugar using energy from sunlight (photosynthesis).

Cacti have economic value as plant novelties, some being driven to near extinction in the wild by unscrupulous collectors. Cacti are now strongly protected by international agreements and local laws. Several *Opuntia* are important agricultural crops, particularly in Latin America. That genus has also provided some seriously invasive species that have wreaked ecological havoc after introduction to new lands by humans.

SAGUARO *Carnegiea gigantea* (Engelm.) Britton & Rose
A.K.A. GIANT CACTUS

QUICK ID **Unique in its region, this tall, thick columnar cactus develops a few massive up-swept, armlike branches as it gets older.**

Stout columnar cactus up to 16 m tall, unbranched at first, later with up to 20 or more branches ("arms"), abruptly upswept, originating well above the base. Arms occasionally rebranch. Single trunk 30–75 cm diam. **STEM SURFACE** Grayish green; on old plants often lustrous grayish near the base. Ribs 12–30, 2.5–3.5 cm tall, tapered from base to edge. **AREOLE** Broadly elliptic, about 12 mm diam., spaced about 12 mm apart; spines needlelike, gray or with a pink tinge, 15–30, spreading or deflexed, longer ones to 3.5 cm long. **FLOWER** Borne near the tip of the stem, 5–6 cm diam., nocturnal but remaining open the following day, with the odor of a ripe melon. Sepaloids greenish with whitish margins, 2–2.5 cm long; petaloids white, about 2.5 cm long; stamens may be more than 3,400 per flower; stigmas cream, slender, about 12 mm long. May–Jun. **FRUIT** Fleshy, ellipsoid or obovoid, 5–7.5 cm long, scaly but otherwise smooth, dehiscent along 3 or 4 vertical lines, exposing juicy red flesh and tiny black seeds.

HABITAT/RANGE Native. Warm sites on mountainsides, alluvial fans, and valley floors, 200–1,300 m; s. Ariz. and immediately adjacent Calif. to nw. Mexico.

SIMILAR SPECIES The **Organ Pipe Cactus** (*Stenocereus thurberi* [Engelm.] Buxb.) of sc. Ariz. and adjacent Mexico branches from the base and is better considered a large shrub than a tree (though in Mexico it may have a short trunk). It has spiny, ribbed cylindric stems, 12–20 cm diam., rarely branched, up to 7 m tall or more, with 10–50 stems in a large cluster.

SAGUARO

Notes Saguaro (sah-WAH-ro) is derived from a Native American name. This is the most massive cactus north of the Mexican border and also is the Ariz. state flower. This sole species of *Carnegiea* is found only on the Sonoran Desert. It is often placed in an inclusive genus, *Cereus*, which has a large, undetermined number of species ranging from s. North America to s. South America.

Saguaros usually began their lives in the association of an established "nurse plant," which affords shade and some protection from rabbits and rodents. They grow very slowly at first, elongating more rapidly later, and live perhaps 150–200 years. They are popular ornamentals, but may not be transplanted from public lands without permit. Under suitable conditions Saguaros may flower at about 15 years old. Roots are very shallow and widely spreading, intercepting water from the slightest showers. The pleats of the stem allow expansion as water is absorbed, and when fully hydrated the plant is 80–90% water, of which 60% may be lost in the desert heat without damage.

The Saguaro has been, and even today remains, important in the subsistence of indigenous peoples. The fruit, the pitahaya (pi-TAI-ya), ripens in Jun. and Jul.; the flesh is eaten fresh, stored as preserves, or fermented into an alcoholic beverage. A butter is made from the seeds. The woody ribs are used in the construction of shelters and other items.

■ *CYLINDROPUNTIA*: CHOLLAS

There are about 35 species of *Cylindropuntia* in North America, about 20 in the West. Several have been introduced in South America and Africa. Species occur from low deserts to the lower portion of piñon–juniper woodland, usually well below 2,000 m elevation. Species of cholla (CHOY-yah) are common in the arid lands of w. North America. They range from low shrubs to small trees, the populations often increasing as grass is removed from the soil.

STEM SEGMENT One season's branch growth produces a stem segment, marked by a joint at the base. These segments may be firmly fixed or very easily detached; they will root in soil and make new plants. Features of the youngest segment, terminal on the branch, are important in identification. The youngest segment usually is covered with tubercles. When the stem segments are very young, real leaves are evident, each a small cylindric-tapered green structure spreading from the base of a new areole.

Saguaro

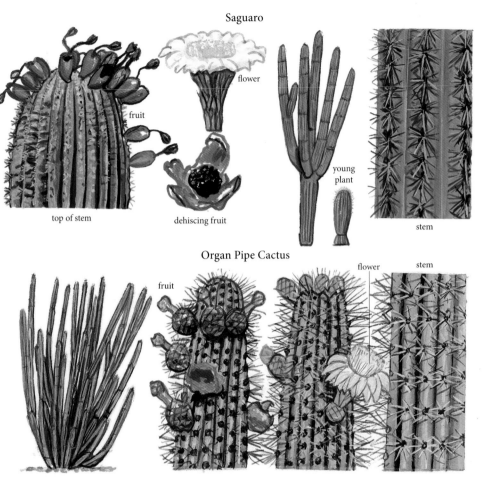

top of stem

flower

fruit

dehiscing fruit

young plant

stem

Organ Pipe Cactus

fruit

flower

stem

AREOLE Scattered over the surface of a stem segment are clusters of barbed spines emanating from a small circular to oval point, the areole, near the top of a tubercle. The areole is covered with woolly hairs (referred to as "wool" in the species descriptions). At the upper edge of the areole, or in a crescent around the upper portion, are small, barbed bristles called glochids, easily detached and painfully annoying when stuck in the skin. Younger spines are covered with a sheath, tight or baggy, which is easily pulled off. **FLOWER** Usually showy in chollas. Bisexual, radial, borne singly or in clusters near the tip of a stem segment, each with numerous parts. Greenish sepaloids at the top of the fruit intergrade with colorful petaloids toward the center of the flower. There are many stamens, which will curl inward when the filaments are touched. The several long stigmas spread from the style at the center, topping the inferior ovary. **FRUIT** Usually egg-shaped,

wider near the top. May be dry or fleshy, covered with tubercles (tuberculate) or not, and may or may not be spiny. Particularly if sterile, fruits may root and form new plants when dropped to the ground.

Species of cholla often readily hybridize, confounding identification. Some species, probably of hybrid origin, are sterile or nearly so, reproducing primarily by rooting of stem segments or fruits that lie on the ground. For the most part, particularly in rangelands, chollas are seen as undesirable weeds, increasing in numbers, the detached stem segments sticking in the mouths and hides of livestock. Several species are commonly cultivated in xeriscape plantings. Once the fleshy material of the stem has weathered away, the remaining wood forms a cylinder with an unusual netlike pattern of perforations. These "canes" are often used in the making of novelty items. *Cylindropuntia* was once considered to be part of *Opuntia*.

PEACH SPRINGS CANYON CHOLLA
Cylindropuntia abyssi (Hester) Backeb.

Shrub or small tree to 1 m tall. **STEM SEGMENT** Cylindric, 8–14 cm long, 1.8–2.5 cm diam.; tubercles prominent, 6–15 mm long. **AREOLE** Elliptic, 5–7 mm long; wool white to gray; spine sheaths silvery white; spines 10–15, erect to spreading, whitish to yellowish tan, aging gray, 18–38 mm long; glochids pale yellow, mostly 1.5 mm long. **FLOWER** Petaloids pale to greenish yellow, 1.5–2 cm long; stamens and stigmas yellowish. Mar.–Jun. **FRUIT** Tuberculate, dry and dull yellow at maturity, spineless or with 1–2 short spines. **HABITAT/RANGE** Native. Limestone in desert scrub, 500–800 m; Peach Springs Canyon, nw. Ariz.

BUCKHORN CHOLLA *Cylindropuntia acanthocarpa* (Engelm. & J.M. Bigelow) F.M. Knuth

QUICK ID This cholla has red stamen filaments, stem segments 2–3.5 cm diam., often loose spine sheaths, and dry and usually spiny fruits.

Gray-green shrub or small tree, 1–4 m tall, crown spreading; trunk short. **STEM SEGMENT** More or less cylindric, 12–50 cm long, 2–3.5 cm diam.; tubercles narrow, mostly 20–30 mm long. **AREOLE** Circular to elliptic, 5–6 mm long; wool white to tan; spine sheaths golden to silvery, often loose; spines 6–30, deflexed to spreading, whitish, yellowish, tan, or reddish, becoming black, 1.5–3 cm long; glochids 0.5–2 mm long, in small tufts. **FLOWER** Petaloids purple-red to yellow, sometimes greenish to brownish, 2.5–4 cm long; stamens with dark red filaments, yellow anthers; stigmas 5, white to light green. Mar.–Jun. **FRUIT** Tuberculate, dry, pale brown at maturity, 2.5–4 cm long, spines numerous, spreading.

HABITAT/RANGE Native. Sandy or gravelly soil, 300–1,300 m; se. Calif. to sw. Utah and se. Ariz.

SIMILAR SPECIES Staghorn Cholla is shrubby and has flowers in a wider range of colors, stem segments 1–2 cm diam., and spineless fruits.

PENCIL CHOLLA *Cylindropuntia arbuscula* (Engelm.) F.M. Knuth

QUICK ID Stems are slender on this densely branched cholla with bronzy flowers and yellowish- to reddish-tinged spineless fruits.

Similar to Desert Christmas Cactus, but stems 5–13 mm diam. **FLOWER** 17–20 mm diam., green- or orange-bronze; Apr.–Jun. **FRUIT** Pale green, sometimes tinged reddish, yellowish near tip, 20–50 mm long, spineless.

HABITAT/RANGE Native. Desert flats and slopes, 300–1,000 m; Ariz., n. Mexico.

PEACH SPRINGS CANYON CHOLLA

BUCKHORN CHOLLA

PENCIL CHOLLA

Buckhorn Cholla

flower

stem

flowers

flower

fruit

Pencil Cholla

flower

fruit

flower

TEDDYBEAR CHOLLA *Cylindropuntia bigelovii* (Engelm.) F.M. Knuth

QUICK ID Often forming thickets, this erect cactus has short, stubby easily detached stem segments covered in golden spines.

Miniature tree, 1–3 m tall, the trunk extending the full height of the plant. Branches short, stubby, densely covered in golden spines when young, spines blackish when older. **STEM SEGMENT** Ellipsoid, readily detached, 7–15 cm long, 3–6 cm diam.; tubercles prominent, oval at base, 6–9 mm long. **AREOLE** Elliptic-triangular, 5–6 mm long, 3–6 mm apart; wool cream to brownish, aging gray; spine sheaths straw-colored or whitish, not loose or baggy; spines 6–15, conspicuous and dense, spreading in all directions, interlacing with spines of adjacent areoles and obscuring surface, pale yellow to reddish, becoming dark brown, 1.5–3 cm long; glochids 3–4 mm long, yellowish to reddish, in a broad crescent. **FLOWER** Petaloids pale green, or yellow streaked with lavender or tipped with red, 1–2 cm long; stamens with green filaments and orange anthers; stigmas 5, light green. Mar.–Jun., sometimes flowering again in Sep. **FRUIT** Strongly tuberculate, more or less obovoid, moderately fleshy, 12–40 mm long, with a few deciduous spines.

HABITAT/RANGE Native. Rocky or gravelly ground, often on south-facing hillsides, 30–900 m; s. Calif. to sc. Ariz.

SIMILAR SPECIES Chain-fruit Cholla also has easily detached stem segments, but its branches are widely spreading, its flowers pinkish, and its fruits more or less smooth and hanging in chains.

Notes "Teddybear," referring to the plant's aspect, sends completely the wrong message: This is one of the nastiest cacti of the Southwest. Stem segments detach and stick in flesh with the slightest touch; detached segments on the ground fasten themselves to shoes or pants legs. A "lucky" victim can extract the segment from the body by lifting it with a comb; a less fortunate person must cut the barbed spines and pull them with pliers. Reproduction by seed is rare; most plants are derived from detached rooted segments.

SILVER CHOLLA *Cylindropuntia echinocarpa* (Engelm. & J.M. Bigelow) F.M. Knuth

A.K.A. GOLDEN CHOLLA

QUICK ID This much-branched cholla has dry, very spiny, almost burlike fruits.

Much-branched gray-green shrub or small tree, 1–1.5 m tall. **STEM SEGMENT** Cylindric, 3–12 cm long, 1–2.5 cm diam.; tubercles oval at base, 4–15 mm long. **AREOLE** Broadly elliptic, 4–4.5 mm long; wool white to tan, aging gray; spine sheaths baggy, silvery with golden tips; spines 10–20, spreading, interlaced and obscuring stem, whitish to pale yellow, brown, or pink, 2–4 cm long; glochids yellow, 3–4 mm long, in a broad crescent. **FLOWER** Petaloids greenish yellow, outer often streaked with red, 20–23 mm long; stamens with greenish-white or yellow filaments, sometimes bronzy, anthers yellow; stigmas 5, whitish, cream, or light green. Mar.–Jun. **FRUIT** Tuberculate, dry and tan at maturity, with dense spreading spines on upper half.

HABITAT/RANGE Native. Sandy soils, 300–1,000 m; s. Calif. to sw. Utah, w. Ariz.

SIMILAR SPECIES Buckhorn Cholla is often larger, and its stamens have red filaments.

TEDDYBEAR CHOLLA

SILVER CHOLLA

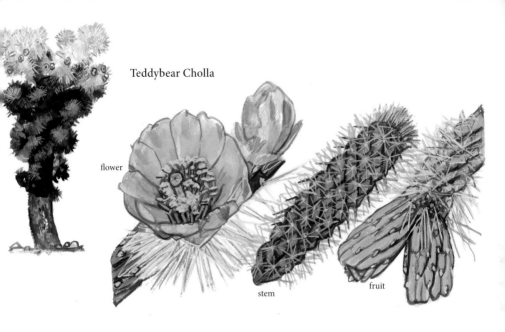

Teddybear Cholla

flower

stem

fruit

Silver Cholla

weathered branch

stem

flower

CHAIN-FRUIT CHOLLA *Cylindropuntia fulgida* (Engelm.) F.M. Knuth
A.K.A. JUMPING CHOLLA

QUICKID This small, densely branched tree cholla is immediately recognized by its fruits, which hang in chains, and flowers that are pink or magenta.

Very spiny small tree or shrub, 1–3 m tall, with many widely spreading branches producing an irregular, rounded crown. **STEM SEGMENT** Cylindric or narrowly ellipsoid, 5–16 cm long, 2–3.5 cm diam., easily dislodged ("jumping" on anyone who brushes by); tubercles prominent, oval at base, 9–19 mm long. **AREOLE** Roughly triangular, 5–7 mm long; wool gold to tan, aging blackish; spine sheaths silvery to straw-colored, baggy; spines 0–18, spreading, pink, yellowish, or reddish brown, aging brown, 2–3.5 cm long, when numerous often interlaced with spines of adjacent areoles; glochids straw-colored, 2 mm long, few in a small tuft or on rim of areole. **FLOWER** Petaloids 5–8, pink, magenta, or white streaked with pink, 12–16 mm long; stamens with pink filaments, cream anthers; stigmas 5, pinkish. Apr.–Sep. **FRUIT** Smooth, fleshy, gray-green, spineless, 2.5–3 cm long, proliferating in branching, hanging chains up to 60 cm long; often 6–15 or more fruits in a chain, a branching complex with 20 or more.

HABITAT/RANGE Native. Sandy or gravelly flats or slopes, 1,200–1,800 m; s. Ariz., nw. Mexico, apparently occasionally growing beyond this region but not establishing.

SIMILAR SPECIES Teddybear Cholla also has easily detached stem segments but is much more spiny and has single fruits. Buckhorn Cholla has firmly attached segments and spiny fruits. Coastal Cholla, found in s. Calif. and southward, has fruits that are solitary or in chains of 2–5.

Notes Flowers open in the late afternoon, and often wither before dawn. The slightest contact with a stem joint will dislodge it, the joint now adhering to the passerby, hence the alternate common name Jumping Cholla. The fruits were harvested by Native Americans, who had favored groves with particularly large fruits. Cattle relish the fruits. Fruits may persist on a plant for 1 or 2 decades. In a complex of chains, one fruit adds 1 or 2 more at its rim, the proliferating chain swaying in the wind and finally breaking. The fallen fruits may establish new plants, as will fallen stem segments, sometimes producing impenetrable colonies of plants.

TREE CHOLLA *Cylindropuntia imbricata* (Haw.) F.M. Knuth

QUICKID This tree cholla has spines that are not dense, magenta flowers, and yellow fruits.

Small gray-green tree or shrub, 1–5 m tall; branches widely spreading, forming a ragged, round crown. **STEM SEGMENT** Cylindric or narrowly ellipsoid, firmly attached, 10–40 cm long, 2–4 cm diam.; tubercles prominent, sharply raised, elongate, 2–5 cm long. **AREOLE** Elliptic, 5–8 mm long; wool yellow to tan, aging black; spine sheaths silvery to dull tan, usually yellow-tipped; spines mostly 8–15, sometimes to 30, spreading, not obscuring stem, tan, reddish, or pink, sometimes silvery, aging gray, 1–4 cm long; glochids pale yellow, 0.5–3 mm long, in a dense tuft. **FLOWER** Petaloids reddish purple, 2.5–4 cm long; stamens with filaments greenish at base, pink near tip, anthers yellow; stigmas 7–8, pale green or cream. May–Aug. **FRUIT** Tuberculate, more or less fleshy, yellow, 2.5–4.5 cm long, with 18–30 areoles but spineless or nearly so at full maturity; tubercles about equal in length, or those near base of fruit longer.

CHAIN-FRUIT CHOLLA

TREE CHOLLA

Chain-fruit Cholla

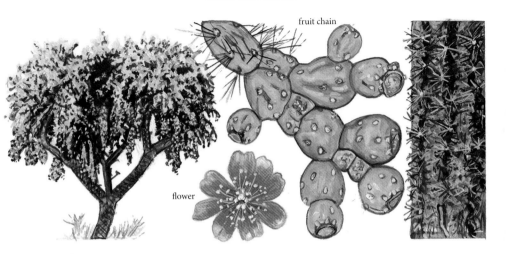

fruit chain

flower

Tree Cholla

fruit

flower

young stem segments with vestigial leaves

HABITAT/RANGE Native. Sandy or gravelly soils, mostly in grassland or remnants of grassland, 1,200–1,800 m; w. edge of Great Plains from s. Colo. and sw. Kans. to Tex., west to se. Ariz.

SIMILAR SPECIES Cane Cholla has smaller tubercles and denser spines on the stem segments, fruits with 28–50 areoles, and longer tubercles near the tip of the fruit.

Notes This is the first tree cholla the traveler sees when heading west across the Great Plains. Plants more easily reseed, and the stem segments easily root, on the open ground as grass is removed by intense grazing. Tree Cholla hybridizes and intergrades with Cane Cholla in sc. N.M. Cactus Wrens (*Campylorhynchus brunneicapillus*) commonly nest in this cactus.

MUNZ CHOLLA   *Cylindropuntia munzii* (C.B. Wolf) Backeb.

QUICK ID Munz Cholla has dry, spineless tan fruits that have numerous long glochids, and flowers with yellow-green inner petaloids tinged pale reddish maroon, contrasting with the green stamen filaments.

Small tree or treelike shrub, 2–5 m tall. **STEM SEGMENT** Easily detached, 4–16 cm long, 12–25 mm diam.; tubercles 1–2 cm long. **AREOLE** Roughly circular, 5–7 mm long; wool tannish gray; spine sheaths yellowish, baggy; spines 9–14, spreading, 1.2–3 cm long; glochids 0.5–2 mm long, forming a crescent between the bases of 2 adjacent tubercles. **FLOWER** Petaloids yellow-green and tinged with red or maroon, 8–15 mm long; stamen filaments green, anthers yellow; stigmas cream. Apr.–Aug. **FRUIT** Tuberculate, dry, tan, with numerous long glochids; spines drop after flowering.

HABITAT/RANGE Native. Gravelly or sandy areas, 300–700 m; se. Calif.

DESERT CHRISTMAS CACTUS
Cylindropuntia leptocaulis (DC.) F.M. Knuth

QUICK ID This densely branched cholla has slender stems, yellowish-green flowers, and spineless yellow to red fruits.

Shrub or small tree to 0.5–1.8 m tall, or taller when supported by surrounding shrubs. **STEM SEGMENT** Cylindric, 2–8 cm long, 3–5 mm diam., usually with very short, easily detached branches that diverge at right angles; tubercles form low, linear ridges, drying as elongate wrinkles. **AREOLE** Elliptic, 1.5–3.5 mm long; wool white to yellow, aging gray; spines usually 0–1, 2.5–5 cm long, spreading, red-brown, with a whitish coat; spine sheaths gray

to yellow, often reddish at the tip; glochids brownish, few, 1–5 mm long. **FLOWER** Petaloids yellowish green, sometimes bronze, often tipped red, 6–12 mm long; stamens and stigmas greenish yellow. Mar.–Oct. **FRUIT** Smooth, fleshy, usually red, sometimes yellow, spineless, 1–2.5 cm long.

HABITAT/RANGE Native. Desert scrub, grassland, piñon–juniper woodland, 40–1,500 m; w. Ariz. to Okla., Tex., n. Mexico.

SIMILAR SPECIES Pencil Cholla has thicker stems and larger, greenish fruits that are yellowish near the tip or are blushed with red. Diamond Cholla has low, short diamond-shaped tubercles and pale orangish flowers.

Notes Fruits mature in winter, giving the plant its common name.

COASTAL CHOLLA   *Cylindropuntia prolifera* (Engelm.) F.M. Knuth

QUICK ID This is the only cholla in its region with fruits in chains. Flowers are red-purple.

Small, compact tree or shrub to 1–2.5 m tall. **STEM SEGMENT** Easily detached, 4–15 cm long, 3.5–5 cm diam.; tubercles 12–25 mm long. **AREOLE** Roughly circular, 4–7 mm long; sheath yellow to rust-brown; spines 6–12, spreading, 1.2–3 cm long; glochids 0.5–2.5 mm long, forming a crescent. **FLOWER** Petaloids red-purple, to 2 cm long; stamens with yellow-green filaments tinted magenta near the tip, anthers yellow; stigmas yellow to white. Apr.–Jun. **FRUIT** Smooth or somewhat tuberculate, fleshy, green, spineless, usually sterile, solitary or in erect to hanging chains of 2–5.

HABITAT/RANGE Native. Fine soils near the coast, 0–300 m; s. Calif., Baja Calif.

MUNZ CHOLLA   DESERT CHRISTMAS CACTUS   COASTAL CHOLLA

Munz Cholla

flower

stem

Desert Christmas Cactus

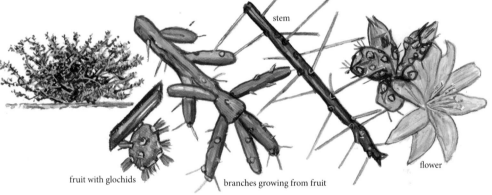

stem

flower

fruit with glochids

branches growing from fruit

Coastal Cholla

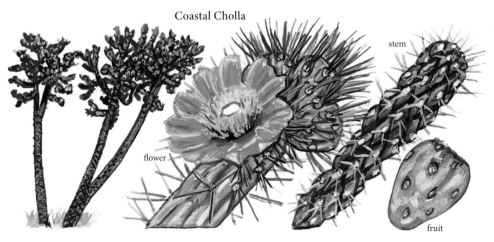

stem

flower

fruit

DIAMOND CHOLLA *Cylindropuntia ramosissima* (Engelm.) F.M. Knuth

QUICK ID Very slender stems with low, short diamond-shaped tubercles and spiny, burlike fruits distinguish this cholla.

Similar to Desert Christmas Cactus, but stem segments 4–10 mm diam. and tubercles low, convex, diamond-shaped, 4–8 mm long. **FLOWER** Petaloids apricot to bronze and blushed with rose, 6 mm long. Apr.–Aug. **FRUIT** Tuberculate, dry, tan, spiny and burlike, 15–30 mm long.

HABITAT/RANGE Native. Sandy soil, deserts, 30–1,100 m; s. Calif., s. Nev., w. Ariz., nw. Mexico.

CANE CHOLLA *Cylindropuntia spinosior* (Engelm.) F.M. Knuth
A.K.A. WALKINGSTICK CACTUS

QUICK ID This cholla, common in sw. N.M. and s. Ariz., has dense, interlaced spines, red-purple flowers, and strongly tuberculate yellow fruits.

Similar to Tree Cholla, but on the stem segments the spines are denser and interlaced, and the tubercles are crowded and 5–15 mm long. **FRUIT** 28–50 or more areoles; tubercles longer near the tip of the fruit.

HABITAT/RANGE Native. Desert plains and grasslands; 300–2,000 m; s. Ariz. to c. N.M. and nw. Mexico.

STAGHORN CHOLLA *Cylindropuntia versicolor* (Engelm. ex J.M. Coult.) F.M. Knuth

QUICK ID The slender stems, in combination with 6–8 spines per areole and spineless fruits, help identify this species.

Small tree or wide-spreading shrub, 1–4 m tall, openly branched. **STEM SEGMENT** Narrow-cylindric, 4–18 cm long, 1–2 cm diam.; tubercles narrowly elongate, 10–25 mm long. **AREOLE** Rounded, 4 mm long; spine sheaths grayish to yellowish, tipped with brown, soon shed; spines 6–8, spreading, interlaced, 10–18 mm long; glochids 1 mm long, in small tufts. **FLOWER** Petaloids red, magenta, yellow, orange, green, or bronze, 20–25 mm long; stamen filaments yellow-green, anthers yellow; stigmas whitish. Apr.–Jun. **FRUIT** Somewhat tuberculate, leathery, yellowish green, tinged reddish, usually spineless, 2–4.5 cm long, sometimes a few in chains.

HABITAT/RANGE Native. Deep sandy soil, 600–1,300 m; sc. Ariz., nw. Mexico.

DIAMOND CHOLLA

CANE CHOLLA

STAGHORN CHOLLA

Diamond Cholla

stem

flowers

fruit

Cane Cholla

stem

flowers

fruit

Staghorn Cholla

stem

flower

fruit

flower

■ *OPUNTIA*: PRICKLYPEARS

There are about 150 species of *Opuntia*, all native to the Americas, with about 30 in the West and only a few treelike. Several have been spread throughout warm regions of the world. Species occur from low deserts to rocky outcrops in forested regions, mostly below 2,400 m elevation. Species of pricklypear are the most cold-tolerant of the North American lowland cacti. They are common from s. Canada to South America; northern plants are small and low.

In warm, arid lands, plants range from low, spreading plants to shrubs and small trees. **PAD** One season's branch growth produces an ovate to elliptic or round, flattened stem segment, often called a pad (the term used in this book). The pads' surfaces are usually hairless, but sometimes are minutely hairy (visible with a hand lens). Pads are sometimes mistaken for thick, succulent leaves. Detached pads will root and make new plants. Features of the pad terminal on the branch are important in identification. When the pads are very young, vestigial leaves are evident as small cylindric-tapered green structures ascending from the bases of new areoles. **AREOLE** Scattered in diagonal rows over the surface of a pad are clusters of spines emanating from a small circular to oval point, the areole. Spines are often more frequent and larger in the areoles near the upper part of the pad. The number of areoles in a diagonal row (simply called row here) that passes through the center of the pad is important in identification. The areole is covered with woolly hairs; around the upper portion are small, easily detached, barbed bristles called glochids. **FLOWER** Usually showy, bisexual, radial, borne singly or in rows near the upper edge of a pad, each with numerous parts. Sepaloids at the top of the fruit intergrade with colorful petaloids toward the center of the flower. Yellow petaloids often become orangish as the flower fades. There are many stamens, which will bend inward when filaments are touched. Several long stigmas spread from the style, topping the inferior ovary. **FRUIT** Usually egg-shaped, wider near the top, barrel-shaped, or globose. May be dry or fleshy, is usually smooth except for a few scales, and may or may not be spiny. Fruits may root and form new plants when dropped to the ground.

Species of pricklypear hybridize, making identification difficult. Particularly in rangelands, they are seen as undesirable weeds, but in drought years ranchers may burn off the spines, and livestock will feed upon the pads. Plants are used in water-conserving landscaping and as natural fences; 1 species is widely grown for its edible fruits and pads (*nopal*, which also refers to the plant). Other species have become troublesome, invasive, obnoxious weeds. In Australia, pricklypears have spread with devastating effects on rangelands; they have been controlled there with a caterpillar, the larva of the Nopal Moth (*Cactoblastis cactorum*), from South America. Introduced in Mexico, this moth now threatens *nopal* production there (see Indian-fig Pricklypear). Since arriving in Fla. from the Caribbean and moving inexorably westward, the moth is now a threat to most native North American pricklypears.

RIO GRANDE PRICKLYPEAR *Opuntia aureispina* (S. Brack & K.D. Heil) Pinkava & B.D. Parfitt

Shrub or small tree, 1–1.5 m tall. **PAD** Circular to obovate, pale blue-green to yellow-green, 8–12 cm long. **AREOLE** 6–8 per row, wool blackish to brownish; spines 4–12, spreading, evenly distributed, bright yellow to orange, red-brown at the base, aging tan to blackish, 2–6 cm long; glochids 5 mm long, well spaced. **FLOWER** Petaloids yellow with an orange to red base, 3–4 cm long; stamens yellowish; stigmas green. May. **FRUIT** Dry, tan, spiny, burlike, 3–4 cm long. **HABITAT/RANGE** Native. Limestone desert, 500–600 m; Brewster Co., Tex., and adjacent Mexico.

ENGELMANN PRICKLYPEAR *Opuntia engelmannii* Salm-Dyck ex Engelm. A.K.A. CACTUS APPLE

QUICK ID This pricklypear is recognized by its large pads, usually clear yellow or buff flowers, and spineless, juicy red or purple fruits.

Broad, round shrub or small tree to 2 m tall; trunk short, stout, well branched and bearing many large blue-green to yellow-green pads. **PAD** Circular, obovate, or roughly diamond-shaped, 15–40 cm long (in var. *linguiformis* the pad is tongue-shaped and up to 1.2 m long). **AREOLE** 5–8 per diagonal row; wool tawny, aging black; spines usually 1–6 (up to 12), erect to spreading to deflexed, 1–5 cm long, chalky white but yellow when wet, red-brown at the base; glochids yellow to red-brown, aging gray to blackish, 10 mm long, sparse, in a broad crescent or nearly encircling areole. **FLOWER** Petaloids yellow to buff, sometimes orange or red,

Engelmann Pricklypear

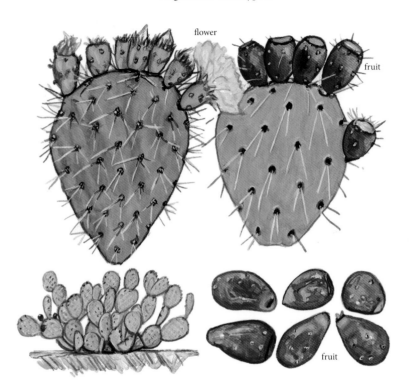

flower

fruit

fruit

3–4 cm long; stamens and styles whitish to cream. Apr.–Jul. **FRUIT** Fleshy, juicy, more or less barrel-shaped, red or purple, smooth, spineless, 3.5–9 cm long.

HABITAT/RANGE Native. Arid grasslands and woodlands, 300–2,700 m; s. Calif. to sw. Utah, c. Tex., and nw. Mexico.

SIMILAR SPECIES Indian-fig Pricklypear, primarily cultivated, is larger and more clearly tree-like, and its glochids are only 2 mm long. Chaparral Pricklypear, of Calif. coastal shrublands, has dense glochids 3–6 mm long in a crescent.

Notes Pads from Engelmann Pricklypear have been moved back and forth across the Southwest, planted, and moved again for centuries by native people, thoroughly mixing the populations. There are several varieties distinguished by pad shape and

spine characteristics. Cow's-tongue Pricklypear (var. *linguiformis* [Griffiths] B.D. Parfitt & Pinkava) has pads that are oval at the base and tapered into a long "tongue" toward the tip. It is very common in cultivation in the Southwest, forming impenetrable fences around properties; it may not occur naturally in the wild. The fruits of Engelmann Pricklypear are edible, with the juice used to make a pleasing jelly.

ENGELMANN PRICKLYPEAR

PANCAKE PRICKLYPEAR *Opuntia chlorotica* Engelm. & J.M. Bigelow

QUICK ID The combination of an erect habit, round bluish-green pads usually with deflexed spines, and fleshy, spineless reddish fruit distinguishes this pricklypear.

Miniature tree or shrub, 0.6–2.5 m tall. **PAD** More or less circular, bluish green, 13–21 cm long. **AREOLE** 1–7 per row; wool tan, aging pale gray; spines 4–12, mostly deflexed, evenly distributed or lacking in lower areoles, light yellow, becoming red-brown or black with age, 2.5–4 cm long; glochids to 14 mm long, crowded in a crescent. **FLOWER** Petaloids yellow, blushed reddish on the outside, 2–3 cm long; stamens and stigmas whitish to pale green. Apr.–Jun. **FRUIT** Fleshy, barrel-shaped, reddish, spineless, 3–6 cm long.

HABITAT/RANGE Native. Deserts to woodlands, 600–2,400 m; se. Calif. to Utah, sw. N.M., nw. Mexico.

INDIAN-FIG PRICKLYPEAR *Opuntia ficus-indica* (L.) Mill.

A.K.A. INDIAN FIG, MISSION PRICKLYPEAR, TUNA CACTUS

QUICK ID A massive treelike cactus with large obovate, few-spined pads bearing small deciduous glochids.

Massive, pale gray-green or green tree, 3–7 m tall; trunk short, 0.3–1 m diam. **PAD** Oblong to broadly obovate, 23–60 cm long. **AREOLE** 5–11 per diagonal row, wool brown; spines 0–6, most near the upper margin, spreading to deflexed, 2–5 cm long, whitish to tan; glochids yellow-brown, 2 mm long, deciduous. **FLOWER** Petaloids yellow to orange-yellow, blushed reddish on the outside, 2.5–5 cm

long; stamens and styles yellow. Apr. **FRUIT** Globose to egg-shaped, juicy, yellow, orange, red, or purple, smooth, spineless, 5–10 cm long.

HABITAT/RANGE Introduced to North America from tropical America; widely planted throughout warmer parts of the world. Cultivated across s. U.S.; escaped at least in s. Calif., s. Ariz., and warmer parts of Tex., 0–300 m.

SIMILAR SPECIES Engelmann Pricklypear is smaller, spiny, and has glochids up to 10 mm long.

Notes Cultivated worldwide in warm areas for the fruit (*tuna*) and pads (each a *nopal*). Spines and glochids are removed from young pads, which are then sliced or diced (*nopalitos*) for salads, pickling, or cooking as a vegetable.

CHAPARRAL PRICKLYPEAR *Opuntia oricola* Philbrick

QUICK ID This cactus, which grows near the coast, is recognized by its dark green pads with deflexed, usually gently curved spines, yellow flowers, and spineless, globose purple fruits.

Shrub or small tree, 1–3 m tall. **PAD** Elliptic to circular, dark green, 15–25 cm long. **AREOLE** 8–10 per row, wool tan to gray; spines 4–16, spreading, larger ones more or less deflexed, usually curved, fairly evenly distributed, yellow, becoming red to black with age, 2–5 cm long; glochids 3–6 mm long, in a dense crescent. **FLOWER** Petaloids yellow, 3–4 cm long; stamens with yellow to orange filaments, anthers yellow; stigmas green. May. **FRUIT** Fleshy, purple outside, pale inside, globose, spineless, 2.5–4.5 cm long.

HABITAT/RANGE Native. Sandy soil in coastal shrublands, 0–500 m; s. Calif., Baja Calif.

PANCAKE PRICKLYPEAR

CHAPARRAL PRICKLYPEAR

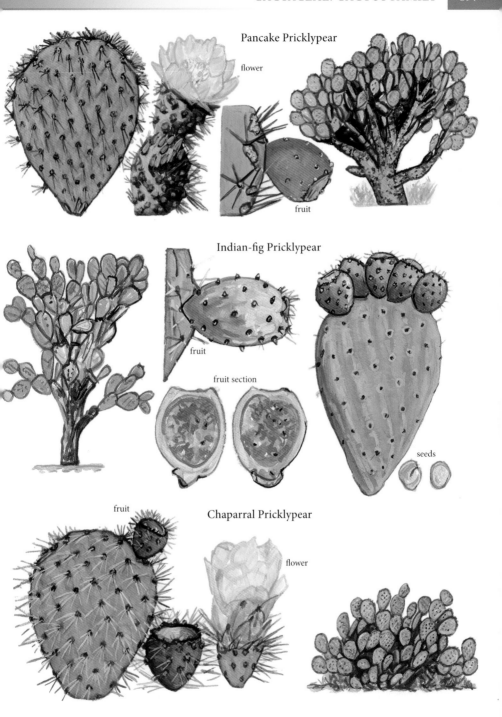

Pancake Pricklypear

flower

fruit

Indian-fig Pricklypear

fruit

fruit section

seeds

fruit

Chaparral Pricklypear

flower

BLIND PRICKLYPEAR *Opuntia rufida*
Engelm.

QUICK ID Fleshy reddish fruit and minutely hairy, spineless bluish-green pads bearing numerous small glochids together distinguish this species within its Big Bend, Tex., range.

Blue-green or gray-green shrub or small tree, 0.5–1.5 m tall. **PAD** Round to kidney-shaped, 7–25 cm long, surface minutely hairy. **AREOLE** 8–13 per row; wool white to tan, aging gray; spines absent; glochids 1–2 mm long, dense, nearly filling areole. **FLOWER** Petaloids pale yellow, 2.5–4 cm long; stamens with whitish filaments, yellow anthers; stigmas green. Mar.–Apr. **FRUIT** Fleshy, red with green flesh, spineless but bearing glochids, 2–3.5 cm long.

HABITAT/RANGE Native. Sandy to rocky soil, 600–1,300 m; Big Bend, Tex., n. Mexico.

Notes The glochids are easily detached and may blind livestock.

PURPLE PRICKLYPEAR *Opuntia santa-rita* (Griffiths & Hare) Rose

QUICK ID This pricklypear of s. Ariz. is distinguished by its round grayish-green pads, purplish in drought or cold conditions, hairless on the surface, and with few or no spines, and its fleshy purplish fruits.

Shrub or small tree, 1–2 m tall. **PAD** Round, gray-green (purplish when stressed), 10–20 cm long. **AREOLE** 6–9 per row, wool tan to brown; spines 0–2, when present mostly on pad margins, deflexed to spreading, yellow to reddish, to 4 cm long; glochids to 5 mm long, in a dense crescent. **FLOWER** Petaloids yellow (the tip sometimes whitish), 2.5–4.5 cm long; stamens with whitish filaments, yellow anthers; stigmas dark green. Apr.–Jun. **FRUIT** Fleshy, purple, spineless, 2.4–4.5 cm long.

HABITAT/RANGE Native. Arid grasslands and woodlands, 700–1,600 m; s. Ariz.; nw. Mexico.

BLIND PRICKLYPEAR   PURPLE PRICKLYPEAR

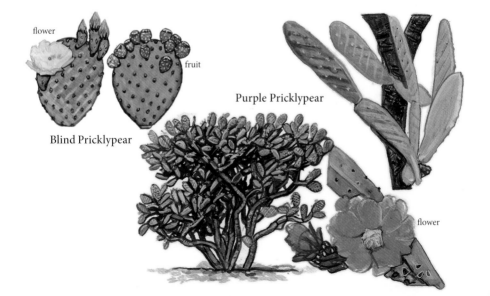

flower

fruit

Blind Pricklypear

Purple Pricklypear

flower

CANNABACEAE: HEMP FAMILY

The hemp family contains 11 genera and about 180 species of shrubs, trees, herbs, and vines, primarily of temperate regions. North of Mexico there are 4 genera and 13 or 14 species, 9 native. One genus in the West produces trees (*Celtis*), which was long included within the elm family (Ulmaceae); recent molecular studies suggest it belongs within Cannabaceae. Marijuana (*Cannabis sativa* L.), a non-native species widely naturalized in the U.S. and Canada, is a family member.

LEAF Woody species of the family are characterized by alternate simple leaves, with 3 primary veins arising from the base. **FLOWER** Small and inconspicuous, unisexual or functionally so, rarely bisexual, ovary superior. **FRUIT** Drupe.

■ *CELTIS*: HACKBERRIES

A genus of 70–100 species distributed nearly worldwide in all but the coldest regions. In the West there are about 4 native and 2 naturalized species.

Mostly deciduous trees. **BARK** Thick, gray, smooth, often developing raised warty corky protuberances on older parts from birds excavating the sweet sap. **LEAF** Alternate, simple, hairy or smooth, the tip pointed, the base round or asymmetric; margins toothed or entire. Three main veins arise from the base of the blade, often raised on the lower surface. **FLOWER** Usually functionally unisexual, a few bisexual, male and female flowers on the same plant, tiny, greenish, borne singly or in small clusters in axils; sepals 4 or 5, separate or slightly joined; petals 0; stamens 4 or 5 and opposite sepals; pistil 1, the ovary superior, 1-chambered. **FRUIT** Small drupe with usually thin flesh.

Hackberries can be distinguished from the elms (*Ulmus*, Ulmaceae) by the lateral leaf veins curving toward the leaf tip as they near the margin, usually unisexual flowers, the drupelike fruit, and rounded seeds. Hackberries provide food and cover for wildlife. Trees often display tight ball-like clusters of twigs (witch's brooms).

NETTLE-TREE *Celtis australis* L.

Deciduous tree to 25 m tall. **LEAF** Lanceolate to lance-ovate, tip slender, pointed; margins sharply toothed except at the base. Upper surface smooth; lower surface softly hairy. Blade 5–15 cm long. **FLOWER** Mar.–Apr. **FRUIT** Purplish to blackish drupe, 11–12 mm diam. **HABITAT/RANGE** Introduced; naturalized in s. Calif. in riparian areas, 15–500 m.

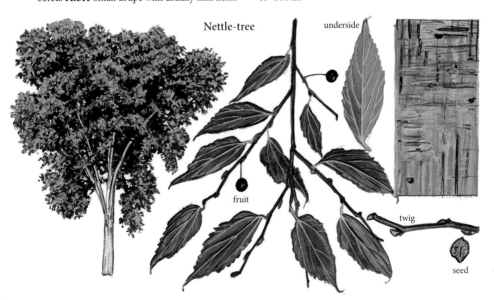

Nettle-tree

underside

fruit

twig

seed

SPINY HACKBERRY *Celtis ehrenbergiana* (Klotsch) Liebm.
A.K.A. DESERT HACKBERRY, GRANJENO

QUICK ID Harshly hairy, ovate to elliptic leaves, commonly toothed at least in the upper half, and small orange drupes help distinguish this hackberry.

More or less deciduous, dense, spiny shrub, or occasionally a tree to 6 m tall. **TWIG** Often zigzagging and thorn-tipped; spines at the nodes often paired, 6–25 mm long. **LEAF** Leathery, harshly short-hairy, ovate to elliptic, tip pointed; margins entire or sparsely and coarsely toothed. Blade 1–4 cm long. **FLOWER** Mar.–May. **FRUIT** Globose to ovoid orange drupe, 6–8 mm diam.

HABITAT/RANGE Native. Arroyos and hillsides, often in thickets or brush, 0–1,200 m; c. Ariz. to s. Tex., also Fla., n. Mexico.

Notes Plants lose their leaves in cold, or slowly drop them with increasing drought in warm areas; the treelike form is more frequent in protected sites and southward. Also widely known as *C. pallida* Torr., a later synonym.

SUGARBERRY *Celtis laevigata* Willd.
A.K.A. HACKBERRY, SOUTHERN SUGARBERRY

QUICK ID This hackberry is distinguished by its alternate simple, evenly long-tapering leaves with mostly entire to irregularly toothed margins; mostly smooth gray bark, roughened by wartlike, corky outgrowths or ridges; and small orange, red, or brown drupes.

Deciduous tree to about 30 m tall; single straight trunk, 1–2.4 m diam. Crown open, spreading, ascending to rounded. **BARK** Gray, smooth at first, becoming pocked with corky ridges or wartlike outgrowths. **TWIG** Slender, gray, hairy at first; buds very small. **LEAF** Usually thin and papery, sometimes moderately thick; lanceolate or rarely ovate, often curved; base rounded or truncate, often asymmetric; tip usually evenly long-tapered to a point; margins entire, sometimes wavy, irregularly toothed, or regularly toothed near the base. Upper surface pale green, hairless, smooth or rough, veins conspicuous, curved toward the blade tip; lower surface pale green. Blade 3–15 cm long, 1.5–8 cm broad, usually more than 2 times longer than broad; petiole 5–15 mm long, slender, hairy. **FLOWER** Yellowish green, tiny; male flowers solitary or in few-flowered clusters at the tips of elongating branches; female flowers usually in leaf axils on developing shoots. May–Oct. **FRUIT** Nearly round brown to orange or reddish drupe, 5–8 mm diam., with 1 stone.

HABITAT/RANGE Native. Floodplains, bottomlands, rocky and alluvial soils along streams, mixed woodlands along river bluffs, ravines, fields, disturbed sites, 0–300 m; widespread through the Southeast, entering the West in w. and c. Tex.

SIMILAR SPECIES Common Hackberry can be distinguished by comparatively broader leaves (about 2 times longer than broad) that are uniformly coarsely toothed from about the mid-blade to the tip. Netleaf Hackberry usually has smaller leaves, often with a shorter point.

CHINESE HACKBERRY *Celtis sinensis* Pers.
A.K.A. JAPANESE HACKBERRY

Deciduous tree to 20 m tall, trunk to 1 m diam. **LEAF** Ovate to ovate-elliptic, tip sharply angled or tapered to a short point. Margins blunt-toothed in the upper half or nearly entire. Upper surface smooth; lower surface softly hairy on the veins, smooth between, the major veins raised. Blade 3–10 cm long. **FLOWER** Feb.–Apr. **FRUIT** Orange-brown to blackish drupe, 5–8 mm diam. **HABITAT/RANGE** Introduced from East Asia; naturalized in s. Calif. in riparian woodland and alkaline grassland, 15–600 m. *Notes* Used as an ornamental; makes handsome bonsai.

SPINY HACKBERRY

SUGARBERRY

Spiny Hackberry

twig

fruit

Sugarberry

fruit

fruit

stones

Chinese Hackberry

fruit

underside

COMMON HACKBERRY *Celtis occidentalis* L.

QUICK ID This species has rough-hairy leaves that are coarsely toothed from mid-blade to the tip, and hard, rounded, 1-stoned, dark orange to purple- or blue-black drupes that often persist through the winter.

Deciduous shrub or usually a tree to 35 m tall; single erect trunk, 25–100 cm diam. Crown low-branching, broad, and rounded. **BARK** Light brown or silvery gray, divided into narrow ridges, deeply furrowed on old trees, often with wartlike, corky protuberances. **TWIG** Slender, greenish, finely hairy, becoming lustrous reddish brown. **LEAF** Thin, leathery, rough to the touch; broadly ovate-lanceolate to triangular, base often very asymmetric, tip abruptly short- or long-pointed; margins entire at the base, coarsely and conspicuously toothed from about the mid-blade to the tip. Upper surface light or bluish green; lower surface paler, hairy on the veins. Blade usually 5–14 cm long, 1–9 cm broad, about 2 times longer than broad; petiole to about 2 mm long, hairy. **FLOWER** Greenish, tiny, usually solitary in the axils of upper leaves. Mar.–May. **FRUIT** Ellipsoid or rounded orange-red or dark purple drupe, 7–13 mm diam., with 1 whitish stone, shriveling and persisting through the winter.

HABITAT/RANGE Native. Woodlands on floodplains and hillsides, 0–1,800 m; widespread in c. and ne. U.S., barely entering c. and e. Canada, entering the West on the Great Plains.

SIMILAR SPECIES Sugarberry has evenly long-tapering, mostly lanceolate leaves. Netleaf Hackberry has smaller leaves, with the margins entire or sparsely toothed above the middle.

LINDHEIMER HACKBERRY *Celtis lindheimeri* Engelm. ex K. Koch

QUICK ID This hackberry has leaves that are densely white-hairy beneath.

Tree to 12 m tall, trunk to 1.5 m diam. **TWIG** Hairy when young. **LEAF** Leathery, ovate to lance-ovate, tip pointed, base rounded to cordate; margins entire or with a few teeth. Upper surface dark green, rough; lower surface whitish with dense soft hairs. Blade 4–9 cm long, 2–5 cm broad. **FLOWER** Mar.–May. **FRUIT** Light brown drupe 7–10 mm diam. **HABITAT/RANGE** Native. Ravines, brushy areas, 100–200 m; Edwards Plateau, Tex.; n. Mexico.

Lindheimer Hackberry

underside

NETLEAF HACKBERRY *Celtis reticulata* Torr.

QUICK ID The ovate leaves are smaller than in most hackberries; mature fruits are reddish or reddish black.

Deciduous tree usually to 10 m tall. Trunk often crooked, low-branching, to 30 cm diam.; crown broad, irregular, with crooked branches. **BARK** Gray and smooth when young, thick when older, sometimes smooth, but more often with irregular warty, corky protuberances. **TWIG** Red-brown, hairy, and with pale lenticels, aging to gray and hairless. **LEAF** Thick, ovate, with 3 main veins at

COMMON HACKBERRY

LINDHEIMER HACKBERRY

NETLEAF HACKBERRY

Common Hackberry

fruit

underside

twig

stone

leaf variation

twig

underside

fruit section

Netleaf Hackberry

fruit

the base, the base round or heart-shaped and asymmetric, the tip narrowed to a sharp point; margins usually entire or sometimes with a few teeth. Upper surface dark green or gray-green, rough-hairy; lower surface smooth or rough-hairy, with soft yellowish hairs along the larger veins, the veins raised in a netlike pattern. Blade usually 3–7 cm long, 2–4 cm broad; petiole 3–8 mm long. **FLOWER** Mar.–Jun. **FRUIT** Globose, glossy drupe, 7–10 mm diam., at first yellowish, progressing to red-brown to reddish black, hanging on a slender stalk 1–1.5 cm long.

HABITAT/RANGE Native. Canyons, riverbanks, washes, slopes, 300–2,000 m; Wash. to Colo. and Kans., south to Mexico.

SIMILAR SPECIES Common Hackberry has often larger, more consistently toothed leaves.

Notes The conspicuous raised veins on the lower surface of the leaf give the species its common name but do not readily distinguish it. The sweet fruit is an important winter resource for birds and small mammals.

CELASTRACEAE: BITTERSWEET FAMILY

The bittersweet (or staff tree) family consists of a diverse assemblage of about 98 genera and 1,200 species of mostly shrubs, trees, and lianas, widespread in temperate and tropical regions. About 10 genera are native north of Mexico, 5 of them containing trees. Several species have been introduced.

LEAF Simple, deciduous or evergreen, alternate or opposite. **FLOWER** Radially symmetric, usually bisexual, small, sometimes with a short hypanthium at the base; 4 or 5 sepals and 4 or 5 petals, or sometimes petals absent. Stamens 3–5, attached at the edge of a conspicuous nectar disk. Ovary superior, or mostly inferior when embedded in a disk. **FRUIT** Capsule (often with conspicuously swollen chambers), achene, berry, drupe, or nutlet. Seeds, often 1 per chamber, often winged or covered by a brightly colored aril.

The family produces ornamental plants, oils, timber, and dye, and an Old World species (Khat, *Catha edulis*) yields a narcotic alkaloid.

CRUCIFIXION THORN *Canotia holacantha* Torr.
A.K.A. CANOTIA

QUICK ID This odd leafless grayish-green arid-land tree has a broomlike habit and pointed, ellipsoid red-brown capsules.

Unkempt grayish-green shrub or small tree, 2–9 m tall, with a broad, ragged crown of strongly ascending branches and thorn-tipped twigs. Trunk may be 60 cm diam. or more in large old specimens, branching low to the ground, where it is often surrounded by broken fallen branches and twigs. **BARK** At first green, becoming pale brownish gray and smooth, later shallowly and longitudinally fissured. **TWIG** At first very flexible, soon stiff, hairless, with pale flecks of wax in grooves, and areas of crowded, dark red-brown glands just above nodes. **LEAF** Scalelike, triangular, 1–1.5 mm long, quickly deciduous. **FLOWER** Small, many in branched clusters 1–3 cm long scattered along branches, the individual stalks beneath each flower jointed

near the middle; sepals 5, 1–2 mm long; petals 5, whitish, oblong, recurved, 5–6 mm long; stamens 5, erect; ovary superior, 5-chambered. May–Jul., sometimes into Oct. **FRUIT** Ellipsoid capsule, 12–14 mm long, with a slender, tapered, sharp beak 7–8 mm long, red when young and fleshy, red-brown when woody and mature, splitting near the tip, becoming blackish brown and persisting until the following spring.

HABITAT/RANGE Native. Dry hillsides and arroyos, 600–1,500 m; Ariz., nc. Sonora, Mexico (in early exploration reported from extreme se. Calif. and sc. Utah, but not since).

SIMILAR SPECIES Spiny Allthorn (*Koeberlinia spinosa*, Koeberliniaceae), palo verdes (*Parkinsonia*, Fabaceae), and Smoketree (*Psorothamnus spinosus*, Fabaceae) have similar habits. These and *Castela emoryi* (Simarubaceae), also called Crucifixion Thorn, are distinguished under Spiny Allthorn (p. 334).

Notes There are only 2 species of *Canotia*, leafless shrubs and trees restricted to arid lands of sw. North America. Crucifixion Thorn has little use, though in its native habit it serves to help control erosion. This species has been known for more than 150 years. The other species, from nc. Chihuahua in n. Mexico, was discovered in 1972.

CRUCIFIXION THORN   WESTERN BURNINGBUSH

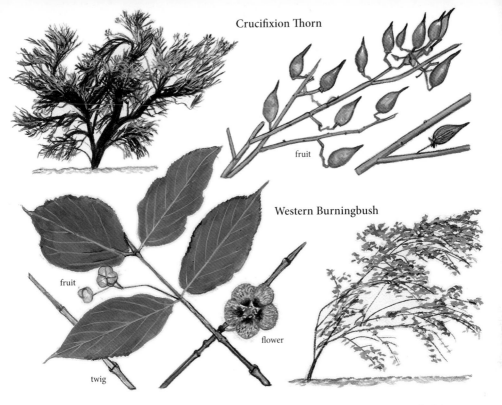

Crucifixion Thorn

fruit

Western Burningbush

fruit

flower

twig

WESTERN BURNINGBUSH *Euonymus occidentalis* Nutt. ex Torr.

A.K.A. WESTERN WAHOO

QUICK ID Opposite, toothed leaves and hanging purplish flowers, few in a very open cluster, help identify this species.

Deciduous, usually a shrub, sometimes a small tree, 2–6 m tall, with a round crown and smooth greenish-gray bark. **TWIG** Slender, more or less 4-angled, hairless, often climbing through other vegetation. **LEAF** Opposite, thin, flat or convex, ovate to obovate, tip usually tapered to a slender point, base truncate to bluntly angled; margins finely toothed. Upper surface green and lustrous, with the veins often impressed. Blade 3–14 cm long; petiole 3–15 mm long. **FLOWER** In hanging, open clusters of 1–7, on threadlike stalks. Sepals 5, 1–1.5 mm long, rounded; petals 5, rounded, 5 mm long, greenish to purplish, often purple-spotted; stamens short, stubby, attached to the edge of a 5-lobed disk 3 mm diam.; ovary embedded in disk. May–Jul. **FRUIT** Deeply 3-lobed capsule, 6–12 mm wide, splitting to reveal a single large seed in each lobe, brown under its fleshy aril.

HABITAT/RANGE Native. Moist, shaded ravines and flats in woods, mostly near the coast, 20–2,000 m; sw. B.C. to sw. Calif.

SIMILAR SPECIES Dogwoods (*Cornus*) also have simple opposite leaves, but their leaf veins are in parallel arcs, and the leaf margins are not toothed.

Notes In the West there is only a single native species of *Euonymus*, a primarily north-temperate genus of 130–170 species of trees and shrubs, a large number native to East Asia. These are the spindletrees or burningbushes, so called because of the use of the wood in Europe for making spindles or in reference to their brilliant autumn foliage. Our species, for example, has attractive orange-red autumn leaves; it is of conservation concern in Ore., Wash., and B.C. There are 2 varieties: Var. *occidentalis*, with leaves tapered to a slender point and with greenish twigs, grows from c. Calif. north to B.C.; var. *parishii* (Trel.) Jeps., with blunt or round-tipped leaves and whitish twigs, grows in the mountains of sw. Calif. Burningbush (*E. alatus* [Thunb.] Siebold), introduced and invasive in e. U.S., has leaves tapered at both ends, and flowers with 4 white petals. It was once reported in wc. Mont., but has not been recorded since.

MAYTEN *Maytenus boaria* Molina
A.K.A. MAITEN

Evergreen broad-crowned tree, 2–15 m tall, resembling a weeping willow; trunk to 80 cm diam. **LEAF** Alternate, leathery, lanceolate, narrowly angled at both ends, margins finely and sharply toothed, light green, blade 1.5–5 cm long. **FLOWER** Tiny, greenish white, 1–5 in small clusters in leaf axils; petals 5, 1.5–3 mm long; ovary superior; stigma with 2–4 spreading lobes. Apr.–May. **FRUIT** Capsule hairless, flattened-globose, 6–9 mm diam., opening by 2 valves. **HABITAT/RANGE** Introduced from Argentina and Chile; used as a landscape tree in Calif., where it shows potential for being invasive, germinating prolifically after brush fires. *Notes Maytenus* is a genus of about 200 species of trees and shrubs, mostly from the tropics of the Southern Hemisphere.

CORNACEAE: DOGWOOD FAMILY

The number of genera included in the Cornaceae has varied widely in different classifications. In a recent classification, followed here, the family consists of 2 genera and 85 species widespread in north-temperate and tropical regions. One genus, *Cornus*, occurs naturally in North America.

Hairs on the plant surface are often T- or Y-shaped, with 2 projecting ends attached in the middle, often lying very flat. **LEAF** Simple, usually deciduous and opposite. **FLOWER** Radially symmetric, bisexual or unisexual; when unisexual, on the same or separate plants, or mixed with bisexual flowers. Sepals, petals, and stamens usually number 4 each; ovary inferior, with 1–4 chambers. **FRUIT** Drupelike or a berry.

The family is probably best known for its numerous widely cultivated, handsome ornamentals. Lumber is obtained from a few Asian species. The tough, hard wood has also been used to make farm implements, butchers' skewers, and other sharp objects.

■ *CORNUS*: DOGWOODS

Dogwoods, also called cornels, form a genus of about 65 species of trees and shrubs; only 2 species are small and nearly herbaceous. They are found primarily in moderately to very moist situations across much of the Northern Hemisphere. There are 20 species in North America, 3 introduced as ornamentals and subsequently escaping. In the West, 1 native species is a handsome tree; several others are shrubs that occasionally become small trees.

LEAF Usually deciduous and opposite, the lateral veins commonly in paired, nearly parallel arcs, converging toward the leaf tip. **FLOWER** Small, radially symmetric, in small branched clusters, umbels, or compact heads. Umbels or heads may be surrounded by showy petal-like bracts. Sepals, petals, and stamens each usually number 4; ovary inferior, 2-celled, with a swollen disk on top. **FRUIT** Drupelike, the stone 2-celled.

Opposite leaves with a few pairs of arching veins are characteristic of dogwoods. The compact clusters of tiny flowers with 4 petals and an inferior ovary also help identify the genus. When leaves are torn gently crosswise, the 2 halves will remain connected as delicate threads formed as water-conducting cells stretch and are pulled from the veins, helping to distinguish dogwoods from other opposite-leaved shrubs and trees (the "*Cornus* test"). In the West, dogwoods are one of the few genera that contribute red hues to autumn foliage.

There are 3 major groups of dogwoods: flowering dogwoods, with compact heads of stalkless flowers surrounded by large, showy bracts; cornels with small umbels of yellowish flowers surrounded by quickly deciduous small bracts; and shrubby dogwoods, with small branched flower clusters lacking bracts. Bark from dogwoods has been used to make a brown dye. The supple twigs are woven into baskets. The fruits are an important food source for birds. Several species are grown as handsome ornamentals for their flower clusters with spectacular bracts, red autumnal foliage, and colorful fruits on bare yellowish to reddish twigs in winter.

Mayten

flowers

dehiscing fruit

Roughleaf Dogwood

flowers

fruit

ROUGHLEAF DOGWOOD *Cornus drummondii* C.A. Mey.
A.K.A. WHITE CORNEL, CORNEL DOGWOOD, SMALL FLOWER DOGWOOD

QUICK ID This species is recognized by the combination of white fruit and opposite leaves with the upper surface rough to the touch; it occurs along the eastern margin of our range.

Deciduous thicket-forming shrub or small tree, 5–10 m tall. **TWIG** Mostly hairless, grayish, brown, or reddish brown. **LEAF** Opposite, narrowly ovate to lanceolate or elliptic, the tip abruptly tapered to a moderately long point, 3 or 4 pairs of lateral veins, margins entire. Upper surface green and rough-hairy; lower surface whitish-hairy. Blade 3–12 cm long. Autumn foliage orangish. **FLOWER** Tiny, white, in round-topped clusters 4–7.5 cm wide; 4

petals, 4–6 mm long. May–Jun. **FRUIT** Globose, white, 5–6 mm diam.

HABITAT/RANGE Native. Thickets, woodland margins, 50–800 m; mostly Midwestern, barely entering the West in Nebr., Kans., and Tex.

Notes At least 40 species of birds feed upon the fruit.

ROUGHLEAF DOGWOOD

BROWN DOGWOOD *Cornus glabrata*
Benth.
A.K.A. SMOOTH DOGWOOD

QUICK ID This dogwood has nearly hairless leaves with 3 or 4 pairs of lateral veins and white to bluish fruits.

Deciduous thicket-forming shrub or small tree, 1.5–6 m tall. **TWIG** Mostly hairless, brown to red-purple. **LEAF** Opposite, lanceolate to elliptic, margins entire, 3 or 4 pairs of lateral veins; upper surface gray-green, paler below, almost hairless. Blade 2–5 cm long. Autumn foliage bright red. **FLOWER** Tiny, dull white, in compact, branched, roundish clusters 2.5–4.5 cm wide; 4 petals, 5 mm long. May–Jun. **FRUIT** Globose, white to bluish, 8–9 mm diam.

HABITAT/RANGE Native. Moist areas, often along streams, 50–1,550 m; sw. Ore. to s. Calif.

PACIFIC DOGWOOD *Cornus nuttallii*
Audubon ex Torr. & A. Gray
A.K.A. WESTERN FLOWERING DOGWOOD, MOUNTAIN DOGWOOD, WESTERN DOGWOOD

QUICK ID The opposite leaves with entire or wavy margins and impressed, parallel, lateral veins, and the tight flower clusters with large white bracts or brilliant red fruits identify this tree.

Deciduous shrub or tree to 20 m tall; trunk usually straight, branching low to the ground in open-grown trees. Crown narrow to broad, fairly open, the branches gently curving upward and producing attractive sprays of fresh yellow-green leaves accented by bright white floral bracts. **BARK** Thin, gray-brown, often tinged reddish, smooth when young, on older parts divided into thin, small, close-fitting scales. **TWIG** Youngest twigs green, covered with grayish appressed hairs, the hairs decreasing in density with age, the twigs becoming reddish purple and ultimately light red-brown and smooth, marked by conspicuous crescent-shaped leaf scars. Terminal buds pointed, 8 mm long, covered by 2 light green scales that become thicker and dark purple just before leaf emergence, flanked by 2 pairs of side buds. **LEAF** Opposite, thin, elliptic-ovate, usually tapered to a slender, narrow point, about 5 pairs of arcing, parallel lateral veins; margins flat and entire or slightly wavy. Upper surface yellow-green, with short, stiff hairs that lie flat, veins impressed; lower surface paler, somewhat woolly. Blade 4–12 cm long, 3–8 cm broad; petiole 5–10 mm long. Autumn foliage brilliant red or orange. **FLOWER** Tiny, pale yellowish, 25–40 in a dense, hemispherical head surrounded by 4–7 bright white to pinkish-tinged, petal-like, elliptic to ovate, abruptly acute bracts, 2–7 cm long. Apr.–Jun., beginning as the leaves expand. **FRUIT** Tightly clustered in a head, individual fruits generally ellipsoid but often misshapen and angular because of crowding, 10–15 mm long, bright red to red-orange, crowned by 5 tiny blackish sepals.

HABITAT/RANGE Native. Deeply to partially shaded forests, or along forest margins, 0–2,100 m; sw. B.C. to s. Calif., isolated in ec. Idaho, where it is of conservation concern.

SIMILAR SPECIES Alders (*Alnus*, Betulaceae) are somewhat similar but have alternate leaves with toothed margins. No other western tree has large, showy white bracts around the flower heads; the only other western dogwood with such bracts is the ground-hugging Bunchberry (*C. canadensis* L.).

Notes This is the provincial flower of British Columbia. Trees are popular as ornamentals, especially near the coast, where sunlight does not burn them. Band-tailed Pigeons (*Patagioenas fasciata*) relish the fruits. Trees are highly susceptible to, and slowly killed by, dogwood anthracnose, an introduced disease caused by the fungus *Discula destructiva*.

BROWN DOGWOOD

PACIFIC DOGWOOD

RED-OSIER DOGWOOD

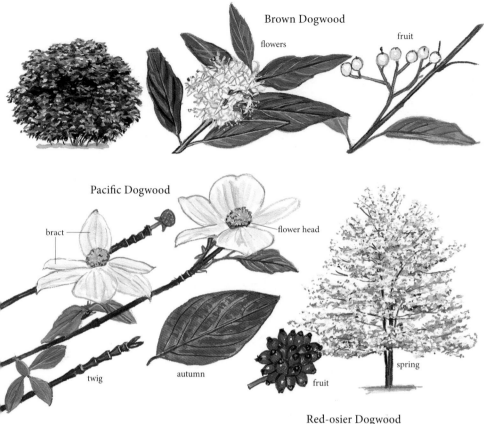

Brown Dogwood

flowers

fruit

Pacific Dogwood

bract

flower head

twig

autumn

fruit

spring

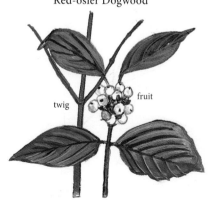

Red-osier Dogwood

twig

fruit

RED-OSIER DOGWOOD *Cornus sericea* L.

A.K.A. CREEK DOGWOOD, AMERICAN DOGWOOD

QUICK ID Finely hairy or nearly hairless leaves with 5–7 pairs of lateral veins and white to bluish fruits distinguish this widespread dogwood.

Deciduous many-stemmed, thicket-forming shrub, or rarely a small tree, 1–6 m tall. **TWIG** Often minutely hairy, deep red, the pith white and about ⅓ the diameter of the twig. **LEAF** Opposite, broadly ovate to oblong-lanceolate, abruptly tapered to a narrow point, 5–7 pairs of veins; margins entire; upper surface dark green and lightly hairy or smooth; lower surface paler and hairless or minutely hairy. Blade 4–12 cm long. Autumn foliage purplish red. **FLOWER** Tiny, dull white, in nearly flat-topped clusters 2–4 cm wide; 4 petals, 2–4 mm long. May–Jul. **FRUIT** Globose, white to somewhat bluish, 8–9 mm diam.

HABITAT/RANGE Native. Moist areas, often along streams, 50–2,700 m; Alaska to Lab., south to ne. U.S., in the West south to Calif., Ariz., N.M., nw. Mexico.

BLACKFRUIT DOGWOOD *Cornus sessilis* Torr. ex Durand
A.K.A. BLACKFRUIT CORNEL

QUICK ID Restricted to n. Calif., this dogwood is distinguished by small, quickly dropping, usually yellow-margined brownish bracts around the flowers, and fruits that mature to shiny black-purple.

Deciduous shrub or small tree, 1–5 m tall. **TWIG** Mostly hairless, grayish or yellow-brown. **LEAF** Opposite, elliptic to obovate, 3–5 pairs of veins; margins entire. Upper surface light green, mostly hairless; lower surface hairy, with hairs mostly appressed, and tufts of soft hairs in the vein axils. Blade 4–9 cm long. Autumn foliage red. **FLOWER** Tiny, yellowish, few in hairy umbels about 2 cm diam. Bracts 4, lanceolate, 1 cm long, greenish brown and usually with yellow margins, quickly dropping. Mar.–Apr. **FRUIT** Ellipsoid, 10–15 mm long, first whitish, then yellow, red, and finally shiny black-purple.

HABITAT/RANGE Native. Moist areas, 150–1,550 m; n. Calif.

Blackfruit Dogwood

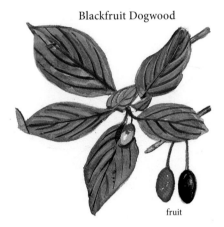

fruit

BLACKFRUIT DOGWOOD

EBENACEAE: EBONY FAMILY

The ebony family is a tropical and warm temperate group of primarily trees and shrubs consisting of 4 genera and about 500 species. About 90 percent of the species are in the large genus *Diospyros*, the persimmons and ebonies.

LEAF Simple, often leathery, alternate and commonly 2-ranked, with nectar glands on the lower surface. **FLOWER** Few in a cluster, or solitary. Usually unisexual, the sexes on separate plants. Sepals 3–7, joined, usually persistent and enlarging at the base of the fruit; petals 3–7, joined, forming an urn-shaped corolla. Stamens mostly number 6–20 or more, replaced by staminodes in female flowers; ovary usually superior, with 3–8 chambers. **FRUIT** Berry, astringent until very ripe.

The family provides valuable hardwoods, some ornamentals, and various fruits.

■ *DIOSPYROS*: EBONIES AND PERSIMMONS

Diospyros is a large tropical or warm temperate genus containing about 480 species, nearly half of which are found on the Malay Archipelago. Two species occur naturally in the U.S. at low to moderate elevations; 2 others have been introduced.

Persimmons and ebonies are deciduous or more or less evergreen shrubs or trees, often with black and gritty bark. **LEAF** Alternate, simple. **FLOWER** Usually unisexual, the sexes usually on separate plants. Small, radially symmetric, in few-flowered

Texas Persimmon

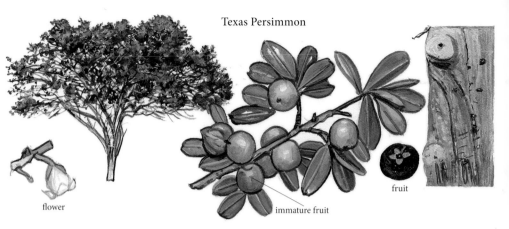

fruit

flower

immature fruit

clusters, or solitary. Sepals 3–7, joined, usually persistent and enlarging beneath the fruit; petals 3–7, joined, tips often recurved or contorted. Stamens 15 or 16; ovary superior, with several cells. **FRUIT** Large, several-seeded berry.

Diospyros supplies many valuable hardwoods, including the famous black ebony of commerce, and numerous edible fruits. In the tropics, leaves of 1 species are used for cigarette papers, the sticky fruit of another is used to caulk boats, and the fruit of a third is a source of black dye for silk.

TEXAS PERSIMMON *Diospyros texana*
Scheele
A.K.A. MEXICAN PERSIMMON, BLACK PERSIMMON

QUICKID The smooth, peeling grayish bark is distinctive, as are the black fruits and the urn-shaped cream flowers with 5 recurved petal lobes.

Evergreen or deciduous slow-growing shrub or small tree, 2–16 m tall; trunk to 50 cm diam.

TEXAS PERSIMMON

Crown narrowly round, with many erect, crooked branches. **BARK** Thin, pale gray, smooth, peeling to expose new whitish or pinkish bark. **TWIG** At first hairy and grayish, later brown and smooth. **LEAF** Alternate, simple, leathery; oblong or obovate, tip rounded and often notched, base abruptly tapered to a narrow angle, margins rolled under. Upper surface dark green, mostly hairless; lower surface pale, densely hairy. Blade 2–5 cm long, 1–3 cm broad; petiole very short, thick, hairy. **FLOWER** Unisexual, the sexes on separate trees, in few-flowered small clusters, creamy white, urn-shaped, 8–12 mm long, hairy on the outside, petals curved back. Feb.–Jun. **FRUIT** Berry, lightly hairy, black when ripe, globose, with a little point at the tip, 2–2.5 cm long, containing 3–8 hard, large triangular, bright red seeds.

HABITAT/RANGE Native. Deep rich or rocky soils of river bottoms and hills, 0–1,350 m; southern half of Tex., south to ne. Mexico.

Notes Leaves are deciduous on plants in the northern portion of the range, and are persistent or tardily deciduous to the south. Trees are grown as ornamentals, particularly for the attractively patterned bark. The fruit, once ripe, is sweet and juicy. Seeds are distributed by animals, readily germinating when free of all pulp. As grasses are reduced by grazing in Tex., mesquites invade rangeland and act as focal points for animals; soon Texas Persimmon follows, forming dense thickets, and may become a serious problem for ranchers. The wood is spectacular, the heartwood black, often streaked with yellow, the sapwood yellow. It has been used for engravers' blocks, tool handles, and decorative items.

COMMON PERSIMMON *Diospyros virginiana* L.

QUICK ID This persimmon is recognized by its alternate simple leaves with entire margins and often with blackish spots on the upper surface, and the large orange berry crowned by large, flaring sepals.

Deciduous tree or robust shrub, usually 15–20 m tall, sometimes forming thickets; trunk erect, to about 1 m diam. Crown round, branches usually crooked. **BARK** Gray-brown and shallowly fissured on young trees, becoming dark gray to nearly black and roughly divided into small squarish blocks. **LEAF** Alternate, simple, ovate or elliptic, tip usually abruptly contracted to a short point, margins entire. Upper surface lustrous green, often with blackish spots, hairless; lower surface paler, grayish green, mostly hairy. Blade 7–15 cm long, 3–8 cm broad; petiole 7–10 mm long, often with glands along the upper surface. **FLOWER** Unisexual, the sexes on separate trees; 1–2 cm long, corolla creamy white or greenish yellow. Apr.–Jun. **FRUIT** Orange berry,

round to slightly elongate, sometimes depressed at the top, 4–5 cm diam.

HABITAT/RANGE Native. Fields, woodlands, bottomlands, along roadsides, 0–1,100 m; much of the e. U.S., extending west into c. Tex., occasionally planted for its fruit in warmer parts of the West.

Notes The fruit pulp is astringent and unpalatable during ripening, becoming sweet when fully ripe. It is used for making puddings, cakes, and a rural beer.

COMMON PERSIMMON

ELAEAGNACEAE: OLEASTER FAMILY

Elaeagnaceae is a small family of stiffly branched, often thorny shrubs and trees. There are 3 genera and 45–64 species, primarily from the Northern Hemisphere, extending south into Australia.

Foliage and twigs are covered by small silvery or golden scalelike hairs that often impart a grayish hue to the plant. Plants are deciduous or evergreen. **LEAF** Opposite or alternate, simple, with entire margins. **FLOWER** Bisexual or unisexual, on separate plants or intermixed, radially symmetric, with no petals; 2–8 sepals; 4 or 8 stamens are at the top of an elongate hypanthium; at the base inside is a superior 1-celled ovary. **FRUIT** Drupelike, commonly yellow, tan, or red, the fleshy or mealy hypanthium surrounding a single achene.

Several species are grown as ornamental shrubs or trees or as windbreaks.

■ *ELAEAGNUS*: OLEASTERS

There are about 67 species of *Elaeagnus*, most from Eurasia, growing at low to moderate elevations. One species is native to North America; at least 4 have been introduced, and 2 are considered invasive.

The trees and shrubs of this genus usually have leaves, twigs, flowers, and fruits covered with minute flat silvery or brownish scales. **LEAF** Simple, usually alternate. **FLOWER** Bisexual, or unisexual

and then usually intermixed with bisexual flowers, lacking petals. Sepals and petals each usually 4. **FRUIT** Drupelike, with a single achene.

Plants are grown as ornamentals and windbreaks. Fruits are a valuable resource for wildlife, particularly birds, and minor use is made of the wood by humans. Species fix atmospheric nitrogen in a symbiotic interaction with bacteria (genus *Frankia*) in the roots, and they tolerate mineral, often saline soils, making them valuable in mine reclamation.

flower

Common Persimmon

spring

flowers

fruit

flowers

Russian Olive   underside   immature fruit

RUSSIAN OLIVE *Elaeagnus angustifolia* L.

A.K.A. OLEASTER

QUICK ID Minute silvery scales on leaves and young twigs, and the flowers and yellowish mature fruits distinguish this plant.

Deciduous, thorny shrub or small tree, 3–14 m tall, with a round crown of ascending branches; trunk 1 to several, erect or ascending, up to 65 cm diam. **BARK** Dark brown, smooth when young, fissured and shredding when older. **TWIG** Slender, flexible, often thorny or thorn-tipped, at first silvery-scaly, becoming lustrous green, then reddish brown. **LEAF** Alternate, simple, narrowly oblong, lanceolate, or oblanceolate; margins entire. Upper surface grayish green, mostly scaly; lower surface very densely silvery-scaly. Blade 4–10 cm long, 1–3 cm broad; petiole about 2 mm long, silvery. **FLOWER** Bisexual (or with some male flowers intermixed with bisexual flowers), very fragrant, small, borne in clusters in leaf axils. Hypanthium tubular, 4–6 mm long, topped by 4 spreading sepals, yellow or yellow-green on the upper surface, silvery-scaly externally. May–Jul. **FRUIT** Drupelike, broadly oval, 1.2–2 cm long, surface scaly, especially when young, lustrous and yellow or tan when mature (sometimes blushed with red), the flesh mealy.

HABITAT/RANGE Introduced from w. Eurasia; bottomlands, low areas, meadows, tolerant of saline soil, 0–2,400 m; much of U.S. and s. Canada.

SIMILAR SPECIES Autumn Olive has leaves with a bright green upper surface and entire, wavy margins, and its fruit is reddish, with juicy pulp.

Notes Russian Olive has escaped from cultivation and become an aggressive, weedy tree, displacing native vegetation. It is difficult to eradicate once established.

AUTUMN OLIVE *Elaeagnus umbellata*
Thunb.
A.K.A. JAPANESE SILVERBERRY

Deciduous, densely thorny shrub or small tree, 4–10 m tall. **LEAF** Alternate, simple, margins wavy; blade 4–10 cm long, 2–4 cm broad; densely silvery-scaly when young, upper surface becoming bright green as scales wear off; lower surface whitish, retaining the dense whitish scaly covering, usually also with some brown scales. **FLOWER** Similar to Russian Olive, but male and female flowers are found among bisexual flowers on separate plants. May–Jul. **FRUIT** Globose to somewhat elongate, juicy, deep pink to red, more or less scaly. The mature fruit is edible, dries well, and has a high lycopene content. **HABITAT/RANGE** Introduced from East Asia. Open disturbed areas, 0–150 m; sporadic in the Northwest; invasive in the East.

SEA-BUCKTHORN *Hippophae rhamnoides* L.
A.K.A. SEABERRY

Deciduous thorny shrub or small tree, 3–8 m tall; crown rounded, dense or spreading. **LEAF** Alternate, narrowly linear, margins entire, surfaces vested with silvery scales; blade 2.5–8 cm long, stalkless. **FLOWER** Unisexual, the sexes on separate plants, tiny, yellow, produced in spikes (male) or clusters in leaf axils (female), prior to new leaf growth. Mar.–Apr. **FRUIT** Drupelike, globose or ellipsoid, 6–10 mm long, bright orange, persisting through winter. **HABITAT/RANGE** Introduced from Eurasia; a colonizer of open habitats in Alta., Sask., and Que., at low to moderate elevations (to 5,200 m in Eurasia). *Notes* Plants are cultivated as ornamentals, for soil stabilization and nitrogen enrichment, and for the nutrient-rich juice from the abundant fruits. There are perhaps 7 species in the genus, all native to Eurasia.

SILVER BUFFALOBERRY *Shepherdia argentea* (Pursh) Nutt.
A.K.A. THORNY BUFFALOBERRY

QUICK ID The narrow, opposite leaves, silvery on both surfaces, and spine-tipped branches distinguish Silver Buffaloberry.

Deciduous shrub or small tree to 6 m tall, with rigid ascending or spreading branches tipped with sharp thorns. Trunk short, branched near the ground, 10–30 cm diam. **BARK** Thin, dull gray, with shallow furrows and flat-topped ridges, peeling and shaggy. **LEAF** Usually opposite, simple, thin and leathery; narrowly oblong to oblanceolate, covered with tiny silvery scales that impart a silvery-gray color to the entire plant; scales denser and leaves paler on the lower surface. Blade 2–6 cm long, 5–15 mm broad; petiole 3–12 mm long, slender. **FLOWER** Unisexual, sexes on separate plants, tiny, yellowish, borne in small umbel-like clusters, or female flowers solitary. Male flowers, appearing before leaf emergence, have 4 spreading sepals, 1–2 mm long, brownish on the inside, and 8 stamens. Female flowers have 1 superior ovary enclosed by an egg-shaped hypanthium, nearly closed at the tip, with 8 tiny bumps on the rim. Apr.–Jul. **FRUIT** Drupelike, 4–6 mm long, red with whitish speckles.

HABITAT/RANGE Native. Watercourses, prairies, shrublands, or woodlands, 300–2,000 m; sc. Canada to se. Ore., s. Calif., Utah, nw. N.M., Nebr., widespread in the n. Great Plains, widely scattered elsewhere in the West.

SIMILAR SPECIES Russian Olive (*Elaeagnus angustifolia*) has silvery leaves, but they are alternate, the plants are generally larger, and the flowers are much larger and bisexual.

Notes Common on the n. Great Plains, Silver Buffaloberry is a tough, cold-hardy plant that provides valuable forage for deer, Pronghorn (*Antilocarpa americana*), Elk (*Cervus canadensis*), and Grizzly Bear (*Ursus arctos horribilis*). Grouse, songbirds, and small mammals relish the fruits. Plants are used in multiple-row windbreaks. They fix nitrogen, enriching impoverished soil, and are commonly used in land reclamation. Berries may be used in jellies, and were dried for winter and cooked with meat by Native Americans. There are 3 species of *Shepherdia*, found in cooler regions of w. North America; the other two are shrubby.

SILVER BUFFALOBERRY

fruit

fruit

flowers

Autumn Olive

Sea-buckthorn

fruit

underside

Silver Buffaloberry

underside

fruit

underside

ERICACEAE: HEATH FAMILY

The heath family is a diverse, worldwide assemblage of herbs, shrubs, trees, and even a few vines, common in many habitats, but rare from lowland tropics and, in general, missing from warm or hot deserts. The family's 125 genera and 4,100 species form several rather distinct groups, which have in the past been recognized as separate families. In North America there are 46 genera and 212 species.

Most are green and photosynthetic, but 1 herbaceous group has white, yellow, or red plants that lack chlorophyll and, through intermediary (mycorrhizal) fungi, absorb their nutrients from the soil. **LEAF** Usually alternate, occasionally opposite or whorled, simple, with margins entire or serrate, or reduced to scales in some herbaceous parasitic species. **FLOWER** Usually bisexual, radially symmetric or slightly bilateral, often pendulous, white to brightly colored. Sepals and petals each 4 or 5, nearly separate to almost completely joined from base to tip, the corolla often cylindric or cup-, funnel-, or lantern-shaped. Stamens usually 8–10, the anthers often opening by terminal pores and often bearing 2 projecting awns. The ovary has 2–10 chambers, and may be superior or inferior. **FRUIT** Capsule, berry, or a drupe with 1 to several stones.

The heath family provides blueberries, huckleberries, and cranberries. Many species and hybrids are grown as showy ornamentals. Originally, oil of wintergreen came from the family before it was produced synthetically. Many of the brushy vegetation types of the world (heath, chaparral, maquis or macchia, fynbos, flatwoods) contain numerous species of Ericaceae. Some species of Ericaceae are very poisonous to livestock.

◾ *ARBUTUS*: MADRONES

There are 10 species of *Arbutus* found from w. North America to Central America, and in w. Europe and North Africa, at low to moderate elevations. Three are native in the West.

Members of the madrone (madrona, madroño) genus are easily recognized by their stiff evergreen leaves and distinctive bark. **BARK** Thin, smooth, peeling, reddish to coppery on younger twigs and in most species on large branches and the trunk as well; older bark is gray or brown and checkered. **TWIG** Often hairy; buds pointed, glossy red, with overlapping scales. **LEAF** Alternate, simple, leathery, usually hairless; margins entire or finely toothed. **FLOWER** Bisexual, radially symmetric, whitish or pale pinkish, the 5 petals joined into a lantern-like structure, at the top of which are 5 translucent, bubblelike "windows." Inside are 10 stamens with awned anthers and a single superior ovary with 5 chambers. **FRUIT** Globose reddish berry with a minutely bumpy surface.

Madrones are related to and often grow with manzanitas (*Arctostaphylos*). Manzanita leaves are smaller, the flowers are more consistently pinkish, plants are usually shrubs, and the surface of the berrylike drupe is smooth. Summer Holly (*Comarostaphylis diversifolia*) has bumpy fruits, similar to those of madrones, but they are in raceme-like clusters, and the narrow leaves are usually felty beneath. Madrones often have a large, burl-like root crown that can give rise to a ring of new trees when the original trunk dies or is cut. The contorted branches may rub against one another and eventually self-graft. Fruit development is delayed up to 5 months after pollination, so maturing fruits are often found along with the next season's flowers. One species is used as an ornamental, and all make good firewood, but the fine-grained, easily worked wood is difficult to cure and finds little other use. The berries, though bland, are edible raw or cooked.

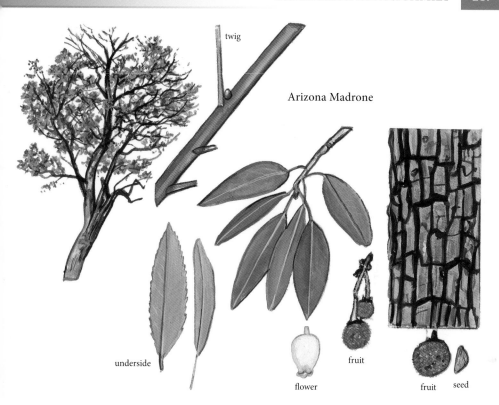

twig

Arizona Madrone

underside

flower

fruit

fruit seed

ARIZONA MADRONE *Arbutus arizonica* (A. Gray) Sarg.

QUICK ID The bark of small branches and twigs is smooth and brick red, but older bark on the larger branches and trunk is persistent and checkered, differing from the smooth bark of other madrones and manzanitas.

Evergreen tree, 3–20 m tall, with 1 to several trunks, 40–60 cm diam., and twigs hairy when young. **BARK** Thin; at first smooth, lustrous, brick red, becoming light gray or reddish gray and checkered with rectangular plates on branches and trunk. **LEAF** Alternate, simple, leathery, hairless; upper surface dark green, glossy; lower surface paler; ovate, base usually tapered, margins entire or finely toothed. Blade 3.5–7 cm long, 1.5–3 cm broad; petiole 2–3 cm long, often reddish. **FLOWER** Creamy white, many in a conical cluster 5–8 cm long; each flower lantern-shaped, 6–8 mm long. May–Jun., sometimes also Aug.–Sep. **FRUIT** Globose orange-red to

blackish-red berry, 6–9 mm diam., covered by tiny wartlike tubercles; borne hanging in clusters.

HABITAT/RANGE Native. Canyonsides and gravelly benches, usually among oaks and pines, 1,500–2,400 m; se. Ariz., sw. N.M., nw. Mexico.

Notes This slow-growing tree is common in the Sierra Madre Occidental of n. Mexico, crossing the border in the isolated mountain ranges ("sky islands") near the Ariz.–N.M. boundary.

ARIZONA MADRONE

PACIFIC MADRONE   *Arbutus menziesii*
Pursh

QUICK ID This is the only tree in its range with smooth, peeling coppery bark.

Evergreen tree, 4–40 m tall, with 1 or 2 crooked, often twisted and leaning trunks up to 1 m diam. Crown broad, the branches contorted and spreading. **BARK** On all but largest parts of the tree, papery thin, smooth, lustrous, coppery red, peeling to expose greenish-gray new bark; where retained on large trunks, bark is checkered and dark gray-brown. **TWIG** Youngest twigs often pale-hairy, soon becoming smooth; terminal buds pointed, 7–9 mm long, reddish brown. **LEAF** Alternate, simple, slightly leathery, flat or slightly convex, usually hairless or nearly so; upper surface dark green, lustrous; lower surface whitish green; elliptic, base usually rounded or indented, margins entire or very finely toothed. Blade 6–13 cm long, 4–7 cm broad; petiole 1–4.5 cm long. **FLOWER** Creamy white, many, spreading to hanging in conical clusters 12–15 cm long, each flower lantern-shaped, 5–6 mm long. Mar.–Jun. **FRUIT** Globose red to orange-red berry, 12–20 mm diam., the surface minutely bumpy; seeds 5, dark brown.

HABITAT/RANGE Native. Open forests, ravines, rocky hills, 0–1,800 m; sw. B.C. to s. Calif.

SIMILAR SPECIES Texas Madrone, which is small and has smaller leaves that are not as pale beneath, is most similar to Pacific Madrone. Arizona Madrone has a tapered leaf base and more widely distributed checkered bark. Neither occurs in Pacific Madrone's range. Strawberry Tree (*Arbutus unedo* L.), a popular ornamental originally from Europe, occasionally persists in abandoned plantings, perhaps escaping but apparently not naturalized, at low elevations in Calif. and near the coast northward to Wash. It is an evergreen shrub or

tree to 15 m tall; leaves elliptic, lustrous dark green above, margins finely toothed, blade 5–10 cm long; flowers creamy white to pinkish, lantern-shaped, 6 mm long, 10–30 in a short, broad, nodding cluster in Sep.–Dec.; fruit a globose orange-red berry, 15–20 mm diam., the surface minutely bumpy, edible and reputedly with narcotic properties.

Notes This distinctive tree is the largest of any in the heath family. Father Juan Crespí, of the Portolà expedition to Monterey, Calif., in the mid-1700s, referred to this tree as *madroño*, recognizing its similarity to the European species *A. unedo*, which he knew by that name. The previous year's leaves yellow in the heat of the summer and progressively fall into autumn, drying on the ground and making silent passage difficult. Madrones often grow with conifers, and the differences in growth between these trees can be readily observed: On a steep slope conifers will grow vertically against gravity, whereas madrones will lean outward, reaching across the shortest distance for light. Seeds are distributed by birds that eat the berries.

TEXAS MADRONE   *Arbutus xalapensis*
Kunth

QUICK ID The smooth, thin, peeling brick-red bark and warty berries identify this as a madrone; the generally rounded or heart-shaped leaf base helps to distinguish it from Arizona Madrone, which has checkered bark occurring more widely on smaller limbs.

Evergreen small tree, 2–8 m tall, often branching near the base; trunk to 20 cm diam. **BARK** Thin, smooth, lustrous, brick red, becoming dark gray or brown and checkered into irregular plates on large branches and trunk. **TWIG** Densely covered with hairs when young. **LEAF** Alternate, simple, leathery, elliptic or slightly ovate, base often rounded

PACIFIC MADRONE   TEXAS MADRONE

Pacific Madrone

flowers

flower

Texas Madrone

flowers

fruit

flower

fruit

or indented; margins entire or finely toothed. Hairless; upper surface dark green, glossy; lower surface paler. Blade 2.5–7.5 cm long, 1.5–4 cm broad; petiole 2–4.5 cm long. **FLOWER** Creamy white or pinkish, many in a conical cluster 5 cm long; each flower lantern-shaped, 5–6 mm long. Feb.–May. **FRUIT** Globose, deep red to blackish-red berry, 6–8 mm diam., covered in tiny bumps; hangs in clusters.

HABITAT/RANGE Native. Rocky hills and slopes, 300–2,200 m; s. N.M., w. and c. Texas, n. Mexico.

Notes This species can be seen in Guadalupe Mountains National Park and Big Bend National Park, Tex., and is common on the state's Edwards Plateau. In the remote Animas Mountains of sw. N.M. it comes into contact, and may hybridize, with Arizona Madrone.

■ ARCTOSTAPHYLOS: MANZANITAS

About 66 species of *Arctostaphylos* occur in North America, Central America, and Eurasia. Of the 62 found in the U.S. and Canada, one (*A. uva-ursi* [L.] Spreng., Bearberry or Kinnikinnik) is circumboreal and the only species in Eurasia. Species occur from sea-level to moderately high elevations.

Manzanitas are usually shrubs, sometimes small trees, distinctive for their leathery leaves and unusual bark. **BARK** Deep rusty red to purplish red, smooth, thin, lustrous. **LEAF** Alternate, simple, hairless or smooth, sometimes glaucous (waxy bloom easily rubbed off, exposing green tissue beneath); margins entire or finely toothed. **FLOWER** Bisexual, radially symmetric, in terminal clusters, whitish or pale pinkish, the 5 petals joined into a cone- or lantern-like structure; stamens usually 10; ovary superior, with 2–10 chambers. **FRUIT** Smooth or hairy, globose reddish berrylike drupe with 1–10 separate or united seedlike stones.

Manzanitas are related to, and often grow with, madrones (*Arbutus*), which are usually trees and have larger leaves, usually creamy-white flowers, and a minutely bumpy surface on the fruit.

The Calif. chaparral is a major vegetation type unique in the world. This shrub formation, composed largely of small-leaved evergreen species of *Adenostoma*, *Arctostaphylos*, *Ceanothus*, *Quercus*, and *Rhus*, readily and periodically burns, the plants composing it adapted to the fires that race through it. Some manazanitas have a basal burl that quickly resprouts new stems after a fire; other species are killed but readily regenerate from the seed bank in the soil. Manzanitas grow on poor soil and are associated with root-dwelling fungi (mycorrhizae) that supply nutrients. The genus has found a home in the diverse climates and topography of Calif., diversifying into at least 54 species that occur only there, some tightly restricted to local, highly mineralized soils. A number of Calif. species are rare and legally protected.

HAIRY MANZANITA *Arctostaphylos columbiana* Piper

QUICK ID The combination of its large size with the sparsely hairy, dark green leaves, densely hairy twigs, drooping flower clusters, and slightly flattened berries helps distinguish this manzanita from others.

Evergreen shrub or small tree, 2–5 m tall. **TWIG** Densely hairy, sometimes also glandular. **LEAF** Lanceolate-ovate, dark, dull green, roughened, sparsely glandular hairy; margins entire or finely toothed; blade 4–6 cm long. **FLOWER** White or pinkish, cone- or lantern-shaped, 6–7 mm long, in slightly drooping clusters 2–3 cm long. Mar.–Jul. **FRUIT** Smooth, semispherical (slightly flattened top and bottom) red berrylike drupe, 8–11 mm diam.

HABITAT/RANGE Native. Chaparral and woodland margins, 0–1,000 m; sw. B.C. to nw. Calif.

BIGBERRY MANZANITA *Arctostaphylos glauca* Lindl.

QUICK ID Bigberry Manzanita has hairless twigs and leaves, with a bluish-green waxy bloom on the leaf surface that easily rubs off, exposing the dark green beneath.

Evergreen shrub or small tree, 1–8 m tall. **TWIG** Usually hairless. **LEAF** Oblong to nearly round, dull whitish blue-green (bloom rubs off); margins entire; blade 2.5–5 cm long. **FLOWER** White or pinkish, cone- or lantern-shaped, 8–9 mm long, in dense clusters 2–3 cm long. Dec.–Mar. **FRUIT** Smooth, globose brownish berrylike drupe, 12–15 mm diam.

HABITAT/RANGE Native. Chaparral, dry woodland, 300–2,000 m; c. Calif. to Baja Calif.

HAIRY MANZANITA

BIGBERRY MANZANITA

Hairy Manzanita

flowers

fruit

Bigberry Manzanita

flowers

fruit

COMMON MANZANITA *Arctostaphylos manzanita* Parry
A.K.A. WHITELEAF MANZANITA, PARRY MANZANITA

QUICK ID This manzanita has leaves the same color (bright green and shiny or with a dull bluish-green waxy coating that rubs off) on both surfaces and hairy along the veins, and a widely branched flower cluster.

Evergreen tree, 2–8 m tall; 1 to several long, crooked trunks, 10–20 cm diam., with or without a large, hemispherical burl at the base. **BARK** Lustrous, rich red-brown, thin and peeling. **TWIG** Hairless, sparsely short-hairy, or glandular. **LEAF** Alternate, simple, leathery, widely ovate to obovate; margins entire. Upper and lower surfaces the same: bright green to whitish blue-green, hairless or hairy. Blade 2–5 cm long, 1–3.5 cm broad; petiole 6–12 cm long. **FLOWER** White or pinkish, many in an abruptly deflexed, spreading-branched cluster, 15–45 mm long; each flower conic to lantern-shaped, 7–8 mm long. Feb.–Apr. **FRUIT** Globose (slightly flattened top and bottom) berrylike drupe, white in early summer, deep red-brown later, 8–12 mm diam., hairy or hairless; hangs in clusters.

HABITAT/RANGE Native. Dry slopes in chaparral and open pine woodland, 100–1,300 m, and readily establishing in old fields and orchards; c. Calif.

Notes Fire adaptation varies in this species: Those with burls sprout after fire; those without burls are killed, and new populations must establish from seed. There are 6 subspecies. Subsp. *roofii* (Gankin) P.V. Wells has a basal burl. The remaining five do not, and vary in fruit and twig pubescence, color of leaves, and fusion of the stones in the fruit. The fruit is edible, pleasantly tart, but when eaten in quantity may cause gastrointestinal disturbance. In the past it was brewed into a cider.

PRINGLE MANZANITA *Arctostaphylos pringlei* Parry subsp. *pringlei*

QUICK ID The glandular hairy, finely roughened, almost round grayish leaves and large pink flower bracts help to distinguish this species.

Evergreen shrub or small tree, 1–5 m tall. **TWIG** Densely glandular hairy. **LEAF** Alternate, simple, elliptic to nearly round, margins entire; gray-green, glandular hairy and also finely roughened; blade 2–5 cm long. **FLOWER** White to pink, lantern-shaped, 6–9 mm long, in simple or 1-branched racemes 1–1.5 cm long; bracts bright pink, lanceolate, 6–10 mm long. Apr.–May. **FRUIT** Finely glandular hairy, ovoid to globose reddish berrylike drupe, 6–10 mm diam.; stones separate.

HABITAT/RANGE Native. Dry hills in brush or woodlands, 1,200–2,600 m; s. Nevada, sw. Utah, much of Ariz., to nw. Mexico.

SIMILAR SPECIES Pink-bracted Manzanita (*A. pringlei* subsp. *drupacea* [Parry] P.V. Wells), usually a shrub, grows in the mountains of sw. Calif., and differs by having stones fused into a single sphere.

STICKY WHITELEAF MANZANITA *Arctostaphylos viscida* Parry

Evergreen shrub or small tree, 1–3 m tall. **TWIG** Usually hairless to densely glandular hairy. **LEAF** 2–5 cm long, ovate to nearly round, dull whitish blue-green (bloom rubs off), hairless or hairy; margins entire. **FLOWER** Pink to whitish, lantern-shaped, 6–7 mm long, in few-branched panicles 1–3 cm long, each flower on a sticky-hairy stalk 8–12 mm long. Feb.–Apr. **FRUIT** Berry brownish or reddish, smooth and hairless, sticky-hairy and rough, or glandular-bristly, globose but slightly flattened on top and bottom, 6–8 mm diam. **HABITAT/RANGE** Native. Chaparral, dry woodland, 30–2,200 m; se. Ore. to s. Calif.

COMMON MANZANITA   PRINGLE MANZANITA

Common Manzanita

seed

flowers

fruit

Pringle Manzanita

flowers

fruit

Sticky Whiteleaf Manzanita

flowers

fruit

SUMMER HOLLY *Comarostaphylis diversifolia* (Parry) Greene
A.K.A. MOCK ARBUTUS, SUMMER-BLOOMING MANZANITA

QUICK ID The round, minutely bumpy red fruit distinguishes this species from other trees in the region except for madrones (*Arbutus*); the leaves, with their grayish-velvety lower surface, differ distinctly from those of madrones.

Evergreen shrub or small tree to 9 m tall; 1 to several trunks about 10 cm diam., often with a large burl at the base. Irregular, round or oval crown with widely ascending branches and gray-hairy twigs. **BARK** Gray-brown, shredding. **LEAF** Alternate, spreading, simple, thick and leathery, narrowly elliptic to narrowly ovate; margins rolled under or not. Upper surface dark green and shining; lower surface grayish and velvety. Blade 3–13 cm long, 1–4 cm broad; petiole 2–20 mm long, gray-woolly. **FLOWER** White, finely hairy, numerous, hanging, usually in racemes 3–14 cm long; 5 petals united into a lantern-shaped corolla 5–8 mm long; stamens 10; ovary superior, 5-chambered. Mar.–Jul. **FRUIT** Globose, minutely bumpy red drupe, 5–7 mm diam., the stones fused together.

HABITAT/RANGE Native. Chaparral near the coast, sometimes partly shaded, 0–600 m; s. Calif., nw. Baja Calif.

Notes There are 10 species of *Comarostaphylis*, all from Mexico and Central America, most from moderate to high elevations in the mountains. Summer Holly is the only one to occur north of the Mexican border, and is the only species that grows below 1,350 m. It is of conservation concern, its populations threatened by suburban encroachment. There are 2 subspecies: Subsp. *diversifolia*, on the mainland from the Los Angeles area southward, has leaves with rolled-under margins; subsp. *planifolia*

SUMMER HOLLY

(Jeps.) G.D. Wallace, from the Channel Islands and the mainland in the Santa Monica Mountains and Santa Ynez Mountains, has flat leaves. These are the northernmost populations of the genus.

■ *RHODODENDRON:* RHODODENDRONS

There are about 1,000 species of *Rhododendron* in North America, Eurasia, n. Malaysia, New Guinea, and n. Australia, usually found in moderately moist areas, from sea-level to high elevations. Diversity is greatest in Southeast Asia. In the West there are 3 native species, two of which sometimes become small trees.

Rhododendrons are evergreen or deciduous woody plants, varying from low creepers to shrubs and small trees, with showy flowers. **TWIG** Twigs are hairy or not, the buds large, with overlapping scales. **LEAF** Alternate, simple, leathery to thin, hairy or not; margins entire or finely toothed. **FLOWER** Bisexual, usually weakly bilaterally symmetric, rarely radial, showy, usually several to many in terminal clusters. Sepals usually 5, slightly joined; petals usually 5, nearly separate to almost completely joined, white or brightly colored; stamens 5–20, included or well exerted from the corolla, the anthers lacking awns; ovary superior, usually 5-chambered. **FRUIT** Elongate capsule that splits longitudinally.

About 700 species of *Rhododendron* are in cultivation, most coming from cool areas of East Asia and the Himalayas. In horticulture, deciduous rhododendrons are called azaleas. Whether the plant is evergreen or deciduous, the clustered, colorful flowers can be spectacular, and many species and hybrids are prized as spring-flowering ornamentals. Some are so valuable that they are dug and stolen at night from gardens. The foliage is toxic, but rarely causes problems for humans or livestock in the West.

PACIFIC RHODODENDRON
Rhododendron macrophyllum D. Don ex G. Don
A.K.A. CALIFORNIA RHODODENDRON, COAST RHODODENDRON

QUICK ID The dark green leathery leaves and clusters of large, showy pink flowers are unique among native western shrubs and trees.

Evergreen shrub or small tree to 9 m tall; trunk to about 10 cm diam. Crown open, loose, with leaves

Summer Holly

flowers

flowers

fruit

flowers

Pacific Rhododendron

flowers

clustered at the branch tips, the twisted branches exposed. **BARK** Thin, dark reddish brown to blackish brown, smooth or furrowed and shredding. **TWIG** At first with matted, glandular hairs, soon mostly hairless. **LEAF** Alternate, simple, leathery, more or less elliptic; margins entire, flat or rolled under. Nearly hairless; upper surface dark green above; lower surface paler. Blade 6–20 cm long, 2.5–7.5 cm broad; petiole stout, 15–25 mm long. **FLOWER** Showy, 10–20 in a large globose terminal cluster; corolla bell-shaped, 2.5–5 cm long, usually pink, sometimes white or deep rose-pink. Apr.–Jul. **FRUIT** Hairy, narrowly ovoid red-brown woody capsule, 1–2.5 cm long, held erect.

HABITAT/RANGE Native. Forests, thickets, edges of forest, 50–1,600 m; sw. B.C. south to nw. Calif.

Notes The state flower of Wash. Though not as compact as some of its relatives, this rhododendron is commonly used as an ornamental.

PACIFIC RHODODENDRON

WESTERN AZALEA *Rhododendron occidentale* (Torr. & A. Gray) A. Gray
A.K.A. CALIFORNIA AZALEA

QUICK ID The large, attractive pastel flowers in clusters and thin yellow-green leaves distinguish this species.

Deciduous shrub or small tree, 1–10 m tall. **LEAF** Thin, hairy, ovate to obovate, yellow-green; margins entire, flat; blade 2.5–11 cm long. **FLOWER** Showy, 3–10 in a cluster, white, salmon, or pink, often with a yellow or orange blotch on the upper lobe, 3–6 cm long. May–Jul. **FRUIT** Erect, oblong, pubescent capsule, 1–2 cm long.

HABITAT/RANGE Native. Moist slopes, thickets, canyon bottoms, bogs, 0–2,700 m; w. Ore. to s. Calif. Widely cultivated.

WESTERN AZALEA

EUPHORBIACEAE: SPURGE FAMILY

This large family of plants, ranging from small herbaceous species to massive trees, is predominantly tropical in distribution. There are more than 200 genera and nearly 6,000 species. About 21 genera and more than 200 species occur in the West.

Many species have milky sap. Most of the species in the U.S. are herbaceous; a few are native shrubs or trees. **LEAF** Alternate, 2-ranked, or opposite, usually simple, but sometimes palmately compound. **FLOWER** Unisexual, the sexes on the same or separate plants; when on the same plant they are often aggregated in a small cup resembling a tiny flower, the cyathium. Sepals may be present; petals are usually lacking. Stamens vary from 1 to many. The ovary has 2 to many chambers, but commonly 3. **FRUIT** Usually a capsule that splits apart along the partitions between chambers (schizocarp).

Many economically valuable products are obtained from the family, among them rubber, castor and tung oils, dyes, timber, and ornamental plants, including Poinsettia (*Euphorbia pulcherrima* Willd. ex Klotzsch). A number of Euphorbiaceae species are planted as ornamentals in the West, several escaping. Two woody species have naturalized; another two may be found escaped or naturalized in warmer parts of the region. **Pencil Rubber Hedge** (*Euphorbia tirucalli* L.), a leafless shrub or small tree with pencil-diameter green stems, is grown as an ornamental in warm regions; it is reported from s. Calif., but probably has not naturalized.

TUNGOIL TREE *Aleurites fordii* Hemsl.

Deciduous small tree with milky sap. **LEAF** Simple, often 3-lobed, with a long petiole, lower surface usually hairy and the sinuses between lobes often having conspicuous glands. **FLOWER** White, about 4 cm diam., with 2 sepals and 5 petals, the petals with reddish veins. **HABITAT/RANGE** Introduced from China; occasionally planted as an ornamental. In some sources it is reported to have escaped in Calif., but it probably has not naturalized there (as it has in the Southeast). *Notes* Also treated as *Vernicia fordii* (Hemsl.) Airy Shaw. There are 5 species of *Aleurites*, all from Southeast Asia. Several commercially valuable oils come from species of the genus, including tung oil from the Tungoil Tree.

underside

Western Azalea

flowers

flowers

Pencil Rubber Hedge

Tungoil Tree

flowers

fruit

seed

CASTOR BEAN *Ricinus communis* L.

Evergreen tree or shrub to 10 m tall in frost-free areas, to 3 m tall and dying to the ground and annual in colder areas. Trunks slender, usually 1, with a few branches in the upper half. **LEAF** Alternate, simple, large, circular in outline, palmately lobed, the 6 or 7 lobes narrowly pointed, margins irregularly toothed. Blade 10–45 cm diam.; petiole stout, usually about as long as the blade. **FLOWER** Tiny, greenish, unisexual, female above the male in dense, pyramidal terminal clusters. Year-round in warm areas. **FRUIT** Three-lobed, usually spiny capsule, each chamber holding 1 large, lustrous black-, gray-, and brown-mottled beanlike seed 9–22 mm long. **HABITAT/RANGE** Introduced from Eurasia; cultivated, naturalized in disturbed places at low elevations, s. Calif. and from s. Tex. to Fla. *Notes* This is the single species of *Ricinus*. Castor oil is pressed from the seeds. Seeds are fatally toxic.

ARROW POISON PLANT *Sebastiania bilocularis* S. Watson
A.K.A. JUMPING BEAN

QUICK ID This shrub or tree bleeds milky sap when the stem is broken. It has tiny yellowish flowers in small spikes and a plump, inversely heart-shaped capsule.

Evergreen many-stemmed shrub, occasionally with few stems and treelike, 2–6 m tall; sap milky.

ARROW POISON PLANT

LEAF Alternate, simple, leathery, smooth, lustrous, bright green to reddish, lanceolate; margins finely toothed; blade 2–6 cm long. **FLOWER** Tiny, greenish yellow, without petals, in spikes 2.5–6 cm long; unisexual, female flowers near the base of the spike with 2 recurved, rough styles; male flowers in the upper part, with 2 stamens. Mar.–Nov. **FRUIT** Two-lobed, plump, inversely heart-shaped capsule, 1 cm wide, each chamber with 1 large, nearly globose brown-and-gray-mottled seed.

HABITAT/RANGE Native. Desert slopes and washes, 300–750 m; Ariz. to nw. Mexico.

Notes The sap is toxic and was once used to stupefy fish and poison arrow tips. One of several species of jumping bean; the seed "jumps" because of the movement of the larva of a tiny moth (*Cydia deshaisiana*) within. *Sebastiana* is a tropical genus of about 100 species, most in Central and South America.

CHINESE TALLOW TREE *Sapium sebiferum* (L.) Roxb.
A.K.A. POPCORN TREE

Deciduous shrub or tree, 6–17 m tall, exuding milky sap when the twigs and leaves are broken. **TWIG** Glaucous at first, becoming tan, usually with scattered circular orange lenticels. **LEAF** Alternate, simple, ovate or elliptic, tip abruptly narrowed to a slender point; margins entire. Midvein yellowish, turning reddish in autumn. Blade 3–6 cm long; petiole with a pair of glands at the point of blade attachment. **FLOWER** Unisexual, male and female flowers yellowish, intermingled in a spike-like cluster to 20 cm long. Apr.–Jun. **FRUIT** Three-lobed capsule, splitting to reveal 3 dull white seeds. **HABITAT/RANGE** Introduced from East Asia; naturalized in moist areas at 0–300 m in Calif., occasionally escaping in the Southwest. Potentially highly invasive. *Notes* The genus contains 20–25 species from warm areas of the world. The species is also called *Triadica sebifera* (L.) Small.

Castor Bean

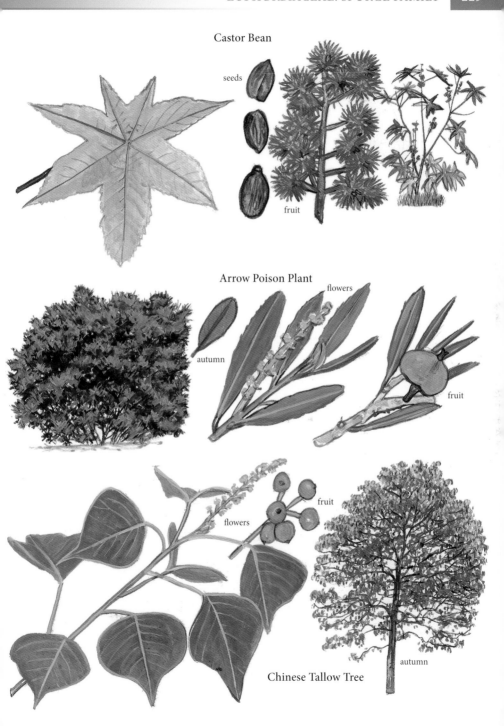

seeds

fruit

Arrow Poison Plant

flowers

autumn

fruit

Chinese Tallow Tree

flowers

fruit

autumn

FABACEAE: BEAN OR PEA FAMILY

With approximately 730 genera and 19,000 species, the bean family is the 3rd largest plant family, following the sunflower (Asteraceae) and orchid (Orchidaceae) families. Fabaceae is worldwide in distribution, and species are found in all habitats. More than 45 genera and 110 species of trees occur north of Mexico, from the hot arid Southwest and humid Southeast northward. The family is commonly divided into 3 major groups, subfamilies Caesalpinioideae, Mimosoideae, and Papilionoideae. For the most part, each subfamily is easily recognized by the structure of the corolla and stamens in the flower. The species text for the family is organized by subfamily; each subfamily is introduced with a brief description.

LEAF Usually alternate, pinnately or bipinnately compound in most species; apparently simple in some by reduction to 1 leaflet (unifoliolate); sometimes leaflets are absent and the petiole is flattened, enlarged, and leaflike (a phyllode). At night or during hot periods leaflets may fold together, apparently a water conservation mechanism. Species with glands on the leaves often attract ants, which may attack insects or animals that would otherwise feed upon the plant. In Fabaceae with compound leaves, whether they are once, twice, or thrice compound, the leaflike structure is a leaflet. In a once pinnately compound leaf the leaflets are arranged along a central axis, the rachis, which begins where the petiole ends, at the 1st leaflet at the base of the pinnately divided blade. A bipinnately compound leaf is divided into primary segments that attach to the rachis, and each primary segment has its own leaflets and its own central axis, the rachilla, to which the leaflets are attached. Occasionally leaves may be tripinnate, with primary and secondary segments, each with their own rachillas.

FLOWER The Fabaceae flower is fundamentally arranged in multiples of 5, except for the single simple pistil, which develops into the legume. The flowers differ among the 3 subfamilies; they are illustrated and further described in the subfamily introductions. **FRUIT** The fruit, the unifying feature for the family, is a legume. The pea pod is a good example of this type of fruit. It is 1-chambered, derived from a superior, simple ovary, with 2 rows of seeds hanging from the upper suture; when mature it is dry and elastically dehisces (splits) along the upper and lower sutures. From this prototype various types of legumes have evolved, some with few seeds, some indehiscent, some breaking into 1-seeded sections.

The family is also known as the Leguminosae, an old name derived from early European words for "vegetable" and "plant with a seed pod." Fabaceae is one of the most economically important families for humankind. It provides many edible seeds and vegetables, forage for livestock, high-quality lumber, sources of dye, spectacular ornamentals, and habitat and food for wildlife. Many members of the family are well known for their ability to fix atmospheric nitrogen and improve soil fertility. *Rhizobium* bacteria reside in root nodules and use atmospheric nitrogen in their metabolism, making nitrogen available to all living systems through soil enrichment.

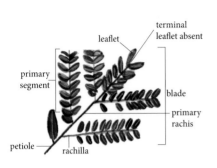

Bipinnately Compound Leaf

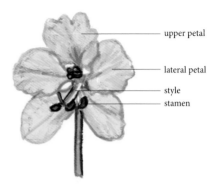

Caesalpinioid Legume Flower
(pp. 231–42)

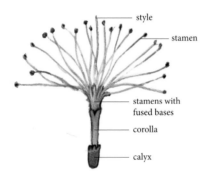

Mimosoid Legume Flower
(pp. 242–67)

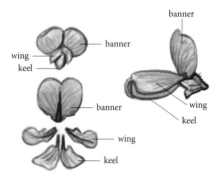

Papilionoid Legume Flower
(pp. 268–275)

SUBFAMILY CAESALPINIOIDEAE: SENNAS AND THEIR RELATIVES

Subfamily Caesalpinioideae includes the sennas, cassias, orchid-trees, locusts, redbuds, and relatives. It is primarily tropical and subtropical, consisting mostly of shrubs and trees, and has about 180 genera and 3,000 species. **LEAF** Alternate, usually pinnately compound, sometimes bipinnate, occasionally unifoliolate; many bear glands at the upper end of the petiole and also often on the rachis. Primary segments and leaflets often in pairs; terminal segment or leaflet often absent. **FLOWER** Usually bisexual, more or less bilateral, the upper petal often largest, positioned interior to the lateral petals and covered by them in the bud. Stamens 10 or fewer, separate or mostly united, often opening by terminal pores.

■ *BAUHINIA*: ORCHID TREES

Bauhinia is a genus of about 250 species of trees, shrubs, and woody vines distributed in tropical regions of the world; 5 species (4 trees) occur in North America, 1 native to the West and 1 introduced there. At least 10 species are used ornamentally.

ANACACHO ORCHID-TREE *Bauhinia lunarioides* A. Gray ex S. Watson
A.K.A. TEXAS PLUME

QUICKID The 2-lobed, butterfly-shaped leaves distinguish this species from other western trees.

Deciduous small, unarmed tree or shrub to 4 m tall, with an open, airy, oval crown. **LEAF** Alternate, pinnately compound or unifoliolate, divided or deeply cut into 2 obliquely obovate leaflets or lobes, the leaf appearing butterfly-shaped; margins entire. Blade 1.5–3 cm long, about as wide; petiole 8–15 mm long. **FLOWER** Showy, in congested clusters near the ends of twigs, bisexual, slightly bilateral. Petals 5, ovate, stalked at the base, 13–18 mm long, white or pink; stamens 9 or 10, only 1 functional, all hairy at the base. Mar.–May, sometimes sporadically all year. **FRUIT** Legume flat or twisted, oblong, 3–7 cm long, 1 cm broad, dark brown, leathery, hairless, containing 1–4 seeds.

HABITAT/RANGE Native. Uncommon in limestone canyons at 400–500 m near the Rio Grande east of the Big Bend, Tex.; also n. Mexico.

MOUNTAIN EBONY *Bauhinia variegata* L.
A.K.A. PURPLE ORCHID-TREE

LEAF Cleft only ⅓ the length of the blade. **FLOWER** 7–10 cm diam., the petals white or pinkish to purple, one with a deep purple or yellow streak at the base; mostly winter to early spring, when the tree is leafless. **HABITAT/RANGE** Introduced from tropical Asia; cultivated (and perhaps escaped) in Calif. and s. Tex.; naturalized in Fla.

■ *CAESALPINIA*: CAESALPINIAS

This worldwide tropical and subtropical genus has 70–165 species, varying from climbers to shrubs or trees, unarmed or armed with spines along the stem. In the West most woody species are introduced. They are cold-sensitive and, thus, are found at low to moderate elevations in warm regions.

Most species are evergreen, but leaves may be lost during drought or cold. Plants commonly have stalked glands, and dark, glandular punctuations on leaves and fruits, which may impart an unpleasant odor. **LEAF** Alternate, pinnately or bipinnately compound, leaflets often paired, a terminal leaflet present or not, margins of the leaflets entire. **FLOWER** Showy, slightly bilaterally symmetric, sometimes fragrant, generally in racemes or branched clusters. Sepals 5, commonly cupped, the lower one sometimes also reflexed; petals 5, all usually stalked, upper petal innermost, commonly more colorful than the others,; stamens 10, often showy and protruding. **FRUIT** Legume flat or swollen, often curved, dehiscent or not. Seeds few to several, often comparatively large, in some species toxic.

Caesalpinias are also called poincianas or bird-of-paradise plants. Some are colorful ornamentals. Others provide high-quality lumber used for flooring, cabinetry, and musical instruments. One species, known as Brasil (*C. echinata* Lam.), yields a red dye; the country Brazil received its name from these trees. Large marble-like seeds of some, known as "nickernuts," are used in tropical regions in counting games and for rustic jewelry. In spite of one of the common names for *Caesalpinia* being bird-of-paradise, the florist's Bird-of-paradise (*Strelitzia reginae* Banks ex Aiton) is related to ginger in the order Zingiberales.

ANACACHO ORCHID-TREE   BIRD-OF-PARADISE

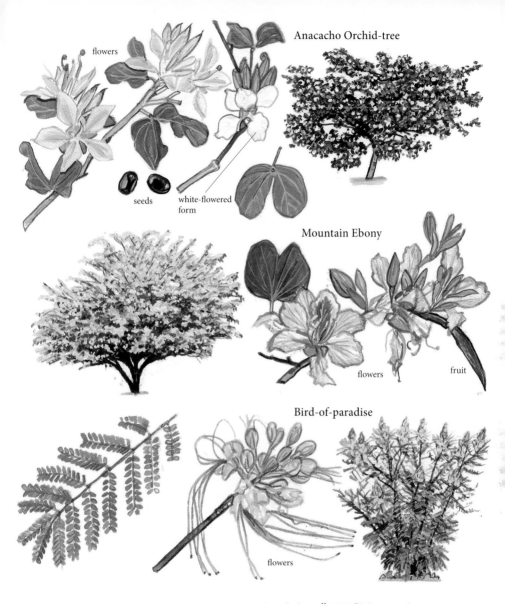

Anacacho Orchid-tree

flowers

seeds   white-flowered
form

Mountain Ebony

flowers   fruit

Bird-of-paradise

flowers

BIRD-OF-PARADISE *Caesalpinia gilliesii* (Wall ex Hook.) D. Dietr.

QUICKID Bipinnately compound leaves and large flowers with yellow petals and bright red stamens together distinguish this shrub or small tree.

Evergreen (deciduous in cold), unarmed, glandular and malodorous, very open shrub or small tree, 1–4 m tall. **LEAF** Bipinnate; primary segments 17–25; leaflets 15–23 per segment, elliptic, 3–8 mm long. **FLOWER** Petals 5, yellow, 2–3.5 cm long, ovate, stalked. Stamens bright red, 8–9 cm long, long-protruding. May–Sep.; flower withers by midday. **FRUIT** Legume oblong, curved, 6–12 cm long, lightly pubescent, spreading.

HABITAT/RANGE Introduced from South America; dry areas, 0–1,400 m; Calif. to Okla. and Tex.

MEXICAN BIRD-OF-PARADISE
Caesalpinia mexicana A. Gray

QUICK ID Deep green bipinnate leaves with oval leaflets 1–2 cm long and spires of yellow bilateral flowers about 2.5 cm diam. distinguish this bird-of-paradise.

Evergreen, or deciduous in colder climates; open, unarmed shrub or tree, 2–9 m tall, with a broad crown, lush foliage, and sprays of brilliant yellow flowers. **LEAF** Alternate, bipinnately compound, blade 4–15 cm long, petiole about ⅓ length of blade; primary segments 3–9, each 2.5–3 cm long; leaflets 6–10 per segment, 1–2 cm long, oval, elliptic or oblong-ovate, deep green above, paler below. **FLOWER** Petals 1–1.5 cm long, stalked, yellow, the upper with a reddish spot near the base; stamens 10, upcurved, barely longer than the petals; 10–30 flowers in a narrowly conical cluster 10–30 cm long. Feb.–Jul. or later. **FRUIT** Legume flat, 5–7 cm long, light brown, leathery, usually with stalked glands.

HABITAT/RANGE Native and introduced. Disturbed areas, 0–150 m; s. Tex. and ne. Mexico; widely cultivated, escaping in sc. Ariz. at 350 m, and perhaps elsewhere.

Notes This primarily Mexican species is widely used as an ornamental in warm areas across the s. U.S., including s. Tex., and its natural range is uncertain.

MEXICAN BIRD-OF-PARADISE

PRIDE-OF-BARBADOS *Caesalpinia pulcherrima* (L.) Sw.
A.K.A. DWARF POINCIANA, BIRD OF PARADISE

Evergreen (or deciduous in light frosts) shrub or small tree 3–5 m tall; trunk 7–13 cm diam., with a broad crown. Branches often armed with scattered prickles 5 mm long. **LEAF** Bipinnate, 15–30 cm long; primary segments 10–20, paired; leaflets 10–24 per segment, oblong, 1–2.5 cm long, 5–10 mm broad. **FLOWER** Five petals, 3–4 cm long, brilliant yellow or orange, often turning red with age, sometimes red with a yellow border; stamens 10, slender, red or yellow, 4–6 cm long. Year-round. **FRUIT** Legume flat, 6–10 cm long, 1.5–2 cm broad. **HABITAT/RANGE** Introduced from tropical America; widely planted in warm regions, occasionally escaping and weakly naturalized in disturbed areas at low elevations in Tex., Ariz., Calif., and warmer parts of the South.

TARA *Caesalpinia spinosa* (Molina) Kuntze
A.K.A. SPINY HOLDBACK

Evergreen shrub or small tree to 2–5 m tall; stems armed with downcurved, broad-based prickles. **LEAF** Bipinnate, to 25 cm long; primary segments 7–21, to 8 cm long; leaflets 6–20 per segment, oval, 1.5–4 cm long. **FLOWER** Petals yellow, fading reddish, the upper petal red-spotted. Flowers in crowded racemes. May–Aug. **FRUIT** Legume oblong, 6–10 cm long, thick and pulpy. **HABITAT/RANGE** Introduced from Peru; established near the coast, 0–50 m, c. and s. Calif.

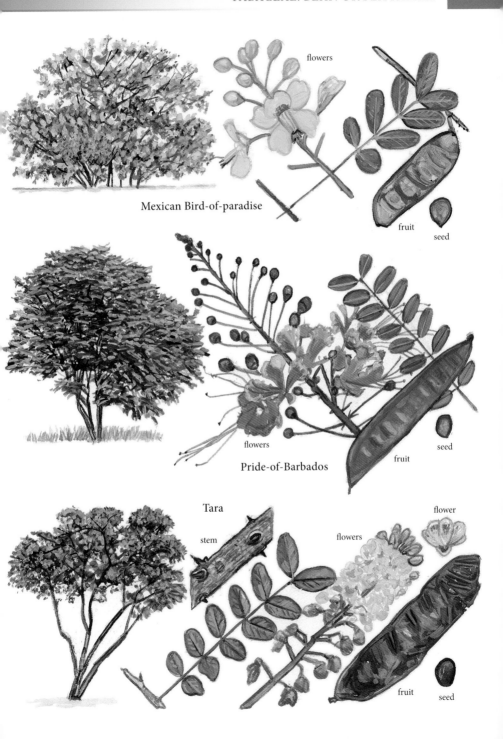

Mexican Bird-of-paradise

flowers

fruit

seed

Pride-of-Barbados

flowers

fruit

seed

Tara

stem

flowers

flower

fruit

seed

CAROB *Ceratonia siliqua* L.
A.K.A. ST. JOHN'S BREAD

Evergreen unarmed tree, 5–17 m tall, with stout, spreading branches and a broad round crown. **LEAF** Alternate, pinnately compound, 10–20 cm long, with 6–10 oval, dark green leaflets, each 2.5–5 cm long. **FLOWER** Usually unisexual, on separate trees; tiny, greenish, in catkin-like racemes on spurs on older branches and trunk, lacking petals; male flowers with 5 stamens; female flowers with 1 pistil with large greenish stigma. Sep.–Oct. **FRUIT** Legume thick, often curved, 10–30 cm long, brown, glossy, hanging in clusters. **HABITAT/RANGE** Introduced widely; has established in s. Calif. near the coast. *Notes Ceratonia*, from sw. Asia and the e. Mediterranean, contains 2 species.

■ *CERCIS*: REDBUDS

A genus of about 8 species from temperate regions, 2 species native to North America. Several from the Old World are planted as ornamentals.

Deciduous trees or shrubs with 1 or multiple trunks, often branching low to the ground. **LEAF** Alternate, unifoliolate, blade distinctly palmately veined, base cordate, margins entire. **FLOWER** Produced in small, few-flowered clusters from the leaf axils, bisexual, bilaterally asymmetric, purplish red, pinkish, or white; petals 5; stamens 10, free. **FRUIT** Legume flattened, stiffly papery, persistent, slowly dehiscent, containing flat, dark seeds.

EASTERN REDBUD *Cercis canadensis* L.

QUICK ID This redbud has broad heart-shaped leaves that taper to a pointed tip, distinguishing it from Western Redbud.

Deciduous unarmed tree, 8–14 m tall, with 1 erect, short trunk to 20–80 cm diam. **BARK** Grayish brown, more or less smooth, becoming finely fissured, with scaly ridges. **LEAF** Alternate, broadly ovate, base cordate or truncate, tip abruptly tapered to a point; veins prominent, 5–7, palmate, arching. Upper surface dull medium or dark green, hairless; lower surface paler, hairless or

hairy throughout. Blade 7.5–12.5 cm long, about as broad; petiole 4–10 cm long, swollen at both ends. **FLOWER** Strongly bilateral, 10–12 mm long; sepals 5, pink to dark magenta, occasionally white; petals 5, light to dark pink or magenta. Mar.–May, prior to the new leaves. **FRUIT** Legume flattened, oblong, 6–10 cm long, to about 1 cm broad.

HABITAT/RANGE Native. Moist or dry woods and slopes, roadsides, 0–670 m; widespread in the East, extending westward to w. Tex.

Notes This and the very similar Western Redbud are planted in the West as ornamentals.

WESTERN REDBUD *Cercis orbiculata* Greene

QUICK ID This redbud may be recognized by the combination of bilateral magenta flowers, broad heart-shaped leaves, usually with a rounded, bluntly angled, or slightly notched tip, and flattened legumes.

Deciduous shrub or small tree, 2–7 m tall, with several slender trunks and a dense round or oval crown. **LEAF** Blade has a rounded or slightly indented tip, rarely bluntly angled or with a small point. **FLOWER** Bright magenta-pink, 11–14 mm long. Feb.–May.

HABITAT/RANGE Native. Foothills, slopes, canyons, 300–1,400 m; sw. Ore., Calif., to s. Utah and c. Ariz.

Notes A spectacularly vivid spring-flowering plant contrasting with the fresh green of grassy hillsides. Sometimes considered a variety of Eastern Redbud, which it resembles.

EASTERN REDBUD

WESTERN REDBUD

Carob

seed

fruit

Eastern Redbud

flowers

fruit

seeds

Western Redbud

flowers

fruit

HONEY LOCUST *Gleditsia triacanthos* L.

QUICK ID This tree is recognized by the pinnate and bipinnate leaves, large, often branched thorns, and long legumes.

Deciduous tree 30–45 m tall, crown broad, open. Single erect trunk, 60–160 cm diam.; it and larger branches are often armed with stout, sharp, strong, usually branched thorns. **LEAF** Alternate, pinnately and bipinnately compound, blade to about 16 cm long, terminal segment and terminal leaflets absent; bipinnate leaves with 2–8 pairs of segments, each with 5–10 pairs of leaflets; pinnate leaves with 10–14 pairs of leaflets. Leaflets elliptic, 1.2–3.5 cm long, margins entire or minutely bluntly toothed. **FLOWER** Unisexual or functionally so, radially symmetric, small, greenish yellow. Apr.–Jun. **FRUIT** Legume large, flat, often curved, twisted, or contorted, 20–45 cm long, 2–4 cm broad, reddish brown or blackish.

HABITAT/RANGE Native. Open woods, 0–600 m; throughout the East, barely entering the West on the Great Plains and in Tex. Thornless forms are often planted as ornamentals. Occasionally naturalized in riparian areas throughout much of the West.

■ *PARKINSONIA:* PALO VERDES

There are 10 species of *Parkinsonia* in warm, dry areas of the world, from sea-level to moderate elevations. For more than 100 years our species have been divided into *Cercidium* and *Parkinsonia*, but recent work indicates there is only 1 genus. All have smooth green bark that carries on most of the photosynthesis once leaves or leaflets have dropped, a water-conservation measure. All species are cold-sensitive. Four species occur in the hot deserts of the West.

Palo verdes are weakly spiny shrubs or small trees, leafless for most of the year. **BARK** Young bark is smooth and green or greenish; older bark is thin, grayish, and more or less scaly. **LEAF** Alternate, bipinnately compound, without a terminal segment; the primary segments with few to many leaflets, usually in pairs, with margins entire. Leaves or leaflets are lost very quickly. **FLOWER** Bisexual, slightly bilateral; sepals 5, fused into a short tube; petals 5, the upper one innermost; stamens 10. **FRUIT** Legume short, swollen at each of the few seeds, leathery, pointed at the tip; slow to split open or indehiscent.

JERUSALEM THORN *Parkinsonia aculeata* L.

A.K.A. RETAMA, HORSEBEAN, MEXICAN PALO VERDE

QUICK ID This tree has green bark and a feathery appearance provided by the long, drooping, linear leaf segments.

Deciduous or nearly evergreen, few-stemmed, diffuse spiny shrub or small tree to 12 m tall. Trunk erect, to 30 cm diam., usually low-branched, the several branches ascending, their tips often drooping, crown roundish. **BARK** Smooth, green, becoming grayish brown or reddish brown and very shallowly fissured. **TWIG** Hairless, with needle-sharp, slightly recurved spines to 2.5 cm long. **LEAF** Alternate, bipinnately compound (rarely pinnate), 20–40 cm long, 6–10 mm broad, with 2–6 linear segments branching from a very short spine-tipped rachis. Leaflets 50–60, widely spaced, linear or oblanceolate, 5–8 mm long, quickly deciduous, leaving the long, slender, slightly flattened, linear, drooping rachillas (which are also deciduous as the season progresses); petiole essentially absent. **FLOWER** In short, congested terminal clusters of racemes, each with 2–15 flowers; corolla about 2 cm diam.; petals 5, yellow; stamens 10. Mar.–Sep., especially after rains. **FRUIT** Legume linear or oblong, nearly round in cross section, often slightly constricted between seeds, 2–10 cm long, 5–6 mm diam.

HABITAT/RANGE Native to Mexico and apparently sc. Ariz. and s. Tex. along the Rio Grande, but now weedy in arroyos and along roadsides, 0–1,400 m; in much of the Southwest, east to Fla.

HONEY LOCUST

JERUSALEM THORN

Honey Locust

flowers

thorn

seeds

fruit

Jerusalem Thorn

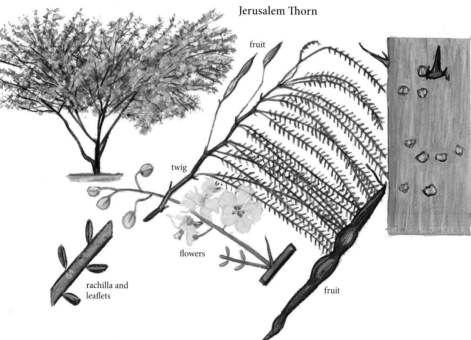

fruit

twig

flowers

rachilla and leaflets

fruit

Notes The leaves may appear to be long, very narrow and once-pinnate because of the very short rachis, which is inconspicuous relative to the long, flattened rachillas. The rachis, which is pointed, becomes hardened and forms the spines of older twigs. The tree is appreciated as an ornamental because of its drought resistance, feathery green foliage, and rapid growth.

BLUE PALO VERDE *Parkinsonia florida*
(Benth. ex A. Gray) S. Watson

QUICK ID This is a mostly leafless bluish-green tree with yellow flowers and many spreading or drooping twigs.

Quickly deciduous spiny tree, 7–12 m tall, with many spreading or drooping twigs. Trunk 10–70 cm diam. Spines at nodes on twigs and smaller branches 2–6 mm long. **BARK** Smooth, bluish green, when older grayish and scaly. **LEAF** Alternate, bipinnately compound, 5–30 mm long; petiole 5–10 mm long; forked into 2 primary segments (sometimes 4 or 6), each with 2–8 ovate to obovate leaflets, 4–8 mm long. Erect glands often on rachises at bases of primary segments and on rachillas between leaflets. **FLOWER** In short racemes of 1–8; corolla 18–25 mm diam.; petals bright yellow, the upper with red splotches near the base. Mostly Feb.–May. **FRUIT** Legume tapering to base and tip, swollen at each of the 1–4 seeds, 2–9 cm long, stiffly leathery, tan; slowly dehiscent or indehiscent.

HABITAT/RANGE Native. Desert washes and flats, 0–1,000 m; se. Calif. to sw. Ariz., nw. Mexico.

SIMILAR SPECIES Foothill Palo Verde has sharply tipped twigs, and leaflets 1–3 mm long. Palo verdes, smoketrees (*Psorothamnus*, Fabaceae), crucifixion thorns (*Castela emoryi*, Simarubaceae, and *Canotia holacantha*, Celastraceae), and Spiny Allthorn (*Koeberlinia spinosa*, Koeberliniaceae) have similar habits. They are distinguished under Spiny Allthorn (p. 334).

FOOTHILL PALO VERDE *Parkinsonia microphylla* Torr.
A.K.A. YELLOW PALO VERDE, LITTLELEAF PALO VERDE

QUICK ID This stubby desert tree is yellow-green and virtually leafless. Its twigs end in a sharp point.

Quickly deciduous shrub or small tree to 8 m tall, with thick limbs and ascending, tangled branches. Twigs end in a sharp point. Trunk commonly 10–30 cm diam. **BARK** Smooth, yellow-green. **LEAF** Alternate, bipinnately compound, 15–25 mm long, petiole absent; blade forked into 2 primary segments, each with 8–14 broadly elliptic to oblong leaflets, 1–2 mm long. Glands clustered at leaf base. **FLOWER** In axillary clusters of 4–8; corolla 12–18 mm diam.; petals pale yellow, spreading, the upper petal white, later turning pale yellow, sometimes orange-flecked. Mar.–May. **FRUIT** Legume tapering to the base and tip, swollen at each of the 1–4 seeds, 4–10 cm long, stiffly leathery, tan; slowly dehiscent.

HABITAT/RANGE Native. Flats, washes, hillsides, 750–1,200 m; se. Calif., s. Ariz., nw. Mexico.

SIMILAR SPECIES Blue Palo Verde is bluish green and has hanging twigs and all-yellow flowers.

Notes This is the most common desert tree in its region, beginning to flower as the Blue Palo Verde finishes. It is slow-growing, maturing in perhaps 100 years and living to 400 years.

TEXAS PALO VERDE *Parkinsonia texana* (A. Gray) S. Watson

QUICK ID Like Blue Palo Verde, this plant has spines along the twigs, but the twigs are usually strongly zigzag and the pods are flattened.

BLUE PALO VERDE

FOOTHILL PALO VERDE

TEXAS PALO VERDE

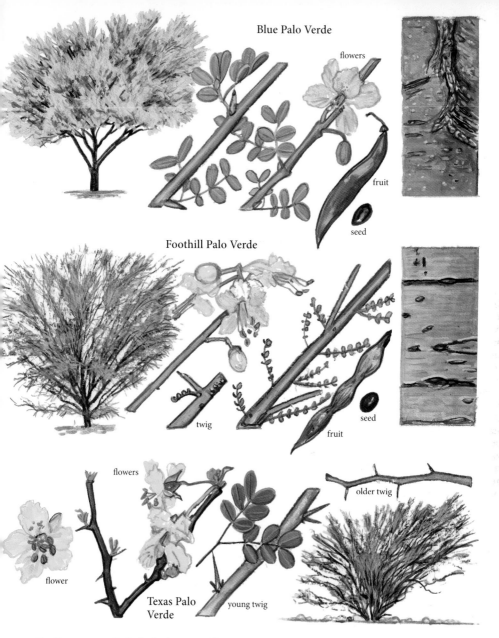

Blue Palo Verde

flowers

fruit

seed

Foothill Palo Verde

twig

seed

fruit

flowers

older twig

flower

Texas Palo Verde

young twig

Deciduous green-limbed shrub or small tree, 1–4 m tall; some branches spine-tipped. **LEAF** Bipinnately compound, 1–2 cm long, petiole about 6 mm long; primary segments 2–6, leaflets 2–6 per segment, broadly oblong, 4–6 mm long. **FLOWER** Corolla about 2 cm wide; petals yellow, upper petal red-spotted. Mar.–Jun. **FRUIT** Pod 3–5 cm long, flattened, tapering at both ends, indehiscent.

HABITAT/RANGE Native; in brush, 0–200 m; s. Tex., ne. Mexico.

Notes There are 2 varieties: in var. *macra* (I.M. Johnst.) Isely, the base of the pod is glabrous, and there are mostly 4–6 primary leaf segments; in var. *texana*, the base of the pod is pubescent, and there are mostly 2 (1 pair of) primary segments.

BUTTERCUP BUSH *Senna multiglandulosa* (Jacq.) H.S. Irwin & Barneby
A.K.A. DOWNY SENNA, GLANDULAR SENNA

QUICK ID **This shrub or small tree has pinnately compound leaves and bright yellow bilateral flowers, the upper petal 2–3 cm wide.**

Deciduous unarmed shrub or small tree to 6 m tall, with a spreading, leafy crown. Twigs, leaf stalks, young leaves, and young pods felty. **LEAF** Alternate, pinnately compound, 4–10 cm long, with 10–18 thick, lightly hairy, elliptic or oblong leaflets, each 1.5–4 cm long, usually with columnar glands between the leaflet pairs. **FLOWER** In clusters of 5–15; bilateral, bright yellow, upper petal broad, 2–3 cm wide; stamens 10, the 3 upper sterile, the fertile stamens opening by the terminal pores. Mostly Mar.–May. **FRUIT** Legume straight or curved, somewhat swollen, 8–12 cm long, 8–12 mm wide, leathery, spreading, indehiscent.

HABITAT/RANGE Introduced as an ornamental from Central and South America; now weedy in many parts of the world, including waste places in c. Calif., 0–100 m.

SIMILAR SPECIES Argentine Senna (*Senna corymbosa* [Lam.] H.S. Irwin & Barneby), a shrub or rarely a small tree, is similar to Buttercup Bush but its pinnate leaves are hairless and divided into only 4–6 leaflets; it is introduced, occasionally escaping from cultivation in c. Tex. and eastward.

Notes The 300–350 species of *Senna*, from tropical and warm temperate regions, range from herbs to shrubs and trees. The genus has been included, at least in part, within *Cassia*.

SUBFAMILY MIMOSOIDEAE: MIMOSAS AND THEIR RELATIVES

This subfamily includes the acacias, wattles, mimosas, tamarinds, blackbeads, and relatives. It largely consists of tropical and subtropical trees and shrubs, and has about 56 genera and up to 3,000 species. **LEAF** Mostly alternate, often bipinnate; many species bear glands on the petiole, rachis, or rachilla. **FLOWER** Usually bisexual, radial, small, and aggregated into heads or spikes. Petals small, not overlapping in bud. Stamens showy, 10 to many.

style
stamen
stamens with fused bases
corolla
calyx

Mimosoid Legume Flower

■ *ACACIA*: ACACIAS

Acacia has about 960 species, mostly in tropical and subtropical regions of the Southern Hemisphere, none native in the U.S. About a dozen tree species originally introduced as ornamentals have naturalized in Calif., as have a few in Fla. Acacias form a very large genus of usually evergreen shrubs and trees that are usually unarmed, but may occasionally bear spines on the stem, or have prickle-tipped leaves. They are most diverse in Australia, where there are hundreds of species.

BARK Usually hard and persistent, often furrowed, and in some species with a commercially significant tannin content. **LEAF** Usually alternate and bipinnately compound, primary segments and leaflets often in pairs and terminal segment absent, or leaf sometimes modified as a phyllode. In species in which mature plants have phyllodes, seedlings and new shoots may have compound leaves or compound segments growing from the tips of phyllodes. In compound leaves, each primary segment has an even number of leaflets, the terminal leaflet absent. **FLOWER** Usually bisexual, small, radial, consisting of 5 inconspicuous sepals and petals, and many separate, showy stamens. Grouped in globose heads or spikes, which are usually aggregated into racemes or branched inflorescences. **FRUIT** Straight, curved, or contorted, usually flat or somewhat swollen, leathery or papery legume, often constricted between the seeds, dehiscing along 1 or both sutures. Seeds usually have an enlarged, colorful, nutrient-rich aril, which forms a cap over the seed or completely covers it. The aril functions in seed dispersal by animals.

Buttercup Bush

fruit

flowers

flower

Argentine Senna

flowers

fruit

fruit

flower

Cootamundra Wattle

flowers

fruit

Acacia previously included about 1,350 species. Recent consensus and ongoing work has placed many of these in smaller genera, among which are *Mariosousa*, *Senegalia*, and *Vachellia*, as considered in this book. Many species of *Acacia* fix nitrogen, enriching the soil. Others have ornamental value. Bark and wood is used in tanning leather. Gums, dyes, oil, and timber are obtained from various species. Glands on the leaves may attract ants that may vigorously defend the plant from other animals. Plants may be very floriferous and showy, popular as ornamentals; the copious pollen, though, is allergenic to many.

COOTAMUNDRA WATTLE *Acacia baileyana* F. Muell.
A.K.A. BAILEY ACACIA

Evergreen unarmed shrub or spreading tree to 6 m tall, similar to Silver Wattle. **LEAF** Bipinnate, with 4–10 primary segments, and 24–40 linear leaflets per segment; glands between segments near tip of rachis. **FLOWER** Bright yellow. Feb.–Apr. **HABITAT/RANGE** Introduced from se. Australia; commonly planted as an ornamental in c. and s. Calif. and occasionally escaping along roadsides and other disturbed areas, 50–300 m.

KNIFELEAF WATTLE *Acacia cultriformis* A. Cunn. ex G. Don

Evergreen shrub or small tree to 5 m tall, with stiff, prickle-tipped leaves. **LEAF** Appearing simple, rounded-triangular, somewhat twisted and oriented vertically on the branch; blade to 2.5 cm long. **FLOWER** Yellow, many in dense globose heads about 1 cm diam., 5–15 heads clustered in a raceme; stamens showy. Mar.–May. **HABITAT/RANGE** Introduced from e. Australia; commonly planted in Calif., occasionally escaping, 50–300 m.

SILVER WATTLE *Acacia dealbata* Link

QUICK ID The bluish-green bipinnately compound leaves with 20–42 primary segments, and 40–130 leaflets per segment, distinguish this species

Evergreen unarmed tree, 6–15 m tall, with feathery bluish-green foliage. The spreading branches form a bluntly conical or rounded crown. Trunk erect, 1 to few, 10–30 cm diam. **BARK** Young bark smooth and gray; older bark hard, brownish black, shallowly fissured. **TWIG** Minutely angled, grayish-pubescent. **LEAF** Alternate, bipinnately compound, blade 7–16 cm long, nearly as wide, petiole short. Primary segments 20–42, overlapping, raised glands present on the rachis between, or immediately below, pairs of primary segments; leaflets 40–130 per segment, each 2–3.5 mm long, oblong, crowded and touching, thin and flexible, bluish green, minutely glandular. **FLOWER** Bright yellow, about 13–42 in globose heads 6–7 mm diam., borne in axillary or terminal sprays of racemes. Feb.–Apr.

FRUIT Legume straight or constricted between the seeds, flat, often slightly contorted, 3–8 cm long, 7–13 mm broad, papery or leathery, hairless, at first silvery blue, becoming reddish brown or blackish, spreading or hanging, dehiscent.

HABITAT/RANGE Introduced from se. Australia; cultivated in sw. Ore. and c. and s. Calif., occasionally escaping, roadsides and disturbed areas, 0–500 m.

SIMILAR SPECIES Cootamundra Wattle has fewer primary leaf segments and fewer leaflets. Green Wattle's leaves are olive green and its twigs are winged. Black Wattle has olive-green leaves, angled twigs, and glands between primary segments and also along the rachis.

Notes Silver Wattle is commonly planted as a fast-growing ornamental, but it suckers aggressively, diminishing its desirability as a street tree. In some parts of the world where it has been introduced it has become invasive. Its pollen is highly allergenic to some individuals.

GREEN WATTLE *Acacia decurrens* Willd.

Evergreen unarmed shrub or spreading tree to 15 m tall, easily confused with Silver Wattle. **TWIG** Hairless, bearing raised winglike ridges. **LEAF** Bipinnate, olive green, with 6–26 primary segments, and 40–80 well-separated linear leaflets per segment; glands on rachis not obvious. **FLOWER** Feb.–Apr. **HABITAT/RANGE** Introduced from se. Australia; cultivated and escaping, mostly near the coast in Calif. in disturbed urban areas, 0–100 m.

Knifeleaf Wattle

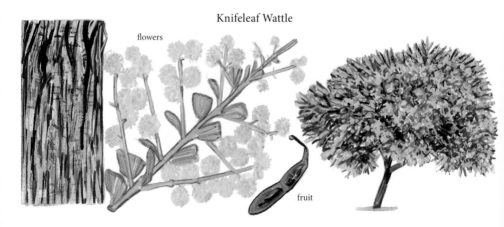

flowers

fruit

Silver Wattle

flowers

fruit

seeds

Green Wattle

Green Wattle

flowers

fruit

leaflet

Cedar Wattle

fruit

CEDAR WATTLE *Acacia elata* A. Cunn. ex Benth.

Evergreen unarmed tree, 7–20 m tall. **LEAF** Bipinnate, deep green; 4–14 primary segments, 3–22 cm long; leaflets 16–40 per segment, well spaced, lanceolate, 1–6 cm long. **FLOWER** Pale yellow to near white, many in globose heads 6–8 mm diam., the heads in loose, branched clusters. Feb.–Apr. **FRUIT** Legume flattish, 8–17 cm long, hairless. **HABITAT/RANGE** Introduced from se. Australia; uncommon, in disturbed areas, 0–100 m, c. and s. Calif.

SYDNEY GOLDEN WATTLE *Acacia longifolia* (Andrews) Willd.

Evergreen unarmed tree to 10 m tall. **LEAF** Appearing simple, more or less lanceolate, 1 edge straighter than other, deep green, 4–20 cm long, 1–3 cm broad, 2 or 3 veins prominent. **FLOWER** Pale yellow, many in paired axillary spikes 2–4 cm long; stamens showy. Jan.–Apr. **FRUIT** Legume slender, linear, round in cross section, constricted between the seeds, 5–10 cm long. **HABITAT/RANGE** Introduced from se. Australia; occasional near the coast, c. and s. Calif., 0–150 m.

BLACK WATTLE *Acacia mearnsii* De Wild.

QUICK ID This wattle has pubescent, bipinnately compound olive-green leaves with 20–36 primary segments, and 50–90 leaflets per segment.

Evergreen unarmed tree, 6–20 m tall, with olive-green foliage in clumps; grayish-pubescent nearly throughout. Trunk 10–60 cm diam.; twigs angled. **BARK** Older bark hard, brownish black, fissured. **LEAF** Alternate, bipinnately compound, olive green, 4–12 cm long, petiole 1.5–2.5 cm long; primary segments 20–36, leaflets 50–90 per segment, 1–4 mm long, short-oblong, crowded and touching. Glands at juncture between 2 paired segments, and often along rachis between segment pairs. **FLOWER** About 20–30 in globose cream-yellow heads 6–10 mm diam.; stamens showy. Feb.–Mar. **FRUIT** Legume straight or constricted between the seeds, flat, 4–15 cm long, papery, reddish brown to black.

HABITAT/RANGE Introduced from se. Australia; disturbed areas, 0–150 m; c. and s. Calif.

SIMILAR SPECIES Silver Wattle has bluish-green leaves and glands on the leaf stalk only at or immediately below the point where the segment pairs are attached.

BLACKWOOD ACACIA *Acacia melanoxylon* R. Br.

QUICK ID Elliptic olive-green leaves with 3–5 veins connected by fine netlike veins help to distinguish this acacia from others.

Evergreen unarmed tree to 20 m tall. Trunk 10–50 cm diam.; crown dense, branches ascending or spreading. **BARK** Older bark hard, furrowed. **LEAF** Alternate, appearing simple, dark, dull green, first grayish hairy, later hairless, ovate-elliptic, usually curved, with 3–5 longitudinal veins connected by fine netlike veins. Blade 7–15 cm long, 5–30 mm broad; petiole 2–5 mm long. **FLOWER** Bisexual, radial, 20–50 in globose cream-yellow to nearly white heads about 1 cm diam., in short racemes of 2–8 heads; stamens showy. Feb.–Mar. **FRUIT** Legume compressed, mostly constricted between the seeds, 5–10 cm long, 5–8 mm wide, leathery, red-brown, curved or curled, dehiscent.

HABITAT/RANGE Introduced from se. Australia; disturbed areas, mostly near the coast, 0–200 m, c. and s. Calif.

SIMILAR SPECIES Golden Wattle, Water Wattle, and Golden-wreath Wattle have only 1 prominent leaf vein. Sydney Golden Wattle has flowers in spikes.

Notes The tree can be invasive. Suckering from the roots may produce large clonal populations.

Sydney Golden Wattle

flowers

seed

dehisced fruit

Black Wattle

seeds

glands on
leaf rachis

flowers

fruit

seed with aril

flowers

fruit

seed

Blackwood Acacia

flowers

Pearl Wattle

fruit

PEARL WATTLE *Acacia podalyriifolia*
A. Cunn. ex G. Don
A.K.A. QUEENSLAND SILVER WATTLE

Evergreen unarmed shrub or tree to 7 m tall. **LEAF**
Appears simple, ovate or widely elliptic, straight,
2–4 cm long, silvery gray and densely covered
with appressed hairs, the midvein prominent and
slightly off center. **FLOWER** Golden yellow, many,
in round heads, 4–8 heads in an axillary raceme
longer than subtending leaf; stamens showy.
Nov.–Mar. **FRUIT** Legume flat, broad, margins
wavy, 4–8 cm long, pinkish gray to silvery blue.
HABITAT/RANGE Introduced from e. Australia;
commonly planted and an occasional escape in s.
Calif., 0–100 m.

GOLDEN WATTLE *Acacia pycnantha* Benth.

Evergreen unarmed shrub or small tree to 8 m tall, similar to Blackwood Acacia. **LEAF** Appears simple, sickle-shaped, with 1 prominent vein; blade 9–15 cm long; petiole 4–8 mm long. **FLOWER** Golden yellow, in globose heads, 10–30 heads in a raceme that is about as long as subtending leaf. Feb. **FRUIT** Legume more or less straight, 5–13 cm long, dark brown, hairless. **HABITAT/RANGE** Introduced from se. Australia; disturbed areas near the coast, 0–200 m, c. and s. Calif. *Notes* This is Australia's floral emblem.

WATER WATTLE *Acacia retinodes* Schltdl.

Evergreen unarmed shrub or small tree to 10 m tall. **LEAF** Appears simple, straight to slightly curved, lustrous, dark green, central vein prominent; blade 3–20 cm long; petiole base 1–3 mm long, gland above base not obvious. **FLOWER** Pale yellow or cream, in globose heads 5–7 mm diam., 5–9 heads in a raceme that is shorter than subtending leaf. Feb.–Mar. **FRUIT** Legumes flat, oblong, more or less straight, without constrictions between the seeds, 3–16 cm long, 6–18 mm broad, brown, papery, glabrous. **HABITAT/RANGE** Introduced from se. Australia; uncommon in disturbed areas near the coast, 0–900 m, c. and s. Calif.; also Fla.

GOLDEN-WREATH WATTLE *Acacia saligna* (Labill.) H.L. Wendl.
a.k.a. Blue-leaf Wattle

Evergreen shrub or small tree to 5 m tall, similar to Golden Wattle. **LEAF** Appears simple, more or less lanceolate, straight or slightly curved, dark green or blue-green, central vein prominent; blade 8–25 cm long; petiole 1–4 mm long, with an obvious gland above the base. **FLOWER** Golden yellow. Mar.–May. **HABITAT/RANGE** Introduced from sw. Australia; disturbed areas near the coast of c. and s. Calif., 0–100 m.

STAR ACACIA *Acacia verticillata* (L'Hér.) Willd.
a.k.a. Prickly Moses

Evergreen straggly shrub or small tree to 5 m tall, armed with narrow, prickle-tipped leaves. **LEAF** Appears simple, linear, stiff, 1–2 cm long, in whorls of 4–7. **FLOWER** Yellow to cream, in axillary spikes, 1–4.5 cm long, with 1–3 heads. Feb.–Apr. **FRUIT** Legume linear, swollen by the seeds, narrower between, 2.5–6 cm long, red-brown. **HABITAT/RANGE** Introduced from se. Australia; escaped, mostly near the coast, c. and s. Calif., 0–300 m.

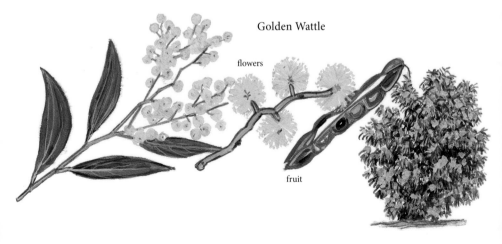

Golden Wattle

flowers

fruit

Water Wattle

fruit

flowers

Golden-wreath Wattle

fruit

flowers

Star Acacia

flowers

■ *ALBIZIA*: ALBIZIAS

A genus of 120–140 species, distributed mostly in tropical or warm regions; 4 in North America, none native. Trees are rapid-growing, providing timber for cabinetry and fuel, and shade for coffee plantations. A number of species are used as ornamentals.

Trees or shrubs, usually unarmed. **LEAF** Alternate, bipinnate; petiole and rachis glandular; leaf segments and leaflets usually in pairs. **FLOWER** Bisexual, or bisexual and unisexual male; calyx usually bell- or funnel-shaped, corolla funnel-shaped with 5 lobes; stamens numerous, joined at the base, the free part extending well beyond the tip of the corolla; inflorescence usually a densely flowered head. **FRUIT** Flat, linear or oblong legume, indehiscent or slowly dehiscent, with rounded or ovoid seeds.

SILKTREE *Albizia julibrissin* Durazz.
A.K.A. Mimosa, Powderpuff-tree

Deciduous tree to about 15 m tall. Single short trunk, often leaning and with several large ascending branches; crown spreading, roughly flat-topped. **BARK** Light gray, smooth to slightly roughened. **LEAF** Bipinnate, with 10–30 primary segments; 30–60 leaflets per segment. Leaflets oblong, 5–15 mm long, 2–4 mm broad; margins entire, upper margin of leaflet more or less straight, lower curved; main vein of leaflet near upper margin. Leaflets fold together at night, possibly a water-conserving mechanism. **FLOWER** Small, tubular, many produced in a showy head, 4–6 cm diam., with a single bisexual flower in the center surrounded by numerous male flowers; stamens about 2.5 cm long, pink and white, showy. May–Jul. **FRUIT** Flattened, straight-sided legume to 20 cm long, 2–3 cm broad, stiffly papery, light brown. **HABITAT/RANGE** Introduced from Asia; disturbed areas, 0–500 m, c. and sw. Calif.; widely planted as a fast-growing ornamental, occasionally escaped elsewhere in the West.

WOMAN'S TONGUE *Albizia lebbeck* (L.) Benth.

Deciduous tree or shrub to 15 m tall; crown spreading, more or less flat-topped. **LEAF** Alternate to subopposite, bipinnate, 15–20 cm long, about twice as broad, usually with 4–8 opposite or subopposite primary segments 5–20 cm long; 6–20 leaflets per segment, each 1.5–6 cm long, 0.5–3.5 cm broad, oblong or narrowly elliptic, main vein off-center, nearer the upper margin of the leaflet. Gland near base of petiole and often between segments. **FLOWER** Small, tubular, 15–40 in a showy head 4–9 cm diam.; stamens about 1.5–3 cm long, white to cream, yellowish in age, showy. Apr.–Sep. **FRUIT** Flat legume, 12–35 cm long, 3–6 cm broad, yellowish brown. **HABITAT/RANGE** Introduced from Asia and widely planted as an ornamental; reported from Calif. and Tex. in disturbed areas at low elevations but probably not naturalized; invasive in Fla.

PLUME ALBIZIA *Albizia lophantha* (Willd.) Benth.
A.K.A. Crested Wattle, Stinkbean

Evergreen unarmed tree or shrub, 5–8 m tall; crown broad, round. **LEAF** Bipinnate, up to 20 cm long, with 14–30 primary segments, each segment with 40–80 oblong, crowded leaflets, each 5–10 mm long. **FLOWER** Small, 40–70 in tight, cylindric, stalked, nodding, axillary spikes 3–8 cm long, about 2.5 cm wide; stamens 95–150 per flower, 1 cm long, greenish cream. May–Jul. **FRUIT** Legume flat, 4–10 cm long, leathery, brown. **HABITAT/RANGE** Introduced from sw. Australia; near the coast, 0–300 m, c. and s. Calif. Sometimes considered to be *Paraserianthes lophantha* (Willd.) I.C. Nielsen.

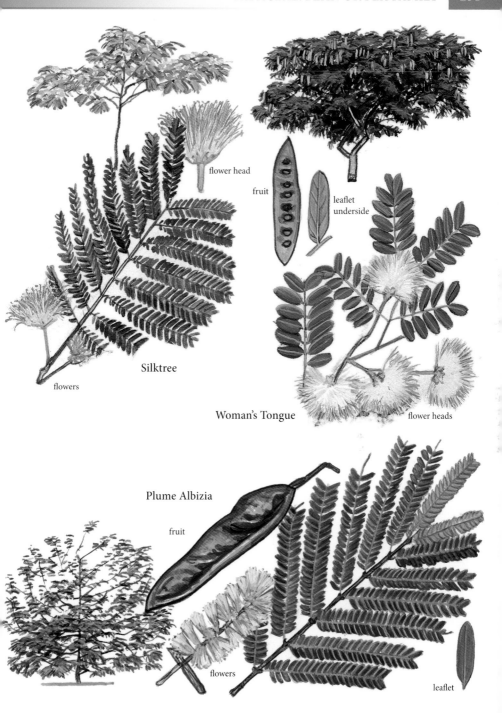

flower head

fruit

leaflet
underside

Silktree

flowers

Woman's Tongue

flower heads

Plume Albizia

fruit

flowers

leaflet

TEXAS EBONY *Ebenopsis ebano*
(Berland.) Barneby & J.W.Grimes
A.K.A. ÉBANO, EBONY BLACKHEAD

QUICK ID This dense, spiny evergreen shrub or tree has bipinnate leaves with few segments and leaflets. Its flowers are in spikes.

Evergreen (or dropping leaves just before flowering or during drought), formidably armed shrub or tree to 9 m tall. Trunk 10–100 cm diam.; dense, round crown of short, forking branches. **BARK** Smoky gray, smooth when young, rough and fissured with age. **TWIG** Zigzag, very flexible, at nodes bearing pairs of sharp spines 6–12 mm long. **LEAF** Alternate, bipinnately compound, dark green and lustrous above, paler below, 3–5 cm long, petiole 8–25 mm long; primary segments 2–6; leaflets 6–12 per segment, 5–12 mm long, oval or obovate. A raised gland occurs between the lowest pair of segments. **FLOWER** Small, bisexual, radial, pale yellow or cream, clustered near the ends of twigs in spikes 2–3 cm long. Sepals and petals tiny; stamens many, showy, about 8 mm long. May–Oct. **FRUIT** Legume straight or curved, 10–30 cm long, hard and thick-walled, dark brown to black, hanging, persisting for a year or more, slow to dehisce; seeds held tightly in compartments.

HABITAT/RANGE Native. Wooded or brushy areas, 0–100 m; s. Tex., Mexico.

Notes *Ebenopsis*, often placed in *Pithecellobium*, is a small Mexican genus of 3 species that occur in thickets and dry tropical woodlands at low elevations. One ranges as far north as s. Tex. Texas Ebony is usually seen as a shrub along roads, or occasionally as a small tree. In remnant woodland along the lower Rio Grande it may be massive. It is also a popular, slow-growing shade tree in regions with minimal winter cold. It is not a true ebony (reserved for *Diospyros* in Ebenaceae). Its dense,

dark red to purplish wood (so heavy it will not float in water) is used for fence posts and high-quality novelty items.

TENAZA *Havardia pallens* (Benth.) Britton & Rose
A.K.A. MIMOSA BUSH

QUICK ID Tenaza has slender, spreading branches and lacy bipinnate leaves with finely hairy leaflets and a single cup-shaped gland between, or just below, the lowest pair of primary segments.

Evergreen or drought-deciduous, lightly armed, lacy shrub, or occasionally a small tree to 10 m tall. Spines 6–16 mm long, in pairs at nodes, best developed on fast-growing parts. **LEAF** Alternate, bipinnately compound, 8–15 cm long, with 6–12 primary segments; leaflets 14–40 per segment, narrow, 3–8 mm long, finely hairy, pale grayish green. Cup-shaped gland between, or just below, the lowest pair of segments. **FLOWER** Small, sweetly scented, globose white heads, 15–20 mm diam., held in branched clusters; stamens many. May–Aug. **FRUIT** Legume straight, flat but bulging at the seeds, 5–13 cm long, velvety or hairless, red-brown, hanging, promptly dehiscing.

HABITAT/RANGE Native. Brushy areas, 0–50 m; s Texas, e. Mexico.

Notes *Havardia*, from warm, dry regions of North America, consists of about 5 species of trees and shrubs.

■ *LEUCAENA*: LEADTREES

There are 22 species of leadtree; all are originally from warm parts of the Americas, but now several species have been planted worldwide throughout the tropics. They are a common component of tropical evergreen and deciduous forests, most losing their leaves in the dry season. In Latin America the trees are grown by rural people for their edible seeds, but caution is advised because seeds of some species are toxic. In the West, 2 species are native and 1 has been introduced. Most species

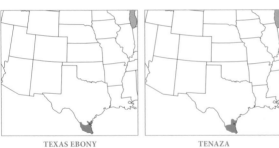

TEXAS EBONY   TENAZA

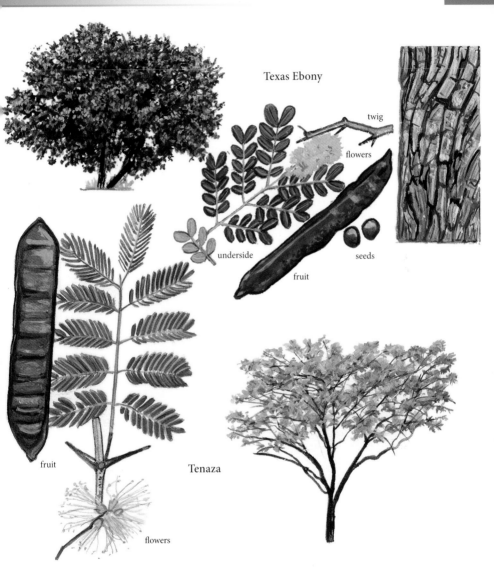

Texas Ebony

twig

flowers

underside

seeds

fruit

fruit

Tenaza

flowers

are cold-sensitive, limiting northern distribution of the genus. In frostless climates plants occur from sea-level to moderate elevations.

Leadtrees are unarmed shrubs or small trees with weak or brittle stems and branches. They are rapid-growing, are an important source of fuel in many tropical countries, and are used as shade trees in coffee plantations. **BARK** Young bark is smooth; older bark is often scaly. **LEAF** Alternate, bipinnately compound, without a terminal segment,

the primary segments in pairs, with few to many pairs of leaflets with entire margins; terminal leaflet absent. Nectar-secreting glands 1 or more on the rachis and sometimes on the rachillas between the leaflets. **FLOWER** Small, radial, and bisexual, aggregated into dense, globose white to yellow heads, the stamens protruding and showy. Calyx narrowly bell-shaped, with 5 teeth; petals 5, small, separate. Stamens 10. **FRUIT** Flat, hanging, dehiscent papery or leathery legume with a stalklike base.

GOLDENBALL LEADTREE *Leucaena retusa* Benth.
A.K.A. LITTLELEAF LEADTREE, LEMONBALL, WAHOOTREE

QUICK ID This shrub or small tree has bipin-nately compound leaves with 4–10 primary segments and 6–16 leaflets per segment

Deciduous or evergreen shrub or small tree to 8 m tall, with an irregular, flattened, broad crown. **BARK** Light gray to brown, smooth when young, later breaking into small, thin scales. **LEAF** Alternate, bipinnately compound, bluish green or bright green, pubescent or glabrous; blade 8–20 cm long, petiole about 2–3 cm long; primary segments 4–10; leaflets 6–16 per segment, oblong to elliptic, 8–25 mm long. Leafstalk glands raised, between most pairs of segments, smaller glands between many pairs of leaflets. **FLOWER** Many, in globose yellow heads, 2–3 cm diam., borne in open, branched clusters or singly on slender stalks. Apr.–Oct., especially after heavy rain. **FRUIT** Legume straight, linear, flat, papery, 8–25 cm long; tapered at the base to a short stalk.

HABITAT/RANGE Native. Rocky limestone, 500–1,700 m; se. N.M., w. Tex., n. Mexico.

SIMILAR SPECIES White Leadtree and Great Leadtree have white to cream flowers and more leaflets per segment.

Notes Goldenball Leadtree is said to be evergreen in references. In the West it is winter-deciduous, which also corresponds to the dry season in its region.

WHITE LEADTREE *Leucaena leucocephala* (Lam.) de Wit
A.K.A. JUMBIE BEAN

Deciduous or evergreen erect shrub or small tree to about 5 m tall; crown spreading. **LEAF** Bipinnate, 8–10 cm long, about 13 cm broad, with 8–18 primary segments. Leaflets 20–40 per segment, oblong, 8–14 mm long, grayish green, folding together at night. **FLOWER** Aggregated in rounded, creamy-white heads, 1–2 cm diam., stalk 2–3 cm long. Year-round. **FRUIT** Legume flat, reddish brown, 8–15 cm long, 2–4 cm broad, in crowded, dangling clusters. **HABITAT/RANGE** Introduced from the West Indies, considered invasive in the U.S.; well established in Fla., naturalized in s. and e. Tex., weedy in urban areas in s. Ariz., planted in Calif., 0–600 m.

GREAT LEADTREE *Leucaena pulverulenta* (Schltdl.) Benth.
A.K.A. MEXICAN LEADTREE

QUICK ID An unarmed tree with feathery, bipinnate leaves, many small leaflets, and flat, stalked pods.

Drought-deciduous, brittle tree, 6–20 m tall; trunk 10–70 cm diam. **BARK** Gray to brown, at first smooth, later broken into narrow scales. **LEAF** Alternate, bipinnately compound, dull green, mostly glabrous; blade 10–25 cm long, 8–10 cm wide, petiole 3–8 cm; primary segments 20–40; leaflets 40–60 per segment, oblong, 4–5 mm long. Leafstalk gland dark, depressed, on the rachis below the 1st segment pair. **FLOWER** Many, in globose white to cream-yellow heads, 1–2 cm diam., borne in open, branched clusters. Mar.–Jun. **FRUIT** Legume straight, oblong, flat, stiffly papery, 8–25 cm long; stalk at base 1–4 cm long.

HABITAT/RANGE Native. Thickets and woodlands, 0–100 m; s. Tex., e. Mexico.

SIMILAR SPECIES White Leadtree has longer and fewer leaflets. Goldenball Leadtree has fewer primary segments and fewer leaflets per segment.

GOLDENBALL LEADTREE   GREAT LEADTREE

Goldenball Leadtree

flowers

fruit

flower head

seeds

fruit

White Leadtree

flower head

seed

Great Leadtree

flowers

LITTLELEAF FALSE TAMARIND
Lysiloma watsonii Rose
A.K.A. FEATHERTREE

QUICK ID This feathery tree is similar to those of *Leucaena*, but the flowers have more stamens, and, in *Lysiloma*, the margins of the pods separate from the sides at dehiscence.

Usually deciduous, widely spreading, unarmed shrub or small tree, 1–3 m tall (to 15 m in Mexico). **LEAF** Alternate, bipinnately compound, without a terminal segment; primary segments 8–18; leaflets 30–66 per segment, oblong, 4–5 mm long, finely hairy on both sides; petiole with a conical gland just below the lower pair of segments, often similar glands between other leaf segments. **FLOWER** Bisexual, tiny, white, in loose clusters of globose heads 1.5 cm diam.; stamens 25–30, 8–10 mm long. Mar.–Apr., and after summer rains. **FRUIT** Straight, flat, oblong legume, swollen around the seeds, stiff-papery, reddish brown, hairless, 12–22 cm long, 1.5–2.5 cm broad, the sides separating from wiry margins at maturity.

HABITAT/RANGE Native; dry, rocky slopes, 850–1,200 m; Rincon Mountains, sc. Ariz., nw. Mexico.

Notes In Arizona this species is damaged by winter cold. *Lysiloma*, the false tamarind genus, comprises about 35 species, mostly of the American tropics. Two species are native to the U.S., one occurring in the West.

LITTLELEAF FALSE TAMARIND

FERNLEAF ACACIA *Mariosousa millefolia* (S. Watson) Siegler & Ebinger
A.K.A. MILFOIL WATTLE, SANTA RITA ACACIA

QUICK ID Fernleaf Acacia is distinguished by the combination of comparatively large leaves with many small leaflets, very short, slender spines (if any), and flowers in spikes.

Semi-deciduous shrub or, rarely, a small tree, 1–3 m tall, retaining petioles and rachises well after the leaflets have fallen. **LEAF** Alternate, bipinnately compound, blade 6–23 cm long; 12–28 segments, terminal segment absent; leaflets 40–74 per segment, 2–4 mm long, hairless above, with appressed hairs beneath; tip narrowly pointed. Stalked, globose gland on rachis between each of 1 or 2 pairs of terminal segments. Spines at base of petiole very slender, 2–3 mm long, often absent. **FLOWER** Cream, tiny, usually in a single axillary spike 3–8 cm long; petals small; stamens many, showy, 4–7 mm long. Jul.–Aug. **FRUIT** Flat, straight, oblong, stiffly papery legume, 7–17 cm long, 1–2 cm broad, yellowish tan, hairless.

HABITAT/RANGE Native; desert grasslands, brush, oak woodland, 1,200–1,700 m; se. Ariz. and adjacent corner of N.M.

Notes *Mariosousa*, a genus of 13 species once included in *Acacia*, occurs mostly in subtropical or tropical Mexico and Central America in shrubby or woodland vegetation at low to moderate elevations.

FERNLEAF ACACIA

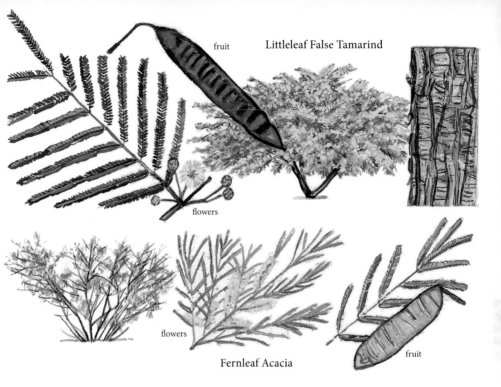

fruit

Littleleaf False Tamarind

flowers

flowers

Fernleaf Acacia

fruit

◼ *PROSOPIS*: MESQUITES

There are about 45 species of mesquite, most occurring in warm, dry regions of the world, many contributing to the diversity of deciduous thorn forests. Three extend naturally northward into warm areas of the West; a fourth has been introduced. American species have been widely introduced throughout the temperate and tropical regions of the world. Cold winters limit their spread.

These long-lived, clump-forming shrubs or short-trunked trees with contorted branches are ubiquitous from e. Tex. to c. Ariz., forming open or dense brushlands and woodlands on flats and hills. The plants are leafless in winter, then in mid-spring leaf out with fresh, bright yellow-green expanding leaves that turn dark green by summer. By late summer clusters of pods hang from the branches, later dropping to the ground. In the winter the zig-zag nature of the twigs is evident, as are the pale, stout, sharp, paired spines at the nodes.
BARK The youngest bark is bright green and smooth, turning red-brown to gray by the end of the 2nd year. Mature bark on the trunk is thick, dark brown to blackish, furrowed and scaly. **LEAF** Alternate, most tightly clustered on spur twigs, bipinnately compound, each leaf with 1 or 2 (occasionally 3) pairs of primary segments forming a V;

terminal segment absent. Each segment has many crowded to well-spaced leaflets; terminal leaflet absent. In the fork between terminal segments, there is usually a small spine. **FLOWER** Bisexual, tiny, radially symmetric, greenish white, aggregated into axillary cylindric spikes a few centimeters long; sepals 5, joined at the base, these and the 5 petals about ½ the length of the 10 protruding stamens. **FRUIT** Legumes usually hanging in clusters, each legume straight or curved, with constrictions between the seeds, or in one of our species, tightly coiled with little indication of constrictions. The pod is very pulpy and sweet. Hard seeds are embedded in the pulp.

Mesquites are very drought-tolerant, their deep roots tapping ground water, their shallow, spreading roots absorbing water from light rains. The seeds require scarification of the seed coat to germinate, and thus trees are common along roadways where seeds may be scratched by passing vehicles. The seeds are also spread by cattle as they feed upon the sweet pods, the undigested seeds passing through the gut to germinate in open spots in grassland. Many hectares of once good rangeland are now covered in continuous noxious brush. The wood is valued for high-quality fuel and lumber, and the flowers produce a fine, light honey. Native peoples used the nutritious pod as a sweetener and a food.

HONEY MESQUITE *Prosopis glandulosa* Torr.

a.k.a. Mesquite, Torrey Mesquite

QUICK ID This is a multistemmed shrub or tree, with forked, bipinnate leaves that have long, well-spaced, oblong, hairless leaflets. The flowers are small and cream, and held in dense spikes.

Deciduous spiny, irregularly round-crowned tree or shrub, 1–10 m tall, sometimes to 15 m, with drooping compound leaves. The trunk is usually low-branching, 10–80 cm diam. **BARK** Young bark greenish brown to gray, soon becoming brown to blackish brown, scaly, and shallowly longitudinally fissured. **TWIG** Zigzag twigs often hairless, often armed at the nodes with 1 or 2 stout, sharp, pale spines up to 5 cm long and 6 mm thick at the base, easily capable of puncturing automobile tires; spines most frequent and largest on rapidly growing stems. **LEAF** Bipinnately compound, flexible, on a hairless, dark green petiole 2–15 cm long, forked into usually 1 pair (rarely 2) of primary segments, each 6–17 cm long. Leaflets 12–20 per segment, spaced 7–18 mm apart, each leaflet narrowly oblong, 1–3.5 (sometimes to 6) cm long. **FLOWER** Many in pale greenish-cream spikes 5–14 cm long and about 15 mm wide. Mar.–Sep. **FRUIT** Pendent, more or less cylindric legume 8–20 cm long, constricted between the 5–18 seeds, fleshy-walled, hairless, straw yellow, often blushed with rose when fresh.

HABITAT/RANGE Native. Arid grasslands to thorn scrub, 0–1,800 m; se. Calif. to w. Mo., s. La., and n. Mexico. Honey Mesquite is a troublesome range weed, and has spread beyond its natural range, particularly to the East (shown on the map by dots added to the periphery of its original range).

SIMILAR SPECIES Screwbean Mesquite has a coiled pod. Velvet Mesquite has finely hairy leaflets. **Smooth Mesquite** (*P. laevigata* [Humb. & Bonpl.

ex Willd.] M.C. Johnst.) has 40–60 close-set leaflets per segment, each leaflet 4–9 mm long; it is known from a single, presumably introduced individual (and its hybrids with Honey Mesquite) in s. Tex.

Notes There are 2 varieties of Honey Mesquite. Var. *glandulosa* has leaflets mostly 30–45 mm long, 8–15 times as long as wide, mostly 12–26 per segment. It is commonly a tree from w. Tex. eastward, but has been widely introduced in the Southwest as an ornamental. Var. *torreyana* (L.D. Benson) M.C. Johnst. has leaflets mostly 15–25 mm long, 5–8 times as long as wide, mostly 20–30 per segment. It is commonly a clumped shrub or small tree from w. Tex. westward.

SCREWBEAN MESQUITE *Prosopis pubescens* Benth.

a.k.a. Screwbean, Tornillo

QUICK ID The combination of forked bipinnate leaves and the unusual, tightly coiled pods hanging in clusters from the twigs is unique.

Deciduous spiny, open, ragged-crowned tree or shrub to 10 m tall; 1 to several trunks to 30 cm diam. **BARK** Young bark greenish brown to gray; when older, dark brown or blackish, thick and fissured into shaggy strips. **TWIG** Long and slender, finely hairy, often with 1 or 2 slender white spines 8–12 mm long at the nodes. **LEAF** Bipinnately compound, flexible, grayish green and minutely hairy; blade 3–8 cm long, petiole 8–15 mm long; usually 1 pair (rarely 2) of primary segments. Leaflets 10–16 per segment, well spaced, each leaflet oblong, 6–15 mm long. **FLOWER** Many in pale greenish-cream spikes 3–8 cm long. May–Jun. **FRUIT** Legume with up to 20 coils, like a tight bedspring, 2.5–5 cm long, 4–6 mm diam., yellow-tan to brown, several in a cluster.

HABITAT/RANGE Native. Along watercourses, outwash fans, road banks, 50–1,700 m; se. Calif. to sw. Utah, eastward to Tex., n. Mexico.

SIMILAR SPECIES Other mesquites in the region also have forked, bipinnate leaves, but the pods are straight. Honey Mesquite has well-spaced hairless leaflets; in Velvet Mesquite they are lightly hairy and close together rather than well spaced.

HONEY MESQUITE   SCREWBEAN MESQUITE

Honey Mesquite

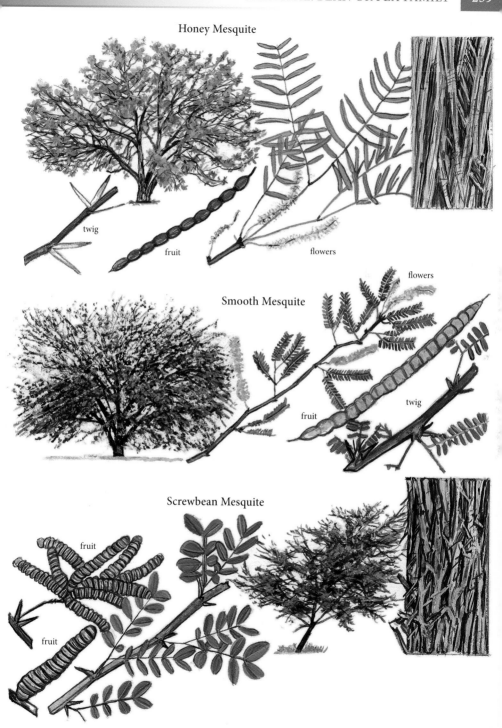

twig

fruit

flowers

Smooth Mesquite

flowers

fruit

twig

Screwbean Mesquite

fruit

fruit

VELVET MESQUITE *Prosopis velutina*
Wooton

QUICK ID This mesquite has bipinnate leaves, usually some with 2 pairs of primary segments, the closely spaced leaflets very finely velvety.

Deciduous spiny tree or large shrub, 9–15 m tall, with a round crown of twisted branches. Trunk low-branching, up to 60 cm diam. **BARK** At first smooth and greenish; later dark brown to blackish, shredding into shaggy strips and flakes. **LEAF** Bipinnately compound, grayish green; blade 7–15 cm long, petiole 1–4 cm long; usually some leaves forked into 2 pairs (sometimes 1 or 3) of primary segments 7–15 cm long; leaflets 28–48 per segment, elliptic-oblong, each 8–13 mm long, almost touching, minutely velvety. **FLOWER** Pale greenish cream, in spikes, very similar to Honey Mesquite. Mar.–May. **FRUIT** Legume, 8–20 cm long, tan, mottled with reddish or black.

HABITAT/RANGE Native. Roadsides, arid grasslands, outwash fans, along watercourses, 200–1,700 m; s. Ariz. to sw. N.M. and nw. Mexico, west to Calif. and s. Nev., where probably introduced.

SIMILAR SPECIES Honey Mesquite has widely separated, hairless leaflets.

■ *SENEGALIA*: CATCLAWS

The genus *Senegalia* contains about 200 species widely distributed in the tropics and subtropics. The 4 species in the West occur from sea-level to moderate elevations in areas with only minimal freezing. The catclaws are evergreen or deciduous (in evergreen species, leaves often lost during drought) shrubs or small trees, ours with curved catclaw-like prickles scattered on the stem, sometimes clustered at the nodes, but true stipular spines are lacking. Instead, stipules are small and not persistent. Species of *Senegalia* were earlier considered to be members of the genus *Acacia*.

LEAF Alternate; in some, 2 or 3 leaves clustered on short spurs; bipinnately compound, primary segments in pairs, terminal segment and terminal leaflet absent; usually at least 1 raised gland on petiole or rachis. **FLOWER** Bisexual, tiny, radial, many in globose heads or spikes, which themselves may be aggregated into racemes or branched inflorescences. Each flower has 4 or 5 inconspicuous sepals and petals, and many showy, separate stamens. Ovary often stalked, with the base of the stalk surrounded by a donut-shaped thickening. **FRUIT** Flattened legume with papery walls, often slowly dehiscent. Unlike *Acacia*, seeds do not have showy arils.

GUAJILLO *Senegalia berlandieri* (Benth.)
Britton & Rose
A.K.A. BERLANDIER ACACIA

QUICK ID Distinguished by curved prickles along the twigs in combination with flowers in globose heads and, on average, a greater number of primary leaf segments and leaflets than other *Senegalia* in the region.

Shrub or small tree to 5 m tall, dropping leaves during drought, usually armed with curved prickles 3–10 mm long. **LEAF** Bipinnately compound, blade 8–15 cm long, with 8–22 or more primary segments, each segment usually with 24–100 (sometimes more) linear leaflets 3–4 mm long; depressed gland near the top of the petiole. **FLOWER** Many, cream, in a globose cluster 10–15 mm diam., the clusters in a branched, conical inflorescence. Nov.–Mar. **FRUIT** Legume, 5–20 cm long, 1–2.5 cm broad, flat, velvety when young, tan to brown when mature.

HABITAT/RANGE Native; limestone flats, hills, 0–850 m; s. Tex., ne. Mexico.

VELVET MESQUITE

GUAJILLO

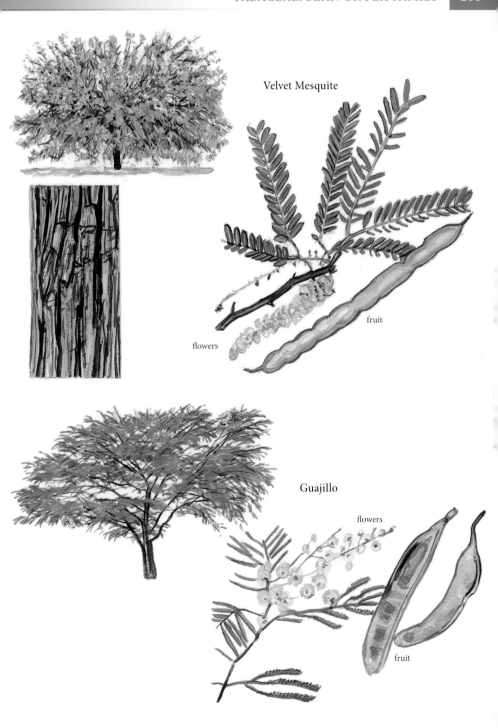

Velvet Mesquite

flowers

fruit

Guajillo

flowers

fruit

CATCLAW ACACIA *Senegalia greggii*
(A. Gray) Britton & Rose
A.K.A. WAIT-A-MINUTE TREE

QUICK ID The flat-based, catclaw-like prickles and cylindric cream flower clusters serve to distinguish this species.

Deciduous prickly shrub or small tree to 1–9 m tall, crooked, stiffly branched. Trunk short, 20–30 cm diam.; crown often broader than tall. **BARK** When mature, thin, grayish to nearly black, shallowly furrowed, with small, thin scales on older trunks. **TWIG** Pale brown to reddish or grayish, finely hairy or glabrous, with formidable scattered recurved, dark brown or gray prickles 3–6 mm long, flat at the base. **LEAF** Alternate or mostly 2 or 3 leaves in clusters on short, scaly spur twigs; bipinnately compound, thin and flexible, grayish green, nearly hairless to densely and finely hairy; blade 2.5–8 cm long, nearly as wide, petiole 4–20 mm long. Primary segments 2–8; leaflets 6–14 per segment, obovate to oblong, 4–6 mm long. A concave gland is present on the rachis at the junction of the lowest pair of primary segments. **FLOWER** Aggregated into dense white to cream-yellow spikes 3.5–7 cm long borne on leafy spur twigs. Apr.–Oct., commonly after rains. **FRUIT** Papery legume, often reddish, hairless, swollen at the seeds and mostly constricted between them, 5–10 cm long, on a slender stalk 2–5 cm long, often twisted and contorted at maturity. Fruits often abundant, spreading or hanging on the tree unopened for most of the winter.

HABITAT/RANGE Native. Gravelly mesas, canyonsides, washes, 100–1,800 m; s. Calif. to sw. Utah, w. Tex.

SIMILAR SPECIES Catclaw Acacia is most easily confused with **Catclaw Mimosa** (*Mimosa aculeaticarpa* Ortega), a common shrub in the Southwest. Its prickles are more numerous and not so prominently flattened or recurved; spurs are lacking or much less obvious; leaves usually have more primary segments and leaflets per segment, the leaflets 1–5 mm long; flowers are white to pink, in globose clusters; there are prickles along the seams of the pod. Texas Catclaw has thickly papery pods that usually are not twisted at maturity.

Notes The prickles on this well-named tree, each resembling a cat's claw, often snag hikers, requiring them to pause to free clothing or skin from the sharp points. There are 2 varieties of Catclaw Acacia: Var. *greggii* has leaves hairless or only slightly hairy and is widespread across Tex.; var. *arizonica* Isely has leaves minutely, densely hairy, often grayish, and occurs from N.M. westward. The varieties apparently intergrade in w. Tex.

ROEMER ACACIA *Senegalia roemeriana* (Scheele) Britton & Rose
A.K.A. ROUNDFLOWER CATCLAW

QUICK ID This species has slender branches, bipinnate leaves with 2–6 primary segments, catclaw prickles, and white balls of flowers.

Evergreen shrub or small tree, 1–4 m tall, with diffuse, weak, slender branches. Trunk to 60 cm diam. **BARK** Bark gray to brown, with small, thin scales when older. **TWIG** Usually armed with abundant short, catclaw-like prickles. **LEAF** Bipinnately compound, blade blocky in outline and V-tipped, 3–10 cm long, petiole about ⅓–½ length of blade. Primary segments usually 2–6; leaflets 6–24 per segment, elliptic or oblong, mostly 5–9 mm long. Glands on petiole or rachis inconspicuous or lacking. **FLOWER** Fragrant, many in globose cream-yellow to greenish-white heads 1 cm diam., arrayed along the branches on stalks 1–3 cm long. Mar.–May, or after rains. **FRUIT** Oblong legume, straight or curved, flat, thickly papery, 5–10 cm long, 2–3 cm wide, reddish, slowly dehiscent.

HABITAT/RANGE Native. Areas of brush on limestone, 300–1,000 m; s. N.M., c. and sw. Tex., n. Mexico.

SIMILAR SPECIES White-thorn Acacia (*Vachellia constricta*) usually has pale, needlelike spines at nodes. The leaves may be divided into few primary segments, but leaflets average 2–6 mm long.

CATCLAW ACACIA

ROEMER ACACIA

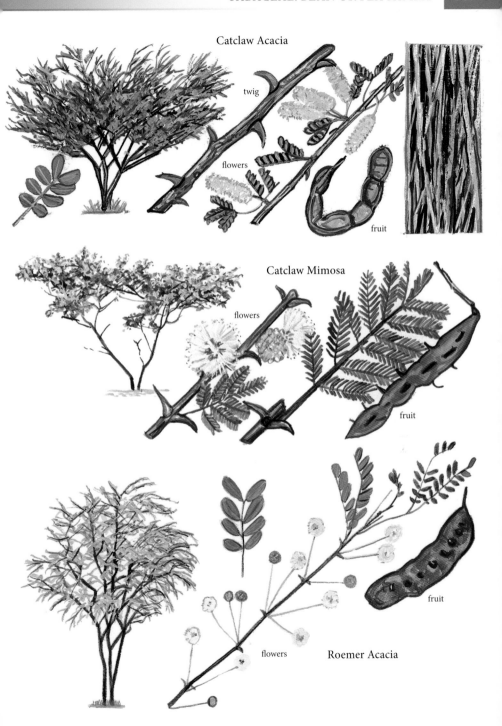

Catclaw Acacia

twig

flowers

fruit

Catclaw Mimosa

flowers

fruit

flowers

Roemer Acacia

fruit

TEXAS CATCLAW *Senegalia wrightii*
(Benth.) Britton & Rose
A.K.A. WRIGHT CATCLAW, UÑA DE GATO

QUICK ID This is very similar to Catclaw Acacia, but its pods are not twisted.

Evergreen shrub or small tree to 9 m tall, the branches armed with catclaw-like prickles 6 mm long. **LEAF** Bipinnate, with 2–4 primary segments, each segment with 4–12 oblong leaflets 5–9 mm long; a stalked gland is present between the lower pair of segments. **FLOWER** Many, in cream-yellow spikes 2–6 cm long. Mar.–May. **FRUIT** Legume flattened, stiffly papery, more or less constricted between the seeds, usually not twisting at maturity, 5–10 cm long, 2.5–3.5 cm broad, reddish.

HABITAT/RANGE Native; brushy slopes and flats, 0–500 m, c. and s. Tex., n. Mexico.

Notes Intergrades with Catclaw Acacia in c. Tex.; sometimes considered a variety of that species.

■ *VACHELLIA*: VACHELLIAS

The genus *Vachellia* has more than 150 species, found in the tropics and subtropics. Six occur in the West from sea-level to moderate elevations in areas with only minimal freezing; of these, three may become trees. Species of *Vachellia* were earlier considered to be in the genus *Acacia*.

Vachellias are generally deciduous shrubs or small trees, usually with paired, mostly straight (in ours) or variously enlarged stipular spines at the nodes. **LEAF** Alternate, bipinnately compound, lacking a terminal segment. Usually there is at least 1 raised gland on the petiole or rachis. **FLOWER** Bisexual, tiny, radial, many, usually in dense globose heads held on slender stalks; near the middle or at the top of the stalk usually is a pair of bracts. Individual flower consists of 4 or 5 inconspicuous sepals and petals, and many separate stamens that form the showy part of flower. **FRUIT** Flat or cylindric legume, with papery or leathery walls, dehiscent or not. The seed rarely has an aril.

WHITE-THORN ACACIA *Vachellia constricta* (Benth.) Seigler & Ebinger
A.K.A. WHITE THORN, MESCAT ACACIA

QUICK ID This arid-land shrub or tree may be recognized by the combination of paired pale spines at the nodes, globose heads of flowers, and 8–12 primary leaf segments.

Deciduous shrub or small tree to 6 m tall, crown open and more or less inversely conical. **TWIG** Often armed at the nodes with paired, straight or very slightly curved white or pale brown spines 1–4 cm long. **LEAF** Alternate, bipinnately compound, blade 2.5–5 cm long, glabrous or more or less hairy; primary segments usually 8–12, leaflets 12–32 per segment, oblong to linear, 2–6 mm long. Glands often between pairs of segments on the rachis and on the petiole. **FLOWER** Many, in dense, globose, bright yellow heads 6–9 mm diam. Mar.–May, and often later after rains. **FRUIT** Slender, hanging, straight to strongly curved legume, usually constricted between the seeds, 4–10 cm long, red-brown, stiffly papery, dehiscent.

HABITAT/RANGE Native. Dry slopes, flats, washes, 450–2,000 m; s. Ariz. to w. Tex. and n. Mexico.

SIMILAR SPECIES Viscid Acacia has leaves appearing varnished, each with only 2–6 primary segments.

TEXAS CATCLAW

WHITE-THORN ACACIA

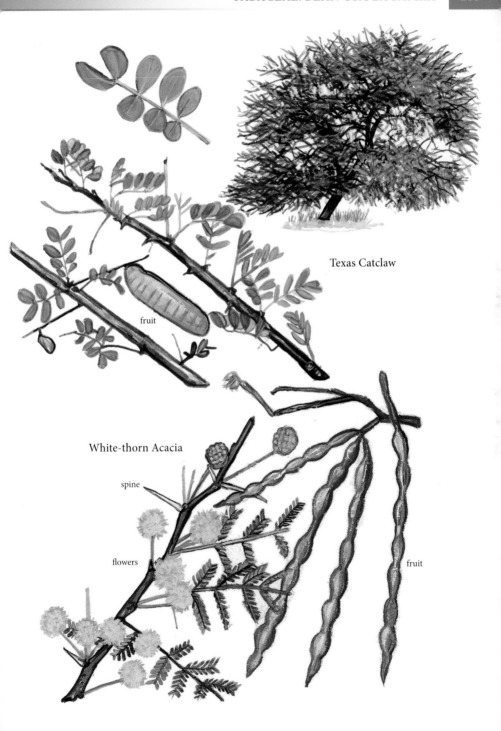

Texas Catclaw

fruit

White-thorn Acacia

spine

flowers

fruit

HUISACHE *Vachellia farnesiana* (L.)
Wight & Arn.
A.K.A. SWEET ACACIA

QUICKID Recognized by the combination of alternate, bipinnate leaves with small leaflets, globular yellow flower clusters, hairy petiole and rachis, and by the leaflets usually having evident secondary venation.

Deciduous shrub or small tree to about 9 m tall, crown round or flattened, usually broader than high, often an inverted cone, very densely branched. Trunks 1 to several, flaring outward, up to 45 cm diam. **BARK** Dark grayish brown, thin, smooth when young, scaly when older. **TWIG** Zigzig, armed at the nodes with paired, straight, pin-like, pale spines to 4 cm long. **LEAF** Often crowded on short spur twigs, bipinnately compound, dark green, hairy; blade 2–10 cm long, petiole 6–10 mm long. Primary segments 4–16, rachis hairy. Leaflets 20–50 per segment, linear-oblong, 3–6 mm long, smaller veins usually evident on the lower surface. Gland often at the middle of the petiole, and another sometimes on the rachis between the upper pair of segments. **FLOWER** Bright yellow, produced in globose clusters 1–1.3 cm in diam.; the clusters on stalks 1.5–3 cm long. Stalks may or may not have small bracts at the middle (represented by a small bump if bracts have dropped). Feb.–Mar. **FRUIT** Flattened, more or less curved, leathery legume, 5–8 cm long, purplish red to blackish, tardily dehiscent.

HABITAT/RANGE Native. Open, disturbed places, woodland borders, 0–1,500 m; Calif. (where apparently introduced) across the South to Fla., south to s. South America.

Notes This widespread group of trees and shrubs is taxonomically complex, provided with many names that attempt to classify the various forms, particularly southward. Plants in the West belong to var. *farnesiana*. Huisache is often called Sweet Acacia because of the pleasingly scented flowers, a source of a fragrance used in many French perfumes. The species is widely cultivated as an ornamental for its dense shade, drought resistance, and aromatic flowers. From Tex. to s. Miss. plants have no bracts on the flower stalks, and venation is not evident on the lower surface of leaflets; these plants are sometimes recognized as Texas Huisache (*Acacia smallii* Isely; name not transferred to *Vachellia*).

VISCID ACACIA *Vachellia vernicosa*
(Britton & Rose) Seigler & Ebinger
A.K.A. STICKYLEAF ACACIA, CHIHUAHUAN WHITETHORN

QUICKID Often found growing with White-thorn Acacia, but easily distinguished by the varnished appearance of the leaves, which have only 2–6 primary segments.

Usually a shrub, sometimes a small tree, resembling White-thorn Acacia but with a more open crown and branches ascending in an unordered zigzag manner. **LEAF** Appearing varnished, with 2–6 primary segments, each with 10–20 leaflets that are 1–3 mm long.

HABITAT/RANGE Native. Dry slopes, flats, washes, 900–1,500 m; se. Ariz. to w. Tex. and n. Mexico.

HUISACHE

VISCID ACACIA

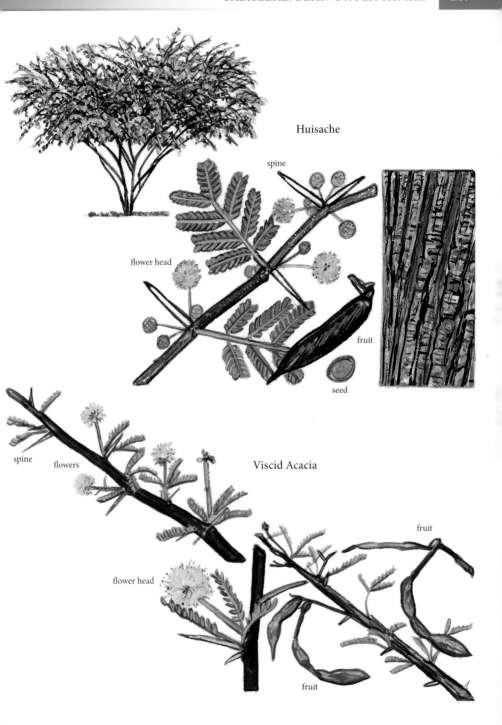

Huisache

spine

flower head

fruit

seed

spine

flowers

Viscid Acacia

fruit

flower head

fruit

SUBFAMILY PAPILIONOIDEAE: PEAS, BEANS, AND THEIR RELATIVES

The subfamily Papilionoideae consists of many herbaceous species in addition to shrubs and trees, and has up to 500 genera and 10,000 species worldwide. It ranges from the hot tropics to cold areas, from wet habitats to dry deserts. Members of the subfamily are usually easily recognized by their typical "pea-like" flowers, or "pea-flowers." **LEAF** Alternate, usually pinnately compound, occasionally unifoliolate and appearing simple by reduction. **FLOWER** Bisexual, strongly bilateral, calyx with 5 united sepals, the tips appearing as teeth on the edge of a deep cup, corolla with 1 large upper petal (banner or standard) held outside the other petals. At the side are 2 lateral petals (wings). In the center toward the bottom of the flower are 2 petals, together called the keel, that are more or less joined

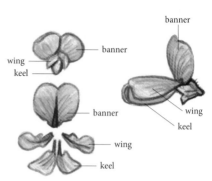

Papilionoid Legume Flower

along their lower edge, enveloping the stamens and the pistil. Stamens are commonly in a group of 9 joined by their filaments, with the 10th stamen uppermost and free; or all may be fused or all free.

SIBERIAN PEA TREE *Caragana arborescens* Lam.

Deciduous, stiffly branched, more or less armed shrub or small tree up to 5 m tall. **LEAF** Alternate or on short spur branches, pinnately compound, light to dark green, hairy to nearly hairless, 4–10 cm long; stipules and rachis tip often spiny. Leaflets 8–12, elliptic to obovate, 5–25 mm long, 5–15 mm wide; terminal leaflet absent. **FLOWER** Yellow, 15–20 mm long, in clusters in the leaf axils. Apr.–Jun. **FRUIT** Legume oblong, compressed but swollen, 6–10 cm long, thick and pulpy, reddish, splitting with a "pop" when ripe. **HABITAT/RANGE** Introduced; may be expected anywhere in cold climates across the continent. *Notes Caragana* is a genus from n. Asia with about 80 species. Early settlers brought Siberian Pea Tree to n. North America for food, fuel, fiber, and dyes, for use in windbreaks, and as an ornamental.

MESCALBEAN *Dermatophyllum secundiflorum* (Ortega) Gandhi & Reveal

A.K.A. CORALBEAN, TEXAS MOUNTAIN LAUREL, FRIJOLITO

QUICK ID The pinnately compound leathery leaves with round-tipped leaflets, purple pea-flowers, and swollen, pendulous woody pods readily identify this species.

Evergreen shrub or small tree, 1–10 m tall. Trunks usually several, 5–20 cm diam.; crown dense, narrow, the branches upright. **BARK** Dark gray to black, smooth when young; when older, shallowly fissured, with narrow, flat ridges and thin, shredding strips. **TWIG** Greenish when young, at first velvety; later nearly hairless, orange-brown. **LEAF** Alternate, pinnately compound, leathery; blade 6–16 cm long, petiole ¼–⅓ length of blade, grooved on top. Leaflets usually 7–11, terminal leaflet present; each leaflet usually 2.5–5 cm long, elliptic-obovate to oblong, gradually narrowed to the base, bluntly angled or round at the tip, often with a notch or a minute point; margin entire. Upper surface hairy when young, later hairless, dark green and lustrous; lower surface very pale, hairless or minutely hairy. **FLOWER** Showy, blue-purple, 5–15 in a dense, ovoid, drooping terminal cluster 5–10 cm long, each flower 14–16 mm long, on a stalk 1–1.5 cm long; 10 stamens, all free from one another. Banner erect, ovoid to nearly round, notched at the tip, mostly spotted at the base on the inside, its margin crinkled. Mar.–Apr. **FRUIT** Pendulous, plump woody legume, constricted between the seeds and often with slender sterile sections, 2–10 cm long, 1–1.5 cm wide, with 1–4 seeds, felty when young, nearly hairless when mature, indehiscent. Seeds plump, 1–1.5 cm long, red (rarely yellow).

HABITAT/RANGE Native. Rocky ground, usually limestone, in brushy thickets, on slopes, in

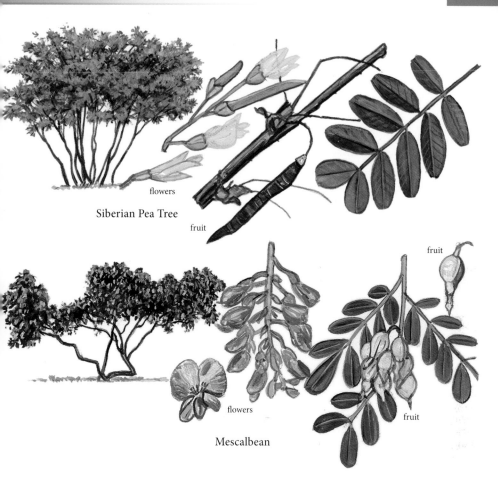

flowers

Siberian Pea Tree

fruit

fruit

flowers

fruit

Mescalbean

canyons, along roadsides, 5–1,500 m; se. N.M., c. and s. Tex., e. Mexico.

SIMILAR SPECIES There are 2 other species of *Dermatophyllum* in s. Ariz. and w. Tex., both shrubs that have slightly flattened pods and smaller leaflets.

Notes The genus *Dermatophyllum* has only 4 species, all occurring in semiarid regions of North America. Until recently, Mescalbean was placed in the larger genus *Sophora* as *S. secundiflora*. Among other features, its woody habit, leathery leaves, and bluish or white flowers distinguish it from *Sophora* species. Mescalbean is a popular but slow-growing ornamental, prized for its drought tolerance, dark evergreen foliage, and bright blue-purple flowers. All parts of the plant are toxic to livestock and

humans. The red seeds are sometimes strung for necklaces, but beware that they are attractive to small children and are toxic when ingested. Indigenous people mixed powdered seeds with mescal to produce intoxication, delirium, and deep sleep.

MESCALBEAN

◼ *EYSENHARDTIA*: KIDNEYWOODS

The kidneywoods comprise a genus of about 15 species of unarmed, mostly deciduous shrubs and small trees primarily of Mexico, but found in brushy areas in dry hills and canyons from sw. U.S. to Central America at moderate elevations. The foliage is gland-dotted, with a resinous, often citrus-like odor.

LEAF Alternate, pinnately compound, with a terminal leaflet; leaflets are usually small and numerous, the margins entire. **FLOWER** Small, bisexual, crowded in narrow spike-like clusters at the ends of branches, white or faintly yellowish, slightly bilateral, the petals more or less equal in size, the banner slightly broader than the other petals. **FRUIT** Hairless, indehiscent, small, usually 1-seeded legume, crowded in a spike. The common name refers to the diuretic properties of the wood.

ARIZONA KIDNEYWOOD *Eysenhardtia orthocarpa* (A. Gray) S. Watson

QUICK ID Dense spikes of small white pea-like flowers with petals rather equal in size to one another and small hanging pods help to identify this shrub or small tree.

Open shrub or small tree to 6 m tall; slowly deciduous during drought or cold. **LEAF** Pinnate, blade oblong, 10–12 cm long; leaflets 21–47, mostly oval, 3–20 mm long. **FLOWER** White, 6–8 mm long, many, in dense spikes 5–10 cm long, the flowers soon spreading or drooping after opening. May–Aug. **FRUIT** Hanging oblong legume, about 12 mm long.

HABITAT/RANGE Native. Dry slopes, ridges, 300–1,500 m; se. Ariz., sw. N.M., nw. Mexico.

TEXAS KIDNEYWOOD *Eysenhardtia texana* Scheele
A.K.A. BEE-BRUSH, VARA DULCE

QUICK ID This kidneywood may be recognized by its dense spikes of small white pea-like flowers with petals rather equal in size to one another, and small, ascending legumes.

Open shrub or rarely a small tree to 5 m tall, slowly deciduous during drought or cold. **LEAF** Pinnate, blade oblong, 3–9 cm long; leaflets 15–47, obovate or elliptic, 4–12 mm long. **FLOWER** White, 5–8 mm long, many in dense spikes 3–10 cm long, the flowers ascending to spreading. Apr.–Sep. **FRUIT** Oblong, incurved, ascending legume, 5–8 mm long.

HABITAT/RANGE Native. Brushy slopes and arroyos on calcareous soils, 10–1,200 m; c. and s. Tex. to c. Mexico.

GOLDEN CHAIN TREE *Laburnum anagyroides* Medik
A.K.A. GOLDEN RAIN TREE, COMMON LABURNUM

Deciduous slender, unarmed tree to 10 m tall, with an irregular crown of slightly drooping twigs. **LEAF** Alternate, palmately compound, with 3 ovate or broadly lanceolate grayish-green leaflets, 3–7 cm long, with appressed hairs; petiole longer than blade. **FLOWER** Bright yellow, 1.5–2 cm long, numerous, in loose, hanging, narrow racemes 10–40 cm long. May–Jul. **FRUIT** Oblong brown legume, finely and lightly hairy, plump and constricted between the seeds, 3–5 cm long, about 5 mm wide, slightly winged on 1 margin, hanging from a short stalk, dehiscing well after maturity. **HABITAT/RANGE** Introduced; widely planted and often escaping, weakly naturalized from Calif. to s. B.C., in moist, often disturbed areas, mostly 0–100 m. *Notes* There are 2 or 3 species of *Laburnum*, all from Europe and w. Asia; this long-lived species is the most commonly cultivated. All parts of the plant are highly toxic.

ARIZONA KIDNEYWOOD

TEXAS KIDNEYWOOD

Arizona Kidneywood

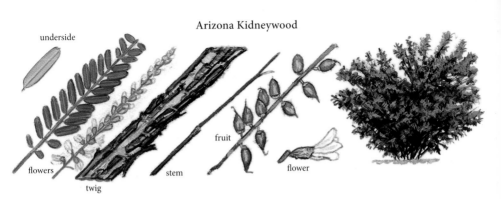

underside

flowers

twig

stem

fruit

flower

Texas Kidneywood

fruit

flowers

immature
fruit spike

Golden Chain Tree

flowers

seeds

fruit

IRONWOOD *Olneya tesota* A. Gray
A.K.A. DESERT IRONWOOD, PALO FIERO

QUICK ID **A desert tree with pinkish pea-like flowers and pinnately compound leaves.**

A slow-growing, often armed tree, to nearly 9 m tall. Evergreen, but may be drought-deciduous, or leaves may drop at flowering time as new leaves emerge. Trunk often 60 cm diam.; crown round, ragged and open. **BARK** Gray, smooth on smaller branches, shredding on older branches and the trunk. **TWIG** May be armed with paired (sometimes single) spines at a node; when present, spines are more or less straight, 6–15 mm long. **LEAF** Alternate or in clusters, pinnately compound, often lacking a terminal leaflet, bluish green, minutely hairy but seemingly hairless until examined with a lens; blade 3–6 cm long, petiole very short. Leaflets 6–25, oblong, 7–20 mm long. **FLOWER** In axillary clusters or short racemes 3–8 cm long. Calyx purple-brown, 4–5 mm long; petals pink to lavender or purple, the banner with a succulent white swelling near the base, a yellow-green nectar guide above the swelling, and a white band highlighting the nectar guide. Later in the day the banner folds back. Apr.–May. **FRUIT** Hairy and glandular, dark red-brown leathery legume, 2–4 cm long, thick, constricted between the 2 or 3 seeds, or often only 1-seeded.

HABITAT/RANGE Native. Dry washes and flats, sometimes on hillsides, 50–900 m; s. Calif., s. Ariz., nw. Mexico.

Notes Along with palo verdes (*Parkinsonia*), ironwoods are iconic trees of the Sonoran Desert, often abundant in desert washes. The wood is dense (heavier than water), with the pale sapwood contrasting with the dark brown heartwood. In Mexico the wood is used for attractive carvings. Trees are now protected by law in the United States. In earlier years trees were nearly extirpated for firewood. Ironwood is sensitive to cold; thus, its presence indicates suitable sites to establish citrus orchards. Seedlings will not establish in areas where temperatures are regularly below −7°C. Trees provide shelter and shade for wildlife, and serve as nurse trees for many species of plants. Domestic and native mammals browse the foliage. Indigenous peoples ate the parched seeds.

SMOKETREE *Psorothamnus spinosus*
(A. Gray) Barneby
A.K.A. SMOKETHORN

QUICK ID **This is an unmistakable thorny small tree with a smoky bluish color and a dense, stiffly twiggy canopy.**

Deciduous small tree or shrub, occasionally reaching 10 m tall. Trunk to 35 cm diam., though usually smaller. Crown ragged and oval, densely and intricately branched, leafless most of the year. **TWIG** Stiff, branching in all directions, covered with dense, low, appressed hairs that bestow the pale bluish-gray color, and sparsely dotted with small round, dark glands that impart a resinous, sweetish odor reminiscent of turpentine. Terminal twigs are modified as long, slender thorns. **LEAF** Alternate, unifoliolate and appearing simple, 5–20 mm long, grayish and gland-dotted, narrowly wedge-shaped, with a blunt tip, leathery, dropping before flowers appear. **FLOWER** Pea-like, borne in short, thorn-tipped racemes of 5–15 flowers. Petals deep blue-purple, 8–10 mm long. Jun.–Jul. **FRUIT** Grayish-hairy and conspicuously gland-dotted, plumply ovoid legume, 7–10 mm long, barely exceeding the calyx, 1-seeded.

HABITAT/RANGE Native. Washes in low, hot desert, about −70–400 m; s. Calif., sw. Ariz., nw. Mexico.

IRONWOOD

SMOKETREE

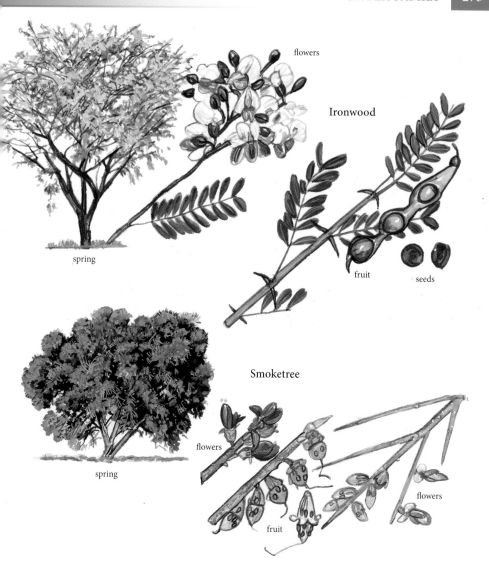

flowers

Ironwood

spring

fruit

seeds

Smoketree

flowers

spring

flowers

fruit

Notes The most treelike of a small genus of thorny desert shrubs and trees, Smoketree is aptly named, its crown reminiscent of a puff of smoke coming from a hot desert wash. There are 8 other species in the genus, all much shrubbier, also grayish green, gland-dotted, odorous, and with purple or bluish pea-like flowers. All are from the hot deserts of w. North America. Smoketree conserves water by dropping its leaves early, photosynthesis then occurring in the stems. The pale hairs reflect heat.

When in bloom the plant may be spectacular, covered in tiny, vivid blue-purple flowers. Seedlings are common in washes after very heavy rains, when tumbling gravel has abraded the seed coat and germination ensues. Seedlings have leaves up to 6 cm long. Other species in the genus may have some or all leaves pinnately compound. All that remains of the pinnate leaf in the Smoketree is the terminal leaflet, the others lost through evolutionary reduction, another adaptation to water conservation.

■ *ROBINIA*: LOCUSTS

There are 4 major species of *Robinia*, all originally confined to the U.S., except for one that ranges a short distance into Mexico. The area of major diversity in this small genus is the Southeast; 1 native and 1 introduced species occur in the West. Locusts are found from sea-level to moderate elevations in forests, openings, and disturbed areas.

Shrubs to moderate trees armed with nodal spines. Clonal reproduction by root suckering is common. **BARK** Brownish gray, not very thick, with shallow longitudinal furrows and often small plates or scales on the flattish ridges. **TWIG** Zigzagging twigs characterize locusts, their nodes with paired spines, or sometimes paired bristles, the latter of which fall from the twig. A terminal bud is absent, and winter buds are hidden under a scalelike covering of the leaf scar between and slightly below the nodal spines. **LEAF** Alternate, pinnately compound, with a terminal leaflet; leaflets are medium-size, oval or elliptic, on a short stalk, the margins entire. **FLOWER** Relatively large and showy pea-like flowers are crowded into short, dense, hanging, tapered racemes. Flower bisexual, bilaterally symmetric, the banner broad and bent partially upward, away from the wings and keel. **FRUIT** Usually pendent legume, thin and stiffly papery, straight, compressed, somewhat constricted between the seeds or not, nearly stalkless, often with a wing along the edge that was oriented upward in the flower. The pod is dehiscent, the inner surface satiny-lustrous.

Differentiation of locust species has been arguable because of hybridization and reproduction by seed, and reproduction of sterile hybrid clones by root-suckering. Because of interfertility among species, and the fertility of hybrids, many horticultural forms have been developed, propagated by grafting and suckers. Some are spineless. Black Locust was brought to early mining towns in the West as a hardy ornamental and has escaped. Locust flowers produce excellent honey.

NEW MEXICO LOCUST *Robinia neomexicana* A. Gray

QUICK ID This mountain shrub or tree has pinnately compound leaves, each leaflet with a tiny point on the rounded tip, and pink pea-like flowers in hanging clusters.

Deciduous shrub or small tree to 8 m tall, often forming thickets on mountain slopes. Trunk erect, 1 to few, 10–20 cm diam. **BARK** When mature, rather thin, light gray-brown, shallowly furrowed, the ridges with small platelike scales. **TWIG** Red-brown, spreading, finely hairy and also glandular when young, becoming nearly hairless by the 2nd year, flecked with small pale lenticels, armed at the nodes with straight or slightly downcurved, paired spines about 1 cm long. **LEAF** Alternate, pinnately compound, thin and flexible, deep green, sparsely covered with appressed hairs, the rachis hairy; blade 10–25 cm long, petiole short. Leaflets 9–21, each leaflet short-stalked, elliptic, 1–3 cm long. **FLOWER** Crowded into hanging, tapered clusters 5–10 cm long, originating in the axils of leaves on twigs of the current year, the stalk and individual flower stalks in the cluster finely hairy and often also glandular. Petals rose to pink or sometimes near-white, 2–2.5 cm long, banner broad, notched at the tip. Apr.–Aug. **FRUIT** Hanging straight legume, flat but swollen at the seeds and mostly constricted between, with a narrow wing along 1 edge, reddish when fresh, brown when dried, stiffly papery, usually hairy but sometimes glabrous, 5–15 cm long, 8 mm wide, dehiscent.

HABITAT/RANGE Native. Mountain slopes, roadsides, waste areas, flats, in openings among conifers, 1,200–2,500 m; se. Calif. and e. Nev. to n. Colo., N.M., w. Tex., and n. Mexico. Reported from n. Utah and Wyo., possibly from cultivated plants.

SIMILAR SPECIES Black Locust is weedy in the West; it has white or creamy flowers up to 20 mm long and hairless pods.

Notes As is true for many members of the bean family, New Mexico Locust fixes nitrogen in the soil. Leaves fold in the evening. The species is among the first to cover hillsides after a fire, declining as later trees shade it out. There are 2 varieties: var. *neomexicana* has a strongly and harshly glandular hairy pod, flower stalks,

NEW MEXICO LOCUST

BLACK LOCUST

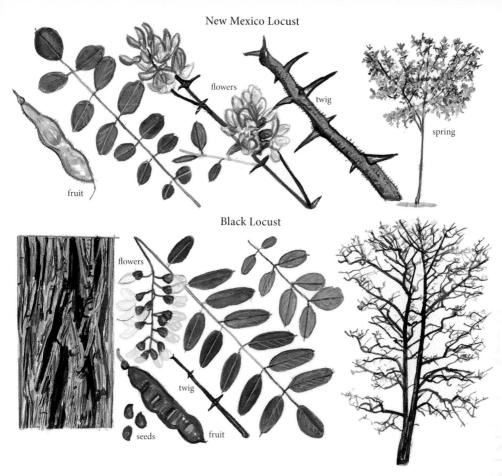

New Mexico Locust

flowers

twig

spring

fruit

Black Locust

flowers

twig

seeds   fruit

and calyx; var. *rusbyi* (Wooten & Standl.) W.C. Martin & C.R. Hutchins ex Peabody has a glabrous pod and hairy but not glandular flower stalks and calyx, and is restricted to w. N.M. and e. Ariz.

BLACK LOCUST *Robinia pseudoacacia* L.
A.K.A. YELLOW LOCUST, LOCUST

QUICK ID This tree is recognized by the combination of white or creamy pea-like flowers, and pinnate leaves subtended by a pair of sharp-pointed spines.

Deciduous tree to about 25 m tall, with an open, irregular crown of ascending branches. Single trunk, erect, straight or crooked, 1–1.5 m diam. **BARK** Gray or dark gray-brown, coarse, becoming deeply furrowed, often developing large forking ridges and large plates. **TWIG** Slender, brittle, reddish brown. **LEAF** Alternate, pinnately compound, blade

20–36 cm long, 4–12 cm broad; petiole averaging about 3 cm long, often subtended by a pair of sharp spines. Leaflets 7–25, thin, 2–6 cm long, 1–2.5 cm broad, elliptic, oblong, or ovate; base rounded or bluntly wedge-shaped; apex rounded, usually with a small tooth at the tip; margins entire. **FLOWER** Fragrant, produced from the leaf axils in an elongate, drooping raceme; flower white or creamy white, the banner with a dull yellow patch; calyx 6–9 mm long, corolla 1.5–2.5 cm long. May–Jun. **FRUIT** Oblong, flat, hairless, stiffly papery legume, 5–10 cm long, about 1 cm broad.

HABITAT/RANGE U.S. native; original range not known with certainty, but probably confined to the s. Appalachians and the Ozark Mountains. Moist woods, stream margins, river bottoms, pastures, fencerows, and disturbed areas, 0–1,900 m; nearly throughout U.S. to s. Canada (also parts of Europe). Widely planted as an ornamental since pioneer times, and possibly disseminated by Native Americans.

FAGACEAE: BEECH OR OAK FAMILY

Fagaceae comprises 9 genera and 600–800 species of trees and shrubs worldwide, naturally occurring mostly in the Northern Hemisphere. Five genera and nearly 100 species occur in North America north of Mexico. Species are absent or rare only in the n. Great Plains, the n. Rocky Mountains, and on the deserts of the Southwest. The oaks (*Quercus*) constitute the family's largest genus native to North America; about 48 species occur in the West, some only as shrubs. *Chrysolepis* and *Notholithocarpus* are strictly western genera, but add only 3 species.

Evergreen or deciduous trees and shrubs. **LEAF** Alternate, simple, and variously lobed, toothed, or entire. **FLOWER** Members of the family are monoecious and characterized by tiny, radial, usually wind-pollinated flowers with a few sepals and no petals; male and female flowers are borne in often separate stiff or flexible catkins on the same plant. Female flowers are much fewer than male flowers. **FRUIT** The family's most distinctive character is the fruit, 1 or more nuts partially or completely enclosed within a scaly or spiny cupule (variously called a cup, cap, or involucre).

Many species of this family are important economically as sources of lumber, fuel, and food, and are also widely used in habitat restoration and as ornamentals. Perhaps no family of woody plants provides more ecological services to a wider array of wildlife. Trees of some species, especially the oaks, may live several hundred years and grow to be very large. When growing within cities and towns, such ancient matriarchs are often revered, named, and even protected by ordinance.

GIANT GOLDEN CHINQUAPIN
Chrysolepis chrysophylla (Douglas ex Hook.) Hjelmq. **var.** *chrysophylla*
A.K.A. Golden Chinquapin, Giant Chinquapin, Golden Chestnut, Goldenleaf Chestnut

QUICK ID In this tree, the lanceolate leaves are golden beneath, and the fruit is enclosed in a spiny bur.

Evergreen shrub or tree. When a tree, to about 45 m tall, and when large usually has 1 straight trunk 1–2 m diam., unbranched for ½–⅔ its length. Crown pyramidal or rounded, usually dense, with spreading branches. **BARK** Thin, smooth and dark gray with pale blotches on young branches; on older parts brownish or reddish, deeply fissured between broad ridges, the fissures more intensely colored. **TWIG** Terminal bud absent; pseudoterminal bud (axillary bud of the youngest leaf) egg-shaped, with 2 unequal outer scales enclosing several overlapping inner scales. Twigs covered by tiny golden scales when young, becoming dark reddish brown and smooth with age. Buds clustered near twig tip, light brown, egg-shaped to nearly spherical, finely hairy on edges of scales; end bud 5–7 mm. Pith yellow and star-shaped in cross section. **LEAF** Alternate, simple, thin, leathery, flat, lanceolate, narrowly tapering to the tip; margins entire, often slightly wavy. Upper surface dark green, lustrous, with sparse scalelike hairs, smooth; lower surface covered with minute golden or brownish scales. Blade usually 5–15 cm long, 1.5–5 cm broad; petiole 5–12 mm long. **FLOWER** Small, unisexual, with 5 or 6 tiny separate tepals, borne in narrow, ascending, fishy-smelling spikes, 4–7.5 cm long, some spikes with only male flowers; others may have inconspicuous female flowers at the base; male flower cream, usually with 12 exserted stamens. Apr.–Aug. **FRUIT** Usually 3 to several nuts (sometimes fewer) enclosed in a burlike cupule; each nut light brown, 8–12 mm long, 3-angled or round in cross section. Cupule spherical, densely covered with branched spines 1 cm long, splitting by 4 divisions to release nuts. Nuts biennial, maturing late summer to autumn.

HABITAT/RANGE Native. Mixed evergreen or conifer forests, 0–2,000 m; c. Calif. to wc. Wash., mostly in the Coast and Cascade ranges.

Giant Golden Chinquapin

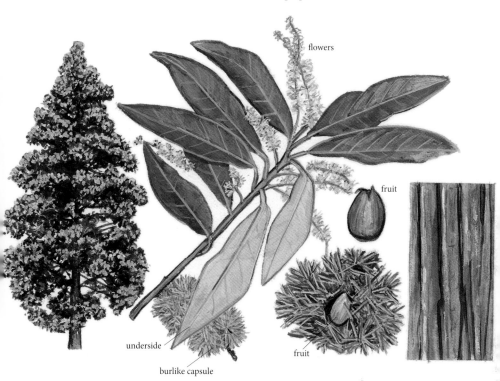

flowers

fruit

underside

burlike capsule

fruit

SIMILAR SPECIES California Bay (*Umbellularia californica*, Lauraceae) has similar leaves, but they are green on both sides, not golden beneath, and have a strong odor similar to the spice bay leaf. Tanbark Oak (*Notholithocarpus densiflorus*), which bears acorns, also has lanceolate leaves, but its leaf margins are toothed and the lower surface is covered by pale wool when young.

Notes The common name is often spelled "chinkapin." Two species comprise the small genus *Chrysolepis* of the Pacific Coast states, the other a shrub. *Chrysolepis chrysophylla* var. *minor* (Benth.) Munz, a shrub of open ridges and slopes, has leaves folded upward along the midrib. The fishy odor of the catkins attracts midges as pollinators. Burs, similar to those of the "true" chinquapins (*Castanea*) of e. U.S., are locally called "porcupine eggs." The nuts are edible but difficult to extract. Trees are occasionally used for lumber and ornamental plantings. Giant Golden Chinquapin is susceptible to chestnut blight, a fungal disease caused by *Cryphonectria parasitica* that has virtually exterminated the American Chestnut (*Castanea dentata* [Marsh.] Borkh.).

GIANT GOLDEN CHINQUAPIN

TANBARK OAK *Notholithocarpus densiflorus* (Hook. & Arn.) Manos, Cannon & S.H. Oh

A.K.A. CALIFORNIA TANBARK OAK, CHESTNUT OAK, PEACH OAK, BUR OAK, SOVEREIGN OAK

QUICK ID Tanbark Oak has toothed lanceolate leaves, densely hairy on the underside at first, nearly hairless later, and large acorns with shaggy-burry caps. Twigs are round, not 5-sided as in many oak species.

Evergreen shrub or tree to 25 m tall, occasionally taller. Forest-grown trees usually with a single long, straight trunk 0.2–1.5 m diam., clear of branches for ½ the length; open-grown trees shorter, with low branches. Crown narrowly oval or pyramidal in forest-grown trees to broad and round in open-grown trees, usually dense, the branches ascending or spreading. **BARK** Mottled gray, thin and smooth on younger growth; thick with widely spaced furrows on older trunks and branches, the broad, flat ridges cut by narrow cross-seams and checks into smooth, squarish plates. **TWIG** Densely rusty-woolly with star-shaped hairs when young, later smooth and reddish brown. Terminal buds 6–8 mm long, egg-shaped, covered in tawny pubescence. **LEAF** Alternate, simple, thick and leathery to brittle; convex, lanceolate or oblong, usually pointed at the tip; margins more or less rolled, with low, regular, sometimes obscure teeth. Upper surface light green, at first covered with star-shaped hairs, later hairless and shiny; lower surface densely tawny-hairy when young, nearly hairless in older leaves, pale greenish or bluish, with tufts of original hairs remaining in the axils of veins. Blade usually 6–14 cm long, 2–8 cm broad; petiole 12–20 mm long. **FLOWER** Tiny, but conspicuous en masse, borne in narrow, ascending or drooping whitish spikes, 8–10 cm long, near the branch tips. Some spikes have only male flowers; others may have inconspicuous female flowers at the base. Individual flowers have 4–6 small separate tepals. Jun.–Aug. **FRUIT** Acorn, 2–3.5 cm long, on a stalk 1–2.5 cm long. Nut yellowish brown, globose to broadly cylindric-tapered. Cup cup-shaped, 7–10 mm deep, 20–30 mm wide, covering ⅕–¼ of the nut; scales brown, hairy, narrowly finger-like and tapered, spreading or bent back toward the stalk, the tip often hooked. Acorns biennial, maturing late summer to mid-autumn.

HABITAT/RANGE Native. Redwood and mixed evergreen forest, 0–1,500 m; s. Calif. to sw. Ore., mostly in the Coast Ranges, but local in the c. Sierra Nevada.

SIMILAR SPECIES California Bay (*Umbellularia californica*, Lauraceae) has similar leaves, but they lack teeth, are green on both sides, and have a strong, spicy odor. Giant Golden Chinquapin (*Chrysolepis chrysophylla*) also has entire leaves, but they are golden- or brownish-scaly on the underside. Silverleaf Oak (*Quercus hypoleucoides*) of the Southwest has dense white to pale tawny hairs on the lower surface of leaves (margins rarely with a few teeth); the scales of the small acorns are smooth and flat. European Turkish Oak (*Q. cerris*) has long, soft-shaggy scales on the cup, but its leaves are deeply lobed. Bur Oak (*Q. macrocarpa*) has long, fringelike scales only around the rim of the cup.

Notes There is only 1 species in *Notholithocarpus*, and it is found only in the Pacific Coast states. Until recently, this was considered the only North American species of the large Southeast Asian genus *Lithocarpus*. New evidence indicates it is best placed in its own genus. Even though it has an acorn, which apparently evolved independently from that of *Quercus*, Tanbark Oak is more closely related to chinquapins (*Castanea*, *Chrysolepis*) and their allies. Its bark was once used for tanning leather, and many trees were logged for that resource alone. Acorns germinate readily in the shade and grow into understory trees in coniferous forests. The trunk arises from a subterranean burl, which produces many sprouts when the tree is removed, as by fire or logging. The devastating fungal disease sudden oak death was first detected in 1995 in Tanbark Oak (see *Quercus* for further discussion).

TANBARK OAK

Tanbark Oak

fruit

flowers

seedling

fruit

underside

■ *QUERCUS*: OAKS

Quercus comprises about 450 species worldwide. About 200 species occur naturally in the Western Hemisphere, nearly 100 north of Mexico. They occur in semiarid scrub, oak woodlands, open savannas, and in mixed forests from sea-level to moderately high elevations.

Evergreen or deciduous shrubs and trees, ranging from ankle-high shrubs to large, majestic trees. **BARK** Varies from scaly to furrowed or blocky and can be helpful in identification. **TWIG** Terminal bud and several lateral buds clustered at the twig tip, usually egg-shaped, protected by several overlapping scales. **LEAF** Alternate, simple; terminal leaves often closely crowded and appearing whorled. Leaf margins may be entire, coarsely toothed, or pinnately lobed. Shape, size, and margins of leaves are variable, depending upon age, position on tree, shading, and genetic variation (including hybridization). **FLOWER** Tiny and individually inconspicuous. Radial, with 4–6 separate or fused tepals. Unisexual (plants monoecious, having both male and female flowers) and produced in unisexual catkins. Male catkins may be long, slender, and pendent, borne in clusters usually at the base of emerging shoots. Female flowers in short single- to several-flowered spikes in the axils of developing leaves. **FRUIT** An acorn, a specialized structure where a thin-shelled nut rests in a cup (variously referred to as an involucre, cap, or cupule) composed of flat or knobby, rarely finger-like, usually appressed scales.

Oaks are wind-pollinated and produce copious pollen in the spring, allergenic to many sufferers. Lumber, cork, tannins, and dyes come from oaks. The acorns provide human, wildlife, and livestock food. Sudden oak death, a disease resulting from a recently introduced fungus, *Phytophthora ramorum*, is lethal to many species; other species carry the fungus but are not killed. The pathogen is spreading, often moving with shipments of western plants. With regard to North American forests this may turn out to be one of the most disastrous of plant pathogens.

Oak Taxonomic Sections

North American oaks are divided into 3 groups, commonly referred to as black (or red) oaks, intermediate (or golden) oaks, and white oaks, and are presented in that order in this book. These groups are formal taxonomic sections. The sections differ primarily in wood anatomy, leaf form, characteristics of the acorn cup and interior of the acorn shell, and the time required for fruit maturation.

RED OR BLACK OAKS: SECTION LOBATAE

There are about 195 species of red or black oaks, all strictly North American. They usually have reddish wood and interior bark (giving the name "red oaks"). **BARK** Hard, dark gray or nearly black, often rough, but not scaly. **LEAF** With bristles at least at the apex and at the tips of the lobes. **FRUIT** Acorn, usually requiring 2 years to develop. Cup has smooth, lightly hairy scales; inside of shell silky or velvety over its entire surface.

This section begins with species that have broad lobed leaves and progresses to species with small unlobed leaves.

CALIFORNIA BLACK OAK *Quercus kelloggii* Newb.
A.K.A. KELLOGG OAK

QUICK ID The large leaves with large, bristle-tipped lobes, and the long, narrow-pointed tips on the acorn cup scales identify this tree.

Deciduous tree to about 25 m tall, usually with a single straight trunk, 0.5–1 m diam. Crown oval or round, more or less open, with stout, spreading branches. **BARK** Dark brown to blackish, smooth when young, later with deep fissures and broad, irregular ridges and plates. **TWIG** Red-brown and hairy when young, usually hairless by end of 2nd year. Terminal buds chestnut brown, ovoid, pointed, 4–10 mm long, hairless or with a few hairs on the scale margins. **LEAF** Alternate, simple, thin, flexible, flat, ovate to broadly obovate in outline. Margins deeply cut on each side into 3–5 major pointed lobes; lobes often expanded near the tip, which may be cut into several points, each point with a bristle. Upper surface dark green, smooth, lustrous; lower surface paler, hairless or finely pubescent, with tufts of hairs in vein axils. Blade 6–20 cm long, 4–14 cm broad; petiole 1–6 cm long. **FRUIT** Acorn, 2–3.5 cm long, short-stalked. Nut brown, oblong or elliptic in outline. Cup saucer-shaped to deeply bowl-shaped, 13–27 mm deep, 20–28 mm wide, covering ⅓–½ of the nut; scales light brown, thin, mostly hairless, the tips acute to long and narrowly tapered, loose, especially around the margin of the cup. Acorns biennial, maturing late summer to early autumn.

HABITAT/RANGE Native. Often in mixed forests, 300–2,400 m; west of the Cascade Range and the Sierra Nevada from w. Ore. to s. Calif.

SIMILAR SPECIES Unique in the West; some eastern red oaks entering our area in Tex. have very similar leaves, but none has the large, deep-cupped acorn with long, narrow-pointed cup scales.

CALIFORNIA BLACK OAK

SHUMARD OAK

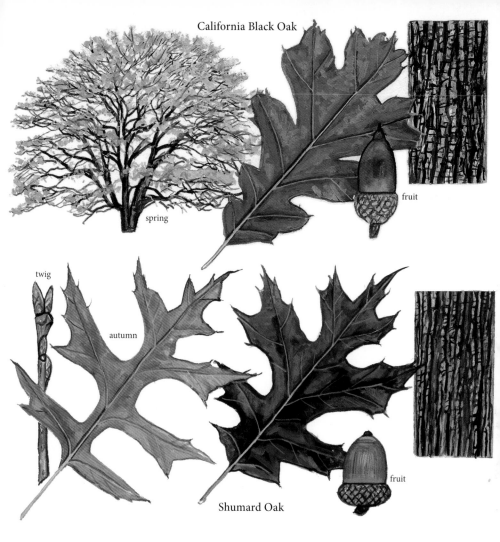

California Black Oak

fruit

spring

twig

autumn

fruit

Shumard Oak

Notes When California Black Oak grows in groves, most trees are of a single age class, the result of sprouting after fire. In natural stands, trees must be about 30 years old or older before they produce viable seed, and they continue to produce abundant seed until they are 200 years old or more; trees may live 500 years.

SHUMARD OAK *Quercus shumardii* Buckley

QUICK ID This oak has deeply lobed leaves with the lobes widest near their tips, hairless terminal buds, and shallow acorn cups enclosing ⅓ of the nut or less.

Deciduous tree to 40 m tall. **LEAF** Broadly elliptic or obovate, hairless except for tufts of hairs in the vein axils below; lobes deep, 4 or 5 per side, widest near their tips, each ending with several small bristle-tipped points. Blade 7–20 cm long; petiole 2–6 cm long. **FRUIT** Acorn, 1.5–3 cm long; cup 1.5–3 cm wide, hairless inside or with a ring of hairs at the center, covering ¼–⅓ of the nut.

HABITAT/RANGE Native. Moist low areas, 200–300 m in the West; se. U.S., entering sc. Tex.

BUCKLEY OAK *Quercus buckleyi* Nixon & Dorr

QUICK ID This oak is restricted to Tex. and Okla. in limestone hills. It has sharply lobed leaves with the lower surface hairless except for inconspicuous tufts in the vein axils.

Deciduous tree to 15 m tall. **LEAF** Hairless or with minute tufts of hairs in the vein axils below; lobes deep, 2–4 per side, each often with secondary lobes tipped with bristles, 12–35 bristles per leaf. Blade 5.5–10 cm long; petiole 2–4.5 cm long. **FRUIT** Acorn, 1.2–1.8 cm long, cup covering ⅓–½ of the nut.

HABITAT/RANGE Native. Rolling limestone hills; Okla. to c. Tex.

SIMILAR SPECIES Shumard Oak (*Q. shumardii*) is often smaller and has smaller leaves.

SOUTHERN RED OAK *Quercus falcata* Michx.

QUICK ID The leaf, with its U-shaped base in combination with the extended, often curving (sickle-shaped), straplike terminal lobe, is diagnostic.

Deciduous tree, typically to 30 m tall. **LEAF** 1–3 tapering lobes per side, terminal lobe longest, lower surface lightly hairy. Blade 10–30 cm long; petiole 2–6 cm long. **FRUIT** Acorn, cup shallow; nut orange-brown, 1–1.5 cm long.

HABITAT/RANGE Native. Sandy upland sites, 0–300 m in the West; e. U.S. Reported in some references to barely enter c. Tex. from the east, where it is perhaps confused with Buckley Oak (*Q. buckleyi*).

GRAVES OAK *Quercus gravesii* Sudw.
A.K.A. CHISOS RED OAK

QUICK ID Found only in mountains in w. Tex. and adjacent Mexico, Graves Oak has shiny, nearly hairless leaves with pointed lobes and a petiole usually less than 2.5 cm long.

Deciduous tree to 13 m tall. **LEAF** Narrowly elliptic to ovate in outline, hairless (sometimes tufts of hairs in the vein axils below), with 2–4 narrowly pointed lobes per side. Blade 4.5–14 cm long; petiole usually 5–25 mm long. **FRUIT** Acorn, 9–16 mm long, cup 7–12 mm wide.

HABITAT/RANGE Native. Rocky canyons in desert mountains, above 1,200 m; w. Tex. and n. Mexico. Hybridizes with Emory Oak (*Q. emoryi*).

EMORY OAK *Quercus emoryi* Torr.
A.K.A. BLACK OAK, LIVE OAK

QUICK ID The leaves of this oak are small, glossy, elliptic to oblanceolate, stiff, often convex, and spine-tipped, with entire or spiny-toothed margins and the lower surface hairless except for conspicuous tufts in the vein axils.

Evergreen (deciduous in dry periods) tree to about 15 m tall, rarely to 25 m; trunk short, branched, to 1 m diam. Crown round, broad, dense, with stout, rigid, spreading branches; lower branches may droop. **BARK** Smooth and gray when young, aging dark brown to nearly black, rough, deeply fissured into oblong plates and cross-checked into tightly attached scales. **TWIG** Red-brown and pubescent when young, becoming darker and hairless. Terminal buds reddish brown, oval in outline, often with a pointed tip, 2.5–6.5 mm long, hairless but for a tuft of hairs at the tip, or pubescent in the upper half.

BUCKLEY OAK   SOUTHERN RED OAK   GRAVES OAK

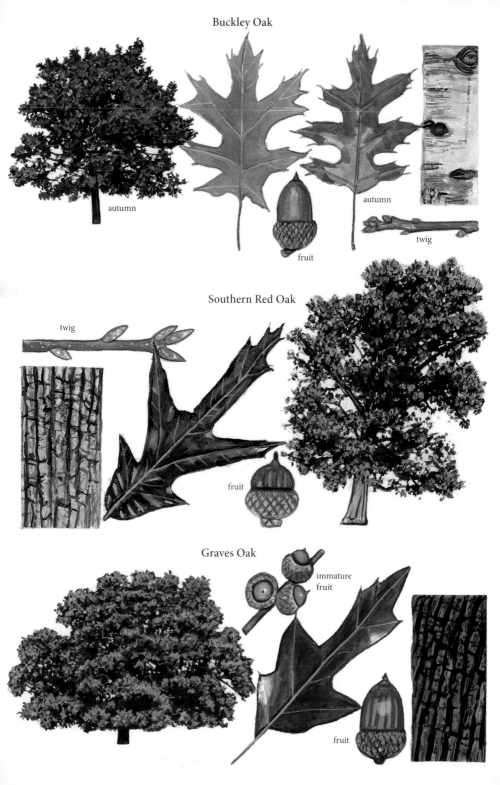

Buckley Oak

autumn   autumn

fruit   twig

Southern Red Oak

twig

fruit

Graves Oak

immature fruit

fruit

EMORY OAK *continued*

LEAF Alternate, simple, thin, stiff, flat or some-what convex, ovate, elliptic, oblong or oblanceolate. Margins entire or with 1–6 spine-tipped teeth along each edge; apex spine-tipped. Upper surface dark green, shiny, smooth, hairless or with a few hairs along the midrib; lower surface paler, hairless except for tufts of hairs in the vein axils, veins slightly raised. Blade usually 3–9.5 cm long, 1.5–4.5 cm broad; petiole 1–7 mm long. **FRUIT** Acorn, 1–1.8 cm long, stalkless to short-stalked. Nut dark chestnut brown or nearly black, oblong to elliptic in outline. Cup cup-shaped, 5–7 mm deep, 7–12 mm wide, covering ¼–½ of the nut; scales light brown, thin, sparsely or densely hairy, tightly appressed. Acorns annual, maturing mid-summer to early autumn.

HABITAT/RANGE Native. Common in canyons and valleys, often in brush or with piñon, juniper, and other oaks, 1,300–2,500 m; w. Tex., across s. N.M., to nw. Ariz., and into n. Mexico.

SIMILAR SPECIES In Toumey Oak (*Q. toumeyi*) and Sonoran Scrub Oak (*Q. turbinella*) the lower leaf surface is finely hairy or golden-glandular and the acorn cups have knobby scales.

Notes The acorns are sweet and edible, a staple for indigenous peoples, even chewed as a confection by the Tohono O'odham. They are relished by wildlife and domestic livestock. Where distributions overlap in Texas, Emory Oak may hybridize with Chisos Oak (*Q. graciliformis*) to form *Q. × tharpii* C.H. Mull. and with Graves Oak (*Q. gravesii*) to form **Robust Oak** (*Q. × robusta* C.H. Mull.). When trees are cut or removed by fire, Emory Oak can vigorously sprout from its roots or stump.

WATER OAK *Quercus nigra* L.

QUICK ID The highly variable but usually spatulate leaves with tufts of grayish hairs in the vein axils on the lower surface help identify this species.

Deciduous tree to 30 m tall. **TWIG** Hairless. **LEAF** Variable, many wedge-shaped, broadest in the distal half and with 1–3 forward-pointing lobes on each side, hairless except for small tufts of hairs in the vein axils below. Blade 3–15 cm long; petiole 2–9 mm long. **FRUIT** Acorn, 9–14 mm long.

HABITAT/RANGE Native. Moist lowlands and dunes, 0–50 m in the West; se. U.S., possibly entering our area near Corpus Christi, Tex.

BLACKJACK OAK *Quercus marilandica* Münchh.

QUICK ID This oak may be recognized by the combination of the dark green upper surface and orange-brown lower surface of the leaves, and the tawny-hairy buds.

Deciduous tree to 20 m. **TWIG** Pubescent. **LEAF** Generally wedge-shaped, or forming a blocky T or Y with a lobe between the arms, the base narrow; lower surface minutely rough-hairy and sometimes brownish. Blade 7–20 cm long; petiole 5–20 mm long. **FRUIT** Acorn, 1.2–2 cm long, the cup covering ⅓–½ of the nut.

HABITAT/RANGE Native. Woods, old fields, rocky outcrops, 0–300 m in the West; e. U.S., entering our area in ec. Tex. Hybridizes with numerous other *Quercus* species.

EMORY OAK

WATER OAK

BLACKJACK OAK

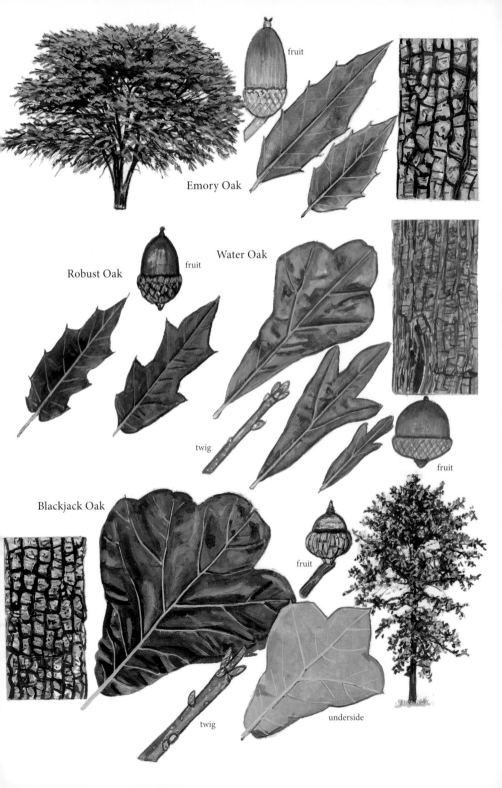

Emory Oak

fruit

Robust Oak

Water Oak

fruit

twig

fruit

Blackjack Oak

twig

fruit

underside

LATELEAF OAK *Quercus tardifolia*
C.H. Mull.

Small evergreen tree. **LEAF** Long, broadly elliptic or obovate, with 3 or 4 forward-pointing teeth on each side; upper surface hairy when young, almost hairless later, the lower surface with easily detached star-shaped hairs. Blade 5–10 cm long; petiole 1–2 cm long. **HABITAT/RANGE** Native. Rare at 2,000 m in the Chisos Mountains, Tex. Perhaps a hybrid between Emory Oak (*Q. emoryi*) and the Mexican *Q. hypoxantha* Trel.

MADREAN WILLOW OAK *Quercus viminea* Trel.
A.K.A. SONORAN OAK

Evergreen tree to 12 m tall. **LEAF** Drooping, narrowly lanceolate, entire or with a few slender, tapered teeth in the upper half, mostly hairless (sometimes with tufts of hairs in the vein axils near the base on the lower side). Blade 3.5–6 cm, long; petiole 2–5 mm long. **HABITAT/RANGE** Native. Dry hills; common in nw. Mexico, in our region known from a few records at 1,480–1,750 m in mountains of sc. Ariz., where it hybridizes with Emory Oak (*Q. emoryi*).

CHISOS OAK *Quercus graciliformis*
C.H. Mull.

QUICK ID Drooping leaves, hairless except for tufts in the vein axils on the lower surface, identify this oak, which is known only from the Chisos Mountains, Tex.

Deciduous tree or shrub to 8 m tall. **LEAF** Drooping, lanceolate to narrowly elliptic, entire or with up to 4 or 5 narrow, forward-pointing teeth on each side; upper surface hairless except along the midrib; lower surface sometimes with tufts of hairs in the vein axils. Blade 4.5–9 cm long; petiole 1–2 cm long. **FRUIT** Acorn, 9–18 mm long.

HABITAT/RANGE Native. Rocky canyons, 1,600–1,700 m; Chisos Mountains, Tex.

SILVERLEAF OAK *Quercus hypoleucoides* A. Camus
A.K.A. WHITELEAF OAK

QUICK ID Leaves that are lanceolate to narrowly ovate, dark green on the upper surface and densely white- or tawny-felty on the lower surface distinguish this oak.

Evergreen tree to 20 m tall, usually with a single trunk 0.3–5 m diam., or a robust, dense, rounded shrub. Crown round, oval, or narrow and inversely conical, usually dense, with slender, spreading branches. **BARK** Dark gray and smooth on young trees or branches, becoming blackish and deeply furrowed on older trees. **TWIG** Red-brown, pubescent when young, later hairless. Terminal buds 2.5–4.5 mm long, light chestnut-brown, oval in outline, hairless except for hairs along the scale margins, and sometimes with a tuft of hairs at the bud tip. **LEAF** Alternate, simple, rather thick and leathery, flat, lanceolate elliptic, narrowly ovate to occasionally ovate. Margins often rolled under, entire or with a few low, forward-pointing teeth, especially near tip. Upper surface dark green, hairless, lustrous, moderately wrinkled by the impression of the major veins; lower surface felty, with low, densely packed white or pale tawny overlapping branched hairs that obscure the surface, the major veins raised and conspicuous. Blade usually 4.5–12 cm long, 1.5–4 cm broad; petiole 1.5–13 mm long. **FRUIT** Acorn, 8–16 mm long, stalkless or on a short stalk. Nut dark brown and often with slightly darker stripes, oblong to broadly elliptic in outline. Cup deeply cup- or saucer-shaped, 4.5–7 mm deep, 6–13 mm wide, covering ⅓ of the nut or less; scales grayish brown, densely or sparsely pubescent with silvery hairs, round-tipped, appressed. Acorns annual or biennial, maturing in early autumn.

HABITAT/RANGE Native. In wooded canyons and on slopes, 1,500–2,700 m; se. Ariz. eastward to w. Tex., and south into nw. Mexico.

CHISOS OAK   SILVERLEAF OAK

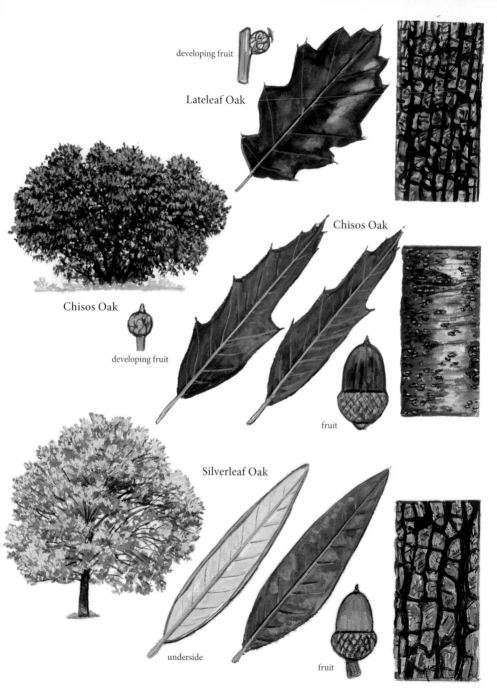

developing fruit

Lateleaf Oak

Chisos Oak

Chisos Oak

developing fruit

Silverleaf Oak

fruit

underside

fruit

SIMILAR SPECIES Within the sw. U.S., Silverleaf Oak is distinct from all other trees by the densely felty white or tawny underside of its leaves.

Notes In the sw. U.S., Silverleaf Oak rarely hybridizes with Emory Oak (*Q. emoryi*) where the two grow in common stands.

COAST LIVE OAK   *Quercus agrifolia* Née
A.K.A. CALIFORNIA LIVE OAK, LIVE OAK

QUICK ID Leaves of this oak are usually convex and holly-like, usually have 5 pairs of veins or fewer, and often have tufts of hairs in the vein axils on the lower surface; its acorns are annual.

Evergreen tree to about 25 m tall; trunks 1 or 2, short, often branched, 0.3–1.2 m (rarely to 4 m) diam. Crown round or low and spreading, usually dense; branches thick, widely spreading, sometimes resting on the ground. **BARK** Gray and smooth when young, becoming blackish brown or black, very thick, with deep furrows and broad, somewhat rounded ridges. **TWIG** Brown or red-brown, at first hairy, later hairless or nearly so. Terminal buds 3–6 mm long, light chestnut brown, egg-shaped or conical, with a few hairs along the scale margins. **LEAF** Alternate, simple, thin, slightly leathery; elliptic, ovate, or oblong, often convex. Margins entire or with a few low, spine-tipped teeth. Upper surface dark green, glossy, the veins slightly impressed; lower surface paler, hairless or with tufts of hairs in the vein axils, the veins raised and conspicuous. Blade usually 1.5–7.5 cm long, 1–4 cm broad; petiole 4–15 mm long. **FRUIT** Acorn, 1.5–3.5 cm long, stalkless or short-stalked. Nut dark chestnut brown, narrowly ovoid or conic. Cup shallowly bowl-shaped to turban-shaped, 9–13 mm deep, 9–15 mm wide, covering ¼–⅓ of the nut; scales light brown, hairless to sparsely pubescent, thin, tips loose. Acorns annual, maturing in autumn, some retained until spring.

HABITAT/RANGE Native. Near the coast and in the Coast Ranges on drier sites on slopes and in valleys, mostly 0–1,400 m; n. Calif. to n. Baja Calif.

SIMILAR SPECIES Interior Live Oak (*Q. wislizeni*) usually has flat leaves with 5 pairs of veins

or more, and its acorns are biennial. Canyon Live Oak (*Q. chrysolepis*) has biennial acorns with thick cups, the scales embedded in hairs; its bark is relatively thin and gray. Holm Oak (*Q. ilex*) has leaves that are yellowish- or grayish-hairy beneath and annual acorns.

Notes This is the only black oak in California that has annual acorns. It is extremely susceptible to sudden oak death. Slow-growing and long-lived, it is a major component of low-elevation oak woodland. Seedling establishment occurs most successfully under shrubs, perhaps reduced by browsing by livestock and native mammals in open areas. It hybridizes with California Black Oak (*Q. kelloggii*) and Interior Live Oak.

INTERIOR LIVE OAK   *Quercus wislizeni* A. DC.
A.K.A. SIERRA LIVE OAK

QUICK ID This oak has leaves that are usually flat, with spiny margins, 5 pairs of veins or more, and often tufts of hairs in the vein axils on the lower surface; its acorns are biennial.

Evergreen tree to 22 m tall; trunk short, branched, to 1.8 m diam. **TWIG** Terminal buds 3–9 mm long, minutely hairy near the tip. **LEAF** Alternate, simple, thin, stiff, flat, oblong to ovate, hairless; upper surface glossy, dark green; lower surface shiny, yellow-green. Margins entire or with 1–8 spine-tipped teeth on each side. Blade 2.5–7 cm long, 2–5 cm broad; petiole 3–20 mm long. **FRUIT** Acorn, 2.1–4.4 cm long, cup covering ⅓–½ of the nut; biennial, maturing midsummer to autumn.

HABITAT/RANGE Native. Coast Ranges and foothills of the Sierra Nevada, 300–1,900 m; Calif. to n. Baja Calif.

COAST LIVE OAK

INTERIOR LIVE OAK

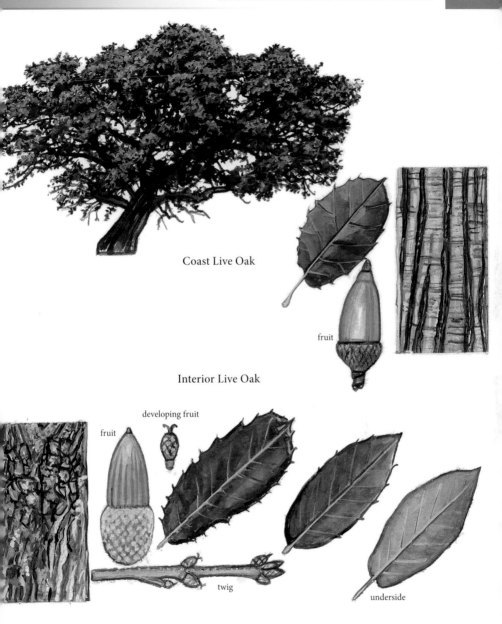

Coast Live Oak

Interior Live Oak

fruit

developing fruit

fruit

twig

underside

SIMILAR SPECIES Coast Live Oak (*Q. agrifolia*) has convex leaves and annual acorns. Some references distinguish Shreve Oak (*Q. parvula* Greene), a shrub or tree to 17 m tall, with leaves 3–9 cm long, dull olive green below; it is found in dry habitats near the c. Calif. coast below 1,000 m.

INTERMEDIATE OAKS: SECTION PROTOBALANUS

There are 5 species of intermediate oaks, 4 of which are found in w. U.S. They have pale tan wood, and bark that is grayish and scaly. **LEAF** Lacks bristles (but sometimes with a small spine on the teeth tips). **FRUIT** Biennial acorn, the cup with knobby scales embedded in velvety, often golden hairs (hence the alternative vernacular name "golden oaks"); inside of acorn shell sparsely to densely hairy.

PALMER OAK   Quercus palmeri Engelm.
A.K.A. DUNN OAK

QUICK ID This shrub or small tree has widely diverging, rigid twigs and acorns with the edges of the scales joined, the united scales forming rings around the cup.

Evergreen shrub or small tree to 3 m tall. **TWIG** Rigid, diverging at 65–90°. Terminal buds 1.5–3 mm long, ovoid, hairless. **LEAF** Alternate, simple, thin, stiff, wavy, elliptic to round, each side with 0–5 triangular spine-tipped teeth; spines often exceeding 1 mm. Upper surface grayish green; lower surface pale bluish green (often obscured by golden glandular hairs). Blade 2–4 cm long; petiole 2–5 mm long. **FRUIT** Acorn, 2–3 cm long; cup scales mostly hidden by yellowish wool, scale edges joined, the scales in rings around the cup; acorns biennial, maturing in autumn.

HABITAT/RANGE Native. Slopes, in thickets and brush, 700–1,800 m; c. and s. Calif., Ariz., sw. N.M., n. Baja Calif.

SIMILAR SPECIES Similar shrubby white oaks in s. Calif. and Ariz., including Sonoran Scrub Oak (*Q. turbinella*) and Ajo Mountain Scrub Oak (*Q. ajoensis*), have annual acorns, the cups with

separate scales, and usually narrower leaves with shorter spines.

Notes The rigid twigs and spiny leaves make thickets of Palmer Oak almost impenetrable.

CANYON LIVE OAK   Quercus chrysolepis Liebm.
A.K.A. MAUL OAK, GOLDCUP OAK, LIVE OAK

QUICK ID The combination of usually spine-tipped leaves, often spiny-toothed on the margins, with a pale or golden lower surface, and acorns with a thick velvety, knobby-scaled cup distinguishes this common oak.

Evergreen tree to 35 m tall, or a shrub. One to several trunks to 1–3 m diam.; in forest-grown trees usually 1 straight trunk, branching high above the ground; in open-grown trees trunk(s) short, often contorted, with low branches. Crown dome-shaped, usually dense; branches widely spreading. **BARK** Light gray to gray-brown, thin and smooth when young, on larger trunks developing furrows, with small appressed, flaking scales on ridges. **TWIG** Flexible, diverging at 60° or less from the branch, golden-velvety when young, the velvet fading to gray by the 2nd year, later mostly hairless. Terminal buds 2–8 mm long, brown, conical; scales with a few hairs along the margins. **LEAF** Alternate, simple, thin, moderately stiff, ovate or oblong; flat, convex, or somewhat rolled; usually sharply spine-tipped. Margins entire or with low, spine-tipped teeth. Upper surface dark or yellowish green, moderately lustrous, smooth; lower surface waxy bluish white, sometimes obscured by golden glandular hairs, often with taller, branched grayish hairs. Blade 2–7 cm long, 1–3.5 cm broad; petiole 3–14 mm long. **FRUIT** Acorn, 1.5–3 cm long; stalk absent or to 1 mm long. Nut red-brown, oval or elliptic in outline. Cup saucer-shaped, 4–10 mm deep,

PALMER OAK

CANYON LIVE OAK

Palmer Oak

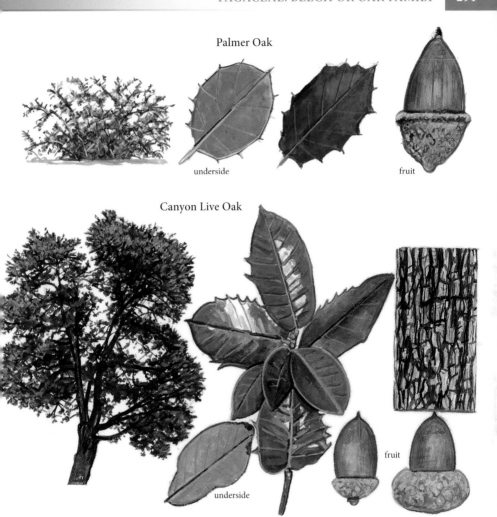

underside

fruit

Canyon Live Oak

underside

fruit

1.5–4 cm wide, covering ¼–⅓ of the nut, thick, the rim often corky and swollen; scales embedded in silvery or golden velvety hairs, only the scale tips visible. Acorns biennial, maturing in mid-autumn.

HABITAT/RANGE Native. Forested canyons, slopes, open areas, 200–2,600 m; sw. Ore., Calif., Ariz. to sw. N.M., nw. Mexico.

SIMILAR SPECIES Easily confused with Sonoran Scrub Oak (*Q. turbinella*) and Toumey Oak (*Q. toumeyi*), but these have smaller leaves, and smaller, annual acorns, with cup scales not embedded in hairs. Coast Live Oak (*Q. agrifolia*) and Interior Live Oak (*Q. wislizeni*) have dark, deeply furrowed mature bark, the underside of the leaves green and hairless (sometimes with tufts of hairs in the vein axils), and acorn cups with thin, distinct scales.

Notes This is among the most variable of western oaks, ranging from stately tall trees in old-growth forests to low multistemmed shrubs in chaparral. Acorn-bearing twigs may not produce new growth in the 2nd season after pollination and, thus, acorns may appear annual. Canyon Live Oak hybridizes with other intermediate oaks. Populations in se. Ariz. and sw. N.M. are hybridized with Palmer Oak (*Q. palmeri*).

CHANNEL ISLAND OAK *Quercus tomentella* Engelm.

Evergreen tree to 20 m. **TWIG** Rather rigid, 3–4 mm diam., branching at 45°. **LEAF** Brittle, oblong-lanceolate to elliptic, wavy, more or less convex, lower surface whitish or brownish hairy; margins often rolled under, teeth 8–12 per side. Blade 7–10 cm long; petiole 7–10 mm long. **FRUIT** Acorn, 2–3 cm long. **HABITAT/RANGE** Native. Canyons, in the U.S. only on the Channel Islands of s. Calif.; also n. Baja Calif.

CEDROS ISLAND OAK *Quercus cedrosensis* C.H. Mull.

Evergreen creeping shrub to a tree 5 m tall. **TWIG** Flexible; buds 1 mm long. **LEAF** Lanceolate to round, hairless; lower surface bluish green; margins entire or with a few irregular spine-tipped teeth. Blade 6–20 mm long; petiole 1.5–2.5 mm long. **FRUIT** Acorn, 1.5–2.2 cm long, cup 8–12 mm wide. **HABITAT/RANGE** Native. In brush, 100–1,800 m; a Baja Calif. species, in the U.S. known only from Otay Mountain, San Diego County, Calif.

WHITE OAKS: SECTION *QUERCUS*

There are about 200 species of white oaks occurring across much of the Northern Hemisphere. White oaks have pale tan wood, and bark that is grayish and scaly (sometimes very pale and near-white, this and the pale wood giving the name "white oaks"). **LEAF** Usually lacks spines (or sometimes has small flexible bristles on the teeth tips). **FRUIT** Acorn, developing in 1 year. Cap with knobby, pubescent scales; inside of shell nearly hairless, or hairy only near the base and tip. This section begins with species that have small unlobed leaves and progresses to species with large lobed leaves.

SONORAN SCRUB OAK *Quercus turbinella* Greene
A.K.A. SHRUB LIVE OAK, SCRUB OAK

QUICK ID Leaves are hairy or glandular and hairy, with spines on the margins about 1 mm long, and the bark is tight and smooth on twigs and branches well over 1 cm diam.

Evergreen, or deciduous in very dry periods. Small tree to about 5 m tall, with 1 to several often branched trunks to 20 cm diam., or a dense, low shrub. Crown round or broader than tall, usually dense, with stiff, ascending or widely spreading branches. **BARK** Smooth and gray on young branches well over 1 cm diam.; light gray, fissured and scaly on older branches and trunks. **TWIG** Brownish or grayish velvety (or more or less hairless) when young, becoming grayish later, ultimately mostly hairless. Terminal buds 1–2 mm long, brown, globose or egg-shaped, minutely hairy. **LEAF** Alternate, simple, thin and stiff, flat or wavy, ovate or elliptic. Margins thickened, entire or with a few pointed-triangular spine-tipped teeth, spines 1–1.5 mm long. Upper surface grayish or bluish green, dull or lustrous, hairless or sparsely pubescent, smooth; lower surface grayish green with branched hairs, or yellowish or golden with glandular hairs, veins slightly raised. Blade usually 2–4 cm long, 1–2 cm broad; petiole 1–4 mm long. **FRUIT** Acorn, 1.5–2 cm long, on a stalk 1–4 cm long. Nut light brown, egg-shaped. Cup shallowly cup-shaped or hemispheric, 4–6 mm deep, 8–12 mm wide, covering ¼–½ of the nut; scales grayish or yellowish hairy, moderately thickened, tips appressed, rounded, nearly hairless and reddish brown. Acorns annual, maturing in mid- to late summer.

HABITAT/RANGE Native. On dry slopes, commonly among piñon and juniper, 800–2,000 m; se. Calif., s. Nev., and sw. Utah, to sw. Colo., N.M., w. Tex., and n. Mexico.

SIMILAR SPECIES Toumey Oak (*Q. toumeyi*) has golden glandular hairs on the undersides of the leaves, but few or no branched hairs, twigs 1 cm diam. have bark breaking into scales, and acorns are on stalks up to only 2 mm long. Ajo Mountain Scrub Oak (*Q. ajoensis*) lacks hairs and glands on the leaves.

Notes Acorns mature coincident with the onset of summer rains. California populations once known as *Q. turbinella* are now realized to represent separate, closely similar species, some of which may be occasionally treelike and are reviewed on p. 296.

SONORAN SCRUB OAK

Channel Island Oak

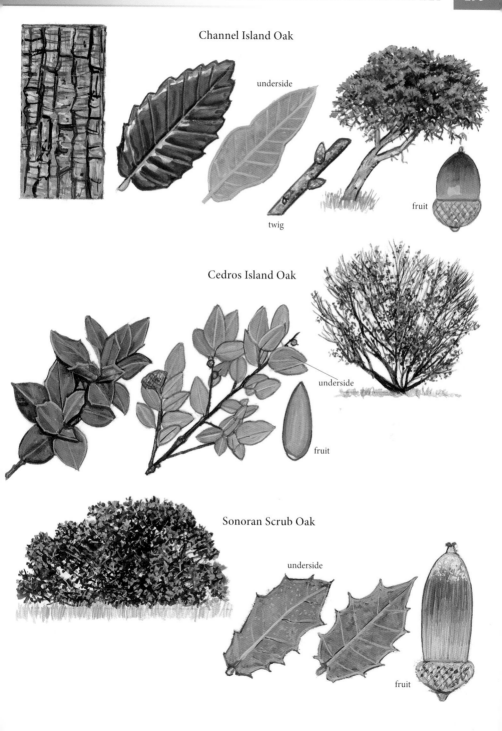

underside

twig

fruit

Cedros Island Oak

underside

fruit

Sonoran Scrub Oak

underside

fruit

TEXAS LIVE OAK *Quercus fusiformis*
Small

A.K.A. SCRUB LIVE OAK, WEST TEXAS LIVE OAK

QUICK ID This oak has thin, rather stiff, lanceolate to elliptic leaves, glossy above, and whitish beneath with low, matted hairs; and pointed acorns, 2–3 cm long, on a stalk 3–30 mm long.

Semievergreen, the leaves falling in spring and immediately replaced as new leaves appear. Tree to 12 m tall with 1 to several short trunks, or a rhizomatous, thicket-forming shrub. Crown dense and broad on larger trees; branches stout, spreading and ascending. **BARK** Dark brown to nearly black, furrowed, blocky, with scaly ridges. **TWIG** Gray or golden gray, felty, often nearly hairless by the 2nd year, or hairs mostly persistent. Terminal buds about 1–3 mm long, glossy brown to reddish, subglobose to egg-shaped, hairless or margins of scales hairy. **LEAF** Alternate, simple, thin and slightly leathery, mostly flat, lanceolate to oblong-elliptic. Margins entire or with 1–3 low teeth. Upper surface green or dark green, smooth, lustrous, more or less hairless; lower surface whitish, covered by low, overlapping branched hairs, the veins inconspicuous. Blade usually 2–9 cm long, 1.5–4 cm broad; petiole 2–8 mm long. **FRUIT** Acorn, 2–3 cm long, 1–3 borne on a stalk 3–30 mm long. Nut brown and often with slightly lighter stripes, thickest near the middle; often barrel-shaped, pointed at the tip (rarely rounded). Cup goblet-shaped, tapered at the base, 8–15 mm deep, 6–12 mm wide, covering ¼–½ of the nut; scale tips narrowly pointed and reddish brown. Acorns annual, maturing late summer to autumn.

HABITAT/RANGE Native. On rocky hills in open woodlands and brush, and in grasslands, 0–500 m; sw. Okla. to s. Tex.

SIMILAR SPECIES Southern Live Oak (*Q. virginiana*) is usually a large tree with widely spreading branches that often sweep the ground, and with acorns mostly 1.5–2.5 cm long, the apex rounded or bluntly pointed.

Notes Texas Live Oak sometimes is considered a variety of Southern Live Oak, as *Q. virginiana* Mill. var. *fusiformis* (Small) Sarg. The two thoroughly intergrade along the s. Tex. coast and from the Brazos River to the Edwards Plateau. Along the coast in s. Tex., leaves average broader and more rounded (blade 3.5–9 cm long, 2–8 cm broad; petiole 2–8 mm long), and acorns are barrel-shaped and blunt, suggesting intergradation with the more southerly *Q. oleoides* Schltdl. & Cham.

SOUTHERN LIVE OAK *Quercus virginiana* Mill.

QUICK ID This oak has thin, rather stiff, lanceolate to elliptic leaves, glossy above, and pale beneath with low, matted hairs; and acorns rounded or blunt at tip, often less than 2 cm long, on a stalk 1–2 cm long.

Evergreen tree to 20 m tall. Usually a single trunk, often massive and branching low to the ground. **LEAF** Usually elliptic, sometimes slightly wider toward the tip. Upper surface lustrous, dark green; lower surface covered by a dense mat of pale gray hairs. Blade 2–10 cm long, 2–5 cm broad; petiole usually less than 1 cm long. **FRUIT** Acorn 1–2.5 cm long. Cup goblet-shaped, 8–15 mm deep, covering ⅓–½ of the nut; nut barrel-shaped, with a rounded or blunt tip.

HABITAT/RANGE Woodlands and hammocks, 0–100 m; se. U.S., barely entering our range near Corpus Christi, Tex.

Notes This magnificent oak of the boulevards of southern cities is similar to Texas Live Oak (*Q. fusiformis*), differing as discussed in that account. Some authorities consider the 2 oaks to be 1 species with slightly different eastern and western races.

TEXAS LIVE OAK   SOUTHERN LIVE OAK

underside

Texas Live Oak

fruit

fruit

Southern Live Oak

HOLM OAK *Quercus ilex* L.
A.K.A. HOLLY OAK

Evergreen tree to 12 m, rarely taller. **LEAF** Broadly lanceolate to ovate, upper surface dark green and mostly hairless, lower surface finely grayish- or yellowish-hairy; margins entire or with a few low teeth. Blade 2.5–8 cm long; petiole 1–2.5 cm long. **FRUIT** Acorn, 1.5–2. cm long, cup with flat scales. **HABITAT/RANGE** Introduced from the Mediterranean region; grown as an ornamental and sparsely naturalized near developments in s. Calif., 50–400 m.

CHANNEL ISLAND SCRUB OAK
Quercus pacifica Nixon & C.H. Mull.

Semievergreen shrub or tree to 5 m tall. **LEAF** Ovate to oblong in outline, with 0–5 low, irregular teeth per side; upper surface green, glossy, and more or less hairless; lower surface waxy, pale green, with sparse, low, stellate hairs. Blade 1.5–4 cm long; petiole 2–5 mm long. **FRUIT** Acorn, more or less stalkless. **HABITAT/RANGE** Native. Brush and dry woodlands, 0–300 m; Channel Islands, s. Calif.

CALIFORNIA SCRUB OAK *Quercus berberidifolia* Liebm.

QUICK ID The common scrub oak, this species has irregularly toothed, small bicolored leaves, the upper surface green, the lower paler, and an acorn about ⅔ as wide as long, its tip rounded.

Semievergreen shrub, rarely a tree, to 4 m. **LEAF** Elliptic to nearly round, upper surface dull green and glossy, lower surface pale greenish with scattered stellate hairs and yellow glandular hairs; margins irregularly toothed, with minute spines at the blade tip and on teeth tips. Blade 1.5–3 cm long; petiole 2–4 mm long.

HABITAT/RANGE Native. Chaparral and coastal sage; much of lowland Calif. below 1,800 m.

AJO MOUNTAIN SCRUB OAK *Quercus ajoensis* C.H. Mull.

QUICK ID This shrub or small tree has small spiny-margined bluish-green leathery leaves that are hairless or nearly so when mature.

Evergreen shrub, rarely a tree, to 3 m tall. **LEAF** Narrowly ovate, ovate or oblong, bluish green, leathery, hairless or nearly so when mature, flat or wavy near the margins, margins with 4–6 teeth, each tipped by a spine; lower surface papillose (with the pebbled texture of a football surface, visible under a 20× lens). Blade 1.5–3.5 cm long; petiole 2–4 mm long. **FRUIT** Acorn, 1.2–1.5 cm long.

HABITAT/RANGE Native. Igneous slopes, 500–1,500 m; sw. Ariz. and adjacent Mexico. Hybrid populations believed to involve Ajo Mountain Scrub Oak and Toumey Oak (*Q. toumeyi*) occur in s. N.M., and others involving Sonoran Scrub Oak (*Q. turbinella*) and Gambel Oak (*Q. gambelii*) occur in s. Utah.

California Scrub Oak

fruit

CALIFORNIA SCRUB OAK   AJO MOUNTAIN SCRUB OAK

Holm Oak

underside

fruit

new shoots, early spring

Channel Island Scrub Oak

fruit

Ajo Mountain Scrub Oak

new leaves

underside   fruit

GRAY OAK *Quercus grisea* Liebm.

QUICK ID Small leaves, usually entire-margined and less than 4 cm long, finely grayish-felty on both the upper and lower surfaces, and buds with yellowish hairs at least on the outer scales, distinguish this widespread southwestern oak.

Evergreen, or deciduous in very dry periods. Tree, usually under 10 m tall, with 1 or 2 often branched trunks to 1 m diam. Crown oval to broader than tall, usually dense, with spreading branches. **BARK** Gray or dark gray, smooth on small branches; on older trunks with rather straight furrows and narrow, scaly ridges. **TWIG** Sparsely or densely tan- or grayish-felty, later nearly hairless. Terminal buds 1–2 mm long, dark reddish brown, egg-shaped to nearly globose, yellowish pubescent with branched hairs at least on the outer scales. **LEAF** Alternate, simple, thin, slightly leathery, flat, elliptic, oblong, or ovate. Margins entire or with a few low teeth, especially near the apex, often slightly rolled under. Surfaces grayish-felty with minute branched hairs; upper surface dull gray-green, veins not impressed; lower surface sometimes a little paler, the veins slightly raised but inconspicuous. Blade usually 2–4 cm long, 1.5–3 cm broad; petiole 3–10 mm long. **FRUIT** Acorn, 1.2–1.8 cm long, stalkless or on a stalk to 3 cm long. Nut light brown, narrow to broadly ovoid. Cup deeply goblet- or cup-shaped, 4–10 mm deep, 8–15 mm wide, covering ⅓–⅔ of the nut; scales densely gray-felty, moderately thickened, the tips appressed, blunt, mostly hairless and reddish. Acorns annual, maturing in autumn.

HABITAT/RANGE Native. Moderately dry valleys and on slopes usually derived from igneous rock, commonly with piñon and juniper, 1,200–2,700 m; c. Colo. to w. Ariz., N.M., w. Tex., and n. Mexico.

SIMILAR SPECIES Mohr Oak (*Q. mohriana*) has leaves with a nearly hairless, dark green upper surface and a grayish-hairy lower surface. Arizona White Oak (*Q. arizonica*) has leaves usually with toothed margins, the lower surface with conspicuously raised veins.

Notes Trees may lose leaves during dry springs. Gray Oak hybridizes extensively with Arizona White Oak, often making identification problematic. Hybrids with Gambel Oak (*Q. gambelii*), and their derivatives, are very common and are known as Wavyleaf Oak (*Q. × undulata*).

TOUMEY OAK *Quercus toumeyi* Sarg.

QUICK ID Small, stiff leaves, with entire or few-toothed margins, dark green and glossy above, paler and often with golden glandular hairs beneath, in combination with acorns only 8–15 mm long on stalks 1–2 mm long, help identify this southwestern tree.

Evergreen shrub or small tree to 7 m tall; trunk short, often branched near the ground, to 30 cm diam.; crown round, dense. **BARK** Becoming scaly on branches as small as 1 cm diam. **TWIG** Terminal buds 1 mm long, egg-shaped, reddish. **LEAF** Alternate, simple, thin, stiff, flat, lanceolate or oblong-elliptic. Margins entire or with a few low, sharply pointed teeth near the tip. Upper surface dark green, glossy; lower surface dull, pale green, sometimes yellowish, with golden glandular hairs and often with whitish branched hairs. Blade 1.5–2.5 cm long, 0.8–1.2 cm broad; petiole 2–3.5 mm long. **FRUIT** Acorn, 8–15 mm long, cup covering ⅓ of the nut; stalk 1–2 mm long. Acorns annual, maturing in late summer.

HABITAT/RANGE Native. Rocky slopes in brush and open woodland, 1,500–1,800 m; sw. Ariz., s. N.M., w. Tex.

GRAY OAK

TOUMEY OAK

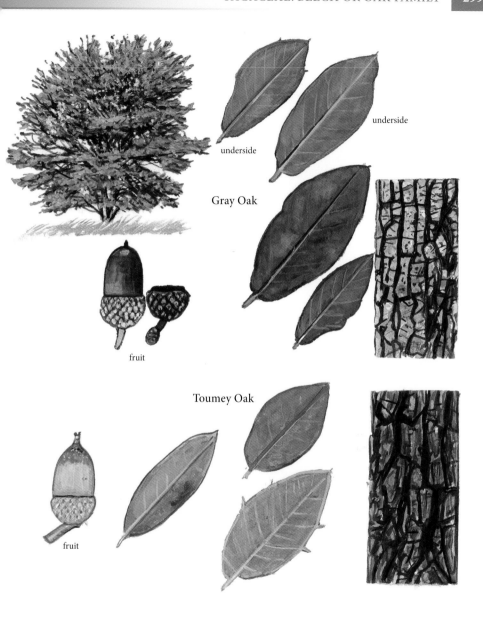

underside

underside

Gray Oak

fruit

Toumey Oak

fruit

SIMILAR SPECIES Forms with toothed leaves resemble Sonoran Scrub Oak (*Q. turbinella*), which
often has hairier leaves and acorns on longer stalks.

Notes In dry periods Toumey Oak may lose its
leaves.

MOHR OAK *Quercus mohriana* Buckley ex Rydb.

QUICK ID This shrub or small tree, common on limestone, has strongly bicolored leaves, darker on the upper surface, and usually hairless, dark red-brown buds.

Evergreen or deciduous shrub or small tree to 3 m tall; when shrubby, commonly grows in patches. **TWIG** Terminal buds 2 mm long, hairless or lightly hairy on the outer scales, dark red-brown, broadly egg-shaped. **LEAF** Alternate, simple, thin, flexible, flat, oblong or elliptic. Margins entire or with up to 5 low teeth on each side, flat or wavy. Upper surface dark green, more or less lustrous; lower surface densely grayish- or whitish-felty with erect, branched hairs. Blade 3–5 cm long, 2–3 cm broad; petiole 2–5 mm long. **FRUIT** Acorn, 8–15 mm long, cup covering ½ of the nut. Acorns annual, maturing midsummer to autumn.

HABITAT/RANGE Native. Arid limestone hills and plains, 600–2,500 m; w. Tex. to w. Okla. and ne. N.M.

Notes This oak hybridizes extensively with Gray Oak (*Q. grisea*) where the 2 species make contact. It also hybridizes with Gambel Oak (*Q. gambelii*); the product is part of the *Q.* × *undulata* complex.

VASEY OAK *Quercus vaseyana* Buckley

QUICK ID Narrow, flat leaves with 3–5 low, blunt teeth on each side, the upper surface dark green and nearly hairless, and the lower paler with small, light hairs, help distinguish this small oak from w. Tex.

Evergreen shrub or small tree to 10 m tall. **LEAF** Narrowly lanceolate to oblong, mostly flat; upper surface dark green and nearly hairless; lower surface with appressed, starlike hairs, giving it a grayish cast. Margin usually with 3–5 low, blunt teeth. Blade 2–6 cm long; petiole 2–5 mm long. **FRUIT** Acorn, about 1.2 cm long, the cup covering ⅕–⅓ of the nut.

HABITAT/RANGE Native. Dry limestone slopes among brush or in arroyos in grasslands, 300–600 m; w. Tex, especially near the Big Bend.

SHIN OAK *Quercus havardii* Rydb.
A.K.A. HAVARD OAK

QUICK ID This mostly shrubby species of deep sands has rather thick, hard leaves with rolled, wavy margins, each side usually with a few low teeth, the upper surface dark green and lustrous, the lower hairy and paler.

Deciduous low shrub or small tree to 4 m tall. **LEAF** Lanceolate to obovate; upper surface dark green, sparsely soft-hairy; lower surface grayish or yellowish green, with low, appressed, branched hairs; margins wavy, rolled under, with a few low teeth on each side. Blade 2–5 cm long; petiole 3–7 mm long. **FRUIT** Acorn, 1.2–2.5 cm long.

HABITAT/RANGE Native. Deep sands, 500–1,500 m; w. Tex., w. Okla., e. N.M. Populations in ne. Ariz. and se. Utah are thought to be hybrids between Shin Oak and both Gambel Oak (*Q. gambelii*) and Sonoran Scrub Oak (*Q. turbinella*).

MOHR OAK   VASEY OAK   SHIN OAK

Mohr Oak

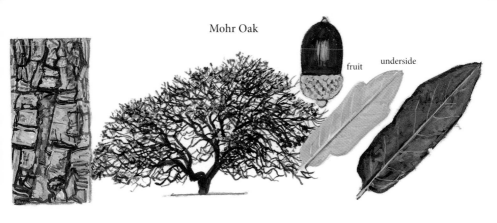

fruit

underside

Vasey Oak

underside

fruit

Shin Oak

underside

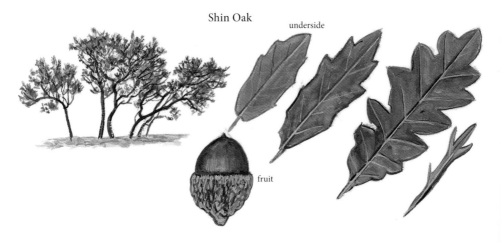

fruit

SANDPAPER OAK *Quercus pungens*
Liebm.

QUICK ID The stiff, leathery leaves of this species have prominently wavy margins with 2–5 coarse teeth on each side; the surfaces are harshly hairy and feel like fine sandpaper.

Evergreen shrub or tree to 6 m tall. **LEAF** Stiff, leathery, wavy, often curved back, elliptic or oblong, with 2–5 coarse teeth on each side, harshly hairy. Blade 1–4 cm long; petiole 3–10 mm long. **FRUIT** Acorn, 1 cm long, on a stalk to 3 mm long.

HABITAT/RANGE Native. Rocky slopes in brush or open woodland, 800–2,000 m; sw. Ariz., s. N.M., w. and sc. Tex.

Notes Leaves may freeze, remaining dried and brown on the twigs for some time.

WAVYLEAF OAK *Quercus* × *undulata*
Torr.

QUICK ID Elliptic to oblong grayish-green leaves with blunt teeth, highly variable on a tree and within a population, help to identify this common, usually shrubby, oak.

Deciduous or semievergreen shrub or tree to 5 m tall, the leaves often withering and remaining on the plant well into winter. **LEAF** Elliptic or oblong, wavy, deeply or shallowly blunt-toothed, softly hairy and usually grayish green. Blade 2–5.5 cm long; petiole 2–3 mm long.

HABITAT/RANGE Native. Dry slopes above 1,000 m; s. Nev. to nc. Utah, e. Colo., Okla., Ariz., N.M., and w. Tex.

Notes Extremely variable and very common, representing hybrids between Gambel Oak (*Q. gambelii*) and any of 6 small-leaved western oaks, most commonly Gray Oak (*Q. grisea*). Parent species may not be in the immediate vicinity.

CHIHUAHUA OAK *Quercus chihuahuensis* Trel.
A.K.A. FELT OAK

Deciduous tree to 10 m tall. **LEAF** Ovate, oblong, or elliptic, green above, paler beneath, velvety with erect hairs, veins conspicuous; margins entire to bluntly toothed or shallowly lobed. Blade 4–8 cm long; petiole 3–5 mm long. **FRUIT** Acorn, 1.4–1.8 cm long; stalk 1.5–6 cm long. **HABITAT/RANGE** Native. Common in Mexico, in our area found only on rocky slopes in w. Tex., at about 1,600 m, where all plants are putative hybrids with Gray Oak (*Q. grisea*) or Arizona White Oak (*Q. arizonica*).

ARIZONA WHITE OAK *Quercus arizonica* Sarg.
A.K.A. ARIZONA OAK, ARIZONA LIVE OAK

QUICK ID The combination of elliptic to oblanceolate, often convex small leathery leaves with entire or few-toothed margins, the upper surface nearly hairless, and the lower lightly hairy and with prominent raised veins, identifies this southwestern tree.

Evergreen, or deciduous in very dry periods. Small to moderate tree to 18 m tall, with 1 or 2 often branched trunks, 0.5–1 m diam. Crown round or broad and irregular, usually dense, with thick, often contorted, widely spreading branches. **BARK** Gray; when young thin, with small appressed scales; later with deep, narrow fissures and broad ridges broken into long, thick, platelike scales. **TWIG** Rusty-velvety at first, fading to gray by the 2nd year, ultimately twigs more or less hairless. Terminal buds about 3 mm long, dull red-brown, egg-shaped, mostly hairless, tip pointed or rounded. **LEAF** Alternate, simple, thin, slightly leathery, flat or convex, elliptic, oblong, obovate, or oblanceolate. Margins usually coarsely few-toothed, especially

SANDPAPER OAK   WAVYLEAF OAK

Sandpaper Oak

fruit

winter

autumn

Wavyleaf Oak

fruit

Chihuahua Oak

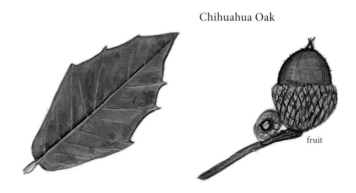

fruit

ARIZONA WHITE OAK *continued*

near the apex, sometimes entire. Upper surface dark or bluish green, moderately lustrous, sparsely and minutely pubescent, veins slightly impressed; lower surface dull or bluish green, pubescent with curly, branched hairs, veins raised, conspicuous. Blade usually 4–8 cm long, 1.5–3 cm broad; petiole 3–10 mm long. **FRUIT** Acorn, 8–12 mm long, on a stalk 1–15 mm long. Nut dark chestnut brown, often striped slightly darker, ovoid to conical. Cup hemispheric or cup-shaped, 5–10 mm deep, 10–15 mm wide, covering about ½ of the nut; scales light brown, densely felty, those near the stalk thickened and rounded; scale tips loose, pointed, nearly hairless, reddish brown. Acorns annual, maturing late summer to autumn.

HABITAT/RANGE Native. Canyons and valleys, often with piñon and juniper, 1,300–2,500 m; w. Tex., across s. N.M., to nw. Ariz. and n. Mexico.

SIMILAR SPECIES Cork Oak (*Q. suber* L.) has gray-fuzzy undersides to the leaves and thick gray corky bark. It is in the taxonomic section *Cerris*, allied to the white oaks. Introduced from Europe, it is known in the West only from cultivated plants. Gray Oak (*Q. grisea*) usually has grayish-hairy, entire-margined leaves with low, much less conspicuous veins on the underside.

Notes In very dry spring seasons all leaves may be lost before new ones appear. Leaf size and pubescence is variable. At high elevations Arizona White Oak may be a shrub. It hybridizes with numerous other white oaks. It is so thoroughly intergradient with Gray Oak that some have considered the two to be a single variable species.

ARIZONA WHITE OAK

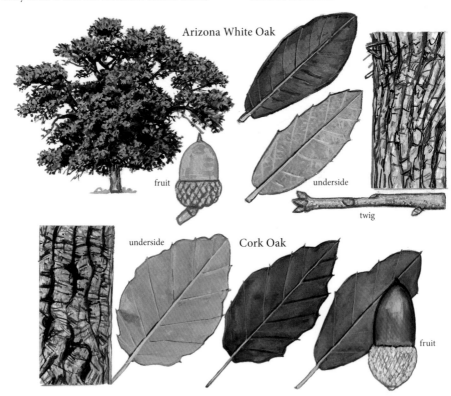

Arizona White Oak

fruit

underside

twig

underside

Cork Oak

fruit

Hybridization

Hybridization is the process by which two organisms with genetics sufficiently different that they are not part of the same population system interbreed and produce offspring. For instance, two tree species may be distinct from one another across their geographic ranges, only to interbreed and intergrade where they come into contact. In another instance a seed might be transported a long distance into a population of a different but related species, and the lone individual that grows from that seed hybridizes with trees of the related surrounding species.

Hybridization is notable in several tree genera, among them the firs (*Abies*), oaks (*Quercus*), locusts (*Robinia*), willows (*Salix*), poplars (*Populus*), crab apples (*Crataegus*), and a number of others. Sometimes the hybridization in the area of contact simply produces a stable zone of intergradation, as is the case between *Abies concolor* and *Abies grandis* in the w. U.S. Outside this zone, environmental differences and distance maintain the differences between the two species. In other instances natural selection stabilizes a new, successful hybrid combination. Complex population systems then may be produced that make identification very difficult. This is the case with crab apples, in which hybrids may faithfully reproduce sexually or asexually, producing a plethora of forms that may be named as species.

A well-known hybrid situation exists among oaks of the sw. U.S. When Gambel Oak (*Quercus gambelii*) came into contact with other white oaks, hybrid populations were often produced. Those persisted, and the hybrids interbred among themselves and the parent species, muddling the differences between the two original parent species. The hybrids were all once considered one species, Wavyleaf Oak (*Q. undulata*), because of similarity in the wavy-edged leaves. We now understand that these are hybrids, and add the mathematical multiplication sign (×) to the name (*Q.* × *undulata*), indicating that this name refers to hybrids.

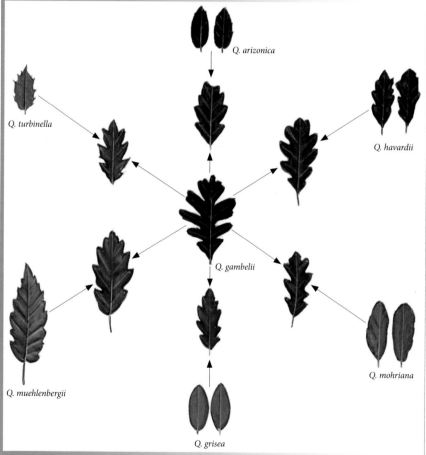

Q. arizonica

Q. turbinella

Q. havardii

Q. gambelii

Q. muehlenbergii

Q. mohriana

Q. grisea

Diagram of leaves from a complex hybridization system in oaks of the sw. U.S. Gambel Oak (*Quercus gambelii*), represented by the leaf in the center, will hybridize with any one of six other white oaks, indicated around the periphery. The hybrids are common; all have similar leaves and are known as Wavyleaf Oak (*Q.* × *undulata*).

MEXICAN OAK *Quercus carmenensis*
C.H. Mull.

Deciduous shrub or tree to 6 m tall. **TWIG** Often red in the 1st season. **LEAF** Obovate; upper surface dark green; lower surface paler, with erect velvety hairs; margins irregularly toothed in the apical half. Blade 3–5 cm long; petiole 2–10 mm long, reddish. **FRUIT** Unknown. **HABITAT/ RANGE** On limestone, among shrubs and trees, 2,070–2,500 m; a Mexican species, known in our region from a single collection in the Chisos Mountains, Tex.

NETLEAF OAK *Quercus rugosa* Née

QUICK ID This oak has broad, stiffly leathery leaves, with the veins strongly raised on the lower surface. No other native western oak has such long acorn stalks.

Evergreen, or deciduous during very dry periods. Dense, stiff shrub or small to moderate tree, usually less than 10 m tall; trunks 1 or 2, often branched, usually to 50 cm diam. Crown round, sometimes irregular, usually dense, with ascending and spreading branches. **BARK** Dark brown to gray, when young thin and smooth, when older furrowed, the ridges with small, thin, tight scales. **TWIG** Rusty-velvety when young, the velvet fading to gray by the 2nd year; ultimately hairless or nearly so. Terminal buds 2–4 mm long, brown, egg-shaped, sparsely pubescent or nearly hairless. **LEAF** Alternate, simple, thick, stiffly leathery, usually convex; ovate, elliptic, nearly round, or sometimes roughly violin-shaped. Margins usually with 5–9 low teeth, some or all bearing a very short spine. Upper surface dark green, lustrous, sparsely hairy, the veins notably impressed; lower surface green or grayish green, sometimes more or less golden with minute glands (glands brown later in season), veins raised, conspicuous, netlike. Blade 3–10 cm long, 2–7 cm broad; petiole to 7 mm long. **FRUIT** Acorn, 1–2 cm long, usually several on a stalk 3–6 cm long. Nut light brown, ellipsoid or egg-shaped, tip bluntly pointed. Cup saucer-shaped to deeply cup-shaped, 5–9 mm deep, 10–15 mm wide, covering ¼–½ of the nut; scales brown, densely felty, often grayish, those near the stalk moderately thickened; tips loosely appressed. Acorns annual, maturing in autumn.

HABITAT/RANGE Native. In wooded canyons and on slopes, 2,000–2,500 m; w. Tex., s. N.M. to c. Ariz., south to Mexico.

SIMILAR SPECIES Easily confused with Arizona White Oak (*Q. arizonica*), which has proportionally narrower, less veiny leaves and very short acorn stalks.

Notes On open slopes Netleaf Oak is often a thicket-forming shrub; in valley bottoms it can be an attractive tree. Southward, in Mexico, trees may be very large, with large ladle-like leaves and acorn stalks up to 13 cm long.

MEXICAN WHITE OAK *Quercus polymorpha* Schltdl. & Cham.

QUICK ID Rare in Tex., this oak has elliptic or ovate leaves, with margins entire or toothed near the tip, glossy and dark green on the upper surface, and the veins raised and conspicuous below.

Evergreen tree to 20 m tall (may lose leaves during dry periods). **LEAF** Slightly leathery, elliptic to ovate, entire or toothed near the tip, mostly hairless; veins 10–14 pairs, curved, the veins and veinlets on the lower surface raised, forming a conspicuous netlike pattern; upper surface dark green, glossy; lower surface light green. Blade 5–10 cm long; petiole 1.5–2.5 cm long. **FRUIT** Acorn, 1.4–2.5 cm long, on a stalk 0.5–3 cm long.

HABITAT/RANGE Native. Forests and dry woods, 400–2,100 m; common in Mexico; in our region known only from a single grove in a wooded river canyon at 400 m in sc. Tex.

NETLEAF OAK

MEXICAN WHITE OAK

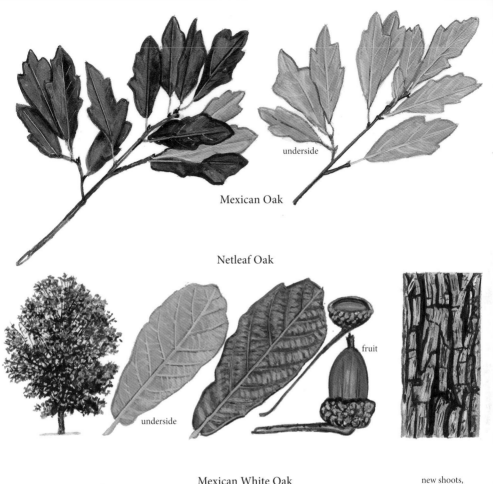

Mexican Oak

underside

Netleaf Oak

underside

fruit

Mexican White Oak

fruit

new shoots,
early spring

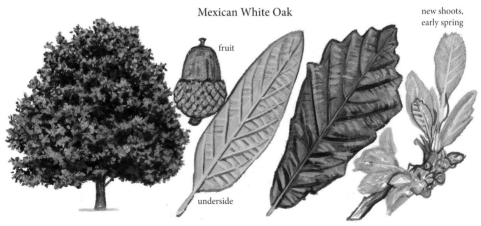

underside

CHINQUAPIN OAK *Quercus muehlenbergii* Engelm.

QUICK ID Unique among western oak trees, this species has leaves with usually 10–14 pairs of parallel veins, each terminating in a marginal tooth.

Deciduous tree 20–33 m tall; trunk single, to 90 cm diam. Crown round, dense. **TWIG** Terminal buds 2–4 mm long, sparsely pubescent, scales with pale margins. **LEAF** Alternate, simple, thin, flexible, flat, obovate to lanceolate; with usually 10–14 parallel veins per side, each terminating at the margin in a forward-curved tooth. Upper surface dark green, lustrous; lower surface pale green to whitish and minutely hairy. Blade 5–15 cm long, 4–8 cm broad; petiole 1–3 cm long. **FRUIT** Acorn, 1.5–2 cm long, cup covering ⅓–½ of the nut. Acorns annual, maturing in early autumn.

HABITAT/RANGE Native. Mixed forests and woodlands, to 2,300 m; mostly e. U.S., extending into the West in c. and w. Tex, and in the mountains along the western edge of the plains of e. N.M.

SIMILAR SPECIES Deer or Sadler Oak (*Q. sadleriana* R. Br.), a shrub of the mountains of nw. Calif. and sw. Ore., also has leaves with numerous parallel veins ending in teeth.

MEXICAN BLUE OAK *Quercus oblongifolia* Torr.
A.K.A. SONORAN BLUE OAK, WHITE OAK

QUICK ID Leaves of this species are smooth and mostly hairless, blue-green, and have usually entire margins.

Evergreen, or semideciduous in very dry periods. Small to moderate tree to 10 m tall, usually with 1 trunk to 50–70 cm diam. Crown round, usually dense, with stout, widely spreading branches. **BARK** Pale gray and smooth on young trees, on older trees closely furrowed, the ridges broken into small, nearly square, flat scales. **TWIG** Brown or reddish brown when young, sparsely or densely velvety, becoming nearly hairless in the 2nd year. Terminal buds about 1–2 mm long, reddish, egg-shaped to nearly spherical, hairless or scales near the base pubescent. **LEAF** Alternate, simple, thin, firm, flat, elliptic or oblong, rarely lanceolate. Margins entire, sometimes undulate, rarely with a few coarse teeth. Upper surface pale green or blue-green, often glaucous, smooth, sparsely pubescent but soon nearly hairless, veins inconspicuous; lower surface slightly paler, at first finely glandular hairy, but soon nearly hairless, the veins slightly raised. Blade usually 3–6 cm long, 1–2.5 cm broad; petiole 2–5 mm long. **FRUIT** Acorn, 1.2–1.7 cm long, on a stalk 1–12 mm long. Nut light brown, egg-shaped or oblong. Cup cup-shaped, 4–12 mm deep, 6–8 mm wide, covering about ⅓ of the nut; scales grayish-felty, those near the base moderately and regularly thickened, the largest 1–1.5 mm wide, scale tips reddish. Acorns annual, maturing in autumn.

HABITAT/RANGE Native. On slopes in grasslands and arid woodlands, 1,300–1,650 m; se. Ariz., sw. N.M., and into n. Mexico.

SIMILAR SPECIES Engelmann Oak (*Q. engelmannii*) has acorn cup scales strongly but irregularly thickened, 1.5–3 mm wide, and the cup averaging wider and deeper.

Notes Along with Emory Oak (*Q. emoryi*), this is a common low-elevation oak in its area. It is so similar to Engelmann Oak of s. Calif. that the two may be a single species. In winter the leaves of Mexican Blue Oak may be pale bluish mauve.

CHINQUAPIN OAK

MEXICAN BLUE OAK

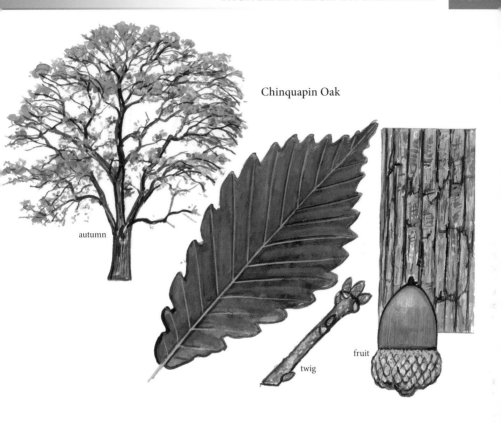

Chinquapin Oak

autumn

twig

fruit

Mexican Blue Oak

fruit

ENGELMANN OAK *Quercus engelmannii* Greene

QUICK ID This oak from s. Calif. has nearly hairless blue-green leaves, and swollen scales up to 3 mm wide on the acorn cup.

Very similar to Mexican Blue Oak (*Q. oblongifolia*), and perhaps the same species. **LEAF** Margins usually with a few low teeth near the tip. Blade 3–7 cm long; petiole 3–4 mm long. **FRUIT** Acorn, 1.5–2.5 cm long (averaging larger than that of Mexican Blue Oak), cup 10–15 mm wide, 8–10 mm deep, scales strongly and irregularly swollen, the largest 1.5–3 mm wide.

HABITAT/RANGE Native. Oak woodlands and margins of chaparral, 50–1,200 m; s. Calif., and n. Baja Calif.

BIGELOW OAK *Quercus durandii* Buckley **var.** *breviloba* (Torr.) Palmer
A.K.A. BASTARD OAK, SHORTLOBE OAK, DURAND WHITE OAK

QUICK ID This oak of dry limestone hills of Tex. and Okla. usually forms thickets, the trees with multiple trunks. Leaves are often cupped upward, the lower surface is silvery, and the margins are entire to shallowly lobed along their length.

Deciduous shrub or tree, 3–5 m tall, often clonal and with multiple trunks to 15 cm diam. **BARK** Gray, shaggy, flaking in strips. **TWIG** Terminal buds 2–3 mm long, broadly egg-shaped, hairless or scales with hairy margins. **LEAF** Alternate, simple, thin, flexible. Often slightly cupped upward, elliptic to obovate; margins entire, wavy or shallowly lobed. Upper surface grayish green, lustrous, mostly hairless; lower surface greenish white, usually with dense, low hairs. Blade 3–12 cm long, 2.5–6 cm broad; petiole 2–6 mm long. **FRUIT** Acorn, 7–15 mm long, nearly as broad, cup covering ¼–½ of the nut. Acorns annual, maturing late summer to early autumn.

HABITAT/RANGE Native. Open woodlands and scrublands, often on limestone, 200–600 m; sc. Okla., c. Tex., ne. Mexico.

Notes Bigelow Oak has been included within *Q. sinuata* Walter, a name whose application is questionable. It has also been considered a species or has been placed as a variety of other species. It intergrades with the more easterly Durand Oak (*Q. durandii* var. *durandii*, replacing it on the Edwards Plateau of Tex.

DURAND OAK *Quercus durandii* Buckley **var.** *durandii*

QUICK ID Durand Oak usually has a single trunk, its leaves are often broader near the tip, the margins are entire, not lobed or with few lobes that are shallow and mostly near the tip, and the blade is bicolored, its lower surface silvery.

Deciduous tree to 25 m tall, with a single straight trunk to 75 cm diam. **LEAF** Variable, from elliptic to obovate to rather kite-, diamond-, or almost wedge-shaped, sometimes with a few very shallow terminal lobes. Blade 5–12 cm long; petiole 3–5 mm long. **FRUIT** Acorn, 7–19 mm long, cup covering ⅓ of the nut.

HABITAT/RANGE Native. Along streams or on fertile hills, 300–400 m in the West; a se. U.S. species barely entering sc. Tex.

ENGELMANN OAK

BIGELOW OAK

DURAND OAK

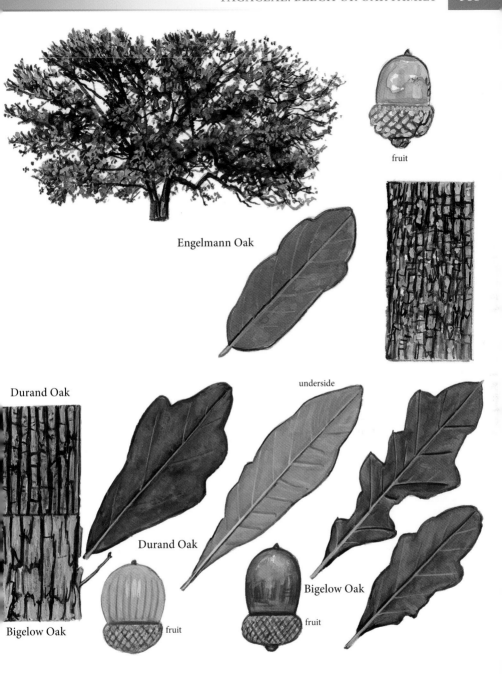

fruit

Engelmann Oak

Durand Oak

underside

Durand Oak

Bigelow Oak

Durand Oak

fruit

Bigelow Oak

Bigelow Oak

fruit

LACEY OAK *Quercus laceyi* Small
A.K.A. Texas Blue Oak

QUICK ID This Tex. oak has thin, entire or shallowly lobed bluish-green leaves that are hairless at maturity.

Deciduous shrub or tree, 5–12 m tall; 1 to several trunks, to 40 cm diam. **BARK** Light gray, papery, scaly. **TWIG** At first hairy, green or brown; later gray and hairless. Terminal buds 1.5–3 mm long, egg-shaped, sometimes pointed, hairless. **LEAF** Alternate, simple, thin, flexible, flat or wavy, elliptic to obovate. Margins entire or shallowly lobed. Bluish green; the lower surface paler, at first lightly hairy, later mostly hairless. Blade 4–9 cm long, 3–6 cm broad; petiole 5–9 mm long. **FRUIT** Acorn, 1.3–1.5 cm long, more or less flattened at both ends, cup covering ⅕–⅓ of the nut. Acorns annual, maturing in autumn.

HABITAT/RANGE Native. Rocky soils in woodlands, 350–600 m; c. Tex. to ne. Mexico.

Notes The foliage is peach or pink in spring, smoky green or bluish in summer, and tan to peach in autumn. Some references show a Tex. range for Bluff Oak (*Q. austrina* Small), a species otherwise from the se. U.S., perhaps based on incorrectly identified Lacey Oak and Bigelow Oak (*Q. durandii* var. *breviloba*).

CALIFORNIA BLUE OAK *Quercus douglasii* Hook. & Arn.
A.K.A. Douglas Oak, Iron Oak

QUICK ID This oak grows on dry slopes throughout much of Calif. It has bluish- or grayish-green leaves with entire to shallowly lobed margins.

Deciduous, with dry leaves remaining for some time; or evergreen in moist, protected sites. Small tree, usually 10 m tall or less, usually with a single trunk to 60 cm diam.; sometimes a shrub. Crown round, often irregular, moderately open, with short, ascending or spreading, contorted branches. **BARK** Smooth and gray at first, later narrowly ridged, scaly, easily flaking. **TWIG** Yellowish, reddish, or grayish velvety when young, ultimately mostly hairless. Terminal buds 3–5 mm long, usually red-brown, egg-shaped to nearly spherical, hairy along the scale margins. **LEAF** Alternate, simple, thin, flexible, flat; oblong, lanceolate, or obovate in outline. Margins entire or shallowly cut into 1–4 lobes on each side, the sinus usually extending less than halfway to the midrib. Upper surface bluish or grayish green, sparsely pubescent; lower surface paler, sparsely or densely pubescent with erect hairs, the veins slightly raised. Blade usually 4–8 cm long, 2–3 cm broad; petiole 2–6 mm long. **FRUIT** Acorn, 2–3 cm long, nearly stalkless. Nut light to dark chestnut brown, narrowly cylindric or egg-shaped, tapered to a point. Cup hemispheric or cup-shaped, 5–10 mm deep, 10–15 mm wide, covering only the base of the nut, the scales grayish felty, thin or those near the base much thickened and rounded. Acorns annual, maturing late summer to autumn.

HABITAT/RANGE Native. Slopes and flats, below 1,100 m; Calif., in the Coast Ranges and around the Central Valley.

SIMILAR SPECIES Valley Oak (*Q. lobata*) grows in deeper soils of valley bottoms and lower slopes; its leaves are dark or grayish green, with sinuses cut more than halfway to the midrib, and with hairs on the underside spreading and interlocked. Oregon Oak (*Q. garryana* var. *garryana*) occurs in mixed forest; its leaf has deep sinuses and erect hairs on the lower surface.

Notes This species is sometimes called "tardily deciduous," because the withered and dried leaves hang on the tree for some time before falling. The wood is hard and brittle, and trees are constantly losing their limbs. Regeneration is inhibited by competition of introduced annual grasses and browsing of young plants by domestic livestock and wildlife.

LACEY OAK   CALIFORNIA BLUE OAK

new leaves, early spring

fruit

Lacey Oak

California Blue Oak

underside

fruit

twig

VALLEY OAK *Quercus lobata* Née
A.K.A. CALIFORNIA WHITE OAK, WEEPING OAK

QUICK ID This is a large oak with drooping branches, deeply lobed leaves with low, interlocked hairs on the underside, and acorns 3–6 cm long.

Majestic deciduous tree to 25 m tall or more, with a single massive trunk to 1 m or more diam. Crown broad, round-topped, rather open, with thick, arching or spreading branches, the tips drooping, often reaching the ground. **BARK** Gray and scaly on young trees, darker on older trees, with deep, narrow, checkered fissures. **TWIG** Yellowish or grayish, rarely reddish, densely or sparsely velvety when young, later mostly hairless. Terminal buds 3–5 mm long, yellowish or light brown, egg-shaped, densely hairy, tip pointed. **LEAF** Alternate, simple, thin, flexible, flat, broadly obovate or elliptic in outline. Margins with 3–5 lobes on each side, the sinuses extending more than halfway to the midrib. Upper surface dark or grayish green, glossy, mostly hairless, smooth; lower surface whitish or light green, densely or sparsely pubescent with low, interlocking hairs, veins slightly raised. Blade usually 5–10 cm long, 3–6 cm broad; petiole 5–12 mm long. **FRUIT** Acorn, 3–6 cm long, more or less stalkless. Nut bright chestnut brown, narrowly barrel-shaped, tapered to a point. Cup hemispheric, deeply cup-shaped or turban-shaped, 1–3 cm deep, 1.4–3 cm wide, covering about ¼–⅓ of the nut; scales densely felty, grayish or cream, those near the stalk thickened and rounded. Acorns annual, maturing in late autumn.

HABITAT/RANGE Native. Valley floors and slopes in grasslands, savanna, and oak woodlands, to 1,700 m; Calif., in and around the Central Valley, the Coast Ranges, and southern mountains.

SIMILAR SPECIES Valley Oak grows with California Blue Oak (*Q. douglasii*), which has bluish-green leaves that are lobed less than halfway to the midrib and have erect hairs on the underside. Oregon Oak (*Q. garryana* var. *garryana*) has deeply lobed leaves similar to those of Valley Oak, but the hairs on the lower surface are erect.

Notes This is the largest of western oaks, and said to be the largest American oak, growing rapidly for the first few years. The massive trees grow far apart in savannas, forming picturesque groves. Large trees, with trunk diam. to 3 m, usually have the trunk rotted and hollow in the center and cannot be accurately aged; some are believed to be 300–500 years old.

OREGON OAK *Quercus garryana*
Douglas ex Hook. **var.** *garryana*
A.K.A. POST OAK

QUICK ID An oak distinguished by the combination of relatively large buds, deeply lobed leaves with yellowish veins and erect, branched hairs on the lower surface, and acorns usually 2.5–3 cm long.

Deciduous tree, 15–30 m tall; usually a single trunk to 1 m diam. Crown round or oval, the branches contorted and gnarled, the tips spreading or drooping. **TWIG** Yellowish or brown, with fine, spreading hairs. Terminal buds yellowish or tan, 6–12 mm long, egg-shaped or both ends tapered, pubescent, often glandular. **LEAF** Alternate, simple, thin, flexible, flat, elliptic, obovate, or nearly round in outline. Margins with 3–5 lobes on each side, the sinuses extending more than halfway to the midrib; larger lobes often with small lobes. Upper surface bright green, lustrous, lightly hairy; lower surface light green or waxy-yellowish, softly hairy with erect, branched hairs. Veins yellowish. Blade 3–12 cm long, 2–9 cm broad; petiole 4–10 mm long. **FRUIT** Acorn, usually 2.5–3 cm long, cup

VALLEY OAK

OREGON OAK

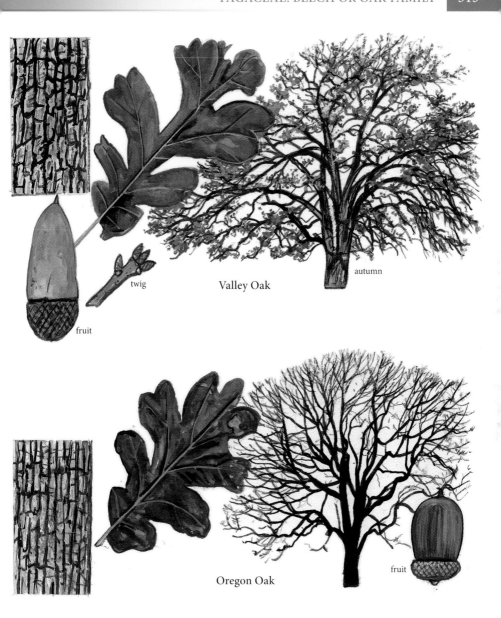

twig

Valley Oak

autumn

fruit

Oregon Oak

fruit

covering ⅓–¼ of the nut. Acorns annual, maturing late summer to mid-autumn.

HABITAT/RANGE Native. Oak woodland and mixed forest, 0–1,900 m; near the coast and in mountains from sw. B.C. to c. coastal Calif.

Notes The species has 2 other varieties, both shrubby. One, var. *semota* Jepson, is often also a small tree to 5 m tall, with several trunks. Its buds are reddish brown, and twigs lack spreading hairs. It occurs from sw. Ore. and n. Calif. southward on the w. slope of the Sierra Nevada.

ENGLISH OAK *Quercus robur* L.
A.K.A. PEDUNCULATE OAK

Deciduous tree to 30 m tall. **TWIG** Reddish brown, hairless. **LEAF** Elliptic to obovate, deeply lobed, hairless or nearly so, the base notched at the petiole and appearing as 2 earlike lobes. Blade 7–15 cm long; petiole 3–6 mm long. **FRUIT** Acorn, 1.5–3 cm long, on a slender stalk 3–8 cm long. **HABITAT/RANGE** Introduced from Europe; often cultivated, perhaps locally naturalized on brushy slopes, lake shores, and disturbed areas, 0–180 m in w. Wash and sw. B.C.

TURKISH OAK *Quercus cerris* L.

Deciduous tree to 40 m tall; trunk to 2 m diam. **LEAF** Oblong-obovate in outline, with 6–12 pairs of lobes. Blade 7–14 cm long, half as broad; petiole 1–2 cm long. **FRUIT** Acorn, 2.5–4 cm long; cup appearing mossy, bearing soft, twisted, bristlelike scales 4–8 mm long. **HABITAT/RANGE** Introduced from Eurasia; occasionally planted and may occur in waste areas in w. Wash and sw. B.C. *Notes* Allied to white oaks, it belongs to the Old World section *Cerris*.

GAMBEL OAK *Quercus gambelii* Nutt.
A.K.A. UTAH WHITE OAK, ROCKY MOUNTAIN WHITE OAK

QUICKID This is the only oak in the Rocky Mountain region bearing deeply lobed leaves with erect, branched hairs on the lower surface.

Deciduous tree, 10–15 m tall, usually with a single trunk to 70 cm diam.; or smaller trees growing from a root mass and forming dense colonies, the trunks about 10 cm diam., or in dense thickets with taller stems in the center. Crown of treelike forms round or oval, with widely spreading branches. **BARK** On older trunks and branches gray, with broad, irregular flat ridges with small, flat scales. **TWIG** Brown or red-brown, pubescent to hairless, becoming gray-brown by the 2nd year, by which time all the twigs are hairless or nearly so. Terminal buds 3 mm long, brown, egg-shaped, sparsely pubescent, becoming nearly hairless. **LEAF** Alternate, simple, thin, flexible, flat; elliptic, oblong, or obovate in outline. Margins lobed more than halfway to the midrib; lobes 4–6 on each side. Upper surface dark green, lustrous, with minute hairs (appearing hairless), smooth; lower surface pale, dull green, sparsely or densely pubescent with erect, branched hairs, the veins slightly raised. Blade usually 6–12 cm long, 4–6 cm broad; petiole 1–2 cm long. **FRUIT** Acorn, 1.2–2 cm long, on a stalk about 1 cm long. Nut light brown, egg-shaped. Cup deeply cup-shaped, 5–8 mm deep, 7–15 mm wide, covering ¼–½ of the nut; scales gray-pubescent, those near the stalk much thickened and rounded. Acorns annual, maturing in early autumn.

HABITAT/RANGE Native. At the upper elevational margin of piñon–juniper woodland and in mixed conifer forest, 1,000–3,000 m; se. Idaho to Utah, Colo. to s. Nev., Ariz., N.M., w. Tex., and n. Mexico.

SIMILAR SPECIES The leaves of Gambel Oak are very similar to those of Valley Oak (*Q. lobata*) and Oregon Oak (*Q. garryana* var. *garryana*), species from the Sierra Nevada and westward.

Notes This is the common deciduous oak in the Rocky Mountain region. In arid areas in Utah and Ariz., Gambel Oak may form dense, low patches of shrubbery that resemble the habit of *Q. havardii* and locally is called Shin Oak like that species. Gambel Oak vegetatively regenerates from a massive underground woody system called a lignotuber. It hybridizes with several other white oaks, producing the shrubby Wavyleaf Oak (*Q.* × *undulata*); see "Hybridization," p. 305.

GAMBEL OAK

English Oak

Turkish Oak

twig

fruit

autumn

fruit

Gambel Oak

fruit

underside

autumn

BUR OAK *Quercus macrocarpa* Michx.
A.K.A. MOSSY-CUP OAK

QUICK ID Bur Oak has deeply lobed, sometimes more or less fiddle-shaped leaves, winged twigs, and large acorn cups with a fringed margin.

Deciduous tree to 30 m tall or more; single trunk to 2 m diam. **TWIG** Develops thin, wing-like corky ridges. **LEAF** Alternate, simple, thin, flexible, flat, elliptic to roughly fiddle-shaped in outline, sides with 4–7 deep lobes, divisions deepest near the middle, lobes broadest in the distal half. Upper surface dark green or gray-green, lustrous; lower surface much paler, with minute star-shaped hairs that lie flat. Blade 7–25 cm long, 1–15 cm broad; petiole 1.5–2.5 cm long. **FRUIT** Acorn, 2.5–5 cm long, cup covering ½ to almost all of the nut; scales at cup margin with soft, flexible awn-like tips to 1 cm long. Acorns annual, maturing late summer to mid-autumn.

HABITAT/RANGE Native. Poorly drained soil, 850–950 m in the West; an eastern species entering the Great Plains from sc. Canada to c. Tex.

Notes The fringe on the cup is short and inconspicuous in the north, and longer and often matted southward. The acorns are the largest of any species north of Mexico.

POST OAK *Quercus stellata* Wangenh.
A.K.A. IRON OAK

QUICK ID The thick, densely yellowish- or grayish-hairy twigs and harsh pubescence on the lower surface of the leaves identify this species; the distinctive cross-shaped leaves of many trees are also distinctive.

Deciduous tree to 20 m tall; single trunk, 30–60 cm diam. Crown round, more or less open, with twisted branches. **TWIG** 3–5 mm diam., densely stellate-hairy with yellowish or grayish hairs; buds 1–4 mm long, sparsely pubescent, egg-shaped, sometimes pointed. **LEAF** Alternate, simple, thick, leathery, usually wavy, more or less obovate, shallowly to deeply lobed, the squarish terminal and middle lobes often diverging at right angles, resembling a Maltese cross, the 2 lower lobes, when present, smaller and distant. Upper surface dark green, lustrous; lower surface yellowish green, rather harshly hairy. Blade 10–18 cm long, 5–15 cm broad; petiole 3–15 mm long. **FRUIT** Acorn, 1–2 cm long, ends rounded, cup covering ⅓–⅔ of the nut. Acorns annual, maturing in autumn.

HABITAT/RANGE Native. Dry sites in prairies and upland woods, mostly below 800 m; an eastern species that enters c. Tex.

Notes The cross-shaped leaves are more apparent in the East; in the West, the lobes often diverge at steeper angles.

SAND POST OAK *Quercus margarettae*
(Ashe) Small

QUICK ID This tree has fairly small leaves, the lower surface velvety with erect hairs, and grayish, hairless mature twigs.

Deciduous shrub or scrubby tree to 8 m tall. **TWIG** Hairless, green or reddish, becoming gray. **LEAF** Obovate in outline, each side with 1–4 lobes, the middle lobe largest; upper surface dark green and mostly hairless; lower surface paler, velvety with erect, branched hairs. Blade 4–8 cm long; petiole 3–10 mm long. **FRUIT** Acorn, 1.5–2.5 cm long, on a short stalk, cup covering ½–¾ of the nut.

HABITAT/RANGE Native. In deep sands, 0–600 m; a se. U.S. species entering c. Tex.

BUR OAK

POST OAK

SAND POST OAK

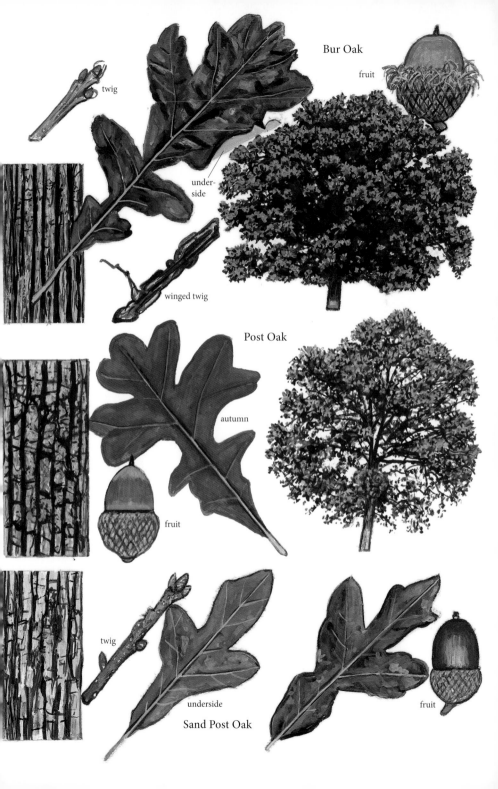

Bur Oak

twig

fruit

under-
side

winged twig

Post Oak

autumn

fruit

twig

underside

fruit

Sand Post Oak

GARRYACEAE: SILKTASSEL FAMILY

Silktassels belong to a small family of shrubs and trees that occur in warm temperate and subtropical regions of w. North America, Central America and the West Indies, and East Asia. Parts or all of the group have been classified with the willow family (Salicaceae), the wax-myrtle family (Myricaceae), or the dogwood family (Cornaceae), or as a separate family with a single genus, and now as a family composed of an American genus, *Garrya*, and an Asian genus, *Aucuba*. The 2 genera together contain about 20 species.

LEAF Evergreen, simple, opposite, those of a pair slightly joined at the base. **FLOWER** Unisexual, in terminal inflorescences, with an inferior ovary. **FRUIT** Dryish drupelike berry. A number of species are used as ornamentals for their attractive foliage, early flowering, or showy fruits.

■ *GARRYA*: SILKTASSELS

There are about 13 species of *Garrya*, all restricted to North America and Central America at low to moderate elevations.

Silktassels are distinguished largely by leaf characters and pubescence, but species intergrade and identification is sometimes difficult. They are evergreen, usually shrubs, sometimes small trees. **BARK** Thin, at first smooth and green, later reddish to brownish on twigs, becoming dark brownish gray and shallowly fissured on larger stems. **TWIG** Four-angled or 4-lined; lenticels small, slit-like or elliptic. **LEAF** Opposite, simple, somewhat leathery, with entire or wavy margins. **FLOWER** Unisexual, the sexes on separate plants, with 0, 2, or 4 perianth parts often fused into a small cup. Male flowers in long, slender, hanging catkins, 3 flowers per bract, each flower with 4 stamens. Female flowers in short hanging or nodding catkins, often with leaf-like bracts that decrease in size toward the tip of the catkin, each flower in a bract. Ovary inferior. **FRUIT** Drupelike berry with a bitter, fleshy interior, a dry, brittle exterior skin, and 1 or 2 seeds.

CHAPARRAL SILKTASSEL *Garrya congdonii* Eastw.

QUICK ID This shrub or small tree is distinguished by its opposite leaves, the younger leaves having dense, fine, wavy, but not feltlike hairs on the underside.

Evergreen yellowish-green shrub or small tree, 1–3 m tall, at first silky-hairy on the twigs, mostly hairless later. **LEAF** Opposite, ovate to obovate-elliptic, convex, margins flat to wavy; upper surface hairless; lower surface with dense, wavy hairs; blade 1.5–7 cm long, 1–3.5 cm broad. **FRUIT** Berry covered with pale hairs, 6–8 mm diam.

HABITAT/RANGE Native. In chaparral, 100–1,200 m; nc. Calif.

WAVYLEAF SILKTASSEL *Garrya elliptica* Dougl. ex Lindl.
A.K.A. COAST SILKTASSEL, QUININE BUSH

QUICK ID Wavyleaf Silktassel has opposite leaves with wavy margins, the lower sides of the leaves with interwoven, feltlike hairs.

Among the western silktassels, this species is the largest and most treelike, particularly in w. Ore., where plants may reach 9 m tall. Crown round, dense, the branches more or less spreading, in layers. **LEAF** Opposite, simple, leathery, flat or convex; elliptic to oval, usually wavy along the margins; margins often rolled under and appearing toothed or lobed. Upper surface nearly hairless, lustrous,

CHAPARRAL SILKTASSEL

Chaparral Silktassel

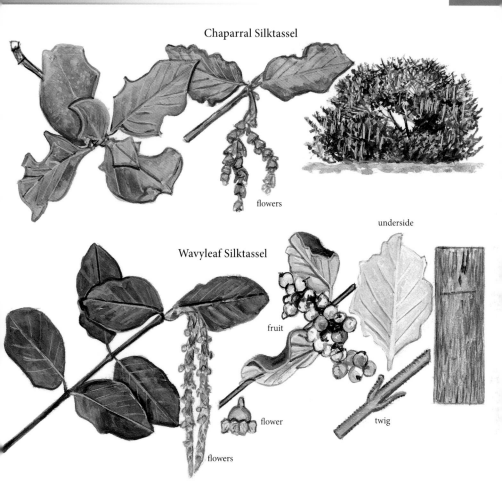

flowers

underside

Wavyleaf Silktassel

fruit

flower

twig

flowers

dark green; lower surface felty with dense, wavy, interwoven hairs. Blade 1.5–11 cm long, 1.5–7 cm broad; petiole 6–12 mm long. **FLOWER** Tiny, the sexes on separate plants in slender, pendulous catkins; male catkins 8–16 cm long, female catkins 5–7 cm long. Dec.–Mar. **FRUIT** Drupelike, globose, 7–11 mm diam., densely white-hairy; fruiting cluster up to 16 cm.

HABITAT/RANGE Native. Sea bluffs, dunes, chaparral, pine–oak woodland not far from the coast, 0–800 m; c. Calif. to w. Ore.

Notes Cultivated as an ornamental near the coast, the male plants are particularly enjoyed for their long, pale pastel green and lavender catkins, which

occur singly or in groups of 2–10, dangling at the ends of the branches. The berries, leaves, and bark are very bitter, giving the plant the alternative common name of Quinine Bush.

WAVYLEAF SILKTASSEL

ASHY SILKTASSEL *Garrya flavescens*
S. Watson
A.K.A. PALE SILKTASSEL

QUICK ID Ashy Silktassel is distinguished by its densely hairy, drupelike berries in combination with opposite leaves that are sparsely hairy on the upper surface.

Evergreen, grayish-green erect shrub or small tree, 1–3.5 m tall, pubescent nearly throughout, with pale, appressed hairs. **LEAF** Opposite, elliptic to obovate-elliptic, flat to more or less convex, margin flat or somewhat undulate; upper surface with few hairs, lower surface densely appressed-hairy; blade 2–7.5 cm long, 1–4.5 cm broad. **FLOWER** Feb.–Apr. **FRUIT** Densely clustered, broadly egg-shaped, 6–8 mm wide, purplish under dense, pale hairs.

HABITAT/RANGE Native. Dry brush and woodland, 650–2,350 m; nw. Calif. to s. Nev., sw. Utah, Ariz., and n. Mexico.

BEARBRUSH *Garrya fremontii* Torr.
A.K.A. FREMONT SILKTASSEL

QUICK ID Both the fruits and the flat opposite leaves of Bearbrush are hairless or nearly so.

Evergreen, yellowish-green erect shrub or small tree, 1–3 m tall. **LEAF** Opposite, oblong-elliptic to oblong-obovate; margins flat, neither rolled under or wavy; upper surface on mature leaves hairless, lustrous; lower surface paler, sparsely hairy; blade 2–12 cm long, 1–7 cm broad. **FLOWER** Jan.–Apr. **FRUIT** Globose, 6 mm wide, buff to purplish or blackish, hairless or nearly so.

HABITAT/RANGE Native. Chaparral, open woodlands, forest, 300–2,300 m; s. Wash., nw. Nev. to s. Calif. and nw. Mexico.

EGGLEAF SILKTASSEL *Garrya ovata*
Benth.
A.K.A. MEXICAN SILKTASSEL

QUICK ID Rather small, simple, opposite leaves help to distinguish this from other trees in the region, and the foliage and twigs being finely hairy when young but less hairy when older helps separate it from Wright's Silktassel.

Evergreen shrub or small tree, 1–6 m tall, pubescent throughout but the density of hairs decreasing with age on the twigs and upper leaf surface. **LEAF** Opposite; narrowly lanceolate, ovate, or elliptic, often with a tiny point at the tip; margin flat or undulate; dull green, upper surface lustrous on older leaves; blade 3–6 cm long, 1.5–4 cm broad. **FLOWER** Mar.–Apr. **FRUIT** Dark purplish to blue-black, 4–8 mm diam., hairless when mature.

HABITAT/RANGE Native. Rocky slopes and ledges in canyons, 350–2,100 m; c. and w. Tex., s. N.M., n. Mexico.

Notes There are 2 varieties of this species in the U.S. Var. *lindheimeri* (Torr.) J. H. Coulter & W.H. Evans, of the Edwards Plateau, Tex., has flat leaves with smooth margins; the more westerly var. *goldmanii* (Woot. & Standl.) B.L. Turner has undulate leaves, the margins rough with minute bumps.

ASHY SILKTASSEL   BEARBRUSH   EGGLEAF SILKTASSEL

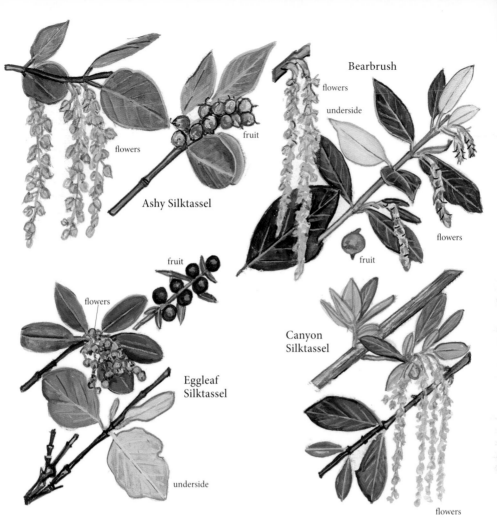

flowers

Ashy Silktassel

Bearbrush

flowers

underside

flowers

fruit

fruit

flowers

Canyon
Silktassel

fruit

flowers

Eggleaf
Silktassel

underside

flowers

CANYON SILKTASSEL *Garrya veatchii* Kellogg

A.K.A. VEATCH SILKTASSEL

QUICK ID The leaves of this silktassel have dense, felty, interwoven hairs covering the lower surface, and margins that are flat or only slightly wavy.

Evergreen erect shrub or small tree, 1–2 m tall. **LEAF** Opposite, lanceolate-elliptic to obovate-elliptic, flat or somewhat convex, tip tapered to a fine point, margins flat to partly rolled under or more or less wavy, green; upper surface hairless, lustrous; lower surface densely pale, felty; blade 2.5–9 cm long, 1–5 cm broad. **FLOWER** Feb.–Apr. **FRUIT**

Globose or broadly egg-shaped, 7–8 mm wide, buff to purple-brown, hairy.

HABITAT/RANGE Native. Chaparral, open woodlands, 250–1,750 m; s. Calif., nw. Mexico.

CANYON SILKTASSEL

WRIGHT'S SILKTASSEL *Garrya wrightii* Torr.

QUICK ID The flat opposite leaves with the margins minutely roughened help distinguish this silktassel from others.

Evergreen shrub or small tree, 1–4 m tall, hairless or nearly so. **LEAF** Opposite, lanceolate to oblong, flat, often with a tiny point at the tip, margin minutely roughened, dull green, surfaces hairless or the lower surface with a few appressed hairs; blade 2–6 cm long, 1–3.5 cm broad. **FLOWER** Mar.–Aug. **FRUIT** Purplish to blue-black, often gray-coated, 6–9 mm diam., hairless when mature.

fruit

Wright's Silktassel

WRIGHT'S SILKTASSEL

HABITAT/RANGE Native. Among boulders, in crevices, on slopes in brush and dry woods, 1,200–2,100 m; w. Tex., s. N.M., Ariz., n. Mexico.

HAMAMELIDACEAE: WITCH-HAZEL FAMILY

The witch-hazel family is small, consisting of about 25 genera and 80 species of temperate and tropical trees and shrubs. It occurs in North America, Mexico, Central America, East Asia, Africa, Australia, and Pacific islands. Two genera and 5 species are native to North America, 1 species barely entering the West. A few species are popular ornamentals. The family is well known for its tendency toward autumn and winter flowering, capsular fruit that sometimes splits forcibly to expel the seeds, and the broad, bluntly toothed leaves. Forked branches of witch-hazel have been used as divining rods, and the leaves, bark, and twigs have been used medicinally.

AMERICAN WITCH-HAZEL *Hamamelis virginiana* L.

QUICK ID This shrub or small tree is easily distinguished by the ovate, scalloped leaves with an asymmetric base and lower surface often bearing star-shaped hairs.

Deciduous shrub or small tree to 8 m tall, with a low-branching, broad, rounded crown of zigzag twigs tipped with naked buds in winter. Trunk erect or leaning, 1 to several, to 30 cm diam. **LEAF** Alternate, simple, 2-ranked, oval or obovate, base asymmetric, tip bluntly pointed, margins scalloped or wavy, lower surface often with at least a few stellate hairs, blade 4–15 cm long. **FLOWER** In small few-flowered clusters along twigs, bisexual, yellow, with 4 pubescent, ribbonlike petals 1–2.5 cm long. Sep.–Dec. **FRUIT** Hairy, 4-pointed, 2-valved greenish or grayish capsule, 1–1.6 cm long.

HABITAT/RANGE Native. In woods on moist slopes and in ravines, 0–1,500 m; e. U.S., barely entering the West on the Edwards Plateau in sc. Tex.

AMERICAN WITCH-HAZEL

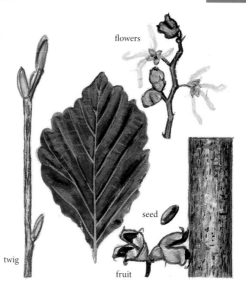

flowers

seed

twig

fruit

American Witch-hazel

JUGLANDACEAE: WALNUT FAMILY

There are 9 genera and more than 60 species of walnuts and their relatives, most of them trees, from Eurasia and the Western Hemisphere; 23 occur in North America, with 7 native species in the West.

LEAF Aromatic, alternate, pinnately compound, usually with a terminal leaflet (odd-pinnate). **FLOWER** Tiny, unisexual, both sexes on the same plant, borne on the previous year's twigs or at the base of the current year's growth; calyx 4-lobed or absent; petals absent. Male flowers have 3–50 stamens; female flowers have a single inferior ovary with 2 usually feathery stigmas. Plants are wind-pollinated. **FRUIT** Resembles a drupe (the fleshy outer part, the husk, develops from an involucre *and* calyx). The hard-walled inner part is the nut with which we are so familiar. The large seed or kernel is oily and often edible.

The family provides valuable hickory, pecan, and walnut lumber. Commercial varieties of pecans and walnuts are grown in extensive orchards in temperate regions of the world for the edible seed within the nut and the oil that can be pressed from the seed. A number of species are grown as ornamentals, enjoyed for their stately form, dense shade, and autumn foliage.

■ *CARYA*: HICKORIES

Carya is genus of 18 species of e. North America, Mexico, and Asia. Of the 11 species in North America, 2 extend their ranges into the West.

Deciduous trees to about 50 m tall. **BARK** Gray, more or less smooth at first, becoming finely or moderately furrowed, the furrows often forming a diamond pattern. **TWIG** Varying greenish to reddish brown, pith solid, bud scales clamlike (valvate) or overlapping (imbricate). **LEAF** Alternate, pinnately compound, terminal leaflet conspicuous. Leaflets 3–21, opposite, usually hairy, hairs sometimes confined to the vein axils of the lower surface. **FLOWER** Unisexual, male and female borne on the same tree, the male flowers in catkins usually on 1st-year twigs, the female flowers in terminal spikes. **FRUIT** Nut, often enclosed in a thick or thin husk, usually splitting at maturity along several sutures; nutshell brown, reddish brown, or tan.

The hickories are widely used and commercially valuable for their nuts, especially pecans. Their wood is valued in applications that require strength and shock resistance, or for its bold grain in cabinetry. Several North American hickories are cultivated for timber in Europe. The nuts are a favored and important wildlife food. Taxonomically, the hickories are divided into 2 groups, those with valvate bud scales and those with imbricate bud scales.

PECAN *Carya illinoinensis* (Wangenh.) K. Koch

QUICK ID Recognized by the combination of alternate, pinnately compound leaves with numerous leaflets, scaly grayish bark, and a distinctive nut.

Deciduous, often large tree, 40–60 m tall, usually with a single trunk to 2.5 m diam.; crown narrowly rounded to vase-shaped. **BARK** Grayish or light brown, often tinged reddish, eventually dividing into narrow, scaly ridges. **TWIG** Purplish brown, more or less hairy, with elongate buff-colored lenticels; bud scales clamshell-like. **LEAF** Alternate, pinnately compound, terminal leaflet conspicuous; blade 15–60 cm long, 15–30 cm broad; petiole 5–9 cm long. Leaflets 5–17, commonly 9 or more, each 8–20 cm long, 2.5–7.5 cm broad; recurved, drooping, lanceolate, base often asymmetrically

wedge-shaped, tip tapered to a long point; margins toothed. Upper surface dark green, usually hairless; lower surface paler, hairless or with scattered hairs along the veins. **FLOWER** Male flowers in slender catkins 12–18 cm long, 5–6 mm diam. Mar.–May. **FRUIT** Nuts 2–10 in a cluster, each rich dark brown, often with darker streaks, ellipsoid, 2.5–4 cm long, released from a husk 3–4 mm thick that splits to the base along 4 narrowly ridged sutures.

HABITAT/RANGE Native. Along streams and in floodplains, 0–600 m; sc. U.S., extending sporadically westward to w. Tex. and ne. Mexico.

SIMILAR SPECIES Nutmeg Hickory has fewer leaflets on average, short-pointed leaflet tips, often shaggy bark, and shorter male catkins.

Notes Pecan is the state tree of Tex. There are many cultivars, which are grown in suitable climates worldwide for the sweet kernel of the nut; such orchards occupy many thousands of acres in the Southwest.

NUTMEG HICKORY *Carya myristiciformis* (F. Michx.) Elliott
A.K.A. SWAMP HICKORY, BITTER WATER HICKORY

QUICK ID Mature tree recognized by the combination of alternate, pinnately compound leaves predominantly with 7 or 9 leaflets, and scaly, exfoliating bark.

Deciduous tree to 35 m tall, 70 cm diam.; crown open, rounded. **BARK** Gray or dark reddish brown, shallowly and irregularly furrowed, separating into long strips or scales. **TWIG** Slender, brown or bronze, hairless, scaly; bud clamshell-like. **LEAF** Alternate, pinnate, blade 30–60 cm long. Leaflets usually 7–9, each 3–17 cm long; ovate, obovate, or elliptic, tip short-pointed, margins finely or

PECAN

NUTMEG HICKORY

Pecan

nut section

nut

nut

splitting fruit

twig

Nutmeg Hickory

twig

fruit

nut

coarsely toothed. Blade surface scaly, with a bronze cast. **FLOWER** Male catkin to about 6 cm long. Apr.–May. **FRUIT** Tan or bronze husk-covered nut, obovoid or ellipsoid, 2–3 cm long, 1.5–2 cm diam.; husks thin, about 2 mm thick, splitting to the base at maturity.

HABITAT/RANGE Native. Moist areas, 0–500 m; scattered in s. U.S. to c. Tex., ne. Mexico; the least common of all hickories.

Notes The common and scientific names refer to the resemblance of the nut to a nutmeg.

■ *JUGLANS*: WALNUTS

There are 21 species of walnuts worldwide, growing from low to moderate elevations; six are native, and several have been introduced to the U.S. but rarely naturalize. Six species occur in the West.

Deciduous large shrubs to large, spreading trees. **BARK** Smooth and gray when young, often fissured and scaly when older. **TWIG** Usually covered with glandular hairs; leaf scars triangular or 3-lobed. Terminal buds bluntly pointed, usually more or less flattened, hairy. Pith cross-chambered, brownish. **LEAF** Alternate, pinnately compound, usually with a terminal leaflet (odd-pinnate), often with a spicy scent; foliage yellowish in autumn. **FLOWER** Unisexual, male and female borne on the same tree; male flowers in pendulous catkins; female flowers solitary, clustered, or in a short spike. **FRUIT** Globose or broadly ovoid nut enclosed in a green husk or rind that dries, blackens, and does not split; nutshells tan to brown or blackish, smooth, grooved, or wrinkled, splitting into 2 halves upon germination. Seed edible, large, oily, wrinkled and lobed.

Walnuts provide economically important nuts, dyes, and valuable dark-hued lumber used in cabinetry, gunstocks, and decorative items. In the wild, the nuts are an important food source for small mammals.

SOUTHERN CALIFORNIA WALNUT
Juglans californica S. Watson
A.K.A. CALIFORNIA BLACK WALNUT

QUICK ID Bluntly pointed or rounded leaflet tips and nearly hairless leaves help distinguish this species from other walnuts.

Deciduous shrub or small tree, 5–9 m tall. Trunk short, 10–30 cm diam., often leaning and low-branching; crown round. **BARK** Grayish, divided into rough plates. **LEAF** Alternate, pinnately compound, terminal leaflet well developed. Leaflets usually 11–15, each 4–9.5 cm long, 16–26 mm broad; narrowly oblong- or lance-elliptic, symmetric or slightly scythe-shaped; tip rounded or pointed; margins finely toothed. Leaf surfaces nearly hairless, without tufts of hairs in the vein axils; surfaces with a few scales, the veins mostly glandular. **FLOWER** Mar.–May. **FRUIT** Globose, 2–3.5 cm diam.; nut nearly globose, depressed on top, 18–25 mm diam., shallowly grooved, smooth between the grooves.

HABITAT/RANGE Native. Hillsides and canyons in moist soil, 30–900 m; coastal hills of s. Calif.

Notes This species is in decline in its native area due to extensive urban development and agriculture. It has been planted outside its range as an ornamental and to help control erosion.

NORTHERN CALIFORNIA WALNUT
Juglans hindsii (Jeps.) Jeps. ex R.E. Sm.
A.K.A. HINDS'S BLACK WALNUT

QUICK ID The nearly smooth nuts and tufts of hairs in the vein axils on the lower surface of the leaves help distinguish this species.

Deciduous tree, 6–23 m tall. Trunk straight, 30–60 cm diam.; crown round. **BARK** Grayish, longitudinally divided into mostly smooth plates. **LEAF** Alternate, pinnately compound, terminal leaflet often smallest. Leaflets usually 13–21, each 7–13 cm long, 2–3 cm broad; narrowly triangular to lanceolate, symmetric or slightly scythe-shaped; tip long-tapered to a slender point; margins toothed. Both leaf surfaces with few hairs along the veins and lower surface with dense tufts of hairs in the vein axils. **FLOWER** Apr.–May. **FRUIT** Globose, 3.5–5 cm diam.; nut broadly ovoid, 24–32 mm diam., smooth or very shallowly grooved.

SOUTHERN CALIFORNIA WALNUT

NORTHERN CALIFORNIA WALNUT

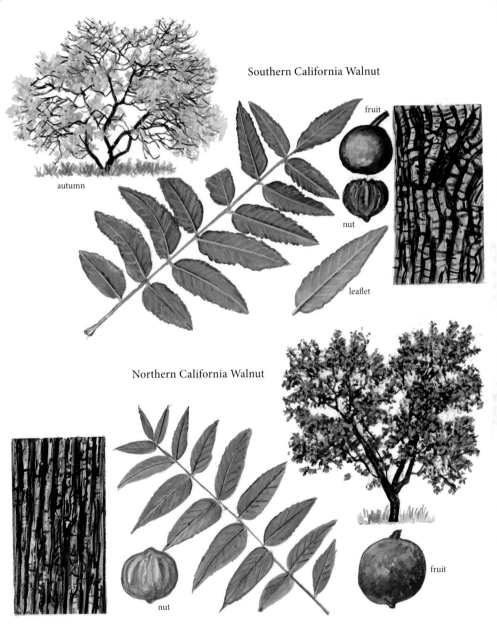

Southern California Walnut

autumn

fruit

nut

leaflet

Northern California Walnut

nut

fruit

HABITAT/RANGE Native. Along streams and on hillsides, 0–300 m; nc. Calif.

Notes This walnut is commonly cultivated as a shade tree, and is used in Calif. orchards as a rootstock on which English Walnut is grafted. The lumber is called claro walnut, particularly when taken from below the graft of an orchard tree, and is highly valued for making figured gunstocks, furniture, and decorative items.

ARIZONA WALNUT *Juglans major*
(Torr.) A. Heller

A.K.A. ARIZONA BLACK WALNUT, NOGAL, NOGAL SILVESTRE

QUICK ID A moderately large tree with alternate, spicy-scented, usually odd-pinnate leaves that have glandular and nonglandular hairs spread across their lower surface, and with a husk-covered nut that is more or less globose and 2–3.5 cm diam.

Deciduous tree, 5–18 m tall, with 1 or sometimes up to a few straight trunks, 0.2–1.3 m diam.; crown round or oval, open to moderately dense. **BARK** Gray-brown and smooth when young, on older trees becoming thick, gray to brownish black, with deep furrows and flat, irregularly cross-checked ridges. **TWIG** Twigs at first finely pubescent with reddish-brown hairs, later nearly hairless and gray. Terminal bud 4–7 mm long, flattened, egg-shaped. **LEAF** Alternate, pinnately compound, the terminal leaflet smaller than others or absent; blade 18–38 cm long; petiole 3–6 cm long. Leaflets usually 9–15, each 6–11 cm long, 15–35 mm broad, on short stalks; lanceolate to ovate, symmetric or scythe-shaped, tip tapered to a slender point, margins prominently saw-toothed. Both surfaces pubescent with gland-tipped hairs, clustered hairs, and sometimes minute scales, upper surface becoming nearly smooth except along the major veins, lower surface remaining pubescent and with tufts of hairs in the vein axils near the leaflet bases. **FLOWER** Apr.–May. **FRUIT** 1–3 nuts per cluster, each husk-covered fruit 2–3.5 cm diam.; husk densely covered by gland-tipped hairs and minute scales. Nut brown or nearly black, 18–27 mm diam., globose, surfaces smooth between deep longitudinal grooves.

HABITAT/RANGE Native. In canyons and along rocky stream beds, 300–2,100 m; s. Ariz., s. N.M., w. Tex., and sporadic in c. Tex. and s. Okla., to n. Mexico.

SIMILAR SPECIES Little Walnut occurs in much of the same area in N.M. and Tex. It has glandular hairs spread across the lower surface of the leaves, and nonglandular hairs limited to the vein axils; its fruit is only 14–23 mm diam.

Notes Arizona Walnut and Little Walnut are very similar, intergrade, and by some are considered varieties of a single species. Along the eastern portion of its range, Arizona Walnut also intergrades with Black Walnut. In all, the flavorful meat is difficult to extract from the thick shell. Squirrels consume the nuts, which at one time were a food source for Native Americans. The wood of the western species is occasionally used for cabinetry, and provides decay-resistant fence posts for western ranchers.

LITTLE WALNUT *Juglans microcarpa*
Berland.

A.K.A. TEXAS BLACK WALNUT, NOGAL, NOGALITO

QUICK ID The small nuts and the glandular, finely pointed leaflets help distinguish this species.

Deciduous shrub or small tree to 10 m tall. Trunk few to many, 10–50 cm diam.; crown round. **BARK** Grayish, deeply fissured, ridges rough. **LEAF** Alternate, pinnately compound, terminal leaflet small. Leaflets usually 11–25, each 5–6 cm long (to 9.5 cm), 8–11 mm broad; lanceolate, often scythe-shaped; tip very slender, long-pointed; margins entire or finely toothed. Leaf surfaces with glandular hairs, and usually with tufts of hairs in the vein axils on the lower surface. **FLOWER** Mar.–Apr., sometimes into Jun. **FRUIT** Globose, 14–23 mm diam.; husk smooth, glandular hairy; nut nearly

ARIZONA WALNUT

LITTLE WALNUT

Arizona Walnut

fruit

nut

Little Walnut

fruit

nut

globose, depressed on top, 11–17 cm diam., the surface smooth between moderately deep grooves.

HABITAT/RANGE Native. Valleys and along rocky stream beds, 200–2,000 m; n. N.M. and sc. Kans. south to ec. Tex. and n. Mexico.

Notes Little Walnut intergrades with Arizona Walnut, making identification sometimes difficult. Trees are planted for ornament and in shelter belts.

BLACK WALNUT *Juglans nigra* L.

QUICK ID This differs from other walnuts in the combination of large round fruits, broader leaflets with the tip tapered to a long point and hairs on the undersurface, and a nutshell that is coarsely warty between the grooves.

Deciduous large tree, 30–50 m tall; single erect trunk to about 2 m diam. **BARK** Light grayish brown or reddish, nearly black at maturity; scaly at first, becoming rough, deeply and irregularly fissured, the fissures often interlacing. **TWIG** Dark brown, pale-hairy, with raised lenticels; bud copiously covered with blond hairs. **LEAF** Alternate, pinnately compound, often appearing even-pinnate due to loss of terminal leaflet; blade to about 40 cm long, 18 cm broad. Leaflets 8–23, each 4–9 cm long, 2–4 cm broad, narrowly ovate or lanceolate, base rounded or wedge-shaped, tip narrowing to a sharp point, margins toothed. Upper surface dark green, venation conspicuous; lower surface paler, shaggy-hairy at least along the veins. **FLOWER** Male flowers in pendent catkins 7–15 cm long. May–Jun. **FRUIT** Globose, 5–8 cm in diam.; nut globose, 4–6 cm diam., nutshell dark brown, longitudinally grooved, coarsely warty between the grooves.

HABITAT/RANGE Native. In woods from floodplains to uplands, 0–1,000 m; an eastern species occasionally naturalized in the West.

Notes Leaflets are all opposite on the rachis, or sometimes a few are not exactly paired. Black Walnut is a frequently cultivated ornamental, especially along roadsides and in parking lots. It is prized for its dark wood.

BLACK WALNUT

ENGLISH WALNUT *Juglans regia* L.

QUICK ID This walnut is recognized by the combination of large, relatively thin-shelled, wrinkled nuts that split open, and mostly 5–9 leaflets with entire (or mostly entire) margins.

Deciduous fast-growing tree to about 25 m tall; single erect trunk to 1.3 m diam. **BARK** Smooth and brownish when young, becoming silvery gray and deeply and irregularly furrowed when older, the furrows separated by broad, flat ridges, often developing a diamond-shaped pattern. **TWIG** Brownish. **LEAF** Alternate, pinnately compound, with a terminal leaflet; blade 25–40 cm long. Leaflets 5–9, each 6–18 cm long, 3–8 cm broad; ovate or elliptic, base broadly wedge-shaped; tip pointed; margins usually entire. Upper surface lustrous green; lower surface paler, hairy in the vein axils. **FLOWER** Male catkins 5–15 cm long. Apr. **FRUIT** Ellipsoid or nearly round husk-covered nut 4–6 cm diam.; nutshell wrinkled.

HABITAT/RANGE Introduced from Asia and brought to Calif. in the 1860s, now cultivated in extensive orchards in the Central Valley; occasionally escapes but rarely lives to maturity, 0–200 m.

Notes English Walnut is grafted on rootstock of native walnuts because of its sensitivity to native pathogens. It hybridizes with Northern California Walnut and Southern California Walnut.

CHINESE WINGNUT *Pterocarya stenoptera* C. DC.

Deciduous fast-growing tree to about 30 m tall. **LEAF** Alternate, pinnately compound, usually evenly pinnate (terminal leaflet absent), winged at least below the upper leaflets. Leaflets mostly 11–21, each 8–12 cm long, 2–3 cm broad; long elliptic or lanceolate, margins toothed. **FLOWER** Male and female flowers in separate inflorescences on the same tree. Apr.–May. **FRUIT** Huskless, 2-winged nutlet, at first emerald green, then brown, 15–80 in a pendulous catkin 20–45 cm long; fruit ellipsoid in outline, the body 6–9 mm long, with 2 erect wings diverging at an angle and running the length of the nutlet, 13–24 mm long, 5–6 mm high. **HABITAT/ RANGE** Introduced; weakly naturalized along streams in the Central Valley of Calif., 0–50 m; also sparingly established in the East. *Notes* There are about 6 species of *Pterocarya* native to Asia.

Black Walnut

twig

fruit

nut

English Walnut

kernel

nut

Chinese Wingnut

fruit

fruit

KOEBERLINIACEAE: ALLTHORN FAMILY

The tiny allthorn family has only 2 species in a single genus, one in arid regions in sw. North America and the other in Bolivia. Plants of both form an interlocked mass of intricately branched, virtually leafless, thorn-tipped twigs.

SPINY ALLTHORN *Koeberlinia spinosa* Zucc.

A.K.A. CRUCIFIXION THORN, CORONA DE CRISTO

QUICK ID Dense thorn-tipped twigs, small whitish flowers with 4 petals, and small globose black berries in combination distinguish this plant.

Deciduous, usually a shrub, sometimes a tree to 8 m tall, with a very short twisted trunk about 15 cm diam.; crown round and dense, forming an interlocked mass of intricately branched, thorn-tipped twigs. **BARK** Thin, at first green and smooth, later grayish and broken into small scales and shallow fissures. **TWIG** Stout, branching at wide angles, mostly hairless, yellow-green, army green or bluish green, rigid, 2–4 mm diam., 2–10 cm long, sharply pointed. **LEAF** Alternate, tiny, scalelike, quickly deciduous. **FLOWER** Small, whitish green, borne in small few-flowered racemes or umbels along the twigs; sepals 4, about 1 mm long; petals 4, ladle-shaped, 4 mm long; stamens 8, the filaments broad in the middle and sometimes resembling the petals; ovary superior, 2-celled, on a short stalk. Feb.–Jul. **FRUIT** Globose, shiny black berry, 5–6 mm diam., containing 1–4 curled, wrinkled seeds.

HABITAT/RANGE Native. On rocky slopes and sandy or gravelly flats, 0–2,100 m; se. Calif. to w. Tex., south to c. Mexico.

SIMILAR SPECIES A number of arborescent plants in the arid Southwest have converged upon the leafless, water-conserving, protective, repeatedly branched, thorny habit. Two others are called Crucifixion Thorn: *Castela emoryi* (Simaroubaceae) flowers often have 7 petals, and the fruit is a ring of drupelike sections; *Canotia holacantha* (Celastraceae) flowers have 5 petals and the fruit is a capsule with a swollen base and a slender pointed tip, which divides into 5 segments. Two other genera in the Fabaceae are also thorny: palo verdes (*Parkinsonia*) have slightly bilateral yellow flowers and hanging pods; and Smoketree (*Psorothamnus spinosus*) has gland-dotted bluish-green twigs, indigo flowers, and small gland-dotted pods.

Notes Plants may form impenetrable thickets and are considered a range pest by southwestern ranchers, but they probably afford some protection from erosion. Birds and small mammals feed upon the berries. The hard, resinous wood is very dense and produces oily black smoke when burned, which was used to fumigate huts by the Seri people of Sonora, Mexico.

SPINY ALLTHORN

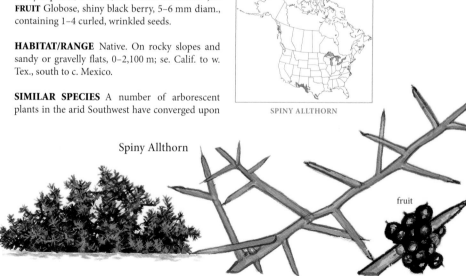

Spiny Allthorn

fruit

LAURACEAE: LAUREL FAMILY

The laurel family contains about 50 genera and 2,500 species, mostly from tropical and subtropical regions. It consists of evergreen trees and shrubs with simple, alternate or opposite leaves (and 1 genus of leafless parasitic climbers). In many species, leaves and other plant parts have cavities that contain highly aromatic oils. There are only 3 native species in the West, two of those barely entering the region from the Southeast.

FLOWER Borne in branched inflorescences; small, radial, bisexual or unisexual, yellow-green to whitish; petals and sepals are not well differentiated, referred to as tepals (references may refer to them as sepals, assuming petals to be absent). Stamens 3–12; commonly 9 are functional. **FRUIT** Ovary is usually superior and develops into a 1-seeded berry or drupe, usually fused to the cuplike base of the tepals.

The family provides the spices cinnamon and bay, camphor and sassafras oils, valuable timber, and the avocado, the last a valuable fruit crop in s. Calif. and s. Fla.

CAMPHORTREE *Cinnamomum camphora* (L.) J. Presl

Evergreen tree to 20 m tall, with a short trunk and dense, round crown. **LEAF** Alternate, simple, ovate to lanceolate, hairless, more or less leathery, giving off a strong camphor odor when crushed. Blade 4–12 cm long, 2–5 cm broad; petiole to 3 cm long. **FLOWER** Bisexual, 1–2 mm diam., with 6 greenish-white or creamy tepals. Apr.–May. **FRUIT** Lustrous black drupe, 8–9 mm diam., borne in a cuplike receptacle. **HABITAT/ RANGE** Introduced from East Asia; disturbed places, 0–150 m, near the coast of c. and s. Calif. *Notes* Camphor is distilled from the wood. There are more than 200 species of *Cinnamomum*, mostly from East Asia. The spice cinnamon comes from this genus.

Camphortree

fruit

new leaf

NORTHERN SPICEBUSH *Lindera benzoin* (L.) Blume

QUICKID The spicy aromatic leaves that increase in size from the base to the tip of the twig are diagnostic.

Deciduous shrub or small tree to 5 m tall. **LEAF** Alternate, simple, lanceolate, aromatic, hairless at maturity above, permanently hairy below (in our var. *pubescens* [Palmer & Steyerm.] Rehder). Blade 6–15 cm long, 2–6 cm broad, increasing in size toward the twig tip; petiole about 1 cm long, usually hairy. **FLOWER** Tiny, unisexual, in several-flowered clusters, borne on separate plants; tepals yellow, deciduous; stamens 9. Mar.–Apr., appearing before leaf expansion. **FRUIT** Ellipsoid, bright red drupe, 8–10 mm long.

HABITAT/RANGE Native. Wooded slopes and rocky areas along streams, 0–1,200 m; much of e. North America, extending westward to c. Tex.

Notes There are about 100 species of *Lindera*, mostly from East Asia; only three occur in the U.S.

REDBAY *Persea borbonia* (L.) Spreng.

QUICKID This tree is distinguished by the combination of lustrous, mildly aromatic, lanceolate, dark green leaves that are whitish beneath, and dark blue or blackish fruit.

Evergreen, usually a small or medium tree to 25 m tall, occasionally a shrub. **LEAF** Alternate, simple, lanceolate, more or less leathery; upper surface lustrous, dark green; lower surface paler and often pale hairy. Blade 2–16 cm long, 1.5–6 cm wide; petiole 1–2 cm long. **FLOWER** Borne in small branched clusters, tiny, bisexual, with 6 greenish or whitish tepals. May–Jun. **FRUIT** Rounded or oblong, dark blue drupe, about 10 mm long, 8 mm diam.

HABITAT/RANGE Native. Moist woodland and stabilized dunes near the coast, 0–100 m; se. U.S., barely entering the West near Corpus Christi, Tex.

Notes There are about 150 species of *Persea* worldwide in the tropics and subtropics. The **Avocado** (*P. americana* Mill.) is widely grown in s. Calif. and has escaped cultivation in s. Fla.

NORTHERN SPICEBUSH

REDBAY

Northern Spicebush

autumn

flowers

fruit

fruit

Redbay

underside

fruit

flowers

Avocado

new leaf

fruit section

CALIFORNIA BAY *Umbellularia californica* (Hook. & Arn.) Nutt.
A.K.A. OREGON MYRTLE, CALIFORNIA LAUREL, PEPPERWOOD, HEADACHE TREE

QUICK ID Smooth, lanceolate, entire evergreen leaves with a pungent spicy odor distinguish this tree.

Evergreen, varying in habit from a large, magnificent straight-trunked tree 45 m tall in the forest, to broad, rounded, short-trunked specimens in the open, to dense, tall shrubby thickets on higher slopes and ridges. Trunk mostly 30–80 cm diam., occasionally to 1 m. Branches strongly ascending in forest trees, more widely spreading on open-grown trees. **BARK** On branches smooth and gray; on older parts dark grayish brown, scaly or warty, and barely ridged. **TWIG** Smooth, round, at first yellow-green, becoming brownish green tinged with red. Twigs bear small naked buds with rolled embryonic leaves. The twig grows continuously during spring and summer, producing new leaves throughout the season, older ones continuously yellowing and falling. **LEAF** Alternate, simple, highly aromatic; lanceolate or ovoid-lanceolate, the margins entire and slightly rolled under. Deep yellow-green or green, hairless and lustrous above, paler and duller below. Young leaves are finely pubescent, this permanent on the lower surface in the var. *fresnensis* Eastw. of c. Calif. Blade 3–10 cm long, 1.5–3 cm broad; petiole 3–6 mm long. **FLOWER** Small, bisexual, radial, pale yellow, aggregated in axillary umbels of 6–10 flowers, the earlier umbels on stalks up to 2.5 cm long, later ones almost stalkless. Tepals 6, rounded, 6–8 mm long. Stamens 9, in 3 concentric rings, the inner 3 stamens with pairs of flattened round orange glands at the base; anthers opening by 4 tiny flaps. An outer, 4th ring consists of 3 tiny sterile stamens. Dec.–Apr. **FRUIT** Drupe, smooth, globose-ovoid, 2–2.5 cm long, at first yellowish green, at maturity dull purplish, the skin and flesh thin, the inner stone large, light brown and thin-shelled, containing 1 seed, borne singly or up to 3 in a group. The flared base of the sepals supports the drupe, resembling a golf ball on a tee.

HABITAT/RANGE Native. Redwood or mixed forests, canyons, open slopes, 0–1,600 m; sw. Ore. to s. Calif.

SIMILAR SPECIES Giant Golden Chinquapin (*Chrysolepis chrysophylla*, Fagaceae) has leaves that are golden-scaly on the underside, and its fruit is spiny. Tanbark Oak (*Notholithocarpus densiflorus*, Fagaceae) has small teeth along the margins of leaves; the fruit is an acorn. Leaves of neither have a spicy odor. **Bay Laurel** (*Laurus nobilis* L.), source of the spice bay leaf, is an occasional waif in Calif., but has not naturalized; its leaf margins are wavy.

Notes This unique species is distinguished from all others in the region by its odor, permeating the air with the scent of bay, but stronger, with overtones of camphor and pepper. It is at first pleasant, but in confined spaces can be obnoxious. This is the only Lauraceae species naturally occurring west of the Rocky Mountains, a remnant of ancient times when other Lauraceae were also present. The trees may live to 300 years, with trunks more than a meter in diameter. The wood is valued for interior cabinetry, furniture, and novelty items, though most commercially harvestable trees are now gone. Leaves have been used to repel fleas in beds. They have also been used medicinally to treat many ailments, including headaches; ironically, their odor also produces a headache in many people. Leaves are sold as the spice California bay; strongly potent, it should be used sparingly. The flesh of the fruit is edible, palatable only for a brief period immediately after maturation.

CALIFORNIA BAY

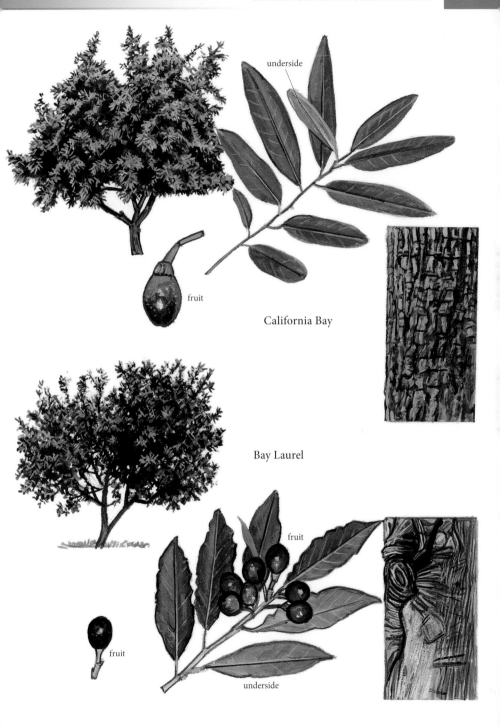

underside

fruit

California Bay

Bay Laurel

fruit

fruit

underside

MALVACEAE: MALLOW FAMILY

The worldwide mallow (or hibiscus) family consists of about 243 genera and 4,225 species of herbs, shrubs, and trees, most diverse in tropical regions. About 250 native and naturalized species occur in North America, most of which are herbaceous. Only 6 tree or treelike species grow wild in the West, two of those introduced. Recent molecular genetic studies have revealed this family to be broader than once construed, and it now includes the chocolate family (Sterculiaceae), to which *Fremontodendron*, *Brachychiton*, and *Firmiana* belonged. Two other newly incorporated families are Bombacaceae and Tiliaceae, the lindens or basswoods; both have species that are grown in the West as ornamentals, and 1 native *Tilia* enters the region from the East.

Several morphological features are characteristic of the family. Mucilage canals are present in soft tissue, resulting in a viscous sap when stems are cut or broken. Hairs in the family are usually branched, often in a treelike pattern (dendritic), sometimes starlike (stellate), or they may form a flattened, ragged-edged disk attached by a central stalk (peltate). Recognition of species is aided by the combination of palmately veined leaves, branched hairs, and stamens fused by their filaments, in many species resembling a little shaving brush in the center of the flower. **LEAF** Usually alternate, simple, often palmately veined and lobed, or palmately compound; the major vein ends at the tip of a marginal tooth. **FLOWER** Usually bisexual, radial, usually with 5 sepals, 5 petals, and 5 to many stamens joined by their filaments into a tube surrounding the superior 2- to many-chambered ovary. Beneath the flower there is often a whorl of several bracts called an epicalyx, which resembles a 2nd calyx. **FRUIT** Variable; in species in the West, most have a capsule that breaks into wedge-shaped segments.

Economically the family is very important, contributing chocolate, okra, durian fruit, balsa wood and other valuable timber, cotton and kapok, and many ornamentals, including hibiscus, one of which, Rose-of-Sharon, or Shrubby Althea (*Hibiscus syriacus* L.), may persist around old habitations.

WHITEFLOWER KURRAJONG
Brachychiton populneum (Schott. & Endl.) R. Br.

Evergreen, rapidly growing tree, 6–20 m tall, the single trunk swollen for water storage. **LEAF** Alternate, simple, 2–6 cm long, 3–9 lobes with long-pointed tips or unlobed, base rounded. **FLOWER** Unisexual, both sexes on the same plant, in loose hanging clusters; calyx bell-shaped, lobes reflexed, 1–2 cm long, pale greenish outside, whitish to pink- or maroon-spotted within, petals absent. Male flower with 18–20 stamens; ovary of female flowers with 5 free segments, upper parts of styles joined. Jun.–Jul. **FRUIT** Stalked, elliptic, flattened brown follicle, 4–7 cm long, with yellow seeds embedded

in prickly fibers. **HABITAT/RANGE** Introduced from Australia; grown as an ornamental in Ariz. and Calif., sometimes escaping in disturbed areas; reportedly naturalized in se. U.S. **Notes** The only species of this genus of about 30 Australian trees found in the U.S.

CHINESE PARASOLTREE *Firmiana simplex* (L.) W. Wight
A.K.A. VARNISH TREE

Deciduous tree to about 20 m tall, the crown of branches mostly clustered at the top, umbrella-like. **BARK** Smooth, green or grayish green. **LEAF** Alternate, simple, palmate, usually with 3 or 5 lobes,

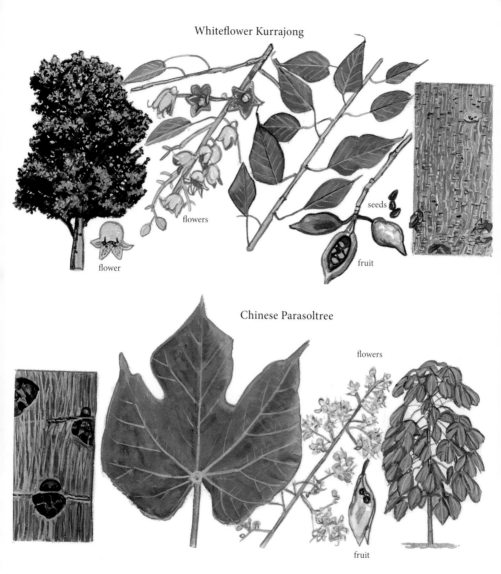

Whiteflower Kurrajong

flower

flowers

seeds

fruit

Chinese Parasoltree

flowers

fruit

the lobe tips sharply pointed. Upper surface dark or bright green, hairless; lower surface paler, softly and densely hairy. Blade 10–30 cm long and broad. **FLOWER** Unisexual, male and female flowers in the same branched cluster 15–60 cm long, some clusters mostly male, others mostly female; sepals greenish white, 7–8 mm long; petals absent; male flower with a thick column topped with a hood-like cluster of fused anthers; female flower with a stalked ovary of 5 pistils and 5 fused stigmas. Jun.–Jul. **FRUIT** Five radiating follicles, opening before maturity into a leaflike structure, exposing up to 4 seeds that hang on the follicle wall. **HABITAT/ RANGE** Introduced from China; cultivated, escaping and naturalized in the East, extending westward to c. Tex. **Notes** Considered invasive in some areas; the only species of this genus of 9 from the Old World tropics that has established in the U.S.

■ *FREMENTODENDRON*: FLANNELBUSHES

Flannelbushes (a.k.a. fremontias) derive their name from the velvety covering of dense branched hairs on the leaves and young twigs. Though technically evergreen, plants may lose many leaves during the summer dry season. **TWIG** At first velvety-hairy, becoming nearly hairless and reddish brown; winter buds lack bud scales. **BARK** Inner bark gelatinous; outer bark gray or reddish gray-brown and smooth when young, on larger trunks becoming rough and fissured, dark blackish brown, sometimes with a reddish tint. **LEAF** Alternate, simple, commonly with 3 main lobes and veins. **FLOWER** Large, solitary, bisexual, radial, lacking petals but with showy yellow or orange petal-like sepals. Stamens 5, large and fleshy, arching outward in the center of the flower, the filaments joined into a tube surrounding a superior ovary with 4 or 5 chambers. **FRUIT** Woody capsule, persisting for months, bristly-hairy, spitting into 4 or 5 segments from the tip downward.

There are only 3 species of *Fremontodendron*, all found in semiarid, rocky areas at low to moderate elevations in Calif. and nw. Mexico. An early pioneer usage of "slippery elm" referred to the gelatinous inner bark, which was once used to make poultices. The nutritious twigs are browsed by cattle and native mammals. A number of horticultural varieties are now available, which grow well in little-watered sandy soil in summer-dry areas. As beautiful as the plants are, detached branching hairs can be irritating to the skin and eyes. The old generic name, *Fremontia*, was replaced for technical reasons.

CALIFORNIA FLANNELBUSH

CALIFORNIA FLANNELBUSH
Fremontodendron californicum (Torr.) Coville
A.K.A. CALIFORNIA FREMONTIA

QUICK ID The large saucer-shaped yellow flowers and palmately lobed leaves distinguish this species.

Evergreen shrub or small tree, 2–9 m tall, branching low on the trunk, the crown open, usually taller than wide, the branches stout, spreading and often nearly reaching the ground. Trunk to 35 cm diam. **TWIG** Long, thick, tough; velvety with branched hairs. **BARK** Dark gray, smooth when young, deeply fissured on the trunk and older branches. **LEAF** Alternate, often on spur branches, simple, thin to leathery, nearly as broad as long, widest at the base, with 1–3 main veins; usually palmately 3-lobed, the lobes with minor secondary lobes, the lobe tips bluntly angled or round. Upper surface dark green, moderately hairy; lower surface densely velvety with pale whitish or rusty hairs. Blade usually 1–5 cm long, 1.5–4 cm broad; petiole stout, 5–15 mm long, stipules 2 mm long. **FLOWER** Showy, usually borne singly, opposite a leaf, or on spurs, 3.5–6 cm diam., saucer-shaped; sepals yellow, sometimes tinged with red near the margins, with silky hairs about 1 mm long in a pit at the base of each sepal. May–Jun. **FRUIT** Ovoid, bristly brown capsule, 2–4 cm long.

HABITAT/RANGE Native. Rocky, poor soil in chaparral or pine-oak woodland, 400–2,000 m; nc. Calif. and c. Ariz., south to nw. Mexico.

SIMILAR SPECIES The closely related Mexican Flannelbush does not branch near the ground, and its sepal pits are hairless.

Notes There are 2 subspecies: subsp. *californicum* is treelike, taller than wide, flowers 3.5–6 cm wide, sepals yellow and sometimes with reddish margins, widespread; subsp. *decumbens* (R.M. Lloyd) Munz, the Pine Hill Flannelbush, is much shrubbier, wider than tall, its flowers about 3.5 cm wide, the sepals orange, coppery, or reddish, and is found only in the s. Sierra Nevada at about 2,000 m.

flowers

flower

underside

California Flannelbush

fruit

flower

fruit

Mexican Flannelbush

MEXICAN FLANNELBUSH
Fremontodendron mexicanum Davidson
A.K.A. MEXICAN FREMONTIA, SOUTHERN FREMONTIA

Evergreen shrub or tree to 7 m tall, not branching close to the ground. Similar to, and sometimes considered a subspecies of, California Flannelbush.

LEAF Stipules 4–5 mm long. **FLOWER** 6–9 cm diam., sepals orange, coppery, or reddish, especially at the base, sepal pits with only a few very short hairs. Mar.–Aug. **HABITAT/RANGE** Native. Rare in chaparral in canyons, 300–1,000 m; s. Calif., n. Baja Calif. *Notes* Critically threatened by fire and habitat loss; only about 100 individuals remain. The species has contributed substantially to cultivated varieties.

THURBER'S COTTON *Gossypium thurberi* Todaro
A.K.A. DESERT COTTON, ALGONDOCILLO, ARIZONA WILD COTTON

QUICKID This distinctive shrub or small tree has deeply lobed palmate leaves and bowl-shaped whitish or cream flowers.

Usually a shrub, but occasionally a small tree to 4.5 m tall, with a broad open crown, the trunk up to 10 cm diam. **LEAF** Alternate, simple, hairless, 5–15 cm long and about as broad, palmately lobed, the 3–5 lobes lanceolate with entire margins. **FLOWER** Bowl-shaped, few in a cluster; petals white or cream, 1.5–2.5 cm long, sometimes with a faint crimson spot at the base. Stamens numerous, the filaments joined in a tube. Aug.–Oct. **FRUIT** Ovoid or round capsule, 10–15 mm long, splitting into 3 segments, each holding a few seeds with few cotton fibers.

HABITAT/RANGE Native. Arid hillsides and along streams, 800–1,400 m, sometimes higher; c. Ariz. to nw. Mexico.

Notes Thurberia Weevils (*Anthonomus grandis thurberiae*), variants of the Cotton Boll Weevil (*A. grandis*), inhabit Thurber's Cotton but do not feed upon bolls of cultivated cotton. Prior to that understanding, the plant was often eradicated around commercial cotton fields in the Southwest. In xeriscapes Thurber's Cotton can be pruned into an attractive tree shape. Of the approximately 40 species of shrubs and small trees in this tropical and subtropical genus, only 2 are native to the continental U.S. (the other in Fla.).

THURBER'S COTTON

AMERICAN BASSWOOD *Tilia americana* L.

QUICKID This distinctive tree is recognized by the combination of 2-ranked, alternate, heart-shaped leaves that are asymmetric at the base, and the long, narrow, leaflike bract that is attached to the lower half of the flower cluster stalk.

Deciduous tree, 18–30 m tall, with a single erect, straight trunk 40–150 cm diam., often clear of branches for at least ½ its height; crown ovoid or rounded. **BARK** Smooth and dark gray on young trees, becoming finely to deeply furrowed with numerous narrow, vertical ridges. **TWIG** Stout, reddish gray, hairy at first. **LEAF** Alternate, simple, 2-ranked, ovate; base heart-shaped, asymmetric; tip abruptly short-pointed; margins coarsely toothed. Upper surface dark yellowish green, hairless, veins conspicuous; lower surface paler, with brownish hairs (in our western plants). Blade 12–15 cm long, 7–10 cm broad; petiole slender, 2.5–5 cm long. **FLOWER** In a few-flowered, open, drooping cluster, the stalk of the cluster attached for about ½ its length to a conspicuous narrow, leaflike bract, 10–13 cm long, each flower bisexual, radially symmetric, fragrant, yellowish white, sepals 5, petals 5, ovary superior with 5 chambers. May–Jul. **FRUIT** Rounded, thick-shelled gray nut about 6 mm broad.

HABITAT/RANGE Native. Rich, deciduous woods, 50–1,500 m; s. Alta. south to c. Tex., widespread in e. U.S.

SIMILAR SPECIES Red Mulberry and White Mulberry (*Morus rubra* and *M. alba*, Moraceae) have similar leaves, but their petioles exude milky sap when broken.

AMERICAN BASSWOOD

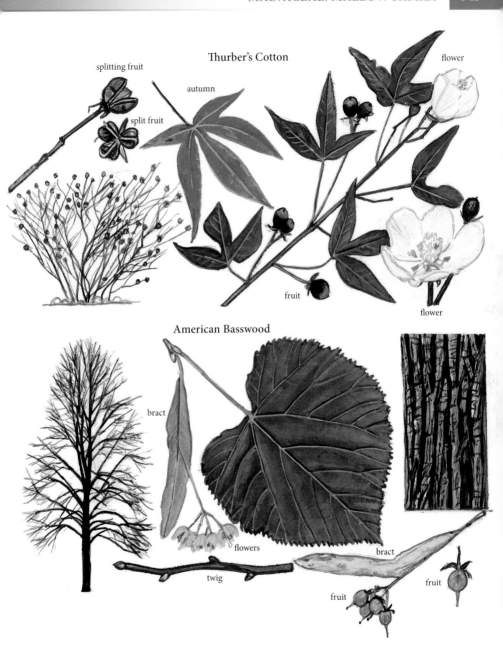

Thurber's Cotton

splitting fruit

autumn

flower

split fruit

fruit

flower

flower

American Basswood

bract

flowers

twig

bract

fruit

fruit

fruit

Notes Tilia is a genus of about 23 species found in temperate and subtropical regions of North America and Asia. Only one occurs in the West, where it is represented, in c. Tex., by *T. americana* var. *caroliniana* (Mill.) Castigl., which has a densely brownish-hairy lower leaf surface. The slightly more easterly var. *americana* has less hairy leaves, the hairs when present often paler.

MELIACEAE: MAHOGANY FAMILY

The mahogany family has about 50 genera and 550–615 species of trees and shrubs distributed mostly in lowlands of the tropics. Leaves are alternate, usually compound, and flowers are usually radial and bisexual, with a superior ovary. Several species produce high-quality timber. Only 1 species is found in the West.

CHINABERRY-TREE *Melia azedarach* L.
A.K.A. PRIDE-OF-INDIA

Deciduous tree to about 15 m tall, with a single erect trunk to 60 cm diam. **LEAF** Alternate, bipinnately or tripinnately compound, blade to 50 cm long and broad; leaflets numerous, 2–7 cm long, 1–2 cm broad, ovate, margins toothed, sometimes deeply cut at the base, the tip abruptly long-pointed. **FLOWER** Fragrant, in a stalked, many-flowered, open panicle to 20 cm long. Sepals 5 or 6, green; petals 5 or 6, pinkish purple, 8–12 mm long; stamens 10–12, forming a purple tube about 8 mm long. Mar.–Jul. **FRUIT** Globose, fleshy yellowish or greenish-yellow multistoned drupe, 1–1.5 cm diam. **HABITAT/RANGE** Introduced from Asia; widely cultivated, establishing in disturbed sites in moderate climates, 0–1,300 m, Calif. to se. U.S. *Notes* Of the 3 species of *Melia*, only this one has naturalized in the West.

MORACEAE: MULBERRY FAMILY

The mulberries, figs, and breadnuts compose a family of about 39–50 genera and 1,100–1,500 species of trees, shrubs, vines, and a few herbs, distributed mostly in tropical and warm temperate regions. Eight genera and about 25 species occur in North America. In the West there is 1 native tree species, and at least 4 more have been introduced. Members of the family have latex-bearing cells in the green tissue that excrete a milky sap when broken, a characteristic that is especially evident when the petiole is severed. The family provides edible figs, mulberries, and breadfruit. Some species produce timber, a number are used as ornamentals, mulberries provide food for silk worms, and natural rubber is prepared from the milky sap of *Ficus*.

LEAF Alternate, simple, with the margins entire or lobed and, in ours, 2-ranked. **FLOWER** Tiny, unisexual, borne on the same or different plants. Flowers usually have 4 or 5 tepals, the male flowers an equal number of stamens, the female flowers usually with a superior ovary that matures 1 seed. **FRUIT** Achene or drupe, usually borne on, or embedded in, a highly modified structure that becomes part of the fruit (the fruiting structure is a multiple fruit). In Osage Orange and the mulberries, the ovaries are at the center of the multiple fruit and the styles directed outward. In *Dorstenia*, a tropical herbaceous or succulent genus occasionally grown as a house plant, the flowers are arrayed on the upper side of a saucerlike structure. In figs, the flowers are all borne inside the vase-shaped fig fruit (syconium), the styles pointing inward, the pistils pollinated by minute wasps.

EDIBLE FIG *Ficus carica* L.
A.K.A. COMMON FIG

QUICK ID The leaves with 3–5 lobes and distinctive fruit (the fig of commerce) are diagnostic.

Deciduous large shrub or small tree, 3–10 m tall. Erect, usually with multiple trunks; crown spreading, irregular. **BARK** Grayish brown, smooth or slightly roughened. **TWIG** Green, hairy. **LEAF** Alternate, simple, ovate or circular, deeply incised with 3–5 broad lobes; base often deeply cordate; tip

flowers

Chinaberry-tree

fruit

fruit

Edible Fig

fruit

bluntly pointed; margins undulate or coarsely and bluntly toothed. Upper surface dark or medium green, with 3–5 palmately arranged veins; lower surface paler; both surfaces rough to the touch from the presence of stiff hairs. Blade 15–30 cm long, equally broad; petiole 8–20 cm long, stout. **FLOWER** Tiny, unisexual, maturing synchronously within a syconium, trees with male and female flowers in each syconium, or syconia on any 1 tree with only female flowers. May–Sep. **FRUIT** Syconium, more or less pear-shaped, fleshy, green, yellow, reddish brown, or purplish, finely hairy, 3–8 cm long, bearing tiny achenes on the inner surface.

HABITAT/RANGE Introduced from Asia; widely planted, persisting around old homesteads and dwellings, naturalizing in warmer parts of the West, 0–1,500 m.

Notes Figs form a diverse genus of about 750 species of trees, shrubs, or woody vines in the tropics and subtropics, where many begin growth as epiphytes. Thirteen species occur north of Mexico, two native in the East, none native to the West. Buds are subtended and enclosed by conspicuous stipules that fall as the leaf emerges, leaving an encircling scar. The fruit is a syconium, derived from a highly modified inflorescence that bears tiny unisexual flowers inside. This is the fig of commerce, which has self-pollinating bisexual trees and unisexual female trees that require cross-pollination; commercial figs develop from female trees or from asexual cultivars that are propagated by cuttings. Minute male and female flowers are scattered across the inside wall of the developing fig. Female flowers are of 2 types, long-stalked with a short style, and short-stalked with a long style. In general, each species of the huge

EDIBLE FIG *continued*

genus *Ficus* depends on 1 species of wasp, and vice versa: Tiny, egg-laden female wasps, bearing pollen, wriggle their way through the opening at the end of the fig, pollinate the female flowers, and deposit eggs. Subsequently, short-styled flowers develop as gall flowers, essentially serving as the incubator for a new crop of male and female wasps; long-styled flowers develop seed. Male flowers and new wasps mature at about the same time. The new, wingless male wasps impregnate the new female wasps, which gather pollen, often by biting into the anthers, and exit the fig through tiny holes chewed by the males, flying to a new fig and renewing the cycle.

OSAGE ORANGE   *Maclura pomifera* (Raf.) C.K. Schneid.

QUICK ID Distinguished by its spiny branches, ovate leaves, and lumpy greenish-yellow, orange-like fruits.

Deciduous shrub or tree to about 25 m tall, often root-sprouting and thicket-forming; trunk erect, 1 or several, to 1 m diam.; crown rounded. **BARK** Dark yellowish brown or orange-brown, furrowed with interlacing ridges, peeling into strips. **TWIG** Bearing axillary spines to 3.5 cm long. **LEAF** Alternate, simple, ovate, elliptic, or broadly lanceolate; base rounded, flat, or broadly tapered; tip abruptly long-pointed; margins entire. Upper surface dark green, lustrous, hairless; lower surface paler, dull, sparsely hairy. Blade 7–15 cm long, 5–8 cm broad; petiole 3–5 cm long. **FLOWER** Unisexual, male and female borne on separate trees; male inflorescence rounded or oblong, 2.5–3.5 cm long, produced on short spur shoots; female inflorescence rounded, 2–2.5 cm long, produced on long stalks from the leaf axils. Apr.–May. **FRUIT** Globose, yellowish green, 7–15 cm diam., composed of densely packed flowers with fleshy calyces, each containing an achene; surface rind-like, resembling an orange.

HABITAT/RANGE Native to the lower Midwest; widely planted, occasionally naturalizing in the West below 450 m on stream banks and in disturbed areas.

Notes This North American native is the only species of *Maclura*.

It is widely planted as a windbreak and natural fence for farmlands, and as a wildlife shelter. The fruit is inedible. Native Americans used the wood for bows, the French giving it the name *bois d'arc*. The bark was used for tanning leather and for producing a yellow dye.

◼ *MORUS*: MULBERRIES

There are about 10 species of *Morus*, widespread in tropical and temperate regions of the world. Three occur in the West, 2 of which are native, all found at low to moderate elevations.

Deciduous shrubs and trees with milky sap. **LEAF** Alternate, simple, often deeply lobed, the margins entire or toothed. **FLOWER** Tiny, borne in unisexual catkins, the sexes on the same or different plants. Male flowers with 4 thin tepals and 4 inflexed stamens; female flowers with 4 thickish tepals, 2 large, 2 smaller, the ovary superior, with 2 styles. **FRUIT** Ellipsoid syncarp resembling a blackberry, an aggregate of achenes each embedded in a juicy, fleshy, beadlike calyx.

Mulberries are edible, their flavor sweetly mild and delicate. Birds relish them. Several species are grown as vigorous ornamentals. Silkworms feed upon mulberry leaves. Though outwardly similar, the blackberry is composed of individual drupelets from a single flower; the mulberry fruit is derived from many small flowers.

WHITE MULBERRY   *Morus alba* L.

QUICK ID This tree is recognized by the combination of alternate, coarsely toothed and often lobed leaves that are lustrous above, and white to dark purple blackberry-like fruit.

Deciduous small tree to about 25 m tall, with a single erect, straight trunk and a broad, spreading

OSAGE ORANGE

WHITE MULBERRY

autumn

fruit

twig

autumn

Osage Orange

White Mulberry

underside

fruit

crown. **TWIG** Smooth, hairless, reddish brown or tan, with scattered lenticels. **LEAF** Alternate, simple, ovate, broadly oblong, or nearly circular, with 0–9 lobes; base rounded, truncate, or cordate; apex and lobe tips abruptly short-pointed; margins coarsely toothed. Upper surface lustrous, dark green, usually smooth; lower surface paler, duller, hairless or with tufts of hairs in the vein axils. Blade 6–16 cm long, 6–10 cm broad; petiole 3–5 cm long. **FLOWER** Pale greenish, male and female flowers in separate catkins on the same or separate plants. Mar.–Apr. **FRUIT** Achene surrounded by a juicy calyx, the individual units grouped in a whitish, pinkish, pale purple, or nearly black ellipsoid cluster, 1–2 cm long.

HABITAT/RANGE Introduced from e. Asia; cultivated, naturalized in woodlands, along watercourses, in disturbed sites and fencerows, 0–1,300 m; throughout much of the U.S. and s. Canada.

SIMILAR SPECIES Dark-fruited forms of White Mulberry (sometimes referred to as *M. alba* var. *tatarica* [L.] Seringe) are easily misidentified as Red Mulberry, but on that species the upper leaf surface has stiff, forward-pointing hairs. The cultivated Black Mulberry (*M. nigra* L.) is also similar, but is usually shrubby and both leaf surfaces are hairy.

LITTLELEAF MULBERRY *Morus microphylla* Buckley

A.K.A. TEXAS MULBERRY, MEXICAN MULBERRY, MOUNTAIN MULBERRY, DWARF MULBERRY

QUICK ID Coarsely toothed, harshly hairy leaves with 3 veins at the base, petioles that exude milky sap when broken, and blackberry-like fruits in combination readily identify this shrub or small tree.

Deciduous shrub or small tree 7–8 m tall, with a broad, irregular crown, the trunk often crooked, up to 20 cm diam.; sap milky, especially in young growth. **BARK** Thin, smooth, tight, light gray, often tinged with reddish, becoming warty, later fissured, with narrow, scaly ridges. **TWIG** Slow-growing, zigzag, light reddish brown to gray, speckled with pale, elliptic lenticels; buds 3–4 mm long, pointed, slightly flattened, dark brown, the 3–5 visible scales lightly hairy, with longer hairs on the margins. **LEAF** Alternate, simple, usually more or less heart-shaped and tapered to a long-pointed tip, often also deeply cut into 3–5 lobes; margins coarsely and irregularly toothed. Dull, dark green, 3-veined from the base, the finer veins forming a delicate network, harshly hairy on both surfaces. Blade 3–7 cm long, about ⅔ as wide; petiole 8–18 mm long. **FLOWER** Tiny, male and female flowers borne in separate pendulous catkins on the same plant. Male catkins white, 1–2 cm long, dropping quickly; Female catkins greenish in flower, 1–1.5 cm long. Mar.–Apr. **FRUIT** Achene surrounded by a juicy calyx, the individual units each 3–4 mm diam., all grouped in an ovoid, dark red to purplish cluster 1–1.5 cm long.

HABITAT/RANGE Native. Canyons, washes, rocky slopes, 200–2,200 m; w. Ariz. to s. Okla. and ec. Tex., n. Mexico.

SIMILAR SPECIES Netleaf Hackberry (*Celtis reticulata*, Cannabaceae) also has harshly hairy leaves with 3 veins at the base, but the margins are usually entire, the sap is not milky, and the fruit is a small round drupe. The closely related Red Mulberry has larger fruits and leaves, the leaves hairless or nearly so.

Notes Native Americans planted Littleleaf Mulberry near villages, eating the fruits and using the wood for bows. Birds also consume the berries. The stamens in the young flower are incurved, cupped in a sepal, the elastic stalk suddenly springing outward when mature, flinging the dry pollen into the air in small puffs.

RED MULBERRY *Morus rubra* L.

QUICK ID Recognizable by the combination of alternate, toothed, and often lobed leaves that are rough to the touch above, and the elongate blackberry-like fruit, typically 3 cm long or more.

Deciduous tree to about 20 m tall, with a single straight trunk and a broad, rounded crown. **TWIG** Smooth, hairless, rarely finely hairy when very young, reddish brown or tan, with scattered lenticels. **LEAF** Alternate, simple, ovate, broadly oblong, or nearly circular, with 0–9 lobes (often lacking lobes on mature trees); base rounded, truncate, or cordate; tip conspicuously and abruptly short-pointed; margins coarsely toothed. Upper surface dark green, roughened by stiff, forward-pointing hairs; lower surface paler, duller, softly hairy. Blade 10–24 cm long, 6–20 cm broad; petiole 1.5–12 cm long. **FLOWER** Pale greenish, male and female in separate catkins on the same or separate trees. Mar.–May. **FRUIT** Achene surrounded by a juicy calyx, the individual units grouped in an ellipsoid, dark red to purplish cluster 2.5–5 cm long.

LITTLELEAF MULBERRY

RED MULBERRY

Littleleaf Mulberry

twig

fruit

seed

Red Mulberry

fruit

twig

HABITAT/RANGE Native of e. U.S. Floodplains, low ridges in bottomlands, slopes, rich moist woods, 0–700 m; enters the West in c. Tex., introduced in s. N.M.

SIMILAR SPECIES White Mulberry, often very similar, is distinguished by its smooth, lustrous upper leaf surface. Littleleaf Mulberry has leaves less than 7 cm long that are harshly hairy on both surfaces, petiole less than 2 cm long, and fruiting catkin to about 1.5 cm long.

MYOPORACEAE: MYOPORUM FAMILY

This family has 4 or 5 genera and 150–200 species, mostly evergreen shrubs or small trees from Australasia. **LEAF** Usually alternate, simple, often gland-dotted. **FLOWER** Usually bisexual and bilateral, calyx with 5 fused sepals and corolla with 5 fused petals; usually 4 stamens, occasionally a vestige of a 5th. The superior ovary has 2 chambers, each containing 1–8 ovules. **FRUIT** Drupe.

Species are grown as ornamentals well beyond their native range, some escaping; a few are invasive. Classification of the family is still unsettled. Recent research indicates that it may be included within the figwort family (Scrophulariaceae), a mostly herbaceous family not otherwise represented by trees in the West.

MOUSEHOLE TREE *Myoporum laetum* G. Forst.

QUICK ID This species has fleshy leaves with embedded oil glands and axillary clusters of bell-shaped white flowers, often maroon-spotted.

Evergreen shrub or small tree to 10 m tall. **LEAF** Alternate, simple, bright green, fleshy, hairless, surfaces speckled with tiny embedded, translucent oil glands; lanceolate to elliptic, base tapered, the edges of the blade continuing down the petiole, usually finely toothed toward the pointed blade tip. Blade 4–14 cm long, 2–5 cm wide. **FLOWER** In small, loose axillary clusters of 2–4 flowers; corolla bell-shaped, 1.5–2 cm diam.; petal lobes 5, white, hairy, often spotted with maroon within. Mar.–May. **FRUIT** Ovoid, pale purple to deep red-purple 2-seeded drupe, 5–10 mm diam.

HABITAT/RANGE Introduced from New Zealand; open areas in grassland and brush, often along streams, 0–450 m, c. and s. Calif., mostly near the coast.

SIMILAR SPECIES Lemonade Sumac (*Rhus integrifolia*, Anacardiaceae) has dark green leathery leaves, flowers ½ the size in dense clusters, and sticky-hairy, slightly flattened drupes.

Notes Myoporum has about 30 species. This rapidly growing, wind- and salt-resistant shrub is planted for its bright green foliage, accented by bronze new leaves, white flowers, and purple drupes. Birds carry seeds to new locations, and the plant has become invasive. The leaves contain liver toxins and may be lethal to livestock.

Mousehole Tree

flowers

fruit

MYRICACEAE: WAX MYRTLE FAMILY

The Myricaceae is a family of 3 genera and 57 species, all but 2 in the genus *Myrica*, found nearly worldwide in temperate or tropical regions. Two genera and 8 native species occur north of Mexico; 1 treelike species occurs in the West.

Evergreen or deciduous shrubs or trees. **LEAF** Alternate, simple, often aromatic. **FLOWER** Small, usually unisexual, borne in axillary catkins, the sexes usually on separate plants. **FRUIT** Drupelike, the surface usually warty.

CALIFORNIA BAYBERRY *Myrica californica* Cham.
A.K.A. PACIFIC WAX-MYRTLE

QUICK ID Evergreen aromatic foliage, narrow leaves with toothed, rolled margins, and short axillary catkins distinguish this species.

Evergreen shrub or tree to 10 m tall, with a narrow, loose crown of ascending branches; trunk to 30 cm diam. Colorless or black dot-like glands on the leaves and twigs produce a spicy aroma. **BARK** Tight, smooth, mottled gray and tan. **TWIG** Stout, rough from elevated leaf scars, loosely hairy at first, later hairless. **LEAF** Alternate, simple, narrowly elliptic or oblanceolate, long-tapered at the base, pointed at the tip; margin usually coarsely toothed and rolled under. Upper surface dark, shiny green; lower surface paler and densely glandular. Blade 4–13 cm long, 1–3 cm broad; petiole 3–10 mm long. **FLOWER** Tiny, in axillary catkins to 3 cm long, unisexual and bisexual flowers on the same plant; male catkins lowest on the branch, mixed female and bisexual above, and often only female near the tip. Stamens 2–22, anthers red-purple, turning yellow; ovary ultimately inferior, with 2 bright red-purple styles. Mar.–Jun. **FRUIT** Dry,

warty, globose drupe, 4–7 mm diam., blackish or purplish brown, sometimes whitish-waxy. Often 2 or 3 ovaries will fuse, making a compound fruit.

HABITAT/RANGE Native. Coastal dunes, marshes, coniferous forest, 0–1,000 m; s. B.C. to sc. Calif.

SIMILAR SPECIES California Bay (*Umbellularia californica*, Lauraceae) also has aromatic evergreen leaves, but they are not toothed, and its drupes are larger and smooth.

Notes Some authorities include California Bayberry in the genus *Morella*, which is differentiated from *Myrica* by position of catkins, size of bracts subtending male flowers, and appearance of fruit.

CALIFORNIA BAYBERRY

underside

California Bayberry

fruit

MYRTACEAE: MYRTLE FAMILY

This family of about 3,000 species is primarily from the Southern Hemisphere, reaching northward into the subtropics of North America and Eurasia. Species occur mostly in dry or moist habitats without frost or where freezes are light and uncommon. In California, *Eucalyptus* is the most well-known genus in the family. About 33 species occur in North America, 8 native.

In habit the myrtle family ranges from straggling shrubs to majestic trees; species are evergreen. **LEAF** Usually opposite, simple, leathery, with margins entire. They often have a spicy or medicinal scent. **FLOWER** Radial and bisexual, usually white, cream, pink, lilac, or red, almost always with numerous stamens, which are often joined together in bundles opposite the petals. A hypanthium forms the base of the flower; attached near the rim are 4 or 5 sepals, the same number of separate petals, and many stamens (in *Eucalyptus* the sepals and petals are fused to make the bud cap). **FRUIT** The ovary is almost always inferior, joined to the hypanthium, forming a berry, drupe, nutlike structure, or capsule, which is often woody and hard.

The family is important for its timber and scented oils. It provides cloves and allspice. Guava is one of the edible fruits in the family. All species in the West are introduced, most of them originally for ornamental use. Primarily in Calif. a number of species have naturalized to a greater or lesser extent, one or two becoming invasive.

■ *EUCALYTPUS*: GUM TREESS

There are 450–500 species of *Eucalyptus*, almost all confined to Australia; a few occur in Malaysia. More than 200 have been introduced throughout the world. They flourish in California, where there are about 10 naturalized species growing from the coast to the interior hills at low elevations.

Eucalyptus is a genus of evergreen plants ranging from dwarf shrubs to massive trees that vie with redwoods as the tallest plants. **BARK** The bark is important in identification, varying from hard, persistent, dark and furrowed to smooth, peeling or flaking, and varicolored in pastel white, cream, salmon, tan, or gray. **LEAF** Arrangement may vary with stage of growth. Leaves of juvenile plants are usually opposite and are often proportionately broader than adult leaves. Adult leaves are initiated from opposite buds, but unequal elongation of the stem between results in alternate arrangement. Blades are simple, leathery, margins entire; the adult leaves, which are described in the following accounts, are most often lanceolate and often curved like a scythe blade. Leaves often hang, or are oriented and structured so that it is difficult to determine "upper" and "lower" sides, which we have not tried to distinguish in the accounts. **FLOWER** Small but often showy, bisexual, radially symmetric, borne singly or in umbellate clusters, the clusters in some arranged in branched panicles. The base of the flower is a leathery hypanthium; in bud the hypanthium has a cap made from completely fused petals and sepals, which is shed as the flower blooms, exposing the many, often colorful stamens. The ovary is inferior, with 3–6 chambers. **FRUIT** Woody capsule, smooth, ribbed or warty, splitting open at the top, with 3 to several small teeth around the rim of the opening.

It has been noted that one can drive the length of the Central Valley in California and never be out of sight of *Eucalyptus*. About a half dozen species not included here spontaneously reproduce in California botanical gardens and may yet join the naturalized flora. This is the most important dicot plantation tree worldwide, valued for timber, wood pulp, and fuel. Oils are extracted from the foliage of some species. Numerous others are grown as ornamentals. Many are invasive and weedy.

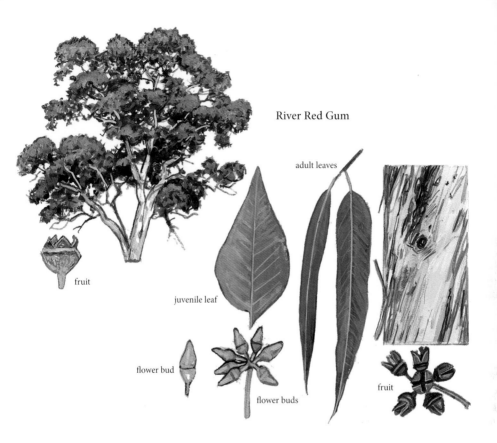

River Red Gum

adult leaves

juvenile leaf

fruit

flower bud

flower buds

fruit

RIVER RED GUM *Eucalyptus camaldulensis* Dehnh.
A.K.A. RED GUM

QUICK ID Recognized by the combination of shredding bark, lanceolate leaves, umbels with 7–11 flowers, and bowl-shaped, 4-toothed woody capsules 5–10 mm long.

Evergreen tree to 25 m tall; branches often hanging in clumps. Trunk short, 1–2 m diam. **BARK** Reddish on twigs; gray and persistent near the base of the trunk; upward and on branches white, pale gray, or buff in patches, shredding in strips or irregular flakes. **LEAF** Leathery, lanceolate, margins entire, light green, hairless. Blade 6–20 cm long; petiole 1–2 cm long. **FLOWER** In axillary umbels bearing 7–11 small white flowers; hypanthium hemispheric, 2–3 mm long; bud cap equally long,

round at base, beaked. Apr.–Jul. **FRUIT** Smooth, bowl-shaped capsule, 5–10 mm long, with 4 broad teeth at the top.

HABITAT/RANGE Introduced from Australia; disturbed areas, 0–350 m, much of Calif., waif in s. Ariz., naturalized in s. Fla.

RIVER RED GUM

LEMON-SCENTED GUM *Eucalyptus citriodora* Hook.

Graceful evergreen tree to 25 m tall. **BARK** Smooth, shed in irregular pieces, powdery whitish or golden when first exposed, tan later. **LEAF** Glossy green, narrowly lanceolate, sometimes curved; blade 10–20 cm long, 1–2 cm wide. **FLOWER** Inflorescence a panicle comprising umbels of 3–5 flowers. Flowers white. Dec.–May. **FRUIT** Urn- or barrel-shaped capsule, 8–15 mm long. **HABITAT/RANGE** Introduced from ne. Australia; very common in Calif., commonly planted along roadsides, occasional escape below 200 m. **SIMILAR SPECIES** Blue Gum, also common, usually has only 1 flower in the leaf axils; its fruits are 4-ribbed, warty, and 2 cm long or more. Forest Red Gum has a hornlike bud cap. *Notes* The oil is used in perfumes and insect repellents.

SUGAR GUM *Eucalyptus cladocalyx* F. Muell.

Straight-trunked evergreen tree, 8–20 m tall; foliage clumped near the branch ends. **BARK** Smooth, shed in large irregular patches, mottled with cream, gray, tan, and brownish orange. **LEAF** Dark green on 1 side, paler on the other, lanceolate, curved; blade 8–15 cm long. **FLOWER** In umbels of 7–11 flowers, usually on leafless sections of the branches. Flowers white to greenish yellow. Apr.–Jun. **FRUIT** Egg- or barrel-shaped, more or less ribbed capsule, 10–15 mm long. **HABITAT/RANGE** Introduced from sc. Australia; coastal urban areas, s. Calif. below 200 m.

SPIDER GUM *Eucalyptus conferruminata* D.J. Carr & S.G.M. Carr

Irregularly branched evergreen shrub or small tree, 1–5 m tall. **BARK** Smooth, shed in short strips, gray or tan. **LEAF** Glossy, light green, 5–9 cm long, 1–4 cm wide, elliptic. **FLOWER** In umbels of 7–10 flowers, stalk flat; bud 5 cm long, cap horn-shaped; flowers joined at the base, yellow-green. Apr.–Jul. **FRUIT** Urn-shaped, 3 cm long, 3 teeth at the top, joined in a cluster 3–6 cm wide. **HABITAT/RANGE** Introduced from sw. Australia; uncommon, disturbed coastal urban areas, below 200 m, sw. Calif. Possibly invasive.

BLUE GUM *Eucalyptus globulus* Labill.
A.K.A. TASMANIAN BLUE GUM

QUICK ID This massive tree has shredding bark, lanceolate leaves, usually 1 flower in the leaf axils, and inverse-pyramidal woody, warty capsules 1–2 cm long.

Massive straight-boled evergreen tree, 15–70 m tall, with large ascending, irregular, slightly crooked branches with hanging leaves. Trunk 2 m or more in diam. **BARK** On trunk and branches smooth, peeling in strips, bluish gray when fresh, becoming yellowish or tan. **TWIG** Squarish when young. **LEAF** Leathery, lanceolate, usually curved, margins entire. Dark green, lustrous, and hairless. Blade 10–30 cm long, 2.5–4 cm broad; petiole about 1–3 cm long. **FLOWER** One, occasionally up to 3, sessile, in the leaf axils. Buds square, 2 cm long, the cap pan-shaped, with a central knob, warty and with a bluish waxy bloom; hypanthium mostly 4-ribbed. Stamens white. Oct.–Jan. **FRUIT** Woody capsule, inversely pyramidal, 1–2.1 cm long, slightly wider, with 4 or 5 sides, prominently ribbed and warty, covered with a bluish waxy bloom, the rim thick, with 4 or 5 horizontally oriented teeth at the top; has a conspicuous indented ring between the cap and hypanthium.

HABITAT/RANGE Introduced from se. Australia; disturbed areas, hillsides, most frequent near coast, below 300 m, much of Calif. in the Coast Ranges.

SIMILAR SPECIES River Red Gum is the other very common eucalyptus in Calif. It has small bowl-shaped capsules 5–10 mm long, and 7–11 flowers in axillary umbels.

Notes Blue Gum is the primary source for eucalyptus oil, most of which is distilled in China. It was introduced to Calif. in the late 1800s as an ornamental and as a potential source for lumber, particularly railroad ties, but the wood is difficult to cure. Elsewhere it is used for construction, fuel wood, and pulp. The tallest flowering plant in Calif., it is so massive that it becomes a problem in most ornamental plantings; the peeling strips of bark are messy. It is invasive, producing nearly pure stands that crowd out and exclude other species. The accumulated leaves and bark provide fuel for fires, the oily leaves exacerbating the problem.

BLUE GUM

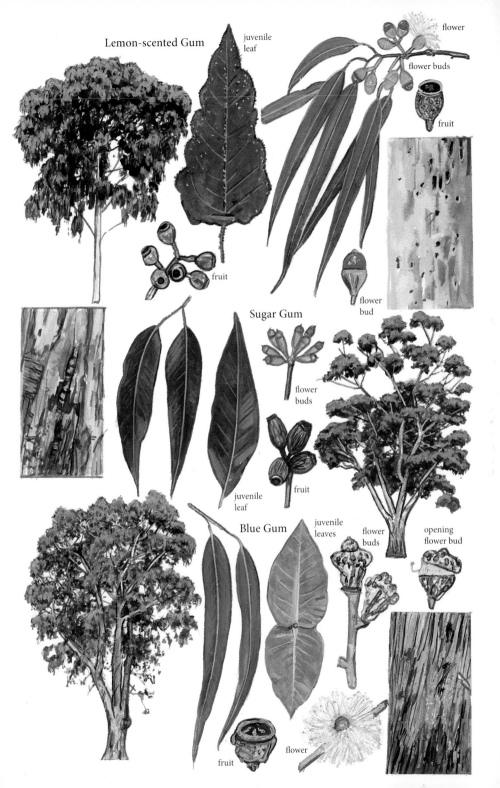

Lemon-scented Gum

juvenile leaf

flower

flower buds

fruit

fruit

Sugar Gum

flower bud

flower buds

fruit

juvenile leaf

Blue Gum

juvenile leaves

flower buds

opening flower bud

fruit

flower

SILVER DOLLAR GUM *Eucalyptus polyanthemos* Schauer

Dense, rounded evergreen tree, 10–25 m tall. **BARK** Smooth, gray or tan, shed in irregular flakes or strips, or persistent, rough, fibrous, brownish gray. **LEAF** Gray-green, blue-green, or silvery, often with a whitish bloom, ovate to round; blade 5–10 cm long. **FLOWER** Inflorescence a repeatedly branched panicle comprising umbels of 5–7 flowers. Flowers white. Dec.–Feb. **FRUIT** Deeply vase-shaped or inversely pear-shaped capsule, 5–6 mm long. **HABITAT/RANGE** Introduced from se. Australia; occasionally escapes in s. Calif. near the coast, below 200 m.

RED IRONBARK *Eucalyptus sideroxylon* A. Cunn. ex Woolls

Evergreen tree 7–25 m tall. **BARK** Hard, furrowed, dark brown to nearly black. **LEAF** Dull green, lanceolate; blade 6–14 cm long, 1–2 cm wide. **FLOWER** In axillary umbels of 5–7 flowers. Flowers pink to red, sometimes white; outer stamens lack anthers. Dec.–Feb. **FRUIT** Blunt egg-shaped capsule, 1 cm long, with 5 teeth inside a swollen rim. **HABITAT/RANGE** Introduced from se. Australia; common landscape plant, naturalized in coastal urban areas, below 200 m, c. and s. Calif.

FOREST RED GUM *Eucalyptus tereticornis* Sm.

Evergreen tree to 25 m tall, very similar to Red Gum. **FLOWER** In umbels of 7–11 flowers. Hypanthium 2–3 mm long, inversely conic to hemispheric; bud cap much like a blunt rhino horn, about twice the length of the hypanthium. Dec.–Feb. **HABITAT/RANGE** Introduced from e. Australia; occasional escape below 200 m in much of Calif.

MANNA GUM *Eucalyptus viminalis* Labill.
A.K.A. RIBBON GUM

Openly branched evergreen tree, 25–50 m tall, with billowy masses of foliage on drooping twigs. **BARK** Smooth, shed in long ribbons, white, gray, or tan. **LEAF** Green, narrowly lanceolate, slightly curved; blade 10–20 cm long, 1–2 cm wide. **FLOWER** In axillary umbels of usually 3 flowers. Flowers white. Jul.–Sep. **FRUIT** Deeply urn-shaped to hemispheric capsule, 5–7 mm long; 3 or 4 ascending teeth at the top. **HABITAT/RANGE** Introduced from se. Australia; occasional escape in s. Calif. below 100 m.

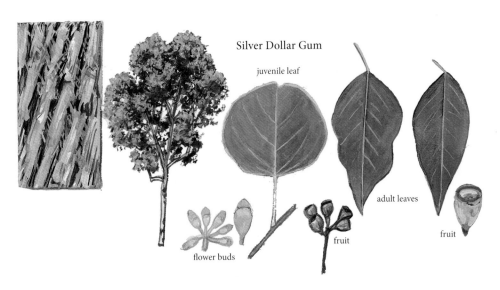

Silver Dollar Gum

juvenile leaf

adult leaves

flower buds

fruit

fruit

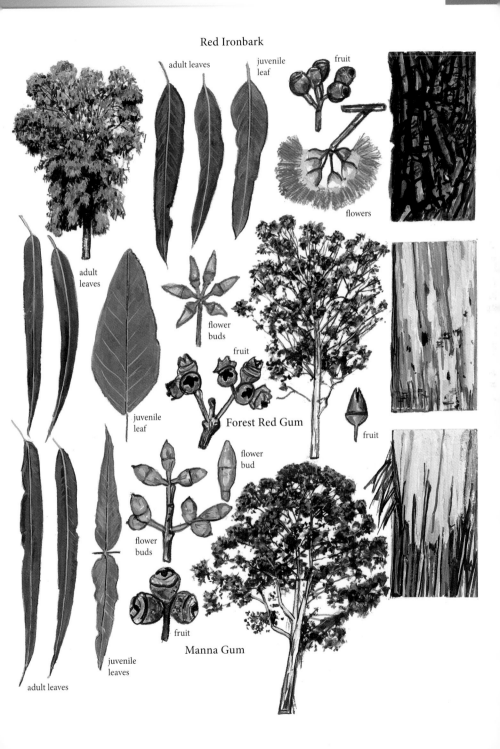

Red Ironbark

adult leaves

juvenile leaf

fruit

flowers

adult leaves

flower buds

fruit

juvenile leaf

Forest Red Gum

fruit

flower bud

flower buds

flower buds

fruit

Manna Gum

juvenile leaves

adult leaves

WHITE PEPPERMINT *Eucalyptus pulchella* Desf.

Evergreen tree 6–20 m tall; main branches erect, twigs weeping. **BARK** Smooth, peeling in strips, freshly exposed bark yellowish, weathering to white or mottled pale gray. **LEAF** Dark green, narrowly linear-lanceolate; blade 5–10 cm long, to 5 mm wide. **FLOWER** In axillary umbels of 9–15 flowers. Flowers white. Dec.–Feb. **FRUIT** Ovoid to cup-shaped capsule, 4–6 mm long. **HABITAT/RANGE** Introduced from s. Tasmania; occasional escape in the San Francisco Bay area, Calif., below 200 m.

AUSTRALIAN TEA TREE *Leptospermum laevigatum* (Gaertn.) F. Muell.

Evergreen shrub or small tree to about 9 m tall, about as wide as high; trunk spreading to erect, curved and twisted; branches tending to arch to the ground. **LEAF** Alternate, simple, oblanceolate to ovate-oblong, stiff, dull bluish gray-green, 3-veined; blade 1–2.5 cm long. **FLOWER** In clusters of 1–3 in the leaf axils, white; calyx lobes 5, silky above; petals 5; stamens about 20, all attached near the rim of a widely cup-shaped hypanthium; ovary mostly inferior. Mar.–Jun. **FRUIT** Many-chambered leathery capsule, 7–8 mm wide, opening at the top. **HABITAT/RANGE** Introduced from Australia and neighboring areas; cultivated as an ornamental and for sand stabilization, occasionally found naturalized along the Calif. coast below 50 m. *Notes Leptospermum* is a genus of 30–70 species of small trees and shrubs native to Australia and neighboring areas.

TEMU *Luma apiculata* (DC.) Burret

Slow-growing evergreen shrub or small tree, 1.5–5 m tall. Trunk erect, twisted and contorted; crown with many branches. **BARK** Smooth, shed in flakes, orange, often with white patches. **LEAF** Opposite, simple, ovate, leathery, glossy, dark green; blade 2–2.5 cm long. **FLOWER** Usually 1 in the leaf axils, 12 mm diam.; sepals 4; petals 4, cream and tinged pink; stamens many in a dense ring; hypanthium broadly vase-shaped. Jul.–Sep. **FRUIT** Dark purple berry, 12 mm wide. **HABITAT/RANGE** Introduced from South America; occasionally naturalized in cool coastal urban areas below 100 m in c. Calif. *Notes Luma* contains 2 species, both from the Andes in Argentina and Chile. This species is a popular bonsai subject.

WEEPING BOTTLEBRUSH *Melaleuca viminalis* (Sol. ex Gaertn.) Byrnes

Evergreen shrub or small tree to about 6 m tall. **LEAF** Alternate, narrowly elliptic, leathery, glossy, dark green or grayish green; blade 2.5–14 cm long. **FLOWER** In dense, more or less drooping, bright red spikes at the ends of the branches, 4–10 cm long, resembling a bottlebrush; the branch often extends as a leafy shoot beyond the inflorescence. Stamens many, showy, extending straight out from the stem, joined together in 5 bundles of 9–14 stamens each. May–Jul. **FRUIT** Hard, persistent capsule enclosed in a persistent cup-shaped hypanthium about 6 mm long. **HABITAT/RANGE** Introduced from Australia; naturalized in disturbed places in s. Calif. below 300 m. *Notes Melaleuca* is a genus of about 150 species of trees and shrubs native to Australia and neighboring areas. This and several other widely cultivated species were formerly included in the genus *Callistemon*.

Weeping Bottlebrush

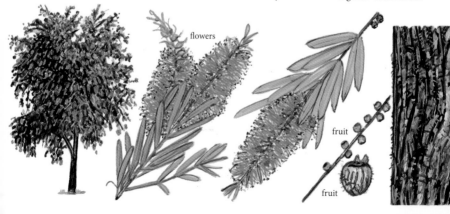

flowers

fruit

fruit

juvenile
leaf

flower
buds

fruit

adult
leaves

fruit

White Peppermint

flowers

fruit

Australian Tea Tree

flower

fruit

flowers

Temu

flowers

fruit

SCRUB CHERRY *Syzygium australe* (J.C. Wendl. ex Link) B. Hyland

Evergreen shrub or small tree, in the wild up to 35 m tall. Branchlets 4-winged or 4-ribbed near the tips, the wings or ribs merging in pairs to form 2 pockets at the next lower node. **LEAF** Opposite, obovate to elliptic, thinly leathery, bronze when young, when mature glossy green above, duller below; blade 3–9 cm long. **FLOWER** In loose axillary or terminal clusters of 3–7 flowers, the buds club-shaped; flower about 12 mm diam.; sepals 4; petals 4, white; stamens numerous. Mostly Apr.–Sep. **FRUIT** Globose or ellipsoid red or purple berry, 14–23 mm long. **HABITAT/ RANGE** Introduced from se. Australia; an ornamental, uncommon below 50 m in canyons and gullies in San Diego County, Calif. *Notes* *Syzygium* is a genus of more than 1,000 species in the Old World tropics.

OLEACEAE: OLIVE FAMILY

The olive family includes about 24 genera and more than 600 species of trees, shrubs, and a few vines distributed mostly in temperate to tropical regions. The family is particularly abundant and diverse in Asia and Australasia. Members of the family occur in a wide range of habitats. About 17 arborescent species, in 4 or 5 genera, occur in the West. Most are native, with a few introduced.

Plants in the family are perennials. They commonly bear minute scales attached by a central stalk (peltate) on the foliage. **LEAF** Deciduous or evergreen, usually opposite, simple to odd-pinnate (with a terminal leaflet), margins entire or toothed. **FLOWER** Usually radially symmetric, calyx small and with 4–15 lobes, corolla with 4–8 lobes; stamens 2–6, arising from near the base of the corolla; single pistil with a 2-lobed stigma; ovary superior. Any one of the series of flower parts may be absent, and flowers may be bisexual, unisexual and mixed with bisexual flowers, all unisexual with the sexes mixed on the same plant (monoecious) or with the sexes separate, borne on different plants (dioecious). In ours, the calyx and corolla, when present, commonly have 4 lobes; the corolla is most often white or yellow. **FRUIT** Drupe, capsule, or samara, usually with 1 seed per chamber.

The **Olive** (*Olea europaea* L.), cultivated in Calif. since the mid-18th century, is a well-known member of the family, the source of the edible olive and the oil extracted from its pulp. Ashes (*Fraxinus*) provide high-quality hardwood. A number of species are used as ornamentals, among them privets (*Ligustrum*) and lilacs (*Syringa*). The **Japanese Tree Lilac** (*S. reticulata* [Blume] H. Hara), naturalized in the Northeast, is reported from Wyo. but probably has not naturalized. With their cheery yellow flowers on otherwise still barren branches, shrubs of the genus *Forsythia* are a welcome harbinger of spring in winter-cold areas.

■ *FORESTIERA:* SWAMPPRIVETS

Forestiera includes nearly 20 species (variably called swampprivets, desert olives, and stretchberries), distributed mostly in the temperate and subtropical regions of the Americas. About 8 species occur in North America north of Mexico; 4 occur in the West. Members of the genus occupy diverse habitats from sea-level to moderate elevations.

Deciduous or evergreen shrubs or small trees with stiff, spreading, hairless or finely hairy twigs, and ragged crowns. **LEAF** Opposite, simple, thin or leathery, linear to obovate; margin entire or toothed. **FLOWER** In small axillary clusters on the preceding year's branches; flowers may be all bisexual, unisexual and bisexual mixed on a single tree, or all unisexual, the sexes mixed or on separate plants. Calyx tiny, bell-shaped, usually with

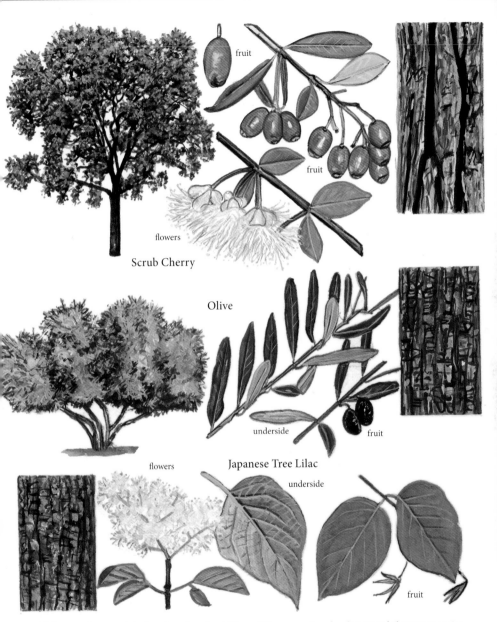

fruit

fruit

fruit

flowers

Scrub Cherry

Olive

underside

fruit

flowers

Japanese Tree Lilac

underside

fruit

4 lobes, or absent; petals 0, or 1 or 2 and quickly deciduous; stamens 1–6; pistil 1, superior, with 2 chambers. **FRUIT** Drupe with thin flesh and a sub-globose, thin-walled, longitudinally ribbed stone.

Species of *Forestiera* are widespread, usually shrubby, and mostly inconspicuous. They have little economic value, but provide browse to native and domestic mammals, which relish them to the point that plants may disappear from rangeland. Birds feed upon the drupes.

TEXAS ELBOW BUSH *Forestiera angustifolia* Torr.

A.K.A. DESERT OLIVE, TEXAS SWAMPPRIVET

QUICK ID Similar to other *Forestiera*, Texas Elbow Bush has small leaves in fascicles, but unlike other species in the region they are linear, with darkish pits beneath.

Evergreen shrub or tree, 1–4 m tall, losing leaves during drought and cold. **TWIG** Densely and minutely hairy. **LEAF** Opposite, simple, leathery, narrow, dark green, hairless or minutely hairy, with tiny darkish pits scattered on the lower surface; margins entire, thickened, sometimes slightly rolled under. Blade usually 4–30 mm long, 1–4 mm broad. **FLOWER** Tiny, in small clusters, bisexual and female on the same plant; anthers dark purple. Jan.–Apr. and Jul.–Sep. **FRUIT** Ovoid drupe, often slightly curved, 5–8 mm long, black, dark blue, or purplish.

HABITAT/RANGE Native. Open sandy, gravelly, or rocky areas, 0–1,400 m; w. and s. Tex. to Mexico.

DESERT OLIVE *Forestiera phyllyreoides* (Benth.) Torr.

QUICK ID Small leaves with entire, rolled-under margins and small, slightly curved purplish-black drupes distinguish this species within its region.

Evergreen (deciduous in drought) shrub or sometimes a small tree to 8 m tall; crown irregular. **BARK** Pale to dark gray. **TWIG** Minutely hairy, stiff, repeatedly branched at wide angles and intertangled. **LEAF** Opposite, mostly clustered on short shoots, lanceolate or oblanceolate, tapered to a very short stalk, the tip narrowly rounded or slightly notched; margins entire, usually rolled under. Surfaces green and finely hairy, upper surface often becoming

sparsely hairy, lower surface without minute darkish pits. Blade 6–25 mm long, 1–4 mm (sometimes to 15 mm) wide. **FLOWER** Bisexual, borne in small clusters of 2–6 flowers; anthers dark purple. Dec.–Mar. **FRUIT** Egg-shaped drupe, slightly curved to one side, 6–10 mm long, purplish black.

HABITAT/RANGE Native. Dry rocky slopes and canyons, 750–1,400 m; s. Ariz., extreme sw. N.M., to c. Mexico.

SIMILAR SPECIES Texas Elbow Bush is very similar but has minute darkish pits on the lower surface of the leaves, and the leaves are sometimes hairless.

NETLEAF SWAMPPRIVET *Forestiera reticulata* Torr.

QUICK ID This species has leaves with flat, usually toothed margins and veins raised on both surfaces.

Evergreen shrub or tree, usually 2–4 m tall. **TWIG** Minutely hairy. **LEAF** Opposite, simple, elliptic, hairless or minutely hairy on both surfaces; upper surface dull green; lower surface paler, without minute dark pits; margins usually toothed; veins pale, opaque, raised on both surfaces and netlike. Blade usually 2–4 cm long, 1–3 cm broad. **FLOWER** Tiny, in small clusters, unisexual on different plants. Mostly Aug.–Sep. **FRUIT** Ellipsoid to obovoid drupe, 5–10 mm long, dark blue or purplish.

HABITAT/RANGE Native. Creek banks, ledges, ravines, often where moist, 300–900 m; sc. Tex.

SIMILAR SPECIES Elbow Bush (*F. pubescens* Nutt.), found from c. Calif. to Colo., Okla., and Tex., and south to Mexico, blooms Jan.–Apr. Its leaves have minute darkish pits on the lower surface and translucent veins.

TEXAS ELBOW BUSH

DESERT OLIVE

NETLEAF SWAMPPRIVET

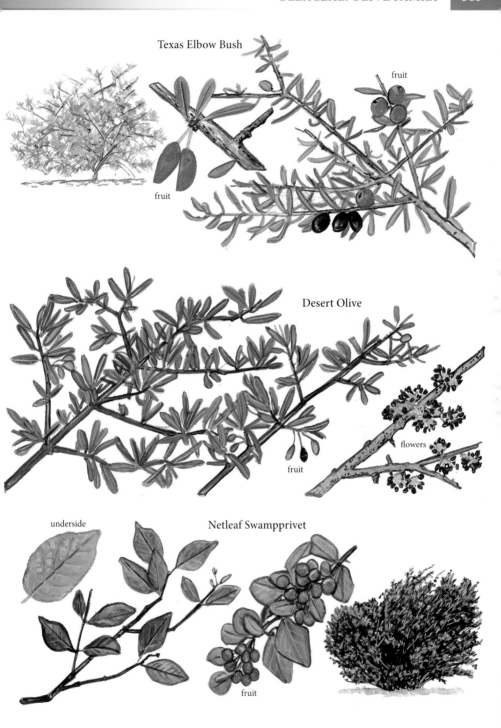

Texas Elbow Bush

fruit

fruit

Desert Olive

fruit

flowers

underside

Netleaf Swampprivet

fruit

■ *FRAXINUS*: ASHES

The genus *Fraxinus* includes 45–65 species distributed mostly in the temperate and subtropical regions of the Northern Hemisphere. About 22 species occur in North America north of Mexico, 20 native and two naturalized; 12 occur in the West. Ashes (a.k.a. fresnos) occupy diverse habitats, from upland forests, dry hillsides, and canyons, to moist valley bottoms and floodplains, and from low to moderate elevations.

Deciduous or evergreen trees or rarely large shrubs, often with a single erect, sometimes massive trunk, sometimes forming clumps with several trunks. Crown rounded, pyramidal, narrow or broad, sometimes with drooping lower branches. **BARK** Usually gray, sometimes blotchy, occasionally reddish brown, often smooth when young, when older sometimes smooth but more often roughened with numerous interlacing furrows and narrow ridges. **TWIG** Usually green at first, passing through tan, brownish, or orange, finally gray when older; hairless or hairy; leaf scars and lenticels conspicuous. **LEAF** Opposite, pinnately compound, with a terminal leaflet (odd-pinnate); leaflets 3–11, sometimes more. **FLOWER** Few to many in axillary, or rarely terminal, panicles; flowers may be all bisexual, unisexual and bisexual mixed on a single tree, or all unisexual, the sexes then on separate plants. Calyx tiny, bell-shaped, with 4 lobes; petals 0, 2, 4, or 6; stamens usually 2; pistil 1, ovary superior. **FRUIT** Samara with a hard, indehiscent, flat or swollen seed body at the base containing a single seed (rarely 2 seeds), with a flat wing extending beyond the tip of the seed body like the blade of a canoe paddle, the wing sometimes with a vertical vane down the middle, the fruit then called "3-vaned." The width and point of origin of the wing on the seed body, and the presence of a 3rd vane, are important in identification.

Ashes are easily recognized by opposite, pinnately compound leaves and a fruit that splits into 2 single-winged samaras. Boxelder (*Acer negundo*, Sapindaceae) and elderberries (*Sambucus*, Adoxaceae) also have large opposite, pinnate leaves, but the fruits differ. Many ashes are important timber trees. The wood is hard, resilient, and shock-resistant, and has been used in the manufacture of baseball bats, boat paddles, and high-quality veneer.

Some species are used as handsome ornamentals, providing rich fall color. All North American ash species are susceptible to the Emerald Ash Borer (*Agrilus planipennis*), an introduced beetle native to e. Asia, and millions of trees have been affected. Mortality rate is 100%. Ash dieback also affects the trees, and is caused by air pollution, drought, and infection by a fungus (*Hymenoscyphus pseudoalbidus*).

Ashes may have minute, centrally attached (peltate) scales, each with a dark dot, on the lower surface of the leaf and sometimes also on the upper surface. In a few species the lower surface of the leaf may also be papillose—that is, minutely roughened with small protuberances, much like the surface of a basketball. Both of these features require a 10× lens for examination.

TEXAS ASH *Fraxinus albicans* S.F. Buckley

QUICK ID Distinguished by opposite, pinnate leaves with an unwinged rachis and 5–7 leaflets that are whitish beneath; the papillose lower surface is unique in western ashes.

Deciduous tree, 6–12 m tall, with a single erect trunk; branches often contorted. **TWIG** Round, light gray, hairless. **LEAF** Opposite, pinnately compound, blade 13–20 cm long, rachis not winged. Leaflets usually 5, broadly elliptic, roundish, or obovate; margins scallop-toothed above the middle. Upper surface dark green, hairless; lower surface often whitish, papillose, usually hairless at maturity. Leaflet blade 3–8 cm long, 2–5 cm broad, stalk 3–10 mm long. **FLOWER** Unisexual, on separate plants; petals absent. Feb.–Mar. **FRUIT** Narrowly elliptic or linear samara, usually 1.5–2.5 cm long. Seed body cylindric, not grooved; wing flat, 3–5 mm wide, arising from near the tip of the body, often minutely notched at the apex.

TEXAS ASH   SINGLELEAF ASH

Texas Ash

seed body

autumn

wing

fruit

fruit

Singleleaf Ash

HABITAT/RANGE Native. Canyons, rocky slopes, riverbanks, 200–400 m; sc. Tex., mostly along the eastern edge of Edwards Plateau, and sc. Okla. to nc. Mexico.

SIMILAR SPECIES Texas Ash is closely related to White or American Ash (*F. americana* L.), a widespread species of the East; the two are often considered a single species. White Ash is generally larger, with thinner, proportionately narrower leaflets (leaflet blade 6–15 cm long, 2–7.5 cm broad).

SINGLELEAF ASH *Fraxinus anomala*
Torr. ex. S. Watson

QUICK ID The opposite leaves with 1 or a few roundish leaflets and the 4-sided young twigs help identify this species.

Deciduous shrub or small tree, 1.5–6 m tall, leaves often persisting well into the cold season. Trunks usually several, short and usually crooked, 12–18 cm diam.; branches often short and crooked, the crown round-topped. **BARK** Gray to brownish, thin, with shallow fissures and narrow, scaly ridges. **TWIG** More or less 4-angled when young, round

when older, dark green to reddish brown at first, gray later, hairy or not; lenticels pale, elevated; leaf scars crescent-shaped. **LEAF** Opposite, simple or pinnately compound. Leaflets 1–7, leathery, light green, each 2–6 cm long, 1.5–5 cm broad, broadly ovate to round; base squarish, bluntly angled, or abruptly tapered to the petiole; tip round or bluntly angled; margins scallop-toothed except in the lower ⅓; lower surface hairless or glandular hairy and black-speckled with minute scales. Petiole 4–40 mm long, sometimes finely glandular hairy. **FLOWER** Many in branched clusters, bisexual, or in some clusters stamens aborted; petals absent. Apr.–May. **FRUIT** Narrowly or broadly ovate samara, usually 1.3–2.6 cm long. Seed body flat; wing flat, 5–11 mm wide, arising from the base of the body and surrounding it, often deeply notched at the apex.

HABITAT/RANGE Native. In brush and conifer forests, on slopes, in canyons and washes, along streamsides, 200–2,600 m; se. Calif. to w. Colo. and w. N.M.

SIMILAR SPECIES Gregg's Ash of w. Tex. also has 1 or few leaflets, but the margins are entire or with only 1–3 teeth on each side in the upper ½, and the twigs are round.

SINGLELEAF ASH *continued*

Notes There are 2 varieties. Var. *anomala* usually has 1 leaflet, occasionally up to 5 on vigorous shoots; it occurs from se. Calif. to w. Colo. and nw. N.M. Var. *lowellii* (Sarg.) Little usually has 5–7 leaflets, occasionally 1; it occurs from se. Calif. eastward, mostly along the Mogollon Rim to wc. N.M. The latter apparently hybridizes with Velvet Ash in sw. Utah.

MEXICAN ASH *Fraxinus berlandieriana* DC.

A.K.A. BERLANDIER ASH

QUICK ID Distinguished by the combination of opposite leaves with 3–5 leaflets on narrowly winged stalks that are usually 3–7 mm long, and a flat or 3-vaned samara with the wing originating in the lower ⅓ of the seed body.

Deciduous tree, sometimes a shrub, 6–12 m tall, usually with a single short trunk 40–50 cm diam.; crown round or oval, branching low to the ground. **BARK** Thick, grayish brown, with deep, interlacing furrows. **TWIG** Round, grayish, usually hairy; leaf scar shallowly hemispheric and shallowly concave across the top. **LEAF** Opposite, pinnately compound, slightly leathery, blade 8–20 cm long, rachis 1.5–4 cm long. Leaflets usually 3–5, each 4–9.5 cm long, 1.5–4 mm broad, on a narrowly winged stalk 3–7 mm long; leaflet blade elliptic, lanceolate, obovate, or roughly diamond-shaped; margins toothed at least in the upper ½, sometimes mostly entire; upper surface gray-green to olive green, glabrous; lower surface paler, hairy along the veins near the base, dark-speckled with minute, dense scales. Foliage brownish to purplish in autumn. **FLOWER** Unisexual, on separate plants, in many-flowered clusters; petals absent. Feb.–Apr. **FRUIT** Oblong-ovate or spatulate samara, 2–4 cm

long. Seed body flattened, with 2 or 3 grooves; wing flat or sometimes 3-vaned (mixed in the same cluster), 4–7 mm wide, gradually arising from the lower ⅓ of the body.

HABITAT/RANGE Native. Wet places, 0–400 m; sc. Okla. through ec. and s. Tex. to ne. Mexico.

SIMILAR SPECIES Green Ash, occurring in the West only in s. Tex., differs subtly: Its leaf scars are broadly oblong-ovate, flat or very shallowly concave across the top; and the wing of the samara originates in the upper ¼ of the seed body.

LEATHERLEAF ASH *Fraxinus coriacea* S. Watson

QUICK ID Opposite, pinnate leaves with usually 5 broad, prominently veined leaflets distinguish this tree.

Deciduous tree, 5–10 m tall, usually with a single trunk 30–40 cm diam.; crown round, with stout, spreading branches. **BARK** Thick, light gray, with fissures and broad, scaly ridges. **TWIG** Round, grayish, hairy at first, usually hairless later. **LEAF** Opposite, pinnately compound, leathery, blade 6–20 cm long. Leaflets 3–7 (usually 5), 2–10 cm long, 2–5.5 mm wide, stalk 5–13 mm long; leaflet blade broadly obovate to more or less round; margins shallowly toothed from near the middle to the tip, teeth often with a tiny point; surfaces yellow-green, hairless or with short, stiff hairs, veins raised and prominent on both surfaces, upper surface shiny, lower with minute scales that appear sunken. **FLOWER** Unisexual, on separate plants, in narrow, many-flowered clusters; petals absent. Apr.–Jun. **FRUIT** Narrowly obovate samara, 2–3 cm long. Seed body more or less cylindric; wing flat, 4–6 mm wide, gradually expanding from near the middle of the body, often notched at the apex.

MEXICAN ASH

LEATHERLEAF ASH

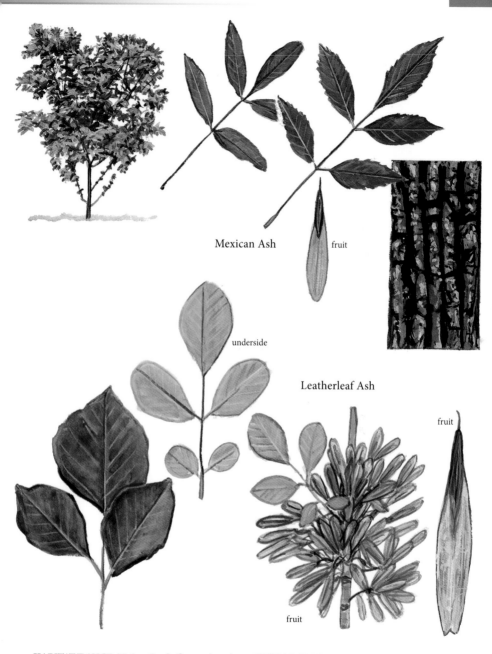

Mexican Ash

fruit

underside

Leatherleaf Ash

fruit

fruit

HABITAT/RANGE Native. Sandy flats and washes, irrigation ditches and riverbanks, desert scrub to dry mixed woodland, 700–2,100 m; s. Calif. to sw. Utah and nw. Ariz., n. Baja Calif.

SIMILAR SPECIES Oregon Ash and Velvet Ash have thinner, slightly more flexible leaflets with veins that are not raised and very short or no leaflet stalks.

FRAGRANT ASH *Fraxinus cuspidata*
Torr.
A.K.A. FLOWERING ASH

QUICK ID The combination of opposite, pinnately compound, dark green leaves, 4-petaled fragrant white flowers, and very flat, oval samaras is distinctive.

Deciduous shrub or small tree, 2–7 m tall. **BARK** Gray, smooth. **TWIG** Round, hairless. **LEAF** Opposite, pinnately compound, blade 4–15 cm long. Leaflets 5–9, each 2–8 cm long, 10–23 mm wide, stalk 3–10 mm long; leaflet blade leathery or thin, narrowly lanceolate, rarely broadly obovate, the tip bluntly angled or long-tapered; margins with sparse, very narrow teeth. Surfaces hairless or with short, stiff hairs; upper surface dark green, lustrous; lower surface dotted with minute scales. **FLOWER** Bisexual, sweetly fragrant, in loose hanging clusters from new tips of branches; petals 4, white, very narrow, 12–16 mm long, joined into a short tube at the base. Apr.–May, sometimes later. **FRUIT** Oval samara, 15–28 mm long. Seed body very flat; wing flat, arising from the lower ¼–½ of the body, usually with a tiny notch at the tip.

HABITAT/RANGE Native. Scattered on dry rocky slopes and streambeds in desert scrub or dry woodland, 800–2,300 m; s. Nev. to w. Tex., nc. Mexico.

Notes Fragrant Ash is the only North American ash with such large, fragrant, showy flowers. There are 2 varieties: Var. *cuspidata* has leaflets with long, slender, tapering tips, and occurs from w. N.M. to w. Tex. and southward; var. *macropetala* (Eastw.) Rehder has leaflets that are bluntly angled or short-tapered at the tips, and occurs from s. Nev. to w. N.M.

TWO-PETAL ASH *Fraxinus dipetala*
Hook. & Arn.
A.K.A. FLOWERING ASH, FOOTHILL ASH, CALIFORNIA SHRUB ASH

QUICK ID The combination of opposite, pinnately compound, dark green leaves, 2-petaled white flowers that are not fragrant, and very flat, oval or spatulate samaras distinguishes this tree.

Deciduous shrub or tree, 2–7 m tall. **BARK** Gray, smooth at first, later with a rectangular pattern of shallow cracks. **TWIG** More or less 4-angled when young, later round, hairless. **LEAF** Opposite, pinnately compound, blade 8–15 cm long. Leaflets 3–9 (usually 5–7), 1.5–4 cm long, 1–2.5 cm wide, usually on a winged stalk 2–7 mm long; leaflet blade leathery or thin, broadly elliptic to elliptic-obovate; margins bluntly toothed, entire near the base, often slightly rolled under. Surfaces hairless; upper surface dark green, lustrous; lower surface dotted with minute scales. **FLOWER** Bisexual, not fragrant, in dense hanging clusters; petals 2, creamy white, ovate, 2.5–4 mm long. Mar.–Apr. **FRUIT** Spatulate or oval samara, 15–28 mm long. Seed body flat; wing flat, 2.5–8 mm wide, arising from near the base of the seed body, often with a notched tip.

HABITAT/RANGE Native. Canyons, rocky slopes, mixed oak woodland in foothills, 100–1,300 m; mostly Calif. to n. Baja Calif., rare in s. Nev., sw. Utah, and nw. Ariz.

GOODDING'S ASH *Fraxinus gooddingii*
Little
A.K.A. LITTLELEAF ASH

QUICK ID Goodding's Ash has pinnate leathery leaves that are mostly clustered near the ends of short shoots.

FRAGRANT ASH   TWO-PETAL ASH   GOODDING'S ASH

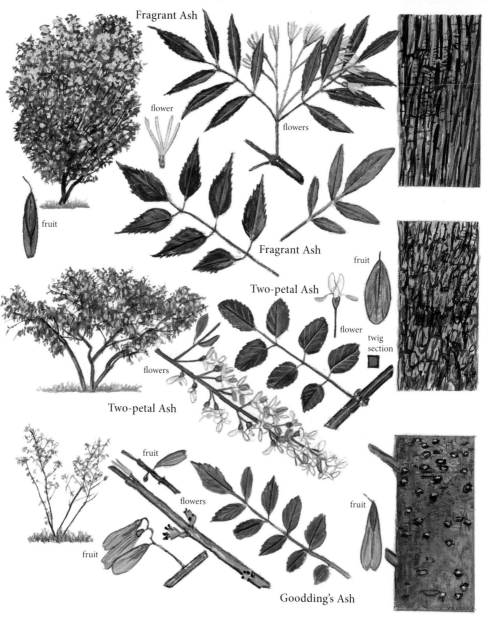

Fragrant Ash

flower

flowers

fruit

Fragrant Ash

Two-petal Ash

fruit

flower

twig section

flowers

Two-petal Ash

fruit

flowers

fruit

fruit

Goodding's Ash

Evergreen shrub or tree, 2–4 m tall, multiple-trunked. Closely related to Gregg's Ash. Young twigs and leaves with loose, multibranched white hairs, becoming mostly hairless later. **LEAF** Opposite but mostly clustered near the tips of short shoots, pinnately compound. Leaflets leathery, usually 5–7 (varying 3–9), 1–2 cm long, 5–18 mm wide, on a winged stalk 0–2 mm long; leaflet blades lanceolate to elliptic-obovate, margins usually with 1–4 pairs of teeth in the upper ½. Leaves yellow and fall at flowering time or during particularly cold winters. **FRUIT** More or less narrowly wedge-shaped samara, usually 1–1.5 cm long. Seed body cylindric; wing flat, 3–4 mm wide, arising from lower ⅓ of the body, tip blunt and shallowly notched.

HABITAT/RANGE Native. Rocky areas, scrub to woodland, 100–1,700 m; se. Ariz., nw. Mexico.

GREGG'S ASH   *Fraxinus greggii* A. Gray
A.K.A. LITTLELEAF ASH

QUICK ID Distinguished by small opposite, pinnately compound leathery leaves with a winged rachis, few leaflets, and small flower clusters.

Evergreen shrub or small tree, 2–4 m tall, often with multiple trunks to 20 cm diam. **TWIG** Round, gray, usually hairless. **LEAF** Opposite, pinnately compound, or occasionally simple, with a narrowly winged rachis. Leaflets usually 1–5, 1–3.5 cm long, 3–9 mm broad, stalkless, narrowly elliptic to obovate or roughly diamond-shaped; margins entire or with 1–3 pairs of teeth in the upper ½, sometimes rolled under. Upper surface dark green, hairless; lower surface paler, black-speckled with minute scales. **FLOWER** Unisexual or bisexual on the same plant, in small few-flowered clusters; petals absent. Mar.–May. **FRUIT** Broadly linear-oblong samara, 14–22 mm long. Seed body more or less cylindric; wing flat, 3–4 mm wide, arising in the upper ¼ of the body, tip rounded to notched.

HABITAT/RANGE Native. Crevices, talus, cliffs, bluffs, canyon bottoms, 400–1,400 m.; w. Tex. near Big Bend, nc. Mexico

Notes Leaves persist until after spring flowering, when new leaves appear. There are 2 varieties: Var. *greggii* has 3–5 leaflets; var. *nummularis* (M.E. Jones) Little, in the U.S. known only from the Chisos Mountains, has 1 leaflet.

GREGG'S ASH

SHAMEL ASH   *Fraxinus uhdei* (Wenzig)
Lingelsh.
A.K.A. TROPICAL ASH

Evergreen tree, 8–25 m tall, with a single trunk to 1.8 m diam. **LEAF** Opposite, pinnately compound. Leaflets usually 5–7, each 4–11 cm long,

1.8–4.5 mm wide; stalk 2–10 mm, not winged; leaflet blade lanceolate, elliptic, or lance-obovate, veins mostly impressed above; margins shallowly and irregularly toothed throughout, or more or less entire. **FLOWER** Lacking petals, in clusters up to 20 cm long. Feb.–Apr. **FRUIT** Samara narrowly oval, usually 3–4.5 cm long; seed body cylindric, narrowly ridged; wing flat, 3–6 mm wide, arising from lower ¼–½ of the body, tip blunt and shallowly notched. **HABITAT/RANGE** Introduced from Mexico; disturbed sites, especially along watercourses, 50–400 m; Ariz., s. Calif.; aggressive weed in Hawaii. **SIMILAR SPECIES** Differs from Oregon Ash and Velvet Ash by the long leaflet stalks and evergreen nature (probably dropping leaves in drought or very cold weather).

GREEN ASH   *Fraxinus pennsylvanica*
Marshall
A.K.A. RED ASH

QUICK ID The combination of wetland habitat, opposite, pinnately compound leaves, and narrowly winged leaflet stalks helps distinguish this species.

Deciduous tree, 12–25 m tall, trunk 30–60 cm diam. Very similar to Mexican Ash. **TWIG** Leaf scar broadly oblong-ovate, flat or very shallowly concave across the top. **LEAF** Opposite, pinnately compound, blade 25–40 cm long. Leaflets 5–9 (usually 7), each 7–11 cm long, 2.5–4.5 cm broad, the short stalk narrowly winged; leaflet blade oval or oblong-lanceolate, sparsely dark-dotted with scales beneath; margins bluntly toothed, mostly above the middle. **FRUIT** Samara with flat wing arising usually in the upper ¼ of the seed body.

HABITAT/RANGE Native. Wet places; in the West found only near Corpus Christi, Tex. below 50 m, widespread in the East, 0–900 m.

GREEN ASH

Gregg's Ash

fruit

fruit

Shamel Ash

fruit

fruit

Green Ash

twig

fruit

OREGON ASH   *Fraxinus latifolia* Benth.
A.K.A. BLACK ASH, WATER ASH

QUICK ID This is the only ash in n. Calif. and the Pacific Northwest. Opposite, pinnately compound leaves and winged samaras distinguish it from other trees in the region.

Deciduous tree, 5–25 m tall, usually with a single straight trunk to 1.2 m diam. Crown oval, narrow or broadly spreading, the branches ascending. **BARK** Young bark pale gray, smooth; older bark thick, dark gray, often with a brownish tinge, deeply cleft by interrupted fissures into broad scaly ridges. **TWIG** Round, tan- or rusty-hairy when young, mostly hairless when older, orange-brown in the 2nd year and flecked with widely spaced pale lenticels, becoming gray when older; leaf scars shallowly hemispheric, shallowly concave on top. **LEAF** Opposite, pinnately compound, thin; leaflets 3–9 (usually 5–7), 3.5–10 cm long, 2.2–4 cm broad, stalkless or nearly so, lanceolate to elliptic or obovate, base bluntly angled or gently narrow-tapered; tip narrowly tapered, bluntly angled, or roundish; margins entire or with widely spaced small blunt teeth in upper ½. Upper surface light green, hairless or mostly so; lower surface paler, usually finely hairy. Petiole finely hairy or hairless. Foliage clear yellow in autumn. **FLOWER** In small, dense, axillary clusters; unisexual, the sexes on different trees; calyx on female flowers deeply lobed; petals absent. Mar.–Apr. **FRUIT** Spatulate or narrowly oval samara, 2–5 cm long; seed body flat to somewhat plump, with multiple fine grooves; wing flat, 6–10 mm wide, arising from lower ¼–½ of body, often shallowly notched at the apex.

HABITAT/RANGE Native. Fertile, moist soil in canyons, on stream banks, along lake shores, from oak–pine woodland and redwood forest to spruce–fir forest, 5–1,200 m; nw. Wash. south to s. Calif., mostly west of the Cascade Range and Sierra Nevada.

SIMILAR SPECIES Leatherleaf Ash in s. Calif. has thick leaves, stalked leaflets, and raised veins on the leaves.

Notes This tree is most abundant and largest in w. Ore. It is occasionally used as an ornamental, and has been introduced to Europe. It sometimes occurs in pure stands, but usually it grows with Red Alder, Bigleaf Maple, California Bay, and Grand Fir. It grows rapidly for the first 75 years or so, then more slowly, living to about 250 years. It is one of the West's more valuable hardwood species, used mostly for fuel, but also for furniture, cabinetry, and at one time tool handles and wagon parts.

VELVET ASH   *Fraxinus velutina* Torr.
A.K.A. DESERT ASH, ARIZONA ASH

QUICK ID Large opposite, pinnately compound leaves with usually 5–7 stalkless or nearly stalkless leaflets that are velvety beneath help distinguish this species.

Deciduous tree, 5–16 m tall, usually with a single straight trunk to 45 cm diam. Crown narrowly oval when young, rounded and spreading when older, the branches spreading-ascending. **BARK** Young bark pale gray, smooth; older bark thick, dark gray to gray-brown, sometimes with a reddish hue, deeply furrowed with longitudinal interlaced fissures, the intervening ridges with small, thin scales. **TWIG** Round, usually velvety-hairy when young, often more or less hairless and gray when older; leaf scars shallowly hemispheric to crescent-shaped, the top shallowly concave, sometimes also notched. **LEAF** Opposite, pinnately compound, slightly leathery. Leaflets 3–9 (usually 5–7), each 3–10 cm long, 1–4 cm broad, stalkless or nearly so, lanceolate to oblanceolate or ovate, base narrowly or widely tapered, tip sharply

OREGON ASH

VELVET ASH

Oregon Ash

fruit

Velvet Ash

fruit

autumn

fruit

angled or tapered to a long, slender point; margins entire or with small blunt or sharp teeth in the upper ½. Upper surface green, hairless, sometimes dotted with scales; lower surface green or whitish and usually finely hairy, or more or less hairless but with hairs along lower part of midrib, and dotted with scales. Petiole usually finely hairy. Foliage clear yellow in autumn. **FLOWER** In small, dense axillary clusters, unisexual, the sexes on different trees; petals absent. Mar.–May. **FRUIT** Wedge-shaped or narrowly obovate samara, 14–33 mm long; seed body more or less flattened to nearly cylindric, shallowly grooved; wing flat, 3–7 mm wide, arising from upper ½–⅔ of the body, bluntly pointed, rounded, or notched at the tip.

HABITAT/RANGE Native. Canyons, stream banks, Ponderosa Pine woods, chaparral, 200–2,100 m; sw. Utah, through Ariz. and N.M. to w. Tex., nw. Mexico.

SIMILAR SPECIES Leatherleaf Ash in s. Calif. has thick leaves, stalked leaflets, and raised veins on the leaves. The introduced Samel Ash has relatively long stalks on its leaflets.

Notes This is a variable species; leaflets are proportionately broader in N.M. and Tex., and more narrowly pointed in Ariz. and Utah. It grows quickly and is a popular ornamental in the Southwest. The wood is used locally for fuel, and at one time for tool handles and wagons.

■ *LIGUSTRUM*: PRIVETS

Privets are all introduced in the U.S., the 45 species in the genus native to Eurasia and Australia. Nine privets have established to a greater or lesser degree in the U.S. Most are clearly shrubs. Seeds are probably spread by birds, which consume the fruits.

GLOSSY PRIVET *Ligustrum lucidum* Aiton

A.K.A. CHINESE PRIVET, TREE PRIVET, WAX-LEAF LIGUSTRUM

QUICK ID Opposite, simple leathery leaves and small funnel-shaped white flowers with 2 stamens distinguish this species.

Evergreen large shrub or small tree, to about 6 m tall, usually with multiple trunks; crown rounded or more or less vase-shaped, with arching or drooping branches. **BARK** Gray or greenish gray, smooth when young, later slightly roughened with corky outgrowths; twig roughened with corky lenticels. **LEAF** Opposite, simple, leathery, often folded upward along the midvein (V-shaped), tip tapering to an elongated point; margins entire. Upper surface lustrous, dark green, hairless; lower surface paler. Blade 6–15 cm long, to about 5 cm broad; petiole 1–2 cm long. **FLOWER** Bisexual, small, greenish white, somewhat malodorous, many borne in panicles 10–20 cm long; tubular base of corolla shorter than or equal to the 4 petal lobes; stamens 2, anthers 1–2 mm long; style extends beyond mouth of corolla tube. Spring to early summer. **FRUIT** Black or blue-black drupe, 4–8 mm long, remaining on the tree for much of the year.

HABITAT/RANGE Introduced from e. Asia; naturalized, often in riparian areas in Calif., 0–1,100 m; also in the Southeast.

JAPANESE PRIVET *Ligustrum japonicum* Thunb.

Similar to, but smaller than, Glossy Privet; usually a shrub to 3 m tall. **LEAF** Usually less than 10 cm long. **FLOWER** In panicles 5–12 cm long; corolla tube is longer than or equal to the petal lobes. **HABITAT/RANGE** Introduced from e. Asia; escaped from cultivation, below 50 m, in Calif.

OVAL-LEAF PRIVET *Ligustrum ovalifolium* Hassk.

Rarely said to be a small tree. **LEAF** Usually less than 10 cm long. **FLOWER** Corolla tube, much longer than the petal lobes, wholly contains the style; anthers 2–4 mm long. **HABITAT/RANGE** Introduced from e. Asia; escaped from cultivation, below 300 m, in Calif.

Glossy Privet

flowers

underside

fruit

Japanese Privet

flowers

stem

fruit

flowers

Oval-leaf Privet

fruit

PAPAVERACEAE: POPPY FAMILY

The poppy family is primarily a Northern Hemisphere collection of about 44 genera and 760 species of mostly herbs, with a few shrubs and small trees. Leaves may be simple or compound; sap is clear, or often white, yellow, orange, or red.

CHANNEL ISLAND TREE POPPY
Dendromecon harfordii Kellogg

QUICK ID A shrub or tree of California's Channel Islands with simple leaves and 4-petaled, bright yellow flowers.

Evergreen large shrub or small tree to 6 m tall. Trunk to 30 cm diam.; crown open, the branches spreading or drooping. **BARK** Pale yellowish gray to nearly white, shredding. **LEAF** Alternate, simple, crowded, leathery, deep green, with clear sap; elliptic to rounded-oblong, tip generally rounded but with a minute point; margins entire. Blade 3–8 cm long, 1.5–4.5 cm broad; petiole 2–3 mm long. **FLOWER** Sepals 2, falling quickly, round, 8–10 mm long; petals 4, bright yellow, obovate, 2–3 cm long; stamens numerous. Mostly Apr.–Jul., but throughout the year. **FRUIT** Narrowly linear, curved capsule, 7–10 cm long, splitting from the base, releasing many small smooth brown or black seeds.

HABITAT/RANGE Native. Brushy slopes, 0–600 m; Channel Islands, s. Calif.

Notes This species is especially common after fire. It is closely related to the smaller mainland shrub **Bush Poppy** (*D. rigida* Benth.), which has similar flowers but narrower leaves, and is common in brush from c. to s. Calif.

CHANNEL ISLAND TREE POPPY

Channel Island Tree Poppy

flower

fruit

flower

splitting fruit

Bush Poppy

flower

underside

branch

fruit

PITTOSPORACEAE: CHEESEWOOD FAMILY

The Pittosporaceae is a family of the Old World tropics, from Africa eastward to the South Pacific, best developed in Australia. The family comprises 6–9 genera and about 200–250 species of shrubs and trees, and a few climbers (the woody climber Australian Bluebell, *Billardiera heterohpylla* [Lindl.] L.W. Crayzer & Crisp is established in Calif.). **LEAF** Alternate, simple, evergreen, often leathery, and usually with entire margins. **FLOWER** Bisexual or functionally unisexual, and then often both bisexual and female flowers on the same plant. Flowers have 5 sepals, 5 petals, often united near the base, and 5 stamens. **FRUIT** The ovary is superior, developing into a capsule or berry, usually with numerous seeds. Two genera, including several species of *Pittosporum*, have escaped and naturalized to some extent in the U.S.

■ *PITTOSPORUM*: CHEESEWOODS

There are about 150 species of *Pittosporum*, most from tropical or moderate, moist climates, all from the Old World. Species are evergreen trees and shrubs. **FLOWER** Usually in umbel-like clusters; flowers have petals adherent at the base, recurved and spreading near the tips. **FRUIT** The ovary has 2 or 3 chambers. The pulp of the capsule is resinous, and the sticky-coated seeds will stick to just about anything (the generic name comes from Greek roots referring to "pitch" and "seed").

A number of species are cultivated throughout temperate regions of the world, some escaping and becoming invasive. An illuminating oil is extracted from seeds and a fragrant oil from flowers. Wood is used locally for lumber, and the elasticity and hardness of some has been valued for bows, war clubs, engraving plates, fishing rods, and golf clubs.

STIFFLEAF CHEESEWOOD
Pittosporum crassifolium Banks & Sol. ex A. Cunn.
A.K.A. KARO PITTOSPORUM, KARO

Evergreen shrub or small tree to 9 m tall; crown open, leaves densest near the ends of branches. **TWIG** Hairy. **LEAF** Alternate, simple, oblong to narrowly obovate; upper surface grayish green, lower surface whitish-velvety; margin thick, rolled under. Blade 4.5–7 cm long. **FLOWER** In terminal clusters of 5–10 flowers; petals about 12 mm long, dark red, curled back. Nov.–May. **FRUIT** Globose or egg-shaped capsule, 1.5–3 cm long, hairy, separating into 3 segments. **HABITAT/RANGE** Introduced from New Zealand; disturbed areas near the coast, 0–200 m; c. and s. Calif. An ornamental tolerant of wind and salt spray.

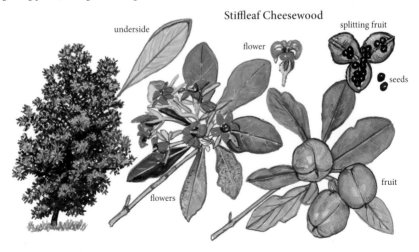

Stiffleaf Cheesewood

underside

flower

splitting fruit

seeds

fruit

flowers

VICTORIAN BOX *Pittosporum undulatum* Vent.

QUICK ID The shiny leaves with wavy margins, sweet-smelling white flowers, and globose orange fruits distinguish this species.

Evergreen tree to 15 m tall, with a dense, broad crown; trunks 1 to several, 10–20 cm diam., with smooth gray bark. **LEAF** Alternate, mostly clustered near branch tips, simple, thin, hairless, shiny; oblong to elliptic-lanceolate, margins wavy. Blade 6–15 cm long, 1.5–4 cm broad. **FLOWER** In small terminal clusters of 5–10 flowers, fragrant; functionally unisexual, both sexes on the same plant. Petals 5, creamy white, 10–15 mm long, curved back. Nov.–Jun. **FRUIT** Globose orange leathery to woody capsule, 10–15 mm long, separating into 2 parts and exposing sticky orange-covered brownish seeds.

HABITAT/RANGE Introduced from se. Australia; disturbed areas near coast, 0–200 m, c. and s. Calif.

Notes This popular ornamental is invasive in moist, frost-free climates worldwide. Leaves produce chemicals that inhibit growth of other plants beneath the tree. Fruit-eating birds spread the seeds widely. Kohuhu (*P. tenuifolium* Gaertn.), to 8 m tall, has dark red to purple flowers, almost hairless leaves with flat, wavy margins, black stems, and a globose fruit 10–12 mm long. It is a waif near the coast in c. Calif. at 0–200 m.

JAPANESE CHEESEWOOD *Pittosporum tobira* (Thunb.) Aiton

Evergreen shrub or small tree to about 12 m tall. **LEAF** Clustered near the ends of branches and appearing whorled; simple, leathery, obovate, tip rounded or slightly notched, margins rolled under. Hairy on both surfaces; upper surface lustrous; lower surface duller velvety. Blade 4–9 cm long. **FLOWER** Several in a terminal cluster; petals 10–12 mm long, white, fading to yellowish. Nov.–May. **FRUIT** Rounded and angular, pale yellow woody capsule, hairy, about 1.2 cm diam., splitting to reveal red seeds. **HABITAT/RANGE** Introduced from e. Asia; a popular garden plant established in Calif., 0–200 m, and se. U.S.

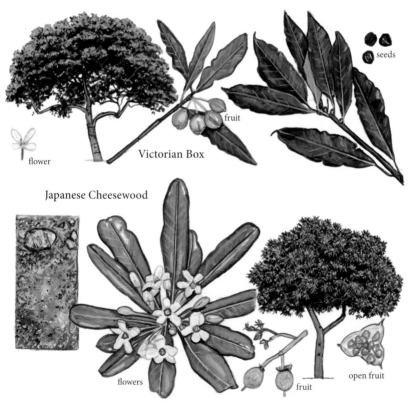

seeds

fruit

Victorian Box

flower

Japanese Cheesewood

flowers

fruit

open fruit

PLATANACEAE: PLANETREE FAMILY

The planetree family contains a single genus, *Platanus*, found in temperate and tropical regions of North America, sc. Europe, and across s. Asia to Indochina.

■ *PLATANUS*: SYCAMORES

The sycamore (or planetree) genus includes 7–10 species of usually deciduous, medium-size to large trees distributed at low to moderate elevations. Four species are found in North America, three native in the West. Another is introduced, and a hybrid is a common ornamental.

BARK Constantly peels in thin, irregular plates, revealing a pale inner bark that ages to grayish tan, producing an attractive mottled pattern on the trunk and large branches; bark at the base of old trees may be thick and fissured. **LEAF** Alternate, simple, usually palmately lobed, the lobes pointed or narrowly angled; margins entire or toothed. Petiole base swollen, surrounding and hiding the axillary bud. **FLOWER** Unisexual, male and female on the same tree, borne in 1 to several dense globose heads that are well spaced along hanging axillary stalks; male inflorescences soon wither and fall. Individual flowers have 3–7 sepals and petals, the male flowers with 3–7 stamens, and the female flowers with a superior ovary of several chambers. Occasionally there is a single male head at the end of an otherwise female flowering stalk. **FRUIT** Each female flower produces a small club-shaped achene with bristles at the base. The ball-like heads of achenes disintegrate from late autumn to early spring, the bristles at the base of the achenes adding loft to the small fruit.

Sycamores are prized as handsome avenue trees. A highly patterned veneer may be cut from the wood. The anomalous *P. kerrii* Gagnep., from Laos, differs from other *Platanus* in its evergreen elliptic, pinnately veined leaves, the petiole not surrounding the bud. Betulinic acid is processed from its bark and is being explored for its medicinal properties, which include facilitating healing, reducing inflammation, and potential anti-cancer properties.

LONDON PLANETREE *Platanus hybrida* Brot.

Similar to American Sycamore but distinguished by its greener bark, narrower and longer leaf lobes (especially on larger leaves), and by fruiting heads often produced 2 to a stalk. **HABITAT/RANGE** Cultivated as a street tree; rarely establishes in the wild.

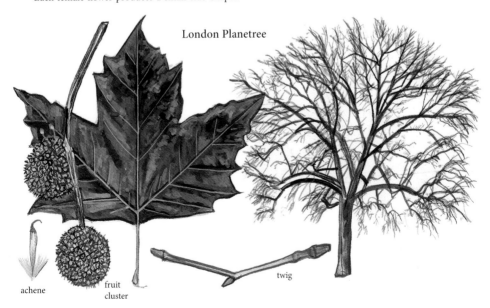

London Planetree

achene fruit cluster twig

AMERICAN SYCAMORE *Platanus occidentalis* L.

QUICK ID Distinguished from other sycamores by its broad terminal lobe on the leaf and the usually single fruiting head dangling on its stalk.

Deciduous tree to at least 50 m tall, usually with a single straight trunk, 1–4 m diam. **BARK** Smooth, brown, mottled, peeling in thin plates to reveal buff, pale green, or creamy-white inner bark; bark often whitish in the crown. **LEAF** Alternate, simple, ovate or circular in outline: 3–5 lobes, lobe tips abruptly short-pointed, sinuses broadly rounded and shallow; base deeply cordate or more or less flat; margins nearly entire or coarsely toothed. Upper surface lustrous green; lower surface usually hairy, at least along the veins and in the vein axils. Blade 6–20 cm long, 6–25 cm broad; petiole 1–5 cm long. **FLOWER** In globose, unisexual heads, usually 1 head, sometimes 2, per stalk. Apr.–May, as the leaves expand. **FRUIT** Achene to about 8 mm long; fruiting head about 2.5 cm diam., dangling on a stalk 8–15 cm long.

HABITAT/RANGE Native. Usually along streams, lakes, and large alluvial rivers, occasionally in uplands, 0–950 m; widespread in the East, barely entering the West in sc. Tex.

CALIFORNIA SYCAMORE *Platanus racemosa* Nutt.
A.K.A. WESTERN SYCAMORE, CALIFORNIA PLANETREE, BUTTONBALL-TREE

QUICK ID Alternate, palmately lobed leaves and chains of dense brown fruiting heads distinguish this tree in its region.

Deciduous medium-sized tree to 15 m tall, rarely to 25 m. Trunks 1 to several, to 2 m diam., erect, leaning, or lying on the ground; crown broad and open, with often contorted, twisting, crooked, spreading large branches. **BARK** To 8 cm thick at the base of the tree, brown, deeply furrowed, with broad, rounded ridges with small flaking scales; younger bark thin, smooth, flaking, mottled, exposing whitish or pale green new bark, becoming yellowish, gray, or brownish, the bark on higher limbs nearly white. **TWIG** Light reddish brown at first, flecked with small lenticels, covered with fine rusty hairs; becoming darker and hairless later. Buds usually all lateral, at first surrounded by leaf bases, later by conspicuous leaf scars, conical, smooth, shining, with 3 caplike scales. **LEAF** Alternate, simple, thickish; with 3–5 palmate, narrowly triangular lobes, mostly longer than wide, basal lobes spreading, not directed toward the petiole, terminal lobe ⅓–½ the length of the blade; sinuses broad and deeply concave, depth of distal sinuses ⅓–⅔ the distance from base of sinus to base of blade; margins entire or with a few small, widely spaced teeth. Upper surface dark green and nearly hairless; lower surface paler and felty-hairy. Blade 10–25 cm long and equally wide; petiole stout, hairy, 2.5–7.5 cm long. **FLOWER** In unisexual globose greenish-yellow to reddish heads, widely spaced on a zigzag hanging axillary stalk; male heads 4 or 5 per stalk, 8–10 mm diam., soon dropping; female heads usually 2–7, about 15 mm diam., on a stalk 15–25 cm long, the heads along the stalk sessile. Feb.–Apr., as the leaves expand. **FRUIT** In dense globose brown heads, 2–2.5 cm diam., each fruit a 4-sided, club-shaped tan achene, 7–10 mm long, with brown bristles at the base ⅔ the length of the achene.

HABITAT/RANGE Native. In canyons and along rivers where moist, often in rocky soil, 0–1,500 m; n. Calif. to nw. Baja Calif.

SIMILAR SPECIES Maples (*Acer*, Sapindaceae) also have palmately lobed leaves, but they are

AMERICAN SYCAMORE

CALIFORNIA SYCAMORE

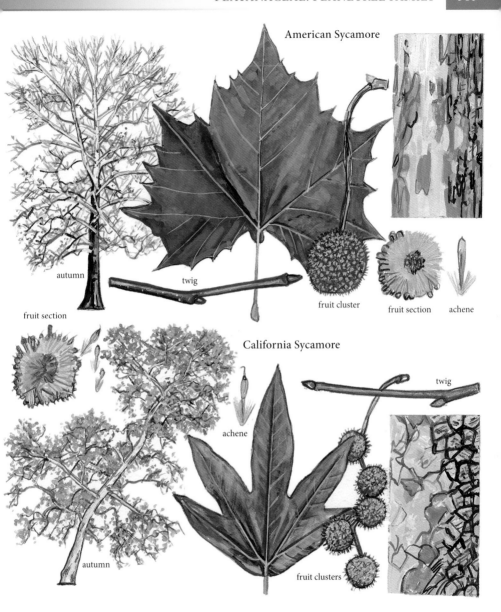

American Sycamore

autumn

twig

fruit section

fruit cluster

fruit section

achene

California Sycamore

twig

achene

autumn

fruit clusters

opposite. The cultivated Eurasian or Oriental Plan-etree (*P. orientalis* L.) is similar, but has coarsely toothed margins on the leaves and fruiting stalks with 3–6 heads. Arizona Sycamore is closely re-lated, but has proportionally longer lobes on the leaves and usually only 2–4 heads on each pistillate (fruiting) stalk.

Notes Trees are often hollow, providing nesting sites for birds. Branches are brittle and readily fall. Along streams, trees provide shade for livestock, but livestock will browse the seedlings. Hairs on the undersides of the leaves are deciduous, float upon the wind, and are irritating to those with sen-sitive respiratory passages.

ARIZONA SYCAMORE *Platanus wrightii* S. Watson

A.K.A. ARIZONA PLANETREE

QUICK ID The terminal lobe of the leaf is almost ⅔ the length of the blade, the lower lobes spread slightly toward the petiole, and the lower leaf surface is sparsely hairy.

This tree, with its massive trunk and attractive large, arching, white-barked branches is so similar to California Sycamore that it is often considered to be a variety of that species. Differences are by degree, and separation by geography. Height, crown, and bark are similar. **LEAF** Alternate, simple; 3–7 palmate lobes, these much longer than wide, the depth of the sinuses equal to or much greater than the distance from the base of the sinus to the base of the leaf (leaves often lobed more than halfway to the base). Terminal lobe ⅔ the length of the blade or more; lowest lobes spreading slightly backward, toward the petiole. At maturity, surfaces not very hairy. Blade 9–25 cm long, sometimes slightly broader; petiole stout, hairy, 3–8 cm long. **FLOWER** Female heads 1–4, borne along a common stalk to 30 cm long, each on an individual stalk to 2 cm long, which when short is often hidden by the developing head. Feb.–May. **FRUIT** 5–8 mm long, the basal hairs ⅔ of, or equal to, the length of the achenes.

HABITAT/RANGE Native. River valleys, along streams, canyon bottoms, 350–2,000 m; Ariz., sw. N.M., nw. Mexico.

SIMILAR SPECIES California Sycamore has proportionately shorter leaf lobes, on average more pistillate heads per stalk (usually 2–7), and leaves that are more persistently velvety beneath.

Notes Trees in Mexico have fruiting heads almost without individual stalks, and the leaves have long, narrow lobes, intermediate between Arizona Sycamore and California Sycamore. As with the more westerly species, leaves turn golden or coppery in the autumn, contrasting with the white bark of the branches.

ARIZONA SYCAMORE

Arizona Sycamore

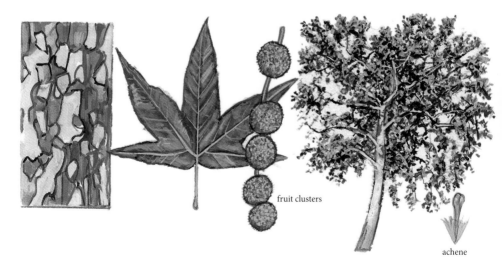

fruit clusters

achene

PROTEACEAE: PROTEA FAMILY

The protea family has 80 genera and about 1,770 species of trees and shrubs, distributed mostly in tropical regions of Australia, Africa, Southeast Asia, and Central and South America. Some are grown as ornamentals in warmer parts of the U.S., appreciated for their showy and complicated flowers; only 1 species is naturalized in North America. The Proteaceae is closely allied with the Platanaceae and is placed taxonomically with the "basal eudicots," which are considered by many systematists to represent the earliest evolutionary lineages of plants with tricolpate pollen (pollen grains with 3 pores).

SILKOAK *Grevillea robusta* A. Cunn. ex R. Br.

QUICK ID **Easily recognized by its deeply divided fernlike leaves and protruding, brilliant orange flowers.**

Evergreen tree, 10–25 m tall; trunk straight, crown narrow. **BARK** Gray, finely fissured, with narrow ridges. **LEAF** Alternate, pinnately compound or simple and deeply incised, somewhat fernlike; leaflets or major divisions 7–19, opposite or alternate, each 3–12 cm long, upper surface dark olive green, lower surface silvery white, usually divided into several narrow lobes; rachis narrowly winged. Blade 15–33 cm long, to 20 cm broad; petiole 4–6 cm long. **FLOWER** Bisexual, more or less bilateral, orange, yellow, or golden yellow, in

1-sided clusters 5–15 cm long; sepals 1.5–2 cm long, fused at first, becoming free, the concave tip of each holding 1 small anther; petals absent; style conspicuous, 1–2.5 cm long, protruding. Mar.–May. **FRUIT** Boat-shaped, 2-seeded silvery-gray or green follicle about 1 cm long, splitting along 1 side at maturity; seeds broadly winged, 10–15 mm long.

HABITAT/RANGE Introduced from e. Australia; escaped and weakly naturalized in canyons in brush, below 450 m, in s. Calif.; also in Fla.

SIMILAR SPECIES Lyontree (*Lyonothamnus floribundus*, Rosaceae) has similar leaves. Its bark is thin and peels in long strips; the flowers are small, white, and radially symmetric; and the follicles are only 3–4 mm long.

Silkoak

flowers

fruit

PUNICACEAE: POMEGRANATE FAMILY

This family contains 1 genus and 2 species from Asia and the Indian Ocean; 1 species, Pomegranate, has escaped or naturalized in North America. The Pomegranate has been grown for food and ornament for centuries and is mentioned in the Bible and Quran. The persistent calyx on the fruit was apparently the inspiration for King Solomon's crown. Recent studies have indicated the Punicaceae could be included within the loosestrife family (Lythraceae).

POMEGRANATE *Punica granatum* L.

Deciduous upright, rounded shrub or small, short-trunked tree, 2–8 m tall, sometimes spiny. **LEAF** Opposite, often clustered on short shoots, simple, lanceolate to oblanceolate or oblong, lustrous green, hairless. Blade 2–9 cm long. **FLOWER** Bisexual, radial, with a tubular reddish fleshy calyx about 2 cm long, 5–9 separate, bright red-orange crinkled petals 15–25 mm long, many stamens, and an inferior ovary. May–Jun. **FRUIT** Round reddish, yellowish, or whitish leathery berry, 5–12 cm diam., crowned at the tip with the remains of the calyx. Seeds numerous, large, embedded in a glistening red edible pulp. **HABITAT/RANGE** Introduced from Asia; cultivated, apparently occasionally escaping in the s. U.S. from Calif. to N.C., 0–500 m.

RHAMNACEAE: BUCKTHORN FAMILY

The buckthorn family includes 50–60 genera and about 900 species of trees, shrubs, and a few climbing vines, widely distributed in temperate to tropical regions. North of Mexico there are about 14 genera, two introduced, and 115 species, 13 introduced. Twenty are trees or are large shrubs that are often arborescent. The genus *Ceanothus* is the largest on the continent, with 60-plus species.

Deciduous or evergreen trees or shrubs, often thorny. **LEAF** Usually alternate, sometimes opposite; venation is often prominently pinnate or palmate. **FLOWER** Radially symmetric, small, bisexual or unisexual, with a hypanthium and often a thick glandular disk; sepals, petals, and stamens number 4 or 5, or sometimes petals are absent. Stamens opposite petals when present, the blade of the petal often enfolding the stamen in young flowers. Ovary superior to inferior. **FRUIT** Drupe or dry fruit that splits into several sections.

The family produces edible fruits, medicines (mostly purgatives), quality lumber, ornamentals, dyes, and charcoal. The crown of thorns worn by Jesus Christ is believed to have been from a member of this family called Jerusalem Thorn or Crown-of-thorns (*Paliurus spina-christi* Mill.).

■ *CEANOTHUS*: WILD LILACS

There are about 55 species of *Ceanothus*, all North American, and 45 species in Calif. alone. The genus occurs from sea-level to high elevations in brush and open woodland. It is called "wild lilac" because the conical clusters of flowers resemble those of true lilacs (*Syringa*, Oleaceae). Most *Ceanothus* are shrubs, some with thorn-tipped twigs. These are often called buckbrush or buckthorn. A few may become small trees. **LEAF** Simple, alternate or sometimes opposite, with 1 central vein or commonly with 3 main veins. **FLOWER** Tiny, sky blue to white, bisexual, with 5 more or less petal-like sepals, a glandular disk, 5 petals shaped like miniature wonton spoons, 5 stamens, and a 3-chambered ovary. **FRUIT** Small 3-lobed capsule.

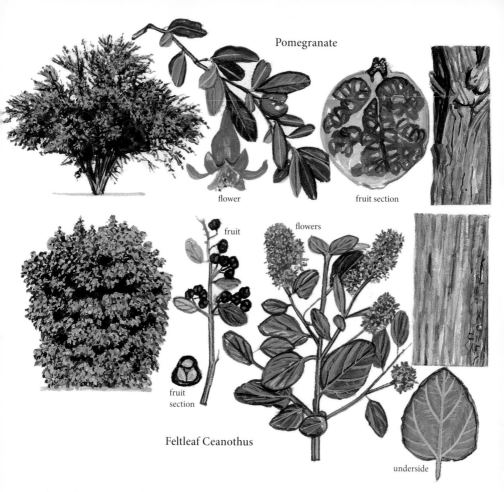

Pomegranate

flower

fruit section

fruit

flowers

fruit
section

Feltleaf Ceanothus

underside

Several species are cultivated as ornamentals. Many species are a major component of chaparral. Hybridization between species is common, adding to difficulty in identification.

FELTLEAF CEANOTHUS *Ceanothus arboreus* Greene

QUICK ID Tiny pale blue flowers in compact arrays and leaves with 3 veins, toothed margins, and a velvety-white lower surface help identify this island species.

Evergreen shrub or small tree, 3–7 m tall; the largest of all *Ceanothus*. **TWIG** Soft-hairy, flexible, round. **LEAF** Alternate, elliptic to broadly ovate, with 3 prominent veins, margins with small teeth; upper surface dull, dark green; lower surface white-velvety. Blade 3–8 cm long, 2–3.5 cm broad.

FLOWER Pale blue, numerous, in branched arrays of conical clusters 5–12 cm long. Feb.–May. **FRUIT** Three-sided capsule, 6–8 mm broad, each lobe with a crest on the back, roughened all over, blackish when mature.

HABITAT/RANGE Native. Chaparral, 0–450 m; Channel Islands, s. Calif.

FELTLEAF CEANOTHUS

CHAPARRAL WHITETHORN
Ceanothus leucodermis Greene

QUICK ID Grayish-green thorn-tipped twigs, 3-veined leaves, and tiny pale blue to white flowers in conical clusters identify Chaparral Whitethorn.

Evergreen shrub or occasionally a small tree, 2–4 m tall. **TWIG** Pale gray to gray-green, stiffly spreading, mostly hairless, thorn-tipped. **LEAF** Alternate, elliptic to ovate, with 3 prominent veins, margins entire or with small gland-tipped teeth; grayish green on both surfaces, sometimes slightly hairy. Blade 1–2.5 cm long, 6–12 mm broad. **FLOWER** Pale blue to white, numerous, usually in simple conical clusters 3–8 cm long. Apr.–Jun. **FRUIT** Three-lobed capsule, 4–6 mm broad, slightly flattened on top, the lobes round, without crests, sticky-varnished.

HABITAT/RANGE Native. Chaparral, at 100–2,100 m, Calif., n. Baja Calif. Often in pure, impenetrable stands, the stiff, thorny branches interlocked with those of adjacent plants.

REDHEART *Ceanothus spinosus* Nutt.
A.K.A. GREENBARK CEANOTHUS, SPINY CEANOTHUS

QUICK ID Greenish spine-tipped twigs, 1-veined dark and shiny leaves with entire margins, and tiny white or pale blue flowers in branched arrays help identify this species.

Evergreen shrub or small tree, 2–6 m tall. Branches ascending, flexible, olive green, hairless or finely hairy. **TWIG** The smallest twigs short, spreading, often thorn-tipped. **LEAF** Alternate, leathery, elliptic to oblong, with 1 prominent vein, margins entire or with tiny teeth near the tip; upper surface shiny, dark green; lower surface paler. Blade 1–3 cm long, 1–2 cm broad. **FLOWER** Pale blue to nearly white, numerous, in branched arrays of conical clusters 4–15 cm long. Feb.–May. **FRUIT** Globose, 3-chambered capsule, scarcely lobed or crested, 4–5 mm broad, sticky-varnished.

HABITAT/RANGE Native. Brushy slopes near the coast, 0–1,200 m; s. Calif., n. Baja Calif.

BLUEBLOSSOM *Ceanothus thyrsiflorus* Eschsch.
A.K.A. BLUEBRUSH

QUICK ID Three-veined, minutely toothed, dark green leaves, with the veins conspicuously raised on the lower surface, and tiny blue flowers in branched arrays identify Blueblossom.

Evergreen prostrate shrub on ocean bluffs to a small tree at forest margins, 0.5–6 m tall. Crown matted, dense, and windswept on exposed bluffs, to ragged and more or less open with ascending branches at forest edges. **TWIG** Hairless, flexible, green, angled when young. **LEAF** Alternate, broadly elliptic to oblong-ovate, margins with small gland-tipped teeth; upper surface shiny, dark green, with 3 major veins impressed; lower surface paler, with a few hairs on the prominently raised veins. Blade 2–4.5 cm long, 1–2 cm broad. **FLOWER** Tiny, blue to pale blue, rarely whitish, numerous, in branched arrays of conical clusters 3–8 cm long. Feb.–Jun. **FRUIT** Subglobose capsule, slightly 3-lobed, 3 mm broad, not crested, glandular-sticky, blackish when mature.

HABITAT/RANGE Native. Brushy or wooded slopes and canyons, 0–600 m; Coast Ranges, sw. Ore. to s. Calif.

Notes Highly variable, with many cultivated forms, some with variegated leaves.

CHAPARRAL WHITETHORN   REDHEART   BLUEBLOSSOM

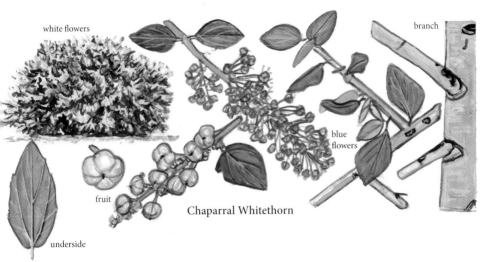

white flowers

branch

blue flowers

fruit

underside

Chaparral Whitethorn

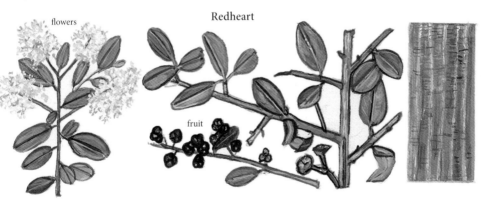

Redheart

flowers

fruit

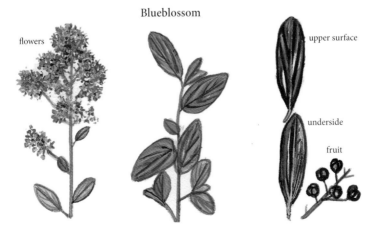

Blueblossom

flowers

upper surface

underside

fruit

SNOWBRUSH *Ceanothus velutinus*
Douglas ex Hook.
A.K.A. TOBACCO BRUSH, MOUNTAIN BALM

QUICK ID Aromatic, finely toothed, 3-veined, bright green leaves, shiny and more or less sticky on upper surface, and tiny white flowers distinguish this species.

Evergreen shrub or small tree, 1–6 m tall, usually with several trunks. **TWIG** Flexible, hairless or minutely hairy, reddish brown. **LEAF** Alternate, spicy-scented, broadly elliptic to ovate, with 3 main veins; margins with many small gland-tipped teeth. Upper surface dark green, shiny, sticky-varnished, often bronze-tinged; lower surface paler and hairless or finely hairy. Blade 2.5–8 cm long, 1–5 cm broad. **FLOWER** Tiny, numerous, white, in branched arrays of conical clusters 3–8 cm long. Apr.–Aug. **FRUIT** Subglobose to more or less triangular, 3-lobed capsule, wrinkled or not, 3–4.5 mm broad, sticky-varnished, not or only slightly crested on top, dark brown when mature.

HABITAT/RANGE Native. Open wooded slopes, 1,100–3,000 m; s. B.C. south to c. Calif., Nev., n. Utah, Colo., S.D.

SNOWBRUSH

■ *CONDALIA*: CONDALIAS

There are about 18 species of *Condalia*, in dry habitats at low to moderate elevations, ranging from North America to South America. Most species are shrubs, all with thorn-tipped twigs; a few species have treelike forms. **LEAF** Simple, alternate on young twigs, in fascicles on short spurs on older branches; veins generally in few pairs, conspicuous or not. **FLOWER** Tiny, greenish, bisexual, stalkless or on very short stalks, with 5 sepals at the rim of a thin glandular disk, 0 or 5 petals, 5 stamens alternate with the sepals, and an ovary with 1 or 2 chambers. **FRUIT** Small drupe, usually with 1 stone.

A blue dye is extracted from the wood of several species. The drupes are edible, though in some species unpalatable. In the Southwest there are several look-alike genera of shrubs and trees with thorn-tipped twigs. Two are leafy and are easily mistaken for *Condalia*. Desert-thorns (*Lycium*, a genus of shrubs in the Solanaceae not covered in this guide), have flowers with usually small trumpet-shaped lavender or greenish corollas and small globose red-orange multi-seeded berries. More subtly distinguished is Lotebush (*Ziziphus obtusifolia*), a relative of *Condalia* covered on p. 400. It has stout grayish thorn-tipped twigs and leaves that are often toothed; the tiny greenish flowers have minute petals that drop early, and a thick, fleshy disk in the center that partially hides the young ovary.

BITTER CONDALIA *Condalia globosa*
I.M. Johnst.
A.K.A. BITTER SNAKEWOOD

QUICK ID The thorn-tipped twigs, leaves with a few prominent veins and borne in fascicles, flowers without petals, and small black drupes help identify this small tree within its region.

Drought-deciduous large shrub or small tree, 4.5–6 mm tall, with an intricately branched round crown; trunks usually several, short, gnarled with age, up to 60 cm diam. **BARK** Smooth and gray when young, when older with interconnecting fissures forming diamond-shaped ridges with flaking scales. **TWIG** Slender, rigid, spreading at nearly right angles, grayish red-brown, sharply tipped with blackish thorns. **LEAF** Thick, narrowly spatula-shaped to oblanceolate, tapered at the base, blunt or round and often notched at the tip, margins entire. Finely hairy, with 2–4 pairs of curved veins, these prominently raised on the lower surface. Blade 5–15 mm long, 3–6 mm broad; nearly stalkless. **FLOWER** Fragrant, 3 mm diam., olive green, shallowly bell-shaped,

BITTER CONDALIA

Snowbrush

flowers

fruit

flower

underside

seeds

Bitter Condalia

fruit

1–8 in leaf axils; sepals 5, triangular, deciduous in fruit, joined to a large fleshy nectar disk; petals absent. Feb.–Apr., and again Oct.–Nov. **FRUIT** Egg-shaped to subglobose drupe, slightly asymmetric, 3.5–5.5 mm long, blackish, very bitter.

HABITAT/RANGE Native. Sandy or gravelly desert flats and washes, 300–750 m; se. Calif., sw. Ariz., nw. Mexico.

Notes The wood, which yields a blue dye, is very hard and valued for firewood; generally all plants have been harvested long ago near settlements. The rigid, protective, thorny branches provide nesting sites for various desert birds.

BLUEWOOD *Condalia hookeri*
M.C. Johnst.

A.K.A. BRASIL, PURPLE HAW, CAPUL NEGRO

QUICK ID The thorn-tipped twigs, few-veined leaves in fascicles, flowers without petals, and small purple or black drupes help identify this small tree

Evergreen or deciduous thicket-forming large shrub or small tree, 6–9 mm tall; trunks usually several, short, often divided near the ground, to 20 cm diam.; crown ragged and round, often broader than tall. **BARK** Smooth, pale gray to reddish brown when young, when older furrowed, with flat ridges breaking into small, thin scales. **TWIG** Rigid, spreading at nearly right angles, gray to brown, sharply tipped with reddish, blackish, or gray thorns. **LEAF** Thin, narrowly spoon-shaped, tapered to a nearly stalkless base, blunt or round at the tip, margins usually entire. Shiny yellow-green, with 3 or 4 pairs of curved veins nearly flush with the finely hairy lower surface. Blade 1–3 cm long, 5–20 mm broad. **FLOWER** 4 mm diam., light olive green, shallowly bowl-shaped, 1–3 in leaf axils; sepals 5, triangular, persistent, joined to a large fleshy disk; petals absent. Year-round in the South, in the warm season northward. **FRUIT** Globose drupe, 5–6 mm diam., shiny, maturing from green through red to purple or black.

HABITAT/RANGE Native. Sandy brush areas, 0–700 m; s. Tex. and ne. Mexico.

Notes The wood, which yields a blue dye, is very hard and valued for firewood. Plants in the northern part of the range turn yellow in autumn, dropping their leaves; to the south they are evergreen. The drupes are sweet, thin-skinned, and fleshy, and are consumed by birds and small mammals; they also make a good jelly.

BLUEWOOD

■ *FRANGULA*: BUCKTHORNS

There are about 50 species of *Frangula*, mostly from the Northern Hemisphere, about 6 in the U.S. and Canada. Five are sometimes small trees in the West, occurring in moist, temperate habitats at low to moderate elevations.

Species of *Frangula* are evergreen or deciduous, thornless or thorny shrubs or sometimes small trees (our species are thornless). Winter buds lack bud scales. **LEAF** Alternate, simple, petiolate, margins entire or with minute teeth. Lateral veins are often conspicuous and impressed on the upper surface, raised on the lower, almost straight near the midrib, and forward-curved near the margins. **FLOWER** Tiny, radial, greenish, bisexual, in small umbel-like clusters in the leaf axils. Five thick, triangular sepals, with a raised ridge on the back, are at the rim of a cup-shaped hypanthium; at the edge of the slightly thickened lining of the hypanthium are 5 minute petals opposite 5 stamens; ovary is mostly inferior, the stigma with a knoblike tip or 3-lobed. **FRUIT** Globose drupe with usually 2 or 3 stones, at first green, then reddish, finally purplish or blackish.

It has long been a source of debate whether *Frangula* and *Rhamnus* should be treated as separate genera, or *Frangula* as a subgenus within *Rhamnus*. Species of *Frangula* have naked winter buds that lack scales, the flowers are bisexual, usually with 5 sepals and 5 petals, the stone remains intact within the fruit, and the seeds are smooth on the back. Species of *Rhamnus* usually have buds with scales, unisexual flowers usually with 4 sepals and 4 petals, the stone splits open within the fruit, and the seed is grooved. Recent work in molecular genetics indicates the 2 genera to be closely related but separate.

In medieval times *Frangula* was thought to protect against demons, headaches, poisons, and witchcraft. Dyes have been extracted from the bark and berries. Wood was used for shoe lasts, nails, and for a high-quality charcoal used in gunpowder; veneer is occasionally produced from larger species. Some species are invasive once introduced, and at least 1 state now prohibits their use as ornamentals. At least 2 species serve as winter hosts for the recently introduced Soybean Aphid (*Aphis glycines*), responsible for considerable crop injury.

Bluewood

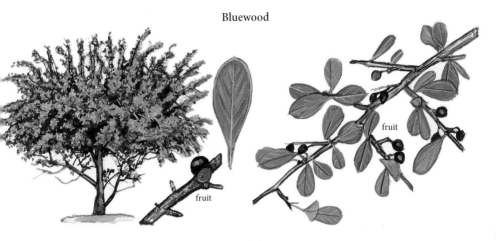

fruit

fruit

Glossy Buckthorn

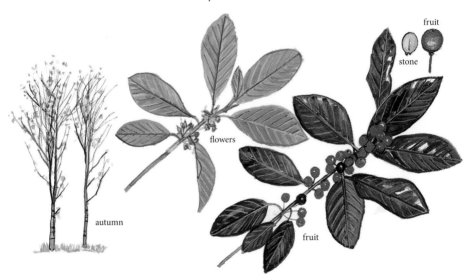

fruit

stone

flowers

autumn

fruit

GLOSSY BUCKTHORN *Frangula alnus* Mill.

A.K.A. ALDER BUCKTHORN

Deciduous shrub or tree to about 7 m tall, often prolifically sprouting from the roots; crown often with stout, erect branches. **TWIG** Thornless, reddish brown, usually hairy. **LEAF** Oblong, oval, or broadly elliptic, the tip usually abruptly short-pointed; margins entire, often somewhat wavy. Upper surface lustrous green with 5–9 pairs of conspicuously parallel lateral veins that arch toward the tip; lower surface dull green. Blade 5–10 cm long. **FLOWER** Creamy green or yellowish green. May–Sep. **FRUIT** Drupe, 5–10 mm diam., purplish black. **HABITAT/ RANGE** Introduced from Europe; moist places, sporadic in a few western states at 850–1,900 m; often invasive in the East. *Notes* Of major military importance in the 15th–19th centuries for producing the best charcoal for gunpowder.

BIRCHLEAF BUCKTHORN *Frangula betulifolia* (Greene) V. Grub.
A.K.A. BIRCHLEAF FALSE-BUCKTHORN, BEECHLEAF FRANGULA

QUICK ID The broad deciduous green leaves, more or less hairy beneath, with parallel lateral veins, and the lustrous dark drupes, distinguish Birchleaf Buckthorn.

Deciduous large shrub or small tree to 6 m tall, with an open round crown; trunks 1 or several, often divided near the ground, to 10 cm diam. **BARK** Thin, gray, dark gray, or gray-brown, often blotchy, smooth or with shallow longitudinal fissures. **TWIG** Finely hairy and green to reddish when young, hairless and gray when older. **LEAF** Alternate, simple, ovate or oblong to obovate (length usually 1.3–1.7 × width), margins with numerous small, sharp teeth. Green, with 7–11 pairs of lateral veins, upper surface lustrous, lower surface more or less hairy. Blade 6–12 cm long, 2.5–4 cm broad; petiole 5–10 mm long. **FLOWER** About 3 mm broad, usually 2–20 in small axillary clusters, the individual flower stalks 4–8 mm long, longer than the common stalk of the cluster about half the time; sepals and petals yellowish green, the petals becoming brown; stigma usually 3-lobed. May–Jun. **FRUIT** Globose drupe, 8–9 mm diam., dark, lustrous purple or black, hairless, usually with 3 stones.

HABITAT/RANGE Native. Moist canyons, often near streams, 1,650–2,300 m; s. Nev., s. Utah, through Ariz. and N.M., to w. Tex. and n. Mexico.

Notes This *Frangula* is very closely related to Carolina Buckthorn, the two perhaps comprising a single species; they intergrade on the w. part of the Edwards Plateau in Tex.

CALIFORNIA COFFEEBERRY *Frangula californica* (Eschsch.) A. Gray

QUICK ID The broad, evergreen leaves, green above and often gray- or white-velvety beneath, with parallel lateral veins, and the lustrous dark drupes, distinguish California Coffeeberry.

Evergreen shrub or small tree, 1–5 m tall. **TWIG** Green to reddish brown, becoming gray, hairless to velvety. **LEAF** Oblong or elliptic, margins entire or with many small teeth. Upper surface dark green to yellow-green, lustrous; lower surface hairless to white-velvety, lateral veins prominent, 7–13 pairs. Blade 2.5–10 cm long. **FLOWER** Tiny, yellowish green, 4–60 in axillary umbel-like clusters up to 2 cm long. Apr.–Jul. **FRUIT** Subglobose to somewhat elongate drupe, 6–12 mm diam., lustrous, blackish, usually with 2 stones.

HABITAT/RANGE Native. Coastal ravines, moist canyons, dry inland slopes, chaparral, open woods, 0–2,500 m; sw. Ore. south to n. Baja Calif., east to s. Nev., Ariz., and sw. N.M.

CAROLINA BUCKTHORN *Frangula caroliniana* (Walter) A. Gray

QUICK ID Carolina Buckthorn has leaves with conspicuous straight, parallel lateral veins that become fainter and strongly curved only as they near the margins; obscurely toothed margins: and reddish to blackish drupes with usually 3 stones.

Deciduous shrub or tree, 10–14 m tall; branches spreading, sometimes arching or drooping near the tips. **TWIG** Reddish brown and hairy, becoming gray and hairless. **LEAF** Broadly oblong to slightly obovate, margins obscurely and irregularly toothed. Upper surface lustrous, dark green, lateral

BIRCHLEAF BUCKTHORN

CALIFORNIA COFFEEBERRY

CAROLINA BUCKTHORN

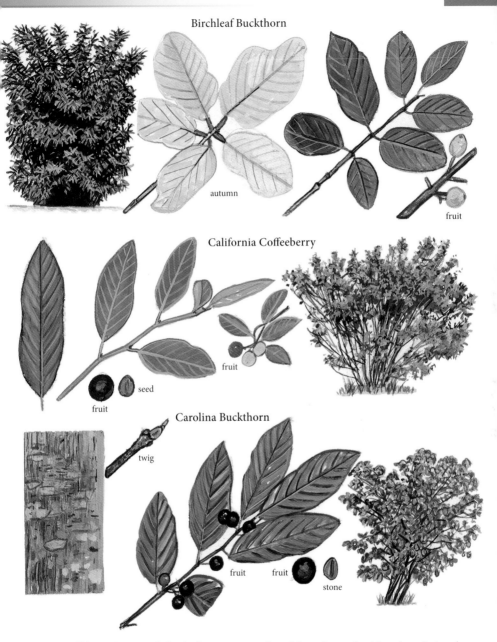

Birchleaf Buckthorn

autumn

fruit

California Coffeeberry

fruit

fruit   seed

Carolina Buckthorn

twig

fruit   fruit

stone

veins parallel, curving toward the tip; lower surface paler, usually at least somewhat hairy. Blade 5–12 cm long, those lowest on the branchlet usually smaller than those above. **FLOWER** Solitary or few in axillary umbels. May–Jun. **FRUIT** More or less globose drupe, about 1 cm long, 3-stoned, black and juicy.

HABITAT/RANGE Native. Calcareous soil in woodlands, 0–600 m; c. Tex. to e. U.S.

CASCARA BUCKTHORN *Frangula purshiana* (DC.) A. Gray

A.K.A. CASCARA, BEARBERRY, PURSH'S BUCKTHORN, CHITTAMBARK

QUICK ID The deciduous leaves with 8–15 prominent parallel veins, straight near the midrib, then curving near the margin, and blackish drupes, distinguish this species within its range.

Usually deciduous large shrub or small tree, 5–15 m tall; trunk straight, 10–50 cm diam.; crown narrow, round, few-branched. In open-grown trees the trunk may be short, 50–75 cm diam., and the branches large and upright. **BARK** Thin, brownish to silvery gray, often with lighter splotches, and with pale vertical stripes, smooth when young, becoming thin-scaly with age. **TWIG** Yellowish green when new, becoming reddish, mostly hairless to finely downy, the tiny buds covered with brownish velvety hairs. **LEAF** Alternate, often clustered and more or less opposite near the twig tips; simple, oblong to oblong-obovate, margins minutely toothed. Lateral veins 8–15 pairs, parallel; upper surface shiny, dark green, veins impressed; lower surface paler and often hairy, veins conspicuously raised. Blade 4–16 mm long, 2–6 cm broad; petiole stout, 5–20 mm long. In autumn, leaves turn pale yellow, sometimes orange, reddish, or purple. **FLOWER** 4–5 mm broad, bell-shaped, yellowish green, 8–40 in small umbel-like axillary clusters; individual flower stalks pubescent, 6–25 mm long, about the same length as the common stalk of the cluster; petals tiny, notched at the tip, each enfolding a stamen. May–Jul. **FRUIT** Globose drupe, 6–14 mm diam., lustrous, blackish, with 2 or 3 stones.

HABITAT/RANGE Native. Roadsides, edges of clearings, understory in open woods, 0–1,600 m; s. B.C. south to n. Calif., east to Idaho and w. Mont.

CASCARA BUCKTHORN

SIMILAR SPECIES Red Alder and White Alder (*Alnus rubra* and *A. rhombifolia*, Betulaceae) are superficially similar and grow in the same area. Their leaves lack parallel veins, and have margins with coarse, irregular teeth; and for much of the year they bear small woody conelike structures. Pacific Dogwood (*Cornus nuttallii*, Cornaceae) has leaves with parallel veins, but the margins are entire; when its leaves are broken and slowly pulled apart, fragile, delicate threads are seen to stretch between the broken edges.

Notes Plant stature and size, thickness, pubescence, and persistence of leaves vary. Where cooler and moister, plants are more often treelike, with thin, large, lightly pubescent, deciduous leaves. Where drier and warmer, plants are shrubby, with thick, smaller, pubescent, semipersistent, or in young plants evergreen, leaves. The bark is intensely bitter, even numbing the taste buds. For centuries it has been peeled and dried to prepare the laxative cascara sagrada; in 2002, the Food and Drug Administration prohibited its sale in over-the-counter medicine because of safety concerns and potential carcinogenic properties. Extracts of fresh bark cause violent vomiting and intense diarrhea. Many tons of bark were once harvested annually, resulting in decline of populations in easily accessible areas. Grouse, Band-tailed Pigeons (*Patagioenas fasciata*), and many other birds and small mammals feed upon the fruits, and deer and Bighorn Sheep (*Ovis canadensis*) browse the twigs and leaves.

COYOTILLO *Karwinskia humboldtiana* (Schult.) Zucc.

A.K.A. DOT-AND-DASH PLANT

QUICK ID Opposite leaves with conspicuous parallel veins, and twigs and leaves marked by tiny black dots and dashes, distinguish Coyotillo.

Shrub or small tree to 8 m tall, deciduous in drought or cold. Flowers, leaves, and young twigs are marked by tiny black dots and dashes. **LEAF** Opposite, elliptic to ovate, margins entire or slightly wavy; lateral veins conspicuous, closely parallel. Blade 2–3.5 cm long. **FLOWER** Small, yellowish, few in axillary clusters. Apr.–Oct. **FRUIT** More or less globose drupe, 6–8 mm long, brownish to black or indigo.

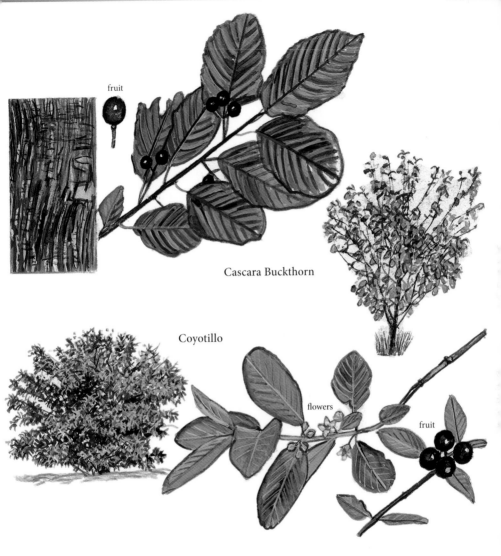

fruit

Cascara Buckthorn

Coyotillo

flowers

fruit

HABITAT/RANGE Native. Dry plains, slopes, brush, 0–600 m; s. Tex. to Central America.

Notes The seed contains a neurotoxin that, several weeks after ingestion, causes ascending paralysis of the limbs. Only 1 species in this genus of 14 species occurs north of Mexico.

COYOTILLO

■ *RHAMNUS*: BUCKTHORNS

There are about 150 species of *Rhamnus*, mostly from the Northern Hemisphere, about 6 native species in the U.S. and Canada, and about an equal number of introduced ones. Three are sometimes small trees in the West, occurring in moist, temperate habitats at low to moderate elevations.

Species of *Rhamnus* are evergreen or deciduous, mostly shrubs, some becoming small trees. Winter buds have bud scales. **LEAF** Simple, alternate or opposite, petiolate, entire or with minute teeth. Lateral veins often conspicuous and impressed above, raised beneath, mostly forward-curved along their entire length. **FLOWER** Tiny, radial, greenish, bisexual or unisexual (with vestigial, nonfunctional parts of the opposite sex), the sexes on separate plants. Usually 4 thin triangular sepals with no ridge on the back attach at the rim of a cup-shaped, thinly lined hypanthium; petals usually absent (especially in female flowers); stamens usually 4; ovary mostly inferior, stigma with 2–4 spreading lobes. **FRUIT** Drupe with usually 2 or 3 stones.

Distinguishing features of *Frangula*, a closely related genus, are discussed on p. 392. Species of *Rhamnus* have provided dyes and medicines.

EUROPEAN BUCKTHORN *Rhamnus cathartica* L.
A.K.A. COMMON BUCKTHORN

QUICK ID This species is recognized by the combination of toothed leaves not exceeding about 2 times longer than broad, usually about 3 pairs of lateral veins strongly curving toward the blade tip, and black drupes with 2 or 3 stones.

Deciduous shrub or tree to about 8 m tall, with 1 short, crooked trunk and a bushy crown with crooked branches bearing stout lateral and terminal thorns 5–55 mm long. **TWIG** Gray, hairless, thorn-tipped, with conspicuous lenticels. **LEAF** Opposite or subopposite, rarely alternate; simple, thin, broadly elliptic or ovate, margins distinctly toothed. Upper surface dull green, lateral veins 2–4 pairs, strongly curving toward the tip; lower surface yellow-green, usually hairless. Blade 4–9 cm long, 3–5 cm broad; petiole 1–4 cm long. Leaves persist on the branch and remain green well into winter. **FLOWER** Unisexual or bisexual, about 5 mm diam., yellowish green, fragrant; male and female usually produced on separate trees. May–Jun. **FRUIT** Globose black drupe, 6–10 mm diam., with 2 or 3 stones.

HABITAT/RANGE Introduced from Europe; cultivated and persisting around homesteads, naturalized in dry, open woods, clearings, fencerows, and roadsides, 0–2,100 m; widespread across the n. U.S. and Canada, reported from Wash., Idaho, and Utah eastward.

Notes Shade-tolerant, fast-growing, and widely regarded as an aggressive invasive species in several northern states and Canada, where its dense shade prevents the establishment of native trees and shrubs. The fruits are reported to be poisonous and nauseating to humans.

DAHURIAN BUCKTHORN *Rhamnus davurica* Pall.

Deciduous shrub or tree to about 10 m tall; crown vase-shaped, with many ascending branches. **BARK** Yellowish brown or reddish brown, smooth, peeling in small flakes. **TWIG** Stout, gray, usually thorn-tipped. **LEAF** Opposite or clustered on short shoots; thin, usually broadly elliptic or ovate, margins toothed, the teeth gland-tipped. Upper surface lustrous, dark green, hairless or hairy, lateral veins 4–6 pairs, impressed, strongly curving toward the tip; lower surface usually hairy on the veins. Blade 4–13 cm long. **FLOWER** Unisexual, yellowish green. May–Jun. **FRUIT** Globose black 2-stoned drupe, 5–6 mm diam. **HABITAT/RANGE** Introduced from Asia; cultivated and escaped, barely entering the West in w. N.D., S.D., and Nebr., at about 600–1,000 m; considered invasive in some eastern states.

ISLAND REDBERRY *Rhamnus pirifolia* Greene

QUICK ID Flowers without petals and with 4 sepals and globose red drupes distinguish this small tree.

ISLAND REDBERRY

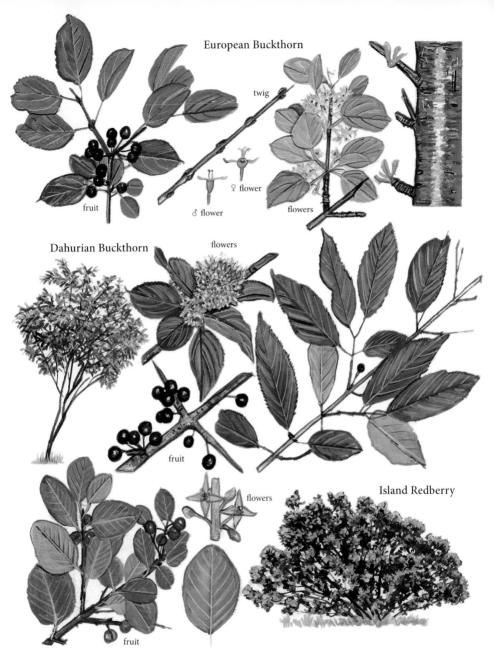

European Buckthorn

fruit

twig

♂ flower

♀ flower

flowers

Dahurian Buckthorn

flowers

fruit

flowers

fruit

Island Redberry

fruit

Evergreen tree to 10 m tall. **BARK** Thin, gray. **TWIG** Purplish, thornless. **LEAF** Alternate, leathery, elliptic, margins entire or toothed, deep green, hairless, lateral veins dark, prominent. Blade 2–5 cm long; petiole 5–10 mm long. **FLOWER** Tiny, yellowishgreen, 1–6 in axillary clusters; individual flower stalks 3–6 mm long. Sepals 4, long-triangular, spreading from the rim of a small hypanthium; petals absent. Mar.–Apr. **FRUIT** Subglobose drupe, 6–12 mm diam., lustrous red, with 2 stones.

HABITAT/RANGE Native. Coastal scrub and chaparral, 10–500 m; Channel Islands, Calif. and islands of nw. Mexico.

■ *ZIZIPHUS*: JUJUBES

There are about 100 species of *Ziziphus* found in the tropics to warm temperate regions in both hemispheres.

Deciduous or evergreen shrubs and trees, usually with stipular spines on at least some branches, 1 spine straight, the other curved, or the pair of spines unequally hooked. **TWIG** Usually zigzag, thorn-tipped or thornless. **LEAF** Alternate, simple, petiolate, mostly oblong or ovate, commonly with 3–5 veins arising from the base. **FLOWER** Small, bisexual, usually yellowish green, in axillary clusters; hypanthium filled with a thick disk surrounding, but not adherent to, the ovary. Sepals, petals, and stamens usually 5, petals falling early; ovary usually 2-celled. **FRUIT** Fleshy drupe with 1 stone.

The genus produces edible fruits, often dried like dates, a tough wood once used in machinery, and fodder for livestock. An alcoholic beverage is made from the fruit of at least 1 species and leaves of some are used for tanning and medicines. Indian Jujube (*Z. mauritiana* Lam.), a Southeast Asia native introduced in Fla. and cultivated in Calif., is harvested for lac (the raw material for shellac), produced by insects that cover and feed upon the branches.

LOTEBUSH *Ziziphus obtusifolia* (Hook. ex Torr. & A. Gray) A. Gray
A.K.A. GRAYTHORN

QUICK ID This much-branched grayish shrub or small tree is recognized by twigs ending in brown-tipped thorns, and small yellowish-green flowers with petals.

Robust deciduous shrub, or occasionally a small tree, to 4 m tall; crown much branched, very thorny, dense, irregular. **BARK** Thin, gray, smooth. **TWIG** Has a grayish waxy bloom; lateral twigs up to 8 cm long, forming a straight or sometimes gently curved, brown-tipped thorn. **LEAF** Alternate or in fascicles, simple, thin or leathery, grayish green, nearly linear to diamond-shaped or ovate, margins often toothed on broader forms, base tapered to a short petiole. Blade 1.2–4 cm long, 2–15 mm broad; petiole 1–5 mm long. **FLOWER** Tiny, 1–15 in axillary clusters; individual flower stalks 1–2 mm long. Sepals 5, triangular, yellow-green, on the rim of a small hypanthium; petals 5, each 1 mm long,

whitish green; stamens opposite petals, on the edge of a thick disk. Apr.–Jul. **FRUIT** Globose to ellipsoid 1-stoned drupe, 5–8 mm diam., dark blue-black, covered with a pale waxy bloom.

HABITAT/RANGE Native. Prairies and dry hills, often with mesquite, 50–1,600 m; s. Calif., Ariz., N.M., to sw. Okla., ec. Tex., n. Mexico.

SIMILAR SPECIES This species is easily confused with the related *Condalia*; the distinctions are given in that genus.

Notes There are 2 varieties: Var. *obtusifolia*, from se. Ariz. eastward, has hairless stems, thin leaves, and a hairless hypanthium; var. *canescens* (A. Gray) M.C. Johnst., of Ariz. and Calif., usually has finely hairy stems, thick leaves, and a hairy hypanthium. Plants provide cover for wildlife, and birds and small mammals consume the fruits. The bark and roots were once used for soap.

LOTEBUSH

COMMON JUJUBE *Ziziphus jujuba* Mill.

Deciduous shrub or tree to 10 m tall; branches in crown greenish, usually drooping. **TWIG** Usually zigzag, thornless, but often bearing paired spines, 1 needlelike, to 3 cm long, the other short and recurved (or spines lacking). **LEAF** Alternate, ovate to oblong, with 3 conspicuous longitudinal veins arising from the base. Blade 3–7 cm long. **FLOWER** Less than 1 cm diam., produced in small clusters in the leaf axils. Apr.–Jun. **FRUIT** Round, juicy red or purplish-red drupe, 2–3.5 cm long, about 2 cm diam., with 1 or 2 stones. **HABITAT/RANGE** Introduced from Eurasia; cultivated for its fruit, occasionally naturalized in n. and c. Tex. and eastward, planted in warmer western states below 1,600 m. *Notes* Earlier sometimes referenced as *Z. zizyphus* (L.) Karst.

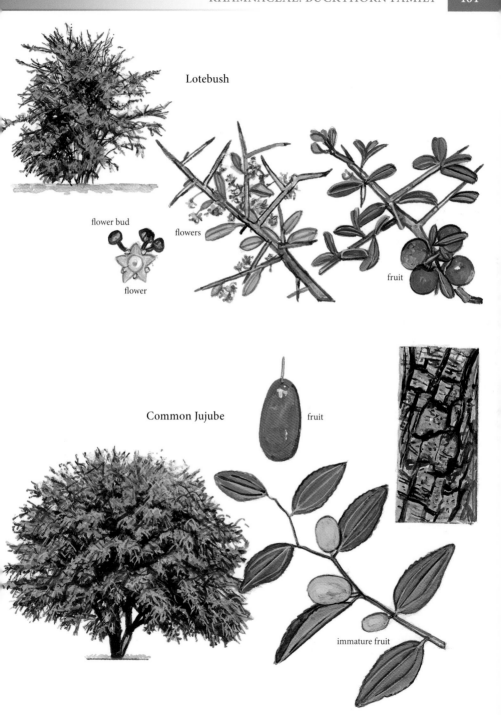

Lotebush

flower bud

flowers

flower

fruit

Common Jujube

fruit

immature fruit

ROSACEAE: ROSE FAMILY

The large and economically important rose family comprises about 120 genera and 3,300 species of herbs, shrubs, and trees worldwide. The family is most diverse in north temperate regions. Species are found in all habitats, from deserts to forests, from sea coasts to alpine tundra. Fifteen genera and more than 70 species of trees of Rosaceae occur in North America north of Mexico, most in the eastern forests, several introduced from Eurasia. The hawthorns (*Crataegus*), a group in which delimitation of species is arguable, constitutes the family's largest woody genus native to North America; it is particularly complex in the East, much less so in the West. Other genera, such as the monotypic *Lyonothamnus* from the Channel Islands of Calif., are very small and only distantly related to other Rosaceae.

LEAF Usually alternate, simple or compound, the margins entire, toothed, or lobed. **FLOWER** Most species in the family have bisexual flowers that are insect-pollinated. Flowers are often large and showy or may be small, showy en masse or, in some cases, inconspicuous. White is the most usual flower color in the wild, but pink and yellow are also common. Flowers are radially symmetric and have a hypanthium or floral cup, on the rim of which are borne 5 sepals, 5 separate petals (petals sometimes absent), and 2 to several times as many stamens as petals. Hypanthium may be free from the ovary, or may be fused to it, in which case the ovary is inferior in position. **FRUIT** Especially diverse, fruits provide distinctive characteristics for classification within the family. Among fruit types are dry capsules (chamise), achenes (bitterbrush), achenes embedded in a fleshy hypanthium (strawberry), drupes (cherries) or an aggregation of drupelets (raspberries), and pomes (apples).

The fruits of the Rosaceae are among the most important of temperate plants, including strawberries, blackberries, raspberries, cherries, apricots, peaches, nectarines, plums, almonds, loquats, apples, pears, and quinces. Many species are popular ornamentals grown for their flowers, such as the rose, flowering quince, flowering cherries, crab apples, and apples, or the vibrant berries of cotoneaster and firethorn. Fruits of numerous Rosaceae are important food for wildlife.

■ *ADENOSTOMA*: CHAMISES

There are 2 species in this genus found only in Calif. and Baja Calif. They occur from low to moderate elevations.

Evergreen erect, unarmed shrubs, sometimes treelike, with resinous heathlike foliage. **LEAF** Numerous, alternate (or in fascicles that are alternate upon the twig), simple, small, linear, with entire margins. **FLOWER** Very small, many, in branched, compact or loose, conical clusters. Each flower bisexual, radial, with 5 sepals, 5 petals, 10 or 15 stamens on a hypanthium that surrounds a single pistil. **FRUIT** Achene, enclosed in the hardened hypanthium.

Adenostoma is a common component of chaparral, a major fire-adapted vegetation type primarily of Calif. Populations are often dense and extensive. Fire burns fiercely across these populations, fueled in part by resinous leaves. New growth soon appears from the woody root crown or basal burl. Leaves on seedlings and new growth from the burl on greasewood are often pinnate, with only 2 to a few linear lobes. The species are capable of hybridizing, but are inhibited from doing so by their different blooming periods. After fire, regeneration from seed is common in Chamise but comparatively rare in Redshank.

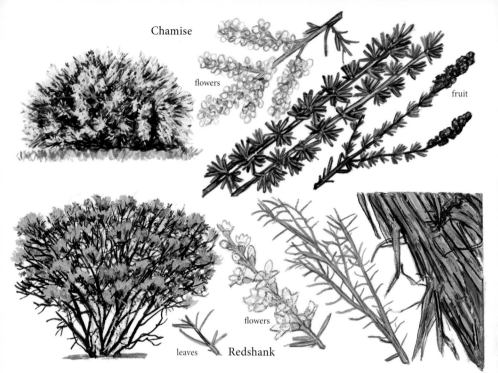

Chamise

flowers

fruit

flowers

leaves

Redshank

CHAMISE *Adenostoma fasciculatum*
Hook. & Arn.
A.K.A. GREASEWOOD

QUICKID Restricted in our area to Calif., this shrub or small tree is distinguished by its small linear leaves clustered in fascicles, in combination with grayish or blackish bark.

Shrub or small tree, 1–4 m tall. **BARK** Gray or blackish. **LEAF** In dense fascicles, dark green, linear, channeled below, 5–13 mm long. **FLOWER** In compact clusters 4–12 cm long; hypanthium 1–3 mm long; petals round to ovate, about 1.5 mm long. May–Jun. **HABITAT/RANGE** Native. Dry slopes and ridges, below 1,850 m; much of Calif. to n. Baja Calif.

REDSHANK *Adenostoma sparsifolium*
Torr.

QUICKID Redshank has threadlike leaves to about 2.5 cm long, and peeling reddish bark.

Erect evergreen shrub or small tree, 2–6 m tall; 1 to few somewhat twisted trunks to 15 cm diam. at the base. Crown open, diffuse, the branches ascending. **BARK** Thin, at first yellowish green, becoming redbrown and peeling in thin, ragged strips. **TWIG** Yellowish green, resinous-glandular. **LEAF** Clustered near branch ends, alternate, simple, flexible, narrowly linear, green and resinous on both surfaces, margins entire. Blade 4–27 mm long. **FLOWER** Tiny, many in a loose cluster 5–10 cm long; petals 5, elliptic, 2 mm long. Hypanthium 1–2 mm long, funnel-shaped, hairless, weakly 10-ribbed. Jul.–Aug. **FRUIT** Achene, about 2 mm long, elliptic, the tip rounded. **HABITAT/ RANGE** Native. Dry slopes in chaparral, often in pure stands, to 2,000 m; s. Calif. to n. Baja Calif. **SIMILAR SPECIES** Chamise has linear leaves in fascicles. *Notes* Individual stems live for perhaps 30 years; the root crown may live 100 years or so.

CHAMISE

REDSHANK

■ *AMELANCHIER*: SERVICEBERRIES

There is no consensus on the number of species in the serviceberry genus. An estimate from the most recent technical treatment is that there are about 25 species in temperate regions of the Northern Hemisphere, about 20 in North America. They are particularly common in moist, semi-open habitats from low to high elevations. Most *Amelanchier* species are clearly shrubs. Classification is difficult because of extensive hybridization and regional variation. And though *Amelanchier* is often difficult to identify to species level, recognition of the genus usually is easy. The prominently veined, rather long-petioled, dull green leaves, toothed in the upper half and borne in fascicles on short spur branches, are distinctive, as are the white flowers with narrow petals and the small purplish or blackish pomes.

Deciduous shrubs or small trees, sometimes erect and with 1 trunk, more often with multiple trunks, often suckering and forming colonies or dense clumps. When treelike, the crown is often oval or round, thick, with erect to spreading branches. **BARK** Generally smooth, thin, often at first reddish, later gray to dark brown, shallowly fissured, and scaly. **TWIG** Slender, round; buds pointed and brown, the inner scales reddish brown as they enlarge. Twigs have a faint odor of bitter almond when crushed. **LEAF** Alternate, borne mostly on short lateral branches, the blade simple, lanceolate to nearly round, thin or slightly leathery, hairy or not at maturity, rather prominently pinnately veined, toothed at least in the upper half. Foliage in the autumn ranges from yellow to orange or red. **FLOWER** Rather showy, borne in short erect or drooping clusters that appear as spring leaves are unfolding. Flowers are bisexual, radial, with 5 sepals, 5 separate petals, 10–20 stamens attached near the top of the hypanthium. **FRUIT** Small globose to barrel-shaped pome, red to purple or black at maturity.

In the West, serviceberries provide good browse for livestock and game animals. Reputedly, through a Cree word (*misaaskwatoomina*) for *A. alnifolia*, the city of Saskatoon derives its name. According to tradition, "shad" in vernacular names (shadbush, shadblow) relates to the genus's early spring flowering, coinciding with when the shad run. Fruits ripen in late spring or early summer, hence one of the many vernacular names, juneberry.

SASKATOON SERVICEBERRY
Amelanchier alnifolia (Nutt.) Nutt. ex M. Roem.
A.K.A. WESTERN SERVICEBERRY

QUICK ID This colony-forming shrub or small tree may be recognized by the combination of round or truncate, toothed leaves that are well developed and usually hairless at flowering, hairy ovary summits, and comparatively large fruits.

Typically a rhizomatous, spreading, clump- or colony-forming shrub, 1–7 m tall, but sometimes a small tree. **LEAF** Alternate, simple, oval to round-squarish, thin to slightly leathery; lower surface pale green or glaucous, finely yellowish-pubescent during expansion, both sides hairless by flowering time; broadly tapered, truncate, or indented at the base; rounded or truncate at the tip; margin toothed mostly above the middle with 2–5 teeth per cm, or entire; veins 8–13 pairs, tips entering teeth. Blade 2–5 cm long, 2.5–5 cm wide; petiole 8–18 mm long. **FLOWER** In erect or ascending clusters of 5–15 flowers, individual flower stalks finely hairy; hypanthium shallowly cup-shaped, 3.5–4 mm diam.; petals oblanceolate, 6–10 mm long; stamens about 20; styles usually 5; ovary summit rounded, densely hairy. May–Jul. **FRUIT** Black or purple pome 10–15 mm diam. Jul.–Aug.

HABITAT/RANGE Native. Moist areas in brush and open woods, 500–2,600 m; c. Alaska to c. Canada, south to Idaho, Colo., Nebr., and Tex.

SIMILAR SPECIES Four other species of serviceberry—Basalt-loving, Cusick's, Many-flowered, and Dwarf shadbush—all closely related to Saskatoon Serviceberry and until recently included within it, also occur in the West. They, too, are usually shrubby, but occasionally may be small trees.

SASKATOON SERVICEBERRY

Saskatoon Serviceberry

spring

fruit

flowers

fruit

autumn

Notes Red-twigged Shadbush (*A. sanguinea* [Pursh] DC.) is mapped by some sources on the n. Great Plains, but recent treatments indicate such records have confused this species, restricted to ne. North America, with western species.

BASALT-LOVING SHADBUSH
Amelanchier basalticola Piper

Shrub or small tree, 1–3 m tall, singled-stemmed or in small clumps. **LEAF** Round or nearly so, hairless by flowering time; margins entire or toothed mostly above the middle with 4–6 teeth per cm; veins 10–13 pairs, tips entering the teeth. Blade 1.5–3 cm long, 1.5–2 cm wide; petiole 7–18 mm long. **FLOWER** Individual stalks hairless. Petals 12–16 mm long; stamens usually 20; styles 4 or 5; ovary summit rounded, hairless or with a ring of hairs at the base of the styles. Mar.–Apr. **FRUIT** Dark purple pome, 9–12 mm diam.; Jun. **HABITAT/RANGE** Native. Mostly on basaltic ledges along rivers; Wash. to Ore. and Idaho.

CUSICK'S SHADBUSH *Amelanchier cusickii* Fernald

Usually a shrub, 1–7 m tall, single-stemmed or in small clumps. **LEAF** Elliptic to rounded, hairless by flowering time; margins entire or toothed mostly above the middle with 3–6 teeth per cm; veins 7–13 pairs, tips entering the teeth. Blade 1.5–5 cm long, 1.5–3 cm wide; petiole 6–22 mm long. **FLOWER** Individual stalks hairless. Petals 16–25 mm long; stamens usually 20; styles 4 or 5; ovary summit rounded, hairless, sparsely hairy, or with a ring of hairs at the base of the styles. Mar.–Jul. **FRUIT** Bluish-black pome, about 10 mm diam. Jun.

HABITAT/RANGE Native. Basaltic ledges and stony soils along streams, on mountainsides; s. B.C. to Ore., east to Mont. and Utah.

MANY-FLOWERED SHADBUSH
Amelanchier florida Lindl.

Shrub or tree, 1–12 m tall, single-stemmed or in small clumps. **LEAF** Oblong to rounded, finely hairy on the lower surface by flowering time; margins entire or toothed mostly above the middle with 4–6 teeth per cm; veins 8–12 pairs, tips entering the teeth. Blade 3–4 cm long, 2–3 cm wide; petiole 10–25 mm long. **FLOWER** Individual stalks finely hairy. Petals 12–15 mm long; stamens usually 20; styles usually 5; ovary summit rounded, densely hairy. Mar.–Jun. **FRUIT** Purplish-black pome, 10–13 mm diam. Jun.–Aug. **HABITAT/ RANGE** Native. Woods, hillsides, roadsides; Alaska to Calif., mostly near the coast.

DWARF SHADBUSH *Amelanchier pumila* Nutt. ex Torr. & Gray

Shrub or small tree, 1–3 m tall, single-stemmed or in small clumps. **LEAF** Oval to rounded, hairless or sparsely hairy on the lower surface by flowering time; margins entire or toothed above the middle with 3–5 teeth per cm; veins 7–9 pairs, tips entering the teeth. Blade 1–5 cm long, 1–2 cm wide; petiole 5–15 mm long. **FLOWER** Individual stalks hairless. Petals 8–12 mm long; stamens 12–15; styles 4 or 5; ovary summit rounded, hairless. May–Jun. **FRUIT** Dark purple pome, 8–9 mm diam.; Jul.–Sep. **HABITAT/RANGE** Native. Mountain slopes and plains, 2,300–3,300 m; Mont. to Ore., south to n. Calif., Utah, and Colo.

UTAH SERVICEBERRY *Amelanchier utahensis* Koehne

QUICK ID This widespread serviceberry has oval to round leaves with 11–13 pairs of veins and toothed margins; the leaf surface remains hairy well into flowering time.

Dense shrub or small tree, 1–5 m tall, often colonial. **LEAF** Alternate, simple, thin, somewhat leathery, oval, obovate, or nearly round; pubescent by flowering time; toothed in the upper half with 3–5 teeth per cm; veins 11–13 pairs, extending into the teeth. Blade 1–3 cm long; petiole 5–18 mm long. **FLOWER** In erect or ascending clusters of 3–6 flowers, individual flower stalks finely hairy; hypanthium cup- or funnel-shaped, 3–4 mm diam.; petals oblanceolate, often wedge-shaped at the base, 6–9 mm long; stamens usually 10–15; styles usually 2–4; ovary summit rounded, densely hairy. Apr.–Jun. **FRUIT** Purplish-black pome 6–10 mm thick.

HABITAT/RANGE Native. Dry rocky slopes, canyons, foothills, below 3,400 m; much of w. U.S., to n. Mexico.

Notes Some phases in Calif. have been called **Pale Serviceberry** (*A. pallida* Greene.)

UTAH SERVICEBERRY

■ *CERCOCARPUS:* MOUNTAIN MAHOGANIES

Mountain mahogany is a small w. North America genus of 8–10 species found in semiarid areas from the w. U.S. to c. Mexico at low to moderate elevations.

Evergreen shrubs and small trees with stiff, contorted, sometimes spinescent branches. **BARK** Thin, rough, brownish gray, fissured. **LEAF** Alternate on new twigs; most are in fascicles on short spurs on older branches. **FLOWER** Small, greenish yellow, 1–3 at ends of short spur branches, radial, lacking petals; sepals 5; stamens 15–45, attached near the rim of a ribbed, funnel-shaped hypanthium, which contains the single superior ovary. Style elongates after pollination. **FRUIT** Slender, pointed achene; style persistent, long-plumose, and twisted, protruding from the hypanthium.

The name "mountain mahogany" was given by Mormon pioneers in reference to the hard reddish wood. *Cercocarpus* roughly translates as "tailed fruit," the feathery style helping in wind dispersal of the fruit. Formal classification of the group is unsettled because of racial differentiation and probable hybridization.

LITTLELEAF MOUNTAIN MAHOGANY *Cercocarpus intricatus* S. Watson

QUICK ID This small shrub or tree has stiff, pointed twigs and small, narrow leaves in fascicles, the leaf margins tightly rolled and the leaf appearing nearly cylindric.

Similar to Curlleaf Mountain Mahogany, but more noticeably spinescent and smaller, to 2.5 m tall. **LEAF** 5–15 mm long, 0.4–1.6 mm wide; margins in-rolled to the midrib, the leaf appearing nearly cylindric. **FLOWER** Hypanthium 4–6 mm long. **FRUIT** Achene about 6 mm long; style plumose, 3–4.5 cm long. Apr.–Jun.

HABITAT/RANGE Native. Dry slopes and rocks, 1,000–3,000 m; se. Calif. to w. Colo., n. Ariz., and nw. N.M.

Notes As the flower ages, the lengthening style sometimes carries the fading sepals and petals from the top of the hypanthium.

LITTLELEAF MOUNTAIN MAHOGANY

Utah Serviceberry

flowers

fruit

spring

Pale Serviceberry

flowers

fruit

Littleleaf Mountain Mahogany

aging flower   young flower

flowers

aging flower

fruit

young flower

fruit

CURLLEAF MOUNTAIN MAHOGANY
Cercocarpus ledifolius Nutt. ex Torr. & Gray

QUICK ID This species has narrow leaves with the margins rolled under and the lower surface whitish-hairy.

Evergreen shrub or small tree, 2–8 m tall; trunks 1 to few, twisted, to 60 cm diam. **TWIG** Stiff, sharp, smooth, first reddish, later grayish. **LEAF** In fascicles, simple, leathery, more or less convex, linear to narrowly oblanceolate; margins entire, rolled under; upper surface dark green, hairless, somewhat resinous; lower surface whitish-hairy. Blade 1–4 cm long, 1.5–10 mm broad; petiole 1–6 mm. **FLOWER** One to several on spur shoots, 8 mm diam.; hypanthium 2.5–15 mm long, white-hairy. May–Jun. **FRUIT** Achene, 7–9 mm long; style plumose, 4–10 cm long.

HABITAT/RANGE Native. Rocky slopes with sagebrush, oaks, pines, 1,000–3,000 m; e. Wash. to sw. Mont., south to s. Colo., nw. Ariz., and s. Nev.

SIMILAR SPECIES The leaves are larger and broader, with more of the underside exposed, than in Littleleaf Mountain Mahogany.

CURLLEAF MOUNTAIN MAHOGANY

ALDERLEAF MOUNTAIN MAHOGANY *Cercocarpus montanus* Raf.

QUICK ID Leaves small, wedge-shaped, the veins in a prominent feather pattern, the tip usually toothed.

Evergreen shrub or small tree, 2–6 m tall; trunk to 30 cm diam. **TWIG** Stiff, smooth, first reddish, later gray. **LEAF** In fascicles, simple, soft or leathery, flat, lanceolate to more or less obovate; base wedge-shaped, tip often round; margins often rolled under, usually toothed around the tip; upper surface dark green, mostly hairless; lower surface hairless to whitish-hairy; veins prominent, 3–10 on each side. Blade 1–6 cm long, 0.5–3.5 cm wide; petiole 2.5–6 mm long. **FLOWER** One to several on spur shoots, 8 mm diam.; hypanthium 3–11 mm long, hairless to hairy. May–Jun. **FRUIT** achene 3–11 mm long; style plumose, 2–9.5 cm long.

HABITAT/RANGE Native. Rocky areas in grasslands, brush or open woods, 0–3,000 m; sw. Ore. to Mont. and sw. S.D., south to n. Mexico.

SIMILAR SPECIES The following are sometimes considered separate species. **Catalina Island Mountain Mahogany** (*C. traskiae* Eastw.) has leaves that are white-hairy beneath and with margins rolled under, and occurs in the Channel Islands, Calif. Birchleaf Mountain Mahogany (*C. betuloides* Nutt.) has leaves that are hairy beneath and with margins short-toothed to more or less entire, and is found in Calif. and sw. Ore. Hairy Mountain Mahogany (*C. breviflorus* A. Gray) has leaves lanceolate to narrowly obovate, with margins mostly entire or with 3–5 teeth, and occurs in Ariz. to w. Tex.

ALDERLEAF MOUNTAIN
MAHOGANY

Curlleaf Mountain Mahogany

underside

flowers

fruit

Alderleaf Mountain Mahogany

flower

flowers

leaf variation

fruit

Catalina Island Mountain Mahogany

fruit and
style base

underside

■ *CRATAEGUS*: HAWTHORNS

There are 150–280 or more species of *Crataegus*, all from the Northern Hemisphere, most from North America. Some have been introduced in the Southern Hemisphere. In the West there are 25–30 species. They occur in most open to wooded habitats from sea-level to moderately high elevations in the mountains.

Well-armed, usually deciduous shrubs and small trees of temperate regions. Branches may be straight or zigzag, and bear long, sharp thorns; in some species the trunk bears branched thorns. **BARK** Thin, brownish or grayish; smooth, scaly and flaking in plates, peeling in strips, or somewhat blocky and corrugated. **TWIG** Buds blunt, scales overlapping. **LEAF** Alternate, simple, narrowly elliptic to broadly ovate, or diamond-shaped, usually more or less lobed, the margins toothed (the teeth sometimes gland-tipped), but usually entire near the petiole. The foliage of many species contributes rich yellows, reds, or burgundies to fall color. **FLOWER** Showy en masse, in few-branched rounded, often drooping, clusters at the ends of branches; flowers bisexual, radial, the parts in 5s; sepals, petals, and stamens borne near the rim of a small hypanthium; petals 5, separate, usually white and roundish; stamens 5–45; styles 1–5, protruding from the opening of the hypanthium. **FRUIT** Small pome, usually more or less globose, containing 1–5 very hard nutlets (technically pyrenes, including the inner wall of the ovary and the seed). The color of mature fruits of hawthorns is important in identification. As the fruit matures it may pass from green through yellows and reds to purples and ultimately black (the mature color—red, purple, or black—is given in this book). Sculpturing of the pyrenes, particularly the back and sides, is also important for identification, but is left for more technical sources.

Fruits are edible and those from some species are used in jellies. Others are not especially palatable. The fruits are the "haws," tracing back to very old European words referring to "hedge" or "pasture." Cultivated forms are prized ornamentals because of the showy spring bloom and the clusters of small red or purple pomes in autumn. Some may persist in plantings or around old homesteads; among them are *C. phaenopyrum* (L. f.) Medik. and *C. mollis* (Torr. & A. Gray) Scheele (information on these may be found in the companion volume, *Trees of Eastern North America*). In areas where winters are mild, hawthorns may keep their leaves until new ones appear in the spring.

Identification and classification of hawthorns is notoriously difficult, sometimes arbitrary, and often subjective, as suggested by the estimated number of species. Hawthorns may reproduce sexually or asexually. By varying in chromosome number they may be reproductively isolated from one another without much genetic change. Most easily hybridize with others. This all leads to a complicated array of populations, some widespread and different from other hawthorn species, some hybrids and intergrades, and some forming uniform local clones barely different from others. In this book, to facilitate identification, western species are arranged beginning with the Northwest, proceeding through the Rocky Mountain region, and ending in the Southwest.

ONESEED HAWTHORN *Crataegus monogyna* Jacq.

QUICK ID The single-seeded fruit separates this species from our native hawthorns.

Deciduous shrub or small tree to about 10 m tall. **BARK** Brown, often with shallow furrows and spiraling ridges. **TWIG** Greenish or reddish brown, densely hairy or hairless; thorns stout, to about 2.5 cm long. **LEAF** Alternate, simple, ovate or triangular; margins deeply divided into several narrow lobes, cut at least halfway to the midrib; upper surface lustrous dark green, hairless; lower surface distinctly hairy, at least on the main veins. Blade 1.25–6 cm long, nearly as broad; petiole 1–3 cm long. **FLOWER** 8–16 mm diam.; petals white, sometimes becoming reddish at maturity; stamens 15–20, anthers pinkish purple. Late spring. **FRUIT** Round, dark or bright red pome, 6–11 mm diam., with a single nutlet.

HABITAT/RANGE Introduced from Europe; found in a wide variety of habitats from sea-level to moderate elevations; naturalized from nw. Calif. to sw. B.C., east to w. Mont., also much of e. North America.

SIMILAR SPECIES Smooth Hawthorn also has deeply divided leaves, but it usually has 2 styles in the flower and 2 nutlets in the fruit.

Notes Numerous horticultural forms and cultivars have been selected from this species, several of which are planted in the U.S. and Canada. Birds eat the pomes and distribute the seeds.

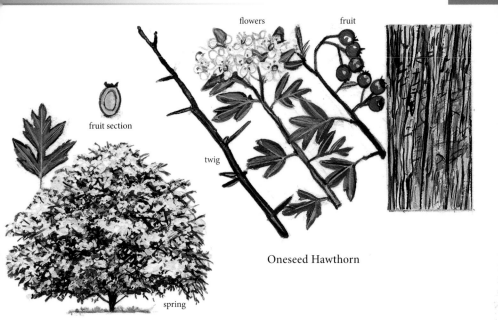

flowers

fruit

fruit section

twig

Oneseed Hawthorn

spring

Smooth Hawthorn

flowers

spring

fruit

fruit section

SMOOTH HAWTHORN *Crataegus laevigata* (Poir.) DC.
A.K.A. WOODLAND HAWTHORN

Thorny deciduous shrub or small tree to 8 m tall. **BRANCH** Thorns few, stout, 1–2 cm long. **LEAF** More or less ovate, hairless except on the veins, usually 3 shallow, blunt lobes near the tip, margins toothed. Blade 1.5–6 cm long; petiole 1–2 cm long. **FLOWER** 12–22 mm diam., stamens 20, anthers purple, styles 2. Inflorescence usually hairless. May. **FRUIT** Hairless, globose red pome, 6–14 mm diam.; nutlets 2. **HABITAT/RANGE** Introduced from Europe; woods, 50 m; San Juan Islands, Wash.

CASTLEGAR HAWTHORN *Crataegus castlegarensis* J.B. Phipps & O'Kennon

QUICK ID This hawthorn has thorns often in 2s or 3s, 10 stamens with pink anthers, and small fruits that are crimson to blackish purple when ripe.

Thorny, deciduous treelike shrub, 2.5–5 m tall. **BRANCH** Thorns 2–3 cm long, often in 2s or 3s. **LEAF** Roundish diamond-shaped, margins sharply toothed, 0–4 low lobes per side; blade 3.5–6 cm long; petiole 7–15 mm long. **FLOWER** 12–15 mm diam.; stamens 10, anthers pink. Inflorescence pubescent. May. **FRUIT** Pubescent, globose crimson to blackish-purple pome, 10–12 mm diam.

HABITAT/RANGE Native. Brush, 300–1,900 m; nw. U.S., s. B.C.

ENDERBY HAWTHORN *Crataegus enderbyensis* J.B. Phipps & O'Kennon

Large, thorny, deciduous shrub or small tree, 5–6 m tall. **BRANCH** Thorns red-brown, curved, 2.5 cm long. **LEAF** Ovate to diamond-shaped, leathery, dark green, appressed-hairy above; margins jagged, sharply toothed. Blade 4–8 cm long; petiole 1–2 cm long. **FLOWER** About 15 mm diam.; stamens 10, anthers cream. Inflorescence spreading-hairy. May. **FRUIT** Pubescent, goblet-shaped burgundy pome, 8–10 mm diam. **HABITAT/RANGE** Native. Open woods, around 400 m; sc. B.C., near Enderby.

PHIPPS HAWTHORN *Crataegus phippsii* O'Kennon

QUICK ID Distinguished by the combination of pink anthers, 10 stamens, lobed leaves, and fruits that are deep purple to black when ripe.

Large, thorny, deciduous shrub or small tree, 5–7 m tall. **BRANCH** Thorns sparse, blackish, curved, 2–4 cm long. **LEAF** Elliptic to ovate-triangular, more or less leathery; upper surface with appressed hairs, lower surface thinly hairy; margins bluntly and shallowly lobed, teeth small, low. Blade 4–8 cm long; petiole 1.5–2 cm long. **FLOWER** 15–22 mm diam.; stamens 10, anthers pale pink. Inflorescence short-hairy. May. **FRUIT** Pubescent, globose, deep purple to black pome, 12 mm diam.

HABITAT/RANGE Native. In brushy areas, 300–850 m; sc. B.C., nc. Wash., nw. Mont.

BLACK HAWTHORN *Crataegus douglasii* Lindl.

QUICK ID This species has short thorns and dark purplish fruits 6–8 mm diam.

Deciduous, usually a shrub 4–6 m tall, rarely treelike to about 8 m tall; trunks 1 or more; crown erect or vase-shaped. **BRANCH** Dark gray, armed with lustrous, short, stout, straight or slightly curved thorns 1–3.5 cm long. **TWIG** Lustrous tan or mahogany-brown. **LEAF** Alternate, simple, elliptic or broadly elliptic; margins coarsely and sharply toothed, sometimes with 2–4 lobes per side, the teeth usually gland-tipped. Upper surface dark green, usually with short hairs; lower surface hairless except for the veins. Blade 4–7 cm long, 2–3 cm broad; petiole 7–15 mm long. **FLOWER** 12–15 mm diam., petals white, circular; stamens 10, anthers pink. May–Jun. **FRUIT** Ellipsoid pome, 6–8 mm diam., dull black or purplish at maturity.

HABITAT/RANGE Native. Moist open woods, along streams, in old pastures and along fencelines, mostly 1,300–2,700 m in the West; common from s. Alaska and wc. B.C. south to n. Calif., Idaho, and Mont., sporadically east to Que. and Mich.

CASTLEGAR HAWTHORN

PHIPPS HAWTHORN

BLACK HAWTHORN

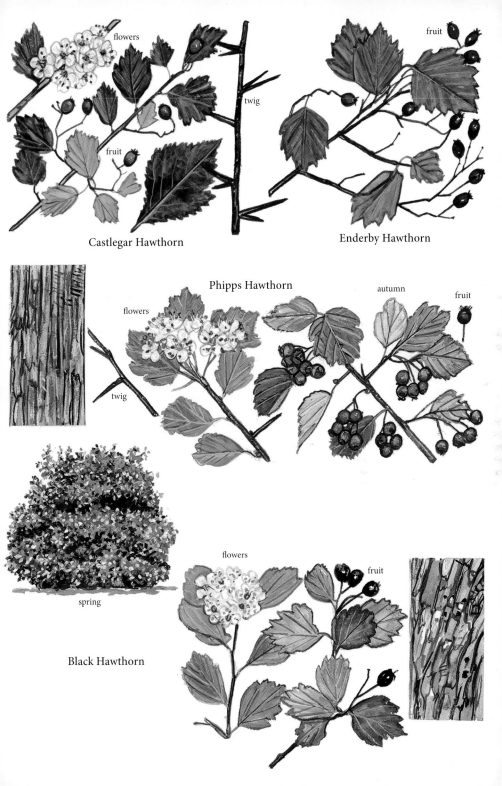

Castlegar Hawthorn

flowers

twig

fruit

Enderby Hawthorn

fruit

Phipps Hawthorn

flowers

twig

autumn

fruit

spring

Black Hawthorn

flowers

fruit

O'KENNON HAWTHORN *Crataegus okennonii* J.B. Phipps

QUICK ID O'Kennon Hawthorn may be recognized by the combination of its comparatively short, brown thorns, thinly hairy or hairless inflorescence, and hairless deep purple to black fruit.

Thorny, deciduous large shrub or small tree, 3–15 m tall. **BRANCH** Thorns about 2 cm long, brown. **LEAF** Elliptic, margins sharply toothed, 0–3 low lobes per side; blade 4–6 cm long; petiole 1–2 mm long. **FLOWER** 15–20 mm diam.; stamens 10–12, anthers pale pink. Inflorescence hairless or thin-hairy. May. **FRUIT** Hairless, globose to goblet-shaped, deep purple to black pome, 8–10 mm diam.

HABITAT/RANGE Native. Streamsides, 250–950 m; sc. B.C. to e. Wash. and nw. Mont.

SUKSDORF HAWTHORN *Crataegus suksdorfii* (Sarg.) Kruschke

QUICK ID The combination of short, dark brown thorns, flowers with 20 stamens that have pink anthers, and hairless fruits that are blackish when mature helps distinguish this species.

Thorny, deciduous shrub or small tree, 3–10 m tall; thorns dark brown, straight or curved, 1–2 cm long. **LEAF** Elliptic-obovate, more or less leathery; upper surface with appressed hairs, lower surface hairless; margins toothed; lobes 0–3, low, blunt.

Blade 3–8 cm long; petiole 7–15 cm long. **FLOWER** 15–17 mm diam.; stamens 20, anthers pink. Inflorescence hairless. May–Jun. **FRUIT** Hairless, globose blackish pome, 10 mm diam.

HABITAT/RANGE Native. Moist areas, 0–1,500 m; Calif. to Alaska, inland to Mont.

FLESHY HAWTHORN *Crataegus succulenta* Schrad. ex Link

QUICK ID The combination of a narrowly winged, nonglandular petiole, thick double-toothed leaves, and comparatively long, stout thorns is characteristic of this hawthorn.

Deciduous shrub or small tree to 7 m tall; older trunks often with stout, compound thorns. **BRANCH** Armed with numerous blackish-brown thorns 3–6 cm long. **TWIG** Hairless at maturity. **LEAF** Thick, firm, mostly obovate, ovate, or broadly elliptic, usually shallowly lobed; margins distinctly and often doubly toothed from below the middle to the tip. Upper surface lustrous, usually hairless at maturity, with conspicuously impressed lateral veins; lower surface paler. Blade 4–8 cm long, 3–6 cm broad; petiole narrowly winged, 1–2 cm long. **FLOWER** Petals white, circular; stamens 20, anthers reddish or pink, rarely white. May–Jun. **FRUIT** Lustrous red pome, 6–12 mm diam.

HABITAT/RANGE Native. Open areas, streamsides, mountain slopes, ridges, 200–1,500 m; an eastern species entering the West on the Great Plains from Colo. to Mont.; also in Utah.

O'KENNON HAWTHORN

SUKSDORF HAWTHORN

FLESHY HAWTHORN

O'Kennon Hawthorn

flowers

fruit

fruit

twig

nutlet

Suksdorf Hawthorn

flowers

flower

fruit

underside

spring

Fleshy Hawthorn

flowers

fruit

autumn

nutlets

FIREBERRY HAWTHORN *Crataegus chrysocarpa* Ashe

QUICK ID The comparatively long thorns and usually permanently pubescent leaves help distinguish this from other western hawthorns.

Deciduous shrub or small tree, to about 8 m tall. Trunk erect, straight, 1 to several, 15 cm diam.; crown narrow, open, ascending. **BARK** Gray-brown or reddish brown, scaly. **BRANCH** Slender, often crooked, armed with slender, straight or slightly curved, lustrous, dark brown or nearly black thorns 3–10 cm long. **TWIG** Usually hairy, yellowish or greenish brown, becoming gray-brown. **LEAF** Alternate, simple, firm at maturity, obovate, rhombic, or broadly elliptic; margins with 2–4 shallow lobes and conspicuous teeth. Upper surface often hairy on young leaves, sometimes becoming hairless at maturity; lower surface hairy on the veins. Blade typically small, varying in size, 2–6 cm long, often at least as broad; petiole 1–2.5 cm long, narrowly winged. **FLOWER** 1–2 cm diam.; petals white, circular; stamens 10 or 20, anthers creamy white, yellowish, or pink. Apr.–Jun. **FRUIT** Rounded red or dark red, rarely yellow, often dark-spotted pome, 6–12 mm diam.

HABITAT/RANGE Native. Open woods, hillsides, stream margins, often in association with rocky, calcareous soils, from low to moderate elevations; east of the Cascade Range from B.C. to Ore., east to e. Canada, ne. U.S., south to n. N.M. and Mo.

Notes This is one of the most variable and wide-ranging North American species of hawthorn. East of the Rocky Mountains it is the most northerly and cold-adapted species.

SHEILA PHIPPS HAWTHORN *Crataegus sheila-phippsiae* J.B. Phipps & O'Kennon

Thorny, deciduous treelike shrub, 3–5 m tall. **BRANCH** Thorns 2.5–4 cm long. **LEAF** Broadly diamond-shaped, margins with small sharp teeth, 3 or 4 sharp lobes per side; blade 4–5 cm long; petiole 1–2 cm long. **FLOWER** 14–19 mm diam.; stamens 20, anthers pink to purplish. Inflorescence hairless. May. **FRUIT** Hairless, globose red to dark burgundy pome, 10–12 mm diam. **HABITAT/RANGE** Native. Open areas, 300–500 m; sc. B.C.

CERRO HAWTHORN *Crataegus erythropoda* Ashe

QUICK ID This hawthorn is distinguished by its short, broad leaves and burgundy pome.

Deciduous, thorny shrub or spreading tree, 2–6 m tall; trunk short, about 10 cm diam. **BRANCH** Thorns shiny, blackish, 2–5 cm long. **TWIG** Hairless, red-brown. **LEAF** Alternate, simple, broadly ovate to diamond-shaped, length about 1.6 × width, lustrous, hairless, with 4 or 5 pairs of veins; margins saw-toothed, often shallowly toward the tip, the teeth gland-tipped. Blade 4–8 cm long, 3–6 cm wide; petiole 1–2.5 cm long. **FLOWER** 15–20 mm diam., 5–10 per cluster; flower stalks hairless, gland-dotted; petals white; hypanthium hairless; stamens about 10, anthers pink to purple. Apr.–May. **FRUIT** Hairless, globose pome, 7–10 mm diam., burgundy when mature.

HABITAT/RANGE Native. Along streams in sagebrush or pine, 1,500–2,700 m; sc. Wyo. to Ariz., N.M.

SIMILAR SPECIES Mountain River Hawthorn has a leaf length more than 2 × width and nearly black pomes. Willow Hawthorn has narrow leaves with 6–9 pairs of veins.

FIREBERRY HAWTHORN   CERRO HAWTHORN

Fireberry Hawthorn

autumn

flowers

fruit

Sheila Phipps Hawthorn

flowers

fruit

nutlet

Cerro Hawthorn

spring

thorn

flower

fruit

fruit

flowers

opening bud

twig

MOUNTAIN RIVER HAWTHORN
Crataegus rivularis Nutt.

QUICK ID This hawthorn, widespread in the West, has long, straight blackish thorns; leaves that are somewhat hairy above but otherwise hairless, with sharply toothed but unlobed margins; and hairless blackish fruits.

Thorny deciduous shrub or small tree, 3–5 m tall. **BRANCH** Thorns blackish, usually straight, 1.5–4 cm long. **LEAF** Elliptic; more or less hairy above, otherwise hairless; margins mostly unlobed, sharply toothed; veins 4 or 5 per side. Blade 3–8 cm long; petiole 1–2.5 cm long. **FLOWER** 14–17 mm diam.; stamens about 10, anthers usually pink. Inflorescence spotted with minute glands. May–Jun. **FRUIT** Hairless, globose blackish pome, 10 mm diam.

HABITAT/RANGE Native. Moist areas, 1,300–3,200 m; Idaho and Wyo. to Ariz. and N.M.

WILLOW HAWTHORN *Crataegus saligna* Greene

QUICK ID Distinguished by its very thorny habit, the thorns blackish; its narrowly elliptic leaves with teeth tipped with red glands; and its flowers with 20 stamens with cream anthers.

Very thorny, deciduous, thicket-forming shrub or small tree, 3–5 m tall. **BRANCH** Thorns 1–3 cm long, blackish. **LEAF** Elliptic, leathery, tip round; margin unlobed, with low, rounded teeth tipped with red glands; veins 6–12 per side. Blade 3–5 cm long; petiole 8–18 mm long. **FLOWER** 10–13 mm diam.; stamens 20, anthers cream. Inflorescence hairless. May. **FRUIT** Hairless, globose blackish pome, 5–8 mm diam.

HABITAT/RANGE Native. Wooded stream banks, 1,800–2,700 m; ne. Utah, w. Colo.; uncommon.

GREEN HAWTHORN *Crataegus viridis* L.

QUICK ID The combination of long, slender blackish thorns, leaves that have 3–5 shallow lobes and are hairless except for tufts in the vein axils on the lower surface, and red or orange fruits helps distinguish this species, found in the West only in c. Tex.

Deciduous shrub or small tree to 12 m tall; trunk often fluted at the base. **BRANCH** Larger branches often lack thorns, smaller branches with slender blackish thorns 3–4 cm long. **LEAF** Elliptic to bluntly diamond-shaped or nearly circular, usually widest near the middle; margins usually with 3–5 shallow lobes, toothed. Upper surface usually dull green, hairless; lower surface paler, usually with tufts of grayish hairs in the vein axils. Blade 2–7 cm long, 2–5 cm broad; petiole 1–5 cm long. **FLOWER** Petals white, 4–8 mm long; stamens 15–20. **FRUIT** Red or orange pome, 5–8 mm diam.

HABITAT/RANGE Native. Wet areas, 0–500 m; se. U.S., barely entering West in c. Tex.

MOUNTAIN RIVER HAWTHORN

WILLOW HAWTHORN

GREEN HAWTHORN

Mountain River Hawthorn

flowers

fruit

fruit

Willow Hawthorn

autumn

flowers

fruit

Green Hawthorn

flowers

leaf variation

fruit

autumn

REVERCHON HAWTHORN *Crataegus reverchonii* Sarg.

QUICK ID Entering the West only in c. Tex., this hawthorn is distinguished by the combination of hairless, rounded or ovate leaves and a comparatively large reddish fruit with 3–5 nutlets.

Deciduous shrub, occasionally a tree to 7 m tall; crown rounded, with slender branches. **LEAF** Obovate to nearly round, firm, stiff, hairless; margins sharply toothed except near the base. Blade 3–4 cm long, nearly as broad; petiole 2–12 mm long. **FLOWER** 8–17 mm diam., petals white, circular; stamens usually 10–15, anthers yellow, pink, rose, or red. Apr.–Jun. **FRUIT** Rounded or oblong red or orange-red pome, 12–22 mm diam.; nutlets 3–5.

HABITAT/RANGE Native. Thickets in rocky prairies, on hillsides, or along streams, 100–400 m; barely entering the West in c. Tex., northeast to e. Kans., s. Mo.

COCKSPUR HAWTHORN *Crataegus crus-galli* L.

QUICK ID The combination of nearly hairless, dark green leaves with very short petioles, and dull red fruits with 1–3 seeds helps identify this species, which occurs in the West only in c. Texas.

Deciduous tree to about 10 m tall, usually with a single erect trunk and a broad, rounded crown with rigid branches. **BRANCH** Thorns stout, straight or curved, brown to black, to 15 cm long. **LEAF** Oblanceolate, narrowly obovate, or spatulate, leathery, base wedge-shaped, tip rounded; margins finely toothed at least toward the tip, the teeth often blunt. Upper surface dark green, lustrous, hairless; lower surface paler, hairy on the midvein. Blade

2–8 cm long, 1–3 cm broad; petiole 0–5 mm long. **FLOWER** 10–15 mm diam.; petals white, circular; stamens 10, sometimes 20, anthers whitish, yellowish, pink, or rose. May–Jun. **FRUIT** Round or barrel-shaped, dull red pome, 8–15 mm long.

HABITAT/RANGE Native. In thickets and woodlands, wet areas, pastures, 0–1,500 m; a widespread eastern species entering the West in c. Tex.

TRACY HAWTHORN *Crataegus tracyi* Ashe ex Eggl.

QUICK ID This hawthorn of Texas has unlobed, thin leaves, pink anthers, and a hairy fruit.

Deciduous thorny shrub or spreading tree to 4.5 m tall; trunk to 30 cm diam. **BRANCH** Thorns straight, dark gray, lustrous, 2.5–5 cm long. **TWIG** Pubescent, dark gray by the 2nd year. **LEAF** Alternate, simple, somewhat thin; elliptic, diamond-shaped, or round; upper surface dark green, lustrous, rough short-hairy; lower surface yellow-green and hairy on the veins; veins about 6 pairs; margins unlobed, sharply saw-toothed with gland-tipped teeth. Blade 3–4 cm long, 2–3 cm wide; petiole 3–10 mm long. **FLOWER** 13–17 mm diam., 6–15 per cluster, stalks soft-hairy; petals white; hypanthium base hairy; stamens 10–20, anthers pink. Late Apr.–May. **FRUIT** Globose or ellipsoid orange-red pome, 8–10 mm diam., more or less hairy.

HABITAT/RANGE Native. Rocky stream banks, 300–1,500 m; w. and sc. Tex., ne. Mexico.

SIMILAR SPECIES Gregg Hawthorn has thicker leaves; Turners Hawthorn has lobed leaves and purple anthers.

Notes W. Tex. plants have 10 stamens, sc. Tex. plants usually 20.

REVERCHON HAWTHORN

COCKSPUR HAWTHORN

TRACY HAWTHORN

Reverchon Hawthorn

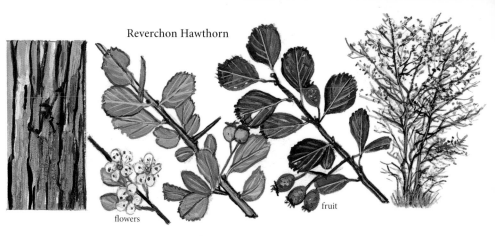

flowers

fruit

Cockspur Hawthorn

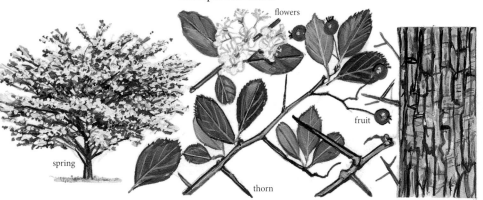

flowers

fruit

spring

thorn

Tracy Hawthorn

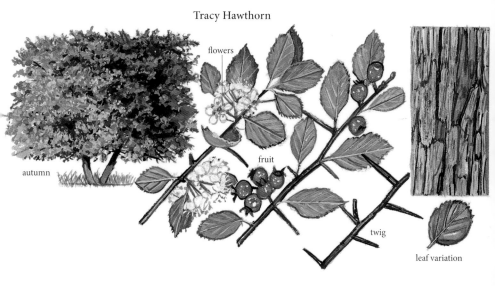

flowers

fruit

autumn

twig

leaf variation

GREGG HAWTHORN *Crataegus greggiana* Eggl.

QUICKID Broad, somewhat leathery, hairy leaves, small flowers, and hairy fruits characterize this hawthorn of Texas.

Deciduous, very thorny shrub or spreading tree, 3–6 m tall; trunk short, 4–15 cm diam. **BRANCH** Thorns, shiny, blackish, 2.5–5 cm long. **TWIG** At first matted-hairy and brownish, later hairless and gray. **LEAF** Alternate, simple, more or less leathery; broadly ovate to diamond-shaped, dull; upper surface sparsely rough short-hairy when mature, lower surface hairy on the veins; veins 5–6 pairs; margins unlobed or with 2–4 shallow lobes, finely and doubly saw-toothed, teeth gland-tipped. Blade 2.5–7.5 cm long, 3–6 cm wide; petiole 6–12 mm long. **FLOWER** 10 mm diam.; 3–8 per cluster, stalks hairy; petals white; hypanthium hairy; stamens 10, anthers pink to purple. Apr. **FRUIT** Hairy, globose pome, brick red when mature, 7–11 mm diam.

HABITAT/RANGE Native. In brush, pastures, or woodland, 300–700 m; Edwards Plateau, Tex., ne. Mexico.

SIMILAR SPECIES Tracy Hawthorn grows in much the same area in c. Tex. It is distinguished by leaves that are on average larger, thin, not leathery, and have coarse teeth on the margins.

TURNERS HAWTHORN *Crataegus turnerorum* Enquist

QUICKID Restricted to sc. Tex., this hawthorn has comparatively long thorns, hairless leaves, 10–15 stamens with deep purple anthers, and a hairless red fruit.

Thorny shrub or tree, 1.5–4.5 m tall. **BRANCH** Thorns 2–5.5 cm long. **LEAF** Ovate to elliptic, hairless; margins doubly saw-toothed in upper half; blade 2.5–8 cm long; petiole 3–10 cm long. **FLOWER** 15–20 mm diam.; stamens 10–15, anthers deep purple. Inflorescence hairless. Apr.–May. **FRUIT** Hairless, globose red pome, 10–14 mm diam., not quite as long.

HABITAT/RANGE Native. Shaded streamsides, 300–1,500 m; sc. Tex.

WOOTON HAWTHORN *Crataegus wootoniana* Eggl.

QUICKID The combination of sharply toothed leaves with 3 or 4 pointed lobes per side; long, stout, gently curved thorns; and hairless, shiny red fruits distinguishes this hawthorn, found only in s. N.M.

Thorny deciduous shrub or small tree to 3 m tall **BRANCH** Thorns slightly curved, red-brown, 4 cm long. **LEAF** Ovate, base truncate or broadly wedge-shaped; margins sharply toothed, 3 or 4 pointed lobes per side; blade 3–5 cm long; petiole 1–2 cm long. **FLOWER** 10–12 mm diam.; stamens 10, anthers pink. Inflorescence hairless. Apr.–Jun. **FRUIT** Hairless, ellipsoid, shiny red pome, 8 mm diam.

HABITAT/RANGE Native. Streamsides, pine forests, 2,000–3,000 m; sw. N.M.

GREGG HAWTHORN   TURNERS HAWTHORN   WOOTON HAWTHORN

Gregg Hawthorn

flowers

fruit

Turners Hawthorn

twig

fruit

flowers

Wooton Hawthorn

flowers

fruit

twig

bud

autumn

TOYON *Heteromeles arbutifolia* (Lindl.) M. Roem.
A.K.A. CALIFORNIA HOLLY, CHRISTMAS BERRY, HOLLYBERRY

QUICK ID This red-fruited evergreen shrub or small tree has simple, sharply saw-toothed, lanceolate or oblanceolate leaves.

Evergreen unarmed shrub or tree to 10 m tall; when treelike with a short trunk to 30 cm diam. Crown round, ragged, with many ascending branches. **BARK** Thin, gray. **TWIG** Slender, dark reddish, pubescent when young, hairless later. **LEAF** Alternate, simple, ascending, leathery; lanceolate to oblanceolate, tapered at both ends, margins sharply and finely saw-toothed. Upper surface dark green and shiny; lower surface paler, duller. Blade 4–11 cm long, 2–4 cm wide; petiole 1–2.5 cm long. **FLOWER** Small (about 6 mm diam.), numerous, in branched round or flat-topped terminal clusters 10–15 cm wide; petals 5, white, roundish, 2–4 mm long; stamens 10, in 5 pairs opposite sepals; hypanthium inverse-conical, fleshy, 2–3 mm long, slightly narrower; ovary inferior, bearing 2 or 3 styles. Jun.–Jul. **FRUIT** Globose or somewhat pear-shaped, bright red pome, 5–10 mm diam., with 2 or 3 cells and 2 brown seeds per cell; sepals are persistent, incurved over top of pome.

HABITAT/RANGE Native. Common in chaparral, also in oak woodland or mixed conifer forest, 0–1,300 m; Calif. and Baja Calif.

SIMILAR SPECIES Other chaparral and woodland species may have lanceolate leaves, but none is sharply saw-toothed.

Notes Beginning in mid-autumn, Toyon produces colorful displays of brilliant red berrylike pomes that persist through winter, contrasting against the dark green foliage of chaparral shrubs. It was once

TOYON

harvested extensively for its berries during the Christmas season; Calif. law now affords the species protection. The berries are edible, astringent, and contain small quantities of cyanogenic compounds (which are destroyed by cooking). Black Bear (*Ursus americanus*), Coyote (*Canis latrans*), Raccoon (*Procyon lotor*), and many species of birds feed upon the berries.

QUINCE *Cydonia oblonga* Mill.

Deciduous shrub or small tree to 6 m tall; crown rounded. **LEAF** Alternate, simple, ovate or oblong; base tapered, rounded, or cordate; margins entire. Upper surface dark green, lower surface densely pale-hairy. Blade 5–10 cm long; petiole 8–20 mm long, subtended by a conspicuous stipule. **FLOWER** 4–5 mm diam.; petals 5, white to pale pink; stamens 20; styles 5. May–Jun. **FRUIT** Pear-shaped to globose yellow pome, fragrant, many-seeded, very hairy when young, less so later, 8.5–12 cm long. **HABITAT/RANGE** Introduced from the Middle East; occasional on old farms and ranches, sometimes slightly naturalized at low to moderate elevations; scattered across the U.S. *Notes* There is 1 species of *Cydonia*, native to the Middle East; it may be the "apple" of biblical temptation. Quince was transported by settlers, its fruit providing pectin for jams and jellies.

LOQUAT *Eriobotrya japonica* (Thunb.) Lindl.
A.K.A. JAPANESE PLUM

Evergreen shrub or small tree, 3–7 m tall. **TWIG** Stout, densely rusty-hairy. **LEAF** Alternate, simple, leathery, obovate or elliptic, wedge-shaped at the base, tapered at the tip; lateral veins parallel, often impressed, each terminating in a tooth at the margin. Upper surface dark green, lustrous, hairless; lower surface paler, densely rusty-felty. Blade 15–25 cm long; petiole about 7 mm long, hairy. **FLOWER** 10–15 mm diam.; petals 5, oval to circular, white or creamy white, fragrant; borne in hairy, branched terminal clusters. Mar.–May. **FRUIT** Pear-shaped to oblong yellow, orange, or whitish pome, 3–4 cm long, with 1 or 2 large seeds. **HABITAT/RANGE** Introduced from e. Asia; cultivated and escaped, 0–300 m; coastal c. Calif. southward, c. Tex., east to Fla. *Notes* *Eriobotrya* is a genus of about 30 species native to e. Asia.

Toyon

flowers

fruit

seed

Quince

flower

fruit

fruit section

seed

twig

Loquat

fruit

fruit section

LYONTREE *Lyonothamnus floribundus*
A. Gray
A.K.A. CATALINA IRONWOOD, CATALINA ISLAND
IRONWOOD

QUICK ID Lyontree has leaves that are dark and shiny on the upper surface and may be simple and entire-margined or finely toothed, or compound with large teeth; the bark is shaggy, peeling, and reddish, weathering to gray.

Evergreen unarmed tree or shrub, 4–15 m high; 1 to several trunks; crown dense, narrow, becoming broader with age or in the open. **BARK** Thin, peeling in long strips, the fresh bark reddish, weathering to silvery gray. **TWIG** At first pale orange and pubescent, later bright reddish, smooth, and shiny. **LEAF** Opposite, simple, palmately compound, or pinnately compound, leathery; when simple (subsp. *floribundus*), linear to oblong, margins entire to minutely scalloped or toothed, sometimes lobed near the base; when compound (subsp. *aspleniifolius* [Greene] P.H. Raven), ovate in outline, the primary leaflets 3–7, linear, divided into 10–15 pairs of forward-pointing, more or less triangular, broad-based secondary leaflets. Upper surface dark green and glossy; lower surface paler, pubescent. Blade 7–21 cm long; petiole 1–3 cm long. **FLOWER** Small, numerous, in flat-topped, loose terminal clusters, 10–20 cm wide. Each flower with 5 roundish white petals 4–5 mm long and about 15 stamens; hypanthium deeply cup-shaped, about 4 mm long, pubescent inside and out. Jun.–Jul. **FRUIT** Two woody follicles, splitting on their inner surface, 3–4 mm long, each usually containing 4 brown seeds.

HABITAT/RANGE Native. Found especially on north-facing slopes and in canyons, in chaparral and oak woodland, 20–500 m; only on the Channel Islands of Calif. (subsp. *floribundus* on Santa Catalina Island; subsp. *aspleniifolius* on Santa Cruz, Santa Rosa, and San Clemente islands).

LYONTREE

Notes This rare species has no known close relatives in the world. It is occasionally used as an ornamental in Calif. but is difficult to start from seeds or cuttings. In the wild it receives conservation protection, and reproduction by seed has been facilitated by removal of feral goats from its habitat. The subspecies thoroughly intergrade. As alluded by the name "ironwood," the wood is hard and heavy, but the rarity of the tree precludes commercial use. Fossils of *Lyonothamnus* are known from now arid regions of sw. U.S., the present populations representing relicts from a wider distribution.

■ *MALUS*: APPLES AND CRAB APPLES

The apple genus, containing 25–55 species, is found naturally in temperate North America and in Eurasia. Most species occur in moderately moist areas from sea-level to moderate elevations. There is only 1 native species in the West.

Deciduous shrubs or trees, occasionally semievergreen; often very twiggy; commonly with spur branches, rarely thorny. **BARK** Smooth when young, becoming rough, scaly, and flaking at maturity. **TWIG** Hairy or hairless, often reddish brown, usually unarmed, sometimes the spur branches sharp-tipped and thornlike; buds egg-shaped, scales overlapping, the inner enlarging as the bud matures, marking the base of the twig with obvious ring-like scars. **LEAF** Alternate, simple, toothed or slightly lobed; stipules threadlike, soon deciduous. **FLOWER** Showy, white to pink or carmine, borne in umbel-like clusters on spur shoots, radial, bisexual, sepals 5, petals 5, separate, stamens 15–50, all borne on the rim of a hypanthium; hypanthium with free funnel-shaped top and bulbous lower portion that is fused to the ovary; ovary inferior, with 2–5 chambers. **FRUIT** Pome, the wall fleshy (without the stone or grit cells of the pear, *Pyrus*), the layer surrounding the seeds resembling stiff parchment. Seeds chestnut brown, lustrous, 1 or 2 per chamber.

The apple is probably the most important temperate fruit, entering cultivation some 6,000 years ago from a species still persisting in the w. Himalayan region, spreading at first along the ancient Silk Road. Dwarf rootstocks were discovered in w. Asia around 300 B.C. There are now perhaps 7,500 cultivars throughout the world. Those with fruits 5 cm or less in diam. are usually called crab apples. The earliest apple orchard in North America is believed to have been near Boston, established in 1625. Apples are very closely related to pears, and sometimes

Lyontree

flowers

fruit

leaf
variation

seeds

Japanese Flowering Crab Apple

flowers

spring

fruit

both are placed in the same genus (*Pyrus*). Apples must cross-pollinate, so the orchard industry relies on commercial bee enterprises.

JAPANESE FLOWERING CRAB APPLE
Malus floribunda Siebold ex Van Houtte

Deciduous tree, 4–8 m tall; crown rounded, densely branched, branches arching, often drooping with age. **TWIG** Hairy at first, later hairless. **LEAF** Ovate-elliptic to oblong-ovate, usually wedge-shaped at the base, pinched to a pointed tip; margins sharply and coarsely toothed. Upper surface lustrous, dark green; lower surface hairy at first, later hairless. Blade 4–8 cm long; petiole 1.5–2.5 cm long. **FLOWER** 2.5–4 cm diam., fragrant; petals 5, deep pink to reddish in bud, opening white or pale pink; stamens numerous; styles 5. Mar.–Apr. **FRUIT** Globose pome, yellowish, often blushed red, or red, about 1 cm diam. **HABITAT/RANGE** Introduced from e. Asia; cultivated and sporadically escaped in the U.S., perhaps in w. Ore. *Notes* There are numerous cultivars.

WESTERN CRAB APPLE *Malus fusca*
(Raf.) C.K. Schneid.
A.K.A. OREGON CRAB APPLE, PACIFIC CRAB APPLE

QUICK ID This crab apple bears its flowers and pomes in clusters; plants are not armed with thorns.

Deciduous thicket-forming shrub or small tree, 3–12 m tall; trunk to 45 cm diam.; crown spreading. **BARK** Thin, pale red-brown to grayish brown at maturity, with large peeling, plate-like scales. **TWIG** Slender, spreading, when new covered by crinkled hairs; after the 1st winter hairless, shining, reddish; later becoming dark brown flecked with well-spaced pale lenticels; short, stiff, spurs bearing leaves, flowers, and fruits develop on older twigs. Buds egg-shaped, chestnut brown, 1–3.5 mm long, scales overlapping, the inner scales becoming reddish. **LEAF** Alternate, simple, firm, broadly lanceolate to ovate-oblong, broadly tapered or rounded at the base, pointed or pinched to a narrow point at the tip; major veins conspicuously raised, the minor veins making a netlike pattern; margins toothed, sometimes also shallowly few-lobed; green and mostly hairless above, paler and soft-hairy beneath. Foliage is scarlet or orange in autumn, making this one of the few western trees adding red to the mostly yellow and green autumn forest palette. Blade 3–10 cm long, 1.5–4 cm wide; petiole 2.5–3.5 cm long, stiff, soft-hairy. **FLOWER** Borne in round or flattish umbel-like clusters of 5–12 flowers. Individual flowers showy, bisexual, radial, 16–22 mm diam., delicately fragrant, carried on a hairy stalk 2–3 cm long. Petals 5, white or pale pink, obovate, with short, broad stalk. Stamens about 20, shorter than petals; anthers yellow. Hypanthium hairless or downy. Apr.–Jul. **FRUIT** Barrel- or egg-shaped (broad end often near the tip) pome, reddish purple or blackish, less commonly yellowish; 10–16 mm long, borne in clusters on drooping stalks; flesh thin, mealy, sour.

WESTERN CRAB APPLE

HABITAT/RANGE Native. Moist woods, low places, often forming thickets near the mouths of rivers, 0–800 m; near the coast from Alaska to n. Calif.

SIMILAR SPECIES This is the only native crab apple in the West, its oval fruits unique in North America. It resembles a hawthorn, but the plants are not thorny.

COMMON APPLE *Malus pumila* Mill.
A.K.A. PARADISE APPLE

QUICK ID The non-thorny twigs, densely hairy buds, unlobed leaves with a hairy lower surface, and large fruit are diagnostic.

Deciduous medium-size tree, 6–13 m tall, 30–140 cm diam.; single short, erect trunk, usually branching low to the ground; crown dense, broad, rounded; branches crooked, spreading or ascending, often with an abundance of short spur shoots. **BARK** Usually smooth when young, becoming grayish and peeling to reveal a smooth reddish inner bark; young and mature bark sharply contrasted. **TWIG** Stout, lacking thorns, finely hairy, especially when young; terminal bud egg-shaped, densely hairy, bearing short spur shoots. **LEAF** Typically clustered near the ends of spur shoots, simple, firm; oval or elliptic, usually broadly wedge-shaped at the base, tip bluntly or sharply pointed, margins finely toothed. Upper surface dark green, hairy at first, becoming hairless; lower surface paler, hairy. Blade 4–10 cm long, 3–6 cm broad; petiole 1.5–3 cm long, stout, hairy. **FLOWER** 2.5–4 cm diam., sepals 5, green, hairy; petals 5, pinkish white or white; stamens numerous; styles 5. May–Jun. **FRUIT** Globose or slightly ellipsoid pome, green at first, becoming red or yellow, 7–10 cm long, 5–9 cm diam.

HABITAT/RANGE Introduced from Eurasia; cultivated, now widely and sporadically naturalized in fields, along roadsides and fencelines, and near old homesites, 0–1,500 m; throughout much of the U.S., but rarely naturalizing in the Great Plains states.

SIMILAR SPECIES Japanese Flowering Crab Apple and Western Crab Apple have much smaller fruits; in the latter the twigs are more or less thorny.

Notes This is the apple of commerce. Thousands of cultivars have been selected based on fruit color, taste, and size. Fruits of escaped seedlings and untended plants are often of lesser quality.

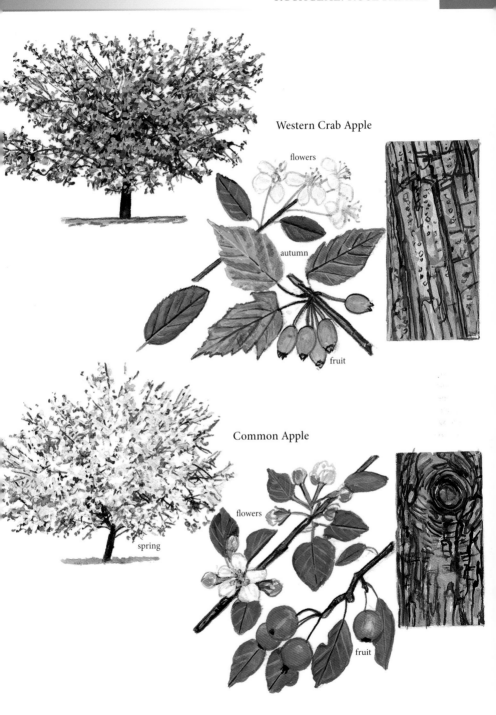

Western Crab Apple

flowers

autumn

fruit

Common Apple

spring

flowers

fruit

■ *PRUNUS*: CHERRIES, PLUMS, PEACHES, AND APRICOTS

There are more than 200 species of *Prunus*, found nearly worldwide in temperate areas, and most abundant in north temperate regions and the Andean region of South America. They occur in open woods, woodland margins, stream banks, bottomlands, dunes, pastures, old fields, and roadside thickets, and are especially common in disturbed sites at low to moderate elevations. Major relationships within the genus are under study, and within the genus the number of species is unsettled. Only about a half-dozen species are native to the West. The combination of glands near the top of the petiole, toothed leaves, showy flowers, abundant fruit, and crushed twigs with the odor of bitter almond helps distinguish the genus. In general, the cherries have true terminal buds projecting from the ends of the twigs and usually lack sharp-tipped spur branches, while plums have offset or axillary buds and usually sharp-tipped spur branches.

Deciduous or evergreen shrubs or trees of moderate size, mostly erect, with 1 or multiple trunks; several species sucker from the roots or base and form distinctive clonal thickets. **BARK** On young trees smooth, occasionally finely fissured, reddish brown or grayish; at maturity often becoming scaly, furrowed, or broken into small plates, often darker, sometimes blackish, a few species exfoliating in curly plates; several species with horizontal lenticels, especially evident on young trees. **TWIG** Reddish brown or grayish, hairy or not, often with a grayish skinlike covering that peels off; usually with the odor of bitter almond when crushed. Long branches often bear short shoots, thorny or not. **LEAF** Alternate, simple, thin or leathery, linear or lanceolate, often clustered near the tips of short shoots; margins usually toothed, the teeth often glandular; petiole hairy or not, usually 1 or more glands near the upper end of the petiole or at the blade margin near the petiole attachment. **FLOWER** One or many, borne in often showy racemes, corymbs, or umbellate fascicles, typically opening in spring, with or before leaf emergence, usually bisexual (when unisexual, plants dioecious); petals 5, white, pink, or dark pink, circular, elliptic, or obovate; stamens 10–30; ovary 1, free from the usually deciduous hypanthium. **FRUIT** Globose or egg-shaped drupe, hairy or not; yellowish, reddish, dark purple, or black at maturity; with a single stone.

The genus is economically important for fruits and nuts, spirits, seed oils, flowering ornamentals, folk medicines, and cabinetry wood.

AMERICAN PLUM *Prunus americana* Marshall
A.K.A. WILD PLUM

QUICKID Within the region, this is the only *Prunus* with thorny twigs and hairless leaves.

Deciduous thicket-forming shrub to small, erect tree to 5 m tall; trunk to about 20 cm diam. **BRANCH** Often bears short thorn-tipped shoots when young. **BARK** Young bark smooth, reddish brown, with conspicuous horizontal lenticels, becoming tan, gray, or nearly black, conspicuously scaly, flaking off in curly plates. **TWIG** Hairy or hairless, sometimes thorn-tipped on short leafy shoots. **LEAF** Alternate, simple, elliptic to obovate or narrowly ovate, base rounded or wedge-shaped, tip abruptly pinched to a point; margins coarsely and sharply single- or double-toothed, the teeth broad at the base and abruptly pinched to a narrow, glandless tip. Upper surface hairless, lower surface hairless or hairy along the midvein and lateral veins. Blade 4–12 cm long, 2–5.5 cm broad; petiole 4–19 mm long, usually hairy, rarely hairless, lacking glands. **FLOWER** 20–25 mm diam.; petals white, often becoming pink with age. Apr.–Jun. **FRUIT** Globose or ellipsoid red, orange, or yellowish drupe, 1.5–3 cm diam., hairless, often glaucous; stone flattened, smooth.

HABITAT/RANGE Native. Forest margins, valleys, along streams, near old homesteads, 1,200–2,100 m; in the West, primarily in the Rocky Mountain region from Mont. to N.M., eastward throughout much of the e. U.S.

Notes Carried to many places in the West by pioneers. About 260 horticultural forms have been derived from American Plum, underscoring the variability across its expansive range.

CHICKASAW PLUM *Prunus angustifolia* Marshall
A.K.A. SANDHILL PLUM, SAND PLUM

QUICKID The spiny habit and small upfolded leaves with gland-tipped teeth on the margins serve to distinguish Chickasaw Plum within the region.

Deciduous thicket-forming shrub or small tree to about 6 m tall; trunks usually multiple, occasionally to 50 cm diam. **BARK** Dark reddish brown or grayish, splitting but not peeling with age. **TWIG**

American Plum

flowers

stone

stone

young twig

flowers

fruit

spring

Chickasaw Plum

older twig

Slender, rigid, slightly zigzag, hairless, the short lateral twigs often thorn-tipped. **LEAF** Alternate, simple, lanceolate, narrowly elliptic, or oblong, usually folded upward and trough- or trowel-like, base wedge-shaped, tip narrowly pointed; margins with fine, blunt teeth tipped with tiny reddish or yellowish glands, often shrinking in size and falling with age, leaving a callus. Upper surface lustrous, bright green, hairless; lower surface duller, usually sparsely hairy, at least along the veins. Blade 1.5–8 cm long, 1–2.5 cm broad; petiole 2–14 mm long, sparsely hairy, rarely hairless, usually lacking glands or with 1 or 2 glands near the blade. **FLOWER** 7–10 mm diam.; petals white; stamens 10–20, filaments white, anthers yellow. Apr.–Jun. **FRUIT** Ovoid or ellipsoid, shiny red or yellow drupe, 1.5–2.5 cm diam., pleasant tasting, ripening in summer.

HABITAT/RANGE Native. Old fields, sandy areas, open woods, fencelines, roadsides, rural homesites, 0–600 m; barely entering the West from Nebr. and N.M. to c. Tex., widely distributed eastward.

fruit

Chickasaw Plum

AMERICAN PLUM

CHICKASAW PLUM

APRICOT *Prunus armeniaca* L.

Deciduous small tree, 5–10 m tall, with a rounded crown and hairless twigs. **LEAF** Alternate, simple, broadly ovate or triangular to nearly circular, base usually rounded, tip often abruptly pinched to a short point; margins with gland-tipped teeth; 1–5 large glands near attachment of petiole to blade. Upper surface hairless, lower surface hairy along the veins. Blade 3–9 cm long, 2–8 cm broad; petiole 12–45 mm long. **FLOWER** 1.5–2.5 cm diam.; petals pink in bud, opening white. Mar.–Apr. **FRUIT** Finely hairy, globose or ellipsoid yellow or orange drupe, 2–6 cm diam., stone not pitted on its surface. **HABITAT/RANGE** Introduced from China; disturbed sites, 0–1,600 m; cultivated and widely escaped in the U.S. *Notes* This is the apricot of commerce; most of those grown for the U.S. market are cultivated in Calif.

SWEET CHERRY *Prunus avium* (L.) L.
A.K.A. Mazzard

QUICK ID This species has double-toothed leaves with a hairy lower surface, a glandular petiole, and shiny red to dark purplish fruit.

Deciduous tree, 9–18 m tall, usually with a single erect, straight or crooked trunk, 30–50 cm diam. **BARK** Mature bark grayish to dark purplish red, fissured, and marked with conspicuous lenticels, peeling in horizontal strips. **LEAF** Alternate, simple, obovate, tip abruptly pinched to a distinctive point; margins with sharp, ascending teeth tipped with glands; 2–5 reddish glands near the top of the petiole. Upper surface dark green with impressed veins, lower surface hairy. Blade 8–15 cm long, 4–6 cm broad; petiole 2–4 cm long. **FLOWER** 2.5–3.5 cm diam., borne in an umbel; petals white, long-stalked. Mar.–May. **FRUIT** Globose to egg-shaped, bright, shiny yellow to red or dark purple-black drupe, about 2.5 cm diam.

HABITAT/RANGE Introduced from w. Asia; widely cultivated for its fruit; commonly escaped across the U.S., less frequently in the Great Plains states, at low to moderate elevations.

SIMILAR SPECIES Similar to Sour Cherry, but that has smaller fruit, smaller leaves, and lacks glands on the petiole.

CHERRY PLUM *Prunus cerasifera* Ehrh.
A.K.A. Myrobalan Plum

Deciduous tree, 4–8 m tall, usually with a single trunk to 35 cm diam.; crown dense, oval, with ascending branches. **BARK** Dark gray, furrowed in age. **TWIG** Purplish, hairless. **LEAF** Green or purplish, elliptic-obovate, base blunt, tip bluntly pointed; margins with blunt, gland-tipped teeth; petiole lacking glands at the top. Upper surface hairless, lower surface hairy along the veins. Blade 3–7 cm long, 1.5–3.5 cm broad; petiole 5–20 cm long. **FLOWER** One or 2 per cluster, 1.5–2.5 cm diam., petals white or pink. Feb.–Apr. **FRUIT** Hairless, globose or ellipsoid purplish-red or yellow drupe, 1.5–3 cm diam. **HABITAT/RANGE** Introduced from Asia; roadsides, stream banks, 0–900 m; escaped from cultivation in several w. states, also e. U.S. *Notes* The purple-leaved form is especially popular in cultivation.

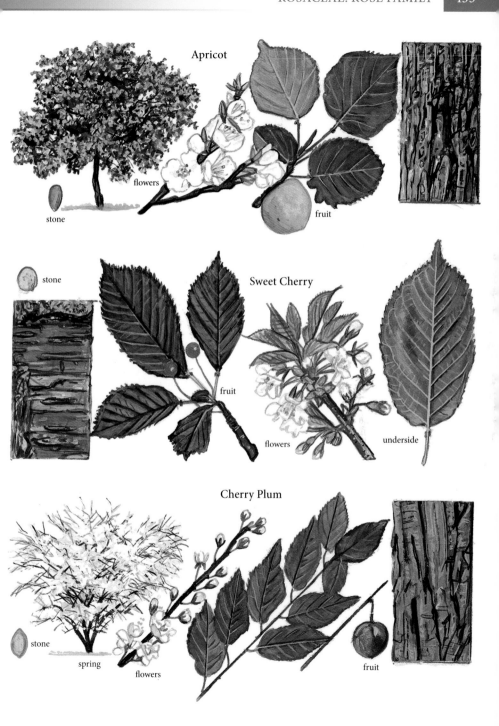

Apricot

flowers

stone

fruit

Sweet Cherry

stone

fruit

flowers

underside

Cherry Plum

stone

spring

flowers

fruit

SOUR CHERRY *Prunus cerasus* L.
A.K.A. PIE CHERRY

Deciduous shrub or small tree to about 6 m tall, with 1 or multiple trunks; crown oval or vase-shaped. **LEAF** Elliptic, oblanceolate, or obovate, abruptly short-pointed; margins sharply double-toothed. Upper surface hairless, lower surface hairy along the veins. Petiole hairless, usually glandless or with poorly developed glands. **FLOWER** Usually 3 per cluster; petals white, 7–9 mm long. Apr.–May. **FRUIT** Drupe bright red, hairless, usually less than 2 cm diam. **HABITAT/RANGE** Introduced from Eurasia; moist, disturbed areas, mostly below 2,000 m; widely cultivated and sporadically escaped across the U.S. *Notes* There are many cultivated varieties.

EUROPEAN PLUM *Prunus domestica* L.
A.K.A. COMMON PLUM

QUICK ID The combination of usually wrinkled leaves with coarsely toothed margins, relatively large fruit, and usually hairy twigs helps distinguish European Plum.

Deciduous shrub or small tree, 2–10 m tall, usually with a single erect trunk; crown dense, round, low-branching. **TWIG** Usually hairy. **LEAF** Alternate, simple, elliptic or obovate, somewhat wavy or wrinkled, base wedge-shaped or bluntly rounded, tip acute or pinched to a point; margins coarsely single- or double-toothed, the teeth blunt and gland-tipped; 0–3 glands near the upper end of the petiole. Upper surface hairless or hairy on the midvein, lower surface hairy throughout. **FLOWER** 1–3 per cluster, 1.5–2.5 cm diam.; petals white, about 1 cm long. Apr.–May. **FRUIT** Hairless, globose or ellipsoid blue-black, green, yellow, or reddish drupe, 1.5–3.5 cm diam.

HABITAT/RANGE Introduced from Eurasia; disturbed sites, escaped from cultivation, 0–1,500 m; scattered throughout much of the U.S., in the West more common in the Northwest.

Notes Included within this species are the yellow-fleshed plums and the Italian prune. The red-fleshed plums of commerce are mostly variants of the Japanese or Satsuma Plum (*P. salicina* Lindl.).

ALMOND *Prunus dulcis* (Mill.) D.A. Webb

Small tree, 4–10 m tall; crown open, spreading. **BARK** Dark, furrowed, hard. **LEAF** Oblong-lanceolate, hairless, 2.5–12 cm long, 5–20 mm wide, broadly wedge-shaped at the base, tip long-tapered to a point, margins finely toothed. **FLOWER** White to pink, 3–5 cm diam. Feb.–Mar., before or with the leaves. **FRUIT** More or less flattened, ovoid drupe, 3–6 cm long; outer layer grayish green, velvety, leathery, splitting and exposing a rough stone (containing the edible seed, or "nut"). **HABITAT/RANGE** Introduced from w. Asia; a waif in c. Calif. or persisting in abandoned orchards in the Coast Ranges; may persist after planting elsewhere in the West.

BITTER CHERRY *Prunus emarginata*
(Douglas) Eaton
A.K.A. OREGON CHERRY, QUININE CHERRY, WILD CHERRY, FIRE CHERRY, WESTERN PIN CHERRY

QUICK ID The flowers and fruits are on long stalks and occur in small clusters; and the leaves usually have a tapered base and margins with fine, blunt, gland-tipped teeth.

Deciduous low, thicket-forming shrub to moderate-size tree, 1–18 m tall, rarely to 30 m; trunk short, straight, 3–35 cm diam. Plants mostly hairless or pubescent throughout. **BARK** Smooth, reddish purple when young, when older becoming gray, with horizontal patches of dark and light gray bands and long orange lenticels. **TWIG** Green, usually pubescent at first, becoming shiny reddish purple, flecked with pale lenticels. Buds chestnut-brown, 3 mm long, pointed; scales overlapping, with translucent edges, inner scales translucent with a reddish tip, up to 10 mm long as bud enlarges. **LEAF** Alternate, simple, thin; elliptic, oblong-obovate, or oblanceolate, base rounded to slender-tapered, tip rounded or pointed; margins finely blunt-toothed, the teeth glandular; 1 or 2 (to 4) large dark glands near the top of the petiole. Upper surface dark green; lower surface paler and usually more densely pubescent. Blade 3–8 cm long, 8–30 mm wide; petiole 5–12 mm long. **FLOWER** 8–12 mm diam., delicately fragrant, 3–10 in short, branched, rounded clusters,

BITTER CHERRY

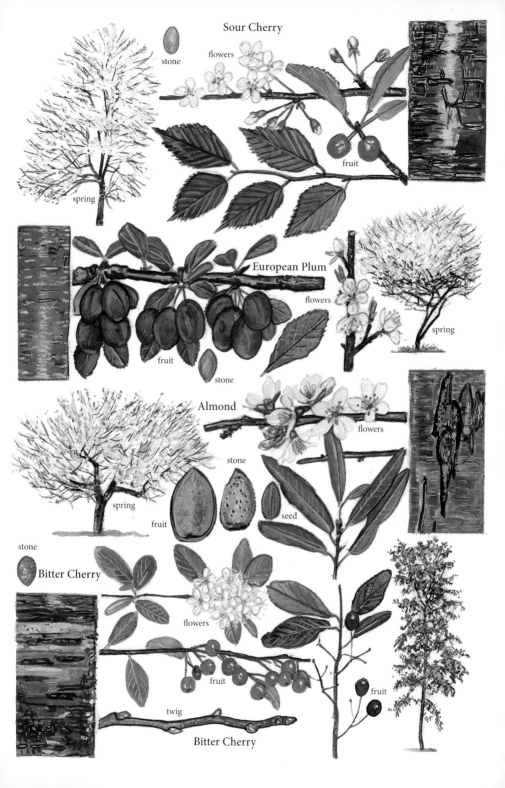

Sour Cherry

stone

flowers

fruit

spring

European Plum

flowers

fruit

stone

spring

Almond

flowers

stone

fruit

seed

spring

stone

Bitter Cherry

flowers

fruit

fruit

twig

Bitter Cherry

BITTER CHERRY *continued*

appearing before or with the leaves. Petals white tinged with green, obovate, rounded or notched at the tip; stamens about 20, with dark anthers; hypanthium funnel-shaped, 2.5–3.5 mm long, orange inside. Apr.–Jun. **FRUIT** Small globose drupe, 8–12 mm long, hanging at the ends of slender stalks in a cluster, red early in maturity, later nearly black, the flesh thin, bitter, and astringent; stone 3 mm long.

HABITAT/RANGE Native. Moist areas, often where open and disturbed, 0–2,700 m; sw. Canada to Ariz. and N.M.

SIMILAR SPECIES Leaves are gradually tapered to slender point in Pin Cherry, which is from mostly east of the Continental Divide; Chokecherry has flowers and fruits in racemes.

DESERT APRICOT *Prunus fremontii* S. Watson

QUICK ID This desert shrub or small tree native to s. Calif. may be recognized by the combination of intricately branched, often thorn-tipped twigs, flowers with 5 broad white petals, and a small yellowish velvety drupe.

Usually a deciduous, intricately and rigidly branched shrub, 1.5–4 m tall, rarely a small tree. **TWIG** Hairless, often spine-tipped. **LEAF** Roundish to ovate, 1–2 cm long, about as wide or less, finely toothed, hairless. **FLOWER** 10–12 mm diam.; petals 5, white. Feb.–Mar. **FRUIT** Yellowish velvety drupe, ellipsoid, often pointed, creased on 1 side, 8–14 mm long.

HABITAT/RANGE Native. Dry canyons and slopes, 200–1,200 m; s. Calif., Baja Calif.

HOLLYLEAF CHERRY *Prunus ilicifolia* (Nutt. ex Hook. & Arn.) D. Dietr.
A.K.A. ISLAY, EVERGREEN CHERRY

QUICK ID Coarsely toothed leathery leaves and white flowers in dense spikelike clusters serve to distinguish this species.

Compact evergreen, mostly hairless shrub or tree to 9 m tall. **LEAF** Alternate, simple, stiff, oval to roundish; upper surface dark green and shiny, lower surface yellow-green; margins usually coarsely toothed and wavy, the teeth gland-tipped (margins entire on plants from the Channel Islands). Blade mostly 2–5 cm long; petiole mostly 8–12 mm long. **FLOWER** Bisexual, radial, 8 mm diam., few to many in dense spike-like clusters 3–6 cm long; petals white. Apr.–May. **FRUIT** Ovoid drupe, 1.2–1.5 cm long, red to nearly black at maturity, flesh thin, juicy, sweet.

HABITAT/RANGE Native. Chaparral, woodland, 0–1,500 m; Coast Ranges, c. Calif. to Baja Calif.

SIMILAR SPECIES Hollyleaf Redberry (*Rhamnus ilicifolia* Kellogg) has similar leaves but is a shrub that has unisexual flowers with no petals and drupes with 2–4 stones.

Notes Hollyleaf Cherry has 2 subspecies: subsp. *ilicifolia*, with leaves 2–5 cm long, the margins toothed and wavy, and a mainland distribution; and subsp. *lyoni* (Eastw.) P.H. Raven (Catalina Cherry), with leaves 6–12 cm long, the margins entire, and a Channel Islands distribution.

COMMON CHERRY-LAUREL *Prunus laurocerasus* L.

Dense evergreen shrub or small tree to 9 m tall; crown broad, rounded. **LEAF** Elliptic to oblong, 3–13 cm long, 1–3 cm wide, hairless, leathery, entire or toothed in the upper half. **FLOWER** Creamy white, 8 mm diam., many in erect racemes 3–10 cm long. Mar.–May. **FRUIT** Hairless, ovoid purplish-black drupe, 8 mm long. **HABITAT/RANGE** Introduced from se. Europe and nearby Asia; disturbed areas, mostly below 200 m; B.C. to Calif.

DESERT APRICOT   HOLLYLEAF CHERRY

Desert Apricot

flower

immature fruit

fruit

spring

Hollyleaf Cherry

flowers

fruit

flowers

Common Cherry-laurel

fruit

fruit

PORTUGAL CHERRY-LAUREL *Prunus lusitanica* L.

Very similar to Common Cherry-laurel. **LEAF** Oblong to oblong-ovate, petiole often reddish. **FLOWER** White, in spreading racemes 15–25 cm long. May–Jun. **FRUIT** More or less conical, dark purple drupe, about 8 mm long. **HABITAT/RANGE** Introduced from sw. Europe and nw. Africa; woods, fields, mostly below 200 m; Wash. to n. Calif. *Notes* Considered invasive in the Northwest. The fruit, inedible to humans, is relished and spread by birds, and plants easily establish in shaded woods.

MAHALEB CHERRY *Prunus mahaleb* L.

Deciduous small tree to about 10 m tall. **TWIG** Densely pubescent. **LEAF** Oval to nearly circular, the tip pinched to a sharp point; margins finely toothed with blunt glandular teeth; 1 or 2 reddish glands near the top of the petiole. Upper surface lustrous, dark green; lower surface paler, hairy on the midvein. Blade 2.5–5 cm long; petiole 5–20 mm long. **FLOWER** Borne in axillary racemes of 10 or fewer flowers 3–4 cm long. Individual flowers about 18 mm diam.; petals white, circular. Apr. **FRUIT** Hairless, globose black or reddish black drupe, about 8 mm diam. **HABITAT/RANGE** Introduced from Eurasia; disturbed areas, chaparral, bluffs, riverbanks, 0–1,100 m; sporadically escaped from cultivation, B.C. and Mont., south to s. Calif., n. Utah, n. Colo., e. U.S. *Notes* Introduced for budding stock for commercial cherries; the wood is used for cherrywood pipes.

MEXICAN PLUM *Prunus mexicana*
S. Watson
A.K.A. BIGTREE PLUM

QUICK ID The combination of leaves with a hairy lower surface and coarsely, sharply toothed margins, and hairy twigs and flower stalks, helps distinguish Mexican Plum, which enters the West only in c. Tex.

Deciduous tree, 3–12 m tall, usually with a single erect trunk to 45 cm diam.; crown open, irregular, rounded. **TWIG** Hairless when mature. **LEAF** Alternate, simple, thickish, elliptic to oblong or obovate, base usually rounded, tip abruptly pinched to a point; margins coarsely double-toothed, the teeth sharp, not gland-tipped; petiole usually hairy, with 1–4 glands near the top. Upper surface hairless, lustrous yellow-green, veins impressed; lower surface densely hairy. Blade 6–12 cm long, 3–7 cm broad; petiole 4–18 mm long. **FLOWER** Up to 4 per cluster, 20–25 mm diam.; petals white, sometimes fading to pink. Mar. **FRUIT** Rounded or ellipsoid red or dark blue drupe, usually glaucous, 1.5–3 cm diam.

HABITAT/RANGE Native. Open areas, 10–400 m; sc. U.S. to n. Mexico, barely entering the West in c. Tex.

MEXICAN PLUM

Portugal Cherry-laurel

flowers

fruit

Mahaleb Cherry

fruit

stone

flowers

spring

fruit

Mexican Plum

flowers

fruit

spring

EUROPEAN BIRD CHERRY *Prunus padus* L.

QUICKID Identified by the combination of sharply toothed leaves, the teeth without glands, small black fruit, and smooth bark.

Deciduous large shrub or medium-size tree, 9–12 m tall, usually with a single erect trunk; crown low-branching, rounded, with ascending branches. **BARK** Gray, smooth to finely roughened. **LEAF** Alternate, simple, obovate or elliptic, base wedge-shaped, tip abruptly pinched to a point; margins finely and sharply toothed, without glands; petiole hairless or finely hairy, with 1–4 glands near the upper end. Upper surface dull, dark green; lower surface grayish, usually hairless except for tufts of hairs in the vein axils. Foliage turns yellow or bronze in autumn. Blade 5–13 cm long, 2.5–5 cm broad; petiole 8–20 mm long. **FLOWER** In erect or drooping racemes of 5–15 flowers 8–15 cm long. Individual flowers 8–14 mm diam., petals white. Apr.–May. **FRUIT** Globose black drupe, 4–8 mm in diam.

HABITAT/RANGE Introduced from Eurasia; escaped from cultivation, 0–1,700 m; established in the Pacific Northwest, the Northeast, and adjacent se. Canada.

SIMILAR SPECIES Very similar to Chokecherry, but the petals of European Bird Cherry average 6–9 mm long (2.5–4 mm in Chokecherry), and the sepals are 1.2–2 mm long, with the length greater than width (0.7–1 mm in Chokecherry, the length about equal to the width).

PIN CHERRY *Prunus pensylvanica* L. f.
A.K.A. Fire Cherry

QUICKID Easily identified among the cherries by the red twig and long-tapering or pointed, lanceolate, finely toothed leaf.

Deciduous shrub or small tree, 8–12 m tall, usually with a single erect, straight trunk 20–25 cm diam.; crown open, rounded, with slender, ascending or spreading branches. Often produces suckers from the root crown, especially following injury. **BARK** Reddish brown, lustrous, with numerous well-spaced horizontal lenticels; at maturity fissured and peeling in papery plates. **TWIG** Slender, lustrous reddish at first, becoming reddish brown; marked by orange lenticels; with an almond odor when crushed. **LEAF** Alternate, simple, lanceolate, thin, often folded upward from the midvein; base tapered or rounded; tip long-tapering, often curved near the point; margins finely, sharply, and unevenly toothed, teeth gland-tipped; petiole with 1–3 glands near the upper end. Upper surface lustrous yellow-green, hairless; lower surface paler, hairless. Foliage turns red, maroon, or orange in autumn. Blade 2.5–14 cm long, to about 5 cm broad; petiole 1–2 cm long. **FLOWER** In clusters of 2–8. Individual flowers 1–1.2 cm diam., petals white; stamens conspicuous, 15 or more. Apr.–Jun. **FRUIT** Rounded, bright red drupe, 6–8 mm long; stalk slender, 1.5–2 cm long; ripens mid- or late summer.

HABITAT/RANGE Native. Roadsides, fields, clearings and similar disturbed areas, 0–2,800 m; across much of the southern half of Canada, sporadically south in the Rocky Mountains to sc. Colo. and south to n. Ga. in e. U.S.

SIMILAR SPECIES The long-tapering, narrower leaf distinguishes Pin Cherry from Black Cherry, which has elliptic, medium-width leaves; and Chokecherry, whose shorter, wider leaves have an abruptly pointed tip.

Notes Plants in the Rocky Mountains and n. Great Plains are mostly shrubby, with leaves often shorter than 6 cm. This fast-growing, short-lived cherry favors disturbance. Seeds are dispersed widely by birds, remain viable for many years in the soil, and germinate quickly following fire or mechanical disturbance. Pin Cherry is intolerant of shade and is overtopped and soon displaced by canopy trees in a restored or maturing forest.

PEACH *Prunus persica* (L.) Batsch

Deciduous shrub or small tree, 3–10 m tall, usually with a single erect trunk; crown open, with usually ascending branches. **TWIG** Hairless. **LEAF** Alternate, simple, lanceolate, long-elliptic, or narrowly oblanceolate, often folded upward from the midrib, base wedge-shaped or

PIN CHERRY

European Bird Cherry

flowers

fruit

Pin Cherry

flowers

fruit

twig

Peach

flowers

stone

fruit section

bluntly rounded, tip long-tapering, often pinched to a point; margins finely and bluntly toothed, teeth gland-tipped; petiole often with 1–4 glands near the upper end, hairless. Surfaces bright green, hairless. Blade 4–15 cm long, 2–4.5 cm broad; petiole 5–15 mm long. **FLOWER** Single or in clusters of 2. Individual flowers 2–4 cm diam., petals rich pink. Feb.–Apr. **FRUIT** Globose yellowish or orange drupe, often blushed red, usually hairy, 4–8 cm diam., stone pitted on the surface. **HABITAT/RANGE** Introduced from China; waste places, 0–2,300 m; scattered across much of the U.S. *Notes* This is the peach of commerce; escaped plants are often shrubby.

CREEK PLUM *Prunus rivularis* Scheele
A.K.A. HOG PLUM

QUICK ID This wild plum has leaves that are typically greater than 2 cm broad, somewhat folded and trough-shaped, and with gland-tipped marginal teeth, glandular petioles, and flowers that open before or with leaf emergence.

Deciduous shrub, or rarely a small tree, to 8 m tall in the West, with a rounded crown and erect branches. **TWIG** Hairless, with numerous lenticels. **LEAF** Alternate, simple, lanceolate or narrowly oblong or elliptic, thin, usually folded upward and troughlike, base rounded or wedge-shaped, tip acute or pinched to a point; margins toothed, the teeth blunt, gland-tipped; petiole sparsely hairy, with 1–4 glands near the top. Upper surface light green, lustrous, hairless; lower surface paler, hairless or hairy along the veins. Blade 4–11 cm long, 1.5–5 cm broad; petiole 7–20 mm long. **FLOWER** In clusters of 2–4. Individual flowers 12–16 mm diam., petals white. Mar. **FRUIT** Hairless, globose, bright red, orange, or yellowish drupe, 1.2–2.5 cm diam.

HABITAT/RANGE Native. Thickets, woodland margins, stream banks, 200–1,000 m; much of e. U.S., extending westward to w. Tex. and se. Colo.; apparently introduced in Calif.

SIMILAR SPECIES Wild Goose Plum (*P. munsoniana* W. Wight & Hedrick) is now considered a larger form of Creek Plum.

BLACK CHERRY *Prunus serotina* Ehrh.

QUICK ID The combination of narrow leaves that have numerous veins flush with the lower surface and incurved marginal teeth, long flower clusters, and the hypanthium persistent on developing fruit helps distinguish this species.

Deciduous tree, 15–40 m tall; usually a single erect trunk to 80 cm diam. (to 150 cm in East), usually straight in forest-grown trees, sometimes crooked in open-grown trees; crown cylindric, usually with conspicuously drooping leaves. **BARK** Reddish brown, mostly smooth and with narrow, horizontal fissures when young, becoming gray or grayish black and conspicuously blocky at maturity. **TWIG** Slender, green at first, becoming reddish brown, hairless or densely hairy, with a bitter almond aroma when crushed; terminal bud 4–6 mm long, egg-shaped, reddish brown, darkest at the tip. **LEAF** Alternate, simple, more or less leathery, narrowly elliptic, oval, or oblong; margins finely and conspicuously toothed with gland- or callus-tipped incurving teeth; 1–6 glands near the upper end of the petiole. Upper surface lustrous green, hairless; lower surface paler, hairless, except the lower portion of the midvein often hairy. Veins 15–30 per side, flush with the lower surface. Foliage yellow or salmon-orange in autumn. Blade 2–15 cm long, 2.5–4 cm broad; petiole 4–20 mm long. **FLOWER** Borne in raceme of 18–90 flowers 10–12 cm long. Individual flowers about 6 mm diam., petals white, stamens 15 or more; hypanthium persistent upon developing fruit. Mar.–Jun. **FRUIT** Globose drupe, red at first, turning lustrous purplish black, 7–10 mm diam.

HABITAT/RANGE Native. Moist areas, margins of woods, open places, 0–2,500 m; Ariz. to central Tex., widespread in the East.

SIMILAR SPECIES Chokecherry has leaves with 6–13 veins per side, raised on the lower surface, and marginal teeth that are ascending or spreading; and the hypanthium soon drops from the developing fruit.

Notes Black Cherry has several varieties. In the West, most plants are Southwestern Black Cherry (var. *rufula* [Woot. & Standl.] McVaugh), with leathery leaves mostly 2–6 cm long and petioles 4–10 mm long. From c. Tex. eastward, var. *serotina* is common, with membranous leaves mostly 4–14 cm long and petioles 10–23 mm long. Measurements vary and the varieties intergrade.

CREEK PLUM   BLACK CHERRY

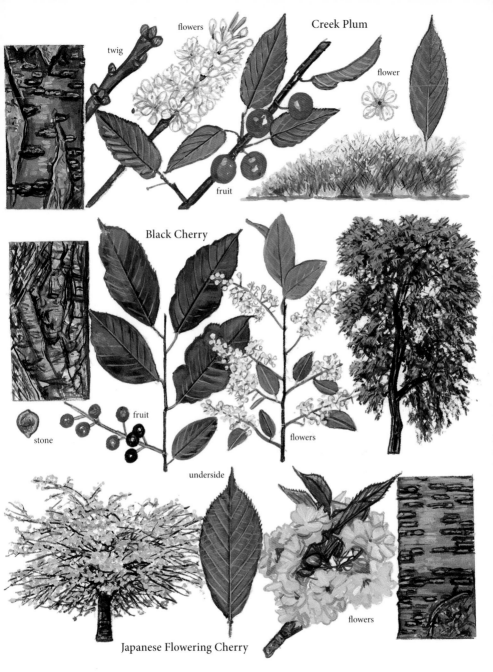

Creek Plum

twig

flowers

flower

fruit

Black Cherry

stone

fruit

flowers

underside

flowers

Japanese Flowering Cherry

JAPANESE FLOWERING CHERRY
Prunus speciosa (Koidz.) Nakai

Deciduous tree, 3–10 m tall. **LEAF** Hairless, ovate-lanceolate, pointed at tip; margins sharply toothed; 2–4 glands at top of petiole. Blade 5–13 cm long, 2.5–6.5 cm wide. **FLOWER** White or pink, 2–4 cm diam., 2–5 in short racemes. Apr.–May. **FRUIT** Blackish drupe, 8–10 mm long. **HABITAT/RANGE** Introduced from e. Asia; open woods, 0–100 m; c. Calif.

KLAMATH PLUM *Prunus subcordata* Benth.

A.K.A. PACIFIC PLUM, WESTERN PLUM, SIERRA PLUM

QUICK ID **A short, crooked, usually thorny tree with red young twigs, small white flowers on spurs, and purplish or yellow drupes 1–3 cm long.**

Deciduous, usually thorny, thicket-forming shrub on dry sites, to a stocky, crooked tree in deep soil and on valley floors, 4–6 m tall, trunk 10–15 cm diam.; branches stout, spreading at right angles from the trunk, crown broad. **BARK** Gray-brown when mature, deeply furrowed and divided into long, thin plates. **TWIG** Short, rigid, numerous, hairless or minutely hairy; bright red when young, becoming purplish, and when older gray or dark brown, some becoming thorn-tipped; buds egg-shaped, sharply pointed, chestnut brown, the inner scales maturing reddish. **LEAF** Alternate, simple, more or less leathery; ovate to obovate, base wedge-shaped, rounded, or somewhat indented, tip blunt to rounded, margins finely toothed; midrib broad, veins conspicuous. Upper surface dark green, hairless or minutely hairy; lower surface paler, hairy. Leaves turn rich yellow, orange, or red in autumn. Blade 2.5–8 cm long, 12–25 mm wide; petiole 4–15 mm long, usually glandless. **FLOWER** 10–15 mm diam., 1–7 borne at the ends of spurs; hypanthium bell-shaped, 4–5 mm long; petals white, aging pink, obovate; stamens about 30, anthers yellow. Mar.–May, before the leaves appear. **FRUIT** Hairless or minutely hairy, ellipsoid or globose reddish-purple or yellow drupe, 1–3 cm long, hanging at the end of a stout stalk 6–17 mm long, flesh tart to bitter; stone 8–12 mm long, with 2 or 3 low ridges on the sides, winged on 1 suture and grooved on the other.

HABITAT/RANGE Native. In brush and open woods, often with crab apples and hawthorns, 50–1,800 m; Coast Ranges to Cascade Range and Sierra Nevada, Ore. and Calif.

SIMILAR SPECIES Hawthorns have glossy, sharply pointed thorns and fruits with several stones; Western Crab Apple is thornless and has slightly larger flowers with about 20 stamens and pomes with several seeds.

Notes The fruit is edible and makes good preserves, but is highly variable: In some populations fruits are larger, yellow, and sweeter; in others they are smaller, red, and very bitter.

CHOKECHERRY *Prunus virginiana* L.

QUICK ID The combination of bicolored bud scales and broad, elliptic leaves with sharply toothed margins, the teeth conspicuously spreading, helps identify this species.

Deciduous shrub or small tree, 4–10 m tall, 10–15 cm diam., ranging from a single erect or leaning trunk to plants with multiple and usually crooked trunks; crown irregular, narrow to rounded. Plants often sucker from the root crown and form thickets. **BARK** Smooth, dark brown when young, becoming almost black, slightly fissured, lenticels oriented more or less vertically. **TWIG** Slender, green or light brown at first, becoming dark brown, with an almond odor when crushed; buds 6–8 mm long, scales dark brown with paler margins. **LEAF** Alternate, simple, thin, papery; obovate, oblong-obovate, or oval, the tip abruptly pinched to a point; margins finely and sharply toothed, the teeth spreading, usually not gland-tipped; petiole usually with 2 glands near the upper end. Upper surface dark green, hairless; lower surface paler, hairless or hairy. Veins 6–16 per side, raised on the lower surface. Leaves turn yellow in autumn. Blade 5–10 cm long, 3–5 cm broad; petiole about 1 cm long. **FLOWER** Borne in

KLAMATH PLUM

CHOKECHERRY

Klamath Plum

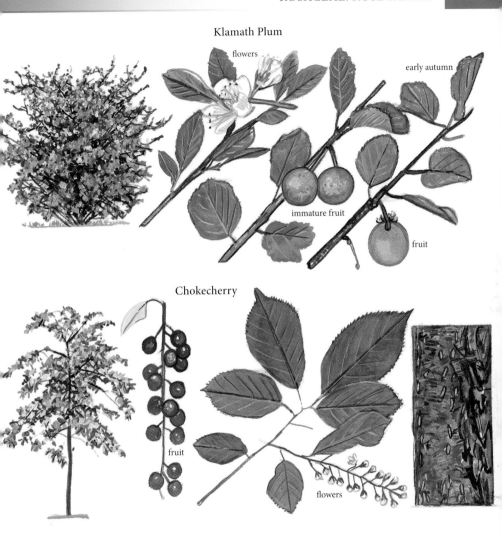

flowers

early autumn

immature fruit

fruit

Chokecherry

fruit

flowers

raceme of 18–64 flowers 4–15 cm long. Individual flowers 8–12 mm diam., petals white, stamens 15–20. Apr.–Jun. **FRUIT** Globose, lustrous red, purple, or black drupe, 6–10 mm diam.

HABITAT/RANGE Native. Open woods, woodland margins, stream banks, usually in moist areas, 0–3,000 m; across much of southern half of Canada, in the West south to s. Calif. and east to w. Tex.; also in much of ne. U.S.

SIMILAR SPECIES Black Cherry has leaves with 15–30 veins per side, flush with the lower surface,

and marginal teeth that are incurved; its hypanthium persists on the developing fruit.

Notes Within the species, there is considerable variation in degree of hairiness, leaf and raceme size, and color of fruits. Two varieties are recognized. More common in western mountains is Western Chokecherry (var. *demissa* [Nutt.] Torr.), with racemes extending 6–11 cm beyond the last leaf subtending a flower, petals 4–7 mm long, and leaf length at least 2 × width. Eastern Chokecherry (var. *virginiana*) has shorter racemes and petals, and leaf length less than 2 × width.

YOSHINO CHERRY *Prunus yedoensis* Matsum.

Deciduous tree, 4–8 m tall. **TWIG** Sparsely hairy. **LEAF** Elliptic, ovate, or obovate, drooping, base rounded, tip abruptly tapering to a point; margins double-toothed, the teeth bristle-tipped and glandular. Upper surface dark green, hairless; lower surface hairy on the midvein and lateral veins. Petiole hairy, sometimes with 1 or 2 glands near the upper end. Blade 5–12 cm long, 2.5–7 cm broad; petiole 1–2 cm long. **FLOWER** In clusters of 2–6 flowers, appearing before the leaves. Individual flowers 15–35 mm diam., floral cup and sepals hairy externally, petals white to pink. Mar.–Apr. **FRUIT** Hairless, globose black drupe, 7–12 mm diam. **HABITAT/RANGE** Introduced from Japan; rarely escaped from cultivation in disturbed sites, persisting in abandoned plantings, 0–200 m; Calif., Wash., East Coast.

STANSBURY CLIFFROSE *Purshia stansburiana* (Torr.) Henrickson
A.K.A. COWANIA, QUININE-BUSH

QUICK ID This dryland species has small lobed leaves in fascicles and produces 4–10 plumose achenes in each flower.

Evergreen, sometimes a small tree to 7.5 m tall. **LEAF** Alternate on new shoots, crowded in fascicles on spurs on older branches, simple, leathery, wedge-shaped or ovate, with 3–7 deep lobes. Upper surface dark green, gland-dotted; lower surface white and felty. Margins strongly rolled under. Blade 6–15 mm long, 6–10 mm wide. **FLOWER**

STANSBURY CLIFFROSE

Fragrant, bisexual, radial, 12–20 mm diam.; sepals 5; petals 5, separate, white to pale yellow; stamens numerous, in 2 rings attached near the rim of a small funnel-shaped hypanthium 4–6 mm long; ovaries several, contained within the hypanthium, each topped by a slender style. Apr.–Jun. **FRUIT** 4–10 slender, pubescent achenes packed in a hypanthium, body 5–7 mm long, topped by a plumose style 2–4.5 cm long.

HABITAT/RANGE Native. Dry foothills and washes, 1,200–2,700 m; se. Calif. across Nev. and Utah to sw. Colo., south into n. Mexico.

SIMILAR SPECIES Mountain mahoganies (*Cercocarpus*) also have plumose achenes, but their leaves have entire margins. Apache Plume (*Fallugia paradoxa* [D. Don] Endl. ex Torr.), a common shrub with similar leaves, has sepal-like bracts between the true sepals and 10 or more achenes in each flower.

Notes The foliage affords good winter browse for game and livestock. There are about 6 species of *Purshia*, all from semiarid regions at moderate elevations in the w. U.S. and n. Mexico. All are evergreen, stiff, and unarmed, with grayish bark peeling in strips; most are shrubs. The genus is named for Frederick Pursh, one of the earliest botanists in North America.

■ *PYRUS*: PEARS

There are about 20 species of pears, all native to Eurasia. They are distinguished from apples and mountain ashes by the tiny, gritty clusters of stone cells within the fleshy part of the fruit.

CALLERY PEAR *Pyrus calleryana* Decne.
A.K.A. BRADFORD PEAR, RED SPIRE

A popular ornamental with a dense, oval crown. **LEAF** Attractive dark green, becoming purplish or scarlet in autumn. **FRUIT** Brown, about 15 mm long. **HABITAT/RANGE** Introduced, cultivated; apparently has escaped in c. Calif. and has naturalized in the East.

Yoshino Cherry

flowers

petal

underside

fruit

fruit

spring

Stansbury Cliffrose

flower

leaves

fruit

Callery Pear

autumn

flowers

fruit

twig

thorn

autumn

COMMON PEAR *Pyrus communis* L.

QUICK ID The ovate, finely scalloped, dark green leaves and pyriform yellowish fruit with stone cells serve to identify this species.

Deciduous tree to about 15 m tall, usually with a single trunk to about 30 cm diam.; crown pyramidal with erect branches when young, the branches becoming spreading, somewhat contorted, and drooping with age. **TWIG** Hairless or nearly so, sometimes thorny, particularly in escaped plants. **LEAF** Alternate, simple, ovate to obovate. Mostly hairless at maturity; upper surface dark green, lower surface slightly paler. Margins finely scalloped. Blade 2–10 cm long; petiole 2–5 cm long. **FLOWER** In few-flowered, round clusters at the ends of short shoots; petals 5, white, 10–15 mm long; stamens 20–30; ovary with 2–5 chambers, each producing 2 seeds. **FRUIT** Obovoid pome, broadest near the tip, often slender near the stalk, 3–15 cm long, pale yellow to brownish, often blushed with red.

HABITAT/RANGE Introduced from Eurasia; cultivated, and sometimes escaped in open areas, thickets, woodland margins, 0–1,600 m; scattered throughout the U.S.

Notes Common Pear is the pear of commerce. Plants in the wild often have small fruits.

■ *SORBUS*: MOUNTAIN ASHES

There are 75–260 species of *Sorbus*, the circumscription of species uncertain. *Sorbus* is confined to the Northern Hemisphere, most frequent in cool, moist habitats, often in poor soils. Species occur from low to high elevations and often establish on open, disturbed ground. Several species are native to the U.S., two of which may be trees in the West.

The mountain ashes (also called rowans and whitebeams) are deciduous shrubs or small round-topped trees with erect to spreading branches. **BARK** Thin, smooth to furrowed and scaly, peeling in plates, light gray to reddish brown, often fragrant. **TWIG** Hairless to velvety; terminal buds relatively large, pointed, with overlapping scales, often gummy. **LEAF** Alternate, simple or pinnately compound and then odd-pinnate (with a terminal leaflet), margins toothed. **FLOWER** Small, bisexual, radial, numerous, in branched, rounded clusters mostly at the ends of branches; sepals 5; petals 5, usually white, rarely pink; stamens 15–20; ovary with 2–5 chambers, more or

less inferior. **FRUIT** Small globose red pome, usually retained on the tree until mid-autumn or winter.

Hybridization within the genus is common, as is the production of viable seeds in the absence of pollination. Species of *Sorbus* hybridize with species of serviceberry (*Amelanchier*) and chokeberry (*Aronia*) to produce the hybrid genera *Amelasorbus* and *Sorbaronia*. Several species are attractive ornamentals, appreciated for their leaves, flowers, and red fruits. Fruits provide food for wildlife when other foods are scarce.

WHITEBEAM *Sorbus aria* (L.) Crantz

Deciduous tree to 15 m tall; crown dense, broad-conical to rounded, branches upswept. **BARK** Gray, with short, shallow fissures. **LEAF** Simple, elliptic, 5–12 cm long, sharply double-toothed, upper surface green and hairless, lower surface bright white and velvety. **FLOWER** Creamy white, 1.5 cm diam., in flattish clusters 5–8 cm diam. May–Jun. **FRUIT** Globose orange-red to scarlet pome, 8–15 mm wide. **HABITAT/RANGE** Introduced from Europe.; disturbed woods; w. Wash. on the San Juan Islands, below 100 m, and perhaps in sw. Mont. at 1,500 m.

EUROPEAN MOUNTAIN ASH *Sorbus aucuparia* L.

QUICK ID This species has red fruit, compound leaves, and nonsticky terminal buds.

Deciduous small tree to about 18 m tall, with a single short trunk to 80 cm diam., crown rounded. **BARK** Smooth on young trees, becoming scaly and gray at maturity. **TWIG** Slender, reddish, hairy at first, becoming hairless with age; buds not gummy. **LEAF** Alternate, pinnately compound, blade 12–25 cm long; petiole to about 2 cm long. Leaflets 9–17, each 2.5–7.5 cm long, narrowly elliptic or lanceolate, tip blunt or acute; margins sharply toothed. Upper surface green, lower surface paler. **FLOWER** About 1 cm diam.; petals white, circular; fragrance unpleasant. **FRUIT** Globose, bright red pome, 8–10 mm diam.

HABITAT/RANGE Introduced from Europe; escaped from cultivation on disturbed sites; scattered across w. U.S. (except the Southwest), below 1,700 m; also in the east.

SIMILAR SPECIES Other western species usually have fewer leaflets or have gummy buds.

Common Pear

flowers

fruit

Whitebeam

flowers

fruit

underside

European Mountain Ash

flowers

fruit

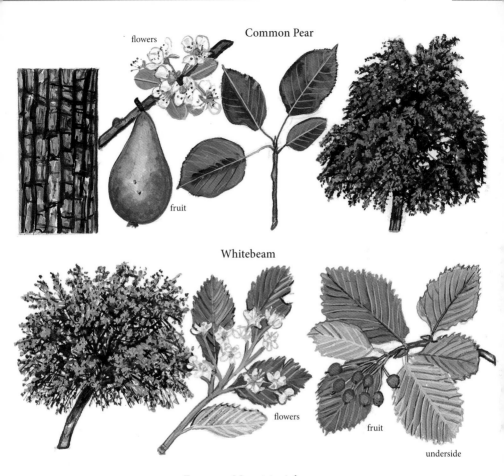

OAKLEAF MOUNTAIN ASH *Sorbus hybrida* L.

Deciduous tree to 3–15 m tall; crown columnar when young, rounded with age, branches ascending. **LEAF** Alternate, usually simple, ovate, 7–12 cm long, 5–8 cm wide; 6–9 deeply cut oval-tipped lobes on each side, the lower pair of lobes often cut to the midrib. Margins sharply toothed. Upper surface lustrous, dark green with impressed veins; lower surface grayish-hairy. Petiole hairy. **FLOWER** White to creamy white, 1–2 cm diam., in round clusters 6–11 cm wide. May–Jun. **FRUIT** Globose, bright red pome, 10–15 mm wide. **HABITAT/ RANGE** Introduced from Scandinavia; cultivated and persisting in abandoned sites, 1,300–1,400 m; Mont. to Utah.

GREENE MOUNTAIN ASH *Sorbus scopulina* Greene

QUICK ID This species has leaves with rarely more than 13 leaflets, and glossy orange or scarlet pomes.

Deciduous shrub or tree to 6 m tall; trunk to 10 cm diam. **TWIG** Sparsely to heavily grayish-hairy, less hairy with age; buds red-brown, gummy, sparsely whitish-hairy. **LEAF** Alternate, pinnately compound; blade 10–23 cm long; petiole 1.5–5 cm long. Leaflets 7–15, thin, 2–8 cm long, less than ⅓ as wide, narrowly elliptic-lanceolate, margins finely toothed. Upper surface dark green, hairless; lower surface paler, sparsely hairy near the midrib. **FLOWER** White, fragrant, about 1 cm wide; 70–200 in branched, nearly flat clusters 3–8 cm broad; hypanthium whitish-hairy. May–Jul. **FRUIT** Globose, glossy orange to scarlet pome, 1 cm diam., in pendent clusters.

HABITAT/RANGE Native. Clearings in woods, 0–3,000 m; Alaska to Calif. and N.M.

Notes Var. *scopulina*, found east of the Cascade Range, has some leaves with 13 leaflets; var. *cascadensis* (G.N. Jones) C.L. Hitchc. (Cascade Mountain Ash), B.C. south, mostly west of the Cascade Range, has usually 11 or fewer leaflets.

SITKA MOUNTAIN ASH *Sorbus sitchensis* M. Roem.

QUICK ID This mountain ash has rusty-hairy buds and young growth, pinnately compound leaves with 7–11 rather blunt-tipped leaflets, and small, bright red pomes.

TWIG Buds hairy, hairs red-brown. **LEAF** Similar to that of Greene Mountain Ash, but with 7–11 thickish, blunt-tipped, oblong leaflets toothed only near the tip (var. *grayi* [Wenz.] C.L. Hitchc.) or toothed for ½–¾ the length (var. *sitchensis*); lower surface with red-brown hairs along the midvein. **FLOWER** In clusters of 15–80. Jun.–Jul. **FRUIT** Pome red but glaucous, with a bluish bloom that is easily rubbed off.

HABITAT/RANGE Native. Moist rich soils along streams or on hillsides, 0–3,000 m; Alaska to Calif., Idaho, Mont.

GREENE MOUNTAIN ASH

SITKA MOUNTAIN ASH

Oakleaf Mountain Ash

Greene Mountain Ash

Sitka Mountain Ash

■ *VAUQUELINIA:* ROSEWOODS

Vauquelinia is a small Southwestern genus, occurring only in the sw. U.S. and n. Mexico. The 3 variable species grow in arid regions at the margins of the deserts, at moderate elevations. The wood is hard, red, and dense; though it is called "rosewood," true rosewood comes from tropical trees in the bean or pea family (Fabaceae).

Evergreen, unarmed shrubs or small trees. **LEAF** Alternate, simple, lanceolate, leathery, with finely toothed margins. **FLOWER** Small, borne in branched, roundish terminal clusters. Bisexual, radial; sepals 5, petals 5, separate, reflexed, and persisting, stamens 15–30, all borne near the rim of a hemispheric hypanthium; ovaries 5, superior, joined by their bases, contained within the hypanthium. **FRUIT** Woody, capsule-like, the 5 chambers joined at the base, each opening along the inner side; 2 seeds in each chamber. Fruits often persist on the plant until spring of the following year.

ARIZONA ROSEWOOD *Vauquelinia californica* (Torr.) Sarg.
A.K.A. TORREY VAUQUELINIA

QUICK ID The finely toothed, lanceolate evergreen leathery leaves and white flowers in rounded clusters characterize this species

Evergreen shrub or small tree, 1–8 m tall, usually with a contorted trunk 3–15 cm diam. Crown ragged, generally oval and dense, with stiff, upright, contorted branches. **BARK** Dark red-brown, thin, at first smooth, later with irregular shallow fissures and small plate-like scales. **TWIG** At first reddish brown, later brown to gray, closely hairy with crinkled hairs or nearly hairless. Bud axillary, minute, pointed, pubescent. **LEAF** Alternate, simple,

ARIZONA ROSEWOOD

leathery, ascending, generally flat, linear-lanceolate to oblong-lanceolate; margins finely toothed, the teeth 2–10 per cm, often gland-tipped, often also somewhat crinkled and inrolled. Upper surface dark green, lustrous, mostly hairless, the midrib impressed; lower surface yellow-green and mostly hairless to densely white-hairy. Blade 4–10 cm long, 1–2 cm wide; petiole stout, 4–14 mm long. **FLOWER** 10–15 mm diam., numerous in branched, rounded clusters aggregated near the branch tips; petals white, oblong-ovate, 3–5.5 mm long; hypanthium hemispheric, about 2–4 mm wide and long, leathery, hairless to pubescent. May–Jun. **FRUIT** Ovoid, erect woody capsule, 4.5–6.5 mm long.

HABITAT/RANGE Native. Rocky canyons and hillsides among shrubs, oaks, piñon, and juniper, 700–2,300 m; s. Ariz. and sw. N.M. to n. Mexico.

SIMILAR SPECIES Other arid-land shrubs may have leathery leaves, but they are broader (some *Prunus*, Rosaceae, and *Rhamnus*, Rhamnaceae) or smaller and entire in species of manzanita (*Arctostaphylos*, Ericaceae). In Desert Willow (*Chilopsis linearis*, Bignoniaceae), the leaves are bright green, soft, flexible, and deciduous, and the flowers are large, white or pink, and snapdragon-like.

Notes There are 4 subspecies, varying, among other attributes, in the density of hairs on the lower side of the leaves. Though named *V. californica*, the species does not occur in the state of Calif., but does occur in Baja Calif. The genus is named for Nicolas Vauquelin, an 18th-century French chemist who discovered beryllium and chromium, and several organic substances common in plants.

SLIMLEAF ROSEWOOD *Vauquelinia corymbosa* Humb. & Bonpl. **subsp. angustifolia** (Rydb.) Hess & Henricks.

QUICK ID Lanceolate leathery leaves with somewhat inrolled, toothed margins and numerous small white flowers in rounded clusters distinguish this arid-land shrub found in w. Tex.

Similar to Arizona Rosewood. **LEAF** Linear or linear-oblong, 6–13 cm long, 5–9 mm wide, but with only 1 or 2 teeth per cm on the margins; lower surface yellow-green, never whitish-hairy. **FLOWER** Jun.–Aug.

Arizona Rosewood

flowers

fruit

fruit

Slimleaf Rosewood

flowers

fruit

HABITAT/RANGE Native. Dry canyons, among brush, usually on limestone or gypsum, 1,050–1,500 m; Mexico, crossing into w. Tex.

Notes Slimleaf Rosewood's narrow leathery leaves with toothed margins are unique in the region. This is the northernmost variety of a Mexican species with 6 varieties, this one distinguished from the others by its narrow leaf blades.

SLIMLEAF ROSEWOOD

RUBIACEAE: MADDER FAMILY

The madder or coffee family contains about 550 genera and 9,000 species of woody to herbaceous plants worldwide, mostly from warm temperate to tropical regions. A few genera and a number of species also occur in cold regions. North of the Mexican border there are 11 genera with trees, 1 genus occurring in the West.

LEAF Opposite or whorled, simple, with stipules fused and joined across the node. **FLOWER** Usually bisexual; radial, often aggregated in clusters. Sepals, petals, and stamens are 4 or 5 each, the petals joined into a usually funnel-shaped corolla. The ovary is inferior, usually 2-celled. Above the ovary is a nectar disk. **FRUIT** Capsule, berry, drupe, schizocarp, indehiscent podlike structure, or occasionally a fleshy fruit formed from several flowers.

The family is best known as the source of coffee (genus *Coffea*). The drugs quinine (*Cinchona*) and ipecac (*Psychotria*), and many ornamental plants, including gardenia (*Gardenia*), come from the family. A red dye from madder (*Rubia*) was important prior to the development of synthetic dyes.

■ *CEPHALANTHUS*: BUTTONBUSHES

There are 6 to nearly 20 species of *Cephalanthus*, depending on varying views of classification, found in warm regions in much of the world. Ours are easily recognized by the opposite or whorled, entire-margined leaves and tight ball-like heads of small flowers. They occur at low to moderate elevations. There are 2 species in the West, 1 barely crossing north of the Mexican border.

Usually deciduous shrubs or trees with thin to deeply furrowed bark. **LEAF** Simple, opposite or 3 or 4 in a whorl, petioles short. **FLOWER** Borne in dense spherical heads at the ends of slender, straight stalks borne terminally or in upper leaf axils. All flowers in a head bloom simultaneously, the stamens projecting like pins in a pincushion. Calyx with 4 or 5 united sepals; corolla trumpet-shaped, with 4 or 5 united petals. Stamens 4. **FRUIT** Ovary 2-celled, forming a schizocarp that ultimately splits from the base upward into 2–4 single-seeded segments.

COMMON BUTTONBUSH
Cephalanthus occidentalis L.
A.K.A. HONEY-BALLS, GLOBE-FLOWERS

QUICK ID This shrub or small tree may be recognized by its simple, opposite or whorled leaves and distinctive creamy-white globular heads of numerous tubular flowers; the calyx of each flower is hairless or nearly so.

Deciduous shrub or small tree, 3–15 m tall. **LEAF** Opposite or in whorls of 3 or 4 per node, lanceolate or elliptic. Upper surface lustrous, dark green; lower surface paler, hairy or not. Blade 6–10 cm long, 1.5–10 cm broad. **FLOWER** In dense spherical heads, 2–4 cm diam. Calyx hairless externally or with a few long white hairs at the base; corolla creamy white, 5–10 mm long, trumpet-shaped, 4-lobed. May–Sep. **FRUIT** Hairless or nearly hairless woody capsule, that of each flower splitting from the base into 2–4 wedge-shaped, 1-seeded nutlike segments, the segments tightly packed in the spherical head.

HABITAT/RANGE Native. Moist places, 0–1,000 m; Calif., s. Ariz., and widespread from w. Tex. across the East.

COMMON BUTTONBUSH

Common Buttonbush

flower head

flower

stem

Mexican Buttonbush

flower head

nutlike segments

fruit head

fruit head

MEXICAN BUTTONBUSH
Cephalanthus salicifolius Humb. & Bonpl.
A.K.A. BOTONCILLO

QUICK ID This shrub or small tree has opposite or whorled leaves and distinctive creamy-white globular heads of numerous tubular flowers; the calyx of each flower is densely white-hairy with appressed hairs.

Deciduous shrub or small tree, 2–5 m tall. **LEAF** Opposite or in whorls of 3, narrowly elliptic to lanceolate, green, shiny, upper surface hairless, lower surface nearly so. Blade 5–12 cm long, 1–2.5 cm broad. **FLOWER** In dense spherical heads, 2–2.5 cm diam. Calyx whitish, with appressed hairs; corolla white, 6–7 mm long, trumpet-shaped, 4-lobed. Mar.–Jul. **FRUIT** Densely and minutely hairy woody capsule, that of each flower splitting from the base into 2–4 wedge-shaped, 1-seeded nutlike segments, the segments tightly packed in the spherical head.

HABITAT/RANGE Native. Wet soil, 0–20 m; near the lower Rio Grande in s. Tex., south to Honduras.

MEXICAN BUTTONBUSH

RUTACEAE: CITRUS OR RUE FAMILY

The citrus or rue family contains more than 150 genera and 900 species in warm regions of the world, the most diverse family in the Southern Hemisphere. A few are native to North America, and several have been introduced to southern parts of the U.S.

Plants are evergreen or deciduous. Most species in the family are woody; some bear thorns, spines, or prickles. **LEAF** Alternate or opposite, pinnately compound (with or without a terminal leaflet), sometimes reduced to 3 leaflets or even to a single leaflet (and therefore unifoliolate), rarely palmate. Dotted with translucent glands loaded with oily chemicals, which impart a bitter taste and skunkish to citrusy odors. Petiole often conspicuously winged. **FLOWER** Flower clusters are terminal, branched, with few to many flowers, or sometimes there is only 1 flower. Bisexual or unisexual; when unisexual, borne on separate plants or not; radial, usually whitish, greenish yellow, or purplish; sepals and petals usually 4 or 5; stamens 4–10 or more; ovary superior, with 4 or 5 chambers. There is usually a nectar disk beneath the stamens and ovary. **FRUIT** Highly variable: samara, schizocarp, drupe, cluster of more or less separate chambers (follicles), or berry (often a hesperidium, a berry with a leathery rind, as in the citrus fruit).

The family is economically very important for its fruits, particularly those of the genus *Citrus*, but also kumquat (*Fortunella*) and white zapote (*Casimiroa*). The essential oils produced in all parts of the plant are used medicinally and in perfumery. A few species provide valuable lumber, and some are used as ornamentals, prized for their foliage or their showy and sometimes delightfully fragrant flowers.

MOUNTAIN TORCHWOOD *Amyris madrensis* S. Watson

QUICK ID Pinnately compound leaves with 5–11 broad, wavy leathery leaflets identify this shrub or small tree of s. Tex.

Unarmed evergreen shrub to small tree, 1–9 m tall. Trunk to 10 cm diam.; bark thin, smooth, gray-mottled. **LEAF** Opposite (or nearly so), pinnately compound, the rachis rough-glandular; leaflets 5–11 (terminal leaflet present), 12–20 mm long, wavy, leathery, elliptic or oval, emitting a citrusy odor when bruised. **FLOWER** Tiny, white to greenish, fragrant, in loose clusters in the leaf axils; petals 4, stamens 8. Mar.–Oct. **FRUIT** Globose or ovoid purplish, red-brown, or blackish gland-pitted drupe, 6–8 mm long.

HABITAT/RANGE Native. Rare in thickets in extreme s. Tex., 0–40 m; ne. Mexico.

Notes Amyris, an American genus of about 30 evergreen species, extends from the s. U.S. to Peru.

SOUR ORANGE *Citrus* × *aurantium* L., pro sp.
A.K.A. SEVILLE ORANGE

Evergreen thorny shrub or small tree. **LEAF** Alternate, unifoliolate, ovate, with a short point at the tip, margins minutely toothed; blade 5–14 cm long, petiole usually conspicuously winged. **FLOWER**

MOUNTAIN TORCHWOOD

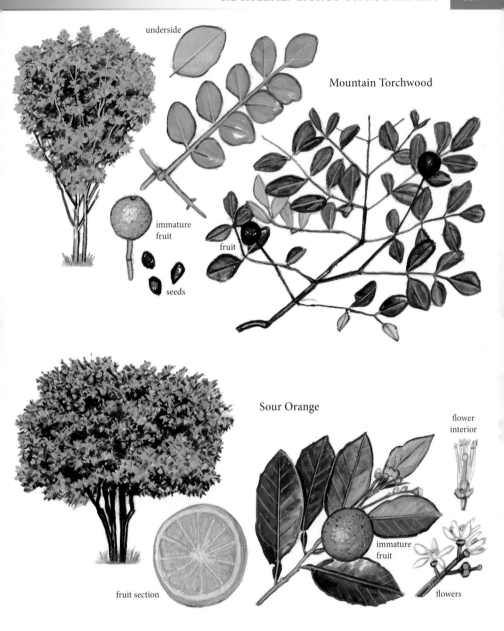

underside

Mountain Torchwood

immature
fruit

fruit

seeds

Sour Orange

flower
interior

immature
fruit

fruit section

flowers

Bisexual and male, borne singly or in clusters in leaf axils, up to 3–4 cm diam.; petals 5, white, recurved; stamens up to 24, yellow. **FRUIT** Round to ovoid, 6–8 cm diam., with a thick, aromatic, bitter, rough-surfaced reddish-orange rind. The pulp is strongly acidic, with few to numerous seeds.

HABITAT/RANGE Cultivated and naturalized in s. Tex. below 100 m, also in Fla. and Ga., perhaps elsewhere. *Notes* Sour Orange is derived from an ancient hybrid between the Shaddock or Pomelo (*C. maxima* [Burm. f.] Merr.) and Tangerine (*C. reticulata* Blanco).

BERLANDIER JOPOY *Esenbeckia berlandieri* Baill.
A.K.A. LIMONCILLO

QUICK ID This rare shrub or small tree of s. Tex. is identified by its lemon-scented alternate leaves with 3 leaflets and its woody 5-lobed capsules.

Semievergreen small tree to 9 m tall. **LEAF** Alternate, lemon-scented, with 3 leaflets, each 3–15 cm long, elliptic, dark green, shiny, nearly hairless. **FLOWER** Numerous, 6 mm diam., cream-white to greenish white, in terminal clusters; May–Jun., Sep. **FRUIT** Usually 5-lobed woody capsule, 2.5–6 cm long, the surface warty; the seeds are elastically ejected.

HABITAT/RANGE Native. Scrub thickets, 5–30 m; extreme s. Tex. to c. Mexico.

Notes The genus contains about 20 species in the American tropics, this the most northerly.

BARRETA *Helietta parvifolia* (A. Gray) Benth.

QUICK ID Opposite, strongly aromatic leaves with 3 leathery leaflets identify this s. Tex. shrub or small tree.

Slender evergreen shrub or small tree to 8 m tall, usually with several trunks branched close to the ground. **BARK** Thin, gray, breaking into plates. **LEAF** Mostly opposite, with 3 leathery leaflets 1–5 cm long, elliptic to obovate, long-tapered to the base, lustrous when mature; upper surface green, lower paler and minutely dotted with dark glands. **FLOWER** Tiny, greenish white, in open-branched clusters in leaf axils; petals 3 or 4. **FRUIT** 10–15 mm long, yellow or tan, consisting of 3 or 4 samara-like segments, each with a vertical net-veined wing on the back.

HABITAT/RANGE Native. Along the Rio Grande near the southern tip of Tex. at about 50 m; Mexico.

Notes *Helietta* is a genus of about 7 species extending from Tex. to South America.

■ *PTELEA*: HOPTREES

Ptelea, with only 2–4 species, is found in warmer regions of the U.S. and Mexico at low to moderate elevations. Taxonomically, the genus is complex, and up to 59 species have been described. Two species occur in the West.

Deciduous shrubs or small trees. **LEAF** Alternate, pinnately compound, with 3 or 5 leaflets. **FLOWER** Small, in branched clusters; sepals, petals, and stamens each number 4 or 5; stamens have hairy filaments; ovary is superior. **FRUIT** Round, flat samara with 2 cells, each with 1 or 2 seeds, and with a papery wing surrounding the central seed body.

Ptelea derives from the Greek name for elm, referring to the outward similarity of the fruits. Trees are grown as ornamentals; the bitter bark has been used medicinally for treating gastrointestinal problems; and fruits were used as a hops substitute in brewing beer. It is the most northerly ranging genus of Rutaceae in North America.

CALIFORNIA HOPTREE *Ptelea crenulata* Greene
A.K.A. WESTERN HOPTREE

QUICK ID Restricted to Calif., this hoptree has 3-parted leaves with a musky aroma when crushed and flat, winged, waferlike samaras borne in ball-like clusters. It so closely resembles Western Poison Oak that you must be careful before touching it (see below).

BERLANDIER JOPOY   BARRETA   CALIFORNIA HOPTREE

Berlandier Jopoy

flowers

fruit

dehiscing fruit

Barreta

fruit

leaf variation

California Hoptree

flowers

fruit

fruit

fruit

Very similar to Common Hoptree, though rarely taller than 5 m. **FLOWER** Pistil in center of flower hairy. **FRUIT** Samara 1–2 cm diam., the seed case thick, half or more the samara diam.

HABITAT/RANGE Native. Open woodland, often in the shade of trees, 50–1,050 m; Calif.

SIMILAR SPECIES Easy to confuse with Western Poison Oak (*Toxicodendron diversilobum* (Torr. & A. Gray) Greene, Anacardiaceae), which may cause severe dermatitis if touched and grows in the same habitat but never is treelike. Western Poison Oak is a shrub or vine, with similar 3-parted leaves, but has round brownish or whitish berries, and leaflets with margins that are scalloped and usually lobed.

COMMON HOPTREE *Ptelea trifoliata* L.
A.K.A. Wafer-ash, Stinking-ash, Skunk-bush

QUICKID The combination of 3-parted leaves with a musky aroma when crushed and flat, winged, waferlike samaras in small clusters distinguishes Common Hoptree. This plant so closely resembles Western Poison Oak and Poison Ivy that you must be careful before touching it (see below).

Deciduous, colony-forming shrub or small tree to about 7.5 m tall, the crown usually broad and spreading. **BARK** Gray-brown, slightly scaly, usually with lenticels and corky ridges. **TWIG** Light reddish brown, decorated with pustular spots. **LEAF** Alternate, pinnately compound; blade 10–18 cm long, about as broad; petiole 4–8 cm long. Leaflets 3 (rarely 5), 1–10 cm long, to about 8 cm broad, the lateral ones stalkless or nearly so, elliptic, obovate, ovate, or broadly lanceolate, margins bluntly or sharply toothed. Upper surface lustrous, dark green; lower surface paler, from hairless to soft-hairy. Releases a musky odor when crushed. **FLOWER** Borne in terminal panicles, bisexual or functionally unisexual (both sexes on the same plant); sepals 4 or 5, tiny; petals 4 or 5, greenish white, 4–6 mm long; stamens usually 4 or 5; ovary superior. Mar.–Jul. **FRUIT** Flat, circular, waferlike samara 1.5–2 cm diam., with 2 conspicuous wings and a body with 1 or 2 seeds; hanging in small clusters as broad as long.

HABITAT/RANGE Native. Canyons, slopes, in brush, woodlands or forest, 0–2,750 m; Ariz., s. Utah, and s. Colo., eastward across much of the East.

SIMILAR SPECIES Some ashes with 3 leaflets are similar, but they have opposite leaves and elongate samaras. Be careful in learning Common Hoptree: The leaves resemble those of Poison Ivy (*Toxicodendron radicans* (L.) Kuntze, Anacardiaceae) and

Western Poison Oak (*T. diversilobum* (Torr. & A. Gray) Greene). In both of these species, which can cause severe contact dermatitis, the 3-parted leaves have margins that are toothed or scalloped and often lobed, and the fruits are brownish or whitish berries. They are usually small shrubs or vines, but may form large bushy clumps.

Notes Common Hoptree is North America's most northerly ranging member of the citrus family. Its amplitude of habitats and elevation has resulted in many genetic races, a number of which have been named as subspecies.

■ *ZANTHOXYLUM*: PRICKLYASHES

Zanthoxylum has more than 200 species in warm regions nearly worldwide; 6 or 7 occur in the U.S.; 3 in the West are occasionally trees.

Deciduous or evergreen shrubs or small trees. **LEAF** Alternate, pinnately compound, terminal leaflet present or absent. **FLOWER** Small, numerous, in branched clusters, bisexual or unisexual, male and female on separate plants; sepals 0–5; petals and stamens 3–5; ovaries superior, 1–5. **FRUIT** Globose bladderlike, gland-dotted follicle, splitting to reveal 1 large, round, glossy black seed.

Zanthoxylum means "yellow wood." One species, West Indian Silkwood (*Z. flavum* Vahl), produces valuable lumber, and has been exploited to the point that the slow-growing trees have been severely reduced in number or extirpated from much of their mainly Caribbean range. Bark, leaves, and fruits of several species, when chewed, produce a mouth-numbing sensation, and were used as a counter-irritant to alleviate pain from toothache (hence the names Toothache Tree and Tickle-tongue or Tingle-tongue for members of the genus). Extracts have also been used to reduce discomfort from varicose veins and rheumatism, and to treat stomach disorders. The fruit of several Asian species is used to produce Sichuan pepper.

HERCULES' CLUB *Zanthoxylum clava-hercules* L.
A.K.A. Southern Prickly-ash, Tickle-tongue

QUICKID One of few species with the combination of alternate, pinnately compound leaves and stout, sharp prickles on the lower trunk, branches, and leaves.

COMMON HOPTREE

Common Hoptree

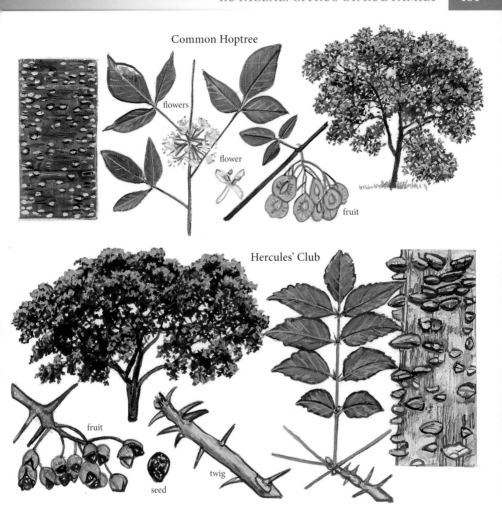

flowers

flower

fruit

Hercules' Club

fruit

seed

twig

Deciduous shrub or tree to 20 m tall, branches and trunk often bearing short, sharp, conical corky-based prickles. **LEAF** Alternate, pinnate, blade 12–20 cm long, rachis often bearing prickles. Leaflets usually 9–13 (full range 5–19), 2.5–7 cm long, on short, winged stalks, stiff, lanceolate or ovate, asymmetric, curved; margins coarsely toothed, with yellowish glands between the teeth. **FLOWER** Mostly in terminal clusters; petals 4 or 5, greenish yellow, 3–4 mm long. Apr.–May. **FRUIT** Globose brownish follicle, rough, pitted, 5–6 mm diam.

HABITAT/RANGE Native. Dunes, disturbed places, woodlands, 0–300 m; barely entering the West in sc. Tex., widespread across the Southeast.

HERCULES' CLUB

LIME PRICKLYASH *Zanthoxylum fagara* (L.) Sarg.
A.K.A. WILD LIME, UÑA DE GATO

QUICKID Recognized by the alternate, pinnately compound leaves with a winged rachis and petiole, and bluntly toothed leaflets.

Evergreen shrub or small tree to 10 m tall; branches often very prickly, with slender, curved prickles (sometimes lacking). **LEAF** Alternate, pinnate, blade 12–20 cm long, the rachis grooved and distinctly winged. Leaflets usually 7–9 (full range 5–13), 7–20 mm long, obovate, elliptic, or nearly round; margins bluntly toothed. Petiole usually winged. **FLOWER** Mostly in axillary clusters; petals 4, yellow-green, 2–3 mm long. Year-round. **FRUIT** Rounded reddish or yellowish follicle, warty, pitted, 3–4 mm long.

HABITAT/RANGE Native. Brush, 0–80 m; s. Tex., c. and s. Fla.

TEXAS HERCULES' CLUB *Zanthoxylum hirsutum* Buckley

QUICKID This pricklyash is distinguished by its leaflets mostly numbering 5–9, and flowers in terminal panicles, each flower with 5 sepals, petals, and stamens.

Deciduous shrub or small tree to 5 m tall; trunk and branches with slender prickles. Twig and leaf rachises hairy and with slender, straight or curved prickles. **LEAF** Alternate, pinnately compound, often smelling of orange peel. Leaflets 5–11, 1–3.5 cm long, glossy yellow-green, elliptic to ovate; margins irregularly scalloped, with glands in notches and somewhat wavy. **FLOWER** In ample terminal panicles, small, greenish yellow; sepals, petals, and stamens 5 each; ovaries 2. Apr.–May. **FRUIT** Hairless, globose reddish-brown follicle, 6 mm diam., usually 1 per flower.

HABITAT/RANGE Native. Brush, edges of woods, fencerows, old fields, 0–850 m; s. Okla., s. Tex., reported from Ark.; ne. Mexico.

Notes A larval host plant for the Giant Swallowtail butterfly (*Papilio cresphontes*).

LIME PRICKLYASH

TEXAS HERCULES' CLUB

Lime Pricklylash

flowers

open fruit

fruit

Texas Hercules' Club

flowers

fruit

open fruit

twig

prickles

SALICACEAE: WILLOW FAMILY

The willow family has 50–60 genera and about 1,000 species of woody plants worldwide. Recent molecular genetic studies show that the mostly tropical Flacourtiaceae belongs in the Salicaceae, considerably expanding our concept of the willow family. Only 1 genus of the old Flacourtiaceae, *Xylosma*, barely enters the West. As construed here, there are 5 genera of Salicaceae in the U.S. (two of them introduced in Fla.).

Members of the family range from diminutive creeping shrubs of cold regions to massive, majestic trees in eastern forests and along southwestern rivers. **LEAF** Usually alternate, simple, and usually toothed. Stipules are often present, sometimes large and leafy. The teeth on the margins of leaves in *Salix* and *Populus* are usually tipped with a persistent spherical gland that arises as an extension of the vein that enters the tooth. **FLOWER** Often borne in unisexual catkins, the sexes on separate plants, or in terminal or axillary clusters. In ours, the perianth lacks petals, and is often reduced to either a small disk or a glandular nectary. Stamens 1–60, the filaments free or partially fused, hairy or not near the base. **FRUIT** In *Populus* and *Salix*, the single ovary usually bears 2 stigmas, and matures into a small capsule, which splits into 2 or 4 segments releasing long-hairy seeds that are carried by the wind. *Xylosma* fruit is a berry.

The wood of larger species in the family is used for lumber, pulp, and occasionally for fuel. Salicaceae species are an important food source for many kinds of wildlife. They quickly revegetate moist disturbed areas, helping to control erosion. A number of species are also popular ornamentals.

■ *POPULUS*: POPLARS, COTTONWOODS, ASPENS

There are 30–35 species of *Populus* native to the Northern Hemisphere from sea-level to the tree-line, but a number have now been spread throughout cooler regions of the world by human activity. There are 8 species native to North America, 5 in the West. Several introduced as ornamentals have escaped and persist clonally, often as hybrids with native species. Poplars, cottonwoods, and aspens are among the best-known deciduous trees of North America. They may form continuous forests in the western mountains and the colder regions of the north, and along southwestern rivers they are important components of riparian woodlands. Some species spread clonally, developing new trees from root shoots. Some clones may cover hectares of ground, all trees similar, all of one sex. The clonal nature of aspen forests is particularly evident when one flies over the western mountains in autumn, when some clones are seen to have lost their leaves, others are deep yellow, another pale yellow, and an adjacent one blushed with orange.

Deciduous small to massive trees. **BARK** Young bark is smooth and pale, in aspens often white; older bark usually is darker, thick, and deeply furrowed between flat, often cracked ridges. **TWIG** Hairy or not; buds conspicuous, with 3–10 scales, often resinous, usually fragrant in poplars and cottonwoods but not fragrant in aspens. **LEAF** Alternate, simple, for the most part toothed, and in some European species lobed. Usually heterophyllous, the leaves from different parts of the season's twig differing in form (in this book leaf descriptions are based on those formed later, midway on the twig or closer to the tip). Autumn foliage yellow. **FLOWER** Very small, unisexual, wind-pollinated, borne in pendulous catkins that expand before the leaves emerge, the sexes borne on separate trees. Perianth modified into a cup- or saucer-shaped floral disk at the base of the flower. Stamens 6–12 in aspens, 12–60 in cottonwoods and poplars. Female flowers have a lobed ovary topped by a short stigma and 2 spreading styles. **FRUIT** Fruiting catkins drooping. Capsules ovoid or globose, splitting into 2 to 4 segments to release the pale seeds, which are covered by long white

underside

fruiting
catkin

White Poplar

down, and waft by the thousands in the air after the leaves mature; capsules are thin-walled in aspens, thick-walled in cottonwoods and poplars.

Populus species provide wood for paper pulp, pallets, boxes, matches, and small utilitarian items. Hybrids are bred for rapid production of biomass, and are planted in large plantations to supply the pulp industry. In Spanish, poplar is *álamo*. In rural areas the wood was once carved for farm implements, water troughs, oxen yolks, and doors, and cut for *vigas* (rafters) and *latillas* (small sections of branches placed over *vigas* to support a mud roof). The bark has been used in tanning, and the resin of the buds was used medicinally. Cultivated, but troublesome as ornamentals due to the tendency of roots to break sidewalks and foundations, and to clog sewage lines.

WHITE POPLAR *Populus alba* L.
A.K.A. EUROPEAN WHITE POPLAR

QUICKID Recognized by the combination of whitish bark on younger parts of the branches and trunk, and leaves usually shaped like those of maples but with a densely whitish-hairy lower surface and petiole.

Deciduous tree, 16–24 m tall; trunk often forked, 50–100 cm diam. Crown large, usually rounded; branches large, with few stout branchlets. **BARK** Smooth and creamy white or grayish on young trees, becoming blackish, furrowed, and deeply pitted, especially on the lower trunk. **TWIG** Stout, green, white-hairy, becoming brownish; buds covered with whitish hairs. **LEAF** Alternate, simple, ovate or palmately lobed to nearly circular; base truncate or broadly rounded; tip bluntly pointed; margins wavy or deeply 5-lobed, with large, bluntly pointed teeth. Upper surface lustrous, dark green, hairless; lower surface white-hairy, becoming nearly hairless. Blade 4–10 cm long, nearly as broad; petiole to about 6 cm long, densely hairy, flattened. **FLOWER** Male catkins 4–8 cm long, stamens 6–16; female catkins 2–5 cm long. Mar.–Jun. **FRUIT** Fruiting catkins 4–8 cm long. Capsule egg-shaped, 3–6 mm long, splitting into 2 parts.

HABITAT/RANGE Introduced from Europe; among the most widely cultivated trees in the U.S. and Canada, escaped and established essentially throughout, less common in southern climes.

SIMILAR SPECIES Native poplars have lanceolate to ovate leaves, hairless or sparsely hairy beneath, in contrast to the strongly bicolored, more or less maple-like leaves of White Poplar.

Notes Considered weedy and invasive in several states, especially in the North.

NARROWLEAF COTTONWOOD
Populus angustifolia E. James
A.K.A. MOUNTAIN COTTONWOOD

QUICK ID Hairless, lanceolate green leaves with finely toothed margins, pendulous catkins, and a large straight trunk help distinguish this species.

Deciduous fast-growing, short-lived tree to 20 m tall; trunk straight, to 70 cm diam. Crown oval, branches ascending or erect. **BARK** At first smooth and light grayish brown, becoming shallowly fissured between broad, flat ridges. **TWIG** Slender, hairless, at first light yellow-green, becoming bright orange-brown during the 1st winter, paler in the 2nd winter, and by the 3rd winter pale gray; terminal buds red-resinous, fragrant, hairless, pointed, usually 6–12 mm long. **LEAF** Alternate, simple, lanceolate, base wedge-shaped to round, tip long-tapered to a point; margins usually finely blunt-toothed (in early leaves usually entire or with 23–35 teeth per side; later leaves with 35–65 teeth per side), thickened, and slightly rolled under. Usually hairless, upper surface shiny green, lower surface paler. Midvein stout, yellowish green. Blade usually 4–8 cm long (up to 14 cm in rapidly growing shoots), 8–25 mm broad; petiole 2–17 mm long (15–20% length of blade), round, and slightly channeled on top. **FLOWER** Male catkins 2–3 cm long; female catkins 4–8 cm long, bearing 35–50 flowers. Floral bracts deeply cut into hairlike brownish lobes. Floral disk shallowly cup-shaped, usually 1–1.5 mm diam. Stamens 10–20, filaments short, anthers large and bright red. Apr.–May, before leaf expansion. **FRUIT** Fruiting catkins up to 10 cm long. Capsule thickly papery, globose to egg-shaped, abruptly pointed, 3–5 mm long, splitting into 2 parts, on an individual stalk 3 mm long.

HABITAT/RANGE Native. Streamsides and moist flats in foothills and mountains, often with willows and alders, 1,350–3,000 m; sw. Alta. south though the Rocky Mountain region from Nev. to the Dakotas and to nc. Mexico.

SIMILAR SPECIES The leaves of Narrowleaf Cottonwood are 2–11 times as long as wide; they are unique among western poplars and strongly resemble those of willows (*Salix*). Willows are ordinarily much smaller, have one non-resinous bud scale, usually erect catkins, and fewer (up to 8) stamens in the male flowers. At its lower elevational edge, Narrowleaf Cottonwood meets western subspecies of the broader-leaved Eastern Cottonwood (*P. deltoides* W. Bartram ex Marshall; leaves 0.8–1.3 times as long as wide) along that species' upper elevational range, producing a common hybrid, **Lanceleaf Cottonwood** (*P. × acuminata* Rydb. pro sp.), which has narrowly ovate-lanceolate leaves (1.4–2 times as long as wide).

Notes The species is occasionally planted as a shade tree and for erosion control. Songbirds will eat the buds, and Beavers (*Castor canadensis*) feed upon the leaves and bark.

NARROWLEAF COTTONWOOD

Narrowleaf Cottonwood

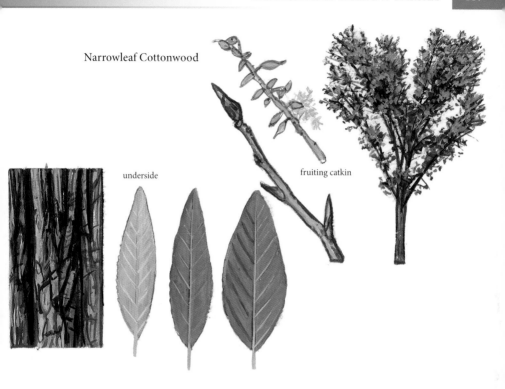

underside

fruiting catkin

Lanceleaf Cottonwood

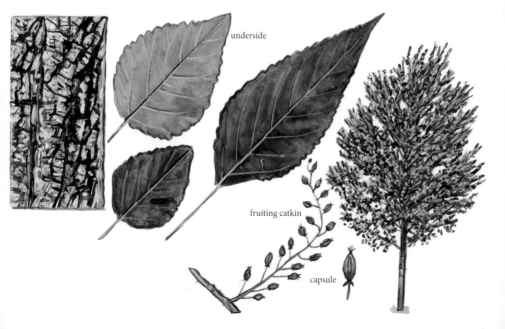

underside

fruiting catkin

capsule

BALSAM POPLAR *Populus balsamifera* L.

A.K.A. HACKMATACK

QUICKID Recognized by the large ovate, bluntly toothed leaves, rounded petiole, and drooping catkins bearing capsules that split into 2 parts.

Deciduous tree, 18–40 m tall, with an erect, slender or massive trunk 30–200 cm diam., sometimes forming multitrunk clones; crown narrow, open, pyramidal, usually with numerous branches. **BARK** Reddish gray, smooth and thin at first, becoming thick and furrowed. **TWIG** Stout, smooth, reddish brown, becoming dark orange, then gray; terminal buds reddish, hairless, resinous; resin fragrant, resembling balsam. **LEAF** Alternate, simple, thin, flexible, usually hairless; ovate or broadly lanceolate, base rounded to cordate, tip long-pointed; margins toothed, teeth mostly rounded. Upper surface lustrous, dark green; lower surface whitish or silvery, usually stained with reddish-orange resin, often with 2 glands near the base. Blade 5–15 cm long, 3–6 cm broad; petiole 1–5 cm long, round in cross section, or slightly flattened in the plane of the blade at the leaf attachment. Turns yellow, or occasionally orange, in autumn. **FLOWER** Male catkins 8–10 cm long, each flower with 20–30 stamens; female catkins 10–13 cm long, bearing 50–70 flowers. Floral bracts deeply cut at the tip, the teeth with fringed tips. Floral disk shallowly cup-shaped, 2–4 mm diam. Mar.–Jun. **FRUIT** Fruiting catkins 10–15 cm long. Capsule egg-shaped, hairless, 3–8 mm long, splitting into 2 parts, almost stalkless.

HABITAT/RANGE Native. Wet, cool, lowlands; stream banks, floodplains, bog margins, moist rocky slopes, sand where the water table is high, montane and boreal regions, 0–3,700 m; scattered in the mountains from sw. Wyo. and c. Colo. northward, throughout Canada to the ne. U.S.; also reported from e. Wash., ne. Ore., and c. Idaho.

SIMILAR SPECIES Balsam Poplar is closely related and similar to Black Cottonwood, with which it hybridizes in the n. Rocky Mountains. The latter has a more spherical capsule that is at least sparsely hairy, and sometimes densely so, and breaks into 3 or 4 sections.

Notes Sometimes referred to as Balm-of-Gilead owing to the alleged healing properties of the fragrant resin on its leaves and buds. This name, however, is more appropriately ascribed to a sterile female clone (cultivar) of Jack Hybrid Poplar (*P. × jackii* Sarg.), a cross between *P. balsamifera* and *P. deltoides* that is distinguished by the combination of large heart-shaped leaves to about 17 cm long, hairy petiole and lower veins; hairless, broadly ovoid capsule; and floral disk 1–3.5 mm diam.

PLAINS COTTONWOOD *Populus deltoides* W. Bartram ex Marshall **subsp.** *monilifera* (Aiton) Eckenw.
RIO GRANDE COTTONWOOD *Populus deltoides* W. Bartram ex Marshall **subsp.** *wislizeni* (S. Watson) Eckenw.

QUICKID The broadly triangular leaves with usually 5–15 small marginal teeth per side help identify this species.

There are 2 western subspecies of *P. deltoides*, which average a little smaller than Eastern Cottonwood (*P. deltoides* subsp. *deltoides*) and differ in features, as described in "Notes," below. Western trees are deciduous, fast-growing, up to 40 m tall, with a spreading crown and a massive trunk sometimes up to 2 m diam. **BARK** Mature bark thick, light tan or grayish, deeply furrowed. **TWIG** Slender, hairless to sparsely long-hairy, at first yellow-brown, becoming tan by the 3rd year; terminal buds greenish, usually 8–15 mm long, fragrantly resinous, densely covered by stiff, short hairs. **LEAF** Alternate, simple, hairless at maturity, broadly triangular; base broadly wedge-shaped, truncate, round, or cordate, bearing 0 or 2 round glands; tip abruptly tapered to a point; margins translucent, with usually 5–15 blunt teeth per side. Blade usually 3–12 cm long (up to 15 cm in rapidly growing shoots), about as broad; petiole 3–9 cm long (roughly equaling blade length), flattened from the

BALSAM POPLAR

PLAINS/RIO GRANDE COTTONWOOD

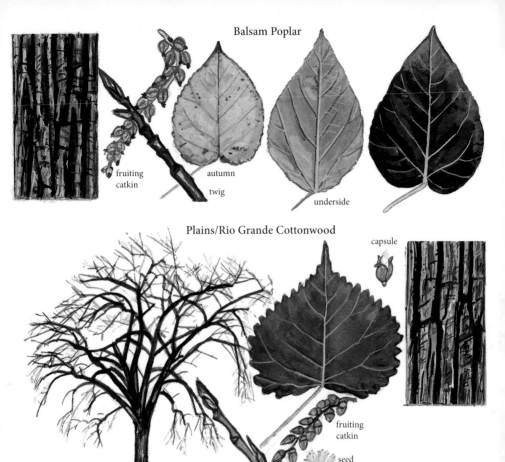

Balsam Poplar

fruiting catkin

autumn twig

underside

Plains/Rio Grande Cottonwood

capsule

fruiting catkin

seed

twig

sides near the blade. **FLOWER** Male catkins 3–5 cm long, each flower with 15–60 stamens, the anthers blunt-tipped; female catkins 5–18 cm long, usually bearing 15–40 flowers. Floral bracts deeply cut and fringed across the tip. Floral disk saucer-shaped, usually 1–4 mm diam. May–Jul., before leaf expansion. **FRUIT** Fruiting catkins 5–24 cm long. Capsule mostly 8–11 mm long, thickly papery, egg-shaped, with a tiny point, splitting into usually 4 parts, on an individual stalk 1–12 mm long.

HABITAT/RANGE Native. Moist places in canyons, on floodplains, near springs and along streams and rivers, 50–2,300 m; e. Wash. to Tex., east across s. Canada and across the U.S. to ne. North America.

SIMILAR SPECIES Fremont Cottonwood often has more stamens, shorter stalks beneath the

capsules, a cup-shaped floral disk 4–7 mm diam., hairless to densely hairy twigs, no glands on the leaf base, and more teeth per side on late leaves. The species are so variable, and so similar, that technical classification has been confused for decades.

Notes Rio Grande Cottonwood (subsp. *wislizeni*) has leaves with a short, narrow-tapered, pointed tip, and no glands at the base, and capsule stalks mostly 8–12 mm long; it occurs in the Rio Grande drainage and adjacent regions from s. Wyo. to se. Ariz., N.M., and w. Tex., to n. Mexico. Plains Cottonwood (subsp. *monilifera*) has long, narrow-tapered tips on the leaves, usually 2 glands on the leaf base, and capsule stalks mostly 1–6 mm long; it occurs widely from the base of the Cascades in e. Wash. to ne. North America, and south through the Rocky Mountain region and the e. U.S. to w. Tex. It is the common cottonwood on the Great Plains.

FREMONT COTTONWOOD *Populus fremontii* S. Watson

QUICK ID The broadly triangular leaves with 20–30 small marginal teeth per side help identify this species.

Deciduous fast-growing, fairly long-lived tree to 30 m tall, with a massive trunk to 3.5 m diam. and a spreading crown. **BARK** At first smooth and light grayish, later pale tan and deeply fissured between narrow, flat, cracked ridges. **TWIG** Slender, hairless to densely yellowish-hairy, at first tan-brown, becoming bone white by the 3rd year; terminal buds tannish-resinous, fragrant, usually densely stiff-hairy, pointed, usually 7–11 mm long. **LEAF** Alternate, simple, hairless or densely hairy, broadly triangular to diamond-ovate; base wedge-shaped, flat, round, or cordate, without glands; tip abruptly tapered to a point; margins translucent, coarsely to finely blunt-toothed (early leaves usually with 3–10 teeth per side; later leaves with 20–30 teeth per side). Blade usually 4–8 cm long (up to 14 cm in rapidly growing shoots), 3–8 cm broad; petiole 1–9 cm long (60–75% length of blade), flattened from the sides near the blade. **FLOWER** Male catkins 3–8 cm long, each flower with mostly 40–60 stamens, anthers blunt-tipped; female catkins 5–10 cm long, bearing usually 15–25 flowers. Floral bracts deeply cut and fringed across the tip. Floral disk broadly cup-shaped, usually 4–7 mm diam. Mar.–Jun., before leaf expansion. **FRUIT** Fruiting catkins to 14 cm long. Capsule 6–11 mm long, thickly stiff-papery, globose, abruptly pointed, splitting into 2–4 parts, on an individual stalk 5–6 mm long.

HABITAT/RANGE Native. Moist places in canyons and on floodplains, 60–2,000 m; sw. U.S. from Colo. and N.M. to Calif.; nw. Mexico.

FREMONT COTTONWOOD

SIMILAR SPECIES Subspecies of *P. deltoides* on average have fewer stamens, longer stalks beneath the capsules, saucer-shaped disks 1–4 mm diam., usually hairless or thinly long-hairy twigs, and usually fewer teeth per side on late leaves.

Notes This is the most common cottonwood in the Southwest west of the Continental Divide. There are 2 subspecies. Subsp. *fremontii* is widespread, its later leaves are about as wide as long, and the twigs are hairless to densely whitish-hairy. Subsp. *mesetae* Eckenw. occurs in w. Tex., its later leaves are longer than wide, and the twigs are usually densely yellowish-hairy. Both subspecies hybridize with *P. deltoides*.

LOMBARDY POPLAR *Populus nigra* L. var. *italica* Münchh.

QUICK ID Recognized by the combination of tapering-columnar form and alternate, often strongly rhombic leaves with toothed margins.

Deciduous tree, 10–20 m tall, erect, often with a massive trunk, low-branching; crown columnar, tapering, branches strongly ascending. **LEAF** Alternate, simple, thick, firm, hairless, widely diamond-shaped (rhombic), margins toothed; blade 5–7 cm long; petiole 2–5 cm long, laterally flattened. **FLOWER** Male catkins to about 8 cm long, stamens 20–55; Mar.–Apr.

HABITAT/RANGE Introduced from Europe (the wild species is widespread in Eurasia); widely planted in the West and persisting, around abandoned farms, fencerows, windbreaks, streams, ponds, 0–2,000 m.

Notes The description applies to a common form of the Black Poplar (*P. nigra* L.) of Eurasia, apparently selected from a male sport in Italy in the 1600s and introduced to the U.S. in the late 1700s. Plants have a tight columnar habit and are primarily male. The few female trees known have a broader crown. Cut twigs are easily rooted in moist soil, and were carried across the West as it was settled, becoming common trees in early mountain towns. Variants of Lombardy Poplar and hybrids with other species can easily be propagated by cuttings and have added to the wealth of ornamental forms, a number of them named.

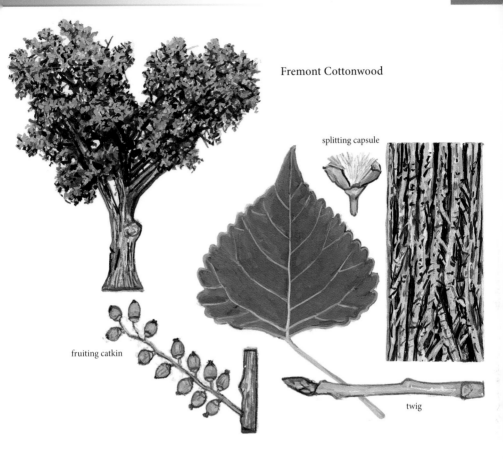

Fremont Cottonwood

splitting capsule

fruiting catkin

twig

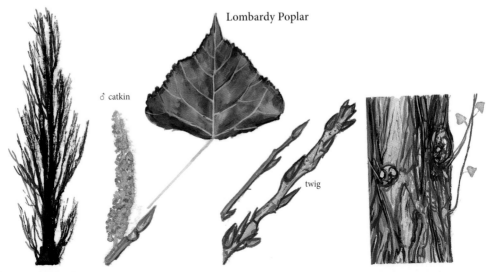

Lombardy Poplar

♂ catkin

twig

QUAKING ASPEN *Populus tremuloides*
Michx.

A.K.A. Trembling Aspen

QUICK ID Recognized by the combination of alternate ovate leaves with finely toothed margins and a petiole flattened from the sides near the blade, smooth yellowish- or creamy-white bark, and a colony-forming habit.

Deciduous tree, 16–35 m tall, with a single usually straight trunk 30–100 cm diam., often forming clonal thickets from the spreading root system. Crown usually branching well above the ground, open, rounded, branches slender. **BARK** Smooth, yellowish- or creamy-white on young trees, becoming grayish and fissured, sometimes developing long, flat ridges. **TWIG** Slender, lustrous reddish brown, hairless, becoming grayish and roughened; terminal buds reddish brown, hairless. **LEAF** Alternate, simple, firm, ovate to circular; base truncate, cordate, or broadly wedge-shaped; tip broadly tapering to a long, slender point or abruptly short-pointed; margins finely toothed, with 25–40 teeth per side. Upper surface lustrous, dark green; lower surface paler and duller, often whitish, usually with 1 or 2 glands near the base. Blade 3–7 cm long, 3–7 cm broad; petiole 1–6 cm long, flattened from the sides near the base. Turns yellow or orange in autumn. **FLOWER** Male catkins 4–8 cm long, stamens 6–12; female catkins 4–8 cm long. Mar.–Jul. **FRUIT** Fruiting catkins 4–12 cm long. Capsule narrowly ovoid, 2–7 mm long, splitting into 2 parts; stalk 1–2 mm long.

HABITAT/RANGE Native. Stream or bog margins, canyons, and mountainsides, 0–4,000 m; common in mountains of the w. U.S. from s. Calif. to w. Tex. and northward, widespread across Canada to Alaska and the ne. U.S., widely scattered in Mexico.

SIMILAR SPECIES The bark is reminiscent of several of the birches, which can be distinguished by leaves with coarsely double-toothed margins and tiny, tightly packed samaras in the fruiting catkins.

Notes Quaking Aspen is the most widely distributed tree in North America. Leaves flutter or quake upon their long, flexible petioles in the slightest breeze. Clones may be large or small, often easily distinguished from one another in autumn by differences in leaf color and time of leaf fall. Individual aspen trees are short-lived, and stands may be replaced by coniferous forest. Nevertheless, the clone may persist by the extensive, nutrient-storing root system, ready to grow vigorously again when fire removes the shading forest. **Eurasian Aspen** (*P. tremula* L.) is closely related to Quaking Aspen, but the leaves usually have slightly larger marginal teeth, and the winter buds are usually minutely hairy. Introduced from Europe and Asia, it is sometimes cultivated in North America and may be found in abandoned plantings, and is sparingly naturalized in the East.

BLACK COTTONWOOD *Populus trichocarpa* Torr. & A. Gray ex Hook.
A.K.A. Balsam Cottonwood, Balm Cottonwood

QUICK ID Lanceolate, finely toothed leaves, dark green above and white to grayish beneath, and a large straight trunk help distinguish this species.

Deciduous fast-growing tree, commonly to 40 m tall, occasionally to 60 m tall; trunk straight, to 1 m diam. (in very large old specimens to 3.1 m diam.). Crown oval, with ascending or erect branches. **BARK** At first smooth and greenish, becoming deeply and regularly furrowed, with sharply defined broad ridges. **TWIG** Slender, densely hairy, at first reddish, gray by the 3rd year, with orange lenticels and large, thick leaf scars; terminal buds red-resinous, fragrant, sparsely hairy or hairless, pointed, usually 6–20 mm long. **LEAF** Alternate, simple, ovate to triangular-ovate, the tip broadly to narrowly angled, margins usually finely blunt-toothed (early leaves 20–50 teeth per side; later leaves with 25–60 teeth per side). Upper surface dark green, hairless; lower surface white, pale gray, or greenish white, often with reddish resin stains, sparsely hairy. Midvein stout, veins often rusty on the lower surface. Blade

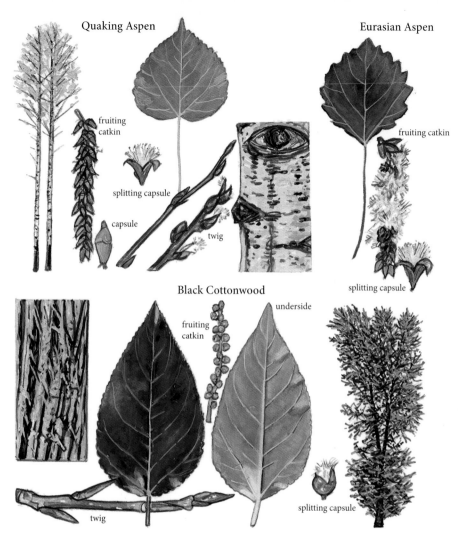

Quaking Aspen

fruiting catkin

splitting capsule

capsule

twig

Eurasian Aspen

fruiting catkin

splitting capsule

Black Cottonwood

fruiting catkin

underside

splitting capsule

twig

usually 5–9 cm long (up to 15 cm in rapidly growing shoots), usually 2–6 mm wide; petiole usually 1–5 cm long, round and slightly channeled on top, at the upper end often swollen and sometimes flattened in the same plane as the blade. **FLOWER** Male catkins 2–5 cm long, each flower with 30–60 stamens, filaments short, anthers large and light purple; female catkins 7–10 cm long, bearing usually 25–50 flowers. Floral bracts deeply cut into pointed, fringed brownish lobes. Floral disk shallowly cup-shaped, usually 4–6 mm diam. Apr.–May, before leaf expansion. **FRUIT** Fruiting catkins up 20 cm long. Capsule 7–9 mm long, thickly papery, sparsely to densely hairy, globose, splitting into 3 or 4 parts, nearly stalkless.

HABITAT/RANGE Native. Moist ground from floodplains to slopes, 0–3,000 m; Alaska south through w. Canada to n. Baja Calif., Utah, and Wyo.

SIMILAR SPECIES Balsam Poplar is similar and Black Cottonwood is sometimes included within it as a subspecies. Balsam Poplar usually has proportionately narrower leaves, with a petiole that is not swollen near the blade, and a capsule that divides into 2 parts.

Notes This is the largest western cottonwood, and probably the largest in the world. Fast-growing hybrids with Eastern Cottonwood are important plantation trees for lumber and pulp.

■ *SALIX*: WILLOWS

The genus *Salix* has about 450 species, mostly in the Northern Hemisphere, about 113 in North America north of Mexico. Nearly 30 in the West are trees or treelike. Occurring from sea-level to beyond timberline, willows are one of the few woody genera to survive on treeless tundra and at very high elevations.

Deciduous or occasionally evergreen, ranging in habit from multistemmed shrubs that sometimes form dense thickets, to trees of moderate size, or in the Arctic and above the tree-line to low woody creepers. **BARK** Generally smooth except on older trunks, where it is variously furrowed, often with scaly ridges. **TWIG** Usually very flexible, hairy or not, often brittle at the very base; a single scale envelops the bud, the scale margins overlapping or fused. **LEAF** Alternate, simple, the margins entire or toothed, flat or rolled under. Dark greenish or reddish glands are present at the top of the petiole in some species. Upper surface usually dull or dark green; lower surface often glaucous, with a silvery-gray bloom that is easily rubbed off. **FLOWER** Unisexual, male and female borne in erect (sometimes slightly drooping) catkins on separate plants. Catkins may appear before the leaves, the male catkins covered in dense, soft grayish hairs prior to blooming (like little kittens, giving the broadly applied name "pussy willow"). In others, catkins bloom with or after leaf emergence. Catkins are borne on slender stalklike branchlets. Perianth present only as a nectary; flowers are both insect- and wind-pollinated. Male flowers have 1–10 stamens; female flowers are borne in the axil of a deciduous or persistent, usually hairy bract, each flower with 1 usually pear-shaped ovary. **FRUIT** Tiny capsule, swollen at the bottom, tapered to a narrow beak at the top, splitting in the upper portion to release the hairy seeds.

It is fair to say that, in North America, where there is moisture there are willows. These pioneer plants quickly occupy newly disturbed ground as the parachute of fine hairs carries, or floats, seeds to newly opened habitats. Twigs that are deciduous from a brittle base may float away, rooting in a new location to form new stands of willows. Willows are important in conservation, quickly colonizing disturbed habitats. Salicin, a component of aspirin, occurs in the bark, and extracts from willow were used by indigenous people to treat toothache, gastrointestinal problems, and dandruff. Twigs were woven into baskets, and split branches were woven into watertight containers, scoops, and fish traps. Slender, straight stems were used for arrow shafts. Willows are important browse for deer, Elk (*Cervus*

canadensis), Moose (*Alces alces*) and domestic livestock. Buds, young shoots, and catkins are consumed by songbirds, ducks, and small mammals. Willow stems and branches are the preferred building material of Beavers (*Castor canadensis*). Several introduced species have numerous horticultural variants, among them Corkscrew Willow (a cultivar of *S. matsudana* Koidz.) and the ever-popular Weeping Willow (*S. babylonica*).

Although the genus is easy to recognize in most instances, willow species are notoriously difficult to separate, often taxing the patience of even the specialist. Willows are variable and they hybridize, resulting in a plethora of forms that makes the delimitation of species tenuous. A combination of leaves, flowers, and fruits is often needed for certain identification, variables affected by time of year and distribution of sexes in a population. Still, leaves alone can be very helpful. Important features include characteristics of the petiole; the shape, color, and distribution of hairs on the leaf blade; and characteristics of the leaf margin.

To help organize the willow species, this section begins with those that have proportionally very narrow leaves and progresses through intermediate forms to species with comparatively broad leaves.

NARROWLEAF WILLOW *Salix exigua*
Nutt.
A.K.A. COYOTE WILLOW, BASKET WILLOW

QUICK ID **This willow is usually thicket-forming and shrubby, with very narrow bluish-green leaves that have appressed silky hairs beneath and margins entire or slightly toothed; usually hairy twigs; and very short stigmas.**

Deciduous thicket-forming shrub or small tree to 10 m tall, with a round-topped crown of slender, ascending or spreading branches; trunks often several, to 13 cm diam. **BARK** Thin, smooth, and gray-brown, becoming longitudinally fissured with age. **TWIG** Yellow- or red-brown, finely hairy to silky with usually spreading hairs. **LEAF** Alternate, simple, narrowly strap-shaped, base wedge-shaped, tip pointed or gradually tapered; margins entire or with tiny, widely spaced, finely pointed teeth, somewhat rolled under. Upper surface bluish green, lustrous, nearly hairless or sparsely silky-hairy; lower surface silvery gray, silky-hairy with appressed or spreading hairs, these thinning with age. Blade 3–14 cm long, 2–8 mm wide (length 10–28 × width); petiole usually 1–5 mm (sometimes to

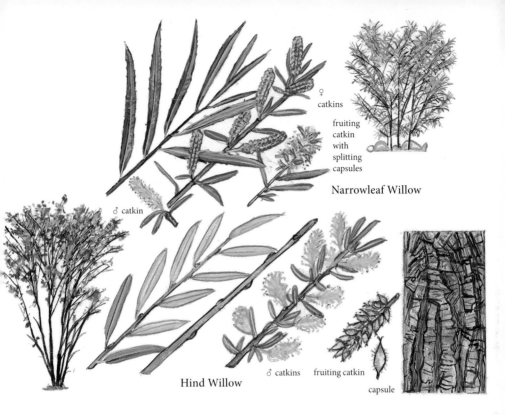

♀ catkins

fruiting catkin with splitting capsules

Narrowleaf Willow

♂ catkin

♂ catkins   fruiting catkin

capsule

Hind Willow

10 mm) long, hairy on upper surface. **FLOWER** Male catkins 1.5–5.5 cm long; stamens 2, filaments hairy in lower half. Female catkins 1.5–7 cm long, 4–12 mm wide, on branchlets 2–55 mm long; bracts deciduous after flowering; pistil 0.2–0.5 mm long, stigmas short and stout, separate and seated nearly directly on the ovary (style and stigmas combined less than 0.6 mm long) Mar.–mid-Jul., after the leaves expand. **FRUIT** Bowling pin-shaped, pale brownish capsule, 4–8 mm long, usually hairless or sometimes with hairy beak; stalk 0–1.5 mm long.

HABITAT/RANGE Native. Moist places, floodplains, shores of lakes and rivers, 600–2,800 m; s. B.C. to s. Calif., east to the western edge of the Great Plains, south to w. Tex.; also n. Mexico

SIMILAR SPECIES Sandbar Willow (*S. interior*) has widely spaced fine teeth on the leaf margins that are not rolled under and the upper surface of the leaf is nearly hairless; it is common and has a range north and east of that of Narrowleaf Willow. Columbia River Willow (*S. columbiana*) has on average longer styles and stigmas, and shorter capsule stalks. Northwest Sandbar Willow (*S. sessilifolia*) occurs west of Narrowleaf Willow in Ore., Wash., and s. B.C.

Notes In late winter and early spring this willow forms attractive dense patches of rich yellowish to reddish twigs. The twigs were woven into baskets by indigenous people. The tree spreads by shoots arising profusely from lateral roots, quickly establishing and covering sandbars. **Hind Willow** (var. *hindsiana* [Benth.] Dorn), from sw. Ore. to s. Calif., at 0–600 m, is sometimes considered a distinct species. It has long-hairy twigs and juvenile foliage; leaves 4–10 cm long, 5–14 mm wide (length 6.5–30 × width); and nearly hairless to very hairy capsules, on stalks 0–0.2 mm long. It may grow to 17 m tall, though is usually no taller than 5 m.

NARROWLEAF WILLOW

SANDBAR WILLOW *Salix interior*
Rowlee

QUICKID This widespread willow is recognized by its thicket-forming habit and narrowly linear leaves that are usually very sparsely hairy and only slightly bluish white beneath.

Deciduous shrub or small tree 4–9 m tall. **LEAF** Linear to strap-shaped; margins flat, with minute well-spaced, fine-tipped teeth. Upper surface yellow-green and hairless or sparsely hairy; lower surface paler, usually sparsely hairy, sometimes hairy to densely silky. Petiole hairless or sparsely hairy on the upper side. Blade 6–16 cm long, 4–11 mm wide (length mostly 11–19 × width). **FLOWER** Male catkins 2–6 cm long. Female catkins 2–7 cm long, on branchlets 3–19 mm long. Apr.–Jul., after the new leaves. **FRUIT** Capsule 5–10 mm long, stalk 0.4–0.8 mm long.

HABITAT/RANGE Native. Common on sandbars, shores, and in other moist habitats, 0–1,800 m; c. Alaska to e. Canada, southward mostly on the eastern side of the Rocky Mountains to c. Tex., lower Mississippi Valley, and ne. U.S.

SIMILAR SPECIES Very similar to, and sometimes considered a subspecies of, Narrowleaf Willow (*S. exigua*), with which it hybridizes on the western Great Plains.

COLUMBIA RIVER WILLOW *Salix columbiana* (Dorn) Argus

QUICKID Restricted to the lower Columbia River and nearby tributaries, this willow has narrow leaves that are silvery gray and sparsely to densely hairy on the lower surface, and silky capsules 3–5 mm long.

Deciduous shrub or tree, very similar to some races of Narrowleaf Willow (*S. exigua*), to 10 m tall. **TWIG** Yellow- to red-brown, pubescent with appressed hairs to hairless. **LEAF** Linear to narrowly elliptic; upper surface green, lower surface silvery gray, both surfaces sparsely silky. Petiole 2–5 mm long, silky-hairy on the upper side, hairs less than 0.5 mm long. Blade 6–12 cm long, 5–17 mm wide (length 6–13 × width), margins with a few small slender-tipped teeth. **FLOWER** Male catkins 2–8 cm long. Female catkins 3.5–9 cm long, on branchlets 1–16 cm long; stigmas flat or broadly cylindric, on a common style (style and stigmas combined 0.8–1.5 mm long). May–Jul. **FRUIT** Somewhat silky-hairy capsule, 3–5 mm long; stalk to 0.3 mm long.

HABITAT/RANGE Native. Sandy areas along the lower Columbia River, below 50 m; Ore., Wash.

SIMILAR SPECIES Northwest Sandbar Willow (*S. sessilifolia*) has petioles that are silky on the upper side, the hairs more than 0.5 mm long.

YEWLEAF WILLOW *Salix taxifolia*
Kunth
A.K.A. YEW WILLOW

QUICKID This dense willow has very narrow, usually finely hairy leaves to 4 cm long, and softly-hairy capsules. It grows in fairly dry habitats near the Mexican border from se. Ariz. to w. Tex.

Deciduous shrub or tree, 2–16 m tall, with stiffly spreading short branches forming a dense round crown; trunk short, to 50 cm diam. **BARK** Light gray to brown, smooth, becoming thick and fissured between interconnecting ridges with small, close scales. **TWIG** Yellow-brown, densely hairy when young. **LEAF** Linear to narrowly oblanceolate, pointed at both ends, dull olive or gray-green,

SANDBAR WILLOW

COLUMBIA RIVER WILLOW

YEWLEAF WILLOW

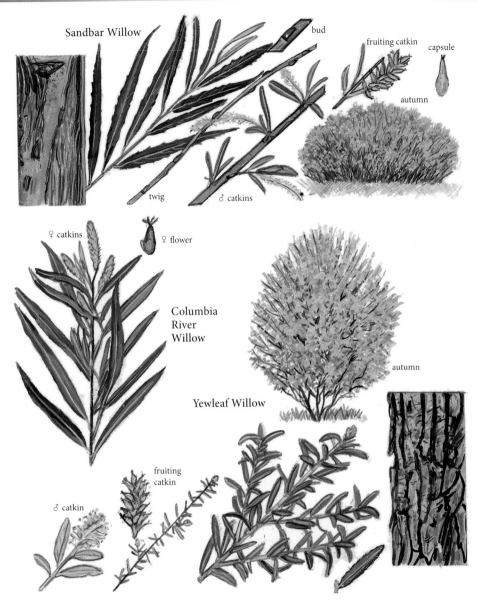

Sandbar Willow

bud

fruiting catkin

capsule

autumn

twig

♂ catkins

♀ catkins

♀ flower

Columbia River Willow

Yewleaf Willow

autumn

fruiting catkin

♂ catkin

hairy; margins flat, entire or with sparse small teeth. Blade 1.5–4 cm long, 1–4.5 mm wide (length 6–25 × width); petiole 0.2–1.5 mm long, hairy. **FLOWER** Male catkins 6–18 mm long, flower with 2 stamens. Female catkins 6–16 mm long, on branchlets usually 8–13 mm long (rarely to 12 cm). Year-round but mostly Mar.–Jun. **FRUIT** Softly-hairy, pale red-brown capsule, 3–6 mm long; stalk to 0.3 mm long.

HABITAT/RANGE Native. Arroyos, floodplains, 400–2,000 m; s. Ariz. to w. Tex., south to Guatemala. Infrequent, slow-growing, in fairly dry habitats for a willow.

DUSKY WILLOW *Salix melanopsis* Nutt.
A.K.A. LONGLEAF WILLOW

QUICKID Distinguished by narrow leaves that are usually dark green above, paler beneath, slightly hairy, and with petioles that are hairless on the upper side, and usually hairless capsules.

Deciduous shrub or tree, 1–5 m tall; similar to, and sometimes considered a subspecies of, Narrowleaf Willow (*S. exigua*), but usually darker green and with proportionately broader leaves. **TWIG** Gray- to dark red-brown, hairy or smooth. **LEAF** Strap-shaped, tapered at both ends; margins flat, usually with a few small slender-tipped teeth. Upper surface dark green; lower surface silvery gray, nearly hairless at maturity. Blade 3–13 cm long, 5–20 mm wide (length 3.5–8 × width); petiole 2–8 mm long, hairless on the upper side. **FLOWER** Male catkins 2–5 cm long. Female catkins 2–6 cm long, on branchlets 4–12 mm long; styles separate, stigmas slenderly cylindric or 2 plump lobes. May–Jul. **FRUIT** Usually hairless capsule, 4–5 mm long; stalk to 0.7 mm long.

HABITAT/RANGE Native. Floodplains, shores, wooded areas, subalpine meadows, 600–3,100 m; sw. Canada to s. Calif., nw. Nev., n. Utah, and c. Colo.

NORTHWEST SANDBAR WILLOW
Salix sessilifolia Nutt.
A.K.A. NORTHWEST WILLOW, SILVERLEAF WILLOW

QUICKID Hairy bluish-green leaves that are 3–8.5 times as long as wide, silky-hairy peti-oles, and hairy capsules on very short stalks help identify this willow.

Deciduous shrub or tree to 8 m tall, trunk 20–25 cm diam. (rarely to 1 m); similar to races of Narrowleaf Willow (*S. exigua*), but with propor-tionately broader leaves. **TWIG** Red-brown, densely hairy. **LEAF** Linear to narrowly elliptic, margins with sparse small teeth; dull bluish green, hairy, densely so below. Blade 4–12 cm long, 8–16 mm wide (length 3–8.5 × width); petiole 1–6 mm long, with long silky hairs. **FLOWER** Male catkins 3.5–4.5 cm long. Female catkins 4–7 cm long, on branchlets 2–3 cm long; stigmas long, slender, flat, or cylindric, on a common style. Apr.–May. **FRUIT** Hairy capsule, 4–5 mm long; stalk 0.1–1 mm long.

HABITAT/RANGE Native. Shores, moist areas, 0–200 m; sw. B.C. to w. Ore.

BONPLAND WILLOW *Salix bonplandiana* Kunth
A.K.A. TOUMEY WILLOW

QUICKID Slender branches, leaves that are sil-very gray beneath, and slender female catkins with persistent bracts help identify this tree.

Semievergreen tree to 13 m tall, with a round-topped crown of slender, ascending or drooping branches; trunks 1 to few, 10–50 cm diam. **BARK** Mature bark dark brown to blackish, with slen-der fissures and broad flat-topped ridges with appressed scales. **TWIG** Yellowish, becoming red-brown, hairless. **LEAF** Alternate, simple, wither-ing on the tree in winter (evergreen in warmer climates); narrowly lanceolate, base wedge-shaped to convex-tapered, tip tapered to a point, margins finely toothed to entire. Upper surface green, lus-trous, hairless or with short ascending hairs; lower surface silvery gray, hairless or with appressed hairs. Blade 6–16 cm long, 7–27 mm wide (length 4.5–11 × width); petiole 4–16 mm long, rarely with spherical glands at the top. **FLOWER** Male catkins 2.5–13 cm long; stamens 3–7, filaments hairy at the base. Female catkins 2.5–5 cm long, 6–12 mm

DUSKY WILLOW

NORTHWEST SANDBAR WILLOW

BONPLAND WILLOW

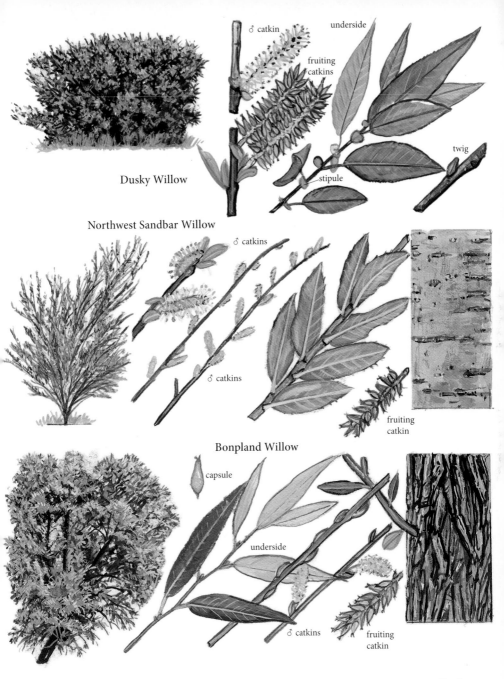

Dusky Willow

Northwest Sandbar Willow

Bonpland Willow

♂ catkin

underside

fruiting catkins

stipule

twig

♂ catkins

♂ catkins

fruiting catkin

capsule

underside

♂ catkins

fruiting catkin

wide, on branchlets 0–10 mm long; bracts persistent after flowering. Mostly Feb.–Apr. but year-round where warm. **FRUIT** Hairless, yellowish to light reddish capsule, pear-shaped, often inversely so, 3–6 mm long; stalk 0.4–2.4 mm long.

HABITAT/RANGE Native. Riparian woodlands, 700–2,000 m; c. Ariz. to Central America.

GOODDING BLACK WILLOW *Salix gooddingii* C.R. Ball
A.K.A. VALLEY WILLOW

QUICK ID Usually yellowish and often brittle twigs, leaves that are green beneath and have toothed margins, and 4–8 stamens in the flowers of male catkins help identify this tree.

Deciduous tree to 15 m tall, sometimes twice that height; trunks 1 to few, often forked at the base, to 1 m diam.; crown loose, irregular, round-topped. **BARK** Mature bark thick, dark gray-brown to black, rough, with deep interconnecting furrows and ridges breaking into plates. **TWIG** Often brittle at the base, yellowish or yellow-green, sometimes red-brown, hairy to almost hairless. **LEAF** Alternate, simple, broadly oblong to linear; base wedge-shaped to convex-tapered; tip tapered to a point or tail-like extension, or simply pointed; margins toothed. Upper surface dull green, lustrous, nearly hairless to short-hairy; lower surface sometimes slightly paler, semilustrous, hairless or with wavy hairs. Blade 7–13 cm long, 1–1.5 cm wide (length 5–12.5 × width); petiole 4–10 mm long, sometimes with globose glands near the blade. **FLOWER** Male catkins 3–8 cm long; stamens 4–8, filaments hairy at the base. Female catkins 3–8 cm long, 6–15 mm wide, on branchlets 2–48 mm long; bracts deciduous after flowering. Late Mar.–Jun., as the leaves emerge. **FRUIT** Pear-shaped capsule, 6–7 mm long, blushed with red, hairless or hairy; stalk 1.2–3.2 mm long.

HABITAT/RANGE Native. Moist meadows, floodplains, shores, 0–1,300 m, sometimes higher; Calif., s. Nev., s. Utah, w. Colo., east across Ariz. and N.M. to sw. Okla. and s. Tex.; nw. Mexico.

SIMILAR SPECIES Red Willow (*S. laevigata*) and Peachleaf Willow (*S. amygdaloides*) have similarly shaped leaves, but they are silvery gray beneath.

Goodding Willow has been considered a variety of the Black Willow (*S. nigra*) of the East; the two meet and intergrade in Tex. and Okla. Black Willow has gray-brown to red-brown twigs.

Notes Twigs that drop may be washed to new sites, where they root and establish new trees. Native Americans used thin splints of the wood to weave watertight baskets, the wood swelling and sealing the basket when wet. Deer and livestock will browse foliage.

BLACK WILLOW *Salix nigra* Marshall

QUICK ID This willow forms a moderately large tree with brittle, usually grayish or reddish twigs; and green leaves that are lustrous above, with the lower surface semilustrous and often slightly hairy in the vein axils and along the main veins.

Deciduous tree, 12–20 m tall, trunk 30–100 cm diam. **TWIG** Gray-brown to red-brown, hairy or hairless, very brittle at the base. **LEAF** Narrowly lanceolate or narrowly linear, margins finely glandular-toothed. Green, upper surface lustrous; lower surface semilustrous and often hairy on the veins and in vein axils. Blade 5–18 cm long, 5–20 mm wide (length 6–13 × width); petiole 2–10 mm long, hairless or hairy on the upper side, bearing spherical glands near the base of the blade. **FLOWER** Male catkins 3–8 cm long; stamens 4–6, filaments hairy at the base. Female catkins 2–7.5 cm long, on branchlets 6–35 mm long; bracts deciduous after flowering. Mar.–Jul. **FRUIT** Capsule 3–5 mm long; stalk 0.5–1.5 mm long.

HABITAT/RANGE Native. Floodplains, sandbars, wet or moist places, 10–1,400 m; widespread in the East, barely entering the West in c. Tex., Okla., and sw. Colo.

SIMILAR SPECIES Similar to, intergrading with, and replaced by Goodding Black Willow (*S. gooddingii*) westward.

GOODDING BLACK WILLOW

BLACK WILLOW

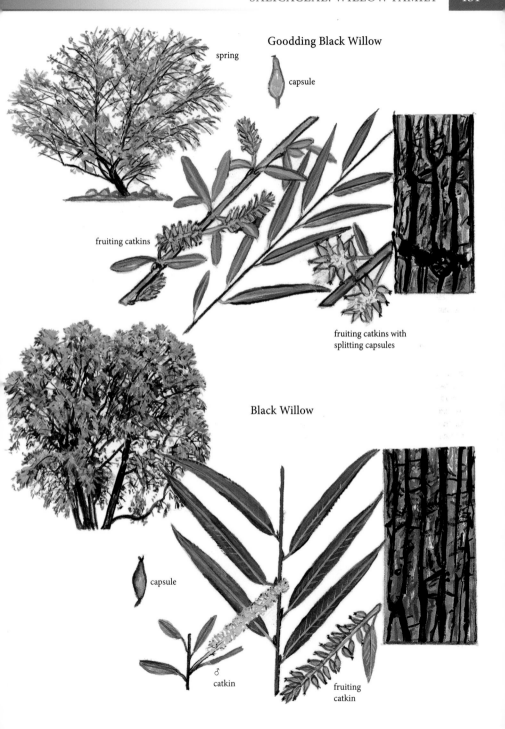

Goodding Black Willow

spring

capsule

fruiting catkins

fruiting catkins with
splitting capsules

Black Willow

capsule

♂
catkin

fruiting
catkin

CAROLINA WILLOW *Salix caroliniana*
Michx.
A.K.A. COASTAL PLAIN WILLOW

QUICK ID Found in the West only in Tex. on the Edwards Plateau, and distinguished by its narrowly lanceolate leaves that are bluish white beneath and finely toothed along the margins, and bracts beneath the female flowers that are deciduous after flowering.

Deciduous tree, 5–10 m tall, trunk 30–40 cm diam. **TWIG** Dull yellow- or red-brown, often hairy. **LEAF** Narrowly lanceolate, margins finely toothed, upper surface green, lower surface bluish white, often hairy on the veins. Blade 5–22 cm long, 1–3 cm wide (length 5–10 × width); petiole 3–22 mm long, hairy on the upper side, with spherical glands near the base of the blade. **FLOWER** Male catkins 3–10 cm long, flower with 4–7 stamens. Female catkins 3–9 cm long, on branchlets 3–35 mm long; bracts deciduous after flowering. Dec.–May. **FRUIT** Capsule 3–5 mm long; stalk 1–5 mm long.

HABITAT/RANGE Native. Floodplains, wet or moist places, 10–600 m; widespread in the East, barely entering the West on Edwards Plateau, c. Tex.

PACIFIC WILLOW *Salix lasiandra*
Benth. **var.** *lasiandra*
A.K.A. WESTERN SHINING WILLOW, WAXY WILLOW, YELLOW WILLOW, WESTERN BLACK WILLOW

QUICK ID This willow has slightly twisted, dark green leaves that are rounded at the base, with the margins finely toothed; a petiole with glands at the upper end; and 3–6 stamens in male flowers.

Deciduous shrub or tree to 11 m tall; trunks often several, crooked or leaning, to 90 cm diam.; crown irregular, round-topped, with erect or slightly drooping branches. **BARK** Mature bark dark gray-brown, thick, with deep furrows and flat, scaly, interconnecting ridges. **TWIG** Sometimes brittle at the base, yellow-, gray- or red-brown, usually initially hairy, later mostly hairless. **LEAF** Alternate, simple, narrowly oblong, lanceolate, or oblanceolate, often slightly twisted or curved, base convex-tapered to rounded, tip tapered to a fine point or tail-like; margins flat, finely toothed. Upper surface dark green, glossy, hairless or sparsely hairy; lower surface often whitish, nearly hairless to hairy with white and sometimes also rusty hairs. Blade 5–17 cm long, 1–3 cm wide (length 3–10 × width); petiole 4–30 mm long, deeply grooved on the upper side, hairless or hairy, with clusters of spherical or thin, flat glands near the junction with the blade. **FLOWER** Male catkins 2–8 cm long; stamens 3–6, filaments hairy at the base. Female catkins persistent through much of the summer, 2–10 cm long, 6–17 mm wide; on branchlets 6–56 mm long; bracts deciduous before the capsule matures. Late Mar.–early Jun., as the leaves expand. **FRUIT** Hairless, pear-shaped, pale brown capsule, 4–11 mm long; stalk 0.8–2 mm long.

HABITAT/RANGE Native. Silt and sand near water, 0–2,700 m; c. Alaska south through w. and c. Canada to s. Calif., w. and se. Utah, s. Colo., ne. Ariz., and n. N.M.

SIMILAR SPECIES In Pacific Willow the bud scale margins are fused together. In Goodding Black Willow (*S. gooddingii*) the scale margins overlap but are not fused, and the leaves are more or less green on both sides. In Red Willow (*S. laevigata*) the bud scales are not fused, the leaves are whitish beneath, but bracts in the female catkin drop shortly after flowering. **Tail-leaf** or **Whiplash Willow** (*S. lasiandra* var. *caudata* [Nutt.] Sudw.) usually has leaves that are green beneath, has only spherical glands on the petiole, and flowers in late May–late Jun.; it occurs in similar habitats to

CAROLINA WILLOW   PACIFIC WILLOW   TAIL-LEAF WILLOW

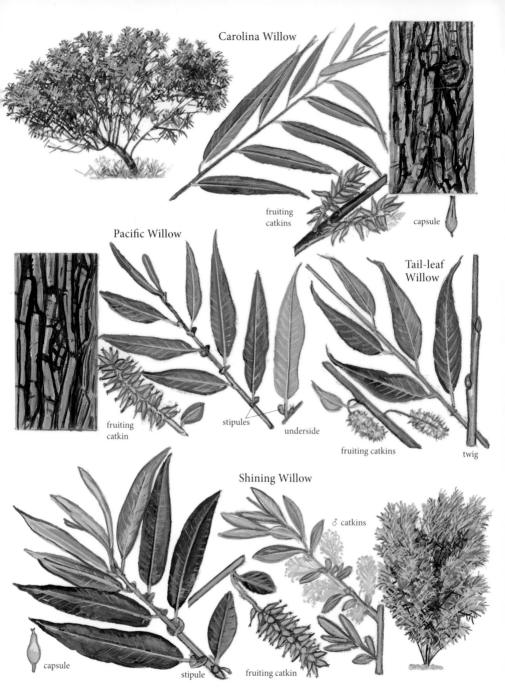

Carolina Willow

fruiting catkins

capsule

Pacific Willow

Tail-leaf Willow

fruiting catkin

stipules

underside

fruiting catkins

twig

Shining Willow

♂ catkins

capsule

stipule

fruiting catkin

Pacific Willow at 30–3,100 m, from c. Alaska to Calif., Nev., Utah and Colo. Pacific and Tail-leaf willows have been considered subspecies within the very closely related, geographically separate

Shining Willow (*S. lucida* Muhl.) of ne. North America, which barely reaches the West on the Canadian central plains and in the Black Hills, S.D.; its leaves are usually not whitish beneath.

ARROYO WILLOW *Salix lasiolepis* Benth.

A.K.A. WHITE WILLOW

QUICK ID Thickish bicolored leaves with rolled margins, petioles longer than 3 mm, female catkins often stalkless or nearly so and with persistent blackish bracts, and hairless capsules help identify this species.

Deciduous shrub or tree, 1.5–10 m tall; trunks 1 to several, 8–18 cm diam.; crown open, round, with slender, erect branches **BARK** Thin, smooth, brown to gray, becoming darker with age, forming shallow fissures and broad ridges. **TWIG** Yellowish to red-brown, lightly to densely hairy, becoming dark and hairless by the 2nd year. **LEAF** Alternate, simple, thick and stiff, narrowly oblong to obovate, base wedge-shaped to convex-tapered, tip pointed to gradually tapered to a slender point; margins entire or with fine, sparse teeth, also slightly wavy and rolled under. Upper surface dark green, lustrous, mostly hairy; lower surface silvery gray, sparsely to woolly-hairy. Blade 3.5–12.5 cm long, 6–32 mm wide (length 2–10 × width); petiole 3–16 mm long, convex to shallowly grooved, hairy. **FLOWER** Male catkins 2–9 cm long; stamens 2, filaments hairless. Female catkins 2–7 cm long, 7–12 mm wide, on branchlets 0–7 mm long; bracts blackish, persistent after flowering; female flower on a stalk to 2 mm long. Jan.–Jun., before the leaves emerge. **FRUIT** Hairless, pear-shaped reddish-brown capsule, 2.5–5 mm long; stalk 1–1.7 mm long.

HABITAT/RANGE Native. Moist places from stream shores to coastal headlands and salt marshes, 0–2,800 m; Wash. to Calif., Ariz., and N.M.; nw. Mexico.

ARROYO WILLOW

TRACY WILLOW *Salix tracyi* C.R. Ball

QUICK ID This willow grows near the coast in nw. Calif. and sw. Ore. Its leaves are silvery gray beneath, with hairs along the midrib.

Deciduous slender shrub or small tree, 1–6 m tall, with 1 to several smooth gray-green trunks and a round crown. **TWIG** Yellow- or red-brown, usually hairless and with a slight grayish bloom, sometimes hairy. **LEAF** Strap-shaped to oblanceolate, pointed at both ends; margins slightly rolled under, entire or with sparse small teeth. Upper surface lustrous green, lower surface silvery-gray; both surfaces hairy, the lower more so. Blade 5–10 cm long, 1.5–3.5 cm wide (length 2–4 × width); petiole 5–11 mm long, velvety above. **FLOWER** Male catkins 2–3 cm long; flower with 2 stamens. Female catkins 2–4 cm long on branchlets 1.5–3 mm long. **FRUIT** Hairless, pale brown capsule, 2.5–3.5 mm long; stalk 1–2.4 mm long.

HABITAT/RANGE Native. Near the coast on sand and gravel bars, floodplains, 90–500 m; nw. Calif., sw. Ore.

SIMILAR SPECIES Closely related to Arroyo Willow (*S. lasiolepis*).

TRACY WILLOW

Arroyo Willow

♂ catkins

underside

fruiting catkin

Tracy Willow

underside

♂ catkins

fruiting catkin

PEACHLEAF WILLOW *Salix amygdaloides* Andersson
A.K.A. ALMOND WILLOW

QUICKID The combination of usually hairless branches, twigs, petioles, and leaves; long-tapering leaf tip; and dull upper leaf surface and bluish-white lower surface help identify this widespread willow.

Deciduous large shrub or small tree, 4–20 m tall; 1 to several trunks to about 40 cm diam. Crown ascending, the branches gray-brown and arching, often with drooping tips. **BARK** Brown, becoming grayish brown, irregularly furrowed, with broad, flat, shaggy ridges. **TWIG** Smooth, slender, flexible, hairless, lustrous yellow or reddish brown with pale lenticels and lustrous buds. **LEAF** Alternate, simple, lanceolate or narrowly elliptic; base narrowly wedge-shaped or tapered, rarely indented; tip long-tapering to a sharp tip; margins finely toothed. Upper surface dull green, hairless, or sparsely hairy along the midvein; lower surface bluish white, hairless. Blade 5–14 cm long, 2–4 cm broad (length 3–6 × width); petiole 7–21 mm long, hairless or finely hairy, with or without glands near the point of leaf attachment. **FLOWER** Male catkins 2–8 cm long; stamens 3–7, filaments hairy near the base. Female catkins 41–110 mm long, 8–16 mm diam., on branchlets 2–3.5 cm long; bracts deciduous after flowering. Apr.–Jun., with the new leaves. **FRUIT** Hairless, pear-shaped reddish or yellowish capsule, 3–7 mm long; stalk 1.5–3 mm long.

HABITAT/RANGE Native. Sandy, silty, or gravelly floodplains, lake margins, marshes, dunes, 60–2,400 m; s. B.C., s. Wash., e. Ore. to w. Tex., northeast to c. and se. Canada and ne. U.S.

SIMILAR SPECIES Carolina Willow (*S. caroliniana*) and Red Willow (*S. laevigata*) usually have hairy twigs.

RED WILLOW *Salix laevigata* Bebb
A.K.A. POLISHED WILLOW, SMOOTH WILLOW

QUICKID Brittle twigs, leaves that are silvery gray beneath, and slender female catkins with deciduous bracts help identify this tree.

Deciduous tree to 15 m tall, with an irregular, round-topped crown; usually 1 trunk, 15–30 cm diam. **BARK** Mature bark dark reddish brown, rough, with furrows and interconnecting narrow, hard ridges. **TWIG** Brittle at the base, yellow- or red-brown, short-hairy or hairless. **LEAF** Alternate, simple, lanceolate to elliptic or narrowly obovate, base wedge-shaped to rounded or cordate, tip tapered to a point or tail-like, margins finely toothed to entire. Upper surface bluish green, lustrous, hairless or with short ascending hairs; lower surface silvery gray, hairless or with ascending white or rusty hairs. Blade 5–19 cm long, 1–3.5 cm wide (length 3–9 × width); petiole 4–18 mm long, sometimes with glands near the base of the blade. **FLOWER** Male catkins 3–8 cm long; stamens 3–7, filaments hairy at the base. Female catkins 3–8 cm long, 6–11 mm wide, on branchlets 3–14 mm long; bracts deciduous after flowering. Mostly Apr.–Jun., sometimes as early as Dec. southward. **FRUIT** Hairless yellowish capsule, pear-shaped, often inversely so, or ellipsoid, 3–6 mm long; stalk 1.4–2.8 mm long.

HABITAT/RANGE Native. Watercourses, lake shores, ditches, other moist areas, 0–2,200 m; s. Ore., Nev., s. Utah south to nw. Mexico.

SIMILAR SPECIES Red Willow has been considered a variety of Bonpland Willow (*S. bonplandiana*), which has hairless twigs and persistent bracts beneath the female flowers.

Notes As is characteristic of willows, this species grows rapidly. Longevity is unknown, but a 50-year-old tree is considered old.

PEACHLEAF WILLOW

RED WILLOW

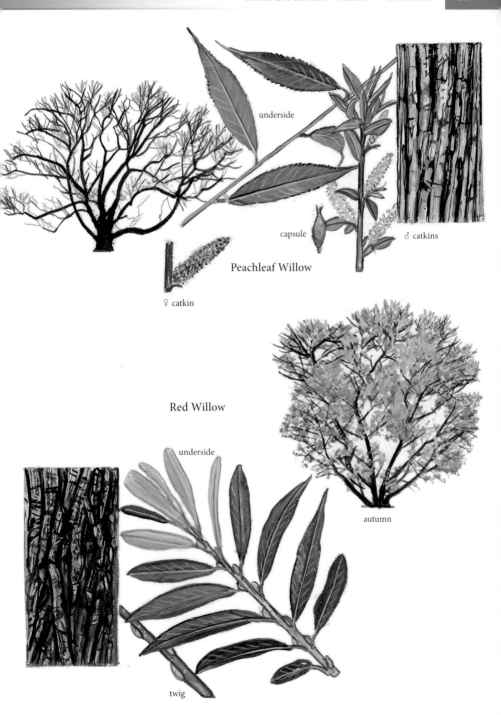

underside

capsule

♂ catkins

Peachleaf Willow

♀ catkin

Red Willow

underside

autumn

twig

WEEPING WILLOW *Salix babylonica* L.

Deciduous low-branching tree, 4–20 m tall; branches strongly drooping, the tips often reaching the ground. **TWIG** Slender, yellow-green or brown, sparsely to moderately hairy. **LEAF** Lanceolate, narrowly oblong, or narrowly elliptic, the tip narrowly long-tapering to an extended point; margins with fine, sharply pointed teeth. Both surfaces dull grayish green, hairless or lightly silky-hairy. Blade 9–16 cm long, 5–20 mm wide (length 4.5–11 × width); petiole 7–9 mm long, hairy below. **FLOWER** Male catkins 13–35 mm long; stamens 2, filaments hairy below. Female catkins 9–27 mm long, on branchlets 0–4 mm long. Feb.–May. **FRUIT** Hairless, pale brown capsule, 2–3 mm long; stalk lacking or nearly so. **HABITAT/RANGE** Introduced; a popular ornamental, rarely naturalized in Calif. below 50 m; widely naturalized in the Southeast. *Notes* Hybrid "weeping willows" more commonly naturalized in Calif. are *S.* × *sepulcralis* Simonk. (*S. alba* × *S. babylonica*), with more densely hairy twigs; and *S.* × *pendulina* Wender. (*S. babylonica* × *S. euxina* V. Belyaeva), with leaves averaging wider.

WHITE WILLOW *Salix alba* L.

QUICK ID Recognized by its drooping branch tips, comparatively large size, and silvery-white appearance when viewed from a distance.

Deciduous fast-growing tree, 10–25 m tall, with 1 or multiple trunks; crown somewhat conical, many-branched, the branches drooping at their tips. **BARK** Brown, becoming deeply furrowed between corky ridges. **TWIG** Slender, flexuous, pendent, yellowish, gray-brown, or red-brown, usually densely hairy. **LEAF** Alternate, simple, narrow, oblong, elliptic or lanceolate; base narrowly wedge-shaped; tip long-tapering to a slender point; margins finely or bluntly toothed. Upper surface dull, sparsely silky-hairy; lower surface silky-hairy, bluish white. Blade 6–11 cm long, 1–2 cm broad (length 4–7 × width); petiole 3–13 mm long, grooved above, bearing pairs or clusters of spherical glands or lobes near the blade. **FLOWER** Male catkins 27–60 mm long; stamens 2, filaments hairy on lower half. Female catkins 3–5 cm long, 4–8 mm diam., on branchlets 3–14 mm long; bracts deciduous after flowering; stigmas joined to a common style. May–Jun. **FRUIT** Hairless capsule, 3–5 mm long; stalk less than 1 mm long.

HABITAT/RANGE Introduced from Europe in colonial times; widely cultivated, naturalized in c. Canada, perhaps sw. Canada, and several western states from Mont. to Ariz.; more widely naturalized in the East.

SIMILAR SPECIES Several other western willows have narrow leaves with the lower surface sometimes or regularly very pale relative to the upper surface: Bonpland Willow (*S. bonplandiana*), Carolina Willow (*S. caroliniana*), Pacific Willow (*S. lasiandra* var. *lasiandra*), Arroyo Willow (*S. lasiolepis*), Peachleaf Willow (*S. amygdaloides*), Satiny Willow (*S. pellita*), Meadow Willow (*S. petiolaris*), and Littletree Willow (*S. arbusculoides*). For positive identification, note stamen number, persistence of bracts on female catkins, leaf margin teeth, glands on petiole, habit, and geography. Others with very pale leaf undersides have leaves that are relatively broader or of a clearly different shape.

Notes This popular ornamental has given rise to numerous cultivars varying in size, crown shape, and foliage, many of which are from hybrids with native species.

Weeping Willow (*Salix babylonica*)

♂ catkins

underside

fruiting catkin

Weeping Willow (*Salix × sepulcralis*)

capsule

♂ catkins

twig

White Willow

♂ catkins

capsule

fruiting catkin

SATINY WILLOW *Salix pellita*
(Andersson) Bebb

QUICK ID This willow is recognized in part by narrow leaves that are strongly bluish white below and lustrous above, and bluish-gray branches.

Deciduous shrub or tree, 3–6 m tall, usually with multiple trunks. **TWIG** Yellow-brown or red-brown, usually strongly glaucous, hairless or finely hairy; branchlets often brittle at the base. **LEAF** Linear to narrowly lanceolate; margins usually rolled under, entire, wavy, or finely bluntly toothed. Upper surface lustrous, usually glossy, hairless or sparsely hairy; lower surface strongly bluish white, usually densely hairy. Blade 4–12 cm long (length 4–11 × width). Petiole 3–14 mm long, hairless or hairy on the upper surface, sometimes with spherical glands near the base of the blade. **FLOWER** Male catkins 2–4 cm long; stamens 2, filaments hairless or hairy at the base. Female catkins 2–8 cm long, 7–17 mm diam., on branchlets 0–7 mm long; bracts persistent after flowering. Apr.–Jun., before leaf expansion. **FRUIT** Sparsely to densely silky capsule, 3–6 mm long; stalk 0.5–1 mm long.

HABITAT/RANGE Native. Usually on moist alluvial soils, 0–800 m; from c. Sask. across e. Canada and ne. U.S.; barely enters the West.

GEYER WILLOW *Salix geyeriana*
Andersson
A.K.A. SILVER WILLOW

QUICK ID Recognized by its grayish appearance, silky-hairy leaves, and short globose catkins.

Deciduous shrub or tree, 1–5 m tall, with 1 to several stems arising from a tight basal cluster. **TWIG** Yellow-, red-, or purple-brown, often with a grayish bloom, hairless to hairy. **LEAF** Narrowly strap-shaped or elliptic, tapered at both ends; margins flat or slightly rolled, entire or with a few teeth; usually silky silvery-hairy, often thinning on the upper surface with age, lower surface silvery gray beneath the hairs. Blade 3–9 cm long, 6–14 mm wide (length 3.5–11 × width). Petiole 2–9 mm long. **FLOWER** Male catkins globose, 1–2 cm long, flower with 2 stamens. Female catkins nearly globose, 1–2 cm long, branchlet 1–8 mm long. Late Apr.–late Jun., with or before leaves. **FRUIT** Moderately silky-hairy capsule, 4–6 mm long; stalk 1–3 mm long.

HABITAT/RANGE Native. Moist areas, 10–3,300 m; s. B.C. south to Calif., Nev., Ariz., and Colo.

MEADOW WILLOW *Salix petiolaris* Sm.

QUICK ID The long, slender, arching purplish stems and branches and open wetland habitat help distinguish Meadow Willow.

Deciduous shrub or multitrunked tree, 1–7 m tall; branches slender, arching, red-brown, purple, or violet, finely hairy, later hairless. **TWIG** Finely hairy, yellow-green or red-brown at first, soon aging to purplish or dark reddish. **LEAF** Narrowly elliptic or lanceolate, margins entire or finely toothed. Upper surface hairless or sparsely hairy; lower surface densely silky-hairy, the hairs bluish white, becoming hairless. Blade 4–15 cm long, 1–3 cm broad (length 5–9 × width); petiole usually hairy. **FLOWER** Male catkins 1–3 cm long; stamens 2, filaments hairy at the base. Female catkins 1–4 cm long, 6–18 mm diam., on branchlets 1–11 mm long; bracts persistent after flowering. Apr.–Jun., with the new leaves. **FRUIT** Finely silky-hairy capsule, 5–9 mm long; stalk 1.5–4 mm long.

HABITAT/RANGE Native. Moist prairies, meadows, openings in woods, 10–2,700 m; nw. Canada southeast to se. Canada and ne. U.S.

SATINY WILLOW   GEYER WILLOW   MEADOW WILLOW

rolled leaf margins

Geyer Willow

underside

Satiny Willow

capsule

fruiting catkins

underside

Geyer Willow

fruiting catkin

Meadow Willow

♂ catkin

capsule

underside

PURPLEOSIER WILLOW *Salix purpurea* L.

Deciduous clonal shrub or shrubby tree, 1.5–5 m tall, usually with numerous erect or arching branches and multiple trunks. **TWIG** Purplish or yellowish brown, hairless. **LEAF** Alternate, sometimes opposite or nearly so, narrowly oblong or oblanceolate, often widest near the apex, hairless; upper surface dark green, lower surface bluish white; margins entire or obscurely toothed toward the sharply pointed tip. Blade 2–10 cm long, 1.5–3 cm broad (length 3–10 × width); petiole 2–7 mm long. **FLOWER** Male catkins 25–33 mm long; stamens 2, filaments joined and hairy at the base. Female catkins 13–35 mm long, 3–7 mm diam., on branchlets 0.5-3 mm long; bracts black or bicolored, persistent after flowering. Mar.–May, before the new leaves. **FRUIT** Densely short-silky, egg-shaped capsule, 2–5 mm long, stalkless or nearly so. **HABITAT/RANGE** Introduced from Europe; cultivated, sparingly naturalized in widely scattered locations in the West, more common in the East.

SITKA WILLOW *Salix sitchensis* Sanson ex Bong.
A.K.A. SILKY WILLOW, COULTER WILLOW

QUICK ID The rough, dark green upper surface and satiny-hairy lower surface of the leaves, and the single stamen in the male flower are distinctive.

Deciduous shrub or tree to 8 m tall; trunks 1 to several, 10–20 cm (rarely 30 cm) diam.; crown much-branched, round-topped. **BARK** Gray, smooth, becoming furrowed and slightly scaly. **TWIG** Yellow-, gray-, or red-brown, densely hairy at least through the 1st year. **LEAF** Alternate, simple, narrowly oblanceolate to obovate; base wedge-shaped to convex-tapered; tip convex-pointed to gently

tapering to a narrow point; margins finely toothed to entire, flat or rolled under. Upper surface dark green, somewhat rough with impressed veins, dull, more or less hairless at maturity; lower surface grayish white and satiny with dense hairs. Blade 3–12 cm long, 2–5 cm wide (length 2–4 × width); petiole 3–13 mm long, velvety. **FLOWER** Male catkins 2–5 cm long; stamen 1, filament hairless. Female catkins 2.5–7 cm long (to 12 cm in fruit), on branchlets 1–9 mm long; bracts brownish, persistent after flowering. Early Apr.–mid-Jun., just before or with leaf emergence. **FRUIT** Hairy, ovoid or pear-shaped capsule, 3.5–5.5 mm long; stalk 0.4–2.4 mm long.

HABITAT/RANGE Native. Coastal dunes, headlands, openings in forests, 0–1,800 m; Alaska to c. Calif., east to c. Alta. and w. Mont.

LITTLETREE WILLOW *Salix arbusculoides* Andersson

QUICK ID This willow has lustrous red-brown twigs, leaves pointed at both ends, shiny green above and white beneath, and silky capsules.

Deciduous thicket-forming shrub or tree to 9 m tall, with 1 to several trunks up to 15 cm diam. **BARK** Gray to reddish brown, smooth. **TWIG** Shiny gray- to red-brown, thinly hairy or hairless. **LEAF** Alternate, simple, narrowly elliptic to lanceolate, tapering at both ends; margins finely toothed, slightly rolled under. Upper surface green, lustrous to glossy, hairless; lower surface whitish, often finely silvery-hairy. Blade 4–8 cm long, 1–2 cm wide (length 5–6 × width); petiole 3–11 mm long, very sparsely hairy to short-hairy on the upper side. **FLOWER** Male catkins 2–4 cm long; stamens 2, filaments hairless. Female catkins 2–4.5 cm long, 6–15 mm wide, on branchlets 0–6 mm long; bracts blackish, persistent after flowering. May–Jul., just before or with the new leaves. **FRUIT** Very densely short-silky, pear-shaped capsule, 4–6 mm long; stalk 0.6–0.9 mm long.

HABITAT/RANGE Native. Lake, stream, and bog margins, forest openings, edges of tundra, 0–2,000 m; Alaska and w. Canada.

Notes This common willow is important browse for Moose (*Alces alces*), deer, Caribou (*Rangifer tarandus*), and smaller mammals.

SITKA WILLOW

LITTLETREE WILLOW

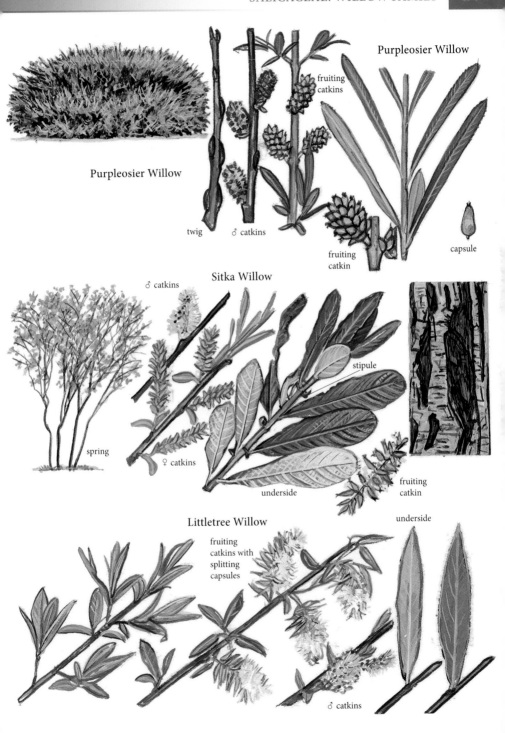

Purpleosier Willow

Purpleosier Willow

fruiting catkins

twig

♂ catkins

fruiting catkin

capsule

Sitka Willow

♂ catkins

stipule

spring

♀ catkins

underside

fruiting catkin

Littletree Willow

underside

fruiting catkins with splitting capsules

♂ catkins

PUSSY WILLOW *Salix discolor* Muhl.

QUICKID Densely hairy male catkins appearing in early spring, strongly bicolored leaves, and short-hairy capsules help identify this species.

Deciduous shrub or rarely a tree, 6–8 m tall, usually with multiple trunks; crown open, with upright branches. **TWIG** Stout, lustrous, red-brown, hairy at first, later hairless, with pale lenticels. **LEAF** Stiff, narrowly elliptic to obovate. Upper surface dark green, dull or slightly lustrous; lower surface whitish, sometimes hairy; margins entire or toothed, especially toward the pointed tip. Blade 3–10 cm long (length 2.5–4.5 × width). Petiole 6–17 mm long, hairy on the upper side. **FLOWER** Male catkins 2–5 cm long; stamens 2, filaments hairless or hairy at the base. Female catkins 2.5–11 cm long, 1–3 cm diam., on branchlets 0–10 mm long; bracts brown to black or bicolored, persistent after flowering. Apr.–May, before the new leaves. **FRUIT** Short-hairy capsule, 6–12 mm long; stalk 1.5–3 mm long.

HABITAT/RANGE Native. Pond and stream margins, moist woods, fens, seepages, 0–2,400 m; scattered from c. Idaho to the Dakotas, widespread across Canada and ne. U.S.

MACKENZIE WILLOW *Salix prolixa* Andersson

QUICKID Strongly bicolored leaves, hairless below, and hairless capsules help identify this willow.

Deciduous shrub or tree, 1–5 m tall. **TWIG** Yellow- or red-brown, hairless to velvety-hairy. **LEAF** Narrowly lanceolate to oblanceolate; margins flat, finely toothed. Upper surface dull green, hairless or lightly hairy; lower silvery gray, hairless. Blade

5–15 cm long, 1–5 cm wide (length 2.5–5 × width); petiole 6–12 mm long, hairy on the upper side or not. **FLOWER** Male catkins 1.5–4 cm long. Female catkins 2–7 cm long, 1–2 cm wide, on branchlets 0.5–6 mm long. **FRUIT** Hairless capsule, 4–6 mm long; stalk 1.3–4.2 mm long.

HABITAT/RANGE Native. Shores, moist places, 100–2,300 m; s. Y.T. and w. N.W.T. south through B.C. and w. Alta. to nw. Calif., n. Idaho, and nw. Wyo.

BALSAM WILLOW *Salix pyrifolia* Andersson

QUICKID This willow occurs in Canada in the West, typically has oval leaves with cordate bases, and is late-flowering.

Deciduous shrub or small tree to 9 m tall. **TWIG** Yellowish green, becoming glossy, lustrous, dark red or reddish brown, hairless. **LEAF** Juvenile leaves membranous and translucent. Mature leaves thick, elliptic, oval, or broadly ovate; base usually cordate, sometimes rounded; tip short-pointed; margins bluntly or sharply toothed, often wavy. Upper surface bright green, lustrous; lower surface bluish white, hairless. Blade 3–10 cm long, 2–5 cm broad (length 1.5–3.5 × width). Petiole 7–20 mm long, hairless or sparsely hairy on the upper side. **FLOWER** Male catkins 2–6 mm long; stamens 2, filaments hairless or sparsely hairy at the base. Female catkins 25–85 mm long, 1–2 cm diam., on branchlets 2–22 mm long; bracts persistent after flowering. May–Jul., just before or with the new leaves. **FRUIT** Hairless capsule, 7–8 mm long; stalk 2–3.5 mm long.

HABITAT/RANGE Native. Moist or wet places, 0–1,600 m; w. Canada and nc. U.S., east to the Atlantic Ocean.

PUSSY WILLOW

MACKENZIE WILLOW

BALSAM WILLOW

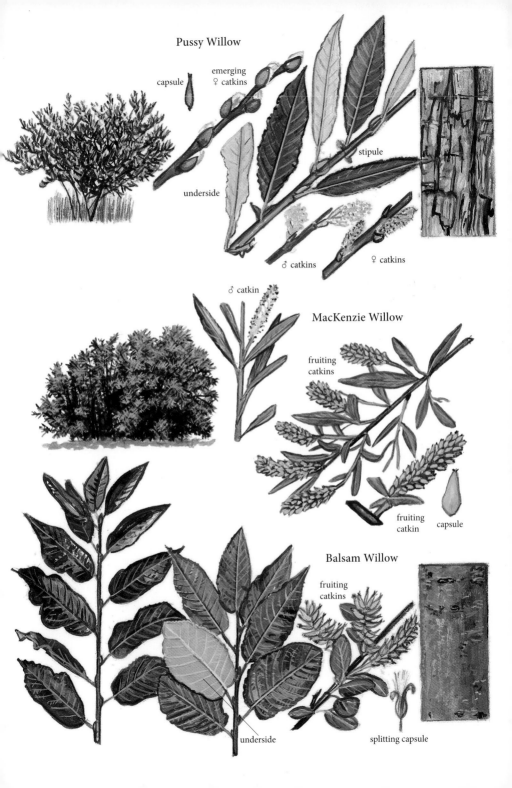

Pussy Willow

capsule

emerging ♀ catkins

stipule

underside

♂ catkins

♀ catkins

♂ catkin

MacKenzie Willow

fruiting catkins

fruiting catkin

capsule

Balsam Willow

fruiting catkins

underside

splitting capsule

SCOULER WILLOW *Salix scouleriana*
Barratt ex Hook.
A.K.A. MOUNTAIN WILLOW, FIRE WILLOW

QUICK ID The hairy (at least when young), stout twigs, broad bicolored leaves with rolled margins, plump male catkins that appear before the leaves, and hairy capsules help identify this species. It is the willow mostly likely to be found well away from streams on mountain slopes.

Deciduous shrub or erect tree to 10 m tall; usually a single trunk, 10–50 cm diam.; crown compact, round. **BARK** Young bark smooth, gray, on branches often whitish; mature bark thin, dull gray to dark gray, with longitudinal fissures and broad, flat ridges. **TWIG** Stout, yellowish, yellowish-brown, or orangish and hairy; becoming dark red-brown by the 2nd year and mostly hairless (hairs retained southward). **LEAF** Alternate, spreading, usually oblanceolate to elliptic, base wedge-shaped to convex-tapered, tip pointed or rounded; margins entire or with widely spaced small teeth, sometimes slightly wavy, rolled under. Upper surface grayish green, moderately to densely hairy; lower surface silvery gray, sparsely to densely hairy, often with rust-colored hairs. Blade 3–10 cm long, 1–4 cm wide (length 2–4 × width); petiole 2–13 mm long, convex or flat and hairy on the upper side. **FLOWER** Male catkins 2–4 cm long, stout; stamens 2, filaments usually hairy at the base. Female catkins 2–6 cm long (to 9 cm in fruit), 1–2 cm wide, on branchlets 0–8 mm long; bracts dark brown or black, persistent after flowering. Late Feb.–mid-Jun., before the leaves. **FRUIT** Long-hairy, pear-shaped capsule, 5–11 mm long, blushed with red; stalk 0.8–2.3 mm long.

HABITAT/RANGE Native. Edges and openings in woods, meadows, subalpine slopes, old burns, disturbed areas, 0–3,500 m; Alaska to w. Man., south to Calif., Ariz., N.M., and S.D.; nw. Mexico.

SIMILAR SPECIES Sitka Willow (*S. sitchensis*), Feltleaf Willow (*S. alaxensis*), and Dune Willow (*S. hookeriana*) all have proportionally broad, bi-colored leaves. Scouler Willow often differs from them in its velvety twigs and petioles, and by having capsules with long, straight silky hairs.

Notes After fires and logging, Scouler Willow often rapidly establishes, forming leafy grayish-green thickets. It is one of the earliest of the "pussy willows," often flowering before snowmelt. Freshly stripped bark has a skunky odor. This is one of several willows that produce "diamond willow" wood, with diamond-like patterns caused by fungi, popular for novelty items and furniture.

FELTLEAF WILLOW *Salix alaxensis*
(Andersson) Coville var. *alaxensis*
A.K.A. ALASKA WILLOW

QUICK ID The broad leaves, felty beneath, with rolled margins, help identify this species.

Semievergreen shrub or tree, 1–3 m tall, with erect or spreading branches; trunk 1 to several, 10–18 cm diam. **BARK** Smooth, gray, becoming furrowed, with scaly plates on the ridges, often with a diamond pattern due to fungal infection. **TWIG** Stout, gray, densely hairy, not silvery-gray beneath the hairs. **LEAF** Alternate, sometimes persisting 1 or 2 years, simple, broadly to narrowly oblong, elliptic, or obovate, base wedge-shaped to convex-tapered, tip bluntly pointed to gradually tapered to a slender point; margins entire or blunt-toothed, rolled under. Upper surface dark green, lustrous, mostly hairy; lower surface white-woolly. Blade 5–11 cm long, 1.5–3.5 cm wide (length 2–4 × width); petiole 3–20 mm long, convex to shallowly grooved, hairy. **FLOWER** Male catkins 2–5.5 cm long; stamens 2, filaments hairless. Female catkins 3.5–9 cm long, 1–2 cm wide, on branchlets 0–13 mm long;

SCOULER WILLOW

FELTLEAF WILLOW

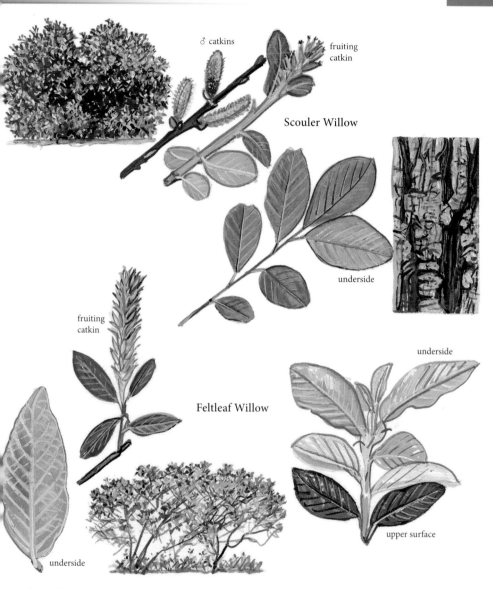

♂ catkins

fruiting catkin

Scouler Willow

underside

fruiting catkin

underside

Feltleaf Willow

upper surface

underside

bracts brown or black, persistent after flowering. Mid-Apr.–mid-Jul., before the new leaves emerge. **FRUIT** Wavy-hairy, pear-shaped capsule, 4–5 mm long; stalk to 0.4 mm long.

HABITAT/RANGE Native. Shores, scree, meadows, 0–2,000 m; boreal Canada, n. Que., west to Alaska, south in the n. Rocky Mountains to ec. B.C. and adjacent Alta; e. Siberia.

Notes This is the northernmost of the tree willows; beyond the tree-line it is a shrub. It is a preferred browse by Moose (*Alces alces*). In many areas it is the only source of firewood. Var. *longistylis* (Rydb.) Schneider, scattered in w. Canada and Alaska, differs in having sparsely hairy, silvery-gray twigs.

BEBB WILLOW *Salix bebbiana* Sarg.

A.K.A. DIAMOND WILLOW, BEAKED WILLOW, GRAY WILLOW

QUICK ID Recognized by the combination of long-beaked capsules and dull green leaves that have impressed veins above and are whitish-hairy beneath.

Deciduous shrub or tree, 1–10 m tall, usually with multiple closely set, upright trunks to about 15 cm diam.; branches upright or ascending, forming an arching or spreading crown. **BARK** Dark reddish brown to yellowish brown or grayish brown, becoming furrowed, often with diamond-shaped fungal patches. **TWIG** Reddish-purple to yellow- or orange-brown, hairy at first, often becoming hairless. **LEAF** Alternate, simple, elliptic, oblong, or obovate, sometimes narrowly so; base broadly wedge-shaped or rounded; tip short-pointed; margins usually entire, or bluntly or sharply glandular-toothed, mostly toward the base. Upper surface dull or moderately lustrous green, hairy or nearly hairless, veins somewhat indented; lower surface bluish white, white-hairy. Blade usually 3–10 cm long, 2–4 cm broad (length 1.7–4 × width); petiole 2–13 mm long. **FLOWER** Male catkins 1–4 cm long, 7–16 mm diam.; stamens 2, filaments hairless or hairy at the base. Female catkins 1.5–8.5 cm long, 1–3 cm diam., on branchlets 1–26 mm long; bracts persistent after flowering. Apr.–Jun., just before the leaves. **FRUIT** Short-silky, long-beaked capsule, broader in the upper half, 5–9 mm long; stalk 2–5 mm long.

HABITAT/RANGE Native. Thickets, forests, stream and prairie margins, disturbed areas, 0–3,300 m; scattered in mountains from Ariz. and N.M. northward, widespread from Alaska to Nfld. and ne. U.S.

DUNE WILLOW *Salix hookeriana* Barratt ex Hook.

A.K.A. BEACH WILLOW, HOOKER WILLOW, COASTAL WILLOW, BIGLEAF WILLOW

QUICK ID This is primarily a coastal willow from n. Calif. northward, with broad leaves that are pale gray and velvety beneath.

Deciduous shrub or tree, 1–8 m tall, with 1 to several trunks 10–45 cm diam. **TWIG** Gray-, yellow-, or red-brown, or purplish, nearly hairless to densely gray-hairy. **LEAF** Elliptic to obovate; margins entire to finely toothed, slightly rolled under. Upper surface pale green; lower surface pale gray, velvety. Blade 3.5–12 cm long, 2–6 cm wide (length 1.5–4 × width); petiole 0.5–3 cm long, hairy on the upper side. **FLOWER** Male catkins 2.5–7 cm long; stamens 2, filament hairy or hairless at the base. Female catkins 4–9 cm long (14 cm in fruit), 1–2.5 cm wide, on branchlets 0–2 cm long; bracts persistent after flowering. Apr.–Jun. **FRUIT** Hairless or hairy capsule, 5–10 mm long; stalk 0.5–2.8 mm long.

HABITAT/RANGE Native. Coastal dunes, marshes, meadows, woods, 0–1,800 m; Alaska to c. Calif.

SIMILAR SPECIES An inland variant in w. Wash. and Ore., sometimes recognized as **Piper Willow** (*S. piperi* Bebb), has prominent stipules, and stems and leaves that become nearly hairless at maturity.

BRUSHHOLLY *Xylosma flexuosa* (Kunth) Hemsl.

A.K.A. CORONILLA

QUICK ID This shrub or small tree from extreme s. Tex. has leaves clustered on short spur branches, the leaf margins coarsely toothed. It differs from other western Salicaceae in its flowers and fruit.

BEBB WILLOW

DUNE WILLOW

BRUSHHOLLY

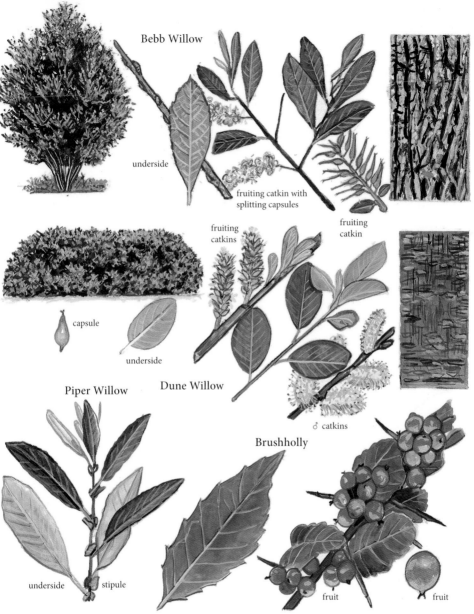

Bebb Willow

underside

fruiting catkin with
splitting capsules

fruiting
catkins

fruiting
catkin

capsule

underside

Piper Willow

Dune Willow

♂ catkins

Brushholly

underside   stipule

fruit

fruit

Evergreen; in the West usually a slender shrub to 2 m tall, occasionally an irregularly branched tree to 12 m tall (especially southward), bearing straight, slender thorns to 3.5 cm long arising from each leaf node. **LEAF** Clustered on short spurs, leathery, elliptic to obovate, coarsely toothed along the margins, dark green (often reddish in autumn). Blade 2.5–6 cm long. **FLOWER** Small, with 5 hairy sepals 1.5 cm long, petals absent, borne in clusters. Year-round. **FRUIT** Globose red berry, 6 mm diam.

HABITAT/RANGE Native. Brush and palm groves, 0–50 m; in extreme s. Tex., south to n. South America.

Notes Sometimes used as a hedge; it belongs to a tropical genus of 80–90 dioecious trees and shrubs.

SAPINDACEAE: SOAPBERRY FAMILY

The soapberry family is a widespread tropical and temperate family of about 150 genera and more than 2,000 species, among which are edible fruits such as litchi (genus *Litchi*) and handsome ornamental shrubs and trees. There are about 15 genera and 54 species of Sapindaceae known from north of Mexico, more than half of which are native. Recent studies have demonstrated that the maples (formerly Aceraceae, with our genus *Acer*) and the buckeyes (formerly Hippocastanaceae, with our genus *Aesculus*) are best placed in the Sapindaceae. In the West there are 11 native species that are shrubs or trees, and 9 introduced tree species that have more or less naturalized. Florida Hopbush (*Dodonaea viscosa* [L.] Jacq.), occasionally a small tree in Fla., is a common shrub on warm slopes in s. Ariz.

The family consists of lianas, shrubs, and trees. **LEAF** Compound, or simple by reduction to 1 leaflet and therefore unifoliolate; alternate or opposite. **FLOWER** Radial or slightly bilateral, often functionally unisexual or sometimes bisexual, with 4 or 5 sepals and usually 4 or 5 petals, 8 or fewer stamens attached to a nectary disk, and a pistil with 2 or 3 chambers. **FRUIT** Diverse: fleshy or dry capsules, drupes, berries, nuts, or samaras. Toxic chemicals such as saponins are present in the leaves, branches, and fruits of a number of species.

◼ *ACER*: MAPLES

There are about 130 species of maple worldwide, 20 in North America, 14 of which are native, five of those native in the West.

Deciduous woody plants, maples range from spreading shrubs to stately trees. **LEAF** Opposite, usually unifoliolate, palmately lobed but in some species pinnate or even pinnately compound. **FLOWER** Unisexual or bisexual, the flower types variously mixed or separate. Borne in small erect, roundish clusters or longer hanging clusters, and often wind-pollinated. Usually with 5 sepals, 5 or 0 petals, a variable number of stamens but most commonly 8, and a superior ovary compressed at right angles to the dividing wall between the 2 chambers. **FRUIT** Paired samara, each (often called a "key") with a swollen 1-seeded base and a broad wing ribbed along its upper edge, thin and paperlike across the surface to the opposite edge. Whirling in the wind, the wing carries the seed, often far from the parent tree, perhaps landing in suitable habitat for a new plant and helping ensure genetic mixing. In the paired samara the upper (ribbed) edges of the wings may be almost parallel or more widely spreading. Straight lines traced along each upper edge will meet at the paired swollen bases, forming an angle (or straight line) adjacent to the samara; this angle is helpful in description and identification.

Maples occur in cool, moist habitats and are widely distributed in the Northern Hemisphere, from sea-level to moderately high elevations. They are among the best-known trees in North America, admired for their beauty, attractively shaped leaves, and their contribution to woodland fall color. A stylized leaf of the eastern Red Maple (*A. rubrum* L.) is a symbol on the Canadian flag. Maples have fine-grained wood that is usually divided into "hard" and "soft." Hard maples, such as Sugar Maple (*A. saccharum* Marshall) and Black Maple (*A. nigrum* F. Michx.), are highly regarded for the fabrication of fine furniture, veneer, and flooring. A number of species are used ornamentally, prized for their shape, attractive leaves, and fall color. Maple syrup is made commercially from Sugar Maple, and can also be made from several other species.

HEDGE MAPLE *Acer campestre* L.
A.K.A. FIELD MAPLE

Deciduous, densely twiggy shrub or small tree, 12–25 m tall. **BARK** Grayish black, somewhat ridged and furrowed. **LEAF** Opposite, unifoliolate, blade 5–10 cm long, with 3–5 round-pointed lobes, each with 0–2 low roundish teeth per side; hairy at least along the veins on the lower surface; yellow in autumn. **FLOWER** Yellow-green, male and female mixed in erect clusters, 4–6 cm diam. Mar.–Apr.,

Hedge Maple

twig

fruit

Vine Maple

autumn

fruit

twig

after the leaves. **FRUIT** Paired greenish samara, 3–4.5 cm long, widely spreading (160–200°). **HABITAT/RANGE** Introduced from Europe; persisting in c. Calif., 0–200 m; also scattered in ne. U.S. and se. Canada.

VINE MAPLE *Acer circinatum* Pursh
A.K.A. MOUNTAIN MAPLE, OREGON VINE MAPLE

QUICK ID The combination of leaves with 7–9 lobes and widely angled paired samaras is unique in western maples.

Deciduous shrub or small tree, rarely to 15 m tall. Trunks 1 to several, 8–30 cm diam. Crown irregular, ragged, open; branches erect, spreading, or sprawling, sometimes rooting where they touch the ground. **TWIG** Bright red-brown. **BARK** Thin, red-brown, mostly smooth, shallowly fissured near the base. **LEAF** Opposite, unifoliolate; 7–9 palmate lobes, the basal lobes smallest; margins sharply toothed. Upper surface yellow-green to dull green; lower surface paler and hairy at least in the vein angles near the leaf base. Blade 3–10 cm long and

broad; petiole 2.5–5 cm long. Foliage brilliant scarlet and yellow in autumn. **FLOWER** Dangling at the ends of slender stalks, 10–20 in loose clusters, male and female in the same cluster; each flower 6–9 mm diam.; sepals reddish; petals heart-shaped, yellowish or whitish green. Apr.–May, after the leaves expand. **FRUIT** Paired samara, 2.5–4 cm long, reddish, maturing yellow-tan, the wings widely divergent (160–210°).

HABITAT/RANGE Native. Usually in the understory of mixed conifer or redwood forest, 0–1,400 m; s. B.C. to c. Calif.

VINE MAPLE

SOUTHERN SUGAR MAPLE *Acer floridanum* (Chapm.) Pax

Deciduous tree to 30 m tall, 60 cm diam. **TWIG** Red-brown, hairless, with conspicuous lenticels. **LEAF** Opposite, unifoliolate, usually with 5 squarish lobes with sharp-pointed tips. Upper surface dark green, lustrous; lower surface whitish, hairy. Blade 3–9 cm long and broad. Foliage red or yellow in autumn. **FLOWER** About 5 mm diam., petals absent, yellow-green, hanging on slender, hairy stalks clustered in the axils of developing leaves, male and female flowers in the same cluster or on separate trees. Feb.–Apr. **FRUIT** Paired samara, 2.5–3 cm long, the wings moderately divergent (45–90°). **HABITAT/RANGE** Native. Moist woods; a southeastern species reported in the West in the Tex. panhandle at 700–800 m.

AMUR MAPLE *Acer ginnala* Maxim.

Similar in habit and fruit to Tatarian Maple; sometimes considered a subspecies or variety within that species. **LEAF** Opposite, unifoliolate; 3 lobes, the middle lobe much the longest; margins double-toothed. Upper surface dark green, shiny; lower surface paler, hairless. Blade 4–10 cm long, 3–6 cm broad; petiole 3–5 cm long. Autumn foliage brilliant scarlet or yellow. **HABITAT/RANGE** Introduced from e. Asia; cultivated, a rare waif in the West, naturalized in the East. Very cold-tolerant.

ROCKY MOUNTAIN MAPLE *Acer glabrum* Torr.
A.K.A. Western Mountain Maple, Dwarf Maple

QUICK ID Leaves on this maple are palmate, usually with 3 lobes separated by very narrow gaps, and with hairless surfaces; the wings of the paired samaras range from nearly parallel to diverging at a right angle.

Hairless deciduous shrub or small tree to 9 m tall. Trunk 20–30 cm diam. Crown narrow, irregular, open, with ascending branches when in the understory, or densely bushy-branched and round when in the open. **BARK** Thin, grayish red-brown, mostly smooth. **TWIG** At first green, soon rich red-brown, later gray. **LEAF** Opposite, unifoliolate, with 3–5 lobes (occasionally divided into 3 leaflets), when undivided the lobes separated by narrow gaps sharply angled at the base, the lobes sometimes again shallowly lobed; margins sharply and irregularly double-toothed. Surfaces hairless; upper surface dark green, lustrous; lower surface paler, the veins yellowish. Blade 1.5–14 cm long, about as broad; petiole from ⅔ to equal the blade length, often red. Foliage red or yellow in autumn. **FLOWER** Functionally unisexual, male flowers have a rudimentary pistil, female flowers have rudimentary stamens, both sexes on the same plant or sexes on different plants, sometimes bisexual flowers on male plants. In pendent clusters about 5 cm long; petals and sepals similar, narrow, 3–8 mm long, yellowish green. Apr.–Jul., with leaf expansion. **FRUIT** Paired samara, 2–3 cm long; rose, turning brown when mature; wings broad, nearly parallel to diverging at 90°.

HABITAT/RANGE Native. Moist areas in mountains, often treelike in the understory of conifer forest, shrubby on open slopes and ridges, 1,200–3,350 m; s. Alaska to c. Calif., se. Ariz., s. N.M.

Notes This maple grows at higher elevations than all other North American maples. Because the trees are small, there is little economic use for the hard, dense wood other than for fuel. Three varieties are currently recognized: var. *glabrum*, leaves mostly 3–6 cm broad, twigs of several seasons red, mainly Rocky Mountains, s. Cascades, and Sierra Nevada; var. *douglasii* (Hook.) Dippel, leaves mostly 6–11 cm broad, twigs of several seasons red, mainly western mountains from Alaska to Ore. and Idaho; and var. *diffusum* (Greene) Smiley, leaves mostly 1.5–4 cm broad, only twigs of current season red, others gray, mainly mountains of Great Basin region.

ROCKY MOUNTAIN MAPLE

fruit

twig

autumn

Southern Sugar Maple

Amur Maple

autumn

fruit

Rocky Mountain Maple

fruit

twig

BIGTOOTH MAPLE *Acer grandidentatum* Nutt.

QUICK ID Opposite leaves with 3–5 palmate lobes, these with a few blunt teeth, distinguish this maple.

Deciduous shrub or small tree to 15 m tall; trunk to 30 cm diam. **BARK** Thin, dark brown, on older portions breaking into plate-like scales. **TWIG** Bright red-brown, hairless, gray in age. **LEAF** Opposite, unifoliolate, thickish; 3–5 bluntly pointed lobes, the middle lobe often narrowed at the base, the gaps between lobes broad; margins with few large, blunt, lobelike teeth or entire. Upper surface dark green, shiny; lower surface whitish, softly-hairy. Blade 5–12 cm long and broad; petiole 3–5 cm long. Foliage yellow, orange, or red in autumn. **FLOWER** Unisexual or bisexual, on the same or separate trees; 6 mm diam., long-stalked, drooping, in essentially sessile clusters; sepals pale greenish, joined at the base; petals absent. Mar.–May, with the leaves. **FRUIT** Paired samara, 1.5–3 cm long, the wings divergent at 5–90°.

HABITAT/RANGE Native. Moist canyons, open slopes, 1,200–2,700 m; e. Idaho to nw. Mexico, se. Okla., c. Tex.

SIMILAR SPECIES Sometimes considered a variety of Sugar Maple (*A. saccharum* Marshall), which has been introduced in the West. Leaves of Bigtooth Maple usually are finely hairy over the entire lower surface, whereas those of Sugar Maple are hairy only along the veins or hairless.

Notes The proportion of male, female, and bisexual flowers in any one tree may change from year to year, apparently depending on moisture. There are 2 varieties of the species: var. *grandidentatum*, leaves with 3–5 bluntly toothed lobes, the middle

lobe constricted at the base, throughout the Rocky Mountains; var. *sinuosum* (Rehder) Little, leaves usually 3-lobed, lobes with entire margins and broad bases, in the mountains near the Mexican border.

BIGLEAF MAPLE *Acer macrophyllum* Pursh

QUICK ID Large opposite leaves with 5 palmate lobes and margins entire or nearly so, or with a few low, blunt teeth, identify this maple.

Deciduous tree to 30 m tall; single trunk often 60 cm diam., but in huge old specimens may reach 1–2 m diam. Crown narrow in forest trees, broad and round in open-grown trees. **BARK** To 2 cm thick, gray to reddish brown, deeply furrowed on older parts, the ridges with small flat plates. **TWIG** At first pale green, becoming bright green or dark red and flecked with pale longitudinal lenticels by the 1st winter, and by the 2nd winter becoming gray. **LEAF** Opposite, unifoliolate, 5-lobed, the lower pair of lobes smallest, the middle lobe sometimes shallowly 3-lobed; margins entire or with a few large irregular, shallow, rounded teeth or low lobes. Upper surface dark, lustrous green, hairless; lower surface paler and finely hairy, at least near the base. Blade 8–30 cm long, usually slightly broader; petiole to 25–30 cm long. Foliage clear pale yellow or yellow-orange in autumn. **FLOWER** Male and female flowers mixed in gracefully hanging clusters 10–15 cm long; sepals and petals greenish yellow, petals 3–7 mm long, sepals slightly longer. Male flowers have 9 or 10 stamens with slender filaments; female flowers with ovary white-hairy at the base, 2 slender styles, and small rudimentary stamens. Apr.–May, after the onset of leaf expansion. **FRUIT** Paired samara, 2.5–3 cm long, mostly green during development, tawny when mature, the wings moderately divergent (50–90°).

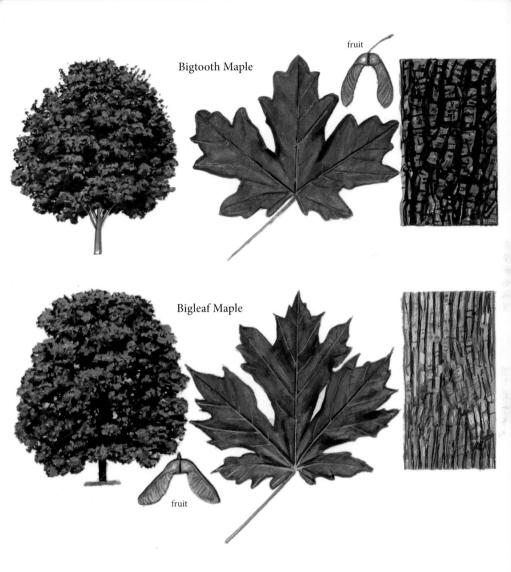

Bigtooth Maple

fruit

Bigleaf Maple

fruit

HABITAT/RANGE Native. Stream banks, canyons, roadsides, in mixed conifer or redwood forests, 0–2,000 m; coastal c. B.C. to s. Calif.

Notes This is the only large maple in the Pacific region and may be the most massive of all maple species. In addition, its leaves, at up to 60 cm long, are the largest of any maple. It is our only native maple with fragrant flowers. The wood is harvested commercially for use in furniture and cabinetry. Some trees may have large hemispherical burls at the base that are valued for their complex and attractive patterns. Maple syrup can be made from the sap. Bigleaf Maple is also used as an ornamental where there is ample space for large mature trees. Wildlife browse on the leaves of saplings, and birds and squirrels feed upon the seeds.

BOXELDER *Acer negundo* L.
A.K.A. Boxelder Maple, Maple Ash

QUICK ID This tree is recognized by the combination of opposite, pinnately compound leaves and paired samara fruit.

Deciduous tree, 12–25 m tall, with 1 or multiple erect trunks 40–90 cm diam. Variable in habit: when crowded by other trees this maple may have a single trunk and narrow crown of ascending branches; in open-grown trees trunks often are divided near the ground into several stout ascending and spreading branches, the crown broad and irregularly rounded; in canyon bottoms sometimes this maple forms impenetrable thickets. **BARK** Smooth, pale gray or brownish on young trees, becoming darker gray and deeply cleft into scaly ridges at maturity. **TWIG** Green, hairless, developing rounded brownish lenticels with age. **LEAF** Opposite, pinnately compound, thin, petiole slender, 3–7 cm long. Leaflets 3–5 (rarely 7–11), each 5–12 cm long, 2.5–6 cm broad; lateral leaflets short-stalked, terminal leaflet on stalk 5–25 mm long. Margins nearly entire or remotely few-toothed. Upper surface light green, lower surface grayish green, somewhat hairy. Autumn foliage yellow. **FLOWER** Unisexual, sexes borne on separate trees; sepals yellow-green, to 2 mm long; petals absent. Apr.–Jun., before or during leaf expansion. **FRUIT** Paired samara, 3–4 cm long, pale brown, the wings moderately divergent (60–90°).

HABITAT/RANGE Native. Stream banks, floodplains, bottomlands, swamp margins, usually where wet, 0–2,400 m; the most widespread of the North American maples, sporadically occurring from c. Canada to Calif., south to s. Mexico; widespread in the East.

SIMILAR SPECIES Elderberries (*Sambucus*, Adoxaceae) and ashes (*Fraxinus*, Oleaceae) have opposite, pinnately compound leaves, but elderberries have small round berries in clusters, and in ashes the samaras are single, not paired.

Notes Boxelder is very fast-growing, and the wood is soft, used for boxes, pulp, and novelty items. Plants persist around old homesites in the West, perhaps reflecting westward expansion—genetic markers from these plants mostly resemble those of plants from the Great Basin. As might be expected in such a widespread species, there are several varieties. Of the many named, three in the West represent intergrading geographic races defined by hairiness: var. *californicum* (Torr. & A. Gray) Sarg., velvety spreading hairs on stems and leaves, west of the Sierra Nevada; var. *arizonicum* Sarg., hairless, glaucous twigs, more common in southwestern mountains; var. *interius* (Britton) Sarg., twigs grayish white with very short hairs, from the Rocky Mountains region.

NORWAY MAPLE *Acer platanoides* L.

QUICK ID This maple has leaves with 5 lobes, petioles that usually exude milky sap when broken, and widely divergent (at nearly 180°) wings of the paired samaras.

Deciduous tree to 30 m tall; single trunk to 1.5 m diam. **LEAF** Opposite, unifoliolate, usually 5-lobed, each lobe narrowly tapering to a fine, hairlike point; margins with a few large, sharp-tipped teeth. Upper surface green, lustrous, hairless; lower surface paler, hairy in the vein axils. Blade 10–20 cm long, equally broad; petiole 8–15 cm long, usually exuding milky sap when broken. Autumn foliage yellow. **FLOWER** Bisexual, 8 mm diam., greenish yellow, in erect, rounded terminal clusters. Mar.–Apr., before leaf expansion. **FRUIT** Paired samara, 3–5 cm long, the wings widely divergent (nearly 180°).

HABITAT/RANGE Introduced from Europe; popular as a street tree, now invasive in many states, releasing chemicals that discourage undergrowth, 0–750 m, nw. U.S.; also in the East.

SIMILAR SPECIES The similar **Sugar Maple** (*A. saccharum* Marshall) is recorded from several western states, where it is grown as an ornamental and may occur as a waif. It has smaller leaves, usually with 5 lobes that are drawn out into slender points, these rounded at the minute tip. The petiole exudes clear sap when broken, and the samaras are nearly parallel or narrowly divergent (5–90°).

BOXELDER

Boxelder

underside

fruit

Norway Maple

fruit

spring

Sugar Maple

♂ flower

autumn

♀ flower

fruit

SILVER MAPLE *Acer saccharinum* L.

Deciduous fast-growing tree to 30 m tall; trunk to 1.2 m diam. **LEAF** Opposite, unifoliolate; 5–7 lobes with 1 to few sharply pointed secondary lobes and a few irregular, coarse, sharp teeth, terminal lobe narrowed at the base. Upper surface yellow-green, lower surface silvery white. Blade 6–15 cm long, equally broad; petiole 4–12 cm long. Autumn foliage yellow. **FLOWER** Small, unisexual, sexes usually in different clusters on the same tree, yellowish green, sepals 5, petals absent. Feb.–May, prior to leaf emergence. **FRUIT** Paired samara, 3–6 cm long, the wings moderately to widely divergent (60–120°). **HABITAT/RANGE** Native to e. U.S. and widespread in the East in riparian woodland, 0–1,500 m; widely planted as an ornamental in the West, a waif or slightly naturalized in several western states.

TATARIAN MAPLE *Acer tataricum* L.

Deciduous shrub, or sometimes a small tree, to 10 m tall, often low-branching, more or less bushy, with a rounded crown. **TWIG** Red-brown, hairless, with numerous lenticels. **LEAF** Opposite, unifoliolate, usually unlobed or irregularly and shallowly lobed, oval to broadly ovate, tip narrowly pointed, margins irregularly double-toothed. Upper surface green, sublustrous, hairless; lower surface paler, hairy along the veins when young, later hairless. Blade 5–10 cm long, 3.5–7 cm broad; petiole 1.5–5 cm long. Autumn foliage red, yellow, or mixed. **FRUIT** Paired samara, 2–3 cm long, wings nearly parallel. **HABITAT/RANGE** Introduced from w. Eurasia; cultivated, a rare waif in the Northwest.

■ *AESCULUS*: BUCKEYES AND HORSE CHESTNUTS

There are 13 species of *Aesculus* in Eurasia and North America. Six are native to the U.S.; one is introduced. In the West, species occur in the Pacific states and Tex. at low elevations.

Deciduous large round-crowned shrubs or small trees, with conical flower clusters borne at the tips of new growth. **TWIG** Buds conspicuous, ovoid, pointed, brown, the terminal bud largest. **LEAF** Opposite, palmately compound, large, about as broad as long, with 5–11 toothed leaflets; petiole often nearly as long as the blade. **FLOWER** Bisexual, or those near the tip of the cluster male, more or less bilateral. Sepals 5, united; petals 4 or 5, separate; stamens 5–8, slender, conspicuously spreading outward from the flower cluster; ovary 1, superior, with 3 chambers, two aborting. **FRUIT** Large, smooth or bluntly prickly leathery capsule, usually bearing only 1 or 2 large globose brown seeds (occasionally up to 3, rarely up to 6).

"Buckeye" may refer to the large round brown seed, reminiscent of a buck's eye. Trees are esteemed for their flowers and attractive foliage. This is our only tree with opposite, palmately compound leaves; other genera with opposite, compound leaves may have some palmate leaves, but these are smaller and bear only 3 leaflets.

CALIFORNIA BUCKEYE *Aesculus californica* (Spach) Nutt.

QUICK ID **This species from Calif. has palmately compound leaves and dense, conical terminal clusters of whitish or pinkish flowers.**

Deciduous large shrub or small tree, 5–12 m tall, with a crown as broad as tall. Trunks 1 to several, 15–50 cm diam. **BARK** Smooth, grayish. **LEAF** Opposite, palmately compound, blade 10–20 cm long, the petiole nearly as long; middle leaflet largest. Leaflets 5–17 cm long, 4–5 cm wide, obovate, tapered to a narrow base; margins finely toothed. **FLOWER** Bilateral, pink or white, sweet-scented, in dense, conical terminal clusters 10–20 cm long. Calyx densely fine-hairy, 2-lobed; petals usually 4, 13–15 cm long, narrowly obovate; stamens 5–7, slender, longer than the petals, anthers orange. May–Jun. **FRUIT** Hanging, broadly pear-shaped, smooth, leathery capsule, 5–8 cm long, usually with only 1 lustrous brown seed 2–3 cm diam.

HABITAT/RANGE Native. Foothills and valleys, 150–1,200 m; Calif.

Notes California Buckeye produces new leaves in early spring; they begin to wither and drop with the onset of the dry season in Jun. Flowers provide nectar for native bees, butterflies, and hummingbirds, but it is toxic to the introduced European Honey Bee (*Apis mellifera*).

CALIFORNIA BUCKEYE

Silver Maple

fruit

winter

Tatarian Maple

fruit

California Buckeye

underside

fruit

flowers

seed

HORSE CHESTNUT *Aesculus hippocastanum* L.

Deciduous tree to 25 m tall, with a broad, round crown and spreading branches curved upward at the tip. **TWIG** Terminal buds sticky. **LEAF** Palmately compound, usually with 7–9 obovate leaflets, each 12–25 cm long, margins irregularly and bluntly toothed. Lower surface usually rusty-hairy near the base when young. **FLOWER** In a conspicuous terminal cluster 20–30 cm long; petals 5, white, with red or yellow spots. May–Jun. **FRUIT** Globose brown, prickly leathery capsule, 5–6 cm diam., with 1–3 lustrous red-brown seeds 2–4 cm diam. **HABITAT/RANGE** Introduced from Europe; moist woods and bottomlands, 0–550 m; w. Ore. and Wash.; widespread in the East.

OHIO BUCKEYE *Aesculus glabra* Willd.
A.K.A. FETID BUCKEYE

QUICK ID This tree has opposite, palmately compound leaves, conical terminal clusters of yellowish flowers, and large prickly capsules.

Deciduous tree, mostly 9–20 m tall, with a broad, round crown and slender spreading branches. **TWIG** Terminal buds powdery-resinous, but not sticky. **LEAF** Palmately compound, usually with 5 ovate or oblanceolate leaflets, each 6–16 cm long, hairless or lower surface hairy, margins finely and irregularly toothed. **FLOWER** In a conspicuous terminal cluster 10–15 cm long; petals 4, pale yellow or greenish yellow. Mar.–May. **FRUIT** Ovoid, light brown, prickly leathery capsule, 2–5 cm diam., with 1–3 lustrous red-brown seeds 2–4 cm diam.

HABITAT/RANGE Native. Moist woods and bottomlands, 0–600 m; c. Tex. to much of e. U.S.

RED BUCKEYE *Aesculus pavia* L.
A.K.A. SCARLET BUCKEYE

QUICK ID This buckeye has opposite, palmately compound leaves with 5–7 leaflets; yellowish flowers in conical terminal clusters; and large, smooth capsules.

Deciduous shrub or tree, rarely to 12 m tall, with a broad, round crown and low, short, crooked, spreading branches that curve upward slightly at the tip. **LEAF** Palmately compound, usually with 5–7 oblong to oblanceolate leaflets, each 6–17 cm long, surfaces hairy or not; margins irregularly and often bluntly toothed. **FLOWER** In a conspicuous terminal cluster 10–25 cm long; petals usually 4, yellow or red. Apr.–May. **FRUIT** Globose, light brown, smooth leathery capsule, 3.5–6 cm diam., usually with 1–3 lustrous brown seeds 2–3 cm diam.

HABITAT/RANGE Native. Woodlands, 0–450 m; c. Tex. through much of the Southeast.

Notes Our plants, of the Edwards Plateau, are yellow-flowered and comprise the var. *flavescens* (Sarg.) Correll; more eastern, red-flowered plants are var. *pavia*.

MEXICAN BUCKEYE *Ungnadia speciosa* Endl.
A.K.A. NEW MEXICAN BUCKEYE, TEXAS BUCKEYE, FALSE BUCKEYE, MONILLA

QUICK ID Pinnate leaves, pink flowers, and 3-lobed fruits with large black seeds serve to identify this species.

Deciduous shrub or tree to 10 m tall, with multiple stems rarely to 20 cm diam. **LEAF** Alternate, pinnately compound, 20–45 cm long (including the petiole). Leaflets usually 5–7, each 6–12 cm

OHIO BUCKEYE

RED BUCKEYE

MEXICAN BUCKEYE

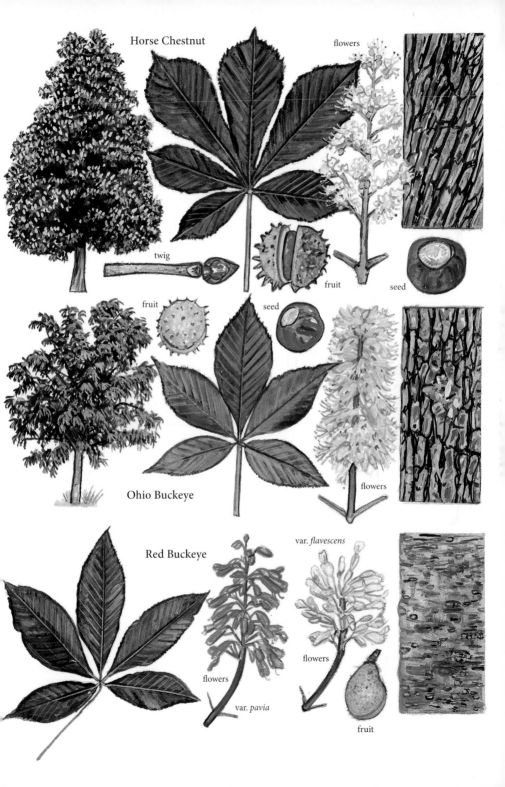

Horse Chestnut

flowers

twig

fruit

seed

fruit

seed

flowers

Ohio Buckeye

var. *flavescens*

Red Buckeye

flowers

flowers

var. *pavia*

fruit

MEXICAN BUCKEYE *continued*

long, 3–5 cm broad, the terminal leaflet on a stalk 6–25 mm long; ovate or lanceolate, with a long, tapering tip, margins finely blunt-toothed. Upper surface dark green, lustrous, hairless; lower surface paler, sometimes finely hairy. **FLOWER** Bisexual and male flowers on the same plant, about 2.5 cm diam., bilateral; calyx bell-shaped, 5-lobed; petals 4, rarely 5, separate, rose-pink, upswept, with a hairy, narrow base; stamens 7–10, attached at the outer edge of a lopsided disk, unequal, exserted, with pink filaments and cherry-red anthers. Mar.–Jun., before or with leaf expansion. **FRUIT** Three-lobed leathery capsule, 3.5–5 cm broad, each chamber splitting to reveal a round, shiny black seed 1–1.5 cm diam.

HABITAT/RANGE Native. Canyons and bluffs, 300–2,000 m; s. N.M. to ec. Tex., ne. Mexico.

Notes There is only 1 species of *Ungnadia*; the fruit and the seeds are reminiscent of those of the buckeyes (*Aesculus*), which at best are distant relatives. The seeds are mildly toxic, causing gastric upset; they may be used by rural children as marbles. Fruits will remain upon the plant for most of the winter.

GOLDENRAIN TREE *Koelreuteria paniculata* Laxm.

Deciduous shrub or tree to 15 m tall; trunk to 50 cm diam.; crown dense, round. **LEAF** Alternate, pinnately to bipinnately compound; blade to 50 cm long. Leaflets 7–18, 5–10 cm long, the longest ones usually near mid-blade; ovate or broadly lanceolate, tip sharply pointed, base truncate, margins coarsely toothed. **FLOWER** Small, yellow, in airy, branched clusters 25–40 cm long; petals 4, reflexed, 5–9 mm long; stamens 8. Jul. **FRUIT** Bladderlike, 3-angled, cone-shaped, hanging papery capsule, 4–6 cm long. **HABITAT/RANGE** Introduced from Asia; weakly naturalized in several western states, particularly Calif. and Tex. **SIMILAR SPECIES** Flamegold (*K. elegans* [Seem.] A.C. Sm. subsp. *formosana* [Hayata] F.G. Mey) is a waif in s. Calif.; it is also sparingly established from e. Tex. to Fla. It has consistently bipinnately compound leaves, 5-petaled flowers, and ellipsoid capsules.

WESTERN SOAPBERRY *Sapindus drummondii* Hook. & Arn.
A.K.A. WILD CHINA TREE, JABONCILLO

QUICK ID This species has pinnately compound leaves with asymmetric entire leaflets, and globose golden fruits.

Slow-growing deciduous large shrub or small tree, 3–15 m tall, with a vase-shaped or round crown of erect or ascending branches. Trunk may be 60 cm diam. in large old specimens. **BARK** On young branches smooth and pale gray; when older, gray or reddish, deeply fissured to expose the pale yellowish inner bark, the long flat ridges flaking into scales. **TWIG** Hairy to hairless, yellowish green to gray, with small, pale lenticels. **LEAF** Alternate, pinnately compound, blade 15–45 cm long. Leaflets 9–19, often alternate on the rachis, 3–10 cm long, 1–2 cm wide, the terminal leaflet smallest; lanceolate, usually sickle-shaped, tapering to a long slender tip, the base rounded and asymmetric, the leaflet broader on the side toward the leaf tip; margins entire. Conspicuously veiny; upper surface yellow-green, hairless; lower surface paler, usually finely hairy. **FLOWER** Unisexual and bisexual flowers in the same cluster, the unisexual male and female flowers on different trees (polygamodioecious); 4–5 mm diam.; numerous, borne in terminal panicles 12–25 cm long; petals 5, white, obovate, tapered to a narrow, hairy base. May–Jun. **FRUIT** Globose, 1-seeded leathery berry, 1–1.5 cm diam., smooth, golden and translucent, becoming darker through autumn, often persisting, shriveled and blackish, through winter.

HABITAT/RANGE Native. Low spots in prairies and along watercourses, 0–1,900 m; c. Ariz. to Kans., Mo., Ark., La., and n. Mexico.

SIMILAR SPECIES Prairie Sumac (*Rhus lanceolata*, Anacardiaceae) has opposite leaflets on a narrowly winged rachis, and small, hairy reddish drupes. Ashes (*Fraxinus*, Oleaceae) and elderberries (*Sambucus*, Adoxaceae) have opposite leaves.

Notes The genus *Sapindus* contains about a dozen species found in warmer regions worldwide. The toxic fruits when mashed in water release saponins, producing a frothy solution that is used by rural people to wash clothes and hair.

WESTERN SOAPBERRY

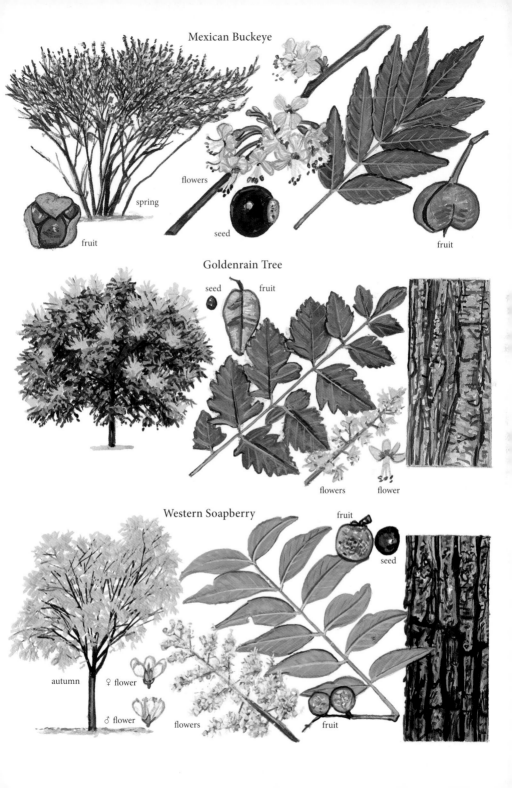

Mexican Buckeye

flowers

spring

fruit

seed

fruit

Goldenrain Tree

seed

fruit

flowers

flower

Western Soapberry

fruit

seed

autumn

♀ flower

♂ flower

flowers

fruit

SAPOTACEAE: SAPODILLA FAMILY

Sapotaceae contains 53 genera and about 1,100 speceis, widespread in the tropics and subtropics. North of Mexico there are 4 or 5 genera and 14–16 species, 11 native. Of those in the West, only the genus *Sideroxylon* sometimes includes trees.

Deciduous or evergreen trees or shrubs characterized by twigs with milky sap and by T-shaped hairs on the foliage, twigs, and elsewhere, the stalk of the T very short, the arms sometimes unequal (visible with a hand lens). **LEAF** Alternate or whorled, on short shoots, margins entire. **FLOWER** Inflorescence usually fasciculate and axillary (in ours), flowers usually radial, bisexual, sepals and petals 4–8 each, stamens 8–16, ovary superior. **FRUIT** Berry.

■ *SIDEROXYLON*: BULLIES

A genus of about 69 species distributed nearly worldwide in the tropics or subtropics, 11 in North America, all native. Western species long considered to be in *Bumelia* are now included in *Sideroxylon*.

Evergreen or deciduous shrubs or trees, often with milky sap. The minute T-shaped hairs on foliage and twigs helps distinguish this genus from other trees and shrubs in the West. **LEAF** Alternate, often in dense fascicles and appearing opposite; simple, margins usually entire. **FLOWER** Bisexual; sepals 4–6; petals 4–6, usually white, creamy yellow, or yellow; usually produced in dense, multiflowered clusters in the leaf axils. **FRUIT** Ovoid, obovoid, or mostly rounded berry, varying from yellow to orange, purplish black, or black, and with 1 or 2 seeds.

SAFFRON PLUM *Sideroxylon celastrinum* (Kunth) T.D. Penn.

QUICK ID This small tree is recognized by the combination of thorn-tipped twigs; fascicled, blunt-tipped leaves, the lower surface hairless and the veins obscure; and small creamy-white flowers borne in clusters at the nodes.

Small, erect but somewhat crooked evergreen tree to about 9 m tall and about 20 cm diam. Crown dense; branches slender, spreading, usually thorn-tipped. **BARK** Nearly black, checkered in age. **LEAF** In clusters, alternate but closely set and appearing opposite; simple, leathery, firm, obovate to elliptic; margins entire, thickened; surfaces hairless, veins inconspicuous. Blade 1–4 cm long. **FLOWER** Tiny, greenish white, 3–15 in a cluster; sepals, petals, and functional stamens each 5, nonfunctional stamens

5, style 2.5–4 mm long. Oct.–Nov. **FRUIT** Ellipsoid, 1-seeded blue-black berry, 6–20 mm long.

HABITAT/RANGE Native. Coastal hammocks, salt flats, salt marshes, gravelly hills, 0–100 m; s. Tex., Fla., to South America.

GUM BULLY *Sideroxylon lanuginosum* Michx.

A.K.A. WOOLLYBUCKET BUMELIA, COMA, WOOLLY BUCKTHORN, FALSE BUCKTHORN, CHITTAMWOOD, IRONWOOD

QUICK ID This shrub or small tree is recognized by its often thorn-tipped branchlets; leaves with a rounded tip, usually felty-hairy lower surface, and veins forming a dense netlike pattern; and fascicle-like clusters of flowers and fruits.

Deciduous, irregular, more or less erect shrub or small tree, 6–15 m tall, about 20 cm diam. Crown of open-grown trees dense and rounded; that of forest-grown trees narrower, open, irregularly branched, and spreading. Branches unarmed or branchlets tipped by a short, stout or slender thorn. **BARK** Reddish brown, narrowly ridged and furrowed, usually with flaky reddish-brown scales, deeply furrowed on old trees. **TWIG** Grayish brown, often thorn-tipped, usually rusty-hairy. **LEAF** Alternate, simple, often in closely set clusters; oblanceolate, obovate, rarely elliptic; base tapered or broadly wedge-shaped; tip usually rounded, sometimes acutely pointed; margins entire. Upper surface lustrous or semilustrous, dark green, hairy at first, soon becoming mostly hairless; lower surface usually conspicuously hairy and feltlike, especially on young leaves, the hairs often sparse on older leaves. Blade 2–8 cm long, 1–4 cm broad; petiole 2–5 mm long, usually hairy. **FLOWER** Up

Saffron Plum

fruit

Gum Bully

twig

flowers

flowers

thorn

immature
fruit

fruit

underside

to 40 in axillary clusters.; sepals usually 5, the lobes erect, 2–3 mm long; petals usually 5, white or creamy yellow, usually divided into 3 segments, only slightly longer than the sepals; stamens 10, of which 5 are fertile with anthers and 5 are sterile and resemble petals; style 1–1.5 mm long. May–Jul. **FRUIT** Obovoid or ellipsoid, lustrous black berry,

6–12 mm long, the style usually persistent at the tip; seed 6–11 mm long.

HABITAT/RANGE Native. Rich, moist upland woods to dry hills, 0–1,800 m; s. Ariz. and sw. N.M., and c. Tex., through much of the Southeast, n. Mexico.

SAFFRON PLUM

GUM BULLY

SIMILAR SPECIES A number of other western trees and shrubs have thorny branches and entire, hairy, dark green leaves, but in those the hairs are not T-shaped as in Gum Bully.

Notes Several subspecies and varieties have been distinguished by leaf size, along with color and density of hairs on flowers and foliage.

SIMAROUBACEAE: QUASSIA FAMILY

The quassia family has about 20 genera and 100 species found in warm regions worldwide. As treated here, the family has 3 genera and 4 species in the U.S. One species has been introduced in the West, a second is native.

Shrubs or trees. **LEAF** Alternate, pinnately compound; sometimes reduced to a single leaflet and appearing to be a simple leaf, or may be lacking. **FLOWER** Small, unisexual (male and female usually on the same plant, some flowers often apparently bisexual, but functionally unisexual), radial, the parts separate, stamens usually 10, carpels united only by their styles. **FRUIT** Clusters of samaras or dry to fleshy drupes. Several species are used as ornamentals.

TREE-OF-HEAVEN *Ailanthus altissima* (Mill.) Swingle
A.K.A. CHINESE SUMAC, COPAL TREE

QUICK ID This weedy tree is recognized by the large compound leaves with opposite and sub-opposite leaflets, at least the lower leaflets toothed or with toothlike lobes near the base, and with a flat, circular gland on the lower surface of each tooth or lobe.

Deciduous fast-growing, often colony-forming tree to about 25 m tall; trunk straight, to 1 m diam. Crown dense, branches ascending and spreading. **BARK** Smooth, light or medium brown, with whitish lenticels, eventually becoming shallowly vertically fissured, the furrows forming pale, discontinuous lines. **TWIG** Stout, smooth, reddish brown, hairy at first, soon becoming hairless. **LEAF** Alternate, pinnately compound, blade 15–90 cm long, to about 30 cm broad; petiole 2–15 cm long. Leaflets to about 41, opposite to slightly alternate, 2–15 cm long, 4–7 cm broad; lanceolate, broadly ovate, often slightly sickle-shaped; base rounded or truncate, often with 1 or 2 toothlike lobes, the tips of which often bear a conspicuous flattened, circular gland on the lower surface; leaflet tip narrowly pointed or abruptly short-pointed; margins otherwise entire or minutely wavy. Upper surface medium green, sometimes purplish when first unfurling; lower surface paler, densely hairy at first, a few hairs usually remaining, at least along the veins. **FLOWER** Unisexual, male and female on separate plants, sometimes mixed with seemingly bisexual flowers; sepals united, cuplike, with 5 minute lobes; petals 5, folded inward and boatlike, greenish yellow, 2–3 mm long; stamens 10, in 2 series of 5 each; pistils 5, fused and appearing as 1, separating in fruit. Apr.–Jul. **FRUIT** Samara, 4–5 cm long, the wings narrowed at the base and tip of the fruit.

HABITAT/RANGE Introduced from Asia; naturalized in disturbed sites and waste places nearly throughout the U.S. to s. B.C. and se. Canada (not in n. Rocky Mountain or n. Great Plains states), 0–2,100 m.

SIMILAR SPECIES At first glance this species might be confused with ashes (*Fraxinus*, Oleaceae), sumacs (*Rhus*, Anacardiaceae), or members of the walnut family (Juglandaceae). However, none of these shares with Tree-of-heaven the combination of colonial habit, alternate leaf arrangement, large teeth with glands on the leaflet margins, and samaras with the wing elongate at each end.

Notes Only 1 species of this largely Asian genus of 10 species has naturalized in the U.S. Tree-of-heaven was introduced in 1784, planted as an ornamental, and moved about the country by settlers and miners, often becoming invasive. This hardy tree withstands dust, smog, poor soil, and lack of care, and is often found crowded against abandoned buildings or sprouting from sidewalk cracks in urban situations. It is mostly free of insect pests, but is easily damaged by wind. Foliage, particularly, has a nutty or burned odor. In Asia, powdered bark was used for intestinal problems. The common and genus names apparently refer to the tree's height.

CRUCIFIXION THORN *Castela emoryi* (A. Gray) Moran & Felger

QUICK ID Numerous leafless, thorn-tipped twigs and persistent starlike woody clusters of fruits distinguish this desert shrub or small tree.

Leafless, densely thorny shrub or small tree to 6 m tall. **TWIG** Numerous, yellowish green to bluish, sharply pointed. **FLOWER** Unisexual, on separate

Tree-of-heaven

fruit

fruit

Crucifixion Thorn

twig

♀ flowers

♂ flower   fruit   fruit

plants, pale yellow to greenish or pinkish, 8–9 mm diam., many in dense clusters 2.5–5 cm long; sepals and petals often 7 each; stamens 12–16 in male flowers, fewer and sterile in female flowers; pistils usually 7, weakly coherent, spreading. Mostly Jun.–Jul. **FRUIT** In starlike clusters of separate drupelike sections 5–7 mm long; becoming dark brown and woody, and sometimes persisting for several years.

HABITAT/RANGE Native. Desert flats and washes, 150–700 m; sw. Ariz., se. Calif., nw. Mexico.

SIMILAR SPECIES The persistent fruits in starlike clusters distinguish *Castela emoryi*

from other leafless, thorny shrubs and trees of the Southwest, including another species known as Crucifixion Thorn (*Canotia holacantha*, Celastraceae), Spiny Allthorn (*Koeberlinia spinosa*, Koeberliniaceae), and Smoketree (*Psorothamnus spinosus*, Fabaceae).

CRUCIFIXION THORN

Notes Castela is a genus of 15 species of shrubs or trees adapted for dry areas of the Americas, mostly with thorn-tipped twigs. Absence of leaves conserves water. The persistent fruits may have been an adaptation to dispersal by now-extinct megafauna, which ate them and distributed seeds ready to germinate after they passed through the gut.

SOLANACEAE: NIGHTSHADE FAMILY

The nightshade family contains 102 genera and about 2,500 species of herbs, shrubs, trees, and vines. The family has a nearly worldwide distribution, but is most diverse in the neotropics. About 31 genera and 175 species occur in North America, of which about 70 species are introduced. Only two produce trees in the West.

LEAF Alternate, usually simple, but often deeply lobed or even compound. **FLOWER** Usually bisexual and radial, usually with 5 fused sepals and 5 fused petals that form a tubular, funnel-shaped, bell-shaped, or more or less flat, star-shaped corolla. There are usually 5 stamens, in a number of genera opening by terminal pores rather than longitudinal slits. **FRUIT** Berry or capsule, the latter sometimes splitting into several compartments at maturity.

Most members of the family are to some degree poisonous. Even so, the family provides vegetables such as bell peppers and chiles (*Capsicum*), tomatoes (traditionally *Lycopersicon*, now in *Solanum*), ground-cherries or tomatillos (*Physalis*), and eggplants and potatoes (*Solanum*). Economically very important is tobacco (*Nicotiana*). Several genera provide ornamentals, including Lady-of-the-Night (*Brunfelsia*), Night-blooming Jessamine (*Cestrum*), Angel's Trumpet (*Brugmansia*), petunias (*Petunia*), and nightshades (*Solanum*). Some *Solanum* are pernicious weeds.

TREE TOBACCO *Nicotiana glauca* Graham

QUICK ID Recognized by its smooth grayish foliage and narrowly tubular, pendulous yellow or greenish-yellow flowers.

Evergreen shrub or tree, 2–8 m tall; trunk slender; crown open, with few branches. **LEAF** Alternate, simple, somewhat leathery; ovate or lanceolate-oblong, base varying from rounded to indented, tip pointed; margins entire, often wavy. Both surfaces hairless, grayish green. Blade 5–25 cm long, 2–7 cm broad; petiole 3–12 cm long. **FLOWER** Bisexual, produced in drooping, many-flowered panicles. Sepals 5, fused into a cuplike calyx 8–12 mm long; corolla tubular, 35–45 mm long, yellow or greenish yellow, flaring into 5 pointed lobes, revealing in the orifice the stigma and anthers positioned in a bulge at the top of the tube. Year-round. **FRUIT** Egg-shaped 4-valved capsule, 10–15 mm long; seeds reddish brown.

HABITAT/RANGE Introduced from South America; escaped and established in sandy and clay soils along stream banks and roadsides, 0–1,100 m; s. Calif., s. Ariz., s. Tex., se. U.S.

Notes The genus *Nicotiana* contains about 95 species of mostly herbaceous plants, less commonly

trees or shrubs. It is largely American, but occurs naturally also in s. Africa, Australia, and the South Pacific. This is the only woody species of the genus in the West. All parts of the plant are extremely poisonous. Several native species of *Nicotiana* were smoked by indigenous people. Various hybrids and races of *N. tabacum* L. yield the tobacco of commerce. Extracts from the leaves may be used as insecticides.

POTATOTREE *Solanum erianthum* D. Don

A.K.A. MULLEIN NIGHTSHADE

QUICK ID The combination of soft-velvety hairs on the branches, leaves, and twigs; large ovate or elliptic grayish-green leaves; star-shaped white flowers; and round yellow berries distinguishes this species.

Evergreen shrub or tree to about 5 m tall; crown dense, rounded. **TWIG** Densely velvety, with branched hairs. **LEAF** Thick, grayish-velvety; ovate, oval, or elliptic; margins entire; blade 10–20 cm long, petiole 5–18 mm long. **FLOWER** 15–18 mm diam., star-shaped, many in branched clusters; corolla lobes white, spreading, narrow-tipped; stamens 5, anthers yellow, to about 3 mm long, erect in the

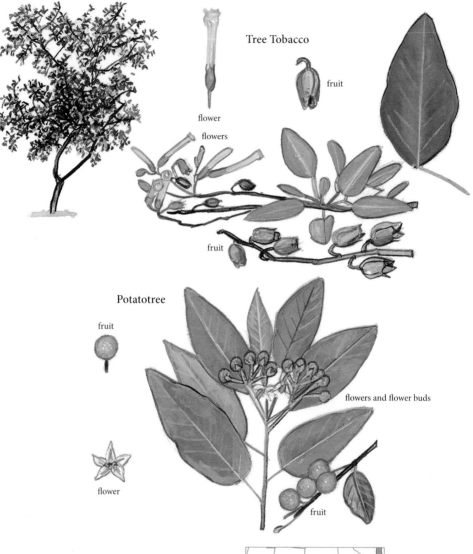

Tree Tobacco

fruit

flower

flowers

fruit

Potatotree

fruit

flowers and flower buds

flower

fruit

center of the flower. Apr.–Oct. **FRUIT** Round yellow berry, 1–2 cm diam.

HABITAT/RANGE Native. Open woods and thickets, 0–50 m; extreme s. Tex., Fla.

Notes Solanum, with 1,200–1,400 species, is distributed mostly in the American tropics. About 65 species occur in the U.S., 35 native. In the West, only this one species is ever treelike.

POTATOTREE

STAPHYLEACEAE: BLADDERNUT FAMILY

Sierra Bladdernut is the only species of Staphyleaceae that may become treelike in the West. The family has 3 genera and 40–50 species of evergreen or deciduous shrubs or trees found primarily in tropical and subtropical parts of the Northern Hemisphere, 23 of which are in *Staphylea*.

SIERRA BLADDERNUT *Staphylea bolanderi* A. Gray

QUICK ID Sierra Bladdernut is easily recognized by its hairless, opposite, pinnately compound leaves, usually with 3 leaflets; drooping clusters of white flowers; and an inflated, football-shaped capsule.

Deciduous shrub, or occasionally a small tree, 2–6 m tall; crown oval, open. **TWIG** Hairless. **LEAF** Opposite, pinnately compound. Leaflets usually 3, each 2.5–6 cm long, 2–4 cm broad; lateral leaflets on stalks 1–2 mm long; terminal leaflet on stalk 6–25 mm long; broadly ovate to round; margins very finely toothed; green, hairless. **FLOWER** Radial, bisexual, several in a drooping cluster 5–10 cm long; sepals 5, narrowly triangular, joined at the base, 8–10 mm long, white; petals 5, narrowly oblong, 10–12 mm long; stamens 5, about twice the length of the petals; ovary superior. **FRUIT** Three-celled, inflated, football-shaped capsule, 2–5 cm long, opening at the top, each cell terminating in a slender "horn"; 1–4 obovoid, light brown seeds per cell, each 5–7 mm long.

HABITAT/RANGE Native. Uncommon on wooded or shrubby slopes, 250–1,700 m; Calif. in northern mountains and western slopes of the Sierra Nevada.

SIMILAR SPECIES The leaves of some ashes (*Fraxinus*, Oleaceae) with few leaflets are similar, but lack the fine teeth, and ash fruits are 1-seeded, long-winged samaras. Common Hoptree (*Ptelea trifoliata*, Rutaceae) has alternate leaves, and the fruit is a disk-like winged samara.

SIERRA BLADDERNUT

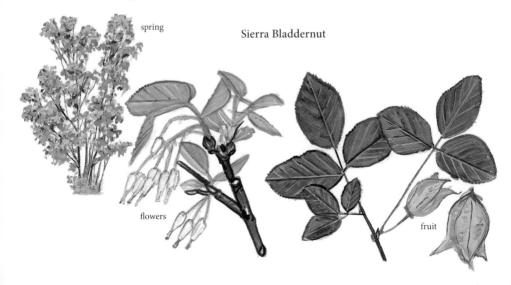

spring

Sierra Bladdernut

flowers

fruit

STYRACACEAE: STORAX FAMILY

The Styracaceae is a family of 11 genera and about 160 species of trees and shrubs of warm regions. The foliage and twigs bear usually stalked, many-branched (stellate) hairs.

SYCAMORELEAF SNOWBELL *Styrax platanifolius* Englem. ex Torr.

QUICK ID This shrub or small tree, in our area only from Tex., has slender branches with leaves about as broad as long, and nodding white flowers with 5 petals and 10 stamens.

Deciduous shrub or small tree to 6 m tall, with slender branches forming an open, irregular crown. **LEAF** Alternate, simple, broadly ovate to nearly round; margins entire, wavy, or with 1 or a few low, blunt, broadly angled teeth. Upper surface hairless and lustrous to stellate-hairy; lower surface sparsely to densely stellate-hairy, veins raised, forming a net-like pattern. Blade 3–10 cm long, about as broad; petiole 6–20 mm long. **FLOWER** 1 or few in a loose pendent cluster 3–6 cm long; calyx bell-shaped, usually with 5 low lobes; corolla white, 12–21 mm long, with 5 softly-hairy, narrowly elliptic lobes gently curved outward; stamens 10, anthers bright yellow. Ovary partly inferior. Apr.–May. **FRUIT** Subglobose leathery capsule, 8–10 mm long, nearly hairless to stellate-pubescent; 1 or 2 brown seeds.

HABITAT/RANGE Native. Streams, canyons, crevices in bluffs, almost always on limestone, 200–1,200 m; c. and w. Tex., nc. Mexico.

Notes Styrax contains about 130 species; 2 occur in the West, of which only this uncommon plant is sometimes a tree. The second western species is Snowdrop Bush (*S. redivivus* [Torr.] L.C. Wheeler), an uncommon shrub to 4 m tall found in the chaparral of Calif.

SYCAMORELEAF SNOWBELL

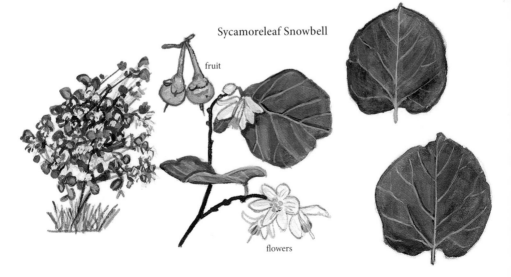

Sycamoreleaf Snowbell

fruit

flowers

TAMARICACEAE: TAMARISK FAMILY

The tamarisk family consists of about 4 or 5 genera of shrubs and trees from Eurasia and Africa. Species are commonly halophytes, occurring in saline or alkaline habitats. **TWIG** Much branched, often green and photosynthetic. **LEAF** Commonly small and scalelike. **FLOWER** Usually tiny, often in branched inflorescences; sepals, petals, and stamens each commonly 4 or 5; ovary superior, 1-chambered, with usually 3 styles. **FRUIT** Capsule containing hairy seeds.

■ *TAMARIX*: TAMARISKS OR SALTCEDARS

Of the approximately 55 species of tamarisk native to the Old World (Eurasia and Africa), about 9 have been introduced to North America, and at least 2 have become aggressively invasive.

Shrubs and trees with fine, wispy, often drooping terminal stems that are grayish green, photosynthetic, and mostly deciduous at the end of a season. **BARK** Brownish or reddish brown, smooth at first, eventually becoming grayish brown and furrowed. **LEAF** Reduced to tiny scales that have salt-excreting glands and thus are sometimes encrusted with white. **FLOWER** Tiny, whitish to pinkish, usually bisexual (when unisexual, male and female on separate plant), borne in racemes that are either single or in branched clusters. Sepals 4 or 5, separate or joined at the base; petals 4 or 5, separate; stamens 4 or 5, attached to the edge of a central nectar disk with 4 or 5 lobes, or immediately beneath it. **FRUIT** Tiny capsule splitting into 3 or 4 segments, with many tiny seeds, each seed with a tuft of hairs at the tip, resembling a minute whisk broom.

The biblical manna may have come from excrescence of insects feeding on tamarisk. Honey producers make a dark, flavorful honey from the flowers. Tamarisk was apparently introduced to the U.S. in the 1850s for ornamental use, for windbreaks, or to stabilize erosion. It raced across the West as an invasive plant in the early 1900s, displacing native vegetation along watercourses, overtaking more than half a million hectares. The Northern Tamarisk Beetle (*Diorhabda carinulata*) and closely related species are now being used for biological control. Tamarisk is deep-rooted, tapping water that other plants may not be able to access, but also has widely spreading roots, which give rise to new plants. The tiny seeds float upon the wind for long distances. Other means of eradication are expensive, requiring chemical and/or mechanical means, and sometimes also the burning of dense stands.

In North America, tamarisks (or saltcedars) occur in places that are wet at least part of the year, such as saline plains, floodplains, roadsides, riverbanks, canyon bottoms, and springs, from low to moderate elevations, in much of the w. and se. U.S. The slender green terminal, often drooping twigs with tiny alternate, scalelike leaves are diagnostic, especially when examined in combination with inflorescences of minute pinkish-white flowers. At first glance *Casuarina*, which has not naturalized in the West, is very similar, but it has scalelike leaves in rings, making a jointed stem, and a small ovoid, rough woody fruiting body.

Tamarix species are differentiated by small differences of the flower, particularly the shape of the nectar disk and attachment of stamens to the nectar disk. Also important is the presence or absence of minute teeth on leaves or sepals, though species are practically impossible to identify without flowers. Flower and leaf features require at least a 10× lens to see. To confound the problem, species will hybridize when in contact with one another, and numbers of floral parts may vary on any one plant. Still, with a lens and persistence, one can usually identify a species, or an intergrade between species. Look at the number of stamens per flower (4 or 5) and the junction of the stamens with the nectar disk in the center of the flower. In this treatment the first species, *T. parviflora*, has 4 stamens. The second group of species, beginning here with *T. gallica*, has 5 stamens with flared bases of filaments confluent with the nectar disk, and no well-defined disk lobes between the filament bases. The third group of species, headed by *T. chinensis*, has 5 stamens with slender filaments, and an abrupt junction between the nectar disk and narrow base of the filament, the disk with well-defined lobes between the filament bases.

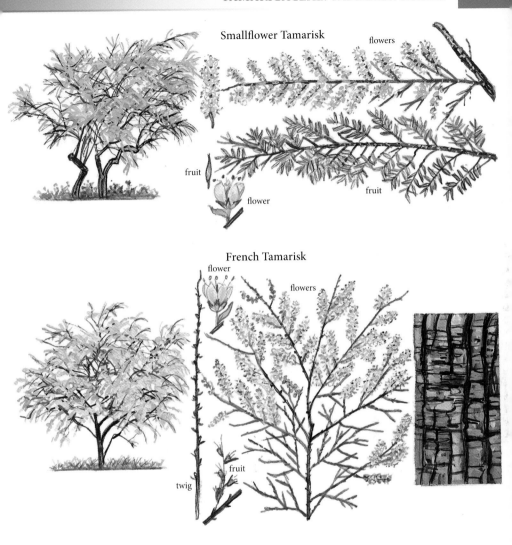

Smallflower Tamarisk

flowers

fruit

fruit

flower

French Tamarisk

flower

flowers

twig

fruit

SMALLFLOWER TAMARISK *Tamarix parviflora* DC.

Shrub or tree to 5 m tall. **LEAF** Slender at the base, and with a long, narrow tip, 2–2.5 mm long. **FLOWER** 4 sepals; 4 petals; 4 stamens, the filaments confluent with the nectar disk. Mar.–Apr. **HABITAT/ RANGE** Introduced; washes, arroyos, road banks, 0–1,300 m; much of c. Calif.; reported from Miss. and N.C.

FRENCH TAMARISK *Tamarix gallica* L.

Bushy shrub or tree to 8 m tall. **LEAF** Narrow, 1.5–2 mm long, with a narrow base. **FLOWER** In loose racemes 2–5 cm long, 4–5 mm wide, the central axis with minute wartlike papillae. Sepals entire; petals elliptic, 1.5–2 mm long, soon falling; stamens 5, each with a narrowly expanded base confluent with the nectar disk. Jun.–Aug. **HABI- TAT/RANGE** Introduced from s. Europe; washes and roadsides, 0–300 m; c. and s. Calif., coastal Tex., and perhaps S.C.

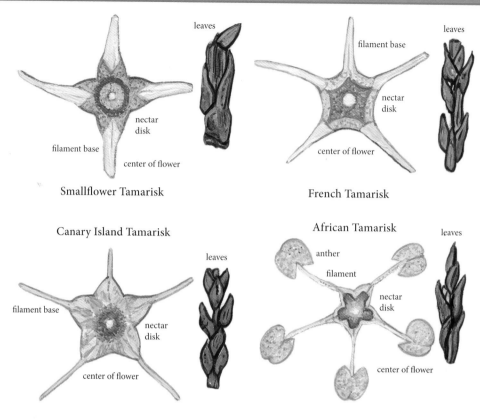

Smallflower Tamarisk

French Tamarisk

Canary Island Tamarisk

African Tamarisk

CANARY ISLAND TAMARISK *Tamarix canariensis* Willd.

Very similar to French Tamarisk, but lacks minute papillae on the axis of the racemes. **FLOWER** Sepals finely toothed; petals obovate, 1–1.5 mm long; stamens 5, each with a broadly expanded base confluent with the nectar disk. Mostly Apr.–Jul. **HABITAT/RANGE** Introduced from w. Mediterranean; reported from Ariz. at 500–600 m; also N.C. to Fla.

AFRICAN TAMARISK *Tamarix africana* Poir.

Small bushy tree. **BARK** Black or dark purple. **LEAF** 1.5–2.5 mm long, margins translucent. **FLOWER** In dense racemes 3–7 cm long, 6–9 mm wide; axis of racemes papillose. Petals ovate, 2.5–3 mm long. Stamens 5, the base of each filament confluent with swollen, roughly conical lobes of the nectar disk. Mar.–Aug. **HABITAT/RANGE** Introduced

the Mediterranean region; occasional in moist areas at low elevations; reported from Ariz. to Tex. (range and identification in the West uncertain).

FIVE-STAMEN TAMARISK *Tamarix chinensis* Lour.

QUICK ID A feathery shrub or tree with minute scalelike leaves, flowers with 5 stamens, the filaments of at least some inserted between the lobes of the nectar disk, and calyx lobes that are not toothed on their margins.

Shrubby tree to 8 m tall; trunks 1 to several, to about 30 cm diam. Crown dense, round, feathery, grayish green, branches spreading or ascending. **BARK** Brownish to black, rough on the trunk. **TWIG** Hairless, the fine terminal twigs green, somewhat drooping. **LEAF** Alternate, scalelike, lanceolate from a narrow base, 1.5–3 mm long. **FLOWER** Minute, in panicles 2–6 cm long, 5–7 m wide,

Canary Island Tamarisk

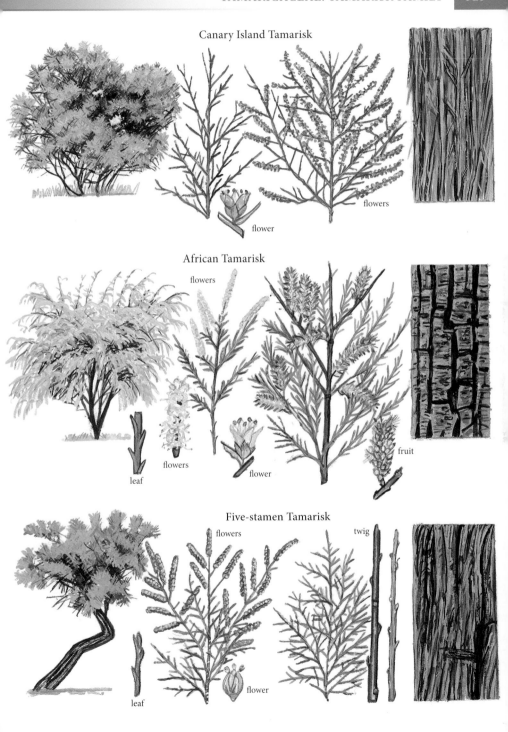

flower

flowers

African Tamarisk

flowers

flowers

leaf

flowers

flower

fruit

Five-stamen Tamarisk

flowers

twig

flower

leaf

FIVE-STAMEN TAMARISK *continued*

mostly on branches of the previous year's growth. Sepals ovate, 0.5–1.5 mm long, entire, tapered to a pointed tip; petals oblong or elliptic, 1.5–2 mm long; stamens 5, filaments slender throughout, some inserted between broad, shallowly notched lobes on the nectar disk, others inserted below the disk between the lobes. **FRUIT** Flask-shaped capsule 3–4 mm long, pointed at the tip.

HABITAT/RANGE Introduced from e. Asia; canyons, riverbanks, springs, salt flats, floodplains, roadsides where there is extra water, 0–1,800 m; widespread in w. U.S. from sw. Canada to nw. Mexico, east to approximately the Mississippi River.

Notes Five-stamen Tamarisk is an aggressive invader of moist, disturbed areas throughout the West, often forming dense, nearly impenetrable thickets. Salt excreted through foliar glands increases the salinity of the soil surface as summer rains wash the leaves, or salt-laden twigs fall to the ground in autumn, making the ground inhabitable for many native plants. In thick stands, the shrubby trees readily carry fires that denude the landscape, followed by even denser tamarisk populations resprouting from root crowns. Disturbance from western agronomic practices seems to increase the potential for infestation by tamarisk species.

SALTCEDAR *Tamarix ramosissima* Ledeb.

As common as, and vegetatively indistinguishable from, Five-stamen Tamarisk, differing in that the sepals are minutely toothed and all stamens attach beneath the nectar disk. **HABITAT/RANGE** Introduced from Asia; probably with a similar range and habitat requirements as Five-stamen Tamarisk, often growing with it, the 2 species apparently hybridizing extensively.

ATHEL TREE *Tamarix aphylla* (L.) H. Karst.

Dense, bushy tree to 25 m tall. **LEAF** 2 mm long, base clasping and completely surrounding the stem (resembling little cups around the branch), stem appearing jointed. **FLOWER** In open panicles, branches slender, 2–6 cm long. Stamens 5, filaments attached between broad, blunt lobes of the nectar disk. May–Nov. **HABITAT/RANGE** Introduced; uncommon on washes, roadsides, 0–200 m; s. Calif. to sw. Utah, also w. Tex.

RUSSIAN TAMARISK *Tamarix aralensis* Bunge

Small bushy tree. **TWIG** With small wartlike papillae. **LEAF** More or less encircling the stem, 1–2 mm long, tip narrow-pointed. **FLOWER** In dense panicles, the slender branches 2–6 cm long, 3–5 mm diam. Sepals irregular-toothed; petals elliptic to ovate, soon falling; base of each filament inserted between broad, rounded lobes of the nectar disk. Mar.–Aug. **HABITAT/RANGE** Introduced from w. Asia; rarely cultivated, not extensively naturalized; reported from Ariz. (range and identification uncertain).

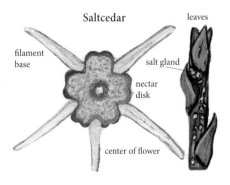

Saltcedar

leaves

filament base

salt gland

nectar disk

center of flower

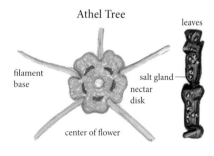

Athel Tree

leaves

filament base

salt gland

nectar disk

center of flower

Saltcedar

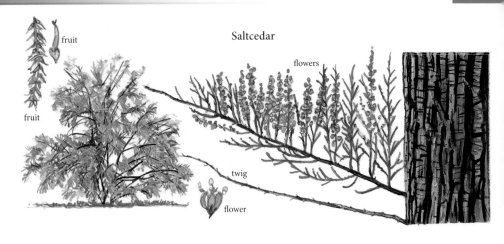

fruit

fruit

flowers

twig

flower

Athel Tree

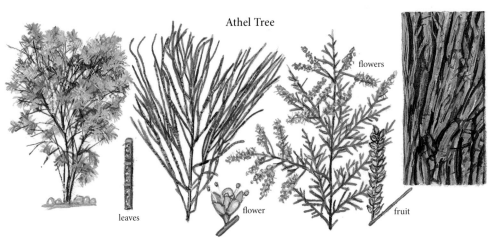

leaves

flower

flowers

fruit

Russian Tamarisk

filament base

leaves

flowers

nectar disk

center of flower

stem

fruit

ULMACEAE: ELM FAMILY

The elm family comprises about 6 genera and 40 species of shrubs and trees distributed nearly worldwide in temperate and warm regions. As traditionally perceived, the family had about 16 genera and 2,000 species and included several genera now placed in Cannabaceae. As the family Ulmaceae is currently understood, only the genus *Ulmus* occurs in the West.

LEAF Alternate, mostly in 2 rows; margins may be toothed or entire, leaf base usually asymmetric. Venation is prominent, consisting of a single midvein with prominent parallel lateral veins. **FLOWER** Tiny and wind-pollinated; petals absent; calyx with 3–9 lobes; stamens opposite sepal lobes and of the same number; pistil 1, with 2 styles or stigmas. **FRUIT** Samara, nut, or drupe.

■ ULMUS: ELMS

Deciduous small to large, single-trunk trees, some reaching stately proportions. **LEAF** Alternate, simple, venation usually prominent, margins variously toothed, base often asymmetric. **FLOWER** Bisexual, small; sepals 3–9, the number and hairiness helpful with identification; petals absent; stamens 3–9, usually matching the sepals in number; inflorescence a fascicle, raceme, or cyme, usually subtended by 2 bracts. **FRUIT** Flattened, winged, 1-seeded samara.

AMERICAN ELM *Ulmus americana* L.

QUICK ID This tree, barely entering the eastern edge of our range, is recognized by the combination of alternate, lustrous, dark green leaves with coarsely double-toothed margins and a strongly asymmetric base; yellowish-white hairs lining the margins of the samara; and narrow, flange-like buttresses at the base of the trunk.

Deciduous tree, 21–35 m tall; single erect, straight trunk, 50–120 cm diam., often with flange-like buttresses at the base. **BARK** Smooth and grayish brown, becoming ashy gray and scaly, with narrow ridges and furrows. **LEAF** Alternate, simple, moderately stiff; obovate to elliptic, base asymmetric, tip usually abruptly pointed; margins coarsely toothed, the teeth usually of 2 sizes. Upper surface dark green, semilustrous, usually hairless, sometimes rough to the touch; lower surface paler, duller, with tufts of hairs in the vein axils. Blade 2–15 cm long, 1–8 cm broad; petiole to about 5 mm long. **FLOWER** In a pendent cluster; sepals 7–9, hairy. Mar.–May, before the leaves. **FRUIT** Stalked samara, 10–12 mm long; sparsely hairy on the surfaces, hairy along the margins, the hairs often yellowish white.

HABITAT/RANGE Native. Moist woods and floodplains, 0–1,400 m; s. Sask. to Tex., east to the Atlantic Coast.

Notes American Elm is subject to the fungal Dutch elm disease, identified in the Netherlands in 1921. The disease is believed to have been imported from Asia and is spread by elm bark beetles (*Scolytus* and *Hylurgopinus*). Disease-resistant cultivars have been developed for landscape use.

AMERICAN ELM

American Elm

flowers

twig

fruit

flower

fruit

fruit

CEDAR ELM *Ulmus crassifolia* Nutt.

QUICK ID This elm, found in the West only in s. Tex., may be recognized by the combination of small alternate leaves that are usually symmetric at the base and have toothed margins, a late-summer and autumn flowering period, and flowers with 6–9 hairy sepals.

Deciduous tree, 24–27 m tall; trunk to about 90 cm diam. Crown with crooked limbs and interlacing branches that often have corky wings. **BARK** Light brown, ridged and furrowed, shedding in scale-like plates. **TWIG** Reddish brown, hairy, stiffish, on some trees with brown corky wings. **LEAF** Elliptic, ovate, or oblong, those at the base of the branch often roughly circular; margins sharply or bluntly toothed. Upper surface dark green, rough to the touch; lower surface shaggy-hairy throughout or only along the veins. Blade 1–5 cm long; petiole 0–2 mm long, hairy. **FLOWER** Sepals 6–9, hairy. Jul.–Oct. **FRUIT** Samara stalked, usually oval, 7–10 mm long; surfaces and margins hairy.

HABITAT/RANGE Native. Riverbanks, low woods, 0–500 m; barely entering the West in s. Tex., east to the Mississippi River Valley.

CEDAR ELM

CHINESE ELM *Ulmus parvifolia* Jacq.
A.K.A. Drake Elm

QUICK ID Recognized by its alternate, simple, mostly single-toothed leaves; elliptic or ovate samaras; and flaking bark mottled with olive green, tan, and brown.

Deciduous tree to about 25 m tall; trunk single, erect, low-branched. Crown open, rounded, somewhat flat-topped. **BARK** Mottled olive green, brown, and tan, flaking into plates, orange-brown where freshly exposed. **TWIG** Brown, hairless or not. **LEAF** Alternate, simple, elliptic to ovate or obovate; base moderately to strongly asymmetric; tip abruptly short- and sharp-pointed; margins finely toothed, the teeth usually of 1 size (sometimes 2 sizes). Upper surface lustrous, dark green, hairless; lower surface paler. Blade 3.5–6 cm long, 1.5–2.5 cm broad; petiole 2–8 mm long. Lateral veins fork 5 or more times between the midvein and margin. **FLOWER** Sepals 3–5, hairless. Aug.–Oct. **FRUIT** Hairless, elliptic or ovate green to light brown samara, about 1 cm long.

HABITAT/RANGE Introduced from Asia; widely planted, naturalized along streams, in wetlands, on roadsides, in disturbed areas, 0–1,200 m; sparsely established from Calif. to Tex. and eastward.

SIMILAR SPECIES Siberian Elm has leaves that are often more than 2 cm wide, and with lateral veins that fork only up to 3 times between the midvein and margin.

ENGLISH ELM *Ulmus procera* Salisb.
A.K.A. English Cork Elm

Deciduous tree to about 40 m tall; crown oval, branches sometimes with corky ridges. **BARK** Grayish brown, deeply furrowed, flaking. **TWIG** Slender, reddish brown, hairy, often rough to the touch, sometimes with corky wings. **LEAF** Broadly lanceolate, elliptic, or ovate, base strongly asymmetric, tip acute, margins with coarse teeth of 2 sizes. Upper surface dark green, rough to the touch; lower surface hairy with tufts in the vein axils. Blade 3–10 cm long; petiole 3–12 mm long, hairy, often rough to the touch. **FLOWER** Sepals 5–8, green, reddish purple, or tan; hairy. Feb.–Mar. **FRUIT** Nearly circular, light brown samara, 9–18 mm long; nearly hairless except near the apex. **HABITAT/RANGE** Introduced from Europe as an ornamental; sometimes persisting and weakly naturalizing near plantings, in Idaho, Ore., Calif., and Nev.; also in the East.

flowers

winged twig

fruit

fruit

Cedar Elm

Chinese Elm

twig

fruit

fruit

English Elm

flower

flowers

fruit

SIBERIAN ELM *Ulmus pumila* L.

QUICK ID This widely naturalized, weedy elm has small leaves and deeply furrowed bark with interlacing ridges.

Deciduous shrub or small to medium tree, 15–30 m tall, with a single erect trunk; crown open, with slender, drooping branches that lack corky wings. **BARK** Gray or brown, deeply furrowed, with interlacing ridges. **TWIG** Slender, brittle, light gray, hairy. **LEAF** Alternate, simple, firm, narrowly elliptic or lanceolate; base symmetric or slightly asymmetric; tip abruptly short-pointed; margins with teeth usually of 1 size. Upper surface dark green, hairless; lower surface paler, hairs usually confined to the vein axils. Blade 2–7 cm long, 2–3.5 cm broad; petiole 2–4 mm long, reddish. Lateral veins fork only up to 3 times between the midvein and margin. **FLOWER** Sepals 4 or 5, hairless. Feb.–Apr. **FRUIT** Hairless, nearly circular yellow-green samara, 10–14 mm long.

HABITAT/RANGE Introduced from Asia; widely naturalized in the U.S. and Canada; roadsides, open areas, fencerows, 0–2,200 m.

SIMILAR SPECIES Chinese Elm has mottled, flaking bark, and leaves usually less than 2 cm broad, the lateral veins forking 5 or more times between the midvein and margin.

Notes Once favored as a fast-growing ornamental tolerant of poor soil and sun, this elm has diminished in popularity because of its poor crown shape, short life, and brittle branches that break in wind. In many areas it has become invasive.

SLIPPERY ELM *Ulmus rubra* Muhl.

A.K.A. RED ELM

QUICK ID Slippery Elm barely enters the West on the c. Great Plains; it has stiff hairs on the upper leaf surface, petiole, and twig, making them rough to the touch.

Deciduous tree, 15–24 m tall; trunk high-branching, 30–60 cm diam.; crown irregular, open, spreading, flat-topped. **BARK** Dark reddish brown to grayish, with flat, nearly parallel, interlacing ridges divided by shallow furrows; inner bark mucilaginous and slippery. **TWIG** Moderately stout, green at first, covered with short, stiff hairs. **LEAF** Obovate, oval, oblong, or elliptic, leaves nearest the base of the twig more nearly ovate; base rounded, occasionally asymmetric; tip abruptly short-pointed; margins with teeth of 2 sizes. Upper surface dark, dull green, very rough because of stiff, erect hairs; lower surface paler, hairs softer. Blade 3–18 cm long; petiole 5–7 mm long, stiffly-hairy. **FLOWER** Sepals 5–9, greenish red, with reddish hairs. Mar.–May. **FRUIT** Oval to nearly circular yellow-green or whitish samara, 8–20 mm long; margins and surfaces hairless.

HABITAT/RANGE Native. Upland woods, mixed forests, 0–900 m; barely entering the West in Nebr. and Kan.; widespread in the East.

SLIPPERY ELM

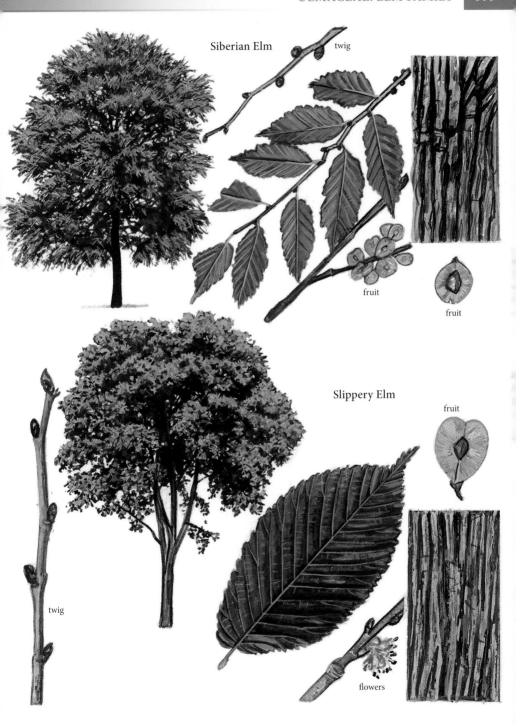

Siberian Elm

twig

fruit

fruit

Slippery Elm

fruit

twig

flowers

VERBENACEAE: VERVAIN FAMILY

As treated here, the vervain family contains about 35 genera and 1,000 species found in tropical and subtropical regions. Recent molecular genetic studies suggest a close relationship between the families Verbenaceae and Lamiaceae (mints), leading some authorities to include the genus *Vitex* (and several other genera) within the mints. The prized hardwood teak (*Tectona*), long allied with the vervains, is now also included within the mint family by many experts.

Several colorful ornamentals come from the family, such as lantana (*Lantana*), and a few species provide herbal teas. The family comprises herbs, lianas, shrubs or trees. **TWIG** At least the young twigs are 4-sided. **LEAF** Opposite or whorled, simple, margins entire to deeply lobed. **FLOWER** In racemes, spikes, or heads. The calyx has 5 joined sepals, and the corolla has 5 joined petals that form a tube with 5 spreading lobes; the corolla is more or less bilateral, the 2 upper lobes sometimes nearly fused and appearing as one. There are usually 4 stamens, and a superior ovary with usually 4 chambers; the stigma has 2 lobes. **FRUIT** Drupe with 2 or 4 stones, or a dry fruit that splits into 2 or 4 nutlets.

BERLANDIER FIDDLEWOOD
Citharexylum berlandieri B.L. Rob.
A.K.A. TAMAULIPAN FIDDLEWOOD, NEGRITO

QUICK ID This small contorted tree from the southern tip of Tex. has 4-sided young twigs and simple opposite leaves, a combination of features unique in its region.

Deciduous unarmed, crooked and contorted shrub or small gnarled tree to 9 m tall, with an irregular crown of heavy, gnarled branches. **BARK** Mottled gray, smooth, tight. **TWIG** Young twigs 4-sided, green, becoming rounded and brownish gray with lighter streaks when older. **LEAF** Opposite, simple, lanceolate to oval or obovate; margins entire or with a few large blunt teeth near the tip. Upper surface light green and hairless, or hairy along the veins or all over; lower surface paler green and finely velvety. Blade 2.5–10 cm long, 2–4 cm broad; petiole

1–10 mm long. **FLOWER** Bisexual, borne in dense spikes 1–10 cm long. Fragrant, 4–5 mm diam., white to cream, slightly bilateral, with 5 lobes flared from a short tube, hairy within the tube near the opening; stamens 4, or sometimes a rudimentary 5th stamen present; stamens and style included within the tube. Feb.–Aug. **FRUIT** Subglobose drupe, slightly 2-lobed, 5–6 mm long, very shiny, fleshy, red-orange at maturity, drying black, containing 2 stones; drupes densely packed in a spike.

HABITAT/RANGE Native. Thickets, dry roadsides, hillsides, 0–100 m; extreme southern tip of Tex.; ne. Mexico.

Notes Of the 2 species of fiddlewood that occur in Tex., this one becomes a tree. There are perhaps 100 species of fiddlewood widely distributed in tropical and subtropical regions of the Americas. The genus name comes from Greek *cithara*, from which we get the word *guitar*; the wood of some species was used for making stringed instruments. Berlandier Fiddlewood is uncommon; fast-growing and heat-tolerant, it is a good ornamental as a specimen tree or in hedges. In contrast to Berlandier Fiddlewood, many other species of fiddlewood have thorn-tipped twigs, and their leaves usually have a pair of glands near the petiole at the base of the blade. Butterflies are attracted to the flowers, and birds relish the fruits. The spikes of red fruits are attractive against the dark foliage. The leaves may develop an orange hue during drought.

BERLANDIER FIDDLEWOOD

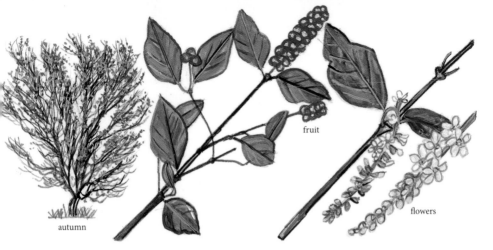

fruit

flowers

autumn

Berlandier Fiddlewood

Golden Dewdrops

fruit

flowers

immature fruit

GOLDEN DEWDROPS *Duranta erecta* L.

Evergreen, usually a shrub, rarely a small tree to about 6 m tall. **BARK** Gray, becoming rough and fissured with age. **LEAF** Opposite, simple, ovate or elliptic, tapering to a short point at the tip; margins entire or toothed above the middle. Upper and lower surfaces dull green, nearly hairless. Blade 1.5–7.5 cm long, to about 2.5 cm broad; petiole to about 3 mm long. **FLOWER** About 1 cm diam.; petals 5, light blue; borne in an elongated raceme 5–15 cm long. Year-round. **FRUIT** Round yellow drupe about 1.3 cm diam. **HABITAT/RANGE** Introduced from the West Indies; escaped from cultivation and naturalized in hammocks, pinelands, disturbed sites, 0–100 m; s. Fla. to e. and s. Tex. *Notes Duranta* is a tropical American genus of about 30 species.

■ *VITEX*: CHASTETREES

This genus of more than 250 species is widely distributed in mostly tropical or subtropical regions of the world. Several species are grown as ornamentals, while others are valued for lumber; two have naturalized in southern parts of the U.S.

Deciduous or evergreen trees and shrubs. **LEAF** Opposite, palmately compound; 3–9 leaflets with margins entire, toothed, or lobed. **FLOWER** Usually perfect, more or less bilateral, small, white, blue, or yellowish, borne in loose to dense racemes or spikes. Sepals 5, joined into a 5-toothed cup or tube; petals joined into a tube that extends beyond the calyx, flared into 5 lobes; stamens 4; ovary superior, 4-chambered, stigma 2-lobed. **FRUIT** Drupe.

LILAC CHASTETREE *Vitex agnus-castus* L.
A.K.A. COMMON CHASTETREE, HEMPTREE

QUICKID The combination of opposite, palmately 5-parted leaves, showy terminal racemes of often lavender flowers, and strongly aromatic foliage distinguishes Lilac Chastetree.

Strongly aromatic deciduous shrub or small tree to about 7 m tall, 10 cm diam., with 1 or several erect trunks; crown rounded, dense. **BARK** Reddish brown or brown, smooth on young trunks, becoming finely fissured and scaly. **TWIG** Four-sided, densely hairy. **LEAF** Opposite, palmately compound; leaflets 3–9, usually 5, thin, about 10 cm long and 3 cm broad, lanceolate, tapering to a sharp tip, margins entire or rarely toothed. Upper surface dull green, hairless, moderately lustrous; lower surface grayish green, finely hairy.

Petiole 1.5–7.5 cm long. **FLOWER** About 1 cm long, corolla lavender, blue, or white; borne in erect terminal clusters 12–18 cm long. Apr.–Oct. **FRUIT** Round, dry, hard drupe containing a 4-chambered stone.

HABITAT/RANGE Introduced from Eurasia; sporadically escaped from cultivation and occasionally naturalized on roadsides, ditch banks, waste places, 0–1,200 m; Tex. eastward.

SIMILAR SPECIES The leaves of other naturalized species of *Vitex* have 3 or fewer leaflets. The palmate leaves of buckeyes (*Aesculus*, Sapindaceae) are much larger, with broader leaflets, and the fruits are large capsules with 1 to few large round seeds.

Notes In the species' native area its twigs were sometimes used in basketwork. The leaves resemble those of hemp (*Cannabis*). The fruits were once substituted for pepper, and the plants have been called Indian Spice, Monk's Pepper, and Wild Peppertree. The white-flowered form has long been considered a symbol of chastity.

CHINESE CHASTETREE *Vitex negundo* L.

Deciduous large shrub or small tree to 5 m tall. **LEAF** Opposite, palmately compound; leaflets usually 3 (sometimes 5), to 11 cm long and about 4 cm broad, lanceolate, margins toothed. **FLOWER** About 3 mm long, 7 mm wide, violet, purple, or bluish; inflorescence to 42 cm long, 15 cm wide. **HABITAT/RANGE** Introduced from China; sporadically escaped from cultivation, 0–100 m; s. Tex. east to Fla.

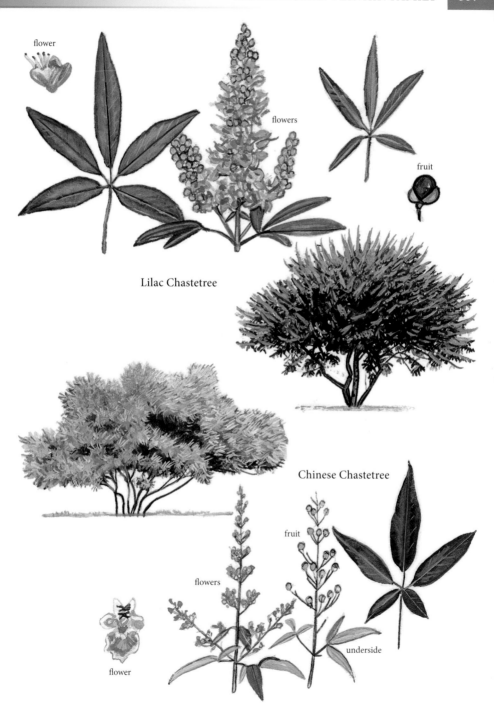

flower

flowers

fruit

Lilac Chastetree

Chinese Chastetree

fruit

flowers

flower

underside

ZYGOPHYLLACEAE: CALTROP FAMILY

The caltrop family contains about 26 genera and nearly 300 species of herbs, shrubs, and a few trees, mostly in tropical or subtropical, often arid regions. About 7 genera and 18 species occur north of Mexico, at least 12 of which are native.

LEAF Opposite (rarely alternate) and pinnately compound. **FLOWER** Radial, bisexual, with 5 sepals and 5 petals, 10 or 15 stamens, and a superior ovary. **FRUIT** Capsule, splitting open to reveal seeds or separating into 5–10 indehiscent sections. Guayacán, one of about 6 species in a genus from the Caribbean and w. Mexico, is the only treelike representative of the caltrop family in the West.

GUAYACÁN *Guaiacum angustifolium*
Engelm.
A.K.A. TEXAS LIGNUM-VITAE, TEXAS PORLIERIA, SOAPBUSH

QUICK ID Opposite, pinnately compound leaves help identify this dense, contorted, evergreen shrub or small tree with small, pinnately compound, dark green leathery leaves.

Evergreen small-leaved shrub or small, densely branched, gnarled, knotty tree to 7 m tall; trunk to 25 cm diam. **BARK** Gray and smooth at first, when older fissured and broken into rough plates. **TWIG** Twigs and branches numerous; new, fast-growing twigs slender; older or slow-growing branches contorted, bearing spur branches. **LEAF** Opposite on new twigs, opposite or in clusters on spur branches, pinnately compound; blade 1–3 cm long; petiole short, pubescent, grooved. Leaflets in 4–8 pairs, each leaflet 5–15 mm long, 2–3 mm broad, linear-oblong; dark, lustrous green, leathery. **FLOWER** Fragrant, borne singly or in few-flowered clusters on slender stalks 1–2 cm long on small spurs or in leaf axils. Sepals 5 mm long. Petals blue-violet to purple or lilac, obovate, often notched at the tip, about 1 cm long. Stamens 10; scale at the base of each filament scalloped. Mar.–Sep., often after rains. **FRUIT** Flattened leathery capsule, hanging

from a stalk, usually with 2 lobes (sometimes 3 or 4), these roughly heart-shaped, each lobe tipped by a point, the central tip of the fruit slender and longer. Seeds large, kidney-shaped, tan, enclosed within a brilliant red, fleshy covering (aril).

HABITAT/RANGE Native. In brush on flats and in arroyos, 0–800 m; w. and s. Tex.; n. Mexico.

Notes Guayacán is a good honey plant and has potential for ornamental use in hot areas. It is often placed in the genus *Porlieria*. The bark may be used to make a gentle soap. The dense, hard wood called lignum vitae comes from tropical species of *Guaiacum*. Creosotebush (*Larrea tridentata* (DC.) Coville), the common army-green shrub of warm deserts from Tex. to Calif., is also in this family.

GUAYACÁN

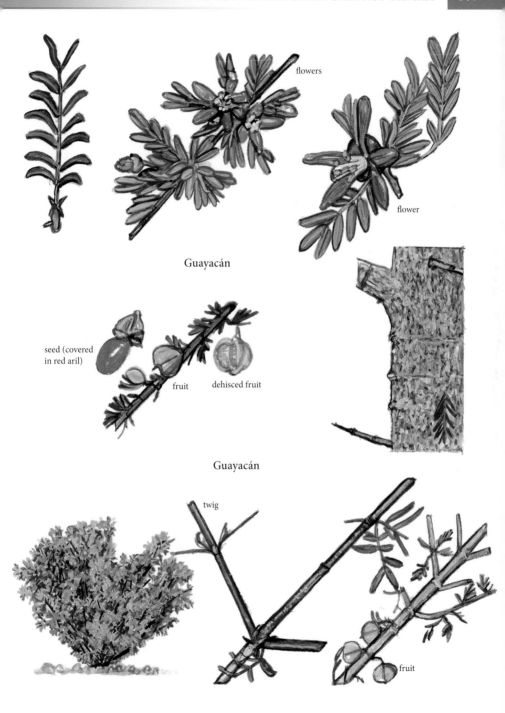

flowers

flower

Guayacán

seed (covered
in red aril)

fruit   dehisced fruit

Guayacán

twig

fruit

■ CREDITS

Figure of Evolution of the Carpel (p. 8), redrawn from P. H. Raven, R. F. Evert, S. E. Eichhorn, *Biology of Plants*, 4th ed. (New York: Worth Pub., Inc., 1986), Fig. 29-10, p. 591.

Illustrations of Coast Redwood tree (p. 53) and Giant Sequoia (p. 54) by Robert Van Pelt.

Figure of Wavyleaf Oak hybrids (p. 305) redrawn from *American Journal of Botany*, vol. 48, no. 3, March 1961, p. 204.

Flowers of *Tamarix* (pp. 524–527) redrawn from B. R. Baum, *The Genus* Tamarix (Israel Academy of Arts and Humanities, 1978).

AUTHORS' ACKNOWLEDGMENTS

This project was originally conceived and presented to Princeton University Press by our editor, Amy K. Hughes. It has been a privilege and delight to work with her. Her ability to coordinate three authors and an artist, interact with the press and production crews, all the while maintaining good humor and patience, has been remarkable and is deeply appreciated. Robert Kirk of Princeton University Press saw the merit in our proposal and from that moment facilitated our efforts at every turn. Kathleen Cioffi, production editor, was always helpful when needed. David and Namrita Price-Goodfellow and their team at D & N Publishing produced the attractive and useful design of the book, and efficiently pushed the project through final production. Susi Bailey skillfully smoothed the rough edges with her copy editing expertise. Finally, Ken Womble, of Florida State University created the range maps, always with a cooperative "can-do" approach. To all these people, we extend deep gratitude for a job well done.

A number of botanists also graciously supplied information that appears in the book; to each and every one of them we extend sincere thanks. Alphabetically, they are: Dr. George Argus, retired from the Canada Museum of Nature, Ottawa, for his help with the difficult willow (*Salix*) genus; Dr. Dan Austin, University of Arizona, provided valuable comment on soapberries (*Sapindus*); Dr. Luc Brouillet, University of Montreal, suggested authors from upcoming volumes of *Flora of North America* who might assist us; Dr. Walter Judd, University of Florida, Gainesville, shared his knowledge and views of leaf morphology in the plant family Sapindaceae; Dr. Guy Nesom, writer, botanist, and publisher of *Phytoneuron*, Fort Worth, Texas, discussed with us problems in the ashes (*Fraxinus*); Dr. James Phipps, University of Western Ontario, helped with the nearly intractable hawthorns (*Crataegus*); Dr. Joseph Rohrer, University of Wisconsin at Eau Claire, provided his manuscript for *Flora of North America* on wild cherries and plums (*Prunus*); Dr. Tom Van Devender, Sky Island Alliance, Tucson, reported to us the rediscovery in the United States of the primarily Mexican Willowleaf Oak (*Quercus viminea*); Dr. James Zarucchi, Missouri Botanical Garden, St. Louis, also suggested authors from upcoming volumes of *Flora of North America* who might assist us; Dr. Peter F. Zika, University of Washington, provided information on some Northwestern introduced trees.

In a project as diverse as this, hundreds of references were required, from the traditional technical taxonomic treatments of certain genera to reviews of plants occurring within a well-defined region. We thank those authors, many now deceased, who contributed so much to our understanding of North American trees. In today's electronic age, we thank the community of supporters and contributors for such listings as Gymnosperm Database, USDA Plants, Angiosperm Phylogeny website, the Biota of North American Program, USGS tree species maps, and scores of other websites; all were used extensively and have proved invaluable sources of information. And finally, to those who we might have inadvertently omitted, we sincerely thank them, noting that their aid, along with that of those above, has contributed to a thorough, concise, and informative gathering of information on trees of North America north of Mexico.

ILLUSTRATOR'S ACKNOWLEDGMENTS

The illustrator wishes to thank Myles Archibald, Julia Koppitz, and staff at Harper Collins, UK, and wishes to thank the following individuals and institutions for their help and support in providing references for the artwork: Marcel Blondeau, Keith Bradley, Judy Gibson of the Botany Department at the San Diego Natural History Museum, Richard R. Halse of the Oregon State Education Department, Roger Hammer, Neal Jackson and Martin Kelsen for technological and moral support, Ron Lance, Jim Phipps, Lulu Rico of the Herbarium Kew Gardens, Adele Smith of the Royal Botanic Gardens, and Sul Ross State University of Texas.

STATE AND PROVINCE ABBREVIATIONS

United States

State	Abbreviation
Alabama	Ala.
Alaska	Alaska
Arizona	Ariz.
Arkansas	Ark.
California	Calif.
Colorado	Colo.
Connecticut	Conn.
Delaware	Del.
Florida	Fla.
Georgia	Ga.
Hawaii	Hawaii
Idaho	Idaho
Illinois	Ill.
Indiana	Ind.
Iowa	Iowa
Kansas	Kans.
Kentucky	Ky.
Louisiana	La.
Maine	Maine
Maryland	Md.
Massachusetts	Mass.
Michigan	Mich.
Minnesota	Minn.
Mississippi	Miss.
Missouri	Mo.
Montana	Mont.
Nebraska	Nebr.
Nevada	Nev.
New Hampshire	N.H.
New Jersey	N.J.
New Mexico	N.M.
New York	N.Y.
North Carolina	N.C.

United States

North Dakota	N.D.
Ohio	Ohio
Oklahoma	Okla.
Oregon	Ore.
Pennsylvania	Pa.
Rhode Island	R.I.
South Carolina	S.C.
South Dakota	S.D.
Tennessee	Tenn.
Texas	Tex.
Utah	Utah
Vermont	Vt.
Virginia	Va.
Washington	Wash.
West Virginia	W.Va.
Wisconsin	Wis.
Wyoming	Wyo.

Canada

Province/Territory	Abbreviation
Alberta	Alta.
British Columbia	B.C.
Labrador	Lab.
Manitoba	Man.
New Brunswick	N.B.
Newfoundland	Nfld.
Northwest Territories	N.W.T.
Nova Scotia	N.S.
Nunavut	Nunavut
Ontario	Ont.
Prince Edward Island	P.E.I.
Quebec	Que.
Saskatchewan	Sask.
Yukon	Y.T.

METRIC–IMPERIAL EQUIVALENTS

25.4 millimeters (mm) = 1 inch
2.54 centimeters (cm) = 1 inch
0.3 meters (m) = 1 foot
1.6 kilometers (km) = 1 mile
0.4 hectares (ha) = 1 acre

Celsius to Fahrenheit:
$°F = 9/5 × °C + 32$

achene A tiny, one-seeded, dry, indehiscent fruit with a hard outer layer.

acuminate Gradually tapered to a slender point, each side concave and often appearing as if pinched together.

adventitious Arising from a site that is more or less unusual, such as roots sprouting from a stem, or branches from the trunk.

aggregate fruit A fruit formed of the adjacent ovaries of a single flower, such as a blackberry.

alluvial Refers to deposits of sand, silt, gravel, and similar material formed by flowing water.

alternate Refers to a leaf arrangement in which only one leaf arises from each stem node. Compare *opposite*.

angiosperm A member of the flowering plants, a group of seed plants that develop seeds within an enclosed ovary.

anther The pollen-bearing structure at the tip of a stamen.

anthesis The time of expansion or opening of a flower; also the period during which the flower is in full bloom.

anthocarp A tiny one-seeded fruit enclosed in a fleshy, leathery, or woody covering derived at least in part from the perianth or receptacle.

apex The tip or distal end of a structure, farthest from the base (adj., *apical*).

apical meristem A small patch of cells at the tip of a stem or root that repeatedly divide, producing cells that differentiate into various cell types of the plant mostly behind the meristem, adding length to the structure.

apophysis The exposed, often thickened portion of a pinecone scale when the cone is closed.

appressed Pressed close to, lying flat against.

arborescent Having a tree form.

areole In the cacti a circular or oval point on the stem from which spines arise (spines sometimes absent, but areole evident), derived from a suppressed, modified branch.

aril An outer covering on some seeds, commonly fleshy, sometimes brightly colored, often derived from the small stalk that connects the seed to the placenta.

ascending In plant habit, oriented upward or forward at an angle, often curving from the base, as in a coconut palm.

axil The angle formed by adjoining vegetative structures such as that between a leaf and the twig from which it grows.

axillary Located in, or arising from, an axil, or angle, usually between a twig and a leaf.

berry A fleshy fruit with few to many seeds within.

bipinnate Refers to a compound leaf that is twice divided, with its primary segments branching from an axis, and each segment divided into separate leaflets along a secondary axis.

bole Tree trunk.

bract A scale or modified leaflike structure, associated with the seed-bearing cone scales of conifers; also found below the bases of some flowers, fruits, and flower and fruiting clusters.

bristle A minute, usually straight and stiff, hairlike extension, often at the tip of a leaf lobe or tooth (also called *awn*).

bundle scar A mark within a leaf scar where a vascular bundle from the leaf entered the twig.

calyx The outermost of the four whorls of parts that make up a flower, formed by the sepals.

carpel The fundamental unit of a pistil, the pollen-receiving, seed-producing part of the flower.

capsule A dry, dehiscent fruit derived from a compound pistil; may have one or several chambers.

catkin A small, usually elongate cluster of highly reduced unisexual flowers, often deciduous as a unit.

chaparral An ecological community of shrubs adapted to dry summers and moist winters, mainly of s. Calif.

compound leaf A leaf with a blade that is divided to the midrib or to the tip of the petiole, thereby separated into smaller individual leaflets, each arising from an axis or central point. Contrast *simple leaf*.

conifer A cone-bearing plant of the gymnosperms order Coniferales, which includes the Cupressaceae and Pinaceae.

cordate In the shape of a heart; with regard to the base of a leaf blade, having two more or less rounded lobes, one on each side of the petiole (resembling the top of a Valentine heart).

corolla The whorl of parts formed by the petals of a flower.

corymb A flat-topped inflorescence in which the flowers mature from the outer edge inward (adj., *corymbose*).

crown The portion of a tree above the trunk formed by the branches and leaves.

cyathium An inflorescence shaped like a small cup and resembling a tiny flower, containing a female flower and several male flowers, the flowers lacking sepals and petals and assumed to be evolutionarily reduced; several *cyathia* (pl.) may be aggregated and surrounded by brightly colored leaves, as in the Poinsettia.

cyme A terminal cluster of successive three-flowered units, the terminal flower of each cluster opening first and arresting further elongation of the cluster's axis, the two successive flowers at ends of branches originating below the terminal flower, the pattern repeated many times, often producing a flat-topped or convex flower cluster (adj., *cymose*).

cypsela An achene-like fruit that develops from an inferior ovary in plants of the Asteraceae.

dehiscent Regarding a dry fruit, splitting or otherwise opening at maturity.

dendritic Like the branching pattern of a tree without a central axis; usually applied to repeatedly branched hairs in plants.

dicotyledon, dicot A member of a group within the flowering plants that usually has two nutrient-storing leaves in the embryo within the seed, netlike leaf venation, and flower parts in multiples of four or five.

dioecious Having the male and female reproductive parts on separate plants.

drupe A fruit, such as a plum, with a three-layered ovary wall consisting of an outer skin over a fleshy layer and an innermost hard, bony layer forming one or more stones, each surrounding one seed.

ellipsoid Referring to a solid (three-dimensional) structure that is oval in outline as viewed from the side.

elliptic In the shape of an oval, the widest part across the middle.

entire In describing margins of leaves (or sepals or petals), indicates the margin is uninterrupted, as by teeth or lobes.

exserted Projecting beyond.

fascicle A small, closely held bundle or cluster (adj., *fasciculate*).

fastigiate Having a narrow, erect form of dense, upright, more or less parallel branches.

female flower A nontechnical term for *pistillate flower*, a flower that lacks functional stamens.

filament The stalk of a stamen.

follicle A dry, podlike fruit derived from a single carpel that splits along one seam to release the seeds.

glabrous Without hairs, usually implying the surface to be smooth.

glaucous Having an impermanent powdery or waxy covering that often imparts a bluish tint, usually easily rubbed off.

glochid In some genera of the cactus family, a small, sharp, barbed bristle on an areole.

grit cell See *stone cell*.

gymnosperm A member of the group of seed plants in which the seeds do not develop within a closed ovary; includes the conifers.

habit A plant's growth form.

hairs Usually slender unicellular or multicellular structures growing from the epidermis of a plant; technically *trichomes*.

halophyte A plant adapted to soil high in salt content.

hesperidium A berry with a leathery rind, such as an orange.

heterophyllous Having more than one form of leaf.

hypanthium An often cuplike structure surrounding the ovary formed by the fused bases of the sepals, petals, and stamens; may be either free or fused to the ovary.

imbricate Overlapping, often forming a pattern like shingles on a roof.

indehiscent Remaining closed at maturity.

inflorescence The flower-bearing portion of a plant, usually referring to a cluster or arrangement.

infructescence The fruit-bearing portion of a plant; the inflorescence in a fruiting stage.

introduced Not native.

involucre A whorl of bracts subtending a flower or flowers, sometimes forming an enclosing structure.

krummholz A forest of subarctic or alpine zones in which the trees are stunted and contorted by climate conditions.

lanceolate A narrow shape much longer than wide, widest below the middle and tapering to a pointed tip, like the head of a spear.

lateral bud A bud that arises along a twig rather than at the growing tip.

lateral vein A side vein that branches from the midvein of a leaf.

leaf scar A mark left on a twig after a leaf drops.

legume The fruit of the Fabaceae, or bean family; a dry pod derived from a simple pistil that splits along two seams.

lignotuber A woody swelling at the root crown containing buds from which new stems may quickly arise, often serving to regenerate stems after a fire.

lenticel A patch of loose, usually pale, corky cells, varying from small dots to short dashes or even long lines, on a twig's surface, allowing the passage of gases into and out of the twig.

locule A chamber within a plant's ovary.

male flower A nontechnical term for *staminate flower*, a flower that lacks a pistil.

mesic Requiring or receiving a moderate amount of moisture; neither excessively wet nor dry.

midvein, midrib A vein that runs down the center of a pinnately veined leaf.

monocotyledon, monocot A member of a group within the flowering plants usually with one nutrient-storing leaf in the embryo within the seed, parallel leaf veins, and flower parts in multiples of three.

monoecious Having male and female reproductive parts in different structures on the same plant.

mucro A tiny, sharp point extending beyond the margin, as at the tip of a leaf (adj., *mucronate*).

multiple fruit A fruit cluster formed of individual fruits of adjacent flowers joined together as a unit, as in the mulberry. Also called a *syncarp*.

mycorrhizae Fungi associated with the roots of a plant, usually both fungi and plant benefiting from the association.

native Originating from a given region.

naturalized Not native to a region but reproducing and persisting there as a population without the aid of horticultural practice.

nectary The gland of a flower that secretes the nectar; also called *nectar gland*.

net-veined Having a fine network of veins.

node The place on a stem where a leaf or leaves attach.

nut An indehiscent one-seeded fruit with a hard outer wall.

nutlet See *pyrene*.

obovate Inversely ovate, with the broader end away from the base and toward the tip.

opposite Refers to a leaf arrangement in which two leaves are attached on either side of a stem node. Compare *alternate, whorled*.

ovate In the outline of an egg, with the broader end at the base, tapering toward the tip.

ovoid An egg-shaped solid, ovate in side view.

ovule A structure that develops into a seed.

palmate In the shape of a hand or a fan, with lobes or veins radiating from a common point.

panicle A large multibranched inflorescence, the secondary branches of which are often racemes (adj. *paniculate*)

papilionaceous Of the Papilionoideae subfamily of the bean family (Fabaceae); often refers to the typical "pea-flower" form.

papillose Bearing minute nipple-shaped or conical projections (papillae).

pedicel The stalk of a flower.

peduncle The stalk of an inflorescence.

peltate Having the stalk attached to the lower surface, rather than the margin, producing a form similar to a thumbtack or mushroom.

perianth The portions of a flower outside the stamens and pistil or pistils, usually consisting of the calyx and corolla, sometimes only the calyx. In some small, often wind-pollinated flowers, the perianth may be absent.

petaloid Resembling a petal in shape, texture, and color.

petiolate Having a petiole, or leaf stalk.

petiole The stalk of a leaf.

phyllode A leaflike structure formed of a flattened, expanded petiole in the absence of leaf blade tissue, often resembling a narrow blade.

pine-needle bundle A sheathed cluster of leaves borne by members of the genus *Pinus*.

pinnate With the pattern of a feather, with a central axis and secondary axes extending from it in a plane on either side; often describes a pinnately compound leaf.

pistil The part of a flower bearing ovules and in which the seeds are produced; consists of a stigma (the pollen-receiving part), style (the sperm-transmitting part), and ovary (containing the ovule).

pistillate Having pistils; the term *pistillate flowers* refers to female flowers.

pith The central tissue within a twig or root, usually soft and more or less spongy, originating from the apical meristem and consisting of thin-walled cells.

pollen Tiny spores of a seed plant that produce sperm or sperm cells that fertilize the ovule.

polygamodioecious Having both unisexual and bisexual flowers on the same individual.

pome A fruit, such as an apple, formed by the thickened, fleshy hypanthium joined to the inferior ovary.

prickle A small, sharp-pointed growth from the surface tissue of the plant.

protogynous Describes a flower in which the female reproductive structure matures before the male parts, inhibiting self-pollination.

punctate Having tiny depressions scattered across the surface.

pustular Having pustules, or blisterlike protrusions.

pyrene The seed-containing stone of a small drupe, such as that of a holly; also called a *nutlet*.

pyriform With the shape of a pear.

raceme A loose (as compared to a *spike*), narrow inflorescence with stalked flowers along an elongate axis (adj., *racemose*).

rachilla In a bipinnately compound leaf, the rachis-like axis of a primary segment holding the leaflets.

rachis In a compound leaf, the central axis along which the leaflets are arranged; begins where the petiole ends, at the first leaflet at the base of the pinnately divided blade.

radicle The root portion of a plant embryo.

remote toothing Teeth that are well separated, not close together, and usually sparse along the margin of a leaf.

reticulate Forming a network.

revolute Rolled downward or backward.

samara A hard, dry, indehiscent fruit with one or more wings, such as that of a maple.

schizocarp A dry fruit derived of multiple carpels that splits open along the partitions between chambers into usually one-seeded sections.

semideciduous Describes plants that lose most but not all of their leaves at the end of the growing season or during dry periods, and occasionally all leaves during particularly extreme conditions.

semievergreen Retaining leaves through the winter (or the dry season) in some circumstances but not in all, usually depending on climate, latitude, or elevation.

sepal A usually flat green unit of the outermost of the four whorls that form a flower, collectively forming the calyx, and usually providing protection to the interior when flowers are in bud. In some plants sepals are colored and more like petals (*petaloid*).

sepaloid With the texture, shape, and color of a sepal.

serotinous Maturing late in the growing season; regarding cones, remaining closed until opened by heat (usually fire) or considerable age and only then releasing seeds.

sessile Lacking a stalk.

short shoots Lateral twigs that grow very slowly and are much shorter than the faster-growing main branch, sometimes appearing as woody stubs, sometime thorn-tipped, and often bearing leaves, flowers, or fruits; also called *spur shoots*.

simple leaf A leaf with an undivided blade; the blade may be toothed or deeply lobed, but not divided to the midrib or tip of the petiole. Contrast *compound leaf*.

spatulate Spatula-shaped; a shape in which the basal portion is very narrow and elongate and the tip is wider and rounded.

spike A tight, long, narrow inflorescence in which the individual flowers lack stalks (adj., *spicate*).

spine A needlelike structure that is derived from a leaf or a portion of a leaf, such as a cactus spine or mesquite spine.

spur shoots See *short shoots*.

stamen The pollen-producing (male) reproductive structure of a flower.

staminate Having stamens; the term *staminate flowers* refers to male flowers.

staminode A sterile stamen.

stellate Starlike, with radiating branches from a common central point of attachment.

stigma In a flower, the tip of the pistil, which serves as the pollen receptor.

stipitate Borne on a stipe, or stalk.

stipule One of a pair of structures at the base of the petiole of a leaf, which are usually small, green, and leaflike, but may be modified into scales, bristles, or spines (called *stipular spines*).

stoma A microscopic pore in the surface of a leaf that allows for the exchange of water vapor and other gases in and out of the leaf (pl., *stomata*).

stone cell A cell with very thick, hard walls, often occurring in clusters as in the flesh of a pear, providing a gritty sensation when eaten; also called *grit cell*.

style The often elongate portion of a pistil between the ovary at the base and the stigma at the tip.

subglobose Nearly globose or spherical.

subopposite Regarding leaf arrangement, technically alternate but so close together as to appear opposite.

subpalmate Not quite palmate but suggestive of a palmate pattern.

subspecies A taxonomic category below the species level designating subgroups of a species that are closely related and capable of interbreeding, but typically do not, usually because of geographic separation. Abbreviated *subsp.* Compare *variety*.

syconium A fruit, characterized by the fig, derived from a highly modified inflorescence that bears tiny unisexual flowers inside.

syncarp See *multiple fruit*.

tepals Refers to perianth parts that are poorly or not differentiated as sepals and petals.

terminal bud A bud that forms at a twig's tip.

thorn A sharp-pointed woody structure derived from, and tipping, a twig.

trifoliolate A compound leaf divided into three leaflets.

tripinnate Refers to a compound leaf that is thrice divided, with its primary segments divided into secondary segments, and each of those divided into individual leaflets.

trunk The main portion of a tree's stem between the roots and the crown; bole.

tubercle A rounded swelling or wartlike protuberance, usually larger than the projections of a papillose texture.

tuberculate Bearing tubercles.

twig The portion of a young branch produced by the current year's growth.

umbel An often flat-topped inflorescence in which the stalks of the individual flowers originate from a common point (adj., *umbellate*)

unifoliolate A compound leaf reduced to, or expressed as, a single leaflet.

valvate Regarding bud scales, meeting at the edges without overlapping, like the halves of a clamshell.

variety A taxonomic category below the species level designating subgroups of a species that are closely related and capable of interbreeding, but typically do not, usually because of geographic separation. Variety is of lower rank than subspecies, but in plants when only one category below species is used, variety and subspecies are conceptually equivalent. Abbreviated *var.* Compare *subspecies.*

waif A stray; a plant that has been introduced and is occasionally found growing naturally, but has not become naturalized or established self-perpetuating populations.

whorled Refers to a leaf arrangement in which three or more leaves are attached at a stem node.

xeriscape Refers to a garden or cultivated landscape designed for minimal use of water.

Abeto del Colorado 60
Abies amabilis 56
Abies balsamea 58
Abies bracteata 56
Abies concolor 60
Abies concolor var. lowiana 60
Abies grandis 60
Abies koreana 64
Abies lasiocarpa 58
Abies magnifica 62
Abies nordmanniana 64
Abies pinsapo 64
Abies procera 62
Abies × shastensis 62
Acacia, Bailey 243
    Berlandier 260
    Blackwood 246
    Catclaw 262
    Fernleaf 256
    Mescat 264
    Roemer 262
    Santa Rita 256
    Star 248
    Stickyleaf 266
    Sweet 266
    Viscid 266
    White-thorn 264
Acacia baileyana 243
Acacia cultriformis 244
Acacia dealbata 244
Acacia decurrens 244
Acacia elata 245
Acacia longifolia 246
Acacia mearnsii 246
Acacia melanoxylon 246
Acacia podalyriifolia 247
Acacia pycnantha 248
Acacia retinodes 248
Acacia saligna 248
Acacia smallii 266
Acacia verticillata 248
Acer campestre 500
Acer circinatum 501
Acer floridanum 502
Acer ginnala 502
Acer glabrum 502
Acer grandidentatum 504
Acer macrophyllum 504
Acer negundo 506
Acer nigrum 500
Acer platanoides 506

Acer rubrum 500
Acer saccharinum 508
Acer saccharum 506
Acer tataricum 508
Adenostoma fasciculatum 403
Adenostoma sparsifolium 403
Adoxaceae 130–133
Aesculus californica 508
Aesculus glabra 510
Aesculus hippocastanum 510
Aesculus pavia 510
Ahuehuete 50
Ailanthus altissima 516
Albizia, Plume 250
Albizia julibrissin 250
Albizia lebbeck 250
Albizia lophantha 250
Alder, Arizona 158
    California 160
    Italian 160
    Mexican 158
    Mountain 157–158, 162
    New Mexican 158
    Oregon 160
    Red 160
    Sitka 162
    Speckled 157, 158
    Western 160
    White 160
Aleurites fordii 226
Algondocillo 344
Aliso 158
Allthorn, Spiny 334
Almond 434
Alnus cordata 160
Alnus incana 157
Alnus incana subsp. rugosa 158
Alnus oblongifolia 158
Alnus rhombifolia 160
Alnus rubra 160
Alnus viridis subsp. sinuata 162
Althea, Shrubby 340
Amelanchier alnifolia 404
Amelanchier basalticola 405
Amelanchier cusickii 405
Amelanchier florida 405
Amelanchier pallida 406
Amelanchier pumila 405
Amelanchier sanguinea 405
Amelanchier utahensis 406

Amelasorbus 448
Amyris madrensis 456
Anacahuite 176
Anacardiaceae 134–148
Anacua 176
Angel's Trumpet 518
Angelica Tree, Japanese 152
Apocynaceae 148–149
Apple, Cactus 194
    Common 428
    Japanese Flowering Crab 427
    Oregon Crab 428
    Pacific Crab 428
    Paradise 428
    Western Crab 428
Apricot 432
    Desert 436
Aquifoliaceae 149–151
Araliaceae 152–153
Aralia elata 152
Araucaria araucana 28
Araucaria bidwillii 28
Araucaria columnaris 28
Araucaria heterophylla 28
Araucariaceae 28–29
Arborvitae, Giant 50
Arbutus, Mock 224
Arbutus arizonica 217
Arbutus menziesii 218
Arbutus unedo 218
Arbutus xalapensis 218
Arctostaphylos columbiana 220
Arctostaphylos glauca 220
Arctostaphylos manzanita 222
Arctostaphylos pringlei subsp. drupacea 222
Arctostaphylos pringlei subsp. pringlei 222
Arctostaphylos uva-ursi 220
Arctostaphylos viscida 222
Arecaceae 112–117
Artemisia tridentata 153
Ash, American 367
    Arizona 374
    Berlandier 368
    Black 374
    California Shrub 370
    Cascade Mountain 450
    Desert 374

Ash *continued*
European Mountain 448
Flowering 370
Foothill 370
Fragrant 370
Goodding's 370
Green 372
Greene Mountain 450
Gregg's 372
Leatherleaf 368
Littleleaf 370, 372
Maple 506
Mexican 368
Oakleaf Mountain 450
Oregon 374
Red 372
Shamel 372
Singleleaf 367–368
Sitka Mountain 450
Texas 366
Tropical 372
Two-petal 370
Velvet 374
Water 374
White 367
Asparagaceae 118–129
Aspen, Eurasian 472
Quaking 472
Trembling 472
Asteraceae 152–156
Athel Tree 526
Avocado 336
Azalea, California 226
Western 226

Baldcypress 50
Montezuma 50
Balm, Mountain 390
Balsam, Canada 58
Barreta 458
Basswood, American 344
Bauhinia lunarioides 232
Bauhinia variegata 232
Bayberry, California 353
Bay, California 338
Bayonetta 128
Bean, Castor 228
Jumbie 254
Jumping 228
Bearberry 220, 396
Bearbrush 322

Beargrass 120
Bigelow 120
Chaparral 120
Bee-brush 270
Betula kenaica 162
Betula neoalaskana 164
Betula occidentalis 164
Betula papyrifera 166
Betula pendula 166
Betula pubescens 168
Betulaceae 156–173
Big Tree 52
Bignoniaceae 172–175
Billardiera heterohpylla 379
Birch, Alaska 164
Alaska Paper 164
Alaska White 164
Black 164
Brown 164
Canoe 166
Downy 168
European White 166
Kenai 162
Kenai Paper 162
Paper 166
Red 162, 164
Resin 164
River 164
Silver 166
Water 164
Weeping 166
Western 164
White 166
Bird of Paradise 234
Bird-of-paradise 233
Bird-of-paradise, Mexican 234
Blackhaw, Rusty 132
Blackhead, Ebony 252
Bladdernut, Sierra 520
Bluebell, Australian 379
Blueblossom 388
Bluebrush 388
Bluewood 392
Boraginaceae 176–177
Botoncillo 455
Bottlebrush, Weeping 360
Boxelder 506
Box, Victorian 380
Brachychiton populneum 340
Brasil 232, 392

Brugmansia 518
Brunfelsia 518
Brushholly 498
Brush, Tobacco 390
Buckeye, California 508
False 510
Fetid 510
Mexican 510, 512
New Mexican 510
Ohio 510
Red 510
Scarlet 510
Texas 510
Buckthorn, Alder 393
Birchleaf 394
Carolina 394
Cascara 396
Common 398
Dahurian 398
European 398
False 514
Glossy 393
Pursh's 396
Woolly 514
Buddlejaceae 178–179
Buddleja saligna 178
Buffaloberry, Silver 214
Thorny 214
Bully, Gum 514
Bumelia, Woollybucket 514
Bunchberry 208
Burningbush 205
Western 205
Bursera fagaroides 180
Bursera microphylla 179
Burseraceae 178–180
Buttercup Bush 242
Butterflybush, Squarestem 178
Buttonball-tree 382
Buttonbush, Common 454
Mexican 455

Cabbage Tree, New Zealand 118
Cactaceae 180–198
Cactus, Desert Christmas 190
Giant 182
Organ Pipe 182
Tuna 196
Caesalpinia echinata 232
Caesalpinia gilliesii 233

Caesalpinia mexicana 234
Caesalpinia pulcherrima 234
Caesalpinia spinosa 234
Caesalpinioideae 231–242
Callistemon 360
Calocedrus decurrens 30
Camphortree 335
Cannabaceae 199–203
Cannabis sativa 199
Canotia 204
Canotia holacantha 204
Capul Negro 392
Caragana arborescens 268
Carnegiea gigantea 182
Carob 236
Carya illinoinensis 326
Carya myristiciformis 326
Cascara 396
Casimiroa 456
Castanea dentata 277
Castela emoryi 516
Catalpa, Northern 174
    Southern 172–174
Catalpa bignonioides 172
Catalpa speciosa 174
Catclaw, Roundflower 262
    Texas 264
    Wright 264
Catha edulis 204
Ceanothus, Feltleaf 387
    Greenbark 388
    Spiny 388
Ceanothus arboreus 387
Ceanothus leucodermis 388
Ceanothus spinosus 388
Ceanothus thyrsiflorus 388
Ceanothus velutinus 390
Cedar, Alaska Yellow 36
    California 30
    California White 40
    Deodar 65
    Desert 46
    Incense 30
    Mountain 40, 42
    Pencil 48
    Port Orford 31
Cedar of Lebanon 66
Cedro 40, 42
Cedro de Incienso 30
Cedro Liso 42
Cedro Rojo 48

Cedrus deodara 65
Cedrus libani 66
Celastraceae 204–207
Celtis australis 199
Celtis ehrenbergiana 200
Celtis laevigata 200
Celtis lindheimeri 202
Celtis occidentalis 202
Celtis pallida 200
Celtis reticulata 202
Celtis sinensis 200
Cephalanthus occidentalis 454
Cephalanthus salicifolius 455
Ceratonia siliqua 236
Cercis canadensis 236
Cercis orbiculata 236
Cercocarpus betuloides 408
Cercocarpus breviflorus 408
Cercocarpus intricatus 406
Cercocarpus ledifolius 408
Cercocarpus montanus 408
Cercocarpus traskiae 408
Cestrum 518
Chamaecyparis lawsoniana 31
Chamise 403
Chastetree, Chinese 536
    Common 536
    Lilac 536
Cheesewood, Japanese 380
    Stiffleaf 379
Cherry, Bitter 434–436
    Black 442
    European Bird 440
    Evergreen 436
    Fire 434, 440
    Hollyleaf 436
    Japanese Flowering 443
    Mahaleb 438
    Oregon 434
    Pie 434
    Pin 440
    Quinine 434
    Scrub 362
    Sour 434
    Southwestern Black 442
    Sweet 432
    Western Pin 434
    Wild 434
    Yoshino 446
Cherry-laurel, Common 436
    Portugal 438

Chestnut, American 277
    Golden 276
    Goldenleaf 276
    Horse 510
Chilopsis linearis 174
China Tree, Wild 512
Chinaberry-tree 346
Chinquapin, Giant 276
    Giant Golden 276
    Golden 276
Chitalpa 175
× *Chitalpa tashkentensis* 175
Chittambark 396
Chittam-wood 134
Chittamwood 514
Chokecherry 444
    Eastern 445
    Western 445
Cholla, Buckhorn 184
    Cane 192
    Chain-fruit 188
    Coastal 190
    Diamond 192
    Golden 186
    Jumping 188
    Munz 190
    Peach Springs Canyon 184
    Pencil 184
    Silver 186
    Staghorn 192
    Teddybear 186
    Tree 188
Christmas Berry 424
Chrysolepis chrysophylla var.
    chrysophylla 276
Chrysolepis chrysophylla var.
    minor 277
Cinchona 454
Cinnamomum camphora 335
Ciprés de Arizona 32
Ciprés Negro 34
Citharexylum berlandieri 534
Citrus × aurantium 456
Citrus maxima 457
Citrus reticulata 457
Cliffrose, Stansbury 446
Coffea 454
Coffeeberry, California 394
Coma 514
Comarostaphylis diversifolia 224
Condalia, Bitter 390

Condalia globosa 390
Condalia hookeri 392
conifers 26–111
Copal Tree 516
Coralbean 268
Cordia, White 176
Cordia boissieri 176
Cordyline australis 118
Cornaceae 206–210
Cornel, Blackfruit 210
  White 207
Cornus canadensis 208
Cornus drummondii 207
Cornus glabrata 208
Cornus nuttallii 208
Cornus sericea 209
Cornus sessilis 210
Corona de Cristo 334
Coronilla 498
Corylus avellana 168
Corylus cornuta 168
Cotinus coggygria 134
Cotinus obovatus 134
Cotton, Arizona Wild 344
  Desert 344
  Thurber's 344
Cottonwood, Balm 472
  Balsam 472
  Black 472
  Eastern 466
  Fremont 470
  Lanceleaf 466
  Mountain 466
  Narrowleaf 466
  Plains 468
  Rio Grande 468
Cowania 446
Coyotillo 396
Crataegus castlegarensis 412
Crataegus chrysocarpa 416
Crataegus crus-galli 420
Crataegus douglasii 412
Crataegus enderbyensis 412
Crataegus erythropoda 416
Crataegus greggiana 422
Crataegus laevigata 411
Crataegus mollis 410
Crataegus monogyna 410
Crataegus okennonii 414
Crataegus phaenopyrum 410
Crataegus phippsii 412

Crataegus reverchonii 420
Crataegus rivularis 418
Crataegus saligna 418
Crataegus sheila-phippsiae 416
Crataegus succulenta 414
Crataegus suksdorfii 414
Crataegus tracyi 420
Crataegus turnerorum 422
Crataegus viridis 418
Crataegus wootoniana 422
Creosotebush 538
Crown-of-thorns 386
Cupressaceae 30–54
Cupressus arizonica 32
Cupressus bakeri 32
Cupressus forbesii 34
Cupressus glabra 32
Cupressus goveniana 34
Cupressus goveniana var.
  abramsiana 34
Cupressus × *leylandii* 36
Cupressus macnabiana 36
Cupressus macrocarpa 34
Cupressus nevadensis 38
Cupressus nootkatensis 36
Cupressus sargentii 38
Cupressus sempervirens 32
Cupressus stephensonii 38
Cycas revoluta 26
Cydonia oblonga 424
Cylindropuntia abyssi 184
Cylindropuntia acanthocarpa
  184
Cylindropuntia arbuscula 184
Cylindropuntia bigelovii 186
Cylindropuntia echinocarpa 186
Cylindropuntia fulgida 188
Cylindropuntia imbricata 188
Cylindropuntia leptocaulis 190
Cylindropuntia munzii 190
Cylindropuntia prolifera 190
Cylindropuntia ramosissima 192
Cylindropuntia spinosior 192
Cylindropuntia versicolor 192
Cypress, Arizona 32
  Baker 32
  Cuyamaca 38
  Forbes 34
  Gowen 34
  Lawson 31
  Leyland 36

  MacNab 36
  Mediterranean 32
  Modoc 32
  Monterey 34
  Nootka 36
  Paiute 38
  Piute 38
  Roughbark 32
  Santa Cruz 34
  Sargent 38
  Shasta 36
  Smooth 32
  Tecate 34

Dagger, Spanish 124, 128
Dasylirion wheeleri 119
Dendromecon harfordii 378
Dendromecon rigida 378
Dermatophyllum secundiflorum
  268
Dewdrops, Golden 535
dicots 130–539
Diospyros texana 211
Diospyros virginiana 212
Dodonaea viscosa 500
Dogwood, American 209
  Blackfruit 210
  Brown 208
  Cornel 207
  Creek 209
  Mountain 208
  Pacific 208
  Red-osier 209
  Roughleaf 207
  Small Flower 207
  Smooth 208
  Western 208
  Western Flowering 208
Don Quixote's Lace 128
Dot-and-Dash Plant 396
Douglas-fir 106
  Bigcone 106
Douglasia Verde 106
Dracaena, Giant 118
Duranta erecta 535

Ébano 252
Ebenaceae 210–213
Ebenopsis ebano 252
Ebony, Mountain 232
  Texas 252

Ehretia anacua 176
Elaeagnaceae 212–215
Elaeagnus angustifolia 213
Elaeagnus umbellata 214
Elbow Bush 364
    Texas 364
Elderberry, Blue 130
    Red 132
Elephant Tree 179
    Fragrant 180
Elm, American 528
    Cedar 530
    Chinese 530
    Drake 530
    English 530
    English Cork 530
    Red 532
    Siberian 532
    Slippery 532
Enebro de Monte 40
Ephedra 26
Épinette Blanche 72
Épinette Noire 72
Ericaceae 216–227
Ericameria parishii 154
Eriobotrya japonica 424
Esenbeckia berlandieri 458
Eucalyptus camaldulensis 355
Eucalyptus citriodora 356
Eucalyptus cladocalyx 356
Eucalyptus conferruminata 356
Eucalyptus globulus 356
Eucalyptus polyanthemos 358
Eucalyptus pulchella 360
Eucalyptus sideroxylon 358
Eucalyptus tereticornis 358
Eucalyptus viminalis 358
Euonymus alatus 205
Euphorbiaceae 226–229
Eve's Needle 124
Eysenhardtia orthocarpa 270
Eysenhardtia texana 270

Fabaceae 230–275
Fagaceae 276–319
Fallugia paradoxa 446
False-Buckthorn, Birchleaf 394
Feathertree 256
Fiddlewood, Berlandier 534
    Tamaulipan 534

Fig, Common 346
    Edible 346–348
    Indian 196
Filbert, European 168
Fir, Amabilis 56
    Balsam 58
    Bristlecone 56
    California White 60
    Caucasian 64
    Desert 106
    Grand 60
    Korean 64
    Noble 62
    Pacific Silver 56
    Red 62
    Rocky Mountain 58
    Santa Lucia 56
    Shasta Red 62
    Silvertip 62
    Spanish 64
    Subalpine 58
    White 60
Firmiana simplex 340
firs, ornamental 64
Flamegold 512
Flannelbush, California 342
    Mexican 343
Forestiera angustifolia 364
Forestiera phillyreoides 364
Forestiera pubescens 364
Forestiera reticulata 364
Fortunella 456
Frangula, Beechleaf 394
Frangula alnus 393
Frangula betulifolia 394
Frangula californica 394
Frangula caroliniana 394
Frangula purshiana 396
Fraxinus albicans 366
Fraxinus americana 367
Fraxinus anomala 367
Fraxinus berlandieriana 368
Fraxinus coriacea 368
Fraxinus cuspidata 370
Fraxinus dipetala 370
Fraxinus gooddingii 370
Fraxinus greggii 372
Fraxinus latifolia 374
Fraxinus pennsylvanica 372
Fraxinus uhdei 372

Fraxinus velutina 374
Fremontia, California 342
    Mexican 343
    Southern 343
Fremontia 342
Fremontodendron californicum 342
Fremontodendron mexicanum 343
Frijolito 268

Gardenia 454
Garrya congdonii 320
Garrya elliptica 320
Garrya flavescens 322
Garrya fremontii 322
Garrya ovata 322
Garrya veatchii 323
Garrya wrightii 324
Garryaceae 320–324
Geiger, White 176
Genévrier des Montagnes Rocheuses 48
Ginkgo 27
Ginkgo biloba 27
Ginkgoaceae 27
Gleditsia triacanthos 238
Globe-flowers 454
Goldenbush, Parish's 154
Golden Chain Tree 270
Golden Rain Tree 270
Goldenrain Tree 512
Gossypium thurberi 344
Granjeno 200
Graythorn 400
Greasewood 403
Grevillea robusta 385
Guaiacum angustifolium 538
Guajillo 260
Guayacán 538
Gum, Blue 356
    Forest Red 358
    Lemon-scented 356
    Manna 358
    Ribbon 358
    River Red 355
    Silver Dollar 358
    Spider 356
    Sugar 356
    Tasmanian Blue 356
gymnosperms 26–111

Hackberry 200
  Chinese 200
  Common 202
  Desert 200
  Japanese 200
  Lindheimer 202
  Netleaf 202
  Spiny 200
Hackmatack 468
Hamamelidaceae 324–325
Hamamelis virginiana 324
Havardia pallens 252
Haw, Purple 392
Hawthorn, Black 412
  Castlegar 412
  Cerro 416
  Cockspur 420
  Enderby 412
  Fireberry 416
  Fleshy 414
  Green 418
  Gregg 422
  Mountain River 418
  O'Kennon 414
  Oneseed 410
  Phipps 412
  Reverchon 420
  Sheila Phipps 416
  Smooth 411
  Suksdorf 414
  Tracy 420
  Turners 422
  Willow 418
  Woodland 411
  Wooton 422
Hazel, European 168
Hazelnut 168
  Beaked 168
Headache Tree 338
Helietta parvifolia 458
Hemlock, Mountain 108
  Western 108
Hemptree 536
Hercules' Club 460
  Texas 462
Heteromeles arbutifolia 424
Hibiscus syriacus 340
Hickory, Bitter Water 326
  Nutmeg 326
  Swamp 326
Hippophae rhamnoides 214

Holdback, Spiny 234
Holly, American 149, 150
  Box-leaf 150
  California 424
  Deciduous 150
  English 150
  Japanese 150
  Possumhaw 150
  Summer 224
Hollyberry 424
Honey-balls 454
Hopbush, Florida 500
Hophornbeam, Big Bend 170
  Chisos 170
  Eastern 172
  Knowlton 170
  Western 170
  Woolly 170
Hoptree, California 458
  Common 460
  Western 458
Horsebean 238
Huata 40
Huisache 266
  Texas 266

Ilex aquifolium 150
Ilex crenata 150
Ilex decidua 150
Ilex opaca 149, 150
Ilex paraguariensis 149
Ilex vomitoria 150
Ironbark, Red 358
Ironwood 172, 272, 514
  Catalina 426
  Catalina Island 426
  Desert 272
Islay 436
Ivy, Poison 460

Jaboncillo 512
Jessamine, Night-blooming 518
Jopoy, Berlandier 458
Joshua Tree 122
Juglandaceae 325–333
Juglans californica 328
Juglans hindsii 328
Juglans major 330
Juglans microcarpa 330
Juglans nigra 332
Juglans regia 332

Jujube, Common 400
  Indian 400
Juniper, Alligator 42
  Arizona 44
  Ashe 40
  California 40
  Cherrystone 42
  Common 40
  Creeping 40
  Drooping 42
  Oneseed 42
  Pinchot 46
  Pinchot's 46
  Redberry 44, 46
  Rocky Mountain 48
  Roseberry 44
  Seaside 48
  Sierra 44
  Southern 48
  Utah 46
  Western 44
Juniperus arizonica 44
Juniperus ashei 40
Juniperus californica 40
Juniperus coahuilensis 44
Juniperus communis 40
Juniperus deppeana 42
Juniperus flaccida 42
Juniperus horizontalis 40
Juniperus maritima 48
Juniperus monosperma 42
Juniperus occidentalis 44
Juniperus osteosperma 46
Juniperus pinchotii 46
Juniperus scopulorum 48
Juniperus virginiana 48

Karee 148
Karo 379
Karwinskia humboldtiana 396
Khat 204
Kidneywood, Arizona 270
  Texas 270
Kinnikinnik 220
Knockaway 176
Koeberliniaceae 334
Koeberlinia spinosa 334
Koelreuteria elegans subsp.
  formosana 512
Koelreuteria paniculata 512
Kohuhu 380

Kurrajong, Whiteflower 340

Laburnum, Common 270
Laburnum anagyroides 270
Lady-of-the-Night 518
Lantana 534
Larch, Alpine 68
  American 66
  European 66
  Subalpine 68
  Western 68
Larix decidua 66
Larix laricina 66
Larix lyallii 68
Larix occidentalis 68
Larrea tridentata 538
Lauraceae 335–339
Laurel, Bay 338
  California 338
  Mountain 144
  Texas Mountain 268
Laurus nobilis 338
Leadtree, Goldenball 254
  Great 254
  Littleleaf 254
  Mexican 254
  White 254
Lemonade-berry 140
Lemonade-bush 140
Lemonball 254
Lentisco 136, 138, 144
Lepidospartum squamatum 154
Leptospermum laevigatum 360
Leptosyne gigantea 154
Leucaena leucocephala 254
Leucaena pulverulenta 254
Leucaena retusa 254
Lignum-Vitae, Texas 538
Ligustrum, Wax-leaf 376
Ligustrum japonicum 376
Ligustrum lucidum 376
Ligustrum ovalifolium 376
Lime, Wild 462
Limoncillo 458
Lindera benzoin 336
Lobatae 280
Locust 275
  Black 275
  Honey 238
  New Mexico 274
  Yellow 275

Lodgepole, Rocky Mountain 100
  Sierra 100
Loquat 424
Lotebush 400
Luma apiculata 360
Lyonothamnus floribundus 426
Lyontree 426
Lysiloma watsonii 256

Maclura pomifera 348
Madrone, Arizona 217
  Pacific 218
  Texas 218
Mahogany, Alderleaf
    Mountain 408
  Birchleaf Mountain 408
  Catalina Island Mountain
    408
  Curlleaf Mountain 408
  Hairy Mountain 408
  Littleleaf Mountain 406
Maidenhair Tree 27
Malosma laurina 136
Malus floribunda 427
Malus fusca 428
Malus pumila 428
Malvaceae 340–345
Manzanita 176
  Bigberry 220
  Common 222
  Hairy 220
  Parry 222
  Pink-bracted 222
  Pringle 222
  Sticky Whiteleaf 222
  Summer-blooming 224
  Whiteleaf 222
Maple, Amur 502
  Bigleaf 504
  Bigtooth 504
  Black 500
  Boxelder 506
  Broadleaf 504
  Dwarf 502
  Field 500
  Hedge 500
  Mountain 501
  Norway 506
  Oregon 504
  Oregon Vine 501
  Red 500

Rocky Mountain 502
  Silver 508
  Southern Sugar 502
  Sugar 506
  Tatarian 508
  Vine 501
  Western Mountain 502
  Western Sugar 504
Marijuana 199
Mariosousa millefolia 256
Mastic Tree, Mount Atlas 136
Mayten 206
Maytenus boaria 206
Mazzard 432
Melaleuca viminalis 360
Mélèze Laricin 66
Melia azedarach 346
Meliaceae 346–347
Mesa Sacahuista 120
Mescalbean 268
Mesquite 258
  Honey 258
  Screwbean 258
  Smooth 258
  Torrey 258
  Velvet 260
Mimbre 174
Mimosa 250
  Catclaw 262
Mimosa aculeaticarpa 262
Mimosa Bush 252
Mimosoideae 242–267
Monilla 510
Monkey-puzzle Tree 28
monocots 112–129
Moraceae 346–351
Mormon-tea 26
Morus alba 348
Morus microphylla 350
Morus nigra 349
Morus rubra 350
Mousehole Tree 352
Mulberry, Black 349
  Dwarf 350
  Littleleaf 350
  Mexican 350
  Mountain 350
  Red 350
  Texas 350
  White 348
Myoporaceae 352

Myoporum laetum 352
Myrica californica 353
Myricaceae 353
Myrtaceae 354–363
Myrtle, Oregon 338

Nannyberry 132
Negrito 534
Nerium oleander 149
Nettle-tree 199
Nicotiana glauca 518
Nicotiana tabacum 518
Nightshade, Mullein 518
Nogal 330
Nogal Silvestre 330
Nogalito 330
Nolina, Bigelow 120
  Chaparral 120
  Giant 122
  Parry 122
Nolina bigelovii 120
Nolina cismontana 120
Nolina erumpens 120
Nolina parryi 122
Notholithocarpus densiflorus
  278
Nutmeg, California 110

Oak, Ajo Mountain Scrub 296
  Arizona 302
  Arizona Live 302
  Arizona White 302, 304
  Bastard 310
  Bigelow 310
  Black 282
  Blackjack 284
  Bluff 312
  Buckley 282
  Bur 278, 318
  California Black 280
  California Blue 312
  California Live 288
  California Scrub 296
  California Tanbark 278
  California White 314
  Canyon Live 290
  Cedros Island 292
  Channel Island 292
  Channel Island Scrub 296
  Chestnut 278
  Chihuahua 302

Chinquapin 308
Chisos 286
Chisos Red 282
Coast Live 288
Cork 304
Deer 308
Douglas 312
Dunn 290
Durand 310
Durand White 310
Emory 282, 284
Engelmann 310
English 316
Felt 302
Gambel 316
Goldcup 290
Graves 282
Gray 298
Havard 300
Holly 296
Holm 296
Interior Live 288
Iron 312, 318
Kellogg 280
Lacey 312
Lateleaf 286
Live 282, 288, 290
Madrean Willow 286
Maul 290
Mexican 306
Mexican Blue 308
Mexican White 306
Mohr 300
Mossy-cup 318
Netleaf 306
Oregon 314
Palmer 290
Peach 278
Pedunculate 316
Post 314, 318
Robust 284
Rocky Mountain White 316
Sadler 308
Sandpaper 302
Sand Post 318
Scrub 292
Scrub Live 294
Shin 300
Shortlobe 310
Shreve 289
Shrub Live 292

Shumard 281
Sierra Live 288
Silverleaf 286
Sonoran 286
Sonoran Blue 308
Sonoran Scrub 292
Southern Live 294
Southern Red 282
Sovereign 278
Tanbark 278
Texas Blue 312
Texas Live 294
Toumey 298
Turkish 316
Utah White 316
Valley 314
Vasey 300
Water 284
Wavyleaf 298, 302
Weeping 314
Western Poison 459, 460
West Texas Live 294
White 308
Whiteleaf 286
oaks, black 280
  intermediate 290
  red 280
  white 292
Ocote Chino 96
Olea europaea 362
Oleaceae 362–377
Oleander, Common 149
Oleaster 213
Olive 362
  Autumn 214
  Desert 364
  False 178
  Mexican 176
  Russian 213
  Texas 176
  Texas Wild 176
Olneya tesota 272
Opuntia aureispina 194
Opuntia chlorotica 196
Opuntia engelmannii 194
Opuntia engelmannii var.
  linguiformis 195
Opuntia ficus-indica 196
Opuntia oricola 196
Opuntia rufida 198
Opuntia santa-rita 198

Orange, Osage 348
  Seville 456
  Sour 456
Orchid-tree, Anacacho 232
  Purple 232
Ostrya chisosensis 170
Ostrya knowltonii 170
Ostrya virginiana 172

Paliurus spina-christi 386
Palma Pita 128
Palm, California Fan 116
  Canary Island Date 113
  Cocos 114
  Date 114
  Desert 116
  Mexican Fan 116
  Queen 114
  Sago 26
  Torbay 118
  Washington Fan 116
Palmella 124
Palmetto, Mexican 114
  Rio Grande 114
Palo Fiero 272
Palo Verde, Blue 240
  Foothill 240
  Littleleaf 240
  Mexican 238
  Texas 240
  Yellow 240
Papaveraceae 378
Papilionoideae 268–275
Paraserianthes lophantha 250
Parasoltree, Chinese 340
Parkinsonia aculeata 238
Parkinsonia florida 240
Parkinsonia microphylla 240
Parkinsonia texana 240
Pea Tree, Siberian 268
Peach 440
Pear, Bradford 446
  Callery 446
  Common 448
Pecan 326
Pepper, False 146
Peppermint, White 360
Peppertree 146
  Brazilian 146
  Chilean 146
  Hardee 146

Longleaf 146
Peruvian 146
Pepperwood 338
Persea americana 336
Persea borbonia 336
Persimmon, Black 211
  Common 212
  Mexican 211
  Texas 211
Peucephyllum schottii 156
Phoenix canariensis 113
Phoenix dactylifera 114
Picea abies 76
Picea × *albertiana* 72
Picea breweriana 70
Picea engelmannii 70
Picea glauca 72
Picea mariana 72
Picea omorika 76
Picea orientalis 76
Picea pungens 74
Picea sitchensis 74
Pin Gris 102
Pinaceae 55–109
Pine, Apache 92
  Arizona 92
  Austrian 104
  Bishop 98
  Blackjack 102
  Bull 94
  Bunya 28
  Canary Island 105
  Chihuahua 96
  Cook 28
  Coulter 94
  Del Mar 96
  Digger 96
  Foothills 96
  Foxtail 80
  Gray 96
  Great Basin Bristlecone
    78
  Idaho 84
  Jack 102
  Japanese Red 104
  Jeffrey 94
  Knobcone 98
  Limber 82
  Lodgepole 100
  Mexican White 84
  Monterey 100

Mugo 105
Norfolk Island 28
Ponderosa 90
Radiata 100
Rocky Mountain Bristlecone
  78
Scotch 102
Scots 102
Shore 100
Soledad 96
Southwestern White 84
Stone 104
Sugar 82
Torrey 96, 98
Umbrella 30
Washoe 91
Western White 84
Whitebark 80
Yellow 90
pines, ornamental 104
Pino Apache 92
Pino Cuatro Hojas 90
Pino de Arizona 92
Pino de Azucar 82
Pino de Coulter 94
Pino de Eldorado 98
Pino de Jeffrey 94
Pino Monoaguja 88
Pino Obispo 98
Pino Real 96
Piñon 86
  Border 88
  Colorado 86
  Four-needle 90
  Mexican 88
  Paper-shell 86
  Parry 90
  Singleleaf 88
  Texas 86
  Twoneedle 86
Piñonero 88
Pinus albicaulis 80
Pinus aristata 78
Pinus arizonica 92
Pinus attenuata 98
Pinus balfouriana 80
Pinus banksiana 102
Pinus canariensis 105
Pinus cembroides 88
Pinus contorta 100
Pinus coulteri 94

Pinus densiflora 104
Pinus discolor 88
Pinus edulis 86
Pinus engelmannii 92
Pinus flexilis 82
Pinus jeffreyi 94
Pinus lambertiana 82
Pinus leiophylla var.
   chihuahuana 96
Pinus longaeva 78
Pinus monophylla 88
Pinus monticola 84
Pinus mugo 105
Pinus muricata 98
Pinus nigra 104
Pinus pinea 104
Pinus ponderosa 90
Pinus quadrifolia 90
Pinus radiata 100
Pinus reflexa 84
Pinus remota 86
Pinus sabiniana 96
Pinus strobiformis 84
Pinus sylvestris 102
Pinus torreyana 96
Pinus washoensis 91
Pirul 146
Pistache, Chinese 138
   Mount Atlas 136
   Texas 138
Pistachio, American 138
   Common 136, 137
   Mexican 138
   Wild 138
Pistacia atlantica 136
Pistacia chinensis 138
Pistacia mexicana 138
Pistacia vera 136, 137
Pittosporaceae 379–380
Pittosporum, Karo 379
Pittosporum crassifolium 379
Pittosporum tenuifolium 380
Pittosporum tobira 380
Pittosporum undulatum 380
Planetree, Arizona 384
   California 382
   Eurasian 383
   London 381
   Oriental 383
Platanaceae 381–384
Platanus hybrida 381

Platanus kerrii 381
Platanus occidentalis 382
Platanus orientalis 383
Platanus racemosa 382
Platanus wrightii 384
Plum, American 430
   Bigtree 438
   Cherry 432
   Chickasaw 430
   Common 434
   Creek 442
   European 434
   Hog 442
   Japanese 424, 434
   Klamath 444
   Mexican 438
   Myrobalan 432
   Pacific 444
   Saffron 514
   Sand 430
   Sandhill 430
   Satsuma 434
   Sierra 444
   Western 444
   Wild 430
   Wild Goose 442
Plume, Apache 446
   Texas 232
Poinciana, Dwarf 234
Poison Plant, Arrow 228
Pomegranate 386
Pomelo 457
Popcorn Tree 228
Poplar, Balsam 468
   Black 470
   European White 465
   Jack Hybrid 468
   Lombardy 470
   White 465
Poppy, Bush 378
Populus × acuminata 466
Populus alba 465
Populus angustifolia 466
Populus balsamifera 468
Populus deltoides 466
Populus deltoides subsp.
   monilifera 468
Populus deltoides subsp. wislizeni
   468
Populus fremontii 470
Populus × jackii 468

Populus nigra var. italica 470
Populus tremula 472
Populus tremuloides 472
Populus trichocarpa 472
Porlieria, Texas 538
Potatotree 518
Powderpuff-tree 250
Prickly-ash, Southern 460
Pricklyash, Lime 462
Prickly Moses 248
Pricklypear, Blind 198
   Chaparral 196
   Cow's-tongue 195
   Engelmann 194
   Indian-fig 196
   Mission 196
   Pancake 196
   Purple 198
   Rio Grande 194
Pride-of-Barbados 234
Pride-of-India 346
Privet, Chinese 376
   Glossy 376
   Japanese 376
   Oval-leaf 376
   Tree 376
Prosopis glandulosa 258
Prosopis laevigata 258
Prosopis pubescens 258
Prosopis velutina 260
Proteaceae 385
Protobalanus 290
Prunus americana 430
Prunus angustifolia 430
Prunus armeniaca 432
Prunus avium 432
Prunus cerasifera 432
Prunus cerasus 434
Prunus domestica 434
Prunus dulcis 434
Prunus emarginata 434
Prunus fremontii 436
Prunus ilicifolia 436
Prunus laurocerasus 436
Prunus lusitanica 438
Prunus mahaleb 438
Prunus mexicana 438
Prunus munsoniana 442
Prunus padus 440
Prunus pensylvanica 440
Prunus persica 440

Prunus rivularis 442
Prunus salicina 434
Prunus serotina 442
Prunus speciosa 443
Prunus subcordata 444
Prunus virginiana 444
Prunus yedoensis 446
Pseudotsuga macrocarpa 106
Pseudotsuga menziesii 106
Psorothamnus spinosus 272
Psychotria 454
Ptelea crenulata 458
Ptelea trifoliata 460
Pterocarya stenoptera 332
Punicaceae 386–387
Punica granatum 386
Purshia stansburiana 446
Pygmy-cedar 156
Pyrus communis 448
Pyrus calleryana 446

Quercus 292
Quercus agrifolia 288
Quercus ajoensis 296
Quercus arizonica 302
Quercus austrina 312
Quercus berberidifolia 296
Quercus buckleyi 282
Quercus carmenensis 306
Quercus cedrosensis 292
Quercus cerris 316
Quercus chihuahuensis 302
Quercus chrysolepis 290
Quercus douglasii 312
Quercus durandii var. *breviloba* 310
Quercus durandii var. *durandii* 310
Quercus emoryi 282
Quercus engelmannii 310
Quercus falcata 282
Quercus fusiformis 294
Quercus gambelii 316
Quercus garryana var. *garryana* 314
Quercus graciliformis 286
Quercus gravesii 282
Quercus grisea 298
Quercus havardii 300
Quercus hypoleucoides 286
Quercus hypoxantha 286

Quercus ilex 296
Quercus kelloggii 280
Quercus laceyi 312
Quercus lobata 314
Quercus macrocarpa 318
Quercus margarettae 318
Quercus marilandica 284
Quercus mohriana 300
Quercus muehlenbergii 308
Quercus nigra 284
Quercus oblongifolia 308
Quercus oleoides 294
Quercus pacifica 296
Quercus palmeri 290
Quercus parvula 289
Quercus polymorpha 306
Quercus pungens 302
Quercus robur 316
Quercus × *robusta* 284
Quercus rugosa 306
Quercus sadleriana 308
Quercus shumardii 281
Quercus sinuata 310
Quercus stellata 318
Quercus suber 304
Quercus tardifolia 286
Quercus × *tharpii* 284
Quercus tomentella 292
Quercus toumeyi 298
Quercus turbinella 292
Quercus × *undulata* 298, 302
Quercus vaseyana 300
Quercus viminea 286
Quercus virginiana 294
Quercus virginiana var. *fusiformis* 294
Quercus wislizeni 288
Quince 424
Quinine Bush 320
Quinine-bush 446

Rabbitbrush, Parish's 154
Redbay 336
Redberry, Hollyleaf 436
Island 398
Redbud, Eastern 236
Western 236
Redcedar, Eastern 48
Western 50
Redheart 388
Redshank 403

Redwood, Coast 52
Sierra 52
Retama 238
Rhamnaceae 386–401
Rhamnus cathartica 398
Rhamnus davurica 398
Rhamnus ilicifolia 436
Rhamnus pirifolia 398
Rhododendron, California 224
Coast 224
Pacific 224
Rhododendron macrophyllum 224
Rhododendron occidentale 226
Rhus copallinum 143
Rhus glabra 140
Rhus integrifolia 140
Rhus kearneyi 142
Rhus lanceolata 142
Rhus microphylla 142
Rhus ovata 144
Rhus virens 144
Ricinus communis 228
Robinia neomexicana 274
Robinia pseudoacacia 275
Rosaceae 402–453
Rose-of-Sharon 340
Rosewood, Arizona 452
Slimleaf 452
Rubia 454
Rubiaceae 454–455
Rutaceae 456–463

Sabal mexicana 114
Sabina 42
Sage, Big 153
Sagebrush 153
Common 153
Saguaro 182
Salicaceae 464–499
Salix alaxensis var. *alaxensis* 496
Salix alba 488
Salix amygdaloides 486
Salix arbusculoides 492
Salix babylonica 488
Salix bebbiana 498
Salix bonplandiana 478
Salix caroliniana 482
Salix columbiana 476
Salix discolor 494

Salix euxina 488
Salix exigua 474
Salix geyeriana 490
Salix gooddingii 480
Salix hookeriana 498
Salix interior 476
Salix laevigata 486
Salix lasiandra var. *caudata* 482
Salix lasiandra var. *lasiandra* 482
Salix lasiolepis 484
Salix lucida 483
Salix matsudana 474
Salix melanopsis 478
Salix nigra 480
Salix pellita 490
Salix × *pendulina* 488
Salix petiolaris 490
Salix piperi 498
Salix prolixa 494
Salix purpurea 492
Salix pyrifolia 494
Salix scouleriana 496
Salix × *sepulcralis* 488
Salix sessilifolia 478
Salix sitchensis 492
Salix taxifolia 476
Salix tracyi 484
Saltcedar 526
Sambucus nigra subsp. *caerulea* 130
Sambucus racemosa 132
Sandpaper Tree 176
Sapin Baumier 58
Sapindaceae 500–513
Sapindus drummondii 512
Sapium sebiferum 228
Sapotaceae 514–515
Scalebroom 154
Schinus longifolius 146
Schinus molle 146
Schinus polygamus 146
Schinus terebinthifolius 146
Sciadopitys verticillata 30
Screwbean 258
Seaberry 214
Sea-buckthorn 214
Searsia lancea 148
Sebastiania bilocularis 228
Senegalia berlandieri 260

Senegalia greggii 262
Senegalia roemeriana 262
Senegalia wrightii 264
Senna, Argentine 242
    Downy 242
    Glandular 242
Senna corymbosa 242
Sequoia, Giant 52–54
Sequoia sempervirens 52
Sequoiadendron giganteum 52
Serviceberry, Pale 406
    Saskatoon 404
    Utah 406
    Western 404
Shadbush, Basalt-loving 405
    Cusick's 405
    Dwarf 405
    Many-flowered 405
    Red-twigged 405
Shaddock 457
Sheepberry 132
Shepherdia argentea 214
Sideroxylon celastrinum 514
Sideroxylon lanuginosum 514
Silkoak 385
Silktassel, Ashy 322
    Canyon 323
    Chaparral 320
    Coast 320
    Eggleaf 322
    Fremont 322
    Mexican 322
    Pale 322
    Veatch 323
    Wavyleaf 320
    Wright's 324
Silktree 250
Silkwood, West Indian 460
Silverberry, Japanese 214
Simaroubaceae 516–517
Skunk-bush 460
Smokethorn 272
Smoketree 272
    American 134
    European 134
Snakewood, Bitter 390
Snowbell, Sycamoreleaf 521
Snowbrush 390
Snowdrop Bush 521
Soapberry, Western 512
Soapbush 538

Solanaceae 518–519
Solanum erianthum 518
Sophora secundiflora 269
Sorbaronia 448
Sorbus aria 448
Sorbus aucuparia 448
Sorbus hybrida 450
Sorbus scopulina 450
Sorbus sitchensis 450
Sotol, Common 119
Spicebush, Northern 336
Spire, Red 446
Spoon, Desert 119
Spruce, Alberta 72
    Bigcone 106
    Black 72
    Blue 74
    Bog 72
    Brewer 70
    Coastal 74
    Colorado Blue 74
    Douglas 106
    Engelmann 70
    Norway 76
    Oriental 76
    Serbian 76
    Sitka 74
    Skunk 72
    Weeping 70
    White 72
spruces, ornamental 76
Staphylea bolanderi 520
Staphyleaceae 520
Stenocereus thurberi 182
Stinkbean 250
Stinking-ash 460
St. John's Bread 236
Strawberry Tree 218
Styracaceae 521
Styrax platanifolius 521
Styrax redivivus 521
Sugar Bush 144
Sugarberry 176, 200
    Southern 200
Sumac, African 148
    Chaparral 144
    Chinese 516
    Evergreen 144
    Kearney 142
    Laurel 136
    Lemonade 140

Littleleaf 142
Mahogany 140
Prairie 142
Prairie Flameleaf 142
Smooth 140
Sugar 144
Texas 142
Tobacco 144
Winged 143
Swampprivet, Netleaf 364
Texas 364
Syagrus romanzoffiana 114
Sycamore, American 382
Arizona 384
California 382
Western 382
Syringa reticulata 362
Syzygium australe 362

Tallow Tree, Chinese 228
Tamarack 66
Western 68
Tamaricaceae 522–527
Tamarind, Littleleaf False 256
Tamarisk, African 524
Canary Island 524
Five-stamen 524–526
French 523
Russian 526
Smallflower 523
Tamarix africana 524
Tamarix aphylla 526
Tamarix aralensis 526
Tamarix canariensis 524
Tamarix chinensis 524
Tamarix gallica 523
Tamarix parviflora 523
Tamarix ramosissima 526
Tangerine 457
Tara 234
Táscate 42, 44
Taxaceae 110–111
Taxodium distichum var.
distichum 50
Taxodium distichum var.
mucronatum 50
Taxus brevifolia 110
Tea Tree, Australian 360
Tectona 534
Temu 360
Tenaza 252

Thorn, Crucifixion 204, 334,
516
Jerusalem 238
White 264
Thuja plicata 50
Tickle-tongue 460
Tickseed, Giant 154
Tilia americana 344
Tobacco, Tree 518
Torchwood, Mountain 456
Tornillo 258
Torrey Vauquelinia 452
Torreya, California 110
Torreya californica 110
Toxicodendron diversilobum 459,
460
Toxicodendron radicans 460
Toyon 424
Tree-of-heaven 516
Tree Lilac, Japanese 362
Tree Poppy, Channel Island 378
Triadica sebifera 228
Tsuga heterophylla 108
Tsuga mertensiana 108
Tungoil Tree 226

Ulmaceae 528–533
Ulmus americana 528
Ulmus crassifolia 530
Ulmus parvifolia 530
Ulmus procera 530
Ulmus pumila 532
Ulmus rubra 532
Umbellularia californica 338
Uña de Gato 264, 462
Ungnadia speciosa 510

Vachellia constricta 264
Vachellia farnesiana 266
Vachellia vernicosa 266
Vara Dulce 270
Varnish Tree 340
Vauquelinia californica 452
Vauquelinia corymbosa subsp.
angustifolia 452
Verbenaceae 534–537
Vernicia fordii 226
Viburnum lentago 132
Viburnum rufidulum 132
Vitex agnus-castus 536
Vitex negundo 536

Wafer-ash 460
Wahoo, Western 205
Wahootree 254
Wait-a-minute Tree 262
Walnut, Arizona 330
Arizona Black 330
Black 332
California Black 328
English 332
Hinds's Black 328
Little 330
Northern California 328
Southern California 328
Texas Black 330
Washingtonia, California 116
Washingtonia filifera 116
Washingtonia robusta 116
Wattle, Black 246
Blue-leaf 248
Cedar 245
Cootamundra 243
Crested 250
Golden 248
Golden-wreath 248
Green 244
Knifeleaf 244
Milfoil 256
Pearl 247
Queensland Silver 247
Silver 244
Sydney Golden 246
Water 248
Wax-myrtle, Pacific 353
Wellingtonia 52
Whitebeam 448
Whitethorn, Chaparral 388
Chihuahuan 266
Wig Tree 134
Willow, Alaska 496
Almond 486
Arroyo 484
Balsam 494
Basket 474
Beach 498
Beaked 498
Bebb 498
Bigleaf 498
Black 480
Bonpland 478
Carolina 482
Coastal 498

Willow *continued*
Coastal Plain 482
Columbia River 476
Corkscrew 474
Coulter 492
Coyote 474
Desert 174
Diamond 498
Dune 498
Dusky 478
Feltleaf 496
Fire 496
Geyer 490
Goodding Black 480
Gray 498
Hind 475
Hooker 498
Littletree 492
Longleaf 478
MacKenzie 494
Meadow 490
Mountain 496
Narrowleaf 474
Northwest 478
Northwest Sandbar 478
Pacific 482
Peachleaf 486
Piper 498
Polished 486
Purpleosier 492
Pussy 494
Red 486

Sandbar 476
Satiny 490
Scouler 496
Shining 483
Silky 492
Silver 490
Silverleaf 478
Sitka 492
Smooth 486
Tail-leaf 482
Toumey 478
Tracy 484
Valley 480
Waxy 482
Weeping 488
Western Black 482
Western Shining 482
Whiplash 482
White 484, 488
Yellow 482
Yew 476
Yewleaf 476
Wingnut, Chinese 332
Winterberry 150
Witch-hazel, American 324
Woman's Tongue 250

Xylosma flexuosa 498

Yaupon 150
Yew, Pacific 110
Western 110

Yucca, Banana 126
Beaked 126
Faxon 124
Hoary 126
Mojave 128
Mountain 126
Sierra Madre 126
Soaptree 124
Soapweed 124
Thompson 128
Torrey 129
Yucca baccata 126
Yucca brevifolia 122
Yucca elata 124, 126
Yucca faxoniana 124
Yucca madrensis 126
Yucca rostrata 126
Yucca schidigera 128
Yucca schottii 126
Yucca thompsoniana 128
Yucca torreyi 129
Yucca treculeana 128

Zanthoxylum clava 460
Zanthoxylum fagara 462
Zanthoxylum flavum 460
Zanthoxylum hirsutum 462
Ziziphus jujuba 400
Ziziphus mauritiana 400
Ziziphus obtusifolia 400
Ziziphus zizyphus 400
Zygophyllaceae 538–539